ECONOMIC AND MILITAR[Y]
OF THE UNITED STATES

● Economic Aid   ○ Military Aid

SWEDEN
NORWAY
DENMARK
GERMAN FED. REP.
BENELUX
ITALY
YUGOSLAVIA
GREECE
AUSTRIA

UNION OF SOVIET
SOCIALIST REPUBLICS

TURKEY   AFGHANISTAN
PAKISTAN
IRAN   NEPAL
SAUDI   INDIA
EGYPT
ARABIA
ETHIOPIA   IRAQ
LEBANON
FR.   ISRAEL
EQUATORIAL   JORDAN
AFRICA   SOMALILAND   THAILAND
BEL.   LAOS
CONGO   MOZAMBIQUE   CAMBODIA
NGOLA   VIETNAM   INDONESIA
MADAGASCAR

RHODESIA &
NYASALAND

KOREA
JAPAN
OKINAWA
IWO JIMA
TAIWAN
PHILIPPINES   GUAM
KWAJALEIN

AUSTRALIA

NEW ZEALAND

NORTH ATLANTIC TREATY 1949		MIDDLE EAST TREATY 1955	SOUTHEAST ASIA TREATY 1954
UNITED STATES	ICELAND	IRAN	UNITED STATES
BELGIUM	ITALY	IRAQ	AUSTRALIA
CANADA	LUXEMBOURG	PAKISTAN	FRANCE
DENMARK	NETHERLANDS	TURKEY	NEW ZEALAND
FRANCE	NORWAY	UNITED KINGDOM	PAKISTAN
GERMAN FEDERAL REP.	PORTUGAL		PHILIPPINES
GREECE	TURKEY		THAILAND
	UNITED KINGDOM		UNITED KINGDOM

AMERICANS IN A CHANGING WORLD

Duquesne University:

Spiritus Est Qui Divificat

AMERICANS IN A CHANGING WORLD

A History of the United States in the Twentieth Century

WILLIAM APPLEMAN WILLIAMS
Oregon State University

In collaboration on the illustrations with
ORDE S. PINCKNEY

HARPER & ROW, Publishers
New York   Hagerstown   San Francisco   London

Sponsoring Editor: John Greenman
Project Editor: Robert Ginsberg
Designer: Ben Kann
Production Supervisor: Marion Palen
Cover Designer: Helen Iranyi
Compositor: Bi-Comp, Incorporated
Printer and Binder: The Maple Press Company
Art Studio: Danmark & Michaels Inc.

Endpaper maps used by permission from William A. Williams, *The Shaping of American Diplomacy*, Chicago: Rand McNally, 1956.

AMERICANS IN A CHANGING WORLD: A History of the United States in the Twentieth Century

Library of Congress Cataloging in Publication Data

Williams, William Appleman.
    Americans in a changing world.

    Includes bibliographies and index.
    1.   United States—History—20th century.   I.   Title.
E741.W55   973.9   77-23649
ISBN 0-06-047125-5

For All of Us

Herein lies the tragedy of the age: not that men
are poor—all men know something of poverty;
not that men are wicked—who is good? Not
that men are ignorant—what is truth? Nay, but
that men know so little of men.

WILLIAM EDWARD BURGHARDT DuBois,
The Souls of Black Folk,
1903.

CONTENTS

NOTES ON UNDERSTANDING AND USING THIS BOOK

Twenty years ago, even less, history textbooks were widely considered to be money machines. There were many students enrolled in history courses, and textbooks were routinely assigned—and even read—as an unquestioned part of the process of doing history. Indeed, history seemed to be a growth industry with a future as unlimited as that of Texas Instruments—or as that of Coca-Cola back in the 1920s.

And of course some publishers and some authors accumulated sizable amounts of money. Even so, the expectations of unlimited expansion were always unhistorical. As with the Florida land boom of the 1920s, the history bonanza collapsed before most historians realized that it was a bubble. The loot had been bagged by a few before the many had finished the first drafts of their manuscripts. And now, in the late 1970s, the historian is fortunate to be offered a contract—let alone be able to build himself even one house with his royalties.

That history raises two questions: Why did it happen; and why, knowing that record, should anyone write another history textbook?

There are several reasons for the recent collapse of history as an influential and profitable academic-publishing enterprise. Allow me to review them without ranking them in any order of importance. (Hopefully, at the end of this book, you will be able to assign your own priorities. That is, as you shall see, the most important aspect of my definition of a good textbook—as well as of being a good historian: you learn how to make your sense out of the data.)

1. History, as with other academic subjects (even including those among the sciences), has always enjoyed and endured the ups and downs of the sine curve. Sometimes it is popular and sometimes it is largely ignored. There is nothing much that the historian can do about that, but the good historians do not worry about it. They understand that it is all part of history. It is rather like being a fish-and-game expert on the Oregon coast: when the salmon run is good, he relaxes and enjoys the summer—but when it is bad, he applies for an unlisted phone number.

2. The recent boom in history was directly and intimately related to American policy toward Cuba and Vietnam and to the broader consequences of defining life in the United States as being centered on policing the world against communism. In the early years after World War II, history enjoyed considerable respect, even popularity, as *the* intellectual discipline that explained how and why it was necessary to define America in terms of containing Russia and expanding the power of the United States.

It was more than a bit crazy. Even so, it was understandable: everyone, including policy makers, wanted an explanation of why he could not come home from the war against the Axis and enjoy life. So many historians told the public that it was a matter of protecting the home fires against the barbarians and of extending the area of freedom. Ultimately, many people began to see that there was, as Frederick Schuman remarked, much room for maneuver between the Bad Red King and the Good White Queen; but for many years American foreign policy was a crusade against communists and other radicals that culminated in campaigns against Cuba and Vietnam. American leaders grossly distorted the heritage of self-determination (and at home as well as abroad). The government first tried to kill Fidel Castro and then it tried to kill Ho Chi Minh—and then it tried to kill the revolutions they led. And then it tried to silence Americans like Martin Luther King, Jr., who asserted that such policies were wrong.

It is not a pleasant story. But the citizens who turned to history as a convenient weapon against such manifestations of American imperialism did not take the time to learn the subtle nuances of the blade they had chosen. For history viewed as an explanation of present wrongs is not sufficient unto any people's needs. What is necessary is a sense of history deep enough to give you ideas about how to move from the past into the future, of how to use what is old in order to create something that is new. And that was lacking.

3. Hence, in a vital respect, the awareness of history evaded history. Which is to say that all too few historians talked or wrote about the central importance of history as a way of learning that we Americans are not unique. They failed to clarify the point that we are basically

just like everyone else. *They* are prejudiced, *we* are prejudiced. *They* are imperial, *we* are imperial. And so on and so forth.

Evading those matters, we continued to consider it a point of honor to view ourselves as different—even as exceptional. Which means that we have not taken advantage of our opportunity (any more than the Russians or the Brazilians have) to develop a more humane way of living with ourselves and others. And so, as many wise people have remarked (oh, so many times), we have not learned from the past in order to move on into a better future.

4. The bulge in undergraduate history enrollments during the late 1950s and early 1960s led most university history departments to emphasize the training of PhDs. That decision had two primary consequences: the active encouragement of the most intelligent and perceptive students to become professionals who concentrated on research and writing books and the related decline of classroom teaching that emphasized helping all students to learn how to do history.

I use the phrase *to do history* in the same way that scientists use the words to describe *doing* physics, or chemistry, or mathematics. One does each of these intellectual disciplines in the same way: you learn the principles, you learn the nature of the raw data, and then you proceed to find and make sense of the hard information.

As far as history is concerned, this means learning how to find, organize, and interpret the information of our human lives. It is a method of acquiring understanding that can be applied to the events of this week as well as to those of the year 1000 B.C. As one develops the skill, moreover, one acquires the ability to see and learn from similar *and* dissimilar situations: if one's sense of history indicates that the present situation is similar to an earlier episode and that option A was tried without success, then one fairly concludes that something else may be more appropriate. And vice versa: if the conditions are different, then choice A may indeed offer the prospect of a creative outcome. It all comes down to learning vicariously about the human condition and thereby increasing the probability of avoiding catastrophe. Hence it violates the spirit of doing history to emphasize the training of a professional elite.

5. The emphasis on producing PhDs had these further results: most of the best professors found themselves spending less and less time with undergraduates as they concentrated ever more on training PhDs; the best graduate students were often very good at teaching undergraduates, but they had to deemphasize that primary activity in order to research and write the books that would attract favorable attention from the leaders of the profession; and so the system produced an elite that became ever more removed from its primary constituency. The result was a self-reinforcing decline in history.

6. Very few leaders of any system respond enthusiastically to major criticisms of their policies and actions. Hence many younger historians whose research did not support the official (and orthodox academic) explanations and interpretations discovered themselves out of favor within the profession and hard put to obtain access to the marketplace of ideas. That meant, despite a short period during which the truly critical spirit can be said to have gained some headway, that most work in history (both written and in the classroom) was prosaic and unchallenging. That contributed to the decline in the serious involvement with history because the clash of ideas is at the center of any intellectual discipline. Without such vitality there is no learning in the true sense and no cerebral (or even emotional) excitement. People turn away because orthodoxy is dull.

7. One of the central themes of this book concerns the way that large corporations increasingly asserted their control over the American political economy during the twentieth century. The economic consequences of that process are obvious: the marketplace came to be dominated by a tiny number of economic oligarchs. The political results are also clear: serious, persistent critics of the corporate system do not become policy makers and do not exert significant, sustained influence on basic decisions.

The corporations also exert tremendous power in cultural—or social—affairs. One thinks, for example, of the blue jeans of antiwar dissent being transformed by the clothing industry into the aqua brushed denim of leisure suits for the middle and upper classes. Or of the way that the angry political lyrics of early rock 'n' roll (or of classic blues or country and western) music were housebroken into the fiddle-faddle now piped into corporate and governmental bureaucracies.

Those examples are as nothing, however, compared with the influence that the corporations have exerted over the nature and content of education. Public education in America has always had two faces: training to service the system versus education in innovation to change the system. It is too simple to define the issue as vocational versus classical education, but those polarities do describe the opposite ends of the spectrum. That tension is inherent in all public or community institutions, as witness the Chinese effort, through the Cultural Revolution, to devise a way out of the dilemma.

One can make an interesting argument that a workable balance between training (or schooling) and innovation (education) was maintained in the United States until about the time of World War I. I am not persuaded by that interpretation because I see much evidence that the balance was tipped toward training in the latter part of the nineteenth century. But, however one decides that issue, there can be no doubt that training became *the* definition of education after World War II.

That shift in values was carried through by the giant corporations with the support or acquiesence of most academic administrators and many professors. The change is simple to describe. The purpose of education (doing history and literature as well as botany and chemistry) is to engage the minds and psyches of people in an ongoing, never-ending intellectual activity that informs and affects *all* aspects of their lives. The objective of training is simply to program people with specific skills for specific jobs.

Let us moot the question of when it happened and concentrate on the process. As the corporations came to dominate the economy, they directly or indirectly defined most opportunities for jobs. The corporations, therefore, had a blunt choice to make: they could support a public system to educate people and then accept the responsibility for training the graduates for various corporation jobs or they could define the public educational system as training (at the expense of the taxpayer) for jobs with the corporations.

The corporations chose the second course. That had many consequences in every intellectual discipline. The study of politics, for example, became ever more an inquiry into the techniques of managerial and bureaucratic administration. And doing history with a critical mind came to be viewed as a disturbing way of raising difficult and inconvenient questions about all aspects of life. It was therefore deemed as incidental at best and something to be discouraged—if not actively opposed. That was accomplished directly by a large relative decline in the funding of the humanities and liberal arts and indirectly by not hiring the graduates of schools and universities that required significant amounts of work in the arts and humanities.

I can only conclude that if history is considered to be that dangerous, then it must be good, and that if it is that ostensibly irrelevant to the corporate political economy, then it must be exceedingly relevant to a richer and more humane life.

If I sound assured in my diagnosis, it is only because I have been through the process. I know whereof I speak. At one point in my career as a historian I became so involved with PhD candidates that I almost lost my relationship with undergraduates. Fortunately, with the help of my children, I caught myself in time, and so, taking a large salary cut, I moved to a university where I could honor my first responsibility: to help undergraduates learn how to do history.

I will never make as much money as I did in those earlier days. I enjoy extra money as much as the next person, but the definition of a teacher, or a professor, is this: a person who reports candidly on the way he or she has found and made sense of the world and in the process offers the students three things: information, a way of making sense out of the data, and hence an example of how one uses one's mind that will help the students make sense of reality for themselves.

As a teacher, I always use two criteria to select the books that I assign to my classes: the authors must provide relevant information and they must reach their conclusions in a way that is different from the way I offer. My objective is to expose the student to at least three or four ways of coming to terms with—and understanding—reality.

This book offers you my way. If it makes sense to you, fine. But make that decision only after you have read and listened to some other ways of fitting all the facts together. And if you choose another way, I salute you even though I disagree with you. I want you to emerge from the experience with *your* sense of history and of America. Hence, on down the line, I expect to learn as much from you as you have from me.

EXPLORATORY READING

An exploratory reading section will follow each chapter throughout the book. It will suggest books and articles that will help you go further into the subjects of each chapter.

The essence of doing history involves studying the records left by the people who thought and acted during any particular period and then trying to reconstruct what they did, how and why they did it, and the consequences of their actions. Hence one of the best ways to use this book is to approach it as a guide to people, ideas, and events, then, when you become particularly interested in one of those aspects, to go to the documents and do some history of your own.

Your teacher should be delighted to guide you into the appropriate government records, private correspondence and memoirs, and other documents that have been published. In addition, many colleges and universities have archives in which you can examine original manuscripts. That is the most exciting kind of research, and you should do some of it even though the available records may pertain only to local or state history. And, for that matter, what seems at first glance to be rather mundane local history often turns out to illuminate the larger story on the national scene. So again, I encourage you to go to the records and do some of your own history.

The challenge of making sense out of the documents has produced many theories of history and even a special discipline known as *historiography*. The following books will introduce you to some of the principal approaches to the problem:

G. Barraclough, *History in a Changing World* (1955)

C. A. Beard, *The Discussion of Human Affairs* (1936)

I. Berlin, *Historical Inevitability* (1954)

M. Bloch, *The Historian's Craft* (1953)

K. E. Boulding, *The Image: Knowledge in Life and Society* (1956)

H. Butterfield, *The Whig Interpretation of History* (1931)

E. H. Carr, *What Is History?* (1961)

R. G. Collingwood, *The Idea of History* (1946)

M. C. D'Arcy, *The Sense of History: Secular and Sacred* (1959)

M. I. Finley, *The Use and Abuse of History* (1975)

P. Gardiner (Ed.), *Theories of History* (1959)

G. Lukacs, *History and Class Consciousness* (1971)

R. S. Lynd, *Knowledge for What?* (1939)

H. Meyerhoff (Ed.), *The Philosophy of History in Our Time* (1959)

The Complete Writings of Thucydides (1934)

WILLIAM APPLEMAN WILLIAMS

AMERICANS IN A CHANGING WORLD

INTRODUCTION
PRELUDE TO SOCIAL TRAUMA: THE ELECTION OF 1892

THE United States entered the decade of the 1890s as a society undergoing ever more rapid transformation from agrarianism to industrialism, and increasingly beset by the many social conflicts caused by such change. The most pervasive source of tension was the economic and political centralization inherent in nineteenth-century industrialization. The marketplace giants like John D. Rockefeller, Andrew Carnegie, and J. P. Morgan were creating a continental economic system increasingly controlled by a small group of people whose decisions affected the rest of the population in every aspect of their lives: from the food they could buy to the jobs they could find to the reading matter and recreation that were available. As a part of that process, the centralizing elite within the upper class sought ever more influence and control over government. That, in turn, consolidated increasing political power in Washington, D.C. For, to create and administer such a system, the basic decisions had to be enforced on a national scale.

The related conflicts between the working class and the owners and managers, and between the middle class and both those groups, were accentuated and complicated by the underlying confrontation between agriculture and industry—between the country and the city. Both those major elements in the political economy were divided within themselves, and some groups in each sector sided with similar elements in the other on various secondary issues. But on the elemental matters—such as the shift and centralization of power into the cities—the agrarians stood as a phalanx against the urbanites.

The central problem for the protagonists of industrialization, workers as well as bankers, therefore, was to devise a program and to find leaders who would attract enough of the agricultural majority to insure their ultimate victory. There was no easy solution. The fluctuating fortunes of both major parties between the elections of 1876 and 1892 made it clear that neither of them had been able to meet that challenge. And the rise and growth of militant agricultural movements, such as the Northern and Southern Alliances and the more diffuse Populist coalition, revealed that metropolitan interests were by no means assured of controlling the process of industrialization in the way that they desired.

I have used two designations—*political economy* and *metropolitan*—that may have surprised or confused you, and hence it seems wise to stop for a few moments and explain what I mean by those terms and how I will employ them throughout the book. Most contemporary economists describe and attempt to explain the economic aspect of life as though it could be separated—or abstracted— from the rest of our existence. That enables them to devise elaborate mathematical explanations of how the economy functions—or fails to function.

But all of us know that the economic side of life is always entwined with our ideas, our dreams, our social position, our politics—in short, with all the rest of our existence. Economics influences politics (even sex) and is in turn affected by those other facets of our lives. The giants of economics, people like Adam Smith, Karl Marx, Rosa Luxemburg, and Joan Robinson, recognized that elementary truth and therefore struggled to integrate politics and ideas into their explanations of the working of the economic system. They used the phrase *political economy* to define the interplay between pure economics and other aspects of life, and that is the way I am using the term in this book.

There is a similar problem with the word *metropolitan*. Most of us commonly use it as a fancy substitute for the biggest cities. And, truth to tell, Adam Smith, writing in the middle of the eighteenth century, was quite content with the term *the city*. That worked for him, for example, in his most famous book, *The Wealth of Nations* (1776), because he was a British political economist writing for people who knew that he meant London. And they further understood that London was *the* center of the new kind of political and economic power as well as being the place name for a large accumulation of people. They recognized, that is to say, that the city of shipping, manufacturing, government, and finance exercised more power than the countryside populated by farmers.

Smith was an honest and candid scholar. He said bluntly that the city—the *metropolis*—enjoyed an inherent, structural advantage over the country. In later years, the term *metropolitan* came to symbolize all those greater powers of the industrial-technological side of the political economy. And, as the capitalist system extended its power throughout the world, as well as within various countries, the term *metropolitan* came to be used as a synonym for the rich and powerful nations that dominated the world political economy.

All those elements of the situation were dramatized during the campaigns and elections of 1892. Secretary of State James G. Blaine was the only politician that year who might have persuaded a majority of the people of the United States to accept metropolitan leadership of the new industrial political economy. He might have built an effective Republican coalition between agricultural and urban businessmen and then arranged enough ongoing compromises between those groups to ease the nation into the new world. Yet, given the severe and racking depression that began in 1893, even he might not have been able to control the maelstrom. In any event, he was trapped as the chief cabinet member in the presidency of Benjamin Harrison, and he became increasingly weary, dispirited, and ill. Harrison was easily renominated as the Republican candidate and campaigned on a generally uninspiring platform, though the delegates did denounce the "inhuman outrages" upon black Americans "in certain Southern States of the Union."

The eastern and southern conservatives who dominated the machinery of the Democratic party turned once again to Grover Cleveland, a man wholly unsuited and unprepared to lead the country through a basic transition of the political economy. He thought that the developing crisis could be dealt with through economy in government; civil service reform; lowering the tariff; laissez-faire economics; opposition to greater participation for women, blacks, and labor; and maintaining the gold standard. The monetization of silver, he warned, would be "dangerous and reckless"—an invitation to "the greatest peril." In summary, Cleveland and his supporters appealed to and defended the past with great verve and zest.

Cleveland's almost obsessive concern with the silver question serves to illustrate a more general aspect of interpreting the raw facts of history. Even at the individual and highly personal level, major confrontations often become displaced—symbolized—by secondary aspects of the crisis. Two people who are living together and who have come to understand their potentially destructive differences often argue about their fundamental incompatabilities (a matter of value systems), for example, in the language of who earns the most money and how it is spent. That also happens on the social level, between two or more groups of people, and just such a debate was well advanced in 1892 in the United States.

The basic clash of values involved two ways of life: an agrarian mode of living that was grounded in decentralized and personal communities, and a new industrial system characterized by the centralization of people, energy, and power in an increasingly homogenized uniformity. The fundamental issue was whether the process of industrialization could and would be controlled according to the principles of community and decentralization. But that was first distorted by the oversimplified rhetoric of the struggle between the city and the country and then further snarled in an emotional argument about the monetization of silver.

The proposal to use silver bullion as money (either as coin or as a reserve of precious metal for paper bills) was almost as old as the country. And, off and on, silver had been an integral part of the monetary system. It became a major issue, however, only after the Civil War, when new silver mines were discovered and opened in the West and when agricultural businessmen began to produce great surpluses of grain and meat for export to Europe and the rest of the world.

By 1892 Cleveland and Harrison had each served a term as president of the United States. James G. Blaine knew that he had more ability and more vision than either. Should he stand aside to let one or the other achieve the presidency for another four years? Bernard Gillam saw Blaine as Shakespeare's Hamlet pondering the dilemma.

HAMLET (J. G. B.): "To be or not to be, that is the question." — From *Judge*.

Reprinted in the *Review of Reviews*, vol. IV, January, 1892, p. 663.

Most eastern urban leaders (and their allies and satellites in the rest of the country) feared that the coinage of silver would lead to inflation, reduce property values, and weaken America's position in the international economic system based in London and using gold as its standard of value. But the silver miners and the farmers argued that the minting of silver would guarantee equitable economic growth by supplying more money at home and by enabling exporters to compete more effectively in world markets which used silver. And, for that matter, a few eastern industrial spokesmen agreed with them.

Silver thus increasingly became *the* symbol for the more basic disagreement and argument about the course of industrialization. Those who favored a monetary system based only on gold were viewed as advocates of allowing an elite to determine the future of the country. On the other hand, those who agitated for silver were damned as ignorant radicals who were determined to obstruct progress and ruin the nation.

Between 1888 and 1892, many angry agriculturalists had come to view the silver issue as the best way to fight the industrialization that was under the control of an eastern minority. Hence, when they were denied the challenge of wrestling with the question of whether or not to support Blaine, who promised support for agriculture as well as industrialism, the militant reformers, who called themselves Populists, adopted a dual strategy. They formed a third party based on western and southern farmers and related businessmen and made overtures for an alliance with urban workers and middle-class citizens. That gave them the hope of becoming a new majority party or of taking control of one of the old parties. Ignatius Donnelly roused them to angry fervor. The nation, he cried, is on "the verge of moral, political, and material ruin. . . . From the same prolific womb of governmental injustice we breed the two great classes—tramps and millionaires."

Then the Populists made their demands. Silver must be accepted on an equal basis with gold as honest money. Postal savings banks must be created as an alternative to the system governed by financial overlords. The secret ballot was essential. Senators should be elected by popular vote. An income tax would be used to pay for state ownership of the railroads and communications systems. And foreign ownership of land should be terminated in order to provide more land for "actual settlers."

The Populist platform sounded more radical than it actually was: the railroad plan, for example, was designed to protect and help the average capitalist against the corporations rather than to open the door to socialism. As a result, the Populist convention finally chose James B. Weaver, a midwestern veteran of the Civil War who had earlier left the Republican party to campaign for an inflationary money policy and to attack the railroads for ignoring their public responsibilities. He was wholly honest, and a good speaker, but he had little vision of a new America. Thus, given the passivity of Harrison and the dullness of Cleveland, the campaign began with rhetoric that was often uninformative and even irrelevant to the fundamental problems before the nation.

Then came the June, 1892, strike by the men who made the steel in Carnegie's plant in Homestead, Pennsylvania. They wanted (and needed) more money and better working conditions, but Henry C. Frick (Carnegie's top assistant) refused to negotiate. He preferred force and hired 300 Pinkerton mercenaries to attack the workers. Men on both sides were killed, but the fight-for-money soldiers failed. So, too, initially, did the militia that the millionaires called upon the state to deliver. So, too, did Alexander Berkman. He was a New York anarchist (and dear friend of Emma Goldman, a courageous radical who helped plan his ventures). He calmly walked into Frick's office and shot and knifed, but failed to kill, the capitalist leader.

The public was uneasy about the reminder of the Haymarket Riot of 1886, but it nevertheless remained generally sympathetic to the workers. Key Republican leaders, recognizing the danger to their campaign, tried to persuade Carnegie to compromise. He refused. Through the use of more force and strikebreakers, Carnegie and Frick destroyed the union, the Amalgamated Association of Iron, Steel, and Tin Workers, and created votes for Pennsylvania Democrats. Then came other strikes: silver miners in Idaho, coal miners in Tennessee, and railroad switchmen in New York. The outcome was the same. Troops were used to defeat the workers, and local Democratic politicians were the principal beneficiaries.

Populist leaders failed to exploit the opportunity to build a coalition with labor, but they did evoke considerable support among agrarian businessmen. Led by William C. Whitney, the Democrats campaigned hard and effectively, blaming the "labor riots, battles, bloodstained fields" on the high tariff, which raised prices for goods, and appealing to the farmer with a similar argument. Even so, and particularly in view of Harrison's passivity, the presidential election was surprisingly close. The popular vote, cast widely for the first time as a secret ballot, gave Cleveland a margin of only 38,961 out of the total of 10,732,125 for both men.

Far from being decisive, the election dramatized the inability of existing metropolitan leaders to direct the new industrial system in an equitable and creative fashion. The Populist effort, which carried five states in the plains and mountains and helped many Democrats to win in the South, further emphasized the failure of the metropolis to assert effective leadership. The congressional voting gave the Democrats numerical control of both houses, though that was modified on some issues by the increased Populist influence. Along with the death of Blaine, the results opened the way for both parties to reorganize around new leaders who understood the nature of the crisis.

EXPLORATORY READING

Some of the most stimulating general interpretations of the tensions that were moving toward a climax by 1892 are offered by:

R. Berthoff, *An Unsettled People: Social Order and Disorder in American Society* (1971)

S. Fine, *Laissez Faire and the General Welfare State: A Study in Conflict in American Thought, 1865–1901* (1956)

R. Ginger, *The Age of Excess* (1965)

J. W. Hurst, *Law and the Conditions of Freedom in the Nineteenth-Century United States* (1956)

H. W. Morgan (Ed.), *The Gilded Age: A Reappraisal* (1963)

———, *Unity and Culture: The United States, 1877–1900* (1971)

B. A. Weisberger, *The New Industrial Society* (1969)

R. H. Wiebe, *The Search for Order, 1877–1920* (1967)

The movers and shakers of industrialization are described, and evaluated in contrasting ways, in these studies:

A. D. Chandler (Ed.), *The Railroads: The Nation's First Big Business* (1965)

T. C. Cochran and W. Miller, *The Age of Enterprise* (1942)

M. Josephson, *The Robber Barons* (1934)

———, *The Politicos, 1865–1896* (1938)

E. C. Kirkland, *Industry Comes of Age* (1961)

O. Lewis, *The Big Four* (1938)

R. D. Marcus, *Grand Old Party: Political Structure in the Gilded Age, 1880–1896* (1971)

G. Myers, *History of the Great American Fortunes* (1910)

H. W. Morgan, *From Hayes to McKinley: National Party Politics, 1877–1896* (1969)

A. Nevins, *Study in Power: Rockefeller* (1953)

G. R. Taylor and I. D. Neu, *The American Railroad Network* (1956)

J. F. Wall, *Andrew Carnegie* (1970)

O. O. Winther, *The Transportation Frontier* (1964)

The results in the city are explored by these writers:

H. David, *History of the Haymarket Affair* (1936)

M. Dubofsky, *Industrialism and the American Worker, 1865–1920* (1975)

M. Meltzer, *Bread and Roses: The Struggle of American Labor, 1865–1913* (1967)

Z. L. Miller, *The Urbanization of Modern America* (1973)

A. M. Schlesinger, *The Rise of the City* (1933)

H. N. Smith (Ed.), *Popular Culture and Industrialization, 1865–1900* (1967)

S. Thernstrom, *Poverty and Progress: Social Mobility in a Nineteenth-Century City* (1964)

N. A. Ware, *The Labor Movement in the United States, 1860–1895* (1929)

And the conflict and consensus among members of the agricultural majority are proved in these works:

L. Atherton, *The Cattle Kings* (1961)

E. Dick, *The Sod-House Frontier* (1937)

H. M. Drache, *The Day of the Bonanza* (1964)

R. F. Durden, *The Climax of Populism* (1965)

G. C. Fite, *The Farmer's Frontier, 1865–1900* (1966)

S. P. Hays, *The Response to Industrialism* (1957)

J. D. Hicks, *The Populist Revolt* (1931)

R. Hofstadter, *The Age of Reform* (1955)

G. H. Miller, *Railroads and the Granger Laws* (1971)

W. T. K. Nugent, *The Tolerant Populists* (1963)

———, *Money and American Society, 1865–1880* (1968)

N. Pollack, *The Populist Response to Industrial America* (1962)

F. Shannon, *The Farmer's Last Frontier* (1945)

W. P. Webb, *The Great Plains* (1931)

C. Vann Woodward, *Origins of the New South, 1877–1913* (1951)

1 THE STRUGGLE TO CONTROL THE EMERGING SYSTEM

THE increasingly urgent need for effective leadership was dramatized by three events in the spring of 1893: the World's Fair, which opened in Chicago on May 1; the financial panic of May 5, which quickly developed into a massive economic depression; and Cleveland's ruthless campaign to defeat the advocates of silver, which further weakened the existing political structure. The fair demonstrated the potential of the rising industrial system. The depression made it clear that the new political economy was dangerously unstable and inequitable. And the president's attitude toward silver revealed his fundamental inability even to imagine the basis for a new political alignment. Hence the problem of control involved two things: the need to regulate, rationalize, and balance the industrial economy and the necessity, in order to accomplish those requirements, to create a political coalition capable of taking such action.

The organization and creation of the Columbian Exposition suggested that the new economy could be organized and directed toward coherent goals, and that hopeful symbolism no doubt helped generate the national enthusiasm and pride in the achievement. Hamlin Garland, the popular and realistic writer about agrarian life, excitedly told his aging parents in Dakota to "sell the cook stove if necessary and come." Another old couple agreed that it had been worthwhile, "even if it did take all the burial money." That was unknowingly a prophetically ironic remark, for despite the fair's use of the frontier theme, the exposition marked the end of America as a predominantly agrarian society.

True enough, the world's largest cheese was on display, but the real drama was created by the largest building, the largest boiler house, the largest piece of forged steel that was part of the largest piece of revolving machinery (the world's largest Ferris wheel—16 stories high), and the largest display of mechanical equipment in operation. As for fun, there was the largest midway (a strip 20 blocks long), which featured such attractions as "Ice Cold French Cider" and a sensuous "dance that will deprive you of a peaceful night's rest for months to come."

The fair did demonstrate that the new industrial system could be coordinated, controlled, and directed for grand purposes. The sandy, marshy, wasting environs of Chicago—"a dismal morass"—had been reclaimed, landscaped, and used to build the celebrated White City. That name suggested a grand metaphor, because after having wrested control of western commerce from Cincinnati and other cities on the eve of the Civil War, Chicago had, in 1871, been blackened by a massive fire that charred the guts of the city.

But, like the phoenix of Egyptian mythology, Chicago arose from its ashes and shortly became the nation's most dynamic meeting point of agriculture, commerce, and industry. It justly boasted itself as the center of the new railroad system, as the home of the McCormicks who dominated the manufacture of agricultural implements, as the hub of a massive steel industry, and as the meat packing center of the world. It was indeed the vortex of violence and hope in which the farm merged with the factory.

Nothing could have been more appropriate than for the fair to be held in Chicago. The architecture, controlled by the always firm and sometimes imaginative hand of Daniel Burnham, combined the old and the new in a way that underscored the need for a decision about the future. He had helped develop the logic of the skyscraper from the steel produced in Illinois as well as Pennsylvania, but he was always afraid of the ruthless aesthetics of that material.

His contemporaries like Louis Henri Sullivan and Frank Lloyd Wright (also of Chicago) were both bolder and more subtle in realizing the potential of the new construction techniques. Even so, Burnham designed the White City with a certain flair: "classicism in the grand manner . . . planning on a prophetically imperial scale . . . [and] power expressed in design, grouping, and form."

But the unavoidable sight of the nearby Chicago slums provided a chilling commentary on the White City—and on the crisis of the evolving urban and industrial system. Black Americans, angry at being excluded from the planning of the fair, discriminated against in employment during its construction, and patronized in various exhibitions, made the obvious pun: it was "the White American's World Fair."

The treatment of women was more subtly ironic. For the grand Women's Building, developed solely by females and clearly demonstrating their talents and abilities, offered a telling commentary on the discrimination against them in everyday life. Chief Red Bull uttered a blunt Indian response to such architecture—"Ugh! Bad medicine." And the anger and unrest of the real America was never far away: Chicago Mayor Carter A. Harrison was assassinated on his way home from the fair; and the governor of Illinois, militant reformer John Peter Altgeld, pardoned three of the Haymarket anarchists shortly after the exposition was opened by President Cleveland.

The president assured everyone on May 1 that the fair would awaken forces that would extend "the welfare, the dignity, and the freedom of mankind," but it did not arouse him from his slumber in the past. Neither did the rumblings of the collapse of the old order. The Philadelphia and Reading Railroad went bankrupt just before Cleveland was inaugurated. Then, four days after the president opened the fair, the National Cordage Company failed and the stock market collapsed.

Cleveland naturally blamed it all on the radicals, the tariff, and the silver purchase act of 1890, which required the government to purchase an inconsequential amount of silver every month. The real causes were far more complex, but he acted on the true faith of the old liners. He called the Congress into special session for the sole purpose of ridding the country of the silver virus.

Not even the discovery of a cancer in the president's mouth unduly delayed the campaign. The day after Cleveland issued his summons (June 30, 1893) for the Congress to convene in special session, a secret operation saved his life. He promptly demanded the repeal of the silver law on August 8, asserting that it was the only way to restore fiscal honesty and stop the slide into a major depression. He got his way on October 30 at the cost of using most of his patronage, isolating himself and other conservative Democrats, and handing the silver issue to the agrarian dissidents.

They maneuvered to capitalize politically on the depression (even as they suffered its consequences) by blaming it on the gold-based monetary system and the greed of its advocates in the United States and England. A more persuasive explanation suggests that the panic and depression involved the major shock of a capitalist marketplace economy reaching the bottom of a long-wave business cycle. The theory about such fluctuations in capitalist economies was developed by N. D. Kondratieff, one of the many impressive young intellectuals active in Russia after the Bolshevik Revolution (and, like most of them, he was exiled in the 1930s). His analysis provides an illuminating overview of what happened during the nineteenth century and what followed during the twentieth century.

Kondratieff concluded that such long cycles last about 50 years. If the depression of the 1890s is viewed as the low point on such a curve, then the Kondratieff theory accurately projects a period of growth peaking in 1918, followed by a decline ending in the early 1940s, and another era of growth through the 1960s. The frequency of wars in the twentieth century undoubtedly modifies any narrow arithmetic application of the theory, but it nevertheless provides a useful guide to understanding what happened after the crisis of the 1890s.

That time of great pain and trouble is thus seen as dramatizing the creation of the steam-and-steel economy—the new industrial system. In the narrower sense, the collapse was caused by the following factors: overexpansion (including inflation) in railroads and other elements of the new industrial system, and in the West; overborrowing by local governments; a decline in the construction industry; a European crisis that led to the withdrawal of investment funds; and a fall in exports.

The results were devastating to individuals, families, and institutions. As they lost their jobs, thousands of men left home in search of work, wandering the country as hoboes, sleeping in parks or jails, taking whatever employment or relief they could find. Some of them, ashamed and totally discouraged, never returned home. There were probably 2.5 million unemployed in the major urban centers during the winter of 1893–1894, and the total for the country rose during 1894 to 20 percent of the labor force. Local relief efforts included breadlines and soup kitchens (promptly termed "Cleveland Cafés"), and Chicago saloons provided up to 60,000 free meals a day; but such efforts barely touched the vast suffering and deprivation.

Congressman William Jennings Bryan—the young crusading Democrat from Nebraska, first elected to the Congress in 1890 during the initial upsurge of agricultural unrest—caught the plight of the farmer in one terse phrase: "Work worn and dust begrimed." Many families were forced off the land, and others hung on only by making great sacrifices and skimping along on survival rations. The natural history of the time, as one observer noted, was "debt, poverty, and despair."

Henry Adams, the grandson of John Quincy Adams and a leading spokesman of the upper class, later recalled similar events among the middle and upper classes. "Men died like flies under the strain, and Boston grew suddenly old, haggard, and thin." Business failures became routine—more than 500 banks had closed by December, 1893, and 15,000 other enterprises had failed during the same months. The value of 33 top-rated stocks declined by $400 million. Within a year, moreover, 156 railroads had gone bankrupt, and by 1897 almost one-third of all railroad mileage was in receivership (and being acquired by the surviving giants).

The widespread economic collapse generated new social and political ferment, as well as strengthened the existing protest movements. Many people were becoming afraid that the entire society might disintegrate, and hence they redoubled their efforts in behalf of what they considered to be the necessary corrective measures. Western farmers, for example, and some urban businessmen stepped up their campaign to remonetize silver, extended their attacks on bankers and large industrialists, agitated for vigorous action by the government to expand export markets, and talked ever more seriously about a new political alignment.

Others in the South went even farther, launching an effort to develop an alliance with the poorest of the poor—the black sharecropping farmers who organized their own movement called the Colored Farmers' National Alliance and Cooperative Union. That action was correctly understood by most southerners (and even some northerners) as a potentially revolutionary development. Hence, even as it began, it was an ambivalent undertaking. No one revealed that more clearly than reform leader Thomas E. Watson of Georgia.

Watson in many ways personified the nation's confusion, fear, and indecision. He was at heart a capitalist who nevertheless favored some drastic—and even potentially radical—reforms to save the system. He wanted more power for the people at home, yet agitated vigorously for the expansion of America's economic and political power throughout the world. And even though he was shrewd enough to understand that the race issue was being used to control *all* the poor—"you are kept apart that you may be separately fleeced of your earnings"—he ultimately turned against the blacks to win some improvement for the whites. But the effort to build such a coalition with blacks was a brave attempt to make the new system more humane and equitable.

The counterattack by southern racists was violent, clever, and effective. The lynchings (there were more than 2500 between 1884 and 1900) served as exclamation points for the warnings to vote the right way or not vote and to stay out of the white man's cafés, toilets, and schools. Faced with the threat of poor whites cooperating with poor blacks, as in North Carolina after the election of 1894, the racists acted with skill and determination. Mississippi had taken the lead in 1890 by imposing a poll tax and a stipulation that a black voter could be challenged to read, understand, and discuss the Constitution to the satisfaction of a white man. Other states promptly followed that example, and in 1898 Louisiana devised a new limitation: black voters whose fathers or grandfathers had not been qualified to vote on January 1,

1867 (none were), were required to meet property or educational regulations (few could).

Benjamin Ryan Tillman of South Carolina, another sometime reformer who demanded a big navy to help expand foreign markets for the farmers, was bluntly defiant: "We took the government away. We stuffed ballot boxes. We shot them. . . ." There were protest riots, as in Wilmington, North Carolina (1898), but the results of that outburst told the general story: 3 whites wounded, 25 blacks wounded—and 11 blacks killed.

Southerners replied to northern and western critics by charging them with living by a double standard. And, in truth, the Supreme Court decision in *Plessy* v. *Ferguson* (1896) was a classic example of sophisticated hypocrisy. Plessy sued the East Louisiana Railway because he was denied a seat in the "white" coach on a trip from New Orleans to Covington. The Court held that he had not been denied any property rights because, as a mulatto, he had no property rights in the white car. Justice John Marshall Harlan filed an eloquent dissent that has yet to be realized: "Our Constitution is color-blind."

The blacks who moved north during the depression did not fare much better. Real estate operator Philip A. Payton, Jr., did try (through the Afro-American Realty Company) to help them find housing in the Harlem section of Manhattan, and Charles W. Anderson, another black politician who held a federal appointment, provided hope and some help. And the National Negro Business League (1900) assisted some blacks in moving beyond menial jobs and in being used as strikebreakers. But most blacks moved only from the bottom of an agricultural economy to the bottom of an industrial economy.

The real power in the business community was wielded by two other groups. The large investment bankers like J. P. Morgan and the giant industrialists like John D. Rockefeller used their power to expand and consolidate their control of the system—and to extend their political influence. And the smaller operators who managed to survive the depression organized themselves in 1895 as the National Association of Manufactures (NAM), to agitate for overseas economic expansion and to control labor unions.

That order of priorities seemed reasonable at the time. The radical elements in the American Federation of Labor (AF of L), which had been strong on the eve of the depression, appeared to have been defeated by the conservative leadership headed by Samuel Gompers, and the railroad engineers seemed to become professionally oriented. The other potential threat, the American Railway Union (ARU) led by Eugene V. Debs, was soon to be mauled by an alliance between the Cleveland administration and another group of businessmen, the General Managers Association, which represented 24 major railroads based in Chicago. Although 469,000 workers had been involved in the strikes of 1894, the number of stoppages had begun to decline—from 1786 in 1891 to 1066 in 1896. For the moment, at any rate, the union problem seemed secondary: workers were hungry, scabs were plentiful, and the conservative AF of L claimed more than half of all organized workers.

RADICALS AND REFORMERS THREATEN THE OLD ORDER

Radical and reform intellectuals posed more immediate trouble for those who were concerned with preserving the old order or establishing the new system based on the corporations. They provided ammunition for the angry agrarians and for dissident members of the middle and upper classes. The silver forces, for example, produced many capable spokesmen. William Jennings Bryan of Nebraska, who had tuned his oratorical skills as a low-tariff advocate in the House of Representatives, became a spellbinder on the virtues of the white metal. He had only one speech, but his variations on the theme would have done justice to a Mozart. Richard Parks ("Silver Dick") Bland, a congressman from Missouri, argued the case with more sophistication, as did others in various magazines like *Arena, Forum,* and *National Bimetallist.* And eastern upper-class spokesmen like Brooks Adams (brother of Henry) were even more intellectually impressive. But it was Bryan and Bland who turned the crowds to silver, even though, as one wit remarked of Bland, they had about as much influence in the Cleveland administration as "the 'p' in pneumonia."

The most dramatic case for silver was made by William H. Harvey of Chicago. Harvey was a one-shot genius who combined, in *Coin's Financial School* (1894), all the ingredients of classic propaganda. His ploy was to use the self-educated country hick as a man who could out-think the metropolitan expert, and on that basis he also preached a militant expansive nationalism and fired salvo after salvo at the upper-class bankers and industrialists.

Other reformers were less flamboyant but almost equally influential. Henry Demarest Lloyd's *Wealth Against Commonwealth* (1894) was a devastating description and analysis of the operations of Standard Oil. Only one major urban newspaper, Joseph Pulitzer's New York *World,* persistently attacked Cleveland on major issues and campaigned against vice and corruption. But writers like William T. Stead (*If Christ Came to Chicago,* 1894) did much to inform and arouse the city populations. There was enough such concern and activity by 1895 to encourage W. D. P. Bliss to edit the *Encyclopedia of Social Reforms.*

Neither moderate reform journals like *The Nation* nor the generally conservative metropolitan press offered impressive counterattacks against the critics. Even William Randolph Hearst, a sometime reformer and politician who launched his newspaper empire by taking over the New York *Journal* in 1895, was mild compared to the Chicago *Prairie Farmer*—let alone Watson's *People's Party Paper*. For that matter, the early realistic playwrights, like James A. Hearne and David Belasco, spoke more forcefully about the nature of the new system—as did artists like Maurice Prendergast and George Luks.

And the new realism in art (even when tinged with mysticism and romanticism) could become, in the mind of a writer like Hamlin Garland, a scalpel to bare the bones of the real America. Garland was a defender (as in *Crumbling Idols,* 1894) of the young radicals like Henry Blake Fuller and Stephen Crane who wrote about poverty, hardship, and the inequities of the new industrial system. But beyond that brave advocacy, Garland's grand theme was the exploitation of the country by the industrial metropolis. He knew at first hand the weary, never-ending struggle of the farmer to avoid failure and presented it unforgettably in *Main-Travelled Roads* (1891), *Prairie Folks* (1893), and *Rose of Dutcher's Cooly* (1895).

Garland's concern (as in *Rose*) with the life of women was not unique. Henry James, the greatest novelist of his era, placed females at the center of most of his impressive works: *Portrait of a Lady* (1881), *The Tragic Muse* (1902), and *The Golden Bowl* (1904). Like Garland and others, James was primarily involved with the basic transitions taking place in American life. His central theme was the way in which the decline of traditional religion left people without a unifying and controlling moral force in their lives and how individuals struggled in that limbo against other people and institutions that could and did destroy them. And he provided, in *The American Scene* (1907), some of the most trenchant criticism of the emerging corporate system.

But James was so deeply concerned with his art and so limited in his practical knowledge that even his admirers were often frustrated. His courage in dealing with a woman's infatuation for a young girl (*The Bostonians,* 1886), for example, lacked the power that it would have had if it had been more naturalistic. It is doubtful, however, that a more forceful treatment would have overturned the prevailing views (and laws) about female sexuality. Only a tiny minority of women were willing in those days to confront that issue.

The reaction against the radical feminists after the Civil War led to repressive legislation against contraceptives and birth control information. Edward Bliss Foote was one of the few (of either sex) who continued to deal with such issues, although Charles Dana Gibson's graphic portrayals of idealized young middle- and upper-class women did not slight their sensuality. Perhaps even more significantly, the eyes and facial expressions of the Gibson Girls carried more than a hint of rebellion against the nonsexual aspects of male domination.

Most American women during the 1890s were more immediately concerned with other issues: poverty, creating homes and raising children, education, and jobs. Farmwives—black and white—were fortunate if they worked only 12 hours a day. In the cities, 25 percent of all black married women had to work if the family was to survive (only 5 percent of white married women were employed outside the home). And by the same date (1900), 20 percent of all unmarried women over 15 were employed—often in circumstances that justified strikes and that sometimes, as in a Chicago glove-making factory, led to strikes.

The vast majority of women activists, however, had accepted the philosophy of mothering society. Julia Ward Howe summarized that outlook in one pithy phrase: "Woman is the mother of the race." That view can of course be criticized on several grounds, but the pragmatic point concerns the extreme difficulty of putting it into practice. For to mother in that sense involves building a community at home and a social movement in the larger world. And, in the broader view, the decision to accept that outlook closed off other options.

In a time of transition, women as well as men needed to clarify and then choose between various alternatives. One was to seek equality within the classic marketplace conception of reality and individualism. A second was to organize as local, regional, and national pressure groups in order to win victories on specific and nonsexually defined issues. A third was to escape into sexuality and other forms of privatization as an individual or as a member of small groups. And a fourth was to devise a new conception of community that would control and humanize the new industrial system and then to build a social movement to realize that vision.

The women who had to work, on the farm or in the city, had little time for theory. Farmwives (and daughters) were partners in a family enterprise that was being pushed to the wall, and they were struggling to survive in the marketplace. Poor city women knew that they would never have a chance to confront the challenge of homesteading. They were concerned with wages and hours and the conditions of the factory and the home.

By accepting women as equal members, farm organizations like the National Grange and the Alliance provided them with political experience that was denied most other American women. But farm women were too preoccupied with their own problems and too geographically diffused to provide significant national leadership. Hence the major female campaigns of the era were dominated by urban middle- and upper-class white women. The long split in the suffrage movement ended in 1893 with the creation of the National American Women's

Suffrage Association, but the moderate allies of Lucy Stone soon won control from the more militant followers of Susan B. Anthony and Elizabeth Cody Stanton. The strategy to win the vote through a constitutional amendment was abandoned in favor of state campaigns, but they proved ineffective and the Congress ignored the issue.

Part of that failure was due to the antisuffrage agitation by women who felt that the emphasis on political action would weaken the home, undercut the effort to mother society, and reduce the effectiveness of pressure group action on specific issues. A related attitude changed the nature of the Women's Christian Temperance Union. Frances Willard had always campaigned for a broad range of reforms—including more natural clothes, kindergartens, and child labor laws—but after she lost control of the organization in 1896, her successors concentrated very narrowly on outlawing booze.

Some temperance advocates did remain active in local reform campaigns, which also gained strength from the expansion of women's clubs throughout the nation. The women's clubs were often derided and discounted (even by feminists), but after a national organization was created in 1890, they became ever more important. The Boston Women's Municipal League and the National Council of Jewish Women (1893) were other groups that helped to win access for females to elementary and secondary education, organized slum improvement associations, and helped working-class women.

The central importance of work in the individual's life was basic to the philosophy of Charlotte Perkins Gilman, who was the outstanding intellectual leader of the women's movement from the end of the nineteenth century until well into the twentieth century. She was severely depressed by family life and, after one child and a divorce, embarked upon a career as a poet and writer. Gilman was attracted by Edward Bellamy's peculiar middle-upper-class mixture of socialism and corporatism (popularized in his best-selling volume, *Looking Backward,* 1888), but after attending the 1896 women's rights convention she concentrated her great energy and ability in the cause of feminist reform.

She was most heavily influenced by Lester Frank Ward, a sociologist who much of the time sounded like a female supremacist. But her almost obsessive concern with economic independence dominated her call to reorganize society so that women could pursue careers in the marketplace. Work was the key to independence and personal fulfillment and was necessary to accomplish the desired improvement of the material conditions of life. She thus advocated, in *Women and Economics* (1898), apartment building collectives to free women (at least some of them) from child rearing and housework. It was a classic middle- and upper-class proposal and contained more than a few contradictions, not the least of which involved the neglect of rural women and Gilman's prudishness about sex.

Gilman was a remarkable person who thought the good marriage involved living in an apartment or boarding out. Here is her comment on her second marriage: "We had 'a home without a kitchen,' all the privacy and comfort, none of the work and care—except for beds and a little cleaning." Her middle-class, evolutionary pseudosocialism was as relevant to the working-class (and nonurban) woman as the idea of a coup d'etat to black sharecroppers in Georgia. But she did provide the basic intellectual captial for the feminist movement as it entered the new industrial society, and she had a refreshing sense of honesty and of her own limits. She terminated her magazine, accurately called *The Forerunner*, after seven years (in 1918) with this remark: "I had said all I had to say."

Not so with President Cleveland. He kept repeating the few things on his mind (and acting on them) until he lost control of a deeply divided party and country. His younger sister was known for "a pre-disposition to women's rights," but Cleveland concentrated on gold, property rights, and a rather subtly imperial foreign policy.

As with other urban leaders, the depression extended and intensified Cleveland's understanding of the importance of exports to the functioning of the American economy. Agricultural businessmen (including Alliance and Populist leaders) had been making that analysis ever since the major depression of the 1870s, but not many industrial spokesmen had stressed the issue until Blaine made it a central part of his political strategy. He sought to build a coalition of farmers and workers under the leadership of urban Republicans, who would control and direct the emerging industrial system.

Blaine's policy involved the negotiation of a network of reciprocal trade treaties designed to open foreign markets for American exports in return for lowering the tariff on related imports. After winning a bitter fight with the high tariff forces within the Republican party led by Congressman William McKinley of Ohio, Blaine put that strategy into operation in 1890–1891. It did expand the market for some exports and in the process attracted the support of an increasing number of western farmers.

CLEVELAND STANDS PAT

Cleveland took a different approach. He was an orthodox free trader who emphasized lowering the tariff on raw materials. That policy, he argued, would lower production costs for American industry, thereby enabling the manufacturers to expand their exports by decreasing their prices. They would in turn increase their production and that would create a larger domestic market for the farmers. As president, Cleveland initiated a campaign to secure the appropriate legislation from the Congress.

He might have had some success in quieter times and if Blaine's policy had not proved effective. But the great turmoil generated by the shift to industrialism, which had been intensified by the massive depression, made it all but impossible to deal with such a central issue in a rational manner. In addition, Cleveland had depleted his patronage fund in fighting his war against silver, and so the members of the House and the Senate squabbled and clawed without effective supervision.

The bill finally maneuvered through the House in 1894 by Congressman William A. Wilson of West Virginia did bear some resemblance to Cleveland's basic idea, but it also antagonized many groups. The American producers of the raw materials placed on the free list were angry, other interests complained that the tariff should have been reduced on other items, and the provision for an income tax tacked on by reformers infuriated some middle-class businessmen as well as the giant industrialists and bankers.

The Senate then proceeded to wreck even that attempt to deal with the issue. As for Cleveland, he did not use his veto power to force the Congress into more responsible action and made no effort to preserve the reciprocity provisions of the Blaine-McKinley legislation. The loss of the markets that had been gained in that way further upset the farmers and urban businessmen, and the reformers erupted in anger when (in 1895) the Supreme Court invalidated the income tax part of the law.

The president gained some temporary support by opposing the various ensuing demonstrations that sought to dramatize the need for relief and positive programs of change. Most middle- and upper-class people were fearful of social unrest and hence were inclined to interpret honest anger—and new ideas—as symptoms of revolution. In truth, as demonstrated by a study of one group in San Francisco, the protesters were typically American: 218 Republicans, 196 Democrats, 240 Populists, and 92 of vague ideological dispositions.

The most famous march was headed by Jacob S. Coxey. He and his followers set out from Ohio to deliver complaints and positive proposals to the government in Washington. They undoubtedly stole a few chickens and pigs on their way to the capital in the spring of 1894, but the saddest part of the story was the failure of anyone in power to take them seriously. Even the Populists looked the other way. But the implementation of Coxey's demand for public works programs could have eased the painful costs of the depression.

Cleveland chose instead to concentrate on maintaining the gold standard in the face of its critics and the economic crisis by government borrowing from the big investment bankers. He went three times to the financiers (1894–1895), who on one of the transactions made a profit of at least $1.5 million. Populists and other reformers were outraged, and the president's narrow conservatism steadily eroded the support he had won through his opposition to organized labor during the strike against the industrial fiefdom dominated by George M. Pullman.

Beginning in 1864, Pullman had devised and patented cars and other devices that enabled railroad passengers to sleep and eat in comfort on long journeys, and those improvements earned him a fortune. He also controlled his labor force as barons once dominated their serfs. His so-called model workers' town was in truth a nightmare—no pets, no gardens, and no griping—that produced additional profits from rent, utilities, and services. Ohio industrialist Mark Hanna, who enjoyed generally good labor relations, summed up the attitude of more enlightened businessmen: "Oh, hell!" he spat out in disgust. "Model——! . . . . A man who won't meet his men halfway is a goddamn fool!"

The workers struck in May, 1894, just after the furor over Coxey's Army, and asked for help from railroad laborers. Debs was initially sympathetic though cautious, but his devastating report to the ARU on conditions at Pullman moved the convention to vote to strike. The union handled mail cars and protected property in the great Chicago rail yards and asked Pullman to arbitrate. The master refused. The railroad owners next won a court injunction (July 2) forbidding interference with interstate commerce. Cleveland and Attorney General Richard Olney then responded quickly and favorably to their request for federal troops without any discussion with Illinois governor Altgeld.

The president, who considered the strike a very "ugly labor disturbance," and Altgeld, who was a vigorous and ambitious reformer, clashed bitterly. The strikers, infuriated by the government's collusion with the owners, attacked railroad property and fought policemen and troops. The strike was broken, Debs was imprisoned, and the union was destroyed. In the immediate aftermath, Cleveland won praise from property conscious members of the middle and upper classes. But the outcome alienated many workers and reformers and on balance further weakened his control of the Democratic party and the country.

He also lost support by his handling of foreign affairs and because his domestic proposals failed to alleviate the depression—or provide significant relief. Many agrarian (and some urban) reformers were incensed over his policy toward the Hawaiian Revolution. The long-established interest and influence of Americans in the islands had been strengthened and extended by the treaty of 1887, which renewed earlier reciprocity agreements and gave the United States the right to construct a major naval base at Pearl Harbor. In that same year the Americans who dominated the sugar industry overthrew the native leadership and established a constitutional monarchy under their influence.

They were hurt badly, however, by the competition encouraged by the free sugar provision of the McKinley-Blaine tariff of 1890 and by the accession to the throne of Queen Liliuokalani. She moved quickly (January 13, 1893) to reestablish native and personal domination. Encouraged by the Harrison administration and aided by the landing of marines (ostensibly to protect life and property), the Americans seized power on January 16 and were recognized by Washington the following day.

They promptly asked to be annexed, though many large planters preferred a protectorate in order to maintain their supply of cheap Oriental labor. President Harrison sent the treaty to the Senate on February 15, but Democrats stalled the issue until Cleveland was inaugurated. He promptly withdrew the treaty on March 9 and ordered an investigation of the revolution. Concluding that the use of the marines had been improper and that annexation was not necessary in this particular case, Cleveland undertook to maintain American domination in a more subtle fashion.

His proposal to restore the queen and the constitution of 1887 would very probably have accomplished that objective. But it was quixotic and impractical unless he was willing to use force against the planter regime. That he refused to do, and he ultimately (on August 7, 1893) recognized their reconstituted government as the Republic of Hawaii. In the meantime, however, his proposal to put the queen back on the throne outraged many agrarians and other reformers.

Their expansion was a blend of marketplace economics and global reformism. "Give the Old Pumpkin Head Hell!" and "Come down on him like a hawk!" were two of the milder reactions. Such militants were not appeased by Cleveland's effective intervention during 1894 against a Brazilian revolution that threatened American economic interests, by Secretary of State Walter Gresham's quietly successful anti-British maneuvers in Nicaragua, or by the president's strong support for a big navy.

The Hawaiian fiasco added more volatile fuel to the anti-Cleveland inferno that had erupted around his antisilver and antilabor policies and his close ties to the bankers. Combined with the continuing severity of the depression, those factors produced a stunning Republican victory in the 1894 congressional elections. McKinley was a key figure in the resurgence. He spoke 23 times in one day in Nebraska during his campaigning, which took him into the South as well as from New England to.Colorado. The Democrats failed to win a single national office in 24 states, and the final tally was 245 seats to 104 seats in the House and 44 to 39 in the Senate. The Populists barely held the congressional seats they had won in 1892, and they lost ground in the South, where conservative Democrats used fraud, intimidation, and racism to demolish the reformers.

Cleveland was done, though he did gain some temporary popularity in 1895 through his nationalistic confrontation with Great Britain during the Venezuelan boundary crisis. The dispute involved the ownership of Point Barima, which controlled the mouth of the Orinoco River and hence economic and military access to the interior of Venezuela. London claimed the area as part of British Guiana and Venezuela had appealed to the United States for support as early as the 1870s.

No significant action was taken, however, until Cleveland announced in December, 1894, that he would try to persuade England to arbitrate the issue. The obvious political consideration—to weaken the Populists with a show of militance—no doubt contributed to the president's action, but the basic explanation lies in the expansionist spirit that had been increasing since the late 1880s and that had been intensified by the depression. Congressmen Leonidas F. Livingston of Georgia and Robert R. Hitt of Illinois made the point with bipartisan bluntness: "This relates to a matter on our continent. Our trade and other relations with those people are involved in this settlement."

Cleveland and Richard Olney (who had replaced Gresham as secretary of state) were adamant: "Today the United States is practically sovereign on this continent, and its fiat is law upon the subjects to which it confines its interposition." British pressure on Venezuela was a violation of the Monroe Doctrine, they added, and hence the United States demanded arbitration. When the English refused, Cleveland asked the Congress to create a commission to settle the matter, adding that it would be "the duty of the United States to resist by every means in its power" any refusal by the British to honor the decision.

That language provoked a war scare among some conservatives, but most Populists and other critics discounted the possibility. "The only war that Mr. Cleveland can engender," scoffed one, "is a war led by the bankers of Wall Street against the commercial and agricultural interests of this country." Watson was derisive: "The war scare is a fake." Henry Demarest Lloyd and others were ready for war to expand trade, to extend liberty, and to weaken Britain as the bastion of the gold standard, but they expected no firm action. They were correct. Troubled by a challenge from Germany in Africa (and from other countries in the Middle East), Britain quietly accepted the ultimate decision of the commission to award Point Barima to Venezuela.

Cleveland's policy toward the Cuban Revolution that erupted in February, 1895, sustained the opposition to his foreign policy. Internal conditions under Spanish rule caused the uprising, but it was triggered by the end of the prosperity which developed on the basis of the reciprocal trade treaty that had been negotiated under the provisions of the McKinley-Blaine tariff. That gave the Cubans a market for their sugar, and western farmers (and others) in turn expanded their exports to the island. The Wilson tariff terminated that relationship and the Cuban economy collapsed.

Agricultural businessmen—large and small—promptly opened a campaign to drive Spain from the island and reestablish the markets. Their attacks on Cleveland clearly displayed the imperial outlook that was developing among many different groups of Americans: free Cuba for markets and to strike a blow for world reform. The mushrooming silverites added that the white metal would open the door to economic supremacy. Bryan was ecstatic: "A silver standard . . . would make us the trading center of all the silver-using countries of the world, and those countries contain far more than one-half of the world's population."

Cleveland instead tried to help Spain repress the rebellion. He ignored the congressional demand (February–April, 1896) to grant belligerent status to the Cuban revolutionaries and to put heavy pressure on Spain to grant independence. The only questions at that point involved who would replace Cleveland as the party's leader and whether or not the reform Democrats could attract enough Populists to win the election.

A tiny group of Cleveland loyalists—the Gold Democrats—made a futile effort to preserve the past. They were overwhelmed, along with others, by the silver advocates. By the time they gathered for their convention in Chicago on July 7, 1896, however, the more perceptive reformers in the party knew that they faced a tough opponent as well as internal difficulties. For the previous month the Republicans had nominated McKinley, who had in turn picked the shrewd and effective Hanna as his campaign manager.

THE CLIMACTIC CAMPAIGN OF 1896

The two men made an impressive combination. McKinley was a late-nineteenth-century man who understood the need to impose a sense of order and direction upon the new industrial system. While they had disagreed on specifics, McKinley had always taken Blaine as his idol and his model. He understood the basic changes that were taking place, dealt fairly with labor, viewed market expansion as the key to agricultural—and the general—welfare, made a public protest against the discrimination against blacks in the South as early as 1888, and was a deceptively effective politician in transcending localism and particularism by arranging compromises designed to build a larger system.

Hanna first met McKinley when the latter was defending union labor, and both respected the working men and women who enabled the system to function—including those who worked the land. Hanna was the kind of broad-gauged capitalist who made the Carnegies, the Rockefellers, the Vanderbilts, and the Fricks of his time shrivel into narrow profit mongers. He was a tough, pithy, candid, cigar-smoking, cane-swinging advocate of organizing the new industrial political economy on the basis of a noncondescending paternalism. Big-corporation capitalism meant big everything else, and hence those who wanted a fair shake should organize themselves and confront power with power.

Ambitious and active in politics since 1880, Hanna was an easy target for cartoonists. They drew him—as they drew J. P. Morgan—as a potbelly covered with dollar signs. McKinely knew better, and he agreed with Hanna's axiom: Never trust a man who is nothing but a businessman in politics—he has no sense of the system. The two men worked so effectively together that they nearly lost it all when the Republican convention of 1892 almost nominated McKinley. As Hanna said, "My God, William, that was a damned close squeak!" His point, of course, was that winning the nomination in 1892 might easily have bankrupted their future before it arrived.

McKinley was always in charge of strategy; indeed, simply always in charge. He was in truth the first charismatic leader of the new system: handsome, courteous, knowledgeable, and ruthless when necessary. McKinley put together a classic package in marketplace politics for the campaign of 1896: gold for the conservative metropolitans and the property conscious middle class, an honest commitment to bimetallism for the marginal silverites, respect and a protective tariff for workers of all kinds, and reciprocity treaties to expand overseas markets. Hanna maneuvered it past the metropolitan diehards during the convention without losing the support of skeptical reformers. Neither the Democrats nor the Populists had comparable leadership, and they underrated the similar appeal of such imaginative conservatism.

The only meaningful alternative to the incipient corporatism of McKinley and Hanna would have been a nationally organized movement for socialism. That did not exist. For that matter, the McKinley-Hanna approach was the first significant political expression of Bellamy's pseudosocialism—in truth, state capitalism—that would later flower in Theodore Roosevelt's New Nationalism, Woodrow Wilson's New Freedom, and Franklin Delano Roosevelt's New Deal.

The Democrats nominated Bryan on the fifth ballot. He was just 36, "a tall, slender, handsome fellow who looked like a young divine." Another young man who campaigned devotedly for him remarked many years later that "Bryan had scrambled eggs for brains." He was not wholly serious, of course, but the judgment does provide an insight into the nature of Bryan's mind. He had all the virtues and limitations of single-mindedness.

He was a Fundamentalist in religion *(the whale did literally swallow Jonah)*, a silverite expansionist, and a spellbinding spokesman for the noble but no longer relevant ideal of a Jeffersonian-Jacksonian community of small businessmen. Bryan was not a reactionary. He simply did not understand that his kind of conservatism was no longer appropriate to the American reality. He was perfectly correct in asserting, in his famous "Cross of Gold" speech that won him the nomination, that the farmer was a businessman, but he failed to understand that the agricultural businessman was becoming a worker who had to forge an alliance with the factory laborer.

The Populists met last on July 22 in St. Louis. They were perplexed, frustrated, angry, unruly, noble, and racked by internal differences. The reformers who opposed making silver the main issue were beaten by others who argued that a victory with Bryan would open the way to other changes. A bit of managerial chicanery helped their cause, but it did not determine the outcome. No Populist could stomach Bryan's Democratic running mate, Arthur Sewell, a conservative easterner, and hence they nominated Watson for vice president. It was a last salute to him and to the original nature of Populism.

The campaign was a parody and a preview. Bryan mimicked the national tours of Harrison in 1891 and McKinley in 1894. He began in Madison Square Garden, went on to Yale University, and finally ended (nearly exhausted) in Minnesota after speaking in 27 states. It was a brave and compelling effort, but it failed. Bryan's only message was silver, and that appealed to few of the urban workers he had to attract in order to win. Watson sulked, becoming each day more of a traditional southerner.

McKinley stayed home. First he wrote a pamphlet known formally as his acceptance speech. It was a reasoned and subtle appeal to crucial groups: markets for agricultural and urban businessmen through reciprocity, a commitment to gold while negotiating for the international remonetization of silver, security for urban workers through tariff protection, and economic recovery and ordered progress for all. Then he settled into the routine of explaining and amplifying those positions to the hundreds of groups that came from all over the country to visit him on his front porch in Canton, Ohio. It was an effective strategy, for although the people trampled his lawn, they returned home as excited and enthusiastic supporters in their own communities.

Hanna managed the rest of the campaign with flair and ruthless efficiency ("Stop blowing and saw wood"). He picked able and dedicated assistants like Charles G. Dawes in Illinois, and collected vast amounts of money to support their efforts with propaganda and hoopla (music, straw hats, and pretty girls). He was thus ready and able to exploit the late-summer upturn in agricultural prices and exports that gave substance to one major campaign theme—McKinley as The Advance Agent of Prosperity.

The McKinley-Hanna operation was successful because it held labor support in urban areas and attracted farmers in crucial midwestern states. McKinley's margin was 5 percent of the popular vote, the largest since 1872, and he entered office with a strong national power base despite a potentially difficult situation in the Senate (34 Democrats, 6 Silverites, 5 Populists, and 1 Independent). His record as an effective moderate suggested that he might well be able to begin creating a social balance within the new political economy, and his victory at the head of an urban-rural coalition seemed likely to restore the confidence that was necessary for economic recovery.

If President McKinley had lived to complete his second term, it is quite possible that he would now be considered an important figure in the reform coalition that dominated American politics during the first years of the twentieth century. Robert M. LaFollette of Wisconsin, one one of the key leaders of that alliance, entered politics as a McKinley supporter and later remarked that he "always felt that McKinley represented the newer view" and "was generally on the side of the public and against private interests."

The president, along with Hanna and other such upper-class leaders, was concerned to provide the kind of leadership that would reunite the country on the basis of fairer shares for all. He understood that he could use the continuing pressure from workers, farmers, and members of the middle class against old-line conservatives, and he counted on those upper-class leaders like Hanna who recognized the need to roll with the sea of change and provide reforms from the top in order to forestall more drastic changes from below.

The defeat of Bryan in 1896 did not end the movement by state legislatures to regulate business. The number of state laws dealing with corporations and trusts in manufacturing and transportation, for example, continued to increase: 29 in 1896, 62 in 1897, 32 in 1898, 100 in 1899, 22 in 1900, and 112 in 1901. Legislation concerning banks and other financial organizations climbed from 83 in 1895 to 128 in 1897, 59 in 1898, 75 in 1899, and 86 in 1901. Led by such men as Frederick L. Cutting of Massachusetts, Zeno M. Host of Wisconsin, and Rean E. Folk of Tennessee, the movement to regulate insurance companies was even more impressive. That campaign produced 130 laws in 1895, 135 in 1897, 162 in 1899, and 168 in 1901. The states also began to extend the practice, begun by Massachusetts in 1862, of taxing insurance companies.

The courts slowly responded to that pressure. The Supreme Court refused, in 1895 (*U.S.* v. *E. C. Knight Co.*), to interfere with the operations of a firm that enjoyed a monopoly in the manufacture of sugar. But in 1897 it ruled, in *U.S.* v. *The Trans-Mississippi Freight Association*, that the 18 railways that operated as a pool were violating the Sherman Anti-Trust Act in fixing rates. During the next year, moreover, the Court extended that approach in an important decision. In *Holden* v. *Hardy* it validated a Utah law limiting the hours that men had to work in mines. In doing so, the Court explicitly held that the theoretically unlimited freedom of contract, which favored the owner or capitalist, had to be modified when there was a significant inequality of bargaining power between the parties.

The Congress also began to act. Several important moves came during the summer of 1898, partially in response to the Republican realization (intensified by Democratic gains in the off-year election) that the party had to react to the protests throughout the country. First came the creation of the United States Industrial Commission to investigate the new political economy and to recommend ways of regulating and controlling its operation for the general welfare. It immediately began a serious study, based on hearings and other research throughout the country, that exerted a continuing influence on the reform movement after its report was published in 1901.

The Erdman Act of 1898 created a system of mediation designed to prevent another railroad crisis like the one caused by the Pullman strike and also made it illegal for employers to require from workers a promise to refuse to join a union (the notorious "yellow-dog" contract) as a condition of employment—though the Supreme Court struck that down in 1908. Another reform measure was the bankruptcy law of July 1, 1898, which made it easier for small- and medium-sized operators to deal with failure in the marketplace by enabling an entrepreneur to declare voluntary bankruptcy.

Combined with the return of prosperity, the enthusiasm for imperial expansion, and McKinley's own effectiveness as a political operator, those positive responses to reform agitation carried the Republicans to victory in the election of 1900. The challenge that McKinley faced in trying to deal with the problem of unifying the country in the face of opposition from the Left and Right was probably better illustrated by the fight within his own party than by the campaign against the Democrats. A number of traditional eastern Republicans, typified by Thomas C. Platt, boss of the party in New York, had justifiably never trusted McKinley's commitment to their hard-line conservatism. But they faced increasing pressure from more sophisticated business leaders and perceptive upper-class aristocrats like Theodore Roosevelt.

Roosevelt had not been particularly bothersome during his short term as New York state assemblyman (1882–1884). But that experience had alerted him to the need for changes, and he was more reformist in his unsuccessful campaign for mayor of New York City in 1886. He maintained that outlook after he became the United States civil service commissioner (1889–1895) and head of the board of New York police commissioners (1895–1897).

Then, after his service in the war against Spain, he was elected governor of New York in 1899, and his reform efforts thoroughly alarmed Platt and other established bosses. Their strategy was to nominate Roosevelt as vice-presidential candidate in 1900. The ploy was obvious: get him out of the way in New York and at the same time sidetrack him to oblivion. The important point is that McKinley accepted Roosevelt's increasing propensity for reform.

The Democrats failed to mount an effective campaign against the McKinley-Roosevelt ticket. Bryan had an appealing running mate in Adlai E. Stevenson, the progressive governor of Illinois, but they did not seize and hold the initiative. Bryan was unable to make an effective issue out of imperial expansion and did not rally the reform groups to his tattered banners of silver and antimonopoly. McKinley won by more than one million popular votes, and by 292 to 155 in the electoral count, and the Republicans took control of both houses of the Congress.

The president moved quickly to maintain prosperity by overseas economic expansion through reciprocity treaties, and he supported the move by Hanna and like-minded businessmen and labor union spokesmen to provide moderate reform leadership for the new political economy. Those men differed among themselves about how much reform was necessary or desirable and about how rapidly it could be introduced, but they were agreed on the general proposition that moderates had to take the lead if further unrest and radical measures were to be avoided.

Some of them, for example, were members of the Social Reform Club of New York City, which in 1898 came out in favor of automatic compensation to workers for industrial injuries. Others were labor leaders like Gompers and other AF of L spokesmen; John Mitchell of the United Mine Workers (UMW); and the heads of the railway brotherhoods, who initially opposed such compensation laws. Despite their differences, they nevertheless discussed such issues, as during the Saratoga Conference of 1898, called to arrange a compromise in support of overseas economic expansion.

They next planned (1899) the Chicago Conference on Trusts. Jane Addams and other more militant reformers sat at the same tables with Hanna and Gompers, but the meeting represented the efforts of upper-class leaders and their allies to maintain their control of the corporate system. The Industrial Commission's preliminary recommendation in 1900 that the federal government should establish a licensing system to control the big corporations spurred such men to action, and behind Hanna's leadership they formalized their loose association in 1901 as the National Civic Federation (NCF).

Their objective was to rationalize and reform and thereby sustain what banker V. Everitt May called "the industrial and commercial structure which is the indisputable shelter of us all." To accomplish that objective, Gompers was willing to work with utility magnate Samuel Insull, George W. Perkins of the House of Morgan, and other key leaders of the corporate community. The consensus was perhaps best illustrated in the organization of the federation's Industrial Department, the central committee created to deal with economic programs and policies. Hanna was made chairman, with Gompers and the banker Oscar Straus selected as vice-chairmen.

McKinley's effort to unify and rationalize the new political economy was terminated on September 6, 1901. He was shot by Leon Czolgosz, an anarchist who acted in desperate opposition to the many inequities of the massive and centralized industrial system and in the conviction that neither the president nor other leaders would make significant changes. Though he rallied briefly, McKinley died on September 14, and old-style conservatives like Platt were confronted with an aristocratic reformer as the leader of their party as well as president.

Roosevelt quickly established himself as a dramatic and often effective upper-class leader. He understood the basic nature of the new corporate system, realized that it required strong and centralized control, recognized the need for various kinds of reforms, and had a firm grasp of the fundamental relationship between domestic and foreign policies. He was, indeed, a conscious and often exuberant imperialist who argued that the United States could not continue as a capitalist political economy unless it moved to control the world marketplace.

His first annual message as president, for example, in December, 1901, stated and developed the need for foreign markets in masterly fashion. America's recent and "highly complex industrial development . . . brings us face to face . . . ," he began, "with very serious social problems." The corporation had asserted its power over the individual businessman as well as the worker. Even so, the corporations had to be treated with "caution" because they were the key to taking "the commanding position in the international business world," a place of "utmost importance" for the future welfare and social harmony of the United States.

Hence it would be necessary, from time to time, to use force against "barbarous or semibarbarous peoples." The world, Roosevelt concluded, must be intergrated into American industrialism. He was doing little more than summarizing an adaptation of an argument that had been developed and expounded by most Americans—agrarian as well as urban—since the first days of the Republic. It had been adjusted to industrialism after the Civil War and in that form had induced—and pressured—McKinley to accept a policy of active imperialism as an integral part of his program to control the new corporate system. Such a combination of reform and expansion was not unique to the United States, but Americans had embraced it with a special enthusiasm. Thus it is necessary to review that process in more detail.

EXPLORATORY READING

The following volumes offer stimulating introductions to the architectural and urban problems that were dramatized by the Chicago World's Fair. The second one is also useful in connection with the Great Strike of 1894.

S. Bass, *The Urban Wilderness: A History of the American City* (1972)

S. Buder, *Pullman: An Experiment in Industrial Order and Community Planning, 1880–1930* (1967)

C. N. Glaab and A. T. Brown, *A History of Urban America* (1967)

C. Tunnard and H. H. Reed, *American Skyline* (1953)

The best sources for the depression are the newspapers and magazines of the time, but for useful analysis consult:

D. R. Dewey, *Financial History of the United States* (1918)

R. Fels, *American Business Cycles* (1959)

M. Friedman and A. J. Schwartz, *A Monetary History of the United States* (1963)

J. A. Schumpeter, *History of Economic Analysis* (1954)

Schumpeter's book will probably strike you as terribly theoretical, and it is, but he had a feel for the dynamics of modern capitalism that was exceptional. Stick with him, and he will tell you much of what you need to know.

Three different approaches to the labor movement are offered by:

L. Adamic, *Dynamite, The Story of Class Violence in America* (1931)

P. S. Foner, *History of the Labor Movement in the United States* (1947 and continuing)

P. Taft, *The A. F. of L. in the Time of Gompers* (1957)

The unhappy story of what happened to the blacks in the South is best told in two volumes by C. Vann Woodward, an extraordinary historian:

Tom Watson (1938)

The Strange Career of Jim Crow (1974)

One can get a feel for the many facets of the protest and reform movement through these volumes:

A. G. Bogue, *Money at Interest: The Farm Mortgage on the Middle Border* (1955)

D. Brown, *The Gentle Tamers: Women of the Old Wild West* (1974)

J. T. Ellis, *American Catholicism* (1969)

J. S. Haller, Jr., *Outcasts from Evolution* (1971)

O. Handlin, *The Uprooted* (1951)

J. Higham, *Strangers in the Land* (1955)

M. A. Jones, *American Immigration* (1960)

J. R. Marcus (Ed.), *Critical Studies in American Jewish History* (1971)

H. F. May, *Protestant Churches and Industrial America* (1949)

M. and L. White, *The Intellectual Versus the City* (1962)

The following books offer various approaches and interpretations concerning the effort to assert some control over the system:

P. E. Coletta, *William Jennings Bryan* (1964)

H. Croly, *Marcus Alonzo Hanna* (1912)

P. W. Glad, *McKinley, Bryan and the People* (1964)

J. R. Hollingsworth, *The Whirligig of Politics* (1963)

R. J. Jensen, *The Winning of the Midwest* (1971)

S. L. Jones, *The Presidential Election of 1896* (1964)

H. S. Merrill, *Bourbon Democracy of the Middle West* (1953)

A. Nevins, *Grover Cleveland* (1932)

If by now you have gone to the library or bookstore and worked your way into some of the books that I have suggested or—better yet—into some of the documents, you will have come to understand two important things about these lists of books.

1. I am skimming the surface in the same way that you skim a rock across the pond—plink-plink-plink—and finally PLOP. I cannot list every relevant book, but many others are listed in the volumes I have mentioned, so the rest is up to you.

2. Most of the books that I suggest you read are written by people who disagree, in one way or another, with what I have to say. I think that is the way it ought to be: I give you my view, and then send you to others who disagree with me. *You do your own history.* History is a way of learning about ourselves as human beings, not something to be memorized.

2 IMPERIALISM AS AN INHERENT PART OF THE NEW POLITICAL ECONOMY

ROOSEVELT had been a vigorous expansionist throughout the 1890s, and in the process he exerted a significant influence on the adoption of an imperial policy. Indeed, he symbolized many of the forces that made imperialism an inherent part of the new political economy. But neither he nor any other individual leader determined the outcome. That was the result of forces beyond the control of any single person. For that matter, the evolution of American imperialism offers a good example of why most historians and other students of human affairs are periodically attracted to the idea of historical inevitability.

It is conceivable that the United States could have developed a different foreign policy as it became the world's most powerful industrial economy, but its traditions, current ideas, and the nature of the new economy made that highly improbable. The reformers were too conservative and the conservatives too unimaginative to embrace anti-imperialism. As that judgment implies, the reformers played a central role in the evolution of American imperialism.

American society was from the beginning vigorously expansionist. The colonies vied militantly over their conflicting claims to vast western lands, almost everyone joined the campaign to push the First Americans ever farther westward (or to kill them), and one of the first military efforts of the Revolution was an attempt to conquer Canada. The political theory underpinning the Constitution, moreover, involved a sophisticated argument that the survival of republican government depended upon expansion. Religious zeal and a secular sense of uniqueness reinforced that theory and generated great psychological intensity. Combined with the more mundane but viscerally powerful factors of escapism, acquisitive ambition, and greed, those ideas and feelings led on to the ruthless conquest of a continent within three generations.

The process acquired a momentum and emotion that carried through the Civil War. And the self-righteousness generated by the conviction of having purified the country of its one flaw—chattel slavery—intensified the sense of mission to extend the virtues of the unique and perfect American Revolution to all mankind. In a similar way, the antebellum economic pressures for expansion were undiminished by the holocaust and were shortly augmented by impulses supplied by industrial and financial groups.

Surely the most interesting—and perhaps the most significant—development involved the way that agricultural businessmen shifted the emphasis of their policy from the acquisition of more land to the opening of ever more overseas markets for their growing surpluses of food and fiber. As is usually the case, there had been earlier indications of what was becoming the new pattern. Mutations—"breakthroughs"—are the sustenance of our human ego (collectively as well as individually), but they are so rare as to tempt one to use the term *unique.* So, while it may deflate our American ego, the truth of it is that the imperialism we developed between 1865 and 1900 was not a breakthrough. Not only had it happened elsewhere, as in England and France, but it was simultaneously emerging in Germany and Japan. It was neither an aberration nor something forced upon Americans by the rest of the world. We can, ironically, take all the credit.

During the years between the end of the Revolution and the sophisticated and nonviolent revolution that replaced the Articles of Confederation with the Constitution (1783–1787), western farmers threatened to secede unless the eastern leaders who were making policy used the power of the government to force Spain to open New Orleans for the free passage of their surplus grain and meat to the markets of the world. It was a tense confrontation that previewed the Civil War.

The descendants of those people became the agricultural businessmen who demanded new and larger foreign markets during the 1870s and 1880s. Nobody went West to contemplate nature or to explore the inner recesses of the soul. People went West to escape the real, imagined, or potential constrictions of society in the East—and to make money. Those two urges—to be free from the demands and responsibilities of a maturing system and to turn a profit—were the determining elements in the foreign policy of the farmers who constituted the majority of Americans as an imperial policy was devised and adopted.

Those people were also viscerally aware of three other elementary facts: their labor fed the cities, their labor produced the surpluses that generated much of the capital for industrialization, and yet they earned far less than those who controlled and directed the emerging system. That knowledge was the engine of their rising concern with reform *and* markets. They wanted more justice and larger profits; it was a simple and powerful combination.

The central importance of foreign markets was dramatized for the farmers by their experience during the depression of the 1870s. Their rapidly rising productivity was beginning to enable them to undersell European competitors before that crisis occurred, and then an unusual combination of events enabled them to dominate British and continental markets. An extended period of wet, cold weather, combined with various plant and animal diseases, almost destroyed European agriculture, and those factors created a vast demand that the Americans were eager and able to supply.

The gigantic expansion of agricultural exports played a vital role in recovering from the depression at home and reinforced the feeling among the farmers that they were crucial to the well-being of the political economy. It likewise underscored the existing argument that exports were the key to prosperity. The experience also convinced key industrial and financial leaders of the validity of that analysis.

Most of those urban spokesmen initially applied the interpretation at the general level: agricultural exports were central to the process of industrialization. But a few of them, particularly David A. Wells, a government intellectual who enjoyed considerable prestige among policy makers, placed exports at the heart of the problem of preserving social and political stability in a time of fundamental change. Wells warned even before the depression that "the poor of the United States under the existing system tend to grow poorer" and concluded that the choice was between ever expanding markets or major social unrest. And still another group, typified by the Rockefellers, was learning that rising surpluses posed the same problem for industrial corporations as for farm businessmen.

Those direct and indirect economic pressures for an expansionist policy were intensified when Europeans retaliated against the influx of American exports. Their tariffs, embargoes, and other measures were designed to protect their own farmers (and decrease the related social unrest in countries like Austria). Combined with the improvement of the climate and other natural forces, such legislation ended the export bonanza enjoyed by American farmers. They in turn began to view those countries, such as England and Germany, as an important part of their difficulties and to agitate for the opening of new markets.

Great Britain bore the brunt of the criticism and anger. Part of that, of course, was a projection of the traditional distrust of London. But it was intensified by the argument about silver. Agricultural leaders came increasingly to feel that the demonetization of silver favored Britain in the international marketplace at their expense and that the Americans who favored the single gold standard were intellectual and economic allies of European conservatives.

In this fashion, the forces of nationalism and reform became forever entangled in the development of an imperial policy. For, according to that argument, prosperity at home became dependent upon using American power to reform the international economic system as well as the domestic political economy. The agriculturalists had thus created an extremely potent combination of economic interest, economic analysis, reform ideology, and political and psychological activism.

That was reinforced, during the late 1880s and early 1890s, by several other developments. The missionary, reforming tradition, which had always been very strong in American society, was reinvigorated by urban spokesmen as well as by the farmers. The philosopher John Fiske had provided one such theory, first in a series of lectures at Harvard in 1869 and then in a book entitled *Outlines of Cosmic Philosophy*. He mixed Christianity and ethnic nationalism with Darwin's theory of evolution and concluded that God was directing the global triumph of Anglo-Saxon institutions and leadership. Fiske may have influenced some leaders like President Harrison through personal associations, and his book, which went through 15 editions after publication in 1874, carried his ideas to a great many Americans.

The Reverend Josiah Strong, a proselytising Congregationalist, was even more effective. He warned that the end of free land, or the frontier, would intensify social unrest and called for an ethical revival that would purify America and rejuvenate the world. Published in 1885, and probably benefiting from the concern created by the depression, his book, *Our Country*, became a fantastic best seller. "Does it not look," he concluded, "as if God were not only preparing in our Anglo-Saxon civilization the die with which to stamp the peoples of the earth, but as if He were also massing behind that die the mighty power with which to press it?"

Though he initially affected a smaller group, Alfred Thayer Mahan, the navy's philosophic strategist, complemented Strong's thesis with the argument that the United States Navy should provide the motive power for American expansion. Often misunderstood as simply advocating a big navy, Mahan actually developed a tightly knit adaptation of the mercantilism of the sixteenth and seventeenth centuries to modern conditions. Inherent in his philosophy was a version of the Christian moral obligation to sustain and improve the well-being of the underdeveloped societies. Such welfare depended upon expansion. And proper functioning of the industrial system depended upon foreign markets, for otherwise it would stagnate and suffer major social upheavals.

By using its economic power to build a merchant marine, by acquiring a network of bases, and by constructing a modern navy, the United States could win and hold the necessary markets. This kind of argument had been advanced, in whole or in part, by a good many Americans before Mahan published *The Influence of Sea Power Upon History* in 1890. But his synthesis was dramatic and persuasive, and it caught the attention of the general public and influenced such rising young politicians as Henry Cabot Lodge and Theodore Roosevelt.

And, in an almost eerie coincidence with the panic of 1893, two other intellectuals offered analyses and interpretations of history that not only pointed toward imperialism but also affected the thinking of many Americans. Brooks Adams saw America at the crossroads of world development. His *The Law of Civilization and Decay* (1894) argued that civilization had moved west until it centered in New York and that the United States must control Asia or lose out to Russia or Japan. Not surprisingly, Adams became a vigorous imperialist—"By God, I like it"—and directly or indirectly influenced men like Roosevelt and McKinley's secretary of state, John Hay.

The other historian was Professor Frederick Jackson Turner of the University of Wisconsin. His argument was less grandiose, but it affected—subtly as well as directly—far more people. Turner's grand analysis of American history (first offered in 1893) came to be called the frontier thesis: The steady westward expansion of the country was what had produced its freedom, prosperity, and welfare. He was not personally as overtly expansionist as Adams, but the imperial implications of his argument exerted a strong influence on the general public—as well as upon Roosevelt and other ambitious young reformers like Thomas Woodrow Wilson (who had studied with Turner at Johns Hopkins University).

Finally, the panic and depression turned ever more urban businessmen toward imperialism. Financiers such as Henry W. Cannon and A. B. Farquhar shared the view of *The Bankers' Magazine* that overseas economic expansion would "keep all our industries permanently employed, as England does, [by] having the world's markets in which to unload any accumulation." Andrew Carnegie and Charles Schwab refined the argument. "The condition of cheap manufacture," Carnegie explained, "is running full." "We are not anxious to sell at low foreign prices," Schwab amplified, "but when our mills are not running steadily we will take anything at any price, even if there is some loss in doing so, in order to keep running." When the NAM was organized in January, 1895, for the purpose of such market expansion, its leaders asked McKinley, then governor of Ohio, to keynote their meeting. He responded with a call for a system of reciprocity treaties to open foreign markets and to supply cheap raw materials.

For their part, the agricultural businessmen continued their own campaign. However they differed on other issues, the National Grange, the National Farmers' Congress, and the Farmers' Alliance agreed on the need for the government to help them find, penetrate, and hold new markets. As the Populist Jerry Simpson of Kansas explained, the farmer felt that "the money question is a part of the great question of trade, or so mixed up with it that you can not separate them." The agrarians also felt, as Bryan and others expressed it, that the United States was so strong that it would not have to go to war to achieve such supremacy. A bold policy would be enough.

AMERICA'S PAST IMPERIALISM PREFIGURES ITS FUTURE IMPERIALISM

That assumption, taken as an article of faith despite all the evidence to the contrary from even its own experience, gave American imperialism a certain kind of quixotic charm for many years. And since it was shared by most urbanites as well as agriculturalists, it engendered an overpowering propensity to blame other societies for any ultimate need to resort to force to accomplish America's self-defined objectives. That process was clearly revealed during the crisis that developed around the Cuban Revolution of 1895 and concurrent events in Asia. While it may seem strange that American policy makers viewed Cuba and China as part of the same imperial problem, there were many historical connections. Indeed, the events of the 1890s offer a classic example of how the past does indeed prefigure the future.

Americans had their eye on Cuba even during the colonial era. As for John Quincy Adams, who belatedly became a powerful antiimperialist, he could never quite agree to let Cuba go its own way. And Henry Clay, in some respects the most eloquent nineteenth-century spokesman for the right of revolutionary self-determination, always insisted that Cuba was the exception that proved the principle. Americans did not talk in that way about *acquiring* China, but they very quickly came to view themselves as having a special and extensive role in the future of The Ancient Kingdom. China offered vast economic opportunities and at the same time posed a major challenge for secular and Christian missionaries.

The two countries began to come together in the public mind during the 1840s, when a campaign to acquire Cuba coincided with an effort to annex Hawaii as the stepping-stone to China. Then, after the Civil

War, the debate about intervening in Cuba's long revolutionary struggle against Spain (1868–1878) took place in the context of renewed efforts to dominate Hawaii and extend the American presence in China.

The issues converged rapidly after the Hawaiian Revolution of 1893 pushed foreign policy into the center of the struggle to control the emerging industrial system. For, in the midst of the heated debate about how best to dominate Hawaii, the Japanese war against China (1894–1895) posed additional problems for Cleveland and other policy makers. They initially thought that the Japanese victory would further American purposes in China, but it quickly became apparent that Tokyo's action had instead suggested the value of similar interventions to Russia and other European powers.

It suddenly appeared possible—if not probable—that China would be carved into colonies to the exclusion of the United States. Hence Cleveland warned the Japanese to go slow, asserted the American right to "equal and liberal trading advantages," and doubled the American fleet in Chinese waters. Those actions previewed the mature and vigorous imperialism that emerged during the next few years.

The process coalesced around the Cuban Revolution that erupted in 1895 in the midst of the Asian troubles. Cleveland's initial response was to use the threat of American intervention to force the Spanish to do whatever was necessary to repress the Cubans. Whatever his other limitations, Cleveland was a rather astute expansionist who understood that it was neither necessary nor particularly desirable to annex a country when it could be brought into the American system through other means. And he realized that Madrid did not want to lose Havana: there was too much profit and prestige involved. Hence he looked forward to a Spanish victory that would leave Cuba open to American economic power and at the same time closed to the influence of, or dominance by, a strong European power.

For an imperialist, that was an ideal solution: effective control and rewards without any troublesome political responsibilities or ideological contradictions between professions of liberty and realities of empire.

But Cleveland encountered two difficulties. The Spanish government, racked by domestic unrest, proved powerless to defeat the able and dedicated Cubans, and agrarian and urban reformers in the United States steadily increased their pressures for military intervention. The critics were seeking the same solution desired by Cleveland—a Cuba free of effective control by Spain yet open to American domination—but argued that military intervention was necessary.

As a result, in the spring of 1896, Cleveland directed the Navy

Department (a vigorous force for expansion in its own right) to prepare a contingency plan for "a war with Spain." The navy responded with a document dated June 1, 1896, that emphasized "the strategic importance of Manila" as well as the requirements for defeating Spain in Cuba. It was a classic example of imperial logic: since Spain controlled the Philippine Islands as well as Cuba and since America had major interests in China, the intelligent course of action was to acquire control of both island territories to further American interests. Cleveland accepted that strategy in October.

He then went before the Congress and the nation in December, despite his humiliating political defeat in the election of November, and warned Spain that time was running out. The United States had "a concern with [Cuba] which is by no means of a wholly sentimental or philanthropic character." There was "a large pecuniary interest." Those economics, which involved ideas about profits as well as the profits themselves, engaged many farmers as well as manufacturers and bankers. As a result, McKinley came under increasing pressure after his inauguration in March, 1897, to free Cuba and integrate it into the American system.

McKinley was firmly committed to economic expansion. He had made that clear during his campaign and underscored the point in his first address as president: the "end in view," he remarked, is "always to be the opening up of new markets." But he did not want a war, feeling instead that peace would generate recovery from the depression and lead on to American predominance in the world marketplace. With that in mind, he warned Spain in June, 1897, that it was essential to suppress or compromise with the Cubans before he was forced to intervene.

Within three months, however, he met with Assistant Secretary of the Navy Theodore Roosevelt to discuss a long memorandum that argued the necessity of war and the wisdom of taking and retaining the Philippines as part of the campaign to free Cuba. China and Cuba had finally converged in the thinking of American leaders, and key congressmen held a similar conversation with the president after Germany seized Kiachow (in China's Shantung Province) on November 18, 1897. During the same period, urban businessmen organized a lobby, ultimately called the American Asiatic Association, to push the government into more aggressive action in China.

The Populists and other agricultural businessmen shared that concern with Asian markets, but they concentrated on the Cuban side of the imperial equation. Their mounting pressure for intervention in the name of freedom and markets increasingly upset many Republican politicians, who felt that the angry farmers might take control of the government away from McKinley. That fear was reinforced by the newspaper campaign that aroused urban citizens. Hearst and Pulitzer had added drumhead journalism to their attacks on vice and corruption, and neither man was averse to war. They used sexually titillating stories to dramatize the cruelty of Spanish policies, presented the revolutionaries as folksy reformers, and berated the government for its lack of missionary zeal.

But McKinley set the stage for the climax by sending the battleship *Maine* to Havana in January, 1898, to underscore his pressure on Spain. He also dispatched "an older and more experienced" man to China, the better to deal with "threatened complications." Then, on February 9, 1898, Hearst's *Journal* published a letter written by the Spanish minister in Washington, Dupuy de Lome, which had been stolen from the mails. His critical remarks about McKinley forced the Spaniard to resign and ignited an angry demand for action.

The de Lome episode was still on the front pages when, at 20 minutes after taps on February 15, 1898, the *Maine* was sunk by explosions, with a loss of 226 men. There was no instantaneous and unanimous outcry for war, but the event significantly increased the tension and did encourage those, like Roosevelt, who had been "hoping and working ardently to bring about our interference in Cuba." Roosevelt labored especially hard on the afternoon of February 25, 1898, while the Secretary of the Navy was ill and absent from his office. His activities were related more to expansion in Asia than to pacifying Cuba. He ordered Commodore George Dewey, commander of the Asiatic Fleet, to "start offensive operations in the Philippine Islands" as soon as hostilities with Spain began. "The deed was done," as Senator Lodge observed, and neither Secretary Long nor President McKinley revoked or modified the order.

The president shortly sent a special emissary to explore the attitude of important businessmen toward war and delivered an ultimatum to Spain. Spain would have to act promptly, even, if necessary, in the view of the United States, grant independence to Cuba, or else Washington would intervene directly. Key businessmen and financiers supported that action because they wanted to settle the issue and get on with economic recovery and overseas market expansion. McKinley then opened the last gate on the road of making war to make peace.

The president's message to the Congress on April 11, 1898, was a public version of his private ultimatum to Spain. The Congress responded on April 19 with a supporting resolution, and McKinley gave Spain four days to acquiesce. Spain accurately interpreted the move as an informal declaration of war. The Congress made it formal on April 23, but it candidly made the action retroactive to April 21, which was three days before Spain took the same action.

Dewey promptly destroyed Spanish naval power in the Pacific during a seven-hour target practice in Manila Bay on the morning of May

1, 1898. Even before he received official confirmation of that victory, McKinley ordered 12,000 troops to embark for the Philippines. Then he turned to the problems inherent in the "establishment of a new political power" in those islands. Finally, on June 11–12, the president opened a drive to annex Hawaii and asked the Congress to authorize a commission to support American economic expansion in China. The debate over Hawaii revolved around the thesis, best stated by a member of the McKinley administration, that "we must have Hawaii to help us get our share of China." By the time annexation was achieved by a joint resolution (July 7), the marines had taken Guam (June 21) as another stepping-stone.

McKinley and other policy makers made it clear from the outset that the Cuban revolutionaries would be excluded from any meaningful share of power or authority. They were even denied a significant part in the victory celebration after the Spanish fleet was destroyed on July 3 and after the 24,000 Spanish troops surrendered in Santiago on July 17. The combat was occasionally exhilarating, at least to enthusiastic volunteers like Roosevelt, but it was not very extensive. American forces suffered 379 battle deaths and 1604 wounded. The most effective enemies were sloppy organization, irresponsibility, and disease: those claimed 5083 American lives.

Spain asked for an armistice on July 22, but it was not signed until the Spanish accepted the loss of the Philippines (August 12). From the American point of view, the Philippine issue was simple to state but difficult to resolve: How much of the Philippines should be retained in order to provide a sound foundation for American economic expansion on the mainland of Asia? McKinley's underlying attitude was revealed in his early remark that "the commercial opportunity . . . inevitably associated with this new opening depends less on large territorial possession than upon an adequate commercial basis and upon broad and equal privileges."

Even so, McKinley soon decided to keep all the Philippines. For one thing, the islands were an economic and social entity that could not be divided on any rational or practical basis. And there was little point in freeing the Philippines or giving them back to Spain if that would lead to more serious troubles in holding Manila against outside challenges.

Those considerations were dramatized by the difficulties in pacifying the Philippines. Native opponents to Spanish rule, led by Emilio Aguinaldo, at first welcomed Americans on the assumption that they were liberating the islands for the Filipinos. Aguinaldo quickly and accurately concluded, however, that the Americans were liberators only so far as the Spanish were concerned. His response, on January 5, 1900, was to rally his countrymen for independence. Armed revolt erupted a month later.

The resulting war against the Filipinos was dirty and inhuman. It did no credit to the United States and seriously weakened its claim that American expansion would extend independence, self-determination, and prosperity to all peoples. The final outcome was clear after the marines won a bloody battle on November 16, 1901, in Ze Gorge on the Sojoton River, but fighting continued into 1905.

The problems involved in ruling the islands, first studied by Jacob Gould Schurman, the president of Cornell University and a religious leader who became a vigorous expansionist, were handed to William Howard Taft (an Ohio politician who had moved into national affairs under Harrison) on April 7, 1900. He terminated military rule outside combat areas on June 21, 1901, and established local governments under a Filipino legislature. The American commission, to which Taft admitted some carefully chosen natives, continued to wield supreme authority, however, and even served as the upper house of the legislature. That general pattern was confirmed by the Congress in the Philippine Government Act of July 1, 1902.

Cuban affairs were handled differently. The Teller Amendment, which had been added to the original war resolution of April, 1898, was a voluntary promise not to keep the island as a colony. The main problems involved reconstruction and establishing direct and indirect limits beyond which the Cubans would not be allowed to move. Within that framework, American economic interests rapidly consolidated a predominant position in the Cuban political economy and organized the island around sugar production. The sanitation and other public health projects, which were the most positive contributions made by Americans, were conceived and directed by Major General William C. Gorgas and Walter Reed.

The reorganization of the Cuban political system was handled by General Leonard W. Wood. After two years of occupation, the Cuban Constitutional Convention codified the new system. Cuba was required (1) to provide land for American bases (such as Guantanamo Bay); (2) to bind itself not to contract any debts beyond its capacity to repay through its ordinary revenues; (3) to agree not to sign any treaty considered by the United States to impair the new position of the island; and (4) to acknowledge the right of the United States to intervene, with force if necessary, to preserve Cuba's status and to maintain law and order. The provisos ultimately became known, collectively and somewhat inaccurately, as the Platt Amendment.

BEGINNINGS OF THE OPEN DOOR POLICY

The process of consolidating American control of the Philippines and Cuba did not significantly distract American leaders from the broader task of evolving and implementing a basic program for the expansion of American economic power into Asia and the rest of the world. That strategy, which came to be known as the Open Door policy, was the outcome of countless discussions among American leaders that began during the 1880s. The central themes emerged very early: American policy is based on "keeping foreign markets open" and securing "equal and liberal trading advantages" (1885); and "we should see to it that as many doors are left open for us as possible" (1888).

Secretary of State John Hay's formal diplomatic notes that brought those ideas together were the result of a combination of circumstances involving the assumptions behind the policy, the American consensus on expansion, and the conditions in Asia. McKinley and Hay judged the moment for action had come in the fall of 1899: America's position in the western Pacific had been established; relations with Germany and Japan had improved; and Great Britain, still worried about the scramble for concessions in China, appeared receptive to a move to keep the competition from erupting into a general war among industrial powers.

On September 6, therefore, Hay asked all interested powers to agree to the following points: (1) all nations should "enjoy perfect equality of treatment for their commerce and navigation within" the various existing spheres of interest; (2) treaty ports and established operations within the spheres would "in no way" be interfered with; (3) the existing Chinese tariff would be applied to the goods of all powers shipped to such treaty ports; and (4) the harbor duties and railroad rates charged by the country holding a sphere of interest would be no higher for other nations than for its own citizens.

Hay returned to the fray on July 3, 1900, in the midst of the Boxer Rebellion, a nationalistic (but conservative) uprising in China that threatened all foreign interests and tempted various nations to impose a kind of administrative colonialism in parts of China. His second effort was designed to commit all the powers to "bring about permanent safety and peace to China, preserve Chinese territorial and administrative entity, protect all rights guaranteed to friendly powers by treaty and international law, and safeguard for the world the principle of equal and impartial trade with all parts of the Chinese Empire." The objective was to obtain a usable (if imperfect) commitment by other powers to the grand strategy of American expansion. In still a third note (1900) Hay made it clear that the United States included investments as well as trade under the provisions of the Open Door policy.

American leaders wanted to establish a framework within which they could use limited force, or merely the threat of force, as a means of maintaining what they considered to be the minimum requirements necessary for America's eventual triumph in the marketplace. They and their successors used force in precisely that fashion: McKinley by sending troops to China during the Boxer Rebellion; Theodore Roosevelt by siding with Japan in its war against Russia and then by sending the Great White Fleet into Japan's home waters; and Woodrow Wilson by sending troops into Siberia. When large-scale force was deemed necessary, as between 1917 and 1919, and 1941 and 1945, it was used to preserve and extend the Open Door policy. In all essential respects, therefore, the United States conducted its foreign affairs within the framework of that policy for more than two generations after it was formulated.

McKinley's dispatch of troops to China in June, 1900, despite the possibility that the action might hurt his chances for reelection, underscores his commitment to an imperial foreign policy. His objectives were to discipline the Chinese and to prevent Germany, Japan, and Russia from using the Boxer uprising to close the open door. The Russians proved the most overtly persistent in trying to establish a large sphere of interest, and the administration cautiously cooperated with Japan in resisting that effort. In the longer view, through reinforcing the existing American antagonism toward Germany and Russia, the Boxer episode subtly influenced later diplomacy.

Other aspects of McKinley's postwar diplomacy were less dramatic. Hawaii was incorporated as a territory and its inhabitants granted citizenship under a law of 1900. The Foraker Act of the same year established a legislative system for Puerto Rico and defined citizenship for the natives in terms of the island rather than of the United States. The problem of the Philippines was handled by defining citizenship in terms of island birth. Voting rights were extended to literate males over 23, and a government headed by Taft as governor-general was established with the expectation that it would prepare the Filipinos for ultimate self-government.

The broad question of American rule over the new acquisitions was tested and partially defined in the courts through a series of suits known collectively as the Insular Cases. The last of those decisions did not come until 1922, but the guidelines were established at the turn of the century. The cases were begun by businessmen, and especially importers, who insisted that the areas were territories and hence part of the economic system of the United States. That status would enable them to avoid paying customs duties. The government broadly agreed with the businessmen's contention that "the significance of the present controversy lies in its commercial aspect," but it maintained that the territories were subject to an almost absolute power of the Congress and that there was nothing automatic about the extension of consitutional rights or guarantees.

A decision by the Supreme Court upheld the power of the Congress to acquire a possession and "keep it like a disembodied shade, in an intermediate state of ambiguous existence." In *Dorr* v. *U.S.* (1904), the Congress was held to have the power to impose import duties as it chose, a ruling that helped to clarify the earlier decision, in *Downes* v. *Bidwell* (1901), that the Constitution was not automatically carried abroad in the process of conquest. The meaning was clear: the metropolis had been given the legal sanction to govern the colonies in accordance with its own conception of everyone's best interests.

Imperialism had ceased to be a major political issue long before those decisions were handed down by the Court, as Bryan discovered when he tried to campaign on that question in the election of 1900. Bryan's best opportunity to defeat McKinley on foreign policy came during the fight in 1899 over ratifying the peace treaty with Spain. The concern about acquiring colonies generated a vocal bipartisan opposition typified by Carl Schurz, a German immigrant who had made a place for himself as a reformer within the Republican party.

Ryan Walker of the New York Times *presented Uncle Sam striding across the world, filling his arms with Puerto Rico, Hawaii, the Philippines, Guam, and reaching for Panama. The "Annexer" was enthusiastically seeking to adopt whatever he could reach.*

THE ANNEXER 'LL GIT YOU UF YOU DON'T WATCH OUT—N.Y. TIMES

Reprinted in *Current Literature*, vol. 36, 1904, p. 174.

He argued that a policy of annexation, or of establishing administrative protectorates, would initiate a process of decline and decay in America itself. It would create a new race problem, subvert republican government by opening the way for the rise of a powerful military interest group inside the government, and lead to further colonialism and wars that would ultimately cost the nation far more than they returned in economic benefits. In any event, Schurz concluded, the benefits of foreign trade could be obtained without acquiring colonies, building a large military establishment, and fighting a sequence of wars. There was some racism in his argument, for he doubted the ability of colored peoples to govern themselves effectively, but the main themes in his attack on colonialism involved moral principles and the logic of the marketplace.

The anticolonial coalition was a heterogeneous combination of urban reformers, New England aristocrats, orthodox conservatives, Populist agrarians, religious groups, radical workers, and southern racists. Despite some of their more inflammatory rhetoric, however, the great majority of them favored overseas economic expansion and the use of American power to influence and reform the world. Save for a tiny (and courageous) handful, they were in truth opposed only to the acquisition of colonies.

But the long, dirty war against the Filipinos (which revealed the nasty side of imperialism far more starkly than the equally effective suppression of the Cuban revolutionaries) gave them a dramatic issue. Perhaps McKinley paid them the most serious kind of respect: a most astute politician, he moved very carefully to build popular support for the annexation of the Philippines before he confronted them in a showdown vote in the Congress.

At that moment of truth, however, Bryan chose to support the annexationist peace treaty in order to end the war and then go on to fight for the independence of the Philippines. His strategy failed, but he may have sensed that the anticolonial coalition was too weak to block the imperial thrust that had emerged by the end of the war. And, in truth, the vast majority of the anticolonialists approved the imperial strategy formulated by McKinley and Hay in the Open Door Notes. A large number of them, including Bryan, later advocated or supported vigorous American intervention in Asia and Latin America. They entertained their own version of the large policy favored by Senator Lodge, Roosevelt, and other overt imperialists—one that concentrated on reforming other societies in the image of America.

The popular enthusiasm for the war against Spain and the general approval of an imperial policy temporarily dampened the agrarian demands for domestic reform. And the shift to an industrial political economy, combined with a period of relative prosperity for the agriculturalists, decreased the importance of farm leadership in that effort. But the concern to improve—and rationalize—American society revived very quickly after the debate over imperialism had been resolved in favor of expansion.

EXPLORATORY READING

The roots of American imperialism are revealed in the following books:

E. R. Johnson (and associates), *History of Domestic and Foreign Commerce of the United States* (1915)

F. Merk, *The Monroe Doctrine and American Expansion, 1843–1849* (1966)

D. M. Pletcher, *The Diplomacy of Annexation* (1973)

H. N. Smith, *Virgin Land: The American West as Symbol and Myth* (1950)

W. Stanton, *The Great United States Exploring Expedition of 1838–1842* (1975)

R. W. Van Alstyne, *The Rising American Empire* (1960)

———, *Genesis of American Nationalism* (1970)

A. K. Weinberg, *Manifest Destiny: A Study of Nationalist Expansionism in American History* (1935)

The transition from the conquest of the North American continent to imperialism is explored in these volumes:

E. P. Crapol, *America for Americans* (1973)

T. Dennett, *Americans in Eastern Asia* (1941)

M. Plesur, *America's Outward Thrust* (1971)

D. W. Pletcher, *The Awkward Years: American Foreign Relations Under Garfield and Arthur* (1962)

H. B. Schonberger, *Transportation to the Seaboard: A Study in the "Communications Revolution" and American Foreign Policy: 1860–1900* (1971)

H. and M. Sprout, *The Rise of American Naval Power* (1939)

S. K. Stevens, *American Expansion in Hawaii* (1945)

T. E. Terrill, *The Tariff, Politics, and American Foreign Policy, 1874–1901* (1973)

W. A. Williams, *The Tragedy of American Diplomacy,* (1962)

———, *The Roots of the Modern American Empire* (1969)

The final evolution of imperialism during the 1890s is nicely reviewed in these studies:

R. L. Beisner, *Twelve Against Empire* (1968)

C. S. Campbell, Jr., *Special Business Interests and the Open Door Policy* (1951)

O. Ferrara, *The Last Spanish War* (1937)

P. S. Foner, *The Spanish-Cuban-American War and the Birth of American Imperialism, 1895–1902* (1972)

T. P. Greene (Ed.), *American Imperialism in 1898* (1955)

J. A. S. Grenville and G. B. Young, *Politics, Strategy, and American Diplomacy: Studies in Foreign Relations* (1966)

D. Healy, *The Imperialist Urge in the 1890s* (1970)

T. Kemp, *Theories of Imperialism* (1967)

W. LaFeber, *The New Empire* (1963)

E. R. May, *Imperial Democracy* (1961)

T. McCormick, *China Market* (1967)

W. Millis, *The Martial Spirit* (1931)

T. G. Patterson (Ed.), *American Imperialism and Anti-Imperialism* (1973)

E. B. Tompkins, *Anti-Imperialism in the United States* (1970)

Hans-Ulrich Wehler, *Der Aufstiegdes amerikanischen Imperialismus* (1974)

L. Wolff, *Little Brown Brother* (1961)

3 CORPORATE POWER PROVOKES RESISTANCE AMONG WORKERS AND INTELLECTUALS

T is fascinating to think seriously about what might have happened in America if key leaders of the agricultural protest movement, say Tom Watson, Jerry Simpson, Mary Ellen Lease, and Bryan, had become Socialists during the late 1880s and early 1890s. One of them might well have become the American Mao Tse-tung of world revolution, adapting the theories of socialism—a philosophy that emerged as a powerful criticism of, and alternative to, European capitalist industrialism—to a situation in which farmers constituted the majority of the population. Given the extensive and visceral anger among average citizens toward the powerful few, such a leader might have created a Socialist society that honored the ideals of Karl Marx in a way that has yet to be done.

Such intellectual play—a sophisticated form of the game of "What if?"—is one of the great virtues of doing history. It was, indeed, one of the favorite stimulants (along with brandy and cigars) indulged by British Prime Minister Winston Spencer Churchill (1874–1965), who engaged in it to keep his mind open to the importance of different ideas—even though he always tried to harness such innovations to the service of his own conservativism. And the most imaginative psychiatrists (such as Robert Jay Lifton in *The Life of the Self,* 1976) make a powerful case that our dreams represent less a regression into (or repression of) our traumas of the past than an effort to move onward into more creative ways of living.

The virtue of the historical approach lies first in providing a foundation for the thoughtful analysis and understanding of *what actually did happen.* Then, informed by an awareness of alternatives, we can transform history from a routine account of what simply occurred into a way of learning about ourselves as human beings. If we imagine and keep in mind the option of a decentralized, Socialist industrial system in America, then we gain important insights into what actually happened—not just into the character of the new centralized and consolidated capitalist order but also into the nature and the limits of the ideas and programs advocated (and in part realized) by the early twentieth-century reformers.

Let us first review, therefore, the nature of the new industrial system. From the fall of 1897 to the spring of 1900, while the country was largely caught up in the crises over Cuba and China, the giant corporations that survived the depression gobbled up many of their weaker competitors. The first such consolidations involved vital consumer industries and resulted in the creation of the Glucose Sugar Refining Company, the International Paper Corporation, the American Thread Company, and the Standard Distilling Corporation. Then, during 1899, while Cuba and the Philippines were being integrated into the American empire, 1028 companies were merged or otherwise consolidated. That activity produced such mammoth corporations as the United States Steel Corporation, the American Tobacco Company, the International Harvester Company, the DuPont Corporation, the Anaconda Copper Company, and the American Smelting and Refining Company. And by 1900, American Telephone and Telegraph had become a $250 million corporation.

The merger movement was powered by the determination to gain more effective control over the market, to establish firm access to raw materials and other supplies, and to defeat competition. It led, on the one hand, to the vertical integration of manufacturing and other operations, from the extraction of raw materials to the distribution and marketing of the finished product, and, on the other hand, to the horizontal extension of power over geographic regions (often the entire nation) and into different but related products (as with razors as well as razor blades or prepared breakfast foods as well as flour).

The changes were initiated by industrialists who understood how the system operated and who saw consolidation and centralization as ways of maintaining and enlarging their profits and power. But the large investment bankers and other financiers rapidly became deeply involved because they agreed with the objectives and because they were needed to provide the vast amounts of capital required to rationalize the economy. They naturally gained considerable direct control, as well as indirect influence, over the resulting system. They took their payment in power as well as in profits, and as a result, the years of

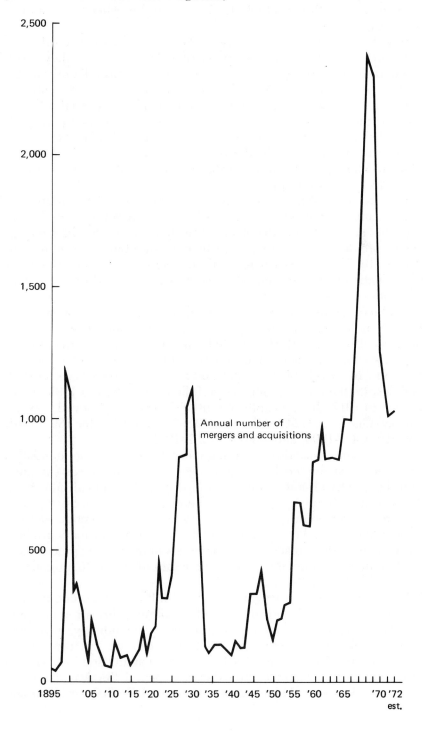

Figure 1   *Acquisitions of manufacturing and mining companies, 1895–1972.*
(Tom Cardamone for *Fortune* Magazine.)

Annual number of
mergers and acquisitions

their greatest authority (1895–1912) came to be called the era of finance capitalism.

Wealthy as they were, the large bankers nevertheless had difficulty accumulating all the necessary capital. As a result, they over-capitalized the combinations formed by mergers, thus inflating values. They also raised prices. They likewise fought each other for control of the great life insurance companies in order to use the capital gathered through the premium payments of millions of individual policyholders. They used their power to win rebates and other special treatment from railroads and struggled for possession of the lines. And they manipulated the contracts between the corporations that they controlled to extract even further profits.

The first wave of major mergers was completed by 1904. About 300 of the giants were capitalized at nearly $6 billion. A mere 29 of them, however, accounted for 40 percent of the total. The centralization was even more dramatically apparent when measured in terms of individual wealth. The richest 1 percent of the population owned 50 percent of the nation's wealth, and 90 percent of it was held by a mere 12 percent of the people.

Productivity also increased. Between 1899 and 1904, for example, the volume of manufacturing jumped 22 percent, and it grew another 30 percent between 1904 and 1909. The output of the entire system, measured on a scale showing progress toward 1929 (100), climbed from 50.7 in 1895 to 55.6 in 1900, and on to 64.4 by 1910. As a result, and despite the population increase from 69.6 million in 1895 to 95.3 million in 1912, the per capita output of the economy moved upward. The average was $424 for the years 1892–1896; $496 for 1897–1901; $569 for 1902–1906; and $608 for 1907–1911.

The economy was also becoming more diversified. The foundation provided by steam, coal, iron and steel, and railroads was extended into the electrical, automobile, petroleum, and chemical industries. There were also changes in steel. The open-hearth process replaced the Bessemer technique as the primary mode of production in 1908; structural steel (and other rolled metals) became the primary product; hydraulic presses replaced steam hammers in the forging process; and total production jumped from 10 million tons to nearly 25 million tons between 1900 and 1910.

The petroleum industry continued its shift from kerosene production to meet the demand for fuel oil, gasoline, lubricating oils, and semifinished products for the expanding chemical industry. Rayon and artificial silk were invented in 1902, for example, and the process developed by Ernest Solvay (a Belgian) for making soda by treating salt with ammonia and carbon dioxide opened the way for many further applications. The electrolytic process brought even more immediate gains. Steel wire, for example, was replaced by copper for the transmission of electricity. And the work of Charles Martin Hall in adapting the technique for refining aluminum created that new industry.

Electrical energy was increasingly used for industrial as well as consumer purposes. The machine tool industry, for example, turned sharply toward electric motors to run its fixed cutting lathes and power presses, as well as its portable tools. On the eve of World War I, electricity supplied the power for over 20 percent of the motors in all manufacturing. And electrical welding, introduced in 1896, was rapidly accepted. In addition, more and more current was needed to run appliances such as fans, irons, stoves, radios, sewing machines, and even washing machines, for lighting cities and homes, and for the small but expanding motion picture industry.

Another dramatic change involved the automobile industry: it quickly became the sixth largest industry in the economy. The first car made for sale was fabricated by the Duryea Motor Wagon Company in 1895, but countless groups working in abandoned barns and sheds as well as in small factories struggled to perfect a reliable car that could be made easily and sold cheaply. The first American victor in that fiercely competitive battle was Henry Ford, who built his first auto during 1892–1893.

Ford's success with his famous end-of-the-century racing car, the "999," encouraged him in 1903 to organize the Ford Motor Company. Refusing to become involved with financiers (he did not trust them), Ford struggled along the edge of failure until he perfected the Model T flivver in 1908. Striving constantly for increased efficiency, he was able within five years to create the kind of continuous-flow production that came to be called the assembly line system and that was steadily applied in other manufacturing industries. It enabled him to produce a reliable product at a low price, and he quickly dominated the automobile market.

The expansion of auto manufacture produced rapid growth in the rubber industry and in other related lines such as batteries, starters, brakes, and drive systems like the one developed in 1914 by Vincent Bendix. Such interdependency based on a major product also developed in the chemical and electrical industries. And all of them created new markets for the construction industry, itself an interrelated combination of cement, steel, lumber, and other seemingly different products and specialized machinery.

The complexity of the new system posed a serious problem for those who controlled its various components, as well as for those who sought to reform and rationalize it to achieve more efficiency and equity. There were three principal aspects of that issue. First, the increasing centralization of economic control in the marketplace. Second, the related concentration of political and social influence. And third, the organization of social and political power capable of controlling the economic power of the giants.

In the broadest sense, Americans had six alternatives for dealing with the massive industrial political economy they had created. One was to leave it alone, acquiescing in the momentum toward monopolies and cartels. That approach was based on the assumption (and faith) that the impersonal workings of the marketplace—the interaction between supply and demand—would produce the general welfare even though the corporations were using their vast power to restrict free competition. Those who favored that course can fairly be called hard-line conservatives, even reactionaries, and they generally opposed all efforts to regulate or reform the system.

A second policy called for the use of governmental power to break up the corporations. The people who advocated the antitrust strategy argued that the key to the general welfare was to be found in restoring and maintaining free competition in the marketplace. They felt that a more activist policy would inevitably transform the government into the largest and most powerful corporation, which would in turn mean the steady decline of individual freedom.

That group poses a problem in nomenclature. The most accurate way of describing them is to call them nineteenth-century liberals, not only for their approach to the new corporate economy but also because many of them supported various social and political reforms. But the term liberal soon came to be used in connection with another group of reformers who advocated increasingly extensive government intervention in the economy. As the hard-line conservatives gradually lost influence, therefore, the nineteenth-century liberals came to be considered conservatives—despite their attitude toward other reforms. The most useful term thus appears to be *antitrust reformers.*

A third approach, the one that came to be called *liberalism,* emphasized the regulation of the corporations. Such corporate liberals asserted that the antitrust policy was a fruitless attempt to turn back the clock. They pointed to the productivity of the corporate system and warned that destroying the new giants would weaken the economy and prevent further material improvements, as well as limiting the power of the United States in the world marketplace. They accepted the essentials of the corporate political economy even as they insisted on the need for government intervention to control and reform the results of that system.

The fourth alternative emphasized the need for labor to organize within the framework of the corporations and thereby limit their power and influence their decisions. That solution, which came to be called *business unionism,* was pushed by the union leadership that accepted the capitalist system, and the key figures were Samuel Gompers, head of the AF of L, and John Mitchell of the UMW. They and like-minded workers felt that the unions could secure vital wage increases and other benefits and at the same time restrain the corporations in other areas. Such people did support additional reforms, but they concentrated on the confrontation between the corporations and the workers.

The fourth and fifth options called for a radical reorganization of the political economy. The Socialist approach, symbolized by Eugene V. Debs, a figure of considerable intellectual ability and great moral power, attracted the most popular support. Debs was a classic nineteenth-century Socialist who accepted the massive, centralized industrial system that had been created by capitalism as given and as necessary to meet the material needs of the people. But he and his followers insisted that it could be operated for the benefit of all only by the government acting through and in response to the political process. And in keeping with the Socialist tradition, Debs supported many political and social reforms that others found too disturbing or dangerous.

The other radical approach, which gained significant support in some parts of the country, was advocated by the International Workers of the World (IWW). That organization was created during a 1905 meeting in Chicago through the merger of the Western Federation of Miners (WFM) and the American Labor Union. Although it had intellectual roots in the European syndicalist tradition, the IWW leaned more to industrial unionism than to a reorganization of the economy along functional lines. It also advocated the abolition of the wage system and the creation of some kind of cooperative economy on a decentralized basis. The key leader was William B. ("Big Bill") Haywood, a tough and charismatic radical who dominated the organization after Daniel DeLeon and his Socialist Labor group were expelled. While the Wobblies' willingness to resort to violence alienated most of the middle and upper classes (and even many workers), it was highly effective in organizing (and helping) unskilled and migratory workers in western agriculture, lumbering, and shipping; and it won a bitter and violent strike on behalf of textile workers in Lawrence, Massachusetts (1912).

The Wobblies were also vigorous, uncompromising defenders (and users) of free speech, and that aspect of their program serves to underscore an important characteristic of most of the other approaches to dealing with the corporate political economy. Whatever their choice for coping with the economic aspects of the new system, the reformers also sought to improve other aspects of life. They sought to reduce the waste of resources, the high rate of industrial accidents, and the fragmentation and depersonalization of work and social relationships. They wanted to improve the treatment of the immigrant and, in a few cases, of the blacks and bring those groups into fuller membership in the society. They tried to obtain more equity in the distribution of the rewards and benefits of the powerful productive system and to treat those who remained poor or otherwise handicapped with more concern and generosity. And they struggled to infuse all aspects of American life with more honesty, equity, and creativity.

SHIFTING COALITIONS STRUGGLE FOR REFORMS

The gradual convergence of those dissimilar approaches into a national campaign to rationalize and reform the system involved a classic combination of the two kinds of political action: push and pull. Every class, agrarians as well as urbanites, was involved in both processes, but it is possible to discern a pattern of activism. Except for the positive attraction (the pull) of socialism as advocated by Debs, the urban working class concentrated—through union organization and strikes—on pushing the conservatives and others into making various reforms.

The white urban middle class acted in a way that was symbolically appropriate to its position in the political economy. On the one hand, it pushed against militant labor and hard-line conservatives, but on the other hand, it pulled by advocating and agitating for a vast array of reforms. As for the upper class, it provided a rough mirror image of the lower class. Its sophisticated leaders recognized the need to offer and act upon a positive program of change. But for many years a strong plurality, if not a majority, of the powerful few pushed back against the workers and the middle class with a kind of mindless negativism.

Hence the reforms that were made were not the result of a social *movement.* They were instead the product of fluctuating *coalitions* among various groups of Americans who cooperated loosely and unevenly to impose some control and rationality on the new industrial system. It is accurate to speak of Progressive*s*, but it is misleading to talk about *a* Progressive *movement.* Had there been a Progressive movement in the true sense of a national convergence of people of all classes, sexes, and colors coming together to transform the corporate system according to the imperatives of a new set of values and procedures, then American society would have undergone far-reaching *structural* change. That did not occur. Instead, various interest groups forged shifting temporary alliances with each other to improve their own position in the corporate political economy.

While the importance of perceptive upper-class leaders like McKinley and Roosevelt should not be underestimated (let alone discounted) in accounting for the mounting momentum for rationalization and reform, it is necessary to emphasize the vigorous push supplied by the lower classes and by various intellectuals of the white middle class. For those groups dramatized the need to make ameliorative changes and hence strengthened such upper-class leaders as Roosevelt, George W. Perkins, and Herbert Croly against the upper-class reactionaries.

The Populists and other agrarian protestors of the 1880s and 1890s undoubtedly deserve credit for generating the initial push for reform, but it is equally true that urban workers sustained that pressure into the twentieth century. It was not simply that the memories of Haymarket and Pullman lived on as nightmares in the minds of corporation executives, though that was a factor; it was that the workers refused to accept the existing conditions of life and labor.

The Socialists, along with the WFM and the IWW, attracted increasing support from the immigrants from southern and southeastern Europe, who after 1900 composed the bulk of the new arrivals. They accounted for 72 percent of the 14.5 million people who came to the United States between 1900 and 1915, when World War I closed off the flow. They found America strange, painful, and difficult. One Slav described the situation in memorable terms: *"My people do not live in America, they live underneath America."*

Low wages and miserable working conditions generated sustained pressure for union recognition and reform. The typical unskilled workers made about $1.50 a day in 1900, or an average of $500 per year. Most of them worked more than ten hours a day, and their real income decreased during those years. Average annual earnings increased, but not enough to match the rise in the cost of living. Between 1890 and 1911, for example, average hourly earnings climbed only from 20 cents to 26 cents per hour. Unemployment and underemployment were also everyday problems throughout the period.

The corporate industrial system also provided an extremely dangerous working environment. Railroads were the worst killers: the average number of deaths per month between 1888 and 1908, for example, was 328. Injuries were likewise high: American railroad workers suffered 11,066 nonfatal accidents in 1903. But other industries were also deadly. At the South Chicago plant of United States Steel, for example, 46 men were killed and 600 injured in 1906. The average annual record for all industry during those years was 35,000 killed and 536,000 injured.

Thus the militance and violence of that time is not difficult to understand. The world of the industrial worker was cramped, dirty, grim, and brutal. Union membership climbed from 447,000 in 1897 to 868,000 in 1900; 2,022,000 in 1905; and 2,687,000 in 1914. There were also many strikes. The high point came in 1903, when there were 3648 stoppages; but there were 1839 in 1900 and 1204 in 1914.

The few instances of ostensibly dramatic improvement did not affect the great majority of workers and did not in truth transform the lives of those who gained the limited benefits. The National Cash Register Company, for example, did attempt to incorporate its workers more fully—and humanely—into the corporation, but playing baseball during the lunch break does not provide a meaningful substitute for having a consequential share in the making of decisions.

In a similar way, Henry Ford introduced an eight-hour day in 1914, guaranteed all regular workers a minimum wage of $5 per day, and offered a profit-sharing plan. The program attracted much attention and praise, but it was not emulated by other entrepreneurs, and it was not the pie in the sky that Ford's publicity claimed. Life on an industrial assembly line was soon recognized to be remarkably similar to the life on an 1885 prairie farm that had provoked the farmers into militant protest activity.

John Mitchell of the UMW understood that point. The worker, he explained, "has made up his mind that he must remain a wage earner. He has given up the hope of a kingdom to come, where he himself will be a capitalist, and he asks that the reward for his work be given to him as a workman." That perception strained relations between capital and labor "almost to the breaking point." Mitchell was not against strikes, as demonstrated by his fierce determination in the coal walkout in 1902, but as one who accepted capitalism, he preferred to find some basis for equitable cooperation.

So did Samuel Gompers, head of the AF of L, who had turned away from Socialist and other radical solutions. He wanted to reform industry by organizing it from within through unionization. The corporation, he argued, "should not be suppressed but regulated and helped to develop constructive control." Gompers was constantly under pressure, however, from those within the union movement who opposed the craft union approach, from radical locals within the AF of L, and from upper- and middle-class spokesmen who argued that he was already too militant. As a result, the Socialists and the IWW continued to gain strength among the workers.

That had been made clear in the returns of the 1900 election. The most astute politicians are in one very limited sense intellectuals who do instant history with the evidence that appears from the last ballot box and the morning newspaper. Their perspective is terribly distorted because it is so short and shifting, but they do recognize a message when it is delivered effectively—either directly or indirectly. Considered superficially, McKinley beat Bryan in 1900 by a comfortable margin: 861,459 popular votes, and 292 to 155 in the electoral college.

But the various dissenters and reformers—from the Prohibitionists to the radicals—attracted 354,166 citizens. That opened the way for serious concern, particularly because Debs did extremely well in his first run as a Socialist and because Hanna and McKinley had to defuse a dangerous confrontation between the working miners and the mine owners. That push began in 1897, when the soft-coal miners (a mere 10,000 strong) went out on strike. Their courage attracted the support of another 90,000 workers, and the operating managers surrendered, settling for an eight-hour day and a rational wage scale.

The next year Mitchell was elected president of the UMW. He was a diffident young man of 28, but whatever his private personality, he quickly established himself as a charismatic and dedicated leader who captured the imagination—and the trust—of the immigrant and native miners (to whom he was fondly known as "Johnny"). It was a remarkable achievement because the men from southeastern Europe (Slavs and Italians) were under enormous pressure to settle for less money than those who had established themselves as Americans—however poor and powerless.

Mitchell had an instinct for the jugular, and he struck quickly and boldly. He called a strike in 1900 and laid his case before the public. The ordinary mine worker earned $250 per year and was forced by the owner-operator to earn that pittance on the basis of paying for his blasting powder, trading at a company store, and loading coal at almost double the rate of the ordinary ton (4000 pounds as against 2400 pounds).

There was no evading it: it was an inexcusable and disgraceful situation, and vast numbers of ordinary citizens who depended upon coal for heat and light supported the workers. Hanna saved the day for McKinley—and for other members of the upper class. He went straight to J. P. Morgan, the financial giant who exercised enormous influence over the mine managers, and persuaded that modern feudal baron to direct his underlings to compromise. They did so, and Mitchell in turn settled for a 10 percent hike in wages.

But he came right back in 1902 to demand more money and recognition of the union. The operators tried to destroy the union by hiring amateur policemen and strikebreakers. That did not work. Neither did the revelation by George F. Baer, the most reactionary owner, of an intimate relationship between the operators and the Almighty. He bluntly asserted that the people to whom "God in his infinite wisdom had given control of the property interests of this country" would protect "the rights and interests of the laboring men." That rousing reactionary sermon did not satisfy the miners and they continued their strike.

Hence Roosevelt, who had succeeded the murdered McKinley, asked Hanna to intercede with Morgan again. This time, however, the financial titan was unable to arrange a settlement. Roosevelt responded by invoking the power of the presidency to arrange a conference between himself, Baer, and Mitchell. The labor leader was conciliatory, but the reactionary capitalist was arrogant and insulting. The president was infuriated by what he termed Baer's insolence and

Strife between labor and management ripped across the nation inside the new century. The problem in the coal fields was particularly fierce. Cooperation between John Mitchell of the mine workers and J. P. Morgan was celebrated by C. J. Bush in the New York World *as the coal flowed again.*

ONLY COMMON SENSE IS NECESSARY—From the *World* (New York).

Reprinted in the *Review of Reviews,* vol. 26, November, 1902, p. 541.

deeply frightened by the possibility that such inflexibility would strengthen the appeal of Debs and socialism. As a result, he told Morgan that he was prepared to use the army to control the mines unless the operators gave way and accepted arbitration.

That carried the day. There were two results. The seven-man board of arbitration awarded the miners another 10 percent wage increase, ordered the creation of an honest weighing system, and forbade discrimination against union members—though the union itself was not recognized. In addition, Roosevelt's handling of the crisis served to accentuate and extend the existing propensity toward centralized power within the system.

In an important sense, of course, that was inherent in the Constitution, which gave the national government enormous power over every state and group. And various earlier leaders, especially Andrew Jackson and Abraham Lincoln, had gone far to consolidate and personalize that power in the presidency. But Roosevelt dramatically focused the issue in the industrial context—the White House versus the corporations—and hence set a precedent for the developing reform campaign.

The conservatives, however, were far from defeated by the outcome of the mine crisis. Among their resources, for example, was the Supreme Court. It seriously weakened the Sherman Anti–Trust Act (*U.S. v. E. C. Knight Co.*, 1895) by drawing an artificial distinction between commerce and industry, invalidated the 1894 income tax, struck down an Illinois law that established a ten-hour day for women, and overturned a Nebraska law that fixed railroad rates. And the NAM turned away from its initial emphasis on overseas economic expansion and concentrated ever more on antilabor activities.

That shift grew out of the union troubles that smaller companies were beginning to experience in cities like Chicago, Louisville, Dayton, and Indianapolis. The critical episode involved James W. Van Cleave, who headed the Buck Stove and Range Company. He filed a suit against the Metal Polisher's Union to stop a boycott of his product. That rallied support from other small- and medium-sized operators like Charles Post, a cereal manufacturer; George Pope, who made bicycles; and David M. Parry, who owned a small factory. Such men elected Parry president of the NAM in 1903, and thereafter the organization concentrated its power against boycotts, the closed shop, and "any interference with employment practices."

The conservatives also advanced a vigorous intellectual defense of their power and prerogatives as property holders. Their basic argument was first developed by Herbert Spencer, the English advocate of Social Darwinism. The key American figure was William Graham Sumner, a talented and powerful figure who became a professor of political and social science at Yale in 1872 after early training and service as an Episcopal minister. Sumner argued that the survival of the fittest meant exactly what it seemed to mean: those who survived and prospered were more qualified than those who failed. He also maintained, in *Folkways* (1907), that the inherent nature of man and the persistence of traditions made it useless to undertake reforms.

AMERICAN ARTISTS AND INTELLECTUALS CHALLENGE THE OLD ORDER

In the realm of art, the conservatives preferred routine derivatives of classical forms. The graphic arts, presided over by the National Academy of Design, favored literal reproductions of a selected part of reality done in subdued tones of middle-range colors and finished with a smooth surface and delicate brushwork. And most American buildings during the Progressive era (and on into the 1930s) were designed as minor variations on the Roman, Georgian, Tudor, Renaissance, Classical, Spanish, and Gothic orthodoxies.

But the intellectual in general, and the artist in particular, is preeminently a person who uses eyes and brain to interpret an ever changing reality, and it is not surprising that artists were among the first Americans to challenge the old order. Not even architecture was immune. Henry Hobson Richardson began, late in the 1880s, to abandon gingerbread decoration and other contrivances in favor of a plain and severe style.

Richardson's revolt was carried forward by Louis Sullivan, one of his disciples, who recognized the fundamental changes that were occurring in the United States and who realized that Chicago offered an unparalleled view of those momentous events. "We are at that dramatic moment in our national life," he explained, "wherein we tremble between decay and evolution."

An office building, he exulted, should be "every inch a proud and soaring thing . . . without a single dissenting line." "What people are within, the buildings express without," he amplified, "and inversely, what the buildings are objectively is a sure index of what the people are subjectively." Caught up in the purity and excitement of his own work, Sullivan may have missed the full truth of that revealing comment. For while his buildings are magnificent art (or sculpture), they also perfectly realize the kind of centralized power that he himself opposed, and they symbolize the way in which the new political economy was making people less human and individual by making them more functional according to its own criteria. An awareness of that disturbing irony may have informed the thought of Frank Lloyd Wright, who was Sullivan's most creative student.

Although Wright designed some striking skyscrapers, his greatest creations were private homes in which he stressed the relationship between the building, the natural materials of the region, and the contours of the site. The result was a marked preference for low, horizontal lines that emphasized the size and importance of man himself. And to maintain his personal independence in the face of modern centralization and bureaucratization, Wright retreated to a neofeudalism based on the community of the master, his family, and his student-disciples.

The architecture of Sullivan and Wright was more independently creative, but the painters and authors probably did more to shake the bastions of conservatism during the formative years of the Progressive coalition. The painter Thomas Eakins and the novelist William Dean Howells began, almost simultaneously in the 1870s, to describe the new system. Eakins created a furor in 1875 with his starkly chilling canvas of a medical operation in progress *(The Gross Clinic)*. And Howells (who became a genteel Socialist) provided a similar shock by depicting, in *The Rise of Silas Lapham* (1885), the cost in human sensibilities and values of becoming a success in the traditional laissez-faire marketplace.

Stephen Crane was another writer who dealt with America in realistic and naturalistic terms. His story about *Maggie: A Girl of the Streets* (1893) was one of the earliest sociological novels about the impact of industrialism on individual lives and was a forerunner of Theodore Dreiser's similar studies of *Sister Carrie* (1900) and *Jennie Gerhardt* (1911). Frank Norris began with *McTeague* (1899), a story of the degeneration and distintegration of a single man. Then in *The Octopus* (1901) and *The Pit* (1903) he revealed how the railroads, the processors, and the speculators took control of the farmers' wheat economy. Dreiser dealt effectively with the overseas expansion of the new industrial and financial system in his powerful studies of *The Financier* (1912) and *The Titan* (1913). And despite many subsequent attempts to portray the world and the life of a giant of the financial corporate system, those novels stand as the most compelling portraits of such a man.

American painters developed their own kind of realism, even though Mary Cassatt, a relatively unremembered artist, won the first major victory for modern American painters by being invited by the French Impressionists to participate in their exhibitions. Theodore Robinson and Robert Henri played key roles in encouraging such realists as Edward Hopper, Everett Shinn, William Glackens, and George Luks.

There was a powerful tension within the realistic and naturalistic approach between the creative thrust of the artist and the requirement to report objectively and impersonally. Frank Norris provided one of the best statements of it, speaking through one of his protagonists in *The Octopus:*

> Just what he wanted, Presley hardly knew. On the one hand, it was his ambition to portray life as he saw it—directly, frankly, and through no medium of personality or temperament. But, on the other hand, as well, he wished to see everything through a rose-colored mist—a mist that dulled all harsh emotion, all crude and violent colours.

Jack London and Dreiser came the closest to revealing the raw power and emotion of the Nietzschean individual. The more general development came through a group of painters that gathered around the leadership of the photographer-artists Alfred Stieglitz and Edward Steichen. Stieglitz was the son of German-Jewish immigrants, and he symbolized not only the upward mobility of that group but also the degree to which it educated Americans in the achievements of Europe. Both Stieglitz and Steichen became masters of photographic art, which involved imposing their own creativity on a machine and a process that by themselves saw everything in flat, two-dimensional, and nonselective terms. The photographer-artist had to assert his own subjectivity if he was to avoid being defeated by his technology.

That proved most difficult to do in connection with motion pictures. The first commercial movie opened in New York City on April 23, 1896, but the form remained a curiosity for almost a decade. The challenge of telling a story was met by Edwin S. Porter in 1903, when he created *The Great Train Robbery.* That film contained the germ of the Western, and the idiom rapidly became a staple of the industry. The business itself quickly developed as a trust, the Motion Picture Patents Company (1909), and after a short period of legal maneuverings it reorganized itself around a few giants like William Fox and the Paramount Studios.

But the major achievements belonged to Mack Sennett and Charles Chaplin, who were great artists of personal and social satire, and to David L. W. Griffith, who was the first American director to handle serious subjects with emotional and artistic success. Griffith also made important technical advances as a director, being the first to use the fade-out, angle shots, close-ups, and soft-focus shots. His tough, realistic, shocking film about Reconstruction, the classic *The Birth of a Nation,* appeared in the same year that Chaplin produced his early masterpiece, *The Tramp* (1915).

Graphic artists learned important ideas and techniques about the nature and uses of light from the photographic process. But many of them, as with Paul Klee, also reacted to the photograph "as a warning against materialistic vision." "The more horrible the world," Klee asserted, "the more abstract our art." That attitude was reinforced by other philosophical, psychological, and scientific discoveries around the turn of the century.

Sigmund Freud's *Interpretations of Dreams,* for example, was published in 1901. In the same year, Max Planck formulated the quantum theory of energy, which stressed the discontinuity of action. Four years later Albert Einstein offered his revolutionary theory of relativity. All of those ideas reinforced the reaction against a fixed, monolithic, depersonalized, and mechanical approach to life.

Subjectivism broke through the tradition that art was based on image making, and it abandoned representation or distorted the object to express insights and ideas and feelings. The Americans who began to hold their own showings in 1908, men like Max Weber, Alfred Maurer, John Marin, and Marsden Hartley, were not as good as Henri Matisse and Pablo Picasso. But they did carry the burden of making the revolution in the United States. Their climactic victory came in the huge show staged at the armory of the Sixty-ninth Regiment of the New York National Guard in December, 1913.

"Before it [the armory show]," one observer remarked, "a painting truly modern was only a rumor." But nobody ignored that vast display of Cubists, Expressionists, Symbolists, Primitive Realists, and Abstractionists—or the showing of conventional items, such as bathtubs, that were designed with particular beauty or style. The exhibition, largely planned and carried through under the direction of Arthur B. Davies, revealed the evolution of modern art as a revolt against the new corporate system as well as against romanticism and orthodox conservatism.

Conservatives like the art writers of the *New York Times* called the show *"pathological"!* And it provoked similar reactions when it was shown in Boston and Chicago. But many Progressive leaders, including Roosevelt, were receptive and friendly despite their reservations and criticism. That was the crucial indicator, for it revealed the artist's important role in the reform agitation.

Eugene Debs was not an artist, let alone a modern one, but he understood the issue:

> When the bread and butter problem is solved and all men and women and children the world around are rendered secure from dread of war and fear of want, then the mind and soul will be free to develop as they never were before. We shall have a literature and an art such as the troubled heart and brain of man never before conceived. . . . We shall have beautiful thoughts and sentiments, and a divinity in religion, such as man weighted down by the machine could never have imagined.

Socialism (and therefore Karl Marx) exerted an important influence on upper-class Progressives. On the one hand, the response it evoked among various other groups of Americans worried and upset men like Roosevelt, Ralph Easley of the NCF, and financier V. Everitt May, all of whom explicitly favored reform as a way to counter socialism. Herbert Croly, an upper-class intellectual who founded the *New Republic* in 1914, candidly remarked that he and his associates viewed reform as being "designed to serve as a counterpoise to the threat of working-class revolution."

Other upper-class reformers drew on Marx in formulating their own analyses of industrial society and in evolving their programs. Walter Lippmann, for example, was initially attracted to socialism. His important book, *Drift and Mastery* (1914), argued that the capitalist industrial system would move toward Marx's revolution unless informed, responsible leaders made the necessary changes and reforms. Walter Weyl insisted even earlier, in *The New Democracy* (1912), that such modifications would serve the best self-interest of the existing system. Weyl moved to the left, however, as he concluded that the people who controlled the system were either unable or unwilling to introduce such reforms.

Brooks Adams, grandson of President John Quincy Adams, was perhaps the most interesting of the upper-class reformers who were influenced by Marx. He had significant direct influence on Roosevelt and Lodge, and through his brother Henry Adams, affected the attitudes and thinking of other leaders such as Oliver Wendell Holmes. Brooks explained the crisis of industrial capitalism in terms of the decline of nerve and intelligence among economic leaders. But he argued in *The Law of Civilization and Decay* (1894) that the solution would not come through a working-class revolution. Instead, upper-class aristocratic leaders would have to take charge and provide the necessary control and direction. And his essays in favor of imperialism, *America's Economic Supremacy* (1897–1900), likewise influenced the foreign policy thinking of many upper-class reformers. So did the similar argument advanced by Croly in *The Promise of American Life* (1909), which also called for a strong, centralized government controlled by an elite.

The influence of Frederick Jackson Turner, which so powerfully informed the outlook of key leaders like Roosevelt and Woodrow Wilson, was part of another intellectual current that also affected the reformers. Turner and Wilson were wide-ranging historians who matured in the seminar system developed at Johns Hopkins University. And that, in turn, was modeled on the program of graduate student training that emerged after 1870 in Germany.

The German influence went far beyond the question of method, however, into the realms of ideas and politics. Infused in part by the Christian doctrine of stewardship, as well as by the need to develop a theory and a program of centralized control for creating and managing a complex industrial economy (and blunting the appeal and rising support for socialism), the German neomercantilism of the 1880s and 1890s engaged the minds of many young Americans who became active reformers.

One important group consisted of young economists like Richard T. Ely, Simon Patten, and E. R. A. Seligman who challenged the orthodox laissez-faire approach of the older professionals such as J. Lawrence Laughlin and John Bates Clark. Most of the reformers had also been affected by the doctrines of the social gospel that the Protestant churches had developed in the 1880s. John R. Commons, for example, with whom Ely worked very closely at the University of Wisconsin, became the first secretary of the American Institute of Christian Sociology in 1893. Even earlier, in 1887, such men joined forces with ministers like Josiah Strong, Lyman Abbot, and Washington Gladden to form the Evangelical Alliance. It is not surprising, therefore, that from its founding in 1885, the American Economic Association represented a close alliance between morality and the new economics of control and regulation.

Another religious thrust entered the Progressive coalition through the ideas and leadership of such men as George D. Herron, professor of Applied Christianity at Iowa State College, and Walter Rauschenbusch, professor of church history at Rochester Theological Seminary. As revealed in Herron's *Social Meanings of Religious Experiences* (1895) and Rauschenbusch's *Christianity and the Social Crisis* (1907), the two men emphasized the New Testament and the community life of the early Christians. They were avowedly anticapitalist and candidly advocated Christian socialism as an alternative to the existing order. "If we can trust the Bible," Rauschenbusch argued, "God is against capitalism, its methods, spirit, and results."

That mixture of the religious and the secular was nicely revealed in the case of Raymond Robins of Chicago. The son of a Confederate officer, Robins first read for the law and then drifted westward, working as a laborer on the waterfront in New Orleans and in the mines of Colorado. He was deeply affected, like many other young men, by Henry George's argument (in *Progress and Poverty,* 1879) for the single tax and by George's insistence that men could improve their environment by collective action.

After a search for gold in Alaska and an intense religious experience while wandering along and snowblind in a terrible blizzard, Robins returned and became a settlement worker in the tough, depressed Seventeenth Ward in Chicago. A dynamic, thoughtful ("Halstead Street is conducive to the study of Marx") and courageous leader, Robins rapidly became a key figure in the affairs of the city. His marriage to Margaret Dreier led him into more extensive cooperation with the Women's Trade Union League, in which his wife played a vital role, and with the reform work of Jane Addams and Ellen Gates Starr.

The religious revival had been partially responsible for Jane Addams' involvement in the reform movement, but she was also reacting to the failure of the leaders of her upper-middle-class and upper-class milieu to correct the abuses of the industrial system. Addams and Starr founded Hull House in Chicago in 1889 as part of their revolt against the idea that "poverty was synonymous with vice and laziness." The same kind of community service activity had been initiated in New York by Stanton Coit in 1886, when his Neighborhood Guild movement opened the University Settlement on the Lower East Side. His work in behalf of child labor laws, adult education for aliens, and the reform of welfare work itself was designed to help people develop and use their own potential. In another approach, people like Edith Abbott began to professionalize the welfare movement in such centers of formal training as the School of Social Service at the University of Chicago.

For that matter, the sociologists provided additional intellectual leadership. Lester Frank Ward and Edward A. Ross, for example, were leading sociologists who argued that evolution was the product of man's intelligence, and Ward's *Dynamic Sociology* (1883) was a call to equalize opportunity through vigorous reform. Albion W. Small, who headed the *American Journal of Sociology* (founded 1895), pushed the same approach by printing devastating exposés of the conditions in and the governments of large cities several years before the popular press began to carry such articles. Louis D. Brandeis, a Kentucky-born and Harvard-educated lawyer, used the insights and the research of the sociologists very effectively. He based many of his legal briefs for reform measures on their contributions, just as he used the work of the economists and the scientific-management leaders to argue that increased efficiency would enable the corporations to lower prices while increasing their profits.

Reform philosophers were led by Charles S. Peirce, William James, and John Dewey. Peirce was trained as a mathematician, but he turned his unusually powerful and imaginative mind to the philosophical and ethical problems arising from the theory of probability. He rejected determinism on the grounds that the universe was evolutionary and that life was governed by the principles of probability (or chance) and continuity. James, who was educated in physiology and anatomy, followed the lead provided by Peirce. His laboratory work in experimental psychology redefined psychology as a discipline studying man's functional response to the environment.

After outlining that approach in *Principles of Psychology* (1890),

James extended the theory of pragmatism in *The Will to Believe* (1897). He argued that there were no deterministic or final truths and that there were no ultimate limits or barriers. The truth of an idea, he maintained, could be known only by its consequences. His work not only reinforced the vigor of the reform movement by assaulting the basis of the status quo but he also helped to arrange an accommodation between religion and science by arguing that faith was real, and hence true, when it satisfied emotional needs. He neglected, however, the truth that the corporation could make an idea consequential regardless of its value in improving human life.

James concentrated on the individual, whereas much of John Dewey's work involved an attempt to reemphasize the social aspects of life (which Peirce tended to stress). Dewey's version of pragmatism, which he developed while teaching at Columbia University, came to be known as *instrumentalism*. He defined reality as a sequence of problems, and his theory of education followed directly from that attitude: children (and adults) should learn by doing, and their intelligence and talents should be directed to altering and reforming society.

As a vigorous advocate of change, Dewey exerted a powerful influence on the reformers. His approach was biased toward defining problems in short-run terms, however, and hence it worked against changes in the structure of the system. Ironically, his sharp attack on abstract theory produced an outlook geared to maintaining the existing system by making periodic adjustments. One brilliant advocate of *pragmatism* named Randolph Bourne finally erupted in embittered anger: almost anything (including war) could be justified in the name of pragmatism, and that kind of reform was in truth the best friend of the established order.

The critical intellectuals also influenced the writing of American history. Socialist Algie Simons was the first to challenge the conservative interpretations, but his seminal work of the 1880s did not attract much general attention. The major impact was made by Charles Austin Beard and James Harvey Robinson of Columbia University, although J. Allen Smith's earlier revisionist study of *The Spirit of American Government* was a major contribution. He argued that the men and women who built the country had been moved by mundane, practical, acquisitive, and even selfish motives and that their ideas often had a direct relationship with their interests. Beard's subsequent study, *An Economic Interpretation of the Constitution* (1913), further opened the door to a more realistic understanding of the system and how it operated.

A similar approach infused the work of Thorsten Veblen in economics and political economy. As editor of *The Journal of Political Economy,* Veblen displayed his mastery of orthodox economics and his ability to do basic research that revealed the essence of capitalism. His first masterpiece, *The Theory of the Leisure Class* (1899), provided a devastating critique of the waste, inefficiency, and inequity of industrial capitalism. Like Beard, who met serious opposition from established academic authorities, as well as from political and economic leaders, Veblen suffered the consequences of his tough, iconoclastic scholarship. But both men did a great deal to sustain the reform spirit.

So did others who applied the same kind of research techniques to the study of the present. Their journalism of the exposé began with the publication of Lincoln Steffens' blast at the city government of St. Louis, "Tweed Days in St. Louis," in the October, 1902, issue of *McClure's Magazine*. The market proved so big and profitable that other magazines, such as *Munsey's* and *Cosmopolitan,* quickly began to print similar articles.

Few, if any, of the authors based their criticism on any broad theoretical or critical outlook such as Marxism. David Graham Phillips, whose study of the connections between senators and the giants of industry and finance *(The Treason of the Senate)* was perhaps the most devastating of all such studies, provided a candid insight into the general attitude: "I am so sick of fraud and filth and lies, so tired of stern realities, I grasp at myths like a child." The muckrakers, as they came to be called after Roosevelt used the term in venting his anger at their constant criticism, nevertheless sparked many specific reforms.

Thomas W. Lawson tore the veil from the machinations of the Amalgamated Copper Company in *Frenzied Finance.* Ida M. Tarbell attacked Standard Oil. Burton J. Henrick explained how the individual helped to provide capital for the giants in *The Story of Life Insurance.* John Moody's review and analysis of the corporations, *The Truth About the Trusts,* and William J. Ghent's more interpretative study, *Our Benevolent Feudalism,* made it clear that individual free enterprise no longer existed in vital areas of the political economy. And the literary power of Upton Sinclair made his novelistic report on the meat packing industry, *The Jungle,* a nightmare of miserable working conditions and labor practices and of unsanitary and dangerous food products.

As typified by the impact of *The Jungle,* the intellectuals played an early, sustained, and significant role in the effort to control and reform the corporate system. They explained the nature of the new political economy to large numbers of people in all classes and thus helped to incite them to action. But so did the militant workers who risked (and often lost) their jobs in a continuing effort to force the conservative members of all classes to share the benefits of the system in a more equitable manner. Without the workers, the intellectuals would have had far less influence. And without the white middle class, which was periodically fearful of the unions and angry with the corporations, the drive for reform would have been defeated—or perhaps have become more radical.

EXPLORATORY READING

If you are intrigued by the nature of the new corporate system and want to do some history in that subject, then go first to the massive—19 volume—government investigation published as the *Report of the Industrial Commission* (1900–1902). The following books, on the other hand, discuss the subject from various points of view:

F. L. Allen, *The Great Pierpont Morgan* (1949)

T. C. Cochrane and W. Miller, *The Age of Enterprise: A Social History of Industrial America* (1968)

E. E. Day and W. Thomas, *The Growth of Manufactures, 1899–1923* (1927)

G. W. Edwards, *The Evolution of Finance Capitalism* (1938)

H. V. Faulkner, *The Decline of Laissez-Faire, 1897–1917* (1951)

E. Jones, *The Trust Problem in the United States* (1924)

E. C. Kirkland, *Industry Comes of Age* (1961)

Z. L. Miller, *The Urbanization of Modern America* (1973)

F. C. Mills, *Economic Tendencies in the United States: Aspects of Pre-War and Post-War Changes* (1932)

J. Moody, *Masters of Capital* (1921)

D. C. North, *Growth and Welfare in the American Past* (1966)

A. J. Noyes, *Forty Years of American Finance, 1865–1907* (1909)

The life of the workers, unorganized as well as those who were members of unions, is likewise revealed in the *Report of the Industrial Commission*. But others have written about it in these ways:

E. Abbott, *Women in Industry* (1910)

D. Brody, *Steelworkers in America: The Non-Union Era* (1970)

R. J. Cornell, *The Anthracite Coal Strike of 1902* (1957)

P. S. Foner, *History of the Labor Movement in the United States* (1947)

R. Hunter, *Poverty* (1972)

W. J. Lanck and E. Sydenstricker, *Conditions of Labor in American Industries* (1917)

D. D. Lescohier and E. Brandeis, *History of Labor in the United States, 1896–1932* (1934)

M. Meltzer, *Bread and Roses: The Struggle. of American Labor, 1865–1915* (1967)

S. Perlman and P. Taft, *A History of American Labor in the United States, 1896–1932* (1935)

L. Wolman, *The Growth of American Trade Unions* (1924)

The best way to get a sense and feel of the intellectual ferment of the time is to read the magazines and books that were published during those years. But some of the most stimulating historical studies have focused on the intellectuals. These will get you started:

D. Aaron (Ed.), *America in Crisis* (1952)

M. W. Brown, *American Painting from the Armory Show to the Depression* (1955)

D. Chalmers, *The Social and Political Ideas of the Muckrakers* (1964)

L. Filler, *Crusaders for American Liberalism* (1939)

C. Forcey, *The Crossroads of Liberalism* (1961)

J. Gilbert, *Designing the Industrial State; The Intellectual Pursuit of Collectivism in America, 1880–1940* (1972)

E. Goldman, *The Rendezvous with Destiny* (1952)

N. G. Hale, Jr., *Freud and the Americans: The Beginnings of Psychoanalysis in America, 1876–1917* (1971)

R. Hofstadter, *The Progressive Historians* (1968)

C. Lasch, *The New Radicalism in America, 1889–1963* (1965)

H. May, *Protestant Churches and Industrial America* (1949)

G. M. Ostrander, *American Civilization in the First Machine Age, 1890–1940* (1970)

C. C. Regier, *The Era of the Muckrakers* (1932)

H. H. Reid, *American Skyline* (1953)

B. Rose, *American Art Since 1900: A Critical History* (1967)

M. White, *Social Thought in America: The Revolt Against Formalism* (1957)

4 THE DYNAMICS OF THE PROGRESSIVE COALITION

THE coal strikes of 1900 and 1902 symbolized the importance of labor unrest in generating action by other classes and groups in the corporate economy. For a time, until about 1905, the disputes evoked a new awareness of and sympathy for the workers among middle-class—and even some upper-class—Americans. Two strikes in 1903, for example, one in Morenci, Arizona, and another at Cripple Creek, Colorado, again involved President Roosevelt as well as the general public.

The Arizona confrontation provoked the conservative governor to ask Roosevelt for troops to insure "peace and order." But it soon became apparent that the union was not threatening the social structure and the president promptly withdrew the soldiers. The opposite occurred in Colorado. The mine owners instituted a campaign of terror against the workers, who in turn asked Roosevelt to send troops to protect them. He refused and was criticized by many people who understood the situation.

In reply, Roosevelt offered a statement that probably articulated the views of a majority of the population. He supported the concept of an open shop but defined it to mean that employment should be open to union members as well as nonunion workers. "I would guarantee by every means in my power," the president explained, "the right of laboring men to join a union and their right to work as union men without illegal interference from either capitalists or nonunion men."

Whether by intuition or by accident, Roosevelt had caught the contemporary feeling of the majority of the middle class, and he knowingly expressed the strategy of his section of the upper class. Both groups wanted a balanced and equitable society that did not threaten their property, power, or prestige. As the workers kept pushing for true equality with the corporations, however, a growing number of conservative capitalists responded with a concerted campaign to break the back of union labor.

That confrontation was filled with contradictions—and hence with ironies. The alliance—sometimes calculated and in other cases coincidental—between the small and large capitalists who were determined to preserve the traditional prerogatives of ownership became increasingly effective. But that forced labor ever more to the left, which in turn pushed other middle- and upper-class people to agitate for further reforms to block the threat of radical changes leading to socialism. And, to complicate the situation even further, some of the most vigorous antiunion leaders were at the same time spokesmen for other kinds of reform.

Encouraged by the coal strike of 1902 and driven by their own miserable conditions, other union workers initiated similar campaigns to improve their lives. There were many, many strikes during the ensuing seven years, but the following list provides a feel for the ferment of the times: the International Association of Machinists struck in 1901; the New York building tradesmen did the same in 1903; the Amalgamated Meat Cutters followed suit in 1904; Chicago teamsters tested their strength against Montgomery Ward in 1905; the Amalgamated Association of Iron, Steel, and Tin Workers carried on a running battle with the owners from 1901 through 1908; and the International Association of Bridge and Structural Steel and Iron Workers waged a similar struggle between 1902 and 1910.

Each of those unions won some victories, but in the end they were defeated. Some of the corporations, such as steel, enjoyed too many advantages: a pool of surplus immigrant labor, enormous amounts of money, and the structure and the precedents of the law. The latter consideration was classically illustrated by the litigation that grew out of the battle between the United Hatters of America and the firm of D. H. Lowe and Company of Danbury, Connecticut. The workers went on strike in 1902 and, as part of their strategy, called for a national boycott of Lowe's hats. He counterattacked by suing each worker for $240,000, basing his charge on a provision of the Sherman Anti-Trust Act that authorized triple damages for anyone injured by a violation of the law. Finally, in 1908, the Supreme Court decided in favor of Lowe. The ruling was a devastating blow to union labor and symbolized the power of property and the rising fears of many middle- and upper-class people.

The steel corporations won their battles more frontally, using lock-outs, force, and strikebreakers. Smaller owners in other industries paid ironic tribute to the giants, banding together to accomplish the same objective. Their use of highly emotional appeals to the ideology of freedom and individualism was belied by their action, but the tactic evoked a positive response among many middle-class Americans. Their activities also provoked violence. The bridge workers, for example, who lived a dangerous and migratory life, were driven to use their knowledge of dynamite.

Those workers had won two nonviolent strikes in 1902 and 1903, and neither settlement threatened the profits of the owners. But the capitalists, led by the National Erectors Association, could not tolerate any modifications of their power and hence hired Walter Drew to organize a counterattack. He was good at his work. He blacklisted union men, cut off suppliers who recognized union labor, hired spies and troublemakers, and refused to negotiate with the union. The bridge workers began in 1908 to respond with force. They used it carefully: none of their first 70 explosions injured any people—and, for that matter, did generally minor damage to property.

But the owners made no compromises. Then two union leaders, Ortie McManigal and J. B. McNamara, destroyed the Los Angeles *Times* plant in October, 1910–and in the process killed 21 people. The upper and middle classes—along with many workers—were appalled, frightened, and outraged. The reaction symbolized the gradual erosion of sympathy engendered by Mitchell and the coal miners. McManigal and McNamara had in effect blasted labor rather than capital.

Three other efforts by labor, aided by violence caused by capitalists, saved the day. The International Ladies Garment Workers Union (ILGWU), moving with sophisticated militance, had slowly improved the initially despicable conditions of employment. But not enough: the owners were calculating, crude, and callous. Then came the great Triangle Fire in New York (1911) that killed 146 people. The court in its wisdom acquitted the property owners of any responsibility, but the public outrage provided vital support for the reformers, who forced the enactment of new labor laws and building codes.

Socialist Eugene Debs spoke to the broader issue: such reforms were helpful, though tragically overdue, but it was necessary to change the system. And Big Bill Haywood delivered the same message to those who struggled for a meager living in the mines and forests of the West. The middle and upper classes could not ignore those messages. Whether out of fear or sympathy, they had to respond. Roosevelt said it all when he revealed his fear that conservatives and the reactionaries like Baer were driving people to Debs. For Debs attracted people of all classes to his vision of socialism. Even farmers.

It was an amazing achievement in American politics, for the American farmer had always been defined by his sense of owning land. Yet the major socialist newspaper, *The Appeal to Reason,* was published in Kansas. Debs understood, even if he did not formally analyze, the changes that were occurring in agriculture.

In some respects, the farmer's condition did improve after the war against Spain. The time of troubles between 1885 and 1900 had forced many marginal operators off the land, and the continued rapid urbanization and industrialization created a rising domestic demand for food and fiber. Production rose about 40 percent between 1900 and 1914, but because of the increase in population there was no vast surplus to depress the market. Prices jumped nearly 50 percent, and gross farm income almost doubled.

The increase in gross farm income was misleading, however, because a good part of it went to the large operators. Another portion had to be reinvested in improvements and current operating costs in order to stay in business. And still another part was lost in the steady inflation during the period. One study of the cost of living, based on an index figure of 100 for 1914, shows an increase from 73 in 1895 to 96 in 1910. Or, looked at in another way, the jump of 100 percent in gross farm income turns out to be far less when translated into average annual earnings for farmers. Excluding agricultural labor, the figures moved from $402 in 1896 to $544 in 1905, and on to $630 in 1910.

Tenancy increased 16.3 percent between 1900 and 1910, and it rose in the corn belt states as well as in the South. Farmers still had to contend, moreover, with the economic power of the processors and the railroads. The dissatisfaction enabled many of the state-level reform movements to draw considerable strength from farmers. The agriculturists wanted short- and medium-term credit to carry them through the period from planting to marketing, or, in case of a poor crop or low prices, across an entire season. They sought similar assistance to finance improvements, called for tighter regulation of the railroads, and agitated for measures to improve their bargaining position with flour millers and other processors.

A powerful attack on the tariff began in Iowa in 1901, for example, and that campaign had much to do with the progressive career of Governor (and later Senator) Albert B. Cummins. Related unrest in Wisconsin, Idaho, Minnesota, and Nebraska produced similar results. Other groups were even militant, such as the members of the National Farmers Union and the Nonpartisan League. Though not formally founded until 1915, the underlying antagonism against the processors and railroads that explained the growth of the league had become apparent as early as the panic of 1907. The demands for state-owned flour mills and control of the railroads were part of a movement to the left. A Nebraska farmer explained it by pointing out that the small operator, the tenant farmer, the sharecropper, and the farm laborer were just as "ripe for socialism" as the factory hand. Debs worked hard to win support among those groups, and a significant portion of his votes after 1900 came from outside the industrial working class.

But the essential dynamism of the Socialist movement came from the urban centers, as illustrated by the effective leadership of Morris Hillquit in New York and Victor L. Berger's organization of the German population of Milwaukee, Wisconsin. Other Socialist leaders attracted similar support in many parts of the country, and by 1912 the Socialist party had elected more than 1000 of its members to public office in well over 300 towns and cities. Such radical political action was one way that immigrants exerted pressure for reform, but they also influenced that process by their very presence—whatever their politics.

The great burst of immigration, which began in 1882 and climaxed in 1907 when 1,285,000 foreigners arrived, shifted in character over those years. The earlier newcomers were largely German and English, but that changed after 1900, when Italians and Russians predominated. Most Americans, including many of the earlier immigrants, considered the latecomers far more difficult to integrate into the new industrial system because of their poverty and cultural differences. There was some substance in that argument, if only because America was a more complex and rapid-paced society in 1907 than in 1890, but the central problem was defined by so many of immigrants arriving in such a short period and settling in a relatively few areas.

In any event, they posed serious practical problems and provoked considerable economic, religious, and ethnic antagonisms. On the one hand, they strengthened the conservative resistance to change and reform (as in the agitation of the Immigration Restriction League), while on the other hand, they spurred many urban reformers like Jacob Riis of New York to great efforts to improve the system. And that clash energized the immigrants themselves, many of whom became reformers.

THE EXCLUSION OF BLACKS AND INDIANS FROM THE PROGRESSIVE COALITION

Black American citizens (perhaps *residents* is the more accurate term) became involved, despite some obvious differences in their circumstances, in a similar process. The great internal migration of blacks to northern industrial centers did not occur until World War I, although a gradual transfer of population began in the 1890s, and so most of them lived a miserable life as wretchedly poor sharecroppers in the South.

The phrase "second-class citizens," which came to be used to describe their situation and status, is in truth a shameful verbal evasion of their miserable lot: desperate poverty, social segregation and personal contempt, political disenfranchisement, and lynchings (death).

Some of them dealt with that horrendous situation by establishing all-black communities in the South as well as in the North. They were shoved into that strategy by the whites, but they understood its potentially creative possibilities: it could generate a powerful sense of social solidarity and strength, and it could create a society that would produce its own leaders. That was viscerally important because most white reformers of all classes were indifferent to the plight of the blacks, and most of the white conservatives were openly antiblack.

The first influential black leader to emerge on the national scene was Booker Taliaferro Washington, born the son of a slave in Virginia. He worked as a miner and janitor while proceeding through various schools, and in 1881 he was asked to organize the training of black teachers in Tuskegee, Alabama. His philosophy and strategy stressed industrial education as the best way to achieve political and social recognition—and power.

That program was supported by some whites in the South as well as the North because it seemingly promised to create a cheap and docile supply of labor for the new industrial system without threatening the economic and political power of the whites. A smaller group of whites honestly felt that vocational training offered the only avenue of progress for the blacks. Such whites tended to overlook, as did more militant blacks, the way that Washington's approach would—over one or two generations—provide the foundation for a black nationalism that could generate social power as well as individual pride and economic improvement.

The leader of the radical blacks was William Edward Burghardt DuBois of Massachusetts. He began as a student of Washington's, and then went on to earn a PhD from Harvard. DuBois was the intellectual peer of any white American leader (and superior to most). Hence he most certainly understood the long-range consequences of Washington's program to educate the blacks so that they could compete on equal terms with other Americans in the marketplace. But he was also shrewd enough to realize that while President Roosevelt's invitation to Washington to have lunch in the White House may well have symbolized an honest sympathy and concern, it also misled everyone into thinking that the problem was being solved.

Thus DuBois broke away from Washington and launched an angry, militant frontal attack on the lynchings, political repression, social abasement, and economic degradation that defined the life of black

Americans. He was the black Debs and Haywood (and in the end became a Communist), and he had a similar effect on white reformers. He was the power behind the Niagara Falls Conference of June, 1905, for example, which issued a ringing manifesto for freedom of speech, suffrage, equal education as opposed to manual training, and social justice—in short, an end to all forms of racism and discrimination.

The need for that kind of toughness was underscored the following year by Roosevelt's handling of the riot in Brownsville, Texas. The president dismissed without honor the entire regiment of black soldiers that was involved and banned all of the men from further military or civil service. The resentment against that arbitrary, drastic, and unjustified action was sustained by the 1908 riot in Springfield, Illinois. The trouble started when a white woman charged a black man with rape. She later retracted the charge, but it made no difference because the mood of terror had been established. The ensuing melee produced two lynchings, as well as the usual beatings and burnings, and it required 5000 militia men to restore order.

A few whites, led by William English Walling, Mary White Ovington, and Oswald Garrison Villard, responded by forming a coalition movement with DuBois and his supporters. They created the National Association for the Advancement of Colored People (NAACP) in 1909. It soon became—even though whites held the top positions—the cutting edge of the fight for black equality. DuBois started a magazine, *The Crisis,* that was a powerful and effective journal of theory and outrage. Two years later Roger W. Baldwin and others organized the National Urban League (NUL), which concentrated on helping blacks find jobs and cope with the difficulties of life in northern cities.

Such vibrant leaders among the Indians—more honorably called the First Americans—had been killed or demoralized during the long war (1863–1900) that defeated those peoples and largely destroyed their cultures. As with the blacks, the First Americans had painfully evolved a sense (and the rituals) of time, place, and pace that could have helped the majority of twentieth-century Americans sustain their own traditions of community and common humanity during the process of urbanization and industrialization. Instead, the First Americans were viewed—and treated—as inferior people who just *possibly* might be transformed into responsible capitalists.

In that respect, and it is an important one, the vast majority of American Progressives dealt with the issue as if it was part of their imperial foreign policy. Indeed, the Dawes Severality Act of 1887 provided an eerie preview of the later treatment of the Filipinos and the Cubans. The purpose of the Dawes law was to destroy tribal life—economic as well as cultural—and transform the First Americans

into proper and responsible individualistic marketplace capitalists settled on small family farms—or into cheap labor in the industrial portion of the economy.

It did largely succeed in subverting tribal life—and hence
community—but it failed to integrate the First Americans into the
pseudocommunity of the corporate industrial system. Part of that failure was due to prejudice and racism, and part of it was explained by
the inherent inability of the capitalist marketplace to function as a new
and better version of community, but the principal difficulty involved
the limited vision of community held by the upper- and middle-class
reformers. The harsh truth of it was (and is) that they had no vision of a
modern industrial *community*. It is possible to argue, with considerable persuasiveness, that it is impossible to create a community out of
a centralized modern industrial and technocratic society: that the reality over powers the vision.

In any event, the First Americans were unable to exert any consequential pressure on any group or class of white Americans that came
together around other issues to form the Progressive coalition. Their
lack of power was clearly revealed by their absence from the struggle
among white Progressives over the issue of conservation. President
Roosevelt personified the contradictory nature of their approach to the
environment. He was a vigorous athlete; so involved, for that matter,
as to lose the sight of one eye in his boxing ring in the White House.
And he loved to play at being a cowboy: charging up San Juan Hill in
Cuba and taking regular vacations on horseback in what remained of
the Dakota Badlands. As an upper-class Massachusetts cowboy, however, he viewed the First Americans as an anachronism. They were
brave and noble but irrelevant to *The Law of Civilization and Decay*.

The cowboy was a romantic, whatever the dreary (and often dangerous) reality of his workaday life, and romanticism was one of the major
elements in the campaign for the conservation of America's natural
beauty and resources. The New England bourgeois entertained a desire to keep America pure (agrarian) even as it became corrupt (industrial). It was at once an irrelevant dream—how to honor the logic of
capitalist industrialism without exploiting resources according to the
imperatives of marketplace profit?—and at the same time a perception
of visceral truth—how to survive, as human beings *or* as capitalists, if
all the resources were considered expendable for short-term pleasures
or profits?

The rational marketplace answer (enlightened self-interest) was to
use much, save some, and regenerate even more. Conservatives of the
old school insisted, of course, that it was all an artificial problem: there
was enough for all forever. They wanted the freedom to cut trees and
dig minerals as fast as they could without any interference from re-

formers, rationalists, or romantics. The romantics wanted to preserve most—if not all—without giving up the benefits of an industrial political economy.

Thus the ongoing battle over conservation provides a revealing insight into the dynamics of the Progressive coalition. Most obviously, the poor people—whatever their color or ethnic origins—were not directly involved. It was a struggle within and between various groups in the upper and middle classes that were acting in the name of—and for or against the interests of—the general public. Roosevelt won an early victory for his approach, which combined a degree of romanticism with the idea of using resources in a rational manner. He effectively supported the Newlands Reclamation Act, passed by the Congress in 1902, which authorized the use of federal funds (taxes) to build dams and in other ways extend the irrigation of arid lands.

Few people then understood the long-range consequences of disturbing, distorting, and ultimately destroying an ancient ecological balance in order to produce profits in the desert. Indeed, if Roosevelt and others had realized that water was a resource that needed to be handled much as forests—by allowing time for nature to replace current usage—the Newlands Act would have been drafted quite differently. But Roosevelt did see that relationship as it affected trees. Using the provisions of the Forest Reserve Act of 1891 and the Newlands Act, he asserted federal control over land in Alaska and various western states in order to block the wild exploitation of timber, coal, and other minerals. "To waste, to destroy, our natural resources," he warned, "to skin and exhaust the land . . . will result in undermining in the days of our children the very prosperity which we ought by right to hand down to them amplified and developed."

The advocates of laissez-faire capitalism, including many miners, timbermen, and power companies, wanted an open field to exploit the resources. The romantics demanded that the forests, in particular, be permanently set aside as monuments to nature and beauty. The conservatives blocked further withdrawals of land in six western states in 1907 through a rider on the Agricultural Appropriations Bill. Acting through Gifford Pinchot in the Department of the Interior, Roosevelt circumvented that maneuver by withdrawing 17 million acres and reserving potential dam sites by designating them as ranger stations before he signed the appropriations law. The opposition was furious and thwarted the president's subsequent bid (1908) to establish a National Country Wildlife Commission and a permanent Inland Waterways Commission.

The cooperation between the reformers in the middle and upper classes that characterized the fight for conservation measures became the basic feature of the Progressive coalition. Both groups were constantly under pressure from the working class (moderate as well as radical members), and they came together with increasing effectiveness to force various changes upon the conservatives and reactionaries, who either did not comprehend the need for adaptation or felt that the existing order could be upheld by power alone. The middle- and upper-class reformers did not always agree, either on the nature or the extent of specific reforms, but by 1908 they had generated a powerful momentum for improving and rationalizing the industrial political economy.

A useful insight into those patterns of conflict and cooperation is provided by the example of the small- and medium-sized businessmen who, even though they were antiunion in labor policy, supported—and even initiated—various other reforms. They were militantly opposed to corrupt ties between business and politics, opposed the ever expanding power of the large corporations, and in many instances favored campaigns for pure-food laws, sanitation improvements, and public health measures. They also led the campaign to rationalize local government. Their approach was expressed very concisely by John H. Patterson, a Dayton manufacturer, as early as 1896: "a city is a great business enterprise," he explained, and he called for reforms to organize its affairs "on a strict business basis."

That attitude led to the commission form of government in which an elected council and a city manager functioned as a board of directors. The big breakthrough came in Galveston, Texas, after a great tidal wave demolished most of the city. The crisis was defined as that of "a great ruined business," and local businessmen established a five-man commission to rebuild the city. Supported by chambers of commerce and other business groups, the idea spread rapidly, first in Texas and then to Des Moines, Iowa (1907), and by 1913 more than 300 cities had adopted that form of government.

The reform campaigns of such men as Mayor Seth Low against Tammany Hall in New York and of Tom Johnson in Cleveland and "Golden Rule" Jones in Toledo also drew strength and leadership from businessmen. All those examples serve to dramatize another important feature of the Progressive coalition. While the middle class was active in such national organizations as the American Association for Labor Legislation and the Consumer's League and became increasingly involved in national political agitation, the real power of the Progressives stemmed from their organization at the local and state levels.

The pattern that evolved was a composite of new city charters, direct primary and recall elections, rate commissions and other regulatory agencies, tax reforms (and even increases), civil service systems, conservation and beautification programs, and antilobby laws. And the result was a group of reform governments spanning the nation. Hiram W. Johnson, who won the governorship in California in 1910, represented the same forces that elected LaFollette in Wisconsin, Cummins in Iowa, Charles Evans Hughes in New York, Hoke Smith in Georgia, Jeff Davis in Arkansas, and Woodrow Wilson in New Jersey.

Urban middle-class women made significant contributions to the reform movement. Some of them learned the weaknesses and failures of the system as a result of working in it (25 percent of all women over 15 were employed in 1910). Along with others who used their leisure to study the nature of the new industrialism, those women agitated for better working conditions, higher pay, and shorter hours. More of the women reformers, however, were primarily concerned with purifying the system of its sins and achieving what they defined as equal treatment for themselves.

Those were the main objectives of the women's clubs that developed after 1900. They were largely antimale on the grounds that men had made a mess of running the affairs of the country and because they kept women in an inferior position. They campaigned for the right to vote, for equality in marriage and property laws, for the protection of minors, for the strict control or prohibition of liquor, and against prostitution. Beyond serving as a conscience and a goad, they offered leadership to lower-class women and worked to relieve the suffering of the poor and handicapped.

Upper-class women also became activists. Margaret Dreier, for example, devoted much of her life to organizing unions among lower-class textile workers. Others supported the female emancipation movement, agitated for reform laws, and encouraged the revolution in art and in letters. And no doubt many of them, in ways that remain unknown to historians, exerted various pressures on their husbands to support (or acquiesce to) reform.

THE DIFFICULTIES IN UPPER-CLASS REGULATION OF THE CORPORATE SYSTEM

As those examples indicate, upper-class reformers were not simply antiradical. The old-fashioned capitalist posed a serious danger because he increased class consciousness among the workers. "Our enemies," Ralph Easley explained in a revealing example of upper-class thinking, "are the Socialists among the labor people and the anarchists among the labor people and the anarchists among the capitalists." The goal, another explained, was to "shape the right kind of regulation" that would block radical proposals *and* prevent a return to laissez-faire.

"Business cannot be successfully conducted," Roosevelt bluntly explained, "in accordance with the practices and theories of 60 years ago." The same point was made by the report that financier J. P. Morgan had nightmares about the return of tooth-and-fang competition. The leaders of the new system wanted order, stability, and efficiency; and their increasing willingness to accept state and even federal regulation was a manifestation of that desire, as well as a way of blocking more drastic measures.

George W. Perkins of the House of Morgan was one of the most effective advocates of reform for stability and efficiency; and Charles G. Bonaparte of Baltimore and Hazen S. Pingree of Detroit were typical of many others who recognized that need. Such men were paternalistic, but honestly paternalistic. Roosevelt, for example, thought that the president was "the steward of the public welfare." "The officers of the great corporation," Perkins remarked in an expression of the same outlook, "instinctively lose sight of the interest of any one individual and work for what is the broadest, most enduring interest of the many."

Had those upper-class leaders been less flexible, the pressures from below might have caused a violent and extensive social explosion. Roosevelt was unusually candid in his first annual message to the Congress in December, 1901. "The tremendous and highly complex industrial development . . . brings us face to face," he warned, "with very serious social problems. The old laws, and the old customs . . . are no longer sufficient." But reform could not go so far as to destroy the corporate system, he explained, because the large corporation must "take the lead in the strife for commercial supremacy among the nations of the world"—"foreign markets [are] essential."

The practical issue, therefore, was defined by how to deal with the "real and grave evils" of the new giants without moving too far toward socialism. Roosevelt asked for power to regulate the railroads, for approval of reciprocity treaties, and for measures to conserve national resources. Traditional conservatives saw the implications of his message and mustered their forces to resist any serious reforms. The president was immediately confronted, therefore, with a division within the upper class that grew increasingly serious and embittered.

That split was bitter in the Senate, where Hanna's approach was resisted by men like Quay, Platt, Aldrich, and Spooner. One influential man in the middle was Senator William B. Allison of Iowa, a Republican who understood the need to accommodate the reformers. Roosevelt had no such allies in the House. First he had to deal with Speaker David B. Henderson, also of Iowa, who was a prorailroad conservative passively following the lead of men like Quay and Platt. His resignation in the face of growing pressure from his own constituents for lower tariffs and railroad regulation, however, proved of no assistance to Roosevelt and the reformers. They were beaten in the ensuing battle to elect a new Speaker. The victor was Joseph G. Cannon of Illinois, a shrewd, ruthless, and effective old-line conservative who opposed reform.

The president encountered similar opposition from many businessmen. The old capitalists were flatly against regulation, and more sophisticated men like Hanna and Morgan differed among

The view of Theodore Roosevelt as a gallant trustbuster was not acceptable to many discerning observers. Several cartoonists attacked the image. C. J. Bush of the New York World *cartooned Roosevelt as the young George Washington in a very different version of the cherry tree myth.*

"I DID IT, DAD, WITH MY LITTLE HATCHET."

—*The New York World.*

Reprinted in *The Literary Digest*, vol. XXVI, March 7, 1903, p. 330.

themselves—and with Roosevelt—over the nature and extent of re-form. Together with Edward H. Harriman, James J. Hill, and the Rockefeller interests, for example, Morgan organized the Northern Se-curities Company in 1901 as a holding company to unify and ra-tionalize the Chicago, Burlington and Quincy Line, the Northern Pacific, and the Great Northern.

Roosevelt viewed the action as a dangerous failure to accept the responsibilities of power and as a challenge to his own leadership and authority. He quietly prepared his attack in the form of an antitrust suit to dissolve the holding company. It produced great anger and dis-may among conservatives, who flayed the president as being "unreasonable"—and worse. But a majority of the country responded favorably, and Roosevelt used that strength (and his later victory in the courts) to outmaneuver such opponents on other issues.

Even so, his first efforts to create the Department of Commerce and Labor as a center for studying and regulating the economy and his call to control railroad rates met stiff opposition from conservatives like Aldrich and Cannon. Such people were equally unmoved by the find-ings and recommendations of the Industrial Commission or by the political gains of the reformers at the local and state levels.

But led by William S. U'Ren, Oregon Progressives won in 1902 their long battle for the initiative and the referendum. The first of those reforms allowed ordinary citizens to place proposals on the general election ballot and the second enabled them to reconsider measures passed by the legislature (and some actions by the governor). And in the same year, Maryland reformers created the first system of work-men's compensation that held employers liable for injuries on the job. That idea spread quickly, and by 1917 all but ten states had passed such laws. The Progressives were on the move: Jeff Davis became governor of Arkansas in 1901; LaFollette triumphed in Wisconsin in 1900; and William R. Stubbs, a reforming Kansas millionaire, was ready to challenge the old-fashioned conservatives in that state.

Roosevelt exploited that kind of pressure to obtain several pieces of reform legislation during 1903: the Expedition Act allowed the Attor-ney General to push antitrust prosecutions through the lower courts to the Supreme Court without the usual delay, and the Congress finally created the Department of Commerce and Labor and also established the Bureau of Corporations, empowered to investigate all firms (except common carriers) that were engaged in interstate commerce.

(It is worth noting, in this connection, that the power to investigate—to demand documents and testimony—is very similar to the process of doing history. Indeed, it dramatizes the value of doing history. For to investigate and learn the facts is the first essential step in the process of making sense of reality and of imagining different ways of organizing reality. Any vigorous congressional investigation produces essential materials for first-rate history.)

The reformers (with some assistance from the more sophisticated conservatives) also passed the Elkins Act. It sought to control rebates by the railroads to large shippers and other discriminations between users of the roads. A number of conservatives, including railroad leaders, supported the bill as a way to blunt the reform agitation and to protect the railroads against the demands by large industrial corporations for special treatment. The law gave published rates the force of law and authorized federal courts to use the power of the injunction against violators. The most dramatic prosecution that flowed from the legislation involved the Standard Oil Company, a notorious exploiter of its powerful position as a shipper. It was fined $29 million in 1907, but in a typical blunting of the reform process, that penalty was later set aside. The Progressives could propose, even legislate, but the conservative courts continued to dispose.

Despite such setbacks, Roosevelt moved into the election of 1904 on a wave of rising strength provided by local and state Progressives. The National Municipal League, organized in 1894, had become an effective agency of reform. Men like Charles R. Crane (the Chicago plumbing millionaire) and Victor F. Lawson (a reform journalist), working with others like Raymond Robins and Jane Addams, were changing the spirit and the earthly realities of Chicago.

And John Randolph Hayes in Los Angeles and James D. Phelan in San Francisco were mayors who broke through the often corrupt, and always conservative, alliance between traditional businessmen and politicians. Reform of the juvenile court system, which began in Illinois in 1899, had spread westward to states like Colorado, where Judge Benjamin B. Lindsey of Denver became a national leader of that movement. And in 1903 LaFollette pushed through a direct primary law, a railroad commission, and income tax legislation.

Roosevelt needed that kind of support. But he was busy helping himself: he handled the corruption in the Post Office, for example, before his enemies could use the scandal against him. Even so, he was engaged in a running battle with the economic giants like Morgan and Hanna who felt that they should run the new corporate system.

The president was unquestionably a certain kind of political magician. He worked effectively with Morgan, for example, in preventing the financial panic of 1903 from becoming a recession (or even a depression). That did not satisfy the upper-class giants. They were inclined to favor Hanna for the presidency, fretting that Roosevelt would lose control of the reformers, mistrusting his aristocratic background, and viscerally upset about the continued growth of the socialist movement.

Hanna had developed significant support among farmers and workers by telling them bluntly to organize against the corporations and bankers. And he might have been an effective president. But he died in February, 1904, and Roosevelt won the Republican nomination without a fight. Then he easily defeated Judge Alton B. Parker, the weak candidate of a deeply divided Democratic party (7.6 million to 5.1 million in the popular vote, and 336 to 140 in the electoral count).

The real surprise of the election was the increased support for Debs. He pulled 402,460 votes, a gain of more than 400 percent over the 94,768 he won in 1900. That jump in Socialist strength—which was based on dedicated organizing at the local level, on the popularity of Debs, and on the growing dissatisfaction with the status quo—exerted a significant and continuing influence on the Progressive coalition. Roosevelt spoke bluntly to that point in his annual message of December, 1904:

> The friends of property must realize that the surest way to provoke an explosion of wrong and injustice is to be shortsighted, narrow-minded, greedy, and arrogant, and to fail to show in actual work that here in this Republic it is peculiarly incumbent upon the man with whom things have prospered to be in a certain sense the keeper of his brother with whom life has gone hard.

The president then asked the Congress to pass legislation limiting working hours and requiring the installation of safety devices on all railroads, to extend the powers of the Interstate Commerce Commission (ICC), to establish a licensing system to regulate large corporations, to control railroad rates, and to initiate a broad program of social welfare measures in the District of Columbia that could then be refined and extended to the entire country.

Roosevelt was supported by reformers throughout the country. The governors of Iowa, Minnesota, and Wisconsin sent a petition to the White House asking for firm action against high railroad rates. Similar agitation developed in the lower Mississippi Valley and throughout the Old South. Even the editors of *The Wall Street Journal* warned that changes had to be made, and Attorney General Philander C. Knox said simply in December, 1904, that railroad rate legislation was "inevitable."

Similar opposition had developed against the large life insurance companies, many of which were coming under the control of the financiers. The work of the Armstrong Investigation in New York (1906–1907) led to tougher regulation. Two upper-class leaders, Elihu Root and Charles Evans Hughes, played key roles in that action and John F. Dryden, who was a state senator as well as president of the Prudential Life Insurance Company, bluntly asked for federal regulation. Within two years, by the end of 1907, 29 of the 42 state legislatures approved new insurance laws. The controls defined the ways that the companies would invest the premiums they collected, prohibitions against lobbying and campaign contributions, and more exacting regulations on company elections and management.

The insurance issue elevated Hughes to the governorship of New York (1906–1910). He promptly instituted the Public Service Commission and initiated a program of developing water power at the state level. A similar story unfolded in Massachusetts, where reform lawyer Louis D. Brandeis headed another investigation of insurance companies (particularly the Equitable Life) that was triggered by the Hughes inquiry in New York. The Brandeis probe, undertaken in his role as attorney for dissatisfied policyholders, led to the creation of a low-cost insurance system anchored in savings banks.

The combined impact of all such pressures, including those from labor unions and the Socialists, prompted even Elbert H. Gary of the United States Steel Corporation, a tough reactionary, to discuss with Roosevelt the best ways of avoiding "extreme remedial legislation." "What we want is stability," he explained, "the avoidance of violent fluctuations." Ralph Easley of the NCF spoke more directly about "the menace of socialism."

The big firms that dominated the NCF began to establish research laboratories as early as 1894 (General Electric), and they took the same approach to social issues. They were against public ownership, but supported regulation, compulsory compensation for injured workers, and similar reforms in other areas. Some of the members of the federation also initiated, or extended, welfare programs in their own corporations. Such industrial noblesse oblige, with its overtones of paternalism, was most apparent in the improvements in working conditions, recreation facilities, and other fringe benefits provided by the National Cash Register Company and by Sears Roebuck and Company.

All such pressures produced four significant pieces of legislation during June 29–30, 1906. The first and most important law was the Hepburn Act. It strengthened the ICC's power over the railroads and extended such regulation to Pullman and express companies, bridges, ferries, oil pipelines, and dock and other terminal facilities. The agency also gained authority to fix just and reasonable maximum rates and was empowered to establish uniform accounting methods for the railroads. The law was weak in failing to fix the value of the railroads, for that would have strengthened the validity of the rates set by the ICC, but it did provide some improvements.

The other legislation included the Immunity Act, which required corporation executives to testify about their firms without invoking the plea of immunity; the Pure Food and Drug Act, which outlawed the production, sale, or transportation of adulterated foods and drugs and forbade fraudulent labeling practices; and the Meat Inspection Act, which provided for the enforcement of sanitary regulations.

Rockefeller and other traditional conservatives launched a bitter counterattack. In addition to charging that such reforms merely whetted the appetite for socialism, they argued that the regulations weakened the economic system by cutting profits and discouraging businessmen from making further capital investments. The combination, they asserted, would cause another depression. An economic downturn did begin in March, 1907, but the reformers were not responsible for the ensuing pain and trouble.

The capitalist marketplace system had never functioned without periodic recessions and depressions, and neither the corporations nor the reformers proved able to prevent such fluctuations. After the stock market panic, business failures increased during the summer of 1907, and the crisis became serious in October when the Knickerbocker Trust Company of New York closed its doors.

Roosevelt again turned to Morgan (and associated economic leaders) for help to prevent a major depression. The financier extracted his payment in a disingenuous fashion. He was then engaged in a maneuver to add the resources (and profits) of the Tennessee Coal and Iron Company to the already vast power of the United States Steel Corporation, and he naturally wanted to avoid any prosecution under the antitrust laws. He therefore sent Roosevelt incomplete (and hence misleading) information about the proposed merger and asked the president to approve the transaction. Roosevelt said yes. Having won that battle, Morgan supplied the capital that stopped the panic from becoming a depression.

The history of that dialogue between Roosevelt and Morgan dramatizes the great virtue of doing history. For the balance of power between those two giants exposes the limits of trying to control and reform a system without challenging its primary center of power. By accepting the essentials of the new political economy based on industrial and financial corporations, the upper- and middle-class reformers revealed themselves as ultimately dependent upon—and hence limited by—the individuals and institutions they were trying to control.

Within that framework, the Progressives moved forward. The panic of 1907 revealed the need for a more reliable and flexible monetary system, and perceptive leaders responded on May 30, 1908, with a stopgap measure known as the Aldrich-Vreeland Act. It authorized national banks to issue money backed by commercial paper and the bonds of local and state governments but did not guard against inflation and other abuses. The law also created the National Monetary

Commission, headed by Senator Aldrich, which ultimately played a central part in the creation of the Federal Reserve System (FRS).

For his part, Roosevelt asked for still more reforms. His annual message of December, 1907, was an extensive catalog of Progressive recommendations: inheritance and income taxes; laws requiring the national incorporation of business firms; measures to control railroad securities and to fix rail rates on the basis of a government evaluation of the roads' assets; and legislation to limit the use of injunctions against labor unions (and to legalize the eight-hour day and workmen's compensation).

The president was pushing and leading: he knew that he would not immediately attain all those objectives. But he did win another battle for conservation. The Congress created the National Conservation Commission, which was designed to support and coordinate the work of the 41 state commissions. Roosevelt's save-to-use program provided federal protection for more than 148 million acres of forest, over 80 million acres of mineral supplies, and at least 1.3 million acres of waterpower sites.

The Progressives were on the move, and Roosevelt sounded another bugle call in his January, 1908, message to the Congress. He ticked off another list of needed reforms and vented his anger at the federal and state courts that had invalidated the system of workmen's compensation in the railroad industry. It was an impressive performance, shortly underscored by the Supreme Court.

Responding to the epoch-making brief prepared by Brandeis, which argued from economic, sociological, and health statistics rather than from legal precedents, it upheld the Oregon law setting maximum working hours for women (*Muller* v. *Oregon*). It also ruled, in *Adair* v. *U.S.*, that railroads could not, as a condition of employment, force workers to forgo their right to join a union. Those decisions reversed the logic that the Court had followed in *Lochner* v. *New York* (1905), when it had struck down a law setting a maximum number of hours (ten) for the working day of bakers in that state.

Roosevelt would have liked nothing better than to stay on in the White House. But he had promised the public in 1904 that he would not campaign for election in 1908, and he honored his word. That was a mistake. He should have gone to the public with a candid explanation of the problem, saying that the choice for Americans was between socialism and sophisticated upper-class leadership. As a historian who has read most of Theodore Roosevelt's letters, memos, and speeches, I think that he understood those options.

Roosevelt was one of those rare aristocrats who understand the need, and have the capacity, to keep moving to the left. They become ever more radical. And, for that reason, he might have asserted a meaningful degree of control over the economy that had come to be dominated by the giant corporations. Without him, however, the middle-class reformers soon reached the limits of their imagination.

EXPLORATORY READING

Begin with these four stimulating—and conflicting—analyses of the Progressive coalition:

R. Hofstadter, *The Age of Reform* (1955)

G. Kolko, *The Triumph of Conservatism* (1963)

J. Weinstein, *The Corporate Ideal in the Liberal State* (1969)

R. Wiebe, *Businessmen and Reform: A Study of the Progressive Movement* (1962)

Next consider these two books about the Socialists and the IWW:

M. Dobofsky, *We Shall Be All* (1969)

D. Shannon, *The Socialist Party of America* (1955)

There are many studies of immigration, but I suggest these to stimulate your own investigations, beginning with a classic novel now in reprint:

P. de Donato, *Christ in Concrete* (1976)

J. Higham, *Strangers in the Land: Patterns of American Nativism, 1860–1925* (1955)

M. A. Jones, *American Immigration* (1960)

H. S. Nelli, *The Italians in Chicago* (1973)

M. Rischen, *The Promised City: New York Jews, 1870–1914* (1970)

The terror and the travail of American blacks are explored in these volumes:

G. Frederickson, *The Black Image in the White Mind, 1817–1914* (1968)

C. F. Kellogg, *N.A.A.C.P., 1909–1920* (1967)

A. J. Lane, *The Brownsville Affair* (1971)

R. W. Logan, *The Betrayal of the Negro: From Rutherford B. Hayes to Woodrow Wilson* (1965)

A. Meier, *Negro Thought in America: 1880–1915* (1963)

E. Rucwick, *W. E. B. DuBois, Propagandist of the Negro Protest* (1969)

D. Southern, *The Malignant Heritage: Yankee Progressives and the Negro, 1901–1914* (1968)

The First Americans have been neglected by historians, as well as by others, but these studies offer a beginning:

R. Burnette and J. Koster, *The Road to Wounded Knee* (1974)

V. V. Deloria, Jr., *Custer Died for Your Sins* (1969)

T. Droeber, *Ishi in Two Worlds* (1961)

H. E. Fey, *Indians and Other Americans* (1959)

W. T. Hagen, *American Indians* (1961)

W. Washburn, *The Indians in America* (1975)

The subject of conservation is complex and subtle. It is difficult to write intelligently about it without being a scientist. Hence I suggest you begin with these two quite different books. The first is science for the ordinary citizen, the second is a history of the struggle within the Progressive coalition:

B. Commoner, *The Poverty of Power: Energy and the Economic Crisis* (1976)

S. Hays, *Conservation and the Gospel of Efficiency, 1890–1920* (1959)

The divisions within the upper class are discussed in:

R. M. Abrams, *Conservatism in a Progressive Era* (1964)

J. M. Blum, *The Republican Roosevelt* (1954)

W. H. Harbaugh, *Power and Responsibility: The Life and Times of Theodore Roosevelt* (1961)

H. G. Holli, *Reform in Detroit* (1973)

Z. L. Miller, *Boss Cox's Cincinnati: Urban Politics in the Progressive Era* (1969)

G. Mowry, *Theodore Roosevelt and the Progressive Movement* (1947)

The beginnings of the middle-class involvement are incisively explored in these studies:

A. F. Davis, *Spearheads for Reform* (1967)

S. Hackney, *Populism to Progressivism in Alabama* (1969)

R. Lubove, *The Progressives and the Slums* (1962)

D. W. Noble, *The Paradox of Progressive Thought* (1958)

R. E. Noble, *New Jersey Progressivism Before Wilson* (1946)

R. B. Nye, *Midwestern Progressive Politics* (1951)

J. Weinstein, *The Corporate Ideal in the Liberal State, 1900–1918* (1968)

5 THE POWER AND THE LIMITS OF REFORM

ROOSEVELT compounded his mistake of not running for reelection in 1908 by choosing William Howard Taft, who had served as his secretary of war from 1904 to 1908, as the Republican leader to carry the banner of reform. Taft had a fine legal mind, which he later exercised with considerable distinction as Chief Justice of the Supreme Court; but he was neither a political leader nor a modern reformer. He was grossly overweight—fatter than fat—and politically (if not personally) lazy. He was, indeed, more than a bit the classic personification of nineteenth-century laissez-faire for a perceptive and talented cartoonist. He preferred to play a poor game of golf than to fight for the changes that were needed to rationalize the new corporate system.

Roosevelt would have served his beloved country far better if he had thrown his presidential influence behind Secretary of State Elihu Root or Charles Evens Hughes, the governor of New York. Both men were tough, sophisticated upper-class leaders with innovative ideas—and the political skill to translate them into laws and policies. They could have sustained the upper-class momentum for reform initiated by Roosevelt and his associates, and they might have carried it forward in a subtle way to form a balanced corporate system at a time when that would have been creative rather than—as it happened a generation later—merely a routine response to another grave emergency.

As you begin to do history, you will develop a feel for the ironies related to a sense of *what might have happened* at those moments known as turning points at which nobody turned, those instants when as a society, as well as in our individual lives, we came to a fork in the road and chose to go on down the path that seemed safe and secure. That is what Roosevelt did, and as a result the old-line conservatives regained some power and influence.

Those men, typified by Senator Aldrich, Speaker of the House Cannon, and James W. Van Cleave, the new president of the NAM, were not true advocates of nineteenth-century laissez-faire. They wanted to preserve—even extend—the power that the corporations had acquired in the process of dominating the relatively open nineteenth-century marketplace. Thus they favored a quasi-monopolistic marketplace and a similar concentration of political power among the spokesmen for the giants. Thus, while they acquiesced in the nomination of Taft, they wrote a Republican party platform that stressed the use of injunctions against labor unions and the necessity of a high tariff to underwrite the profits of American corporations.

The election was dull. Bryan was again nominated by the Democrats, and he came forth against labor injunctions—and for various progressive reforms. Those actions won the endorsement of the AF of L, but neither Bryan's personality nor his conception of reform convinced many Republican progressives to desert their state organizations. He was in truth a leader whose time had come and gone. Taft won decisively (7.7 million votes to 6.4 million). The most significant point was that Debs again increased his vote for president, and local Socialists won more battles for office.

Taft may well have sensed the meaning of those election returns, for once in the White House he offered a classic combination of irony and insight. Both were nicely revealed by this remark: "We must get back to competition," he observed in a candid moment. "If it is impossible, then let us get on to socialism, for there is no way between." But he was too smart (despite his laziness) not to know that there was a middle way. It was the course being defined by the members of the Progressive coalition: accept the corporate system but try to control and reform its power.

The president sensed what Herbert Hoover later sorrowfully learned the hard way. To make piecemeal reforms, *on a continental scale,* demanded a degree of continuous commitment by the ordinary women and men that they were unwilling to make. That approach demanded a break with the tradition of the frontier and individual liberty that was simply too great to expect. Hence Hoover realized that the reformers would ultimately create a centralized bureaucracy without any sense of direction or purpose.

But Taft understood that the Socialists, led by Debs, *did* offer an image and an ideal of a democratic industrial community that just might adapt and sustain the original conception of American representative democracy. And, given the choice between unrestrained corporate power and socialism, the president was saying he would choose democratic socialism. He did not *prefer* it, but he viewed it as the better of those two possibilities. He of course desired to re-create the nineteenth-century ideal.

And so to the final irony. Taft's effort to return to the nineteenth-century dream of laissez-faire capitalism indirectly helped the reformers in their struggle to rationalize the twentieth-century corporate marketplace. He was, in his own way, fighting the giant corporations no less than those who wanted to control and reform the new corporate system. He angered both those groups—let alone the radicals—but he also unintentionally strengthened the Progressives. First he made them angry, which energized their campaign, and then he helped them put the corporations on the defensive.

The president was a mild reformer on some issues. He favored a low tariff, for example, as well as the antitrust strategy against the corporations. He particularly opposed the railroads, arguing that they broke the law, engaged in corrupt practices, and exercised undue influence in the marketplace. And, in a similar vein, he opposed the kind of dictatorial power exercised by Speaker Cannon in the House of Representatives.

Those views initially led some men, like Senators LaFollette and George W. Norris (Republican, Nebraska), to view the president as a potential ally. But Taft opposed organized labor, and he considered the kind of broad regulation advocated by upper-class reformers and other Progressives as fallacious and dangerous. He quickly lost credibility with many reformers, moreover, when he failed to honor his promise to fight Cannon. LaFollette and others who had been ready for battle were isolated without vital influence and patronage.

Taft also backed down on the tariff. Reformers, led by Representative Sereno E. Payne (Republican, New York), won a quick victory in the House and even added a modest inheritance tax to the bill. But special interest spokesmen and conservatives, again led by Senator Aldrich, launched an effective counterattack. Taft acquiesced. The final version of the Payne-Aldrich tariff did lower rates (to an average level of 40.7 percent), but the Progressives were furious over Taft's refusal to fight for the principles he had proclaimed.

Their anger was intensified by the ensuing battle over conservation that developed during the summer of 1909, after Taft appointed Richard A. Ballinger as secretary of interior. Ballinger believed that the resources of the country should be developed largely by private operators without much interference from the government. Pressure for that approach had been intensified by the organization in 1909 of the National Domain League in Colorado and the Western Conservation League in Washington.

Taft lit the fuse when, on the recommendation of Ballinger, he reopened more than one million acres of land that Pinchot and Roosevelt had protected by reserving them as ranger stations. Pinchot retaliated by raising the issue of coal lands in Alaska, which Ballinger had approved for sale to a group of Seattle businessmen who were rumored to be acting in collusion with a syndicate of corporation giants headed by Morgan and Guggenheim.

Taft promptly fired Pinchot as head of the Bureau of Forestry. The resulting congressional investigation of Ballinger's action (1909–1910) cleared him of any corrupt dealings with Morgan and Guggenheim, but it left the public feeling that Taft and Ballinger were opposed to effective conservation. That was not accurate. Taft later appointed a friend of Pinchot (Walter Fisher) as the new secretary of the interior and ultimately reserved more land than Roosevelt.

But the damage was done, and Pinchot led an important group of Progressives into the camp of Senator LaFollette. Other dissenters like Hiram W. Johnson of California, William E. Borah of Idaho, Dolliver and Cummins of Iowa, Joseph L. Bristow of Kansas, Moses Clapp of Minnesota, and Beveridge of Indiana developed a working partnership on many issues with Democrats like Joseph W. Bailey of Texas. Borah and Bailey combined in 1909, for example, to propose a graduated tax on all incomes over $5000. They lost the fight in Congress, but the issue was referred to the states for consideration as a constitutional amendment.

Taft went on alone. He saved over $40 million in the first fiscal year of his administration (July 1, 1909–June 30, 1910) and began an investigation of government spending and a survey of government organization. Then he launched a vigorous antitrust campaign in which he initiated more than twice as many actions as Roosevelt had (90 to 44). It was an honest example of classical nineteenth-century laissez-faire.

The angry insurgents won a major victory on their own, however, when, in March, 1910, behind the leadership of George W. Norris, they defeated Speaker Cannon. They enlarged the Rules Committee, which controlled legislation, from 5 members to 15 members and required them to be elected by the House rather than be appointed by the Speaker. Those changes did not destroy all of Cannon's powers (nor those of subsequent Speakers), but they did restore some degree of democratic government in the House of Representatives.

The president and the reformers next clashed over his proposal to extend regulation of the railroads. The fight was caused in part by the mutual suspicions that had developed during 1909 and 1910, but the real issues involved basic policy differences and control of the party and the Progressive coalition. Taft called in January, 1910, for the special Commerce Court, empowered to handle rate cases; a grant of authority to supervise and regulate railroad securities; and power for the ICC to set rates on its own initiative and to approve some kinds of mergers.

The ensuing struggle between Taft, the reformers, and the conservatives destroyed the original bill. The final version, known as the Mann-Elkins Act of June 18, 1910, was a compromise acceptable to Senator Aldrich and the railroad companies. The Commerce Court was retained, but the proposals for valuation of and control over securities were lost. The ICC was empowered to initiate rate changes and was granted new authority over telephone, telegraph, cable, and wireless companies. It could also suspend new rates introduced by the corporations until they won court approval for their actions. And it was given more power to enforce decisions concerning the differences between rates for long and short hauls. The bill did strengthen the Hepburn Act, and despite their differences with the president, the Progressives voted solidly for the compromise. It did not, however, make the railroads equitable common carriers.

The Congress approved several other reform measures before it adjourned for the elections of 1910. A postal savings system paying 2 percent interest was established on June 25 as an alternative to commercial banks. On the same day, a law was passed requiring candidates in elections for the House of Representatives to file statements on their campaign expenses. That bill was a continuation of the fight against corrupt practices that had won its first victory in 1890 in New York.

By that time, Roosevelt had returned from a long vacation and had reentered politics with a frontal attack on the courts for blocking needed social legislation, by reasserting the wisdom of the strategy of controlling rather than destroying the large corporations, and by issuing a warning to conservatives like Aldrich and Cannon that every citizen "holds his property subject to the general right of the community to regulate its use to whatever degree the public welfare may require."

Combined with the Ballinger-Pinchot fight, those performances opened a gap between Roosevelt and Taft that was never closed. And, together with the defection of the Progressives backing LaFollette, that insured the president's failure to purge the party of reformers in the elections of 1910. The Democrats won control of the House of Representatives and elected 26 governors (including Woodrow Wilson in New Jersey), and the Senate fell under the sway of a coalition of Progressive Republicans and Democrats.

Theodore Roosevelt was lost without the "bully pulpit" of the presidency. He and the office belonged together. To have his "beloved policies" in the possession of others was too much to bear. Barclay pictured his heartbreak in the Baltimore Sun.

ENOCH ARDEN.

"Now when the dead man come to life beheld
His wife his wife no more, and saw the babe
Hers, yet not his, upon the father's knee,
And all the warmth, the peace, the happiness"—
GEE! IT WAS TOUGH!
—Barclay in the Baltimore *Sun.*

Reprinted in *The Literary Digest*, vol. XLIV, April 6, 1912, p. 673.

FOUNDATION OF THE NATIONAL
PROGRESSIVE LEAGUE

The reformers promptly organized to exploit those gains by founding the National Progressive League on January 21, 1911. Led by Senators LaFollette and Jonathan Bourne (Republican, Oregon), they called for the direct election of senators; direct primaries to choose candidates and to elect delegates to the national conventions of both parties; the general acceptance of the initiative, referendum, and the recall; and a federal corrupt-practices act.

Another objective, less publicized but nevertheless apparent, was to secure the 1912 Republican nomination for LaFollette. His drive steadily gathered momentum as he won the support of key Progressive businessmen like Charles R. Crane, the plumbing magnate of Chicago, and on July 17, 1911, the senator formally announced his candidacy. Then Taft and the Supreme Court unintentionally gave Roosevelt the opening he needed to counterattack.

The Court dramatized the debate about how to control the corporations by its rulings in 1911 against the Standard Oil Company and the American Tobacco Company. Standard's national operation was ordered dissolved into regional and functional units, and the tobacco trust was also directed to reorganize itself. Reformers generally applauded the results, but some were upset: one group complained that the Court had decided the cases on the grounds of the reasonableness of the charge against the firms and on the undue control they had exercised over the free marketplace; others were disturbed because the decision was so vague; and still another group was angry because the Court had unilaterally claimed power to make crucial decisions.

Then Taft filed a suit against the United States Steel Corporation, citing its control over the Tennessee Coal and Iron Company as particular proof of its near-monopoly position. That not only upset Perkins of the House of Morgan and other upper-class reformers but it also angered Roosevelt; it implied that he was not a reliable Progressive because he had approved the merger in 1907. Perkins and others of his outlook, as well as many middle-class reformers, sided emotionally and enthusiastically with Roosevelt. That led to a four-way battle for the presidency, the election of Woodrow Wilson, and the development of a Progressive consensus based on accepting the large corporation as the cornerstone of American society.

Taft quickly destroyed his chances for reelection. First he antagonized agricultural businessmen, fishermen, and timber interests by approving a proposed reciprocity treaty with Canada (they feared the competition). Then he vetoed the admission of Arizona as a state because he viewed its constitutional provision for the recall of judges as inflammatory and dangerous. It was a fruitless gesture; Arizona simply removed that clause until after its constitution was accepted on February 14, 1912, and then repassed it as the law of the state.

Despite Roosevelt's increasing support among the Progressive rank and file, Senator LaFollette maintained his position during 1911 as the leading reformer for the Republican nomination. If the two men had combined forces, they might have blocked Taft despite his command of the party organization in the South. But both wanted to be president, and that clash intensified their differences over policy. LaFollette remained committed to the ideal of a competitive marketplace, while Roosevelt reiterated his strategy to use the federal government to regulate and direct the highly integrated political economy created by the giant corporations.

LaFollette's increasing fatigue (and worry about the health of his daughter) led him on February 2, 1912, to make an embittered and somewhat incoherent attack on the press as a mouthpiece of monopoly interests. Roosevelt seized the opening and quickly entered the fight for the Republican nomination. In 13 bitterly fought presidential primary battles, he overwhelmed LaFollette and Taft. Taft still controlled the party machinery, however, and with the aid of old-line conservatives was renominated by the Republican National Convention on the first ballot.

Encouraged by the support of Perkins and by the appeal he had demonstrated in the primaries, Roosevelt launched a third-party campaign. He very probably would have been elected if the Democrats had not nominated Woodrow Wilson. Wilson, the moralistic son of a Virginia minister, quickly abandoned the practice of law for an academic career that culminated (1902) in his being selected as president of Princeton University. Defeated in his efforts to reform the graduate school, he entered New Jersey politics and became a reforming governor who evoked startled and then enthusiastic support from many Democratic Progressives. He was a willful and righteous crusader who believed in strong executive leadership and an expansionist foreign policy.

"Concessions obtained by financiers," Wilson had written in 1907, while serving as president of Princeton, "must be safeguarded by ministers of state, even if the sovereignty of unwilling nations be outraged in the process. Colonies must be obtained or planted, in order that no useful corner of the world may be overlooked or left unused." Wilson also wanted a strong corporate political economy and opposed any drastic use of the antitrust strategy for reforming the system. "The system cannot be suddenly destroyed. That would bring our whole economic life into radical danger."

Business, Wilson explained, "is the foundation of every other relationship, particularly of the political relationship. . . . The question of statesmanship is a question of taking all the economic interests of every part of the country into the reckoning. Just as soon as the business of this country has general, free welcome to the councils of Congress, all the friction between business and politics will disappear."

Roosevelt faced the difficult task of beating a new and exciting leader backed by united party organization. He declared his readiness for the fight by saying he felt like a bull moose. The Bull Moose platform, which Roosevelt preferred to discuss as the New Nationalism, was far more advanced than the one offered by the Democrats. It either described or pointed toward the major reforms of the

Cartoonist John L. De Mar graphically depicted the divided Republican party in the election year of 1912. Railroading was a way of life and many chuckled over the railway car's mischievous wheels. The leading set committed itself to the tracks leading to Taft, while the rear set switched off in the direction of Theodore Roosevelt. This cartoon appeared in the Philadelphia Record.

ACCIDENTS WILL HAPPEN.
—De Mar in the Philadelphia *Record.*

Reprinted in *The Literary Digest,* vol. XLIV, March 23, 1912, p. 277

next 50 years. Minimum wages for women and workmen's compensation were paralleled by calls for social insurance and child labor laws. The initiative, recall, and referendum were extended by demands for the recall of judicial decisions. And Roosevelt's regulative approach to the problems of the political economy was translated into specific demands for a federal tariff commission and a national trade commission.

Wilson shrewdly wooed the antitrust Progressives and the otherwise conservative-minded small businessmen who felt that an attack on the corporation was the best way to avoid being destroyed in the marketplace. The strategy was labeled and merchandized as the New Freedom. That was misleading because it deemphasized Wilson's approval of strong presidential leadership and likewise ignored his belief that the political and social aspects of the new system ought to be integrated into a corporate whole. But it won the support of important Progressives who had previously backed LaFollette. Wilson's refusal to identify himself with organized labor also helped, particularly in the context of the militant IWW strike of 1912 at the Lawrence, Massachusetts, textile mills. The union, which had reached its peak strength of 100,000, won that battle (and important gains for the workers) at the cost of intensifying the opposition to itself and to organized labor in general.

Roosevelt described the talk of restoring competition as "foolish" and "doomed to failure." Wilson was forced in reply to admit that he thought that "society is an organism." "Business," he added, "underlies everything in our national life, including our spiritual life." And, "We cannot go back to the old competitive system." He wanted the "reintegration" of an "atomizing society," and hence "government and business must be associated" under the New Freedom. He was even more candid after he won the election. "We shall deal with our economic system as it is," he admitted early in 1913, "and as it may be modified, not as it might be if we had a clean sheet of paper to write upon."

He was a minority president, even though the Democrats won control of both houses of the Congress. But Debs again doubled his vote, and even more Socialist candidates won local elections. The combined vote for Wilson, Roosevelt, and Debs (11.3 million of 14.8 million) made it clear that the old system was gone, even though it was equally apparent that there was no consensus on how the corporation was to be subjected to humane principles.

Wilson was elected and inaugurated when the vigor and influence of the Progressive coalition was reaching a climax. In social welfare, for example, the principle of providing public assistance to mothers with dependent children had been established in Illinois in 1911, and many states had followed Maryland's lead (1902) in enacting workmen's compensation laws. And Massachusetts, in 1912, extended Oregon's initiative in setting minimum working standards for the employment of women.

As those examples indicate, the local and state reformers had developed a momentum that was affecting national politics and legislation in many areas of policy. Their intellectual leadership and organizational ability and energy had generated a public psychology—a mood—that put the conservatives and reactionaries on the defensive. Even organized labor enjoyed a revival of strength and influence.

Part of that was due to the decision by Gompers to make some accommodation to the appeal of industrial unionism as advocated by Debs and Haywood. Beginning with the building trades in 1907, the AF of L gradually grouped some of its related craft unions into loosely coordinated departments, and by 1912 that policy had been applied to metalworkers, railway unions, and miners. Gompers also began to take a more active role in party politics. He pressured both the Democrats and Republicans in 1908, for example, to adopt platforms supporting the right to organize, the eight-hour day, and the creation of a department of labor in the cabinet—and opposing the use of injunctions against unions.

Those activities, along with the generally prosperous state of the economy, helped increase union membership. The AF of L grew to two million members by 1914, and 70 percent of those workers were in the major industries of railroads, construction, mining, and clothing. The garment workers provided much of the militance during the early years of the revival. Even before the public outrage about the Triangle Fire, for example, the ILGWU waged a bitter and violent strike to win increased wages and the union shop. And the United Garment Workers, led by Sidney Hillman, became a powerful force for social as well as economic reforms.

Under constant pressure from Debs and Haywood, Gompers ultimately adopted much of the labor policy of the Socialists and other radicals. He called on all three candidates in the presidential election of 1912 to support such reforms as government relief for unemployed workers and the 40-hour week. That was eloquent testimony to the influence of the radicals, for Gompers constantly attacked Debs with the same kind of bitter anger and fear displayed by conservative businessmen.

During those same years, moreover, the middle- and upper-class progressives were mustering and using their own power. Prior to Wilson's election, for example, the reformers in the House of Representatives twice passed low-tariff measures, and in February, 1912, they launched (under the leadership of Arsene Pugo of Louisiana) a major investigation of the financial leaders of the corporate political economy. The results of that inquiry made it clear that the large banks and investment firms had established themselves in positions of great influence in the major insurance companies, industrial firms, public utility trusts, railroads—and even in the banking business itself.

Then came a dramatic illustration of how the Progressives had deployed their power at every level of government. They forced the Congress in 1909 to propose a constitutional amendment authorizing an income tax. The battle then moved to the states, and on February 22, 1913, the amendment secured the necessary number of ratifications. Next came the Seventeenth Amendment (May 31, 1913), providing for the direct election of senators. And on March 1, 1913, the ICC gained the power to investigate the property held or used by the railroads in order to provide a basis for setting rates and judging reasonable profits.

President Wilson dramatically appeared before the Congress on April 8, 1913, to ask for new tariff legislation. In keeping with the president's concern to further overseas economic expansion, the resulting Underwood Tariff schedules were designed to improve America's position in the world marketplace, as well as to lower the price of various goods to the consumer. All in all, the rates were lowered to about 30 percent. And, largely through the efforts of Congressman Cordell Hull of Tennessee and a group of Republican Progressives, a graduated income tax taking 3 percent of incomes over $100,000 was included in the legislation.

The bill immediately ran into serious trouble from special interest groups that exerted great pressure on various senators to restore protective rates. The president boldly attacked the lobbyists in a public statement on May 26, and the Progressives launched a Senate investigation of their activities. They won lower rates (by about 4 percent) and an increase in the income tax rate to 6 percent on $500,000. The final bill was signed by Wilson on October 3, 1913.

The president then staffed the Commission on Industrial Relations with large-corporation leaders who controlled the NCF. Next he appointed the same kind of men to the Federal Reserve Board (FRB), created on December 23, 1913, to control the monetary system. The demand for financial legislation had risen steadily after the creation of the Aldrich Commission in 1908. The most militant reformers, who rallied behind Secretary of State Bryan's leadership, wanted a reserve system dominated by the federal government. The more moderate Progressives, along with the conservatives, wanted only to break Wall Street's control by decentralizing the financial and currency system into units largely controlled by private banks.

That battle developed around a bill drafted by Congressman Carter Glass of Virginia that proposed 20 reserve banks, but Wilson insisted upon a proviso for a central governing board that would be dominated by nonbankers. The Bryan group, which included such key adminis-tration figures as Secretary of the Treasury William G. McAdoo and Senator Robert L. Owen, as well as Republican Progressives like LaFollette, promptly and vociferously demanded federal control of the system and asked for a provision enabling the banks to grant short-term credits to farmers.

President Wilson accepted loans to agriculture, approved presiden-tial control of appointments to the central FRB, and agreed that the currency of the new system would be backed by the federal govern-ment. But he refused to make the Federal Reserve Banks into govern-ment banks, and hence the large private interests were assured of ownership and significant influence. The sustained efforts of men like Senator Aldrich and banker Paul W. Warburg convinced the conserva-tives within the financial community that the legislation served their own enlightened self-interest.

WILSON BECOMES A NEW NATIONALIST

Wilson continued his effort to rationalize and balance the political economy by next dealing with the industrial sector. He asked in Janu-ary, 1914, for still more power to regulate railroad rates, to prohibit interlocking directorates, to create a federal trade commission, to provide a clear definition of the phrase "combination in restraint of trade" in the antitrust law, and to impose penalties upon individuals and corporations.

Gompers and other labor spokesmen demanded exemptions for unions from antitrust legislation. Other criticism led the president, working closely with Brandeis, to shift his support to a trade commis-sion bill sponsored by Congressman Raymond B. Stevens of New Hampshire. That legislation created a body empowered to issue cease and desist orders against any firms found guilty of unfair competition. The law (signed September 26, 1914) authorized the commission to demand reports from firms as part of its investigations and to initiate suits against offenders in the federal courts.

The Clayton Anti-Trust Bill suffered from Wilson's concern with creating the Federal Trade Commission (FTC). Labor did not win the exemption it sought, but the law (signed October 15, 1914) did contain a long passage explicitly denying that labor was merely a commodity in the marketplace. The provision limiting the power to issue injunc-tions against unions in labor disputes was a more tangible gain, as was the reiteration of the ruling by various courts that unions and farm organizations were not, as such, illegal combinations.

The Clayton Act specified many unfair practices: interlocking di-rectorates in corporations capitalized at more than $1 million; price manipulations that tended to create a monopoly; and contracts between a producer and a merchant that prevented the seller from offering the products of a competitor. And executives became liable, *as individuals,* for violations, while injured parties could file civil suits for threefold damages, as well as apply for court injunctions.

Wilson at that point confidently told Secretary of the Treasury McAdoo that "the antagonism between business and government is over." And he was even more explicit a few weeks later in his annual message to the Congress on December 8, 1914: "The road at last lies clear and firm before business. It is a road which it can travel without fear or embarrassment. It is the road to ungrudged, unclouded success."

Wilson was not actively interested in the Progressive campaigns to provide more direct assistance to the farmers, to pass a federal child labor law, to grant women full citizenship, to improve the position of blacks, or to deal with the thorny question of immigration. But he did support the Industrial Relations Commission in its thorough investigation of the Colorado coal strike in 1914, and he backed assistance to agriculture through the Smith-Lever Act of May 9, 1914. That law enlarged agricultural extension work conducted through land grant colleges (a similar bill, the Smith-Hughes Act of February 23, 1917, created the Federal Board for Vocational Education).

On the other issues, Wilson was anything but a reform leader. He encouraged discrimination against black workers in the government and did little to help women and children. He was a politician, however, and hence responded to the Republican gains in the midterm elections of 1914. Assistance to agriculture was granted through the Federal Farm Loan Act (July 17, 1916) and the Warehousing Act (August 11, 1916). Farm Loan Banks were created in 12 districts, and they were empowered to make long-term loans (up to 40 years) at interest rates of between 5 and 6 percent. The Warehousing Act established a system of licensed and bonded storage depots that could issue receipts for grain, cotton, tobacco, and wool that could be used as collateral for loans.

Andrew Furseth, president of the International Seaman's Union, who had devoted 20 years of his life to a campaign to improve working conditions at sea, finally won his battle with the support of LaFollette and Congressman William B. Wilson. The main objectives were to free the seamen from their restrictive contracts with the shipowners and to legislate improved safety measures. The president gave way, even though the bill posed problems for America's shipping interests and hence to the overseas economic expansion that Wilson favored. A compromise law was signed on March 4, 1915.

By that time the reformers were increasingly involved in questions

of foreign policy connected with the Mexican Revolution and the outbreak of World War I. The great majority of Progressives favored the
extension of America's economic and political influence throughout
the world, and Wilson, like Roosevelt and Taft, stressed the importance of overseas economic expansion. The war intensified those
problems, and thus did slow the momentum for domestic reform. The
Progressives had always accepted the essential structure of the corporate system; hence, when that appeared to be threatened by Socialists
and other radicals, they rallied to its defense.

That shift in priorities nevertheless obscures a vital point: war or no
war, the reformers were approaching the limits of their outlook. They
were not blocked so much by the war as by their own lack of imagination and vision. The witnesses to that judgment were the black Americans, women, workers, Indians, and poor whites. Their lives had not
been significantly improved by the programs and policies of the Progressive coalition.

The Progressives were not radicals: they were neither Socialists nor
pacifists. If there had been no outbreak of war in Europe (with its
immediate repercussions in Asia and elsewhere), they would soon
have been content with variations upon their orthodox reforms. Even
the ominous economic downturn in 1913—before the outbreak of
war—failed to push them closer to accepting structural changes. They
were capitalists to the core.

Hence the last surge of reform owed less to them than to the radicals
and to those of all classes who did not want to become militarily
involved in the war. The early and general sentiment against military
intervention in Europe forced Wilson to mute his desire to lead
America once again onto the world stage as a redeeming reformer.
That was frustrating to the president, for he was the classic twentieth-
century combination of the missionary and businessman of the
nineteenth century.

But he was also shrewd. He understood that he had to convert the
reformers to his larger vision. Fundamentally, of course, that was not
very difficult. But, in the short run, he had to emphasize domestic
reforms. Make America great so that America could make the world
great. He moved first in January, 1916, by nominating Brandeis for
membership on the Supreme Court. The fight to confirm Brandeis
against the bitter opposition of business groups, other conservatives,
and anti-Semites of all classes led on to a final campaign to fulfill the
Progressive dream.

Wilson personally proposed bills to improve the flood and navigational levees along the Mississippi River, to control corrupt practices in
politics and the bureaucracy, to extend self-government to Puerto
Rico, and—the most astute political move—to provide government

loans to farmers. In the latter case, the president was simply rolling with the punch delivered by the militant and radical agriculturalists.

Led by Arthur C. Townley, an ex-Socialist, the militant Scandinavian and Russian farmers in North Dakota organized the Nonpartisan League in February, 1915, and they rapidly won extensive support in 15 other states. Within a year they were preparing to run a full slate of candidates in many state elections. Their platform proposals suggested a desire to tamper with the structure of corporate capitalism. They called for state banks for farmers, state grain elevators, flour mills, and packing plants (even hail insurance), and publicly funded credits for rural capitalists.

Wilson recognized the challenge. So did Theodore Roosevelt. He tried to use the convention of his diehard Bull Moose party members to frighten the Republicans into nominating him in 1916, but he had already lost to Charles Evans Hughes. Hughes had a solid reputation as a reformer in New York, and Republican leaders offered that to the Progressives. His sound judgments as a member of the Supreme Court were used to attract businessmen and more conservative members of both parties. And his call for strict neutrality appealed to all who did not want to go to war. Though he lacked personal magnetism, Hughes was an attractive candidate, and he almost won the election. His defeat is often explained by the divisions within the Republican party and by various blunders (such as his failure to make a gesture of friendship to the more liberal Hiram Johnson of California). What counted more decisively, however, was the way the Democrats added the peace issue to their revived reform program.

Wilson had seen and acted on the appeal of reform, but he was not responsible for the emphasis on peace that emerged during the convention. He wanted to stress patriotism and preparedness. But the delegates sat on their hands during that part of the keynote address. They forced the speaker, Governor Martin H. Glynn of New York, to emphasize neutrality and peace. Then they demanded to hear Bryan, who had campaigned the country against intervention after resigning as secretary of state over the *Lusitania* crisis.

Whatever his personal reservations, Wilson had no choice but to accept the mandate as a peace candidate. He did so effectively, making speech after speech that reminded the country he had kept American males at home and that strongly implied he would do so in the future. The president and the Democrats in the Congress were also successful on the reform front. His handling of the labor conflict in the railroad industry was the highlight of that effort.

The issue was joined in the spring, when the four railroad brotherhoods (engineers, conductors, firemen, and trainmen) demanded the eight-hour day without any reduction in pay and time and a half for overtime. Management rejected that proposal on June 15, 1916, and a national strike seemed certain. Wilson intervened on August 13, supporting the demand for an eight-hour day. Management spurned that appeal and another made on August 18. With the strike called for September 4, Wilson proceeded to persuade, cajole, and manhandle the Congress. The result, on September 2, was a bill that imposed the eight-hour day and created a commission to review and investigate all problems of the industry. Though it was another move that extended and centralized the power of the federal government over the political economy, the public generally responded favorably to action that ended the threat of a major strike.

The unions, of course, were favorably impressed with Wilson. They had also approved, along with other reformers, the Keating-Owen Child Labor Act of August 8, 1916. That prohibited the interstate shipment of manufactured items that were worked on by children under 14 and of the products of mines and quarries that hired children under 16 years of age. The same groups also supported the Kern-McGillicuddy Act (August 19), which provided a workmen's compensation system for federal employees.

In a similar way, and with the same kind of exquisite political timing, the Wilson administration moved to deal with the question of taxes. The reformers had never been able, between 1901 and 1916, to provide any significant tax relief for the middle and lower classes, who supplied the bulk of federal and state revenues. Those people paid most of the tariff duties and the taxes on tobacco, liquor, and beer that supplied almost $600 million of the total $735 million income in 1901.

That highly inequitable situation was attacked by the Association for an Equitable Federal Income Tax, led by John Dewey, in a campaign that attracted support throughout the South and the West from many of the people who also opposed the preparedness program and intervention. The resulting legislation of September, 1916, won a basic income tax of 2 percent and added a surtax of 13 percent on all incomes over $20,000. It also provided a special tax of 12.5 percent on the gross income of munitions firms and a general tax on the capital, as well as on the profits and surpluses, of corporations.

Wilson then worked the other side of the street. First he compromised with Catholics and others who feared that granting independence to the Philippines in the near future would undercut their positions of power. He approved the creation of an elective legislature but agreed that the United States should decide when the Filipinos were ready to handle their own affairs. Then he turned to the business of courting the corporations.

The president had long opposed the idea of a tariff commission that would set rates on the basis of a sophisticated inquiry into the needs of various groups (importers as well as exporters) in the economy. But he switched his position and approved the idea. It was translated into action, as if to dramatize the compromise, by an amendment to the revenue act. The same method was used to pass antidumping legislation designed to protect American firms, especially the chemical industry, from foreign competition. And to help the corporations win a larger share of foreign markets, Wilson came out strongly in favor of a law to exempt them from antitrust regulations when they combined to compete with England, Germany, and France.

Wilson thus touched all the bases. (That metaphor was commonplace even in 1916 because professional baseball was by then well established as *the* marketplace sport, and politicians were quick to identify with such popular escapes from the harsh realities of corporate America.) He thereby put Roosevelt and the bulk of the Republicans in a difficult position. It was an impressive performance that revealed the ever increasing power of the incumbent president in an ever more centralized political economy.

Roosevelt wanted to reoccupy the White House as a wave wants to meet the shore, but the old warrior was beaten. He had been outflanked. He could go no farther left because Debs controlled that territory, and he could not go back to the right because he knew that ground had become a swamp of irrelevancies. As for Charles Evans Hughes, the Republican nominee, he lacked the charisma to dramatize his sophisticated upper-class progressivism. But he might have been an excellent president, for he understood the issues, honored the basic principles of democracy, and recognized the dangers of Wilson's visceral propensity to handle foreign policy as a crusade.

And he came very close to winning. Indeed, Wilson went to bed thinking that he had lost. But he won by the margin of 3773 votes in California. That enabled him to slip past Hughes in the electoral college by 23 votes: a squeak that would have given most men a sense of humility. But the president proceeded to maneuver the nation into a war that consolidated the power of the corporations. The Progressive coalition was mortally wounded even as it was dying of its own terminal illness.

EXPLORATORY READING

Some of the most stimulating general interpretations of the later years of reform were written by people who participated in the action:

J. Chamberlain, *Farewell to Reform* (1932)

H. D. Croly, *The Promise of American Life* (1909)

W. Lippmann, *Drift and Mastery* (1914)

W. E. Weyl, *The New Democracy* (1912)

Four of the best general studies by later historians are:

J. M. Blum, *Woodrow Wilson and the Politics of Morality* (1956)

E. Goldman, *Rendezvous with Destiny* (1952)

O. L. Graham, Jr., *The Great Campaigns: Reform and War in America, 1900–1928* (1971)

A. K. Link, *Woodrow Wilson and the Progressive Era, 1910–1917* (1954)

The differences among conservatives are revealed in these studies:

R. W. Leopold, *Elihu Root and the Conservative Tradition* (1954)

H. and M. G. Merrill, *The Republican Command, 1897–1913* (1971)

N. M. Wilensky, *Conservatives in the Progressive Era: The Taft Republicans of 1912* (1965)

These volumes open the way to explore the variations within the Progressive coalition:

H. C. Bailey, *Liberalism in the New South: Southern Social Reformers and the Progressive Movement* (1969)

J. D. Buenker, *Urban Liberalism and Progressive Reform* (1913)

K. W. Hechner, *Insurgency: Personalities and Politics of the Taft Era* (1940)

R. M. Lowitt, *George W. Norris* (1963)

G. E. Mowry, *The California Progressives* (1951)

D. G. Noble, *America By Design* (1976)

A. B. Sageser, *Joseph L. Bristow: Kansas Progressive* (1968)

R. F. Wesser, *Charles Evans Hughes: Politics and Reform in New York, 1905–1910* (1969)

Various special topics are examined in these books:

G. Adams, Jr., *Age of Industrial Violence, 1910–1915* (1966)

L. D. Brandeis, *Other People's Money and How the Bankers Use it* (1914)

A. Meier, *Negro Thought in America, 1880–1915* (1963)

J. B. Morman, *The Principles of Rural Credits* (1915)

F. W. Taussig, *Some Aspects of the Tariff* (1915)

H. P. Willis, *The Federal Reserve System* (1923)

I. Yellowitz, *Labor and the Progressive Movement in New York State, 1897–1916* (1965)

6 REFORMERS MARCHING DOWN THE IMPERIAL ROAD TO WAR

WILSON provides an excellent example of the way that most members of the Progressive coalition favored and supported an imperial foreign policy despite their concern with reforming American society. Strongly influenced by Frederick Jackson Turner's frontier thesis, Wilson used it in his own writings to explain American expansion at the turn of the century. He also accepted the necessity of enlarging America's share of the world marketplace and the related kinds of intervention designed to deal with European competitors and to create and maintain the appropriate—and profitable—kind of conditions in the nonindustrial countries. And his Calvinistic zeal for righteous reform produced a crusading, missionary nationalism that led him to view America—and himself—as being responsible for reorganizing the world on the basis of the true principles that had been revealed in the United States.

In some ways, however, William Jennings Bryan, whom Wilson appointed as secretary of state, provides an even more striking illustration of the domestic reformer as vigorous imperial interventionist. Bryan's approach reveals how the late-nineteenth-century agricultural need for ever larger markets influenced the development of America's anticolonial imperialism of the twentieth century. Once he had reluctantly accepted the annexation of the Philippines, he concentrated on the classic kind of marketplace expansion that integrated economic necessity and political reform, arguing that the extension of American power and influence would improve the lives of everyone in the world.

As Bryan wryly remarked after a White House visit with President Theodore Roosevelt, many of those who had once considered him a dangerous radical had come to understand that he was not trying to change the essentials of the system. Roosevelt was slow to recognize that truth for several reasons: his provincialism as a member of the metropolitan elite left him woefully ignorant of the realism of the agricultural majority; as a secular crusader, he was psychologically and intellectually antagonized by the more religiously oriented campaigners like Bryan and Wilson; and, finally, he was in certain important respects less subtle in his understanding of how to expand American power most effectively.

Many of those considerations became apparent shortly after Roosevelt moved into the White House in 1901. The speech that McKinley had prepared for his appearance in Buffalo was meant to be the opening salvo in a major effort to expand the American marketplace through the strategy of reciprocity. Roosevelt understood that approach, but he did not sustain the momentum generated by Blaine and McKinley. He explained his failure by saying that as an emergency president he lacked the political strength to overcome its opponents. Yet even after he had been elected as his own man in 1904, he never fought hard for the policy.

The various special interest groups that opposed reciprocity because they feared it would weaken their control of the American market exerted steady pressure on the Congress (and the public), and the agricultural businessmen, enjoying regular prosperity for the first time in two generations, became far less aggressive in pushing the program. Hence Roosevelt may have been correct in arguing that he would use too much of his political strength in a frontal battle over the issue. It seems more likely, however, that Roosevelt considered reciprocity too routine an issue for the attention of a bold leader who was busy extending American power—it was a secondary matter to be dealt with later.

He understood the economic arguments for expansion and felt and responded to the pressure exerted by various business interests for government assistance throughout the world. Roosevelt often dealt, for example, with George W. Perkins of the House of Morgan, who was a key figure in the conservative wing of the Progressive coalition. Perkins provided a particularly clear summary of that group's outlook in a letter to Roosevelt on August 12, 1905, explaining that he supported various federal regulations of the domestic economy because such a program was "absolutely necessary if the commercial leaders of this country are to go on in their development of our interests, at home and abroad, on a foundation sufficiently strong to endure and bring us to the commanding position to which our people are entitled in the commerce of the world, during the next quarter of a century."

Roosevelt agreed with that argument, but his boxing in the basement of the White House, like his charging horsemanship in Cuba and the Dakotas, suggests that he saw himself as a man who preferred to establish control of a situation and *then* work out the details. He used that approach effectively in some international situations, but it did not prove successful in the Far East.

Roosevelt became president at a time when American exporters of such items as kerosene, cotton, and clocks controlled a large share of the foreign trade in Manchuria, and there was a general feeling and excitement that they would match that achievement in China. There was a growing sentiment among such expansionists, moreover, that Russia rather than Japan posed the greatest danger to their imperial prospects. The anti-Russian sentiment was reinforced by attacks on Russian domestic policies by various reformers and Jewish spokesmen. For himself, Roosevelt viewed Japan as a tacit ally and "a formidable counterpoise to Russia." Within that framework the administration approved the Anglo-Japanese Alliance of February 12, 1902, and felt that it helped it to win a pledge from the Russians in 1903 to keep the ports of Manchuria open to American commerce.

Some expansionists, like Horace N. Allen, who had become American minister to Korea in 1897, opposed the anti-Russian strategy on the grounds that Japan posed the basic—and increasingly active—threat to the Open Door policy. That difference of opinion, which cost Allen his job after he argued it out in a blunt face-to-face confrontation with Roosevelt, served to clarify the fundamental options that were open to American policy makers.

Roosevelt and other leaders had three alternatives in trying to maintain the Open Door policy that was their basic strategy for expanding American commerce and influence. The United States could align itself primarily with China, concentrating on the economic development of that country south of Mukden, Manchuria, and opposing any encroachment by other powers. Having assumed that stance, it could then proceed with the development and extension of American interests in China. But such a course involved the possibility of war, and American leaders sincerely wanted to reap the rewards of imperialism without the cost of war.

Ultimately, of course, the United States did go to war against Japan to uphold the Open Door, but at the turn of the century the policy makers concentrated on the two other possibilities: to work either with Japan or Russia, making some compromises, and to share the economic opportunities in China. In choosing to back Japan, however, Roosevelt thought far less about a partnership than about using Japan against Russia in order to facilitate American predominance.

Japanese leaders thought to play the same game. Roosevelt was rudely awakened to that situation shortly after Japan opened its war against Russia on February 8, 1904, with a surprise naval attack on Port Arthur. When asked by Secretary of State Hay on February 20 to make an unequivocal commitment to the Open Door policy, the Japanese deftly sidestepped the request.

Roosevelt responded with an effort to check Japan, but it did not involve cooperating with Russia. He was in a tight spot, as he admitted in his remark that the best solution would be to let both countries fight until they were exhausted. In a limited sense, that was perhaps the key factor that enabled Roosevelt to win the Nobel Peace Prize for his efforts to end the conflict, for both Russia and Japan had depleted their ready resources in the first stage of the war. At that point, Japan was established in Korea and Manchuria.

Both nations were torn by serious domestic difficulties that weakened their capacity to continue the war. Seeking to consolidate its gains, Japan moved first, appealing to Roosevelt to mediate the conflict and promising to honor the Open Door in Manchuria. While he negotiated with the Russians to accept that approach, Roosevelt arranged a secret understanding with the Japanese (the Taft-Katsura Agreement of July 29, 1905) whereby the United States recognized Tokyo's dominance in Korea in return for Japan's promise to honor American control of the Philippines.

Roosevelt was overly optimistic in thinking that the peace settlement left Russia strong enough to exert "a moderative action" on Japan. The Japanese were solidly entrenched in Korea and southern Manchuria, and many of them were angry that Roosevelt had thwarted their efforts to win a monetary indemnity and possession of all of Sakhalin Island. Such dissatisfaction strengthened the influence of those who wanted to close the door to American competition in Manchuria, and using devious means, the Japanese drastically reduced American economic influence in that region. They also made it clear that they were not willing to collaborate with American businessmen.

The railroad magnate Edward H. Harriman unsuccessfully proposed that kind of cooperation in October, 1905. The Japanese refusal prompted Harriman and other Americans to explore the possibility of working with Russia. One important group of Russian leaders thought that such broad economic collaboration would check Japan and at the same time benefit the United States and Russia. The strategy might not have been successful, but it was never tried.

Roosevelt was not, of course, opposed to helping American economic interests. He was, indeed, trying to establish an American presence throughout the world that would facilitate such economic expansion. And he actively supported the House of Morgan, for example, in its attempts to expand in China. But he was not responsive to the idea of working with the Russians, and they turned away to save what they could through arrangements with the Japanese.

That left Roosevelt standing alone against Japan. His position was further complicated by an outburst of economic and racial opposition to Japanese immigration (particularly in California, where it reached 1000 persons a month in 1906). Responding to the increasingly virulent agitation against the Japanese, the San Francisco school authorities segregated Japanese children and thereby provoked a major crisis.

Typically, Roosevelt wanted to intervene vigorously against the Californians, but political and legal considerations forced him to settle for persuading the school board to change its policy. That did not end the discrimination against the Japanese, but it did help Roosevelt to reach an understanding with Tokyo (the Gentleman's Agreement of 1907) that called for both nations to restrict the emigration of people deemed undesirable by the other.

The crisis provoked a good deal of talk about war early in 1907, however, and Roosevelt became quite worried that the Japanese would misinterpret his willingness to compromise as a sign of weakness. That reinforced his concern over their actions in Manchuria, and he responded by planning and executing the famous world cruise of the Great White Fleet between December, 1907, and February, 1909. Roosevelt thought the display of power made a major contribution to peace, and it probably did play a role in the negotiations of the Root-Takahira Agreement of November 30, 1908, in which Japan and the United States reaffirmed their mutual commitment to maintain the status quo in the Pacific, to honor the Open Door policy, and to support China's independence. But it also antagonized many Japanese, and Roosevelt did not carry through on the understanding either by inducing Japan to collaborate with American businessmen or by cooperating with the Chinese or the Russians. As a result, Japan retained the initiative.

Roosevelt was somewhat more successful in extending the Open Door policy to other areas of the world and in establishing the predominance of the United States in the Western Hemisphere. The European struggle for empire in Africa reached one of its periodic crises during 1904–1905 as France and Germany wrestled for control of Morocco. Germany asked Roosevelt in January, 1906, to arrange an international conference and he agreed, no doubt motivated by his desire to stay front and center on the stage of world politics, as well as by his concern to prevent a European war and to strengthen America's position in Africa.

France won most of the immediate gains during the ensuing April negotiations in Algeciras, Spain, but the United States did succeed in committing the Europeans to the principle of the Open Door in Africa. During the course of that campaign, moreover, American leaders provided a particularly clear exposition of their imperial outlook. The first objective was to win acceptance of the Open Door policy, but that had to be followed by various kinds of intervention to make sure, as Root phrased it, "that the door, being open, shall lead to something, that the outside world shall benefit by assured opportunities, and that the Moroccan people shall be made in a measure fit and able to profit by the advantages" offered by American and European penetration of their society. What that meant, beyond being an expression of the racial and cultural arrogance of American and European spokesmen, was that Morocco and other weak, poor, nonindustrial countries would have to be changed internally so that they would become safe and profitable parts of the imperial marketplace system.

UNITED STATES EXPANSION IN LATIN AMERICA

Except for their continuing involvement in Liberia, American leaders did not assign a high priority to expansion in Africa for several decades. But Roosevelt and his successors were eager and determined to see that the door led to something in Latin America. The United States moved quickly during the winter of 1901–1902 to consolidate its control of the Cuban political economy. That was accomplished by giving Cuban sugar interests a dominant position in the American market in return for opening Cuba to American exports and capital. As a result, Cuba developed as an agricultural colony of the United States even though it was legally a quasi-independent protectorate.

Roosevelt's drive to Americanize any isthmian canal was far more dramatic and classically imperial. He opened his campaign with considerable support, as indicated by the Senate's refusal to accept a new treaty with Britain (signed in 1900) because it did not give the United States absolute control of the project. The British retreated, and the final understanding (signed November 18, 1901) left the United States free to make any canal part of the American coastline.

Roosevelt next moved to reverse the existing sentiment in favor of a Nicaraguan route and to acquire the rights that the French had secured from Colombia for a canal across the Colombian province of Panama. Aided by the vigorous propaganda and lobbying campaigns of William Nelson Cromwell and Philippe Buna-Varilla, the American and French agents of the French company, Roosevelt accomplished his objective: the Congress reversed itself in favor of the Panamanian site.

Colombian leaders, however, refused to fold under Roosevelt's pressure to give over part of their country on such terms. The country was still in the throes of social unrest that had erupted in 1899, and the liberal revolutionaries resented Roosevelt's intervention in support of the conservatives. Others resisted his meddling or simply wanted more money. Roosevelt was ready to take the Panama route by force, but a pro-American revolution erupted in the region on November 3, 1903, and all he had to do was deploy American forces to keep the Colombian government from reasserting its control.

It was a classic example of subversion without overt military action, and hence Roosevelt's later assertion that "I took the canal" is largely true. The United States paid the new government of Panama a lump sum of $10 million and agreed to an annual rent of $250,000 in return for perpetual control (but *not* sovereignty) over the ten-mile-wide canal zone. Roosevelt bitterly opposed paying any compensation to Colombia, arguing that it would be an admission of imperial guilt. Admitted or not, the guilt was there.

Having consolidated American power in Cuba and acquired the canal route, Roosevelt seemed for a time to think that the United States could proceed to extend its position in Latin America without continued intervention. He acted within that framework, at any rate, when Germany and Great Britain used naval power in December, 1902, to convince Venezuela to pay its debts and to treat foreigners with more deference and consideration.

His initial passivity aroused strong public opposition in the United States and upset many expansionist leaders; so Roosevelt again intervened. He brandished the fleet and persuaded the Europeans to arbitrate their claims. That did not solve the problem, however, because the Permanent Court of International Arbitration (established in 1899 and known as The Hague Tribunal) ruled that countries using force were entitled to preferential treatment. The judgment not only angered Americans who had claims against Venezuela but it also established a precedent for the use of force that could easily lead to constant European intervention—and that was viewed as a threat to American predominance in the Western Hemisphere.

Roosevelt responded by asserting that the United States would henceforth handle the disciplinary problems in the Western Hemisphere. "It is our duty," he announced in February, 1904, "when it becomes absolutely inevitable, to police these countries in the interest of order and civilization." "If we intend to say 'Hands Off' to the powers of Europe," he later wrote Secretary of State Elihu Root, "then sooner or later we must keep order ourselves."

His public statement of those sentiments came in his annual message to the Congress in December, 1904, and was quickly labeled The Roosevelt Corollary to the Monroe Doctrine:

Chronic wrongdoing, or an impotence which results in a general loosening of the ties of civilized society, may in America, as elsewhere, ultimately require intervention by some civilized nation, and in the Western Hemisphere an adherence of the United States to the Monroe Doctrine may force the United States, however reluctantly, in flagrant cases of such wrongdoing or impotence, to the exercise of an international police power.

While cast in the idiom of the Monroe Doctrine, the statement was in truth an assertion of American power that could be applied anywhere in the world. And over the ensuing years, it was so applied by subsequent American leaders. In a vital sense, therefore, Roosevelt globalized the Open Door policy as the strategy of the United States in the competition for empire. He divided countries into those that were civilized and those that were not on the basis of whether or not they accepted the world view of Western marketplace capitalism, and he asserted the right and the necessity of the United States to police the dissidents.

Some Americans, and most non-Western peoples, were deeply disturbed over that kind of globalism. Roosevelt's economic and administrative intervention in the Dominican Republic (1903–1904) provoked the Washington Post, for example, to raise the fundamental issue:

The proposition that a government has a right to tax its subjects to provide ships of war and fighting men to collect private debts, or that it has a right to risk the lives of any of its subjects in that kind of warfare is so self-evidently wrong that the simplest statement of it exposes its abhorrent character.

Not enough Americans agreed with that analysis to change the nation's imperial policy, but Roosevelt did retreat a bit when he asked Secretary of State Root to develop a more sophisticated imperial approach. Root was an extremely intelligent and able member of the conservative wing of the Progressive coalition. As secretary of war under McKinley and Roosevelt, he laid the foundation for a modern American army, and in foreign policy he took the long-range view of the American imperial position in the Western Hemisphere. "In the nature of things," he observed, "trade and control, and the obligation to keep order which goes with them, must come" to the United States. Given that outlook, he evolved a policy based on three main points: the United States would not annex any more territory; it would not allow such annexation by any other power; and it would offer help to the Latin Americans, as they were prepared and able to use it, to assist them in becoming part of the American system.

Root began to implement that policy guided by a realistic sense of how long it would take to build such an empire, a willingness and a desire to establish cordial relations with the peoples of the region, and great patience. His tour of South America in 1906 and his visit to

Mexico in 1907, for example, were highly effective in creating a receptive attitude throughout the hemisphere. And his persistent labor to strengthen such organizations as the Pan-American Congress and the Bureau of American Republics and to create the International Court for Central American States pointed toward the institutionalization of the economic and political predominance of the United States.

He recognized the importance of Mexico and persistently tried to collaborate with that nation to stabilize the situation in Central America and thereby open the way for the penetration of American power and the development of the region. With Mexican support and assistance, Root negotiated a general treaty of peace and amity that committed those nations to settle their differences through the Central American Court of Justice, defined Honduras as permanently neutral, obligated each nation to prevent itself from being used as a base for an attack on any of the others, and established the policy of withholding recognition from revolutionary regimes until they honored the electoral process. Not only did that document provide a preview of American policy for the next generations but it also stopped a war on Honduras that was started in July, 1908, by various groups supported by Guatemala.

Cuba proved more troublesome, though the Roosevelt administration did handle the problem without full-scale military intervention. Cuban politics had never been fully stabilized after the withdrawal of American forces in 1902 because the Cubans were simply not accustomed to ruling themselves under a system modeled on that of the United States. Roosevelt finally dispatched William Howard Taft in September, 1906, to rule the island as provisional governor. There was no need to use force; the Cubans were either awed or cowed by the fleet that Roosevelt assembled off Cuban shores.

Given the imperial relationship between the two countries, Taft handled the mob in a reasonably restrained and effective manner. The election laws were thoroughly revised, financial reforms were instituted, and a serious—and partially successful—effort was made to revive the economy. American power and influence in the island were not weakened by those changes (indeed, they were reinforced), and the United States withdrew in 1909 after an election and the installation of a new government. That modest success enabled Roosevelt to leave office without the embarrassment of handing incoming President Taft a crisis in foreign affairs.

William Howard Taft had clarified his foreign policy as early as 1906: "Our surplus energy is beginning to look beyond our own borders, throughout the world, to find opportunity for the profitable use of our surplus capital, [and] foreign markets for our manufactures." The panic of 1907 reinforced those views, and as president, he accepted what he termed in 1910 the responsibility for "active intervention to secure for our merchandise and our capitalists opportunity for profitable investments."

The broad bipartisan support for that policy was expressed in typical imperial rhetoric. "We are engaged in a supremacy war for markets and for trade," explained Congressman Jacob S. Fassett of New York. Congressman David E. McKinley of California stressed the relationship between expansion and social stability at home: "It is most essential that our goods should find a market in order that our manufacturers should remain in operation and our workers remain in steady employment."

Both Taft and Secretary of State Philander C. Knox talked far more explicitly in economic terms than Roosevelt had. They were men of the marketplace, so to speak, and felt neither embarrassed nor guilty about that orientation. They saw economic considerations as both the driving force and the most effective instrument of American expansion, which in turn was essential to the health and security of the domestic political economy.

Seriously committed, as he explained in 1912, to the tactics of using dollars instead of bullets, Taft faced two problems. He first had to find the money that was essential to such dollar diplomacy without violating the principle of private enterprise, an aim that involved negotiations with industrialists and bankers. As Roosevelt had learned, however, putting the money to work often involved the threat or the use of force.

The bankers sometimes claimed that the government forced them to become involved in overseas activities against their will. There was some substance to that charge, but in the broader sense it was a misleading half-truth. The financiers actively sought such opportunities and lobbied for government help. When the government asked them to help reorganize the finances of a country like Honduras in order to lay the basis for further American penetration, therefore, the bankers were really being asked to help the government improve their chances for greater profits. They understood the process, though sometimes they bargained for better terms, or more assistance and protection, or simply concluded that the particular proposal was not worth the effort.

The bankers were quite active, for example, in connection with Knox's effort to implement his policy of "benevolent supervision" in Latin America. In Cuba, that approach was known as "The Preventive Policy," and Knox explained the purpose with commendable candor. It was "to deter the Cuban government from enacting legislation which appears to [us] of an undesirable or improvident character . . . especially if it is likely in any degree to jeopardize the future welfare or revenue of Cuba." The continuing turmoil in the island, which involved a drive for racial equality by Cuban blacks, as well as more traditional conflicts, led to renewed violence. Taft and Knox responded with the navy and the marines, and the threat of even greater intervention served to intimidate the rebels for a few years.

Benevolent supervision was less effective in Central America. An attempt to stabilize Honduras under American authority touched off a civil war in which the existing government was backed by the financiers and Knox while the rebels were supported by the United Fruit Company. The revolutionaries finally triumphed, and the banana corporation became the dominant influence within the country.

But the English outmaneuvered Knox and the bankers, as well as the fruit company, in Guatemala. American influence was not terminated, but it was not extended as rapidly as anticipated by the expansionists. And though Taft's military intervention in behalf of Adolfo Diaz in Nicaragua (1909–1911) led to a treaty establishing American power in that country, the administration encountered effective (though not majority) opposition in the Senate.

That resistance was mounted by a coalition of three groups. Though the Democrats who won the congressional elections of 1910 included many vigorous expansionists, they refused to support Republican imperialism because they expected to take over the White House in 1912 and gain the credit for imperial successes. A second group was composed of Republicans and Democrats who questioned the methods of Taft and Knox: they agreed on expansion, but opposed such regular intervention involving force. A smaller number of people, including some Progressives, as well as Socialists and other radicals, challenged the entire expansionist outlook.

FRUSTRATIONS IN ASIA

Though they won some minor gains, Taft and Knox were largely ineffective in Asia. The administration encouraged and supported American bankers and other entrepreneurs in the international scramble for concessions in China. Their plan was to use the power and the influence of the government to establish American economic power in a commanding position inside the various syndicates (or consortiums) that were organized to exploit the opportunities in that country. They thought, not without reason, that such an approach would provide the leverage to keep the door open for all American businessmen. And Taft's direct pressure on the Chinese government, as well as on other nations, did secure American participation in railroad and currency-reform projects.

But Knox failed in his grandiose attempt to create a multinational syndicate for the development of Manchuria. For one thing, American policy had antagonized Japan and Russia, and the support of those countries was essential to his plan. Beyond that, all the interested parties correctly concluded that it was a scheme to establish the United States in a controlling position. Given that opposition, many of the bankers decided to abandon the project unless the incoming Wilson administration was willing to promise extensive government support.

President Wilson and Secretary of State Bryan were vigorous advocates of American expansion, but they approached foreign policy with a less heavy-handed emphasis on economics. They talked more about extending freedom and democracy, and about reform and brotherhood. Wilson left no doubt, however, that his conception of democracy and reform excluded any changes that would threaten American economic expansion.

"When properly directed," Wilson was fond of observing, "there is no people not fitted for self-government." If that meant that a nation's own leaders were to do the directing in keeping with their society's values and culture, then the statement could only be understood as a commitment to the principle of self-determination. But Wilson and Bryan believed that the United States in general, and themselves in particular, should provide much of the proper direction. That was not self-determination, but rather intervention.

Both men opposed what Bryan termed "pernicious revolutionary activity." Various changes and reforms were necessary and desirable in order to bring other countries into line with the American Way, but it was vital to observe orderly and constitutional procedures. Revolutions must therefore be prevented or aborted, and it was legitimate to use force for those purposes. The Filipinos would ultimately become independent, for example, but only after what Wilson termed "a long apprenticeship" during which they would accept American standards and methods. As Wilson once phrased it during his sustained intervention in the Mexican Revolution, he defined his responsibility as teaching "the South American republics to elect good men."

While he usually discussed American expansion and intervention in such philosophical and political terms, Wilson was deeply concerned with the economic side of the imperial outlook. "I have never admitted the distinction," he pointed out, "between the other departments of life and politics." Hence his idea of being "properly directed" involved creating the conditions "under which all contracts and business and concessions will be safer than they have been."

His acceptance of the expansionism inherent in the frontier thesis that he had learned from Turner became apparent in his 1907 analysis of America's economic situation: "The many sharp struggles for foreign trade make it necessary that we should turn our best talents to the task of dealing firmly, wisely, and justly with political and commercial rivals." He was even more forthright when he spoke to a labor audience during his presidential campaign of 1912:

> We have reached, in short, a critical point in the process of our prosperity . . . . Our domestic market is too small . . . . Our industries have expanded to such a point that they will burst their jackets if they cannot find a free outlet to the markets of the world . . . . Our domestic markets no longer suffice. We need foreign markets.

Wilson dealt with the problems connected with the Open Door policy in Asia within that framework. Many of the bankers involved in various syndicate operations in China wanted Wilson to make an unequivocal (and largely open-ended) commitment to provide government support. They sought assistance in dealing with the Chinese and other members of the consortium and in accumulating the necessary capital. "It is not the bankers themselves who provide the money to finance a foreign loan," explained Willard Straight of the House of Morgan: the bonds are "sold to the public." And the financiers had learned from experience that "the American investor is not willing to buy Chinese bonds unless he believes that the American government will protect him by all possible diplomatic means."

Wilson was more immediately concerned with other aspects of the operation. He was not willing, as he feared the bankers were, to abandon Manchuria to Japan and Russia. And he was worried, as Bryan explained, that the Americans "could not have a controlling voice" in the syndicates. "The president believed," Bryan commented, "that a different policy was more consistent with the American position, and that it would in the long run be more advantageous to our commerce." Wilson thus chose to reassert America's independent support of the Open Door policy for *all* of China: Americans "certainly wish to participate, and participate very generously, in the opening to the Chinese and to the use of the world the almost untouched and perhaps unrivaled resources of China."

Bryan was even more explicit. "This government expects that American enterprise should have the opportunity everywhere abroad to compete for contractual favors on the same footing as any foreign competitor." That approach, along with Wilson's unwillingness to fight California's racist land legislation in 1913–1914, ultimately carried the United States into a blunt confrontation with Japan. That did not come until after the outbreak of World War I, however, by which time Wilson and Bryan had become deeply involved in trying to control and direct events in Central America and Mexico.

THE IMPERIAL PUSH INTO LATIN AMERICA

Given considerable freedom of action, Bryan acted in the Caribbean in keeping with his candid explanation that he intended "to employ every agency of the Department of State to extend and safeguard American commerce and legitimate American enterprises in foreign lands . . . consistent with [the] sovereign rights of other governments." Bryan also viewed Latin Americans as "our political children, which led him to continue the military intervention in Nicaragua that Taft and Knox had initiated and to undertake similar operations in Haiti (July, 1915) and in the Dominican Republic (May, 1916).

The United States, as Bryan explained in talking about Haiti, felt "compelled to take steps necessary to prevent a period of disorder and anarchy, which would menace the rights and property of Americans and other foreigners." Even when order had been restored, however, Bryan made it clear that "the United States will not permit revolutionary methods to be employed." It would "feel at liberty thereafter," Wilson added in a massive contradiction, "to insist that revolutionary changes in the government of the republic be effected by the peaceful processes provided in the Dominican Constitution."

Given that approach, it is hardly surprising that Wilson attempted to control the Mexican Revolution that erupted in 1910 and reached its first climax in 1911, when Francisco I. Madero overthrew Porfirio Diaz. Diaz had dominated Mexico from 1876 as a tough and effective despot, but his pretensions to benevolence for the masses had instead produced extensive favors for a few Mexicans and almost as many foreigners. Louis Para y Pardo characterized the regime in a biting and memorable phrase: "Mexico is the mother of foreigners and the stepmother of Mexicans."

Many Americans were counted among those foreigners. They poured at least a third of all their foreign investments into Mexico between 1900 and 1911 (the sum had reached $1,044,600,000 by the time Diaz was defeated) and were deeply involved in mines, smelters, agricultural lands, railroads, and oil. They were not attracted to Madero, who promptly launched a serious effort to change the old order. His effort generated increasingly determined opposition from the Catholic Church, various business groups, the Diaz political machine, and elements in the army; and he was overthrown and ultimately murdered during a coup (February 9–18, 1913) led by Victoriano Huerta.

Guided by the traditional policy of recognizing de facto governments (and by his own conservatism), President Taft planned to deal with Huerta when he indicated a willingness to compromise on various unsettled issues. Taft and Knox also sensed that Mexico had entered upon a major social upheaval and realized that American intervention could very easily provoke a horrible encounter in which the United States would be confronted by a population motivated by racial and nationalistic emotions. They wanted no part of such a war.

Wilson cared far less for the established rules of recognition than for his opposition to revolutions or for his own dictum that Latin Americans should honor his standards. And, along with Bryan, the president entertained a blithe confidence that American power would intimidate any opposition. As a result, the effort to depose Huerta quickly involved Wilson in a crusade to control the course of the Mexican Revolution.

The president first acted on a plan proposed by various large American corporations that wanted to protect their stakes in Mexico. Led by spokesmen of the Southern Pacific Railroad, the Greene Cananea Copper Company, an oil firm, and Phelps, Dodge and Company, they

Benjamin Robinson of the New York Tribune *compares Woodrow Wilson, with his desire to teach moral principles, to Don Quixote. He attacks the windmill (Mexico) while a doubtful Sancho looks on.*

THE CHARGE OF THE DON
—Robinson in N.Y. *Tribune*

Reprinted in *Current Opinion*, vol. 56, January, 1914, p. 8.

recommended the following strategy: Huerta would be recognized if he accepted the proposal of Venuctiano Carranza (his chief rival) to stop fighting and abide by the result of an election. That approach was supported by Gompers of the AF of L, who backed Carranza. Gompers was not fundamentally opposed to American investments in Mexico; he merely wanted them handled intelligently enough to prevent an influx of competitive Mexican labor into the United States.

Wilson accepted the general idea but modified it in a way that would give him leverage to control the election. He offered such a bargain to Huerta in June, 1913, simultaneously asking all interested foreign powers to put pressure on the Mexican leader—and promising to help Mexico to secure a loan in the United States. The Mexican foreign minister responded to the barely disguised bribe by reading Wilson a lecture on morals and self-determination:

> If even once we were to permit [such intervention] of the United States of America not only would we . . . forgo our sovereignty but we would as well compromise for an indefinite future our destiny as a sovereign entity and all the future elections for president would have to be submitted to the veto of any president of the United States of America. And such an enormity . . . no government will ever attempt to perpetrate . . . . When the dignity of a nation is at stake I believe that there are not loans enough to induce those charged by the law to maintain it to permit it to be lessened.

Huerta responded by aligning himself with English oil interests and establishing himself as a dictator. Wilson was furious. He warned the English (and other powers) to stand aside while he launched a personal vendetta against Huerta. He first made it possible for Carranza to obtain arms and then used an incident as an excuse for a major show of force designed to change the Mexican government.

Wilson had earlier stationed an American naval squadron off Vera Cruz to block arms deliveries to Huerta. Part of the crew of one ship went ashore at Tampico on April 10, 1914, to obtain supplies and for recreation. They landed without permission at a time when Huerta's forces were under siege by Carranza's army and were placed under arrest by a junior officer. When he learned of the action, Huerta's local commander immediately released the Americans and formally apologized to the admiral of the squadron.

In a classic imperial gesture, the admiral insisted upon a 21 gun salute, and the president supported the extravagant demand. Huerta refused to give way, and Wilson asked the Congress on April 20 for authority to use the army and the navy. The next day, before his request was granted, Wilson ordered the navy to occupy Vera Cruz. The Mexicans resisted bravely, suffering 331 killed and wounded, but the Americans quickly captured the town.

In the New York Herald, *W. A. Rogers cartooned Uncle Sam with broom, brush, and a bucket of suds, determined to launder the murky leadership of the Mexican people.*

NOT GOING TO BE ANY WAR—BUT THERE'S GOING TO
BE A FINE HOUSE-CLEANING

Rogers in N.Y. *Herald*

Reprinted in *Current Opinion*, vol. 56, June, 1914, p. 411.

Wilson was immediately confronted by an aroused and hostile Mexico and by a shocked and confused public at home. A minority of Americans wanted full-scale intervention, but the overwhelming majority agitated for peace. The president was reluctant to undertake the occupation of Mexico, but he remained determined to unseat Huerta and control the revolution. He arranged an offer of mediation by Chile, Brazil, and Argentina, with the idea of using it to accomplish both objectives. But Huerta surrendered to Carranza on July 15, and Carranza promptly and bluntly told Wilson that the revolution was its own master.

Wilson did not surrender gracefully. Instead, he encouraged Francisco ("Pancho") Villa, one of Carranza's disaffected generals who appealed to one segment of Mexico's lower class, as a way of bringing pressure on Carranza. But Villa's force was scattered early in 1915, and he turned in desperation to guerrilla warfare and border provocations designed to involve the United States in renewed intervention. As a result, Wilson was faced with serious troubles in Mexico as he tried to cope with what he considered to be the growing threat to American interests and leadership created by the European war.

EXPLORATORY READING

The following studies provide a good introduction to the vast literature on American foreign relations from 1900 to 1917 and at the same time reveal the different ways that historians have interpreted the policies. Most contain helpful bibliographies.

H. K. Beale, *Theodore Roosevelt and the Rise of America to World Power* (1966)

P. Calvert, *The Mexican Revolution, 1910–1914* (1968)

C. S. Campbell, *Anglo-American Understanding, 1898–1903* (1957)

H. F. Cline, *The United States and Mexico* (1953)

R. Daniels, *The Politics of Prejudice: The Anti-Japanese Movement in California* (1962)

G. T. Davis, *A Navy Second to None: The Development of Modern American Naval Policy* (1940)

R. A. Esthus, *Theodore Roosevelt and Japan* (1966)

F. H. Harrington, *God, Mammon, and the Japanese* (1944)

J. Israel, *Progressives and the Open Door* (1973)

B. I. Kaufman, *Efficiency and Expansion* (1974)

A. S. Link, *The New Freedom* (1956)

D. G. Munro, *Intervention and Dollar Diplomacy in the Caribbean, 1900–1914* (1964)

W. L. Neumann, *America Encounters Japan: From Perry to MacArthur* (1963)

H. Notter, *The Origins of the Foreign Policy of Woodrow Wilson* (1937)

C. P. Parrini, *Heir to Empire: United States Economic Diplomacy, 1916–1923* (1969)

H. Schmidt, *The U. S. Occupation of Haiti, 1915–1934* (1964)

W. and M. Scholes, *The Foreign Policies of the Taft Administration* (1970)

R. F. Smith, *The United States and Revolutionary Nationalism in Mexico, 1916–1932* (1972)

C. C. Tansill, *The U.S. and Santo Domingo* (1938)

C. Vevier, *The United States and China, 1906–1913* (1955)

W. A. Williams, *The Tragedy of American Diplomacy,* (1972)

7 ONWARD TO REFORM THE WORLD

AMERICANS were shocked more than surprised by the European war that erupted after the assassination by a Serbian extremist, on June 28, 1914, of Archduke Francis Ferdinand, heir to the Austrian-Hungarian throne. The traditional view of Europe as an undemocratic and less progressive society led most Americans to assume the worst as England and Germany began to organize rival alliances after the turn of the century. Members of the government, and others who followed international affairs, were concerned as early as 1912 that the increasing tension would end in violence. Others assumed that a war would come as a matter of course—the Old World knew no other way.

But instead of developing from a direct imperial confrontation in Africa, the Middle East, or Asia, the fighting came only after five weeks of move and countermove (June 28–August 4) that created an attitude of disgust among Americans. President Wilson's proclamation of neutrality (August 4) and his emotional plea for Americans to be neutral in thought as well as deed reflected the country's dismay and its desire to avoid being drawn into the fighting.

From the outset, however, the preference for remaining on the sidelines was counterbalanced by three factors that ultimately led to armed intervention. First, the war challenged the American outlook and strategy in foreign affairs, which was intimately connected with the nation's approach to domestic matters. The Open Door policy was predicated upon peaceful competition in which the superiority of the

American political and economic system would result in world leadership and prosperity and welfare at home. The war not only disrupted the international system per se but it also raised the clear possibility that the world would be reorganized in new spheres of interest to the detriment of the United States.

Second, the desire to remain aloof was steadily subverted by ethnic commitments to Germany or the Allied Powers (particularly England), by quick judgments on the question of war guilt, by habits of association in personal and business relationships, and by ingrained assumptions about which nations posed the most serious threat to America's power throughout the world. The spoken and written propaganda that immediately began to flow into the United States from the Allies and the Central Powers was more effective in reinforcing such existing attitudes than in changing them. Wilson was no more neutral in thought or feeling than most other Americans. Along with the majority, the president viewed Germany as the more dangerous threat to American interests and wanted the Allies to win. Rather than being neutral, the majority of Americans were nonbelligerents who favored England and France.

Finally, those attitudes and involvements guided early decisions, which in turn made it ever more difficult to control America's increasing involvement on the side of the Allies. Wilson revealed his understanding of those factors in a later (1919) exchange with Senator Porter James McCumber.

"Do you think," the senator asked, "if Germany had committed no act of war or no act of injustice against our citizens that we would have gotten into this war?"

"I do think so," Wilson replied.

"You do think we would have gotten in anyway?"

"I do."

Germany did not embark upon a policy of overt acts of war against the United States until March, 1917, a month after Wilson had broken diplomatic relations. Long before that time, however, between August 4 and December 31, 1914, Wilson and other American leaders had made decisions in the vital areas of economic policy, neutral and belligerent rights, and about America's postwar objectives that pointed the nation toward military involvement.

"The war opened," as financier J. P. Morgan later explained, "during a period of hard times that had continued in America for over a year. Business throughout the country was depressed, farm prices were deflated, unemployment was serious, the heavy industries were working far below capacity, and bank clearings were off." Andrew Carnegie agreed, warning Wilson at the time that the "present financial and industrial situations are very distressing." The seriousness of the situation was accentuated because the reform movement had no clear ideas about how to deal with the problem.

The outbreak of the war intensified the economic crisis. The belligerents began to liquidate their holdings in America to finance the war, and the banking system did not have the capital reserves to meet that demand and at the same time service the domestic economy. As a result, the New York Stock Exchange and the cotton exchange were forced to close. Such grave disturbances in the marketplace forced the administration to intervene in the economy, initiating a collaboration between business and government that continued into the 1970s.

The Wilson administration issued emergency currency that eased the demands for capital, but much less was done for the cotton producers, who lost about 50 percent of the normal value of their 1914 crop. The wheat and tobacco interests were likewise upset, warning that the crisis was "paralyzing" their businesses. And similar reactions came from Standard Oil of New Jersey and southern producers of naval stores (who were in "a very precarious position").

Private economic leaders and government officials agreed that an expansion of exports offered the most promising solution to the crisis. At the outbreak of the war, over 75 percent of America's trade was carried on with the belligerents: 77 percent of its exports, and 75 percent of its imports. But half of the exports and one-third of the imports involved England and the British Empire. In order to revive the economy through exports and remain neutral, therefore, the United States would have needed to treat both groups of belligerents equally and at the same time expanded its trade with other countries.

Wilson did try to enlarge the merchant marine, and he advised businessmen to preempt the trade with South America that had been controlled by Germany and England. "Here are the markets which we must supply," he said, and promised official help: "The government must open these gates of trade, and open them wide; open them before it is altogether profitable to open them or altogether reasonable to ask private capital to open them at a risk."

In action, however, the government gave priority to exploiting the markets offered by the Allies. Great Britain and France immediately began to place orders with American firms, but, not wanting to pay for them by liquidating the empires the war was designed to save, they asked for credits and loans in the United States. Secretary of State Bryan first ruled, on August 15, 1914, that "loans by American bankers to any foreign nation which is at war are inconsistent with the true spirit of neutrality."

Other leaders disagreed. Businessmen and bankers immediately opened a campaign to reverse his decision, basing their argument on the necessity of exports. And the legal counselor in the State Department, Robert Lansing, who was militantly pro-British, pointed out that Bryan's position was not technically correct. Wilson gave way and on October 23–24 drew a wholly artificial distinction between credits and loans that opened the way for the Allies to finance their purchases in the United States. Bryan acquiesced in the reversal, which was made in secret and not announced for many months.

Wilson also retreated in the face of Britain's determined offensive to control world trade in order to strangle the German economy. Wilson asked both belligerents on August 6, 1914, to abide by the Declaration of London (1907), which specified the right of neutrals to continue to trade with and ship to all belligerents in time of war. The Central Powers agreed to do so if the Allies accepted the proposal. Britain refused. Wilson abandoned his effort on October 22, and England promptly (November 3) defined the North Sea as a war area and began to lay mines. That action initiated a general blockade designed to control all trade with Europe—by neutrals as well as belligerents. The next move was an extensive contraband list. Then London used its power over the raw materials produced throughout its empire. Within six months, therefore, the American economy had become deeply involved with the Allied war effort on terms largely specified by Great Britain.

Wilson was far tougher in dealing with Germany over the issue of using the submarine against merchant ships. That problem arose in the wake of the president's response to Britain's decision to arm its merchantmen. Wilson allowed them to enter American ports on the grounds that the weapons were for defense. But he asserted that submarines had to surface in order to inspect ships for contraband, and that left them easy targets for the so-called defensive guns of the merchantmen. His double standard had become apparent.

The point was dramatized on February 4, 1915, when Germany defined the English Channel and other waters surrounding England and Ireland as a war zone and opened submarine warfare in the area in retaliation for Britain's war on neutral trade with Germany. The Germans did not sink an American ship, but Leon C. Thrasher lost his life when the British steamer *Falaba* (carrying 13 tons of munitions) was torpedoed on March 28, 1915. Bryan clearly defined the issue: "I cannot help feeling," he wrote Wilson, "that it would be a sacrifice of the interests of all the people to allow one man, acting purely for himself and own interests, and without consulting his government, to involve the entire nation in difficulty when he had ample warning of the risks which he assumed."

Bryan was giving serious thought to warning Americans that they traveled on belligerent ships at their own risk. But the president was increasingly inclined, with strong encouragement from Lansing, to challenge Germany in a blunt, harsh note condemning submarine warfare. That propensity was strengthened by events in Asia, which increased Wilson's determination to act on his version of American rights and influence throughout the world.

Japan exploited the European conflict to further its ambitions in Asia. It first declared war on Germany (August 23, 1914), to honor the letter of the Anglo-Japanese Treaty. It soon violated the spirit of that agreement, and further challenged the Open Door policy, by occupying the Shantung peninsula. Then, on January 18, 1915, it confronted China with a bill of particulars (known as the Twenty-One Demands) that was designed to reduce China to a colony or protectorate.

Wilson and Bryan responded with a strong reassertion of America's rights and interests. "We shall not have uttered a more important state paper," Wilson exclaimed to Bryan on February 25, 1915, as they began preparing their counterblast. They first made it clear, on March 13, that they were "concerned with the legitimate participation in the economic development of China" and that they considered Japan's action a serious threat to such involvement.

Wilson then underscored the central importance he attached to "the maintenance of the policy of the open door to the world" by issuing a strong public warning to Japan. The United States "cannot recognize any agreement or undertaking which has been entered into between the governments of Japan and China, impairing the treaty rights of the United States and its citizens in China, the political or territorial integrity of the Republic of China, or the international policy relative to China commonly known as the Open Door policy."

Japan began a sophisticated tactical retreat that left it in a powerful strategic position. As for Germany, it continued its submarine warfare. It publicly warned Americans on May 1, 1915, that it was extremely dangerous to travel on belligerent merchant ships. And the following day, the British vessel *Lusitania* was torpedoed and sunk off Ireland. The ship carried contraband, including ammunition, and may have been armed. The loss of life did not blind some American leaders to the belligerent status of the *Lusitania*. General Leonard Wood made the point in a memorable phrase: "You cannot cover 10,000 tons of ammunition with a petticoat." And Bryan clearly understood that a blunt confrontation with Germany would bring the United States to the edge of war.

Lansing was willing to accept that result. He was certain that a German victory would "mean the overthrow of democracy in the world . . . and the turning back of the hands of human progress two centuries." Wilson publicly expressed his similar feelings in an unqualified assertion of American rights and a moral condemnation of submarine warfare. The president's formal protest of May 13, 1915, was tough: it almost demanded that Germany abandon the submarine and asserted that the United States would hold Berlin "to a strict accountability for any infringement"—"intentional or incidental"—of the rights of American shipmasters or American citizens on belligerent merchantmen.

Wilson and Lansing did not take such strong action against the British extension of the Allied blockade on March 1, 1915, and in April allowed the FRB to underwrite further loans to England and France. Germany argued that the involvement of the FRS made the loans governmental instead of private, but Wilson dismissed that logic and also refused to accept Germany's plea of self-defense in the case of the *Lusitania.*

In a brave and unique act, Bryan offered his resignation on June 8, 1915, in protest against a policy that he considered would lead the United States into the war. Wilson immediately accepted the resignation and appointed Lansing as secretary of state. Germany began to modify its position on July 8, 1915, but an acceptable compromise was not arranged until after the *Arabic* was sunk on August 19, 1915. "Liners will not be sunk by our submarines . . . ," the Germans pledged on September 1, 1915, "provided that the liners do not try to escape or offer resistance." This gave the president a victory of sorts, but he still had not resolved the submarine issue. He had merely defined it in such a way that American rights, interests, and objectives had become intimately involved with submarine attacks on belligerent ships. Bryan was right: unless the president changed his outlook, the United States would go to war.

Wilson's handling of the submarine issue deeply confused American thinking about the war. The majority of people, composed of many with pro-German sympathies as well as those who favored the Allies, did not want to join the fighting. They were not isolationists in the sense of withdrawing from the world or from the extension of American influence. They simply preferred not to go to war unless and until they concluded that the United States was directly threatened.

Two smaller groups disagreed. One of them argued for more vigorous intervention. The other maintained that Wilson's policy was placing the country in a position where it would have to risk its prosperity by behaving as a true neutral, back down on its demands concerning the submarine, or go to war.

The antiinterventionists found themselves increasingly on the defensive because they seemed to be pro-German and because their opponents began to mobilize a martial spirit among the population. The National Security League was organized on December 1, 1914, and it was soon working closely with the Army and Navy leagues to prepare for war. The clash with Japan and the *Lusitania* crisis rein-

From his position in the State Department, Secretary William Jennings Bryan fought the drift away from neutrality incurred by the extension of credit to belligerents. Cartoonist Tan of the Providence Journal *placed Bryan in the position of the young maid in Rose Thorpe's poem "Curfew Shall Not Ring Tonight" who saved her sweetheart by muffling the clapper. But Bryan failed.*

"CURFEW SHALL NOT RING TO-NIGHT"
—Tan in Providence *Journal*

Reprinted in *Current Opinion*, vol. 62, April, 1917, p. 229.

forced their argument, which they merchandized in articles, speeches, and books. Their efforts were also aided by two movies produced in 1915. Both *The Battle Cry of Peace* and *The Fall of a Nation* depicted the invasion of the United States by forces that looked remarkably like German infantrymen.

WILSON'S FIRST MILITARY MOVE

Wilson made his first major military move on July 21, 1915, when he asked Secretary of the Navy Josephus Daniels and Secretary of War Lindley M. Garrison to submit expansionist programs for the armed forces. While those were being prepared, the president agreed to a further interlocking of the American economy with the Allied war effort. It was a "serious condition," warned confidential aide Colonel Edward M. House on July 18, 1915. "Unless the Federal Reserve System broadens its basis of credits another month or two will bring about a crisis and almost a complete breakdown of our foreign trade." Secretary of the Treasury William G. McAdoo was equally blunt: "Great prosperity is coming. It is, in large measure, here already. It will be tremendously increased if we can extend reasonable credits to our customers. . . . Our prosperity is dependent on our continued and enlarged foreign trade."

Secretary of State Lansing added his pressure on September 5: the result of failing to approve the necessary changes "would be restriction of outputs, industrial depression, idle labor, numerous failures, financial demoralization, and general unrest and suffering among the laboring classes." The first of many further loans to the Allies ($500 million) was negotiated in October, 1915.

In the same month, the president approved the navy's proposal for a five-year program to build 10 battleships, 16 cruisers, 50 destroyers, and 100 submarines. The army's request to underwrite a vast increase in its might was less sophisticated because it embodied a controversial proposal to replace the National Guard with a continental reserve of 400,000 men. Wilson approved that challenge to the status quo, however, and opened his fight for both recommendations with a major policy speech.

He was immediately answered by an aroused and articulate opposition. The institutional leadership was provided by the League to Limit Armaments, headed by such men as Oswald Garrison Villard, and by the Women's Peace party under the leadership of Jane Addams. Vital support also came from labor and farm organizations. And in Bryan, LaFollette, and House majority leader Claude Kitchin, the movement claimed bipartisan political giants who could hold their own with Wilson. "Talk of the 'national defense' is the sheerest rot," Kitchin roared back at the president on November 18, 1915. "Who is threatening invasion? Who is coveting our territory? Who is seeking the overthrow of our institutions? Who is manifesting a desire to bring us under subjugation?"

The president responded with three speeches and embarked on a tour that carried him as far west as St. Louis. He warned that it might not be possible to stay out of the war and stressed the need for power to enable the United States to lead in "the redemption of the affairs of mankind." And his constant call for a huge merchant marine and navy came to a climax in St. Louis where he cried out for support in building "incomparably the greatest navy in the world."

The proposal to scrap the National Guard, however, ran into heavy opposition from a broad coalition that included both the people who feared a standing army as well as the more narrowly self-interested guardsmen. Secretary of War Garrison resigned over the issue on February 10, 1916, and was replaced by Newton D. Baker, a new convert to preparedness. At that juncture, Wilson was helped by Pancho Villa, who on March 9, 1916, raided Columbus, New Mexico. The reaction was so strong that LaFollette took the lead in passing a joint resolution on March 17 that authorized the president to deploy the army and capture Villa. A week later the House passed a bill that increased the regular army forces to 250,000 men, enlarged the reserves to 261,000, and saved the National Guard (with the proviso that it would be fully integrated into the army in case of emergency or war).

On the following day, March 24, 1916, a German submarine sank the channel steamer *Sussex*. Wilson told the Germans on April 18 that he would break relations unless they accepted his rules on submarine warfare and the next day advised Congress of the gravity of the crisis. Germany recognized the danger and promised on May 4 to honor the visit-and-search procedure in all cases. But the German emperor was angry and bitter over Wilson's failure to force the British to observe basic provisions in international law concerning neutral trade. "Either starve at England's bidding," he wrote in a memo on the American ultimatum, "or war with America! That is, in the name of Wilson's humanity!" And he carefully reserved "complete liberty of decision," as he told Wilson, if the president was unable to induce the British to change their policy.

Wilson replied by deploying his influence to coerce the House to accept the big navy bill that the Senate had passed on July 21, 1916. He had his way on August 15 and a bit later won passage of a law creating the United States Shipping Board. Like the Council of National Defense, created as part of the army bill, the Shipping Board became a central agency in the tighter organization of the economy under the direction of the federal government. Wilson was sucking power into Washington (and the White House) as if he were a corporation executive on a binge of vertical integration.

The success of the president's simultaneous campaign for preparedness temporarily slowed the momentum toward intervention. Many of the people who supported an increase in the army and the navy, for example, were not ready to go to war. And the antiinterventionist groups did not abandon their struggle simply because they lost one round in the battle. There was a general feeling that, whatever the disagreements of the past, the United States was now sufficiently armed to meet any threat to its interests. That was reinforced by Germany's retreat in the *Sussex* crisis.

At the same time, moreover, British actions produced considerable American anger and antagonism. The English were particularly ruthless in repressing the Irish Rebellion of April 24, 1916, and the hostility was intensified when the leaders were quickly executed. Even earlier, on April 13, the British had launched a new economic offensive with the announcement that they were abandoning all distinctions between absolute and conditional contraband in their control of neutral trade. Three months later, on July 18, London blacklisted 85 American firms on the grounds they were aiding the Central Powers. Even Wilson was angered enough by these and other British actions to reconsider Bryan's earlier argument that loans to belligerents were dangerous to American interests.

The president realized that he was in a very difficult position. In and of themselves, neither the preparedness efforts nor the tough verbal protests produced satisfactory results. Bryan's earlier suggestion that the president use his influence to end the war became increasingly attractive as a way to avoid military intervention and at the same time strengthen America's world position. Early in 1916, therefore, Wilson opened negotiations to explore the idea of ending the war by restoring the status quo ante.

But the British refused to participate unless Wilson promised to enter the war if the effort failed, and the president was not willing to make that commitment. Then the Germans drew back in the *Sussex* incident, and the British tightened their economic controls. "We are plainly face to face with this alternative, therefore," Wilson wrote Colonel House on May 16, 1916, "the United States must either make a decided move for peace (upon some basis that promises to be permanent) or, if she postpones that, must insist to the limit upon her rights of trade and upon such freedom of the seas as international law already justifies her in insisting on as against Great Britain, with the same plain speaking and firmness that she had used against Germany. And the choice must be made immediately."

But it was not made immediately. For one thing, Wilson was still involved in trying to control the Mexican Revolution. He sent almost 7000 men well over 300 miles into Mexico in search of Villa. The growing opposition was bluntly expressed by General Hugh L. Scott, chief of staff. "If the thing were reversed," he commented, "we would not allow any foreign army to go sloshing around in our country 300 miles from the border, no matter who they were."

Wilson ignored the advice and reacted strongly in April, 1916, when Mexican regulars clashed with American troops. Another clash ensued on June 20–21, when an American field commander, assuming that the Mexicans would give way, tried to run a bluff. But the Mexicans, as one observer noted dryly, "did not run." They held their ground and won the battle.

The American public responded with strong pressure for peace. Wilson was forced to give way even though he preferred (and was prepared) to try to establish military control throughout northern Mexico. He shifted to a confrontation in Europe. The Allied Economic Conference, held in Paris during the summer of 1916, offered the president a new challenge. Alba B. Johnson, president of the Baldwin Locomotive Works, for example, warned fellow members of the National Foreign Trade Council that the discussions "would increase the difficulties of our struggle for foreign trade." Senator Lodge feared the conference pointed to an effort "to close the gates of trade and commerce upon us in many directions." And Lansing advised Wilson that the "consequent restrictions upon profitable trade . . . will cause a serious if not critical situation for the nations outside the union."

Wilson moved first against Germany. He stopped a proposed loan to that country. Then he protested Germany's use of Belgian forced labor. Next he turned on the Allies, warning financiers and individual investors against buying treasury bills offered by Britain and France. Those moves were interrelated parts of a campaign to bring the belligerents to the peace table under his guidance and influence.

Germany's peace proposal of December 12, 1916, which disrupted Wilson's own efforts, was rebuffed by the Allies shortly after Christmas (December 30). Neither side was willing, having waged war for three years, to stop short of a fight to the finish, and neither was willing to let Wilson stand above the battle and hand down the terms of settlement. Wilson responded on January 22, 1917, with a speech before the Senate making it clear that he was determined to protect and advance his conception of American rights and interests.

"I am proposing, as it were," he announced, "that the nations should with one accord adopt the doctrine of President Monroe as the doctrine of the world . . . . That all nations henceforth avoid entangling alliances." "I am proposing," he concluded, "government by consent of the governed . . . freedom of the seas . . . and that moderation of armaments which makes of armies and navies a power for order." Wilson was telling Americans and the rest of the world that he was preparing to act in order to defend and advance the principles underlying the Open Door policy.

German leaders accurately viewed the United States as the workshop and the bank of the Allies and astutely concluded that Wilson would not sit indefinitely on the sidelines and thereby risk losing all influence on the peace settlement. Hence they decided on January 8, 1917, to reopen unrestricted submarine warfare. Wilson replied by breaking diplomatic relations on February 3, 1917.

The news that Germany hoped, in the event of war, to open a second front through an alliance with Mexico and Japan, was a dramatic but not decisive event. The British provided the information (on February 25) after intercepting and decoding a cable outlining the projected effort. Wilson was of course disturbed, but he knew that a proposal was not an overt act against the United States. He nevertheless released the dispatch to the American people.

THE UNITED STATES ENTERS THE WAR

The president then announced on March 9 that he was arming American merchantmen and ordering them to fire on submarines. Ten days later, March 18, the Germans sank three American ships. The cabinet voted for war on March 20, and Wilson shortly mobilized National Guard units and raised the strength of the navy to its limit of 87,000 enlisted men. He asked the Congress for a declaration of war at 8:30 on the evening of April 2, asserting in a revealing and memorable phrase that "the world must be made safe for democracy." The Senate voted 82 to 6, and the House 373 to 50, and Wilson signed the war resolution on April 6.

Wilson understood full well that intervention would change American society. "Once lead this people into war," he almost sobbed to a friend the night before he spoke to the Congress, "and they'll forget there ever was such a thing as tolerance. . . . The spirit of ruthless brutality will enter into the very fiber of our national life." He was unfortunately correct. Even more unhappily, the president contributed to the extension of that spirit. "When men take up arms to set other men free," he had declared as early as 1911, "there is something sacred and holy in the warfare. I will not cry 'peace' so long as there is sin and wrong in the world." His attitude had not changed. "Woe to the man or group of men," he warned on June 14, 1917, "that seeks to stand in our way in this day of high resolution."

The early effort to enact a broad espionage act met stiff resistance. Progressive Senator William E. Borah of Idaho called it "omnipotently comprehensive" and warned that "no man can foresee what it might be in its consequences." Others agreed, but the administration won the battle. The Espionage Act of June 15, 1917, gave the postmaster general power to exclude what he considered treasonable or seditious material from the mails and provided stiff fines and jail sentences for those found guilty of aiding the enemy or of obstructing the creation or operation of the armed forces. The official federal drive for conformity was reinforced by the efforts of state and local governments and by the activities of various private groups such as the American Defense Society and the National Security League.

The most powerful of those organizations, the American Protective League, was in reality sponsored by Attorney General Thomas W. Gregory and had units operating in 600 cities and towns by the time the Espionage Act became law. Wilson was aware of the strong probability that such activities would become "very dangerous": "I wonder," he commented, in response to vigorous criticism from Treasury Secretary McAdoo, "if there is any way in which we can stop it." There was, of course, but the president was unwilling to fight for a principle that might undercut his imperial ethic.

The ensuing campaign against dissent and criticism, as well as against the small amount of overt opposition to the war, was belligerent and thorough. Thousands of people were abused or jailed. The old-time Populist Tom Watson, for example, wanted to test the Selective Service Act (May 18, 1917) in the courts. But the extremist groups prevented him from raising funds and organizing support for that effort. "The world must be made safe for democracy," he commented bitterly, "even though none is left in these United States."

Newspapers often censored themselves on a voluntary basis. One example documents the point. Explaining his position, Senator LaFollette admitted in St. Paul on September 20, 1917, that "we had at the hands of Germany, serious differences," but then went on to argue that those difficulties did not warrant armed conflict. The Associated Press reported him as having said, "We had no grievances."

Watson and LaFollette, along with other reformers, paid a terrible price for their integrity. The cost was even higher for those who were more radical and militant, especially the IWW and the Socialists. A radical protest parade of 8000 in Boston on July 1, 1917, was attacked by soldiers and sailors. Then attention shifted to the United Metal and Mine Workers strike against the Anaconda Mines in Butte, Montana. Frank Little, an IWW organizer, was dragged behind a car until his kneecaps were scraped off. Then he was hanged. All that in retaliation for a speech. Attorney General Gregory did nothing to stop the hysteria. "May God have mercy on them," he piously remarked, "for they need expect none from an outraged people and an avenging government."

In keeping with that spirit, the Espionage Act was amended on May 16, 1918, to extend the provisions against sedition. Avowedly designed to punish radicals and pacifists, the law led to the arrest of Socialist leaders Eugene V. Debs and Victor L. Berger. There were also mass roundups in Chicago, Detroit, Sacramento, and Kansas City. In one case, the jury required only 55 minutes to convict a group of 96 men. Berger ultimately won his freedom on appeal, but Debs (sentenced to ten years) remained in jail. President Wilson adamantly refused to consider a pardon, and Debs was not released until President Warren G. Harding freed him in 1921.

The wartime atmosphere of righteous conformity and intolerance undoubtedly facilitated the final triumph of the long campaign for Prohibition. The organization that headed the dry campaign after the turn of the century was the Anti-Saloon League (established in 1895), and its militant efforts soon produced striking results. A large majority of Americans (75 percent) lived in dry counties, and half the states had passed prohibition laws. Exhilarated by the momentum of their successes, the leaders of the antibooze war attacked the Congress about the time that the war began.

Their militant pressure produced a test vote in favor of a dry amendment in 1916, and the next year they induced the Congress to prohibit alcohol in the District of Columbia. Then, exploiting the spirit of patriotic duty and sacrifice, and the atmosphere of repressing all actions that might hinder the war effort, the drys mounted a campaign to have the required number of states ratify the constitutional amendment that the Congress had adopted on December 18, 1917.

The Prohibitionists were succeeding because they had persuaded people that their cause was just and that their remedy was necessary. President Wilson thought the same kind of propaganda campaign was required to sell the war. He was probably correct. There were millions of Americans, at least in the spring and summer of 1917, who were not convinced that the United States needed to go to war, and a good many of them felt that the country was becoming involved for reasons (such as the loans by the bankers to the Allies) that were considerably less than just.

To convince such doubters and to reassure those who agreed with him (however reluctantly), Wilson established the Committee on Public Information. He chose George Creel, a journalist who had helped in the campaign of 1916, to manage what was in reality an official propaganda bureau. Creel and his associates were effective. The Germans and their allies were portrayed—directly or by implication—as monstrously evil barbarians out to rape and loot the world and as people who dabbled in minor atrocities when no women or gold were at hand. The Allies, and especially Americans, were pictured as noble and idealistic crusaders engaged in saving—and extending—morality, freedom, democracy, and prosperity.

Arousing the American public proved to be frighteningly easy, but organizing and coordinating the American economy proved almost too difficult. Most of the troubles, failures, and delays were finally overcome, however, and the United States produced and delivered to Europe a massive amount of matériel and contributed an effective combat force. The production of war goods had begun in response to Allied orders in 1914, but it was not until October, 1916, that the first effort was made, through the creation of the Council of National Defense and the Shipping Board, to coordinate and direct the increasingly complex process. As a result, the transition to a warfare economy was plagued by confusion and inefficiency.

The production and allocation of food and fuel were fortunate exceptions to that initially poor performance. The Lever Food and Fuel Control Act of August 10, 1917, created the administrative system, but the key elements in the success were the administrators: Herbert Clark Hoover and Harry A. Garfield. Both men used high prices as an incentive for production ($2.20 per bushel for 1917 wheat, for example) and organized vigorous propaganda campaigns to persuade and cajole the public to decrease consumption.

Hoover provides an excellent example of the extensive interrelationship that developed between the business community and the government. An unusually able and a wealthy mining engineer (with a reformist approach to labor problems), he approved of many Progressive measures and wanted (in part because of his Quaker outlook) to enter public service. The war gave him the opportunity. He quickly made a reputation as the effective head of the American Relief Commission in London and then became chairman of the Commission for Relief in Belgium. When America entered the war, Wilson immediately called him home and the two men developed a close working relationship that carried over into the early postwar years.

Hoover managed the extremely difficult task of feeding the Allies and the military forces and of keeping American civilians healthy while at the same time checking inflation. Wholesale food prices had moved from an index of 100 in 1913 to 180 by August, 1917, but his program limited the advance to 20 points during the next two years.

The financing of the war began with a congressional authorization on April 24, 1917, of a $7 billion bond sale (almost half of which went to the Allies). All in all, counting the campaign in April, 1919, there were five major Liberty Loan drives. But most of the expenses of the war were passed on to future generations. The grand cost was approximately $33.5 billion, but only $10.5 billion was covered by current taxes.

In most other respects, however, mobilization floundered initially. A Senate investigation concluded that the war effort "has almost stopped functioning." Poor management, corporate greed, special privileges, fuel shortages, and bad weather almost paralyzed the railroad system. Wilson took control of the lines on December 26, 1917, and placed them under the authority and direction of Treasury Secretary McAdoo. Working closely with the Fuel Administration, which provided the necessary coal, he ordered most other industries to operate on a reduced schedule while he cleared the massive traffic jam. The Congress then passed (March 21) the comprehensive Railroad Control Act that fixed payments to the companies and created a regional system of government management. Railroad express firms and the inland waterway network were later placed under the same administration.

That pattern of presidential initiative and action was not new, but the extensive use of the procedure during the war greatly extended the centralization and consolidation of power in the executive department. Wilson continued the practice in dealing with the chronic inability of the War Industries Board (WIB) to function effectively. He first called, early in 1918, for a delegation of power to enable him to administer the economy and even provided a draft of the necessary legislation. When the Congress proved recalcitrant, he ignored the legislators and acted on his own. He appointed Bernard Baruch to run the show on March 4, 1918, and gave him wide powers. The enabling legislation, known as the Overman Act, was finally approved more than two months later.

By that time, Baruch had reorganized the WIB around a select group of about 100 businessmen and military leaders. Operating through various committees, the WIB located the required materials, established rules and priorities for production and allocation, and cut inessential operations (as when, for a period in 1918, it held auto production to one-fourth of capacity). All of this helped labor and other groups in the economy by increasing and regularizing production. Labor's direct involvement in the war effort, however, was first handled through two commissions, established in the summer of 1917, that set wages and hours for contracts with the army and the navy.

Unions demanded more general participation and greater benefits, and the administration responded by creating the National War Labor Board (April, 1918) under the leadership of labor lawyer Frank P. Walsh and ex-president Taft. "The right of workers to organize in trade unions and to bargain collectively, through chosen representatives,"

Wilson declared, "is recognized and affirmed. This right shall not be denied, abridged, or interfered with by the employers in any manner whatsoever."

That ideal was not realized, for many firms denied, abridged, and interfered with those rights in many ways. But the government did give some support to labor, which helped the workers make significant—if limited—gains during the war. The AFL, for example, grew from 2 million to 3.2 million members between 1916 and 1920, and other unions enjoyed even greater expansion. Even so, only a minority of workers were organized at the end of the conflict. The eight-hour-day movement gained support, and nearly half the workers in manufacturing were on a 48-hour week by 1919—the steel industry remained a vital exception. Conditions of labor were also improved in many industries. And, as with the farmers, many—but by no means all—workers increased their real income. And certain leaders, particularly Samuel Gompers of the AFL, enjoyed increased prestige and enhanced status.

The government was also active in other areas. The Trading-with-the-Enemy Act of October 6, 1917, for example, gave the president wide powers to control foreign trade. Under its provisions, the War Trade Board licensed imports, embargoed trade with the enemy, and even shared in the allocation of some materials and supplies. That concern to improve America's commercial position in the world marketplace was also apparent in the actions of the Office of the Alien Property Custodian. It seized considerable German property in the United States and sold much of it at very low prices to selected American businessmen, particularly those in the chemical industry.

There was no similar success in aviation. The National Advisory Committee on Aeronautics was created in 1915, but neither it nor the Aircraft Production Board was effective during the war. By the time of the armistice, the United States had delivered the grand total of 1185 planes and 5400 engines for service in Europe. Neither were a match for the products of Germany, France, or England.

American fliers were more effective. They went to Europe long before the United States entered the war and, using French and British planes, produced a distinguished combat record. The first American to become an ace while flying in an American unit was Douglas Campbell of the Ninety-fourth Pursuit Squadron (which used the symbol of the Hat in the Ring). The most famous member of that outfit, and the American ace of aces (26 kills), was Captain Edward Vernon Rickenbacker. Before America entered the war, he was an automobile test driver and a highly successful racer, with a total annual income of about $40,000 from that rapidly expanding industry. He was such an excellent driver that his desire to become a flier was thwarted for many months by General Pershing's determination to keep him as a personal chauffeur.

The transfer was finally arranged by Colonel Billy Mitchell, and Rickenbacker quickly became one of the best pilots of the war. Such men were important in providing aviation leadership after the war. Some, like Mitchell, stayed in the service to organize, build, and train the Army Air Force. Others played a key role, as barnstormers and charter pilots, in creating the basis for commercial aviation. In one of his early novels, *Pylon*, author William Faulkner caught the wild spirit and the danger of their lives—and their impact on postwar America. The real war was not so glamorous.

Fighting in water-filled trenches and laying antisubmarine mines in the cold, violent seas of the North Atlantic was far less romantic than waging personal duels in Nieuport and Spad pursuit planes. That miserable kind of combat was far more important, however, in determining the outcome of the war. The United States did not win World War I. Had France and Britain collapsed, the conflict would have ended before America could have sustained the war on its own—even if the public had been willing to undertake that task. But the United States did provide the psychological, material, and human contribution that enabled the Allies *together* to defeat the Germans in the field.

The navy acted quickly. The first destroyers were on station by July, 1917, and they quickly proved their ability. The navy's key roles in mining the North Sea and in convoying men and matériel, while mundane and almost as boring to the reader as to the participants, were crucial to victory. The navy also transported nearly half of the American Expeditionary Force and almost all of its supplies.

In selecting the commander for the overseas ground forces, the Wilson administration bypassed General Leonard Wood, who was considered by many to be the army's top officer, in favor of Pershing. Wilson apparently feared Wood's reputation for standing up to his superiors and may have been worried by the old friendship between Wood and Roosevelt, who wanted to lead his own contingent against the Germans. The choice was probably unfair to Wood, but Pershing proved as efficient and effective as indicated by his nickname—"Black Jack." He was a stubborn and militant nationalist, a tough and able leader, and a successful field commander. He was determined from the outset to have Americans fight as Americans rather than as random replacements in other Allied units, and he largely won his way.

There was another bitter fight at home before the Selective Service Act was passed on May 18, 1917, and minimum age was set at 21 despite strong pressure from the army to induct men at 19. The first registration (June 5, 1917) went off without riots or other organized resistance, however, and 9.5 million men were processed for possible service. The age bloc was later extended (August 31, 1918) to include all men from 18 to 45. By the end of the war, 2.8 million men had been inducted, and adding the volunteers, the United States mustered a total of 4.8 million men in service.

The first American contingent of 14,500 men was assigned to the Toul sector near Verdun and on October 21, 1917, moved into the line. A German offensive renewed the Allied pressure to integrate American units, but Pershing (and Wilson) insisted on an independent role. They briefly gave way on March 21, 1918, when Germany launched its end-the-war offensive. Some 2000 Americans fought with French and British units to prevent the Germans from breaking through the Somme line and moving on to Amiens (a key supply and rail center) and the English Channel.

These men were insufficient, however, and Pershing agreed (on March 28) to allow other Americans to be used wherever they were needed in the crisis. The Germans nevertheless continued to advance: by April 6 they were in sight of Amiens, and on May 31 they reached the Marne on a 40-mile front. That was the context and the place of the battle of Chateau Thierry, where the American Second Division, along with elements of the Third and Twenty-Eighth divisions, helped the French stop the Germans less than 50 miles from Paris.

Then the Second Division was reinforced by the Fourth Marine Brigade. Advised to leave because a further retreat seemed probable, the marines exploded. "Retreat, hell! We just got here." They recrossed the Marne and won the bloody battle of Belleau Wood (their casualty rate was 55 percent). Farther to the north, the First Division played a similar role in preventing the Germans from consolidating their position before Amiens.

The Germans tried once more, launching a final offensive on July 15, 1918. By that time, 85,000 Americans were in the line that quickly blunted the attack. More than three times that many, 270,000, joined by some French units, opened the counteroffensive on July 18. The ensuing victory, secured by August 6, marked the beginning of the end for Germany. There were many more battles and deaths, as in the bloody engagement at St.-Mihiel between September 12–16 (about 7000 American casualties), but by the end of October the Germans were in full retreat. The end came on November 11, 1918.

Clearly enough, the United States earned its place at the peace table. American soldiers and workers had given President Wilson the opportunity to launch his crusade to "make the world safe for democracy."

EXPLORATORY READING

These volumes deal with the broad significance of the war, the response of various groups of Americans, the war effort itself, and the debate among historians about why the United States entered the conflict:

R. C. Challener, *Admirals, Generals and American Foreign Policy, 1898–1914* (1973)

C. J. Child, *The German-Americans in Politics, 1914–1917* (1939)

R. Gregory, *The Origins of American Intervention in the First World War* (1971)

A. S. Link, *Wilson: Campaigns for Progressivism and Peace, 1916–1917* (1965)

E. May, *The World War and American Isolation* (1959)

W. Millis, *The Road to War* (1935)

F. L. Paxton, *American Democracy and the World War* (3 vols., 1936–1948)

H. C. Peterson and G. C. Fite, *Opponents of War: 1917–1918* (1957)

J. J. Roth (Ed.), *World War I: A Turning Point in Modern History* (1967)

D. Smith, *Robert Lansing and American Neutrality* (1958)

D. M. Smith, *The Great Departure: The United States and World War I, 1914–1920* (1965)

L. Stallings, *The Doughboys* (1963)

C. C. Tansill, *America Goes to War* (1938)

B. Tuchman, *The Guns of August* (1971)

R. F. Weigley, *The American Way of War* (1973)

C. Wittke, *The Irish in America* (1956)

8 TRAUMAS OF CHANGE AND FAILURE

THE triumph over Germany momentarily confirmed the middle class and the new upper class of corporate leaders in their sense of power and achievement and in their satisfaction with the reforms made by the Progressive coalition. The concurrent victory that outlawed booze and the enactment of the Nineteenth Amendment giving women the right to vote on June 4, 1919 (ratified August 26, 1920), reinforced that somewhat smug self-confidence. The war effort against Germany had also served, directly and indirectly, to give some of the poor (black as well as white) a glimpse of what was generally considered to be the good American life: more money, mobility, and creature comforts, and some sense of belonging to the whole while remaining a staunch individualist.

The euphoria was short-lived, for America quickly entered a period of trouble and trauma. President Wilson's unsuccessful effort to create a world system based on the Open Door policy can only be understood within that context. The immediate postwar years were full of turmoil generated by the reemergence of old tensions, by the continuing extension of metropolitan-industrial power over the country areas, and by the intensity of conflicts within the metropolis.

The old society of farmers and small towns fought valiantly to preserve its way of life and even won some battles, but the new urban industrial system won the domestic cultural war. It proved incapable, however, of creating a new community or even a system in which people were able to control the institutions created in their name. The triumphant corporation did not become a responsible and benevolent lord of the industrial manor but instead revealed itself as nothing more than an extremely powerful advocate of marketplace self-interest.

Many workers learned that truth the hard way, and they deemed their struggle to be more important than President Wilson's crusade to

The Eighteenth Amendment was supported by a strange alliance in the 1920s—the bootleggers, whose purse depended upon Prohibition, and the crusaders, whose morality committed them to it. W. A. Rogers drew this cartoon for the Washington Post.

UPHOLDERS OF THE CONSTITUTION
—Rogers in the Washington *Post*

Reprinted in *The Literary Digest*, vol. 81, May 17, 1924, p. 7, © The Washington Post.

reform the world. One such group of day laborers considered going on strike in July, 1919, against the intolerable conditions arbitrarily imposed by their corporation boss, but in the end they chose a more devious revenge. The workers were eight men employed by Charles Albert Comiskey to make profits for him by using their great skills as members of the Chicago White Sox baseball team to defeat other such workers employed by other businessmen.

Baseball began as a game, and across the turn of the century developed as an intriguing Anglo-Saxon variation on the ritualistic drama of the bullfight. It was a classic duel between the pitcher and the hitter, designed at once to provoke and control the spontaneous combustion inherent in such a confrontation. As a game combining the almost tranquilizing peace of a pastoral landscape and the nerve-shattering speed and impact of a stamping press upon a piece of steel, it became by the end of the nineteenth century *the* American game—and so a natural investment for a businessman with a flair for the dramatic.

Most of the early-twentieth-century owners were a New World version of wealthy Old Country sportsmen: the gentlemen robber barons, as it were, of athletics. But increasingly the game came to be played according to the rules of the marketplace—by the percentages. The duel was becoming a ballet too esoteric for the lower-middle- and working-class people whose support had made it into the national pastime. Military intervention in the war further lowered attendance.

That was bad for business; hence the owners, Comiskey in the front rank, agreed among themselves in 1919 to cut wages. Comiskey gave the appearance of being one of the old breed of sportsmen-owners. He had assembled a group of unusually skilled men, like outfielder "Shoeless" Joe Jackson and third baseman George ("Buck") Weaver, who played with such explosive verve that they seemed capable of reviving the game. As it happened, however, that occurred a bit later through the play of George Herman ("Babe") Ruth and his supporting cast known as Murderers Row of the New York Yankees. In the meantime, in a way that symbolized many of the changes that were taking place in America, Comiskey proved himself to be a sportsman becoming a corporation manager.

The White Sox workers knew by July, 1919, that their skill and style had revived attendance and understandably felt that they deserved an appropriate increase in their wages. It seemed both logical and fair, particularly as Comiskey was notoriously tightfisted. He owned the best team in the business but gave his players 25 percent less for meals on the road than the poorest workers received. He paid his best pitcher perhaps $6000 and his number two hurler a miserly $2600—together they were winning more than 50 games a year. He also promised them bonuses they never received and manipulated them so that they could not use their skills to earn the extra money.

And so eight of them conspired, with occasional artistry, to lose the World Series to the vastly inferior Cincinnati Reds. They were angry country boys and bitter working-class kids revenging themselves upon the mighty metropolis. And of course they were taken: first by the gamblers who paid them a pittance (not even the traditional 30 pieces of silver) and then by Comiskey.

The boss handled the business very neatly. He knew before the series was over that his disenchanted workmen had thrown the contest. But he suspended no one, forfeited no game, and during the 1920 season worked his skilled but corrupted artisans as long as he could in order to win another pennant. Along the way, of course, he took certain precautions. His company lawyer deceptively guided the players into making confessions before the grand jury convened to investigate the scandal. The corporation then stole that evidence from the files.

So in the end the workers were acquitted in the trial (to great rejoicing by their loyal fans) only to be banished forever from their labor by Kenesaw Mountain Landis, a judge enthroned as a czar of the industry by the owners in an astute move to protect their investments and profits. In such fashion did they expand and consolidate their control of the business, the workers, and the spectators for the next half century.

Many workers in other industries fought their battles with the strike (there were 3353 in 1918 and 3630 in 1919), and some of them won higher wages and better conditions of labor. The Amalgamated Clothing Workers (ACW), who walked out on November 15, 1918, gained a 44-hour week in the men's clothing industry. A dissident element of 100,000, led by Abraham J. Muste, defied the conservative leadership of the United Textile Workers of America (UTWA) and forced management to grant many of their demands. New England Telephone Company operators struck against the government (which had taken over the lines during the war) and improved their position. Dock workers and longshoremen in New York raised their wages and shortened their hours; and workers on the Milwaukee Railroad, defying their leaders, touched off a strike in Chicago that, even though it failed in the formal sense, induced the corporations to grant a wage increase.

Soft-coal miners, belonging to the UMW and led by John L. Lewis, were particularly embittered. They had given a no-strike pledge as a contribution to the war effort, but the government had ignored them while raising the pay of workers in the hard-coal industry. Their anger rose steadily after the armistice, and finally, in September, 1919, Lewis demanded an end to government control, a six-hour day, a five-day week, and large wage increases. Failing in its efforts to break the union's will, the Wilson administration finally granted significant wage hikes and agreed to arbitrate most of the other grievances.

Other workers lost like the White Sox eight. Boston policemen, seeking only the rudiments of equitable treatment from the city they served and protected, were first ignored by their superiors. After they joined the AF of L, a citizens' committee favored granting most of their requests. But the police commissioner spurned the recommendation and fired 19 men; hence, on September 9, 1919, the rest of the force went on strike. Citizen patrols quickly reestablished effective order in the city, but the leaders of the metropolis retreated into hysteria. Governor Calvin Coolidge mobilized units of the National Guard, refused to negotiate, and justified his actions by proclaiming that there was "no right to strike against the public safety by anyone, anywhere, anytime." That pithy remark thrust Coolidge into the orbit of national politics, but his proposition was in truth based upon a double standard: public employees were to honor the ancient ideal of service to the community, but city fathers were free to deal with them as workers in the marketplace.

Shipyard laborers in Seattle fell victim to the rising hysteria about radicalism. They went on strike in February, 1919, and were promptly

Figure 2   Workers involved and man-days lost in strikes, 1916–1937. (From M. Levin and K. B. Wright, *The Income Structure of the United States,* (Washington, D.C.: The Brookings Institution, 1938, p. 89. Copyright 1938 by the Brookings Institute.)

supported by 60,000 fellow workers. The city stopped functioning for four days. Then Mayor Ole Hansen (with the help of uncritical newspaper editors) terrified the middle and upper classes—and even some of the lower class—by falsely raising the specter of revolution. The strike was broken. Similar tactics were used, along with violence, against the steelworkers in the East.

During the summer of 1918 William Z. Foster began to organize the steel makers for a campaign to force the corporations (and the government) to honor President Wilson's bold words about fair treatment for those who served in the trenches on the home front. Foster was a dedicated and effective radical, a man moving toward Marx's Communist vision of a worker's community as an alternative to the corporation's dominance of the metropolis that was coming to rule the country.

Foster's energy and ability enabled him to overcome the antagonisms created among the workers by differences of skill and ethnic background and culture, and by May, 1919, he mustered 100,000 steelworkers in support of six major demands. Union recognition and collective bargaining were sought in order to obtain an eight-hour day and a six-day week (with no 24-hour shifts), wage increases (with overtime), and the rehiring without prejudice of men who were fired for union activity. Elbert H. Gary, chairman of the board of United States Steel, refused to negotiate, and the strike began on September 22, 1919, when 375,000 men walked off the job.

The owners and the press immediately launched a massive campaign against Foster and others as dangerous radicals and revolutionaries, and the civil rights of the strikers were blatantly violated (particularly in Pennsylvania). The police, reinforced by troops, broke the picket lines (killing 18 strikers and injuring hundreds of others). Then black and white strikebreakers were brought in to restore production. The great effort was defeated long before it was formally ended on January 9, 1920.

The growing paranoia about radicals and revolution, which increasingly poisoned the environment in which Wilson's peace proposals were debated, grew out of many causes and affected almost every aspect of postwar American life. Most Americans had never been receptive to radical ideas (witness abolitionism), and that predisposition was particularly noticeable after the appearance of Communist, Socialist, and syndicalist ideas in the latter part of the nineteenth century.

The IWW generated deep fears and embittered opposition from the outset. And while the Socialism of Eugene Debs had, prior to the onset of the war, begun to establish a significant power base, the party was not revolutionary. In any event, many Americans reacted against its

antiwar stand and approved (or acquiesced in) the Wilson administration's vigorous repressive measures. Antiwar Socialists were
quickly smeared as being pro-German, though of course they were
not, and that in turn made it easy to attack all immigrants as dangerous
radicals who were un-American.

The movement against immigration had begun long before 1917,
but it gained increasing momentum from the misleading connection
with radicalism and from the rising militance of labor at the end of the
war. That in turn reinforced the more general antiforeign feeling that
helped defeat Wilson. The president ironically strengthened that attitude, moreover, by using the argument that radicals were pro-
German in his effort to discredit and oppose the Communists who, on
November 7, 1917, took power in Russia.

WILSON'S ANTIREVOLUTIONARY ACTIONS

The first wartime revolution in Russia, in which liberals overthrew the
czar in February, 1917, was welcomed by many Americans. They
viewed it as another victory for progressive reform throughout the
world, and it may have swayed some of them to support military intervention in the war. And a significant minority initially reacted favorably to the subsequent victory by Lenin, Trotsky, and their
followers.

But Wilson and Lansing (and most other American leaders) were
deeply opposed to the Bolshevik Revolution. They viewed it as a
threat to Western capitalism and to America's power and leadership in
the world. The president was aware that Lenin symbolized and appealed to what Wilson called the global "feeling of revolt against the
large vested interests which influenced the world both in the economic and in the political sphere." But Wilson naturally argued that
"the way to cure this domination was through constant discussion and
a slow program of reform," even as he admitted that "the world at
large had grown impatient of delay."

Short of declaring war, the president did all he could to oppose,
weaken, and overthrow the Bolsheviks. He first attacked them as
pro-German subversives, a move that strengthened the antiforeign and
antiradical feelings in the country. But Lenin's appeal in December,
1917, for a peace settlement that would end autocracy and imperialism
and "guarantee to each nation freedom for economic and cultural
development" could not be ignored. Not at all incidentally, the ongoing Mexican Revolution, as well as the actions of Japan, made it clear
that the revolt against the dominance of Western capitalism was not
limited to Russian Bolsheviks.

The Mexican Constitution of January 31, 1917, was designed to end foreign exploitation of the nation's resources and to protect native workers against all capitalists. Wilson protested those provisions of the document even before it went into effect, calling them "objectionable" and "capricious" and refusing to consider them legitimate. For different reasons, he also became increasingly concerned about Japanese moves, such as the occupation of the Shantung peninsula, that threatened the Open Door policy in China.

Wilson made a major decision in December, 1917, to aid all anti-Bolshevik forces in Russia. Then, on January 8, 1918, he presented his program for peace in answer to Lenin's appeal to the peoples of the world. The president would have offered his proposals even if Lenin had never taken power, but the form and the timing of his Fourteen Points speech were clearly influenced by events in Russia. Wilson provided the key to understanding his plan for the postwar world in an earlier remark made during the crisis with Japan in 1915: he was deeply concerned with "the maintenance of the policy of the open door to the world."

His objective was to commit the peace conference to the principles of that policy and then create an international organization to guarantee that those rules would be honored in practice. Like his predecessors, he was confident that such a system would enable the United States to dominate the global marketplace and lead the way in reforming the world. The central elements of the Open Door policy involved "perfect equality" of economic opportunity, "territorial and administrative integrity," "permanent safety and peace," and American leadership.

Wilson reiterated that framework at the outset of his address. He then elaborated upon the central themes: "absolute freedom of navigation upon the seas"; the "removal, so far as possible, of all economic barriers and the establishment of an equality of trade conditions"; a guarantee "that national armaments will be reduced to the lowest point consistent with domestic safety"; a "free, open-minded, impartial adjustment of all colonial claims"; self-determination for Italy, Austria-Hungary, Romania, Serbia, Montenegro, and minorities in Turkey and Poland. Finally, in a passage that quickly returned to haunt him, Wilson asserted that "the treatment accorded Russia by her sister nations in the months to come will be the acid test of their goodwill."

However reluctantly, Wilson decided a month later (February, 1918) to intervene with force against the Bolsheviks. The timing was influenced by his secondary concern to block Japan's advance in Asia. He first moved to revive the idea of a financial syndicate in the hope that it would open the way for American economic supremacy. Then, between September 6 and November 2, 1917, he negotiated a stopgap agreement with the Japanese. The United States again acknowledged Japan's preeminent position in Korea and Manchuria in return for a renewed commitment to the Open Door and a pledge not to obtain "special rights or privileges in China which would abridge the rights of the subjects or citizens of other friendly states."

The Japanese maintained their pressure. And the Bolsheviks did not collapse. So Wilson intervened. Anti-Bolsheviks were given military and economic aid; American troops were committed briefly to northwestern Russia; and a significant number of soldiers were sent to Siberia *before* the German offensive was stopped. The president unquestionably wanted to intimidate the Japanese, but his primary objective was to overthrow the Bolsheviks.

Wilson made that clear in his remarks during the peace negotiations in Paris. The president was greeted in Europe as a charismatic leader, even though his power had been weakened at home. He appealed on October 25, 1918, for American voters to elect a Democratic Congress in the upcoming election, but they responded by sending a Republican majority to both the House (50) and the Senate (2). The president paid no heed: he sailed for France on December 4, 1918, without a single adviser from the Senate, and the only Republican in his entourage (Henry White) was a secondary figure from the past.

Leaving a country that was moving rapidly into a period of social and intellectual turmoil (and a flu epidemic that killed at least 100,000 people), Wilson presented himself to Europeans as a man with the answers. In private, however, he was plagued by the Bolshevik challenge to his leadership. The question of Poland's boundaries, a central issue involving his commitment to self-determination, was high on the agenda, but the president "suggested that it might be unwise to discuss a proposal of this sort on its individual merits, since it formed a part of the much larger question of . . . how to meet the social danger of bolshevism." Herbert Hoover made the point in classic fashion: "Communist Russia was a specter which wandered into the Peace Conference almost daily."

Granted that major distraction, Wilson was in a strong position. Neither the Russians nor the Germans were present to challenge the president, and the American economic system was the key to the viability of any settlement. Given those circumstances, the president enjoyed the initiative by virtue of his Fourteen Points speech. As a result, and aided greatly by David Hunter Miller and other members of his staff of experts known as "The Inquiry," and by Lord Robert Cecil of Great Britain, Wilson operated effectively in the first round of negotiations.

WILSON AND THE FIGHT OVER THE LEAGUE OF NATIONS

He returned home on February 24, 1919, with a document that combined a settlement with Germany with the essentials of an international organization designed to guarantee the major principles of the Open Door policy. The latter part of the plan, known formally as the Covenant of the League of Nations, was based on three propositions. First, all nations would participate as members of the Assembly in the discussion of vital issues, but the Western metropolitan powers would dominate the final decisions through their permanent membership on the Council. Second, Article 10 bound all members "to respect as against external aggression the territorial and existing independence of all" members. And, third, Article 16 provided for enforcing that commitment through economic or military sanctions—or both. The threat or reality of war in which all members would take part—*collective security*, as it came to be called—would intimidate any potential aggressor or quickly defeat the outlaw.

Wilson said Article 10 was "the very backbone" of the league; without it the organization "would be hardly more than an influential debating society." He was essentially correct in the sense that a commitment to preserve the status quo had to be honored or else it became meaningless, and he chose to stand on that proposition. He was ultimately defeated in the United States by a coalition of critics who argued persuasively that there were important weaknesses—and dangers—inherent in his position.

The president quickly encountered that opposition after he returned to the United States. A working dinner party with powerful members of the Congress on February 26 was marked by sharp exchanges that prompted 37 Republican senators to issue a manifesto against the league covenant as it existed and to call for revision after the peace settlement had been signed. Undaunted and defiant, Wilson returned to France on March 13 only to meet equally determined opposition by the other victorious allies.

Wilson compromised in Paris but remained adamant in America. The French wanted large reparations from Germany and control of some of its vital industrial regions. Italy insisted on a northern boundary at the Brenner Pass, additional territory on the Adriatic Sea, and the port of Fiume. Japan demanded the Shantung peninsula and commitment to racial equality. Wilson backed down. The final treaty, imposed upon the Germans on May 7, 1919, could be defended as a basis for further negotiations, but it was not at all what Wilson had led his supporters to believe that he would secure.

Germany was forced to admit unilateral guilt for the war (an absurd proposition), lost its colonies, was disarmed, and saddled with enormous reparations. France was assured domination of the rich Alsace-Lorraine region and the Saar Basin. Japan remained for an indefinite period in Shantung. Italy acquired all it wanted except Fiume (and got that in 1924). European (and American) colonies remained colonies. The world was not made safe, economically or politically, either for democracy or for the Open Door policy.

As a result, Wilson was a man in serious trouble. He had driven himself extremely hard during the first sessions in Paris. Perhaps then, but certainly during his second trip, he suffered a slight stroke. Then he began to lose his fine sense of political maneuver. His once subtle ruthlessness became increasingly mere defensive aggressiveness, as in an outburst during an argument with his advisers about reparations: "Logic? Logic? I don't give a damn for logic!"

Nor for compromise. Wilson returned home on July 3, 1919, and immediately challenged his domestic critics. His initial position was strong: a large plurality, perhaps even a bare majority, of politically concerned Americans very probably favored joining the League of Nations. That sentiment gave him, despite his defeat in the congressional elections of 1919, a powerful bloc of votes in the Senate. All he needed to do was to isolate his implacable opponents.

One group of those was led by Senator Lodge. He and the president, key figures in their respective parties, were locked in a visceral clash of personalities (and wills), but Lodge's opposition cannot be understood simply as the result of the convergence of the political and the personal. The senator was a classic turn-of-the-century imperialist. America, he cried, had achieved world power independently, "by our own efforts. Nobody led us, nobody guided us, nobody controlled us." He was willing to sign specific treaties for limited purposes, such as military security in Europe, but he was not prepared to abandon the imperial freedom of action. America must remain "master of her own fate."

As chairman of the Senate Committee on Foreign Relations, Lodge first stalled the treaty and the league covenant by holding lengthy hearings. Then he sent the documents to the floor of the Senate encapsulated in a web of amendments designed to extend and confuse the debate. The strategy was effective: it prevented Wilson from capitalizing on his initial support; it forced other leaders to examine the proposition more carefully; it gave other opponents time to develop their own criticisms; it further frustrated an already impatient president; and it immersed the issue in the other troubles of the time.

Even so, Lodge could not have defeated Wilson without the support of two other groups. One was led by Senators Borah, LaFollette, and Johnson, men who had serious reservations about any crusades to reform the world and about the increasing concentration of power in the executive department. They were also deeply committed to the principle of self-determination and for that reason were militantly critical of Wilson's intervention against the Mexican and Bolshevik revolutions and the way the treaty dealt with Germany, China, and colonial societies.

Such critics were further upset by the increasing fervor of the government's attack on radicals. They were not leftists themselves, but they were committed to freedom. Hence they were deeply disturbed when the Supreme Court upheld the conviction (in *Schenck* v. *U.S.*) of a man for distributing Socialist party pamphlets that were against the draft and when it ruled (*Abrams* v. *U.S.*) that a man who had opposed intervention in Russia was not protected by the First Amendment.

Borah summarized the essence of their criticism with considerable eloquence. "The Versailles treaty," he thundered, "is grounded in imperialism. It dismembers nations, divides peoples, and separates races. . . . You must either give them independence, recognize their rights as nations to live their own lives and to set up their own form of government, or you must deny them those things by force." The treaty, he concluded, "does not mean peace, far, very far from it. If we are to judge the future by the past it means war."

The central theme of Borah's argument was echoed by a larger group of leaders who were basically sympathetic to the idea of an international organization, people like Henry L. Stimson, Hoover, and Root. They concentrated on Article 10, and Root provided a devastating criticism:

> If perpetual, [the article] would be an attempt to preserve for all time unchanged the distribution of power and territory made in accordance with the views and exigencies of the Allies in this present juncture of affairs. It would necessarily be futile. . . . It would not only be futile; it would be mischievous. Change and growth are the law of life, and no generation can impose its will in regard to the growth of nations and the distribution of power upon succeeding generations.

Wilson refused to compromise. He launched a national tour on September 4 to rally support, and a week later Borah and Johnson set off after him in a counterattack. Moving at a furious pace, the president almost collapsed in Pueblo, Colorado, on September 25, and a week later (after returning to Washington) he was incapacitated by a severe stroke. He recovered enough to prevent (on November 18) his supporters from reaching any accommodation with his critics, and hence the treaty and covenant were defeated. The fight lingered on into 1920, but the issue had been decided long before Wilson stubbornly vetoed (May 29, 1920) a joint resolution ending the war.

THE ASSAULT ON RADICALS AND BLACKS

The president did not reveal any comparable concern to control the wild assault on aliens and radicals. There were provocations: bombs in the mail, bombs on the front steps of political leaders, the creation of the American Communist party (1919), and many strikes. But the Socialist party, the only potential challenge to the system, was leaderless, deeply divided, and constantly harassed by the national and state governments. Even Senator Borah was under surveillance by a tiny group of spying bureaucrats who later became the nucleus of the awesome Federal Bureau of Investigation (FBI).

That did not satisfy Wilson's attorney general, A. Mitchell Palmer, who had his eye on the White House. Palmer embarked during the late summer of 1919 on a ruthless campaign to tidy up the country. He was particularly concerned to corral aliens, most of whom he considered guilty of "cupidity, cruelty, insanity, and crime." He also considered radicalism a crime, and on December 22, 1919, he deported 249 people (including Emma Goldman and Alexander Bergman) to Russia. A bit later, on January 2, 1920, he staged a night of nationally coordinated mass arrests, conducting raids in 33 cities and taking 2700 prisoners. State and local officials used antisyndicalist laws to harass thousands of others.

Black radicals were likewise weakened by the general assault on the Left, but that problem was a minor aspect of the much broader mistreatment of black Americans during the war and postwar years. The turn-of-the-century migration of blacks from the South into the industrial centers of the Northeast and Midwest accelerated during the war. Industrialists actively recruited them for cheap labor, but poverty and racism were the main reasons for the growing exodus from the South. The blacks usually obtained more money and sometimes gained a sense of pride and self-respect, but they also met sustained hostility among most whites. Racial antagonism and sexual fears were reinforced (and increased) by economic competition.

The first crisis began during May and June, 1917, in East St. Louis. Union leaders protested black immigration to the North, and with classic irrationality they asserted that black men had been encouraged to come north because the war left too few white men for the white women in the city. The first riot was quickly controlled by the militia, but a horrible rampage erupted on July 1 after four whites careened through the black district shooting indiscriminately at people and buildings, The blacks resisted. That was a new development in racial conflict, but they were no match for the white gangs (female as well as male) that roamed the streets for almost 36 hours, killing people and destroying property. Understandably, almost 10,000 blacks left the city.

On July 28, two days after a smaller outburst had killed more blacks in Chester, Pennsylvania, William E. B. DuBois led the massive Silent Protest Parade in New York, and one prominent banner bluntly asked President Wilson why he did not undertake another crusade to "make America safe for democracy." The question became even more pertinent when black soldiers of the Twenty-fourth Infantry were insulted and goaded into violence after white policemen beat and jailed two black military policemen. The furious soldiers killed 17 whites, but the subsequent miscarriage of justice led to the hanging of 13 blacks, and 41 others were imprisoned for life.

The new militance of the blacks—"Shoot Back to Stop Riots"—was strengthened by their contribution to the war effort and by the discrimination they suffered while helping to make the world safe for democracy. The worst treatment occurred in the service battalions and the stevedore regiments, to which most blacks were assigned. When they were given the opportunity, as in the 369th Infantry Regiment, the black soldiers performed as well as any white ones did. The 369th never retreated, was cited for bravery 11 times, and every member was awarded the French Croix de Guerre for gallantry in combat.

In some cases, as in Montgomery, Alabama, and Memphis, Tennessee, the courage and determination of the blacks prevented riots. But lynchings rose from 34 in 1917 to 60 in 1918 and reached 76 in 1919. By the time the fear and fury had run their course, 25 cities had been torn by racial violence. The worst outbreaks came back to back in Washington, D.C., and Chicago. The majority of whites in the capital were either southern or had adopted major features of that outlook, and they had become increasingly concerned by the large influx of blacks during the war.

The fears in Washington about returning black soldiers, whom the whites thought would be "uppity and spoiled by French women," wound the tension even higher. A series of attempted rapes (one was successful) pushed the city to the edge of hysteria, and violence erupted when a white woman was jostled by two blacks. That confrontation, involving a sizable mob led by white soldiers, was controlled by the police. But when a black wounded a policeman (in an unrelated incident), the city exploded. The black community was invaded by mobs and hundreds were injured.

The Chicago riot was more like war. White gangs had been attacking blacks (and killing some) throughout the spring and early summer of 1919, and elements on both sides began to stockpile weapons. Then, on July 27, 1919, a black boy unintentionally drifted across the imaginary line that divided the blue waters of Lake Michigan into black and white. White toughs stoned him to death. That touched off a battle that not even the National Guard could control for 13 days, and there were 38 dead at the end of the horrible assault upon the black community.

As DuBois pointed out, such events—and the government's failure to act—made a mockery of Wilson's crusade for democracy and self-determination. DuBois was deeply angry about the concern of the reformers for immigrants: "There are in the United States today nearly twice as many persons of Negro descent as there are Belgians in Belgium; there are three times as many as there are Irish in Ireland." And he could be scathingly bitter. Either play it straight, he suggested to whites (high and low, left and right) or choose a black, invite her or him home, entertain the stranger, and "then through some quick and painless method kill [the guest]. In that way, in a single day, we could be rid of 12 million people who are today giving us so much concern, or rather so little concern."

A brave and brilliant man (though personally somewhat cold and austere), DuBois was too committed to an ideal of humanity to embrace desperate and irrelevant violence or to drift off into despair and private well-being. He challenged Wilson (through his Pan-African Congress held in Paris during the peace negotiations) to honor his rhetoric about democracy and self-determination; he documented the mistreatment of black soldiers; and he criticized other black leaders who were willing to settle for menial jobs—or reactionary dreams—for their followers.

Chief among the latter was Marcus Garvey, a charismatic West Indian who came to the United States in 1916 after a sequence of misadventures in Jamaica. Garvey was a black nationalist, a marketplace operator, and a leader who captured the imagination of many black Americans. He advocated a version of Black Power, though he affected the costumes of European royalty rather than the raised clenched fist. As the creator and dominating power of the Universal Negro Improvement Association, he presided over a movement that stressed pride ("Up, you mighty race"), visions of a new Africa, and capitalist profits.

He joyously asserted that black is beautiful and happily played the old game of empire. He was serious, even prophetic, but he was doomed. His plans for a power base in Africa foundered on insufficient capital to finance an archaic idea, too much rhetoric (often good), and ignorance of the truth that most blacks were determined to improve their life in America rather than begin over again in an ancient homeland.

DuBois, the classic American radical without a party, attacked Garvey reluctantly but effectively. He granted that Garvey raised the consciousness, self-respect, and awareness of thousands: "a beloved leader." And he agreed that it was conceivable that an alliance between black Americans and black Africans could become a force in world affairs. But not as a Napoleonic empire, and not as a movement without a positive program. Garvey could not answer that kind of criticism. He collected hundreds of thousands of dollars but his ventures failed. He was imprisoned for mail fraud in 1925 and deported two years later.

Many whites viewed that failure as proof of the inherent inferiority of blacks, but they were not confident enough of that analysis to relax and allow nature to take its course. Such people, and there were millions of them in all parts of the country, were the power behind the campaign at the end of the war against all who were not white and Fundamentalist Protestants. That attack took three forms: a revival of the Ku Klux Klan; an assault on immigration; and a religious revivalism that concentrated its power against Freud, Darwin, and other manifestations of a scientific rationality that, if they did not boldly announce that "God is dead," clearly discounted Him as an active participant in daily life.

The Klan was formally reorganized in Georgia (1915) by William J. Simmons, but it failed to attract significant support until after the race riots during and after the war. Then Edward Y. Clarke, a prejudiced, money-hungry promoter, and Hiram Wesley Evans, a dedicated bigot, combined talents to create a force of five million whites that for a time used terroristic methods against blacks, Jews, and Catholics to gain political influence in the North (Indiana) and the West (Oregon), as well as in the South (Texas).

Drawing on the warped ideas of Madison Grant and Lothrop Stoddard, the Klan attacked Western European Jews on religious grounds, blacks and Eastern European Jews with racial arguments, and Catholics as a foreign-dominated political party. Evans could be an effective polemical writer. He was a master of the plain-folks ploy—accepting the put-down of being called a rube and a hick and turning it into an advantage. Foreigners were welcome if they became Americans; Jews, embraced if they amalgamated; and Catholics, accepted if they Americanized their religion. He even admitted that blacks were present as a problem because of the early mistake of the white man and added that the blacks should be allowed to realize their limited abilities.

The movement provoked a severe and ultimately effective counterattack, but not before it had tortured and murdered some of its enemies—and swindled its members. The Baltimore *Sun* exposed a reign of horror in Louisiana, and the New York *World* bared the gory details of similar events in the North. Grand Dragon David C. Stephenson was ultimately convicted of second-degree murder in Indiana. But even though the membership declined rapidly (to about 9000 in 1930), the Klan left a legacy of hate and violence that poisoned American society for another two generations.

The related attacks on Jews and Catholics reinforced the rising clamor to restrict or end immigration. That campaign had begun in the 1890s and from the outset was fueled by religious antagonisms and the

The ghostly presence of the Ku Klux Klan put reason to flight so easily that the nation was embarrassed. Neither the Democratic nor the Republican party offered sturdy resistance. Rather, each fled ignominiously, as Daniel Fitzpatrick noted in the St. Louis Post-Dispatch.

BOO!
—Fitzpatrick in the St. Louis *Post-Dispatch*

Reprinted in *The Literary Digest*, vol. 81, May 17, 1924, p. 7.

fear of socialism. President Cleveland vetoed a bill imposing a literacy test in 1896, as did Taft and Wilson. But the Congress overrode Wilson's second veto and in 1918 banned anarchists and other radicals.

The war drastically reduced immigration, from 1,218,480 in 1914 to 110,618 in 1918 and 141,132 in 1919. Those statistics were naturally used by those who wanted to close the door (just as the prohibition of liquor was presented as the highest form of patriotism). A serious case for limited immigration could be made (and sometimes was) on the grounds that uncontrolled population growth was irrational and that the nation needed time to deal with the social tensions created by the large influx of people after the late 1880s.

Most of those who agitated for restriction, however, appealed to fear and prejudice. Their first success was the passage of the quota law of May 19, 1921, which limited annual immigration from any country to 3 percent of those who had arrived in 1910 (with a maximum of 357,000). Then, on May 26, 1924, that basic allowance was cut in half and further reduced for people in Eastern and Southern Europe. The Fundamentalist leaders of the country should have been relieved by such drastic restrictions, but they generally behaved as if the danger had somehow become even greater.

Two of the most charismatic leaders of religious fundamentalism, William S. ("Billy") Sunday and Aimee Semple McPherson, were old-time evangelists with a flair for modern innovations. They leaned heavily on Dwight L. Moody, who had led a revival in the 1870s, but they added a profitable sense of how to exploit the radio and subtle sexuality. Aimee preached The Four Square Gospel with all the innuendoes of her considerable physical attractiveness, with lights and staging that were the envy of movie and theater producers, with a bit of early group therapy ("everyone take the hand of five others all around front and back"), and with her grasp of the euphoria of mutual true confessions:

> I was loaded down with sin,
> But my Saviour took me in.

Aimee had a genius for combining sex and salvation in a Fundamentalist experience. (Sunday was also very good, but not quite in Aimee's class.) In the end, however, she became too brazen and lost her flock by scooting off for a vacation with her lover in the guise of being kidnapped.

While Aimee made a profitable business out of Fundamentalism, Bruce Barton (later chairman of the board of the advertising firm Batten, Barton, Durstine, and Osborn) did well for himself by explaining how embracing the teachings of Jesus could make one a better and more successful businessman. Presenting The Carpenter as "the founder of modern business," Barton argued that service was the key to the Scripture and the key to profits. The rules were elementary:

1. Whoever will be great must render great service.
2. Whoever will find himself at the top must be willing to lose himself at the bottom.
3. The big rewards come to those who travel the second, undemanded mile.

The aging giant of Fundamentalism, William Jennings Bryan, won a Pyrrhic victory for his cause just before he died. He was the classic embodiment and spokesman of the faith that was summarized effectively by William B. Riley, president of the World Christian Fundamentals Association. The words of the Bible, Riley explained, were "verbally inspired by God" and were "of supreme and final authority." The true Christian "insists upon the plain intent" of those words: they "are not individual opinions that can be handed about at pleasure."

For Riley and Bryan, and uncounted others, the Darwinian theory of evolution was a "poison" that produced a fatal "epilepsy." That conviction led Bryan to his famous confrontation with Clarence Darrow. As an associated prosecuting advocate of the biblical version of creation, Bryan spoke for the State of Tennessee in a well-staged trial (1925) against a schoolteacher named John Scopes who had knowingly violated the law by exposing his students to the theory of evolution.

Darrow appeared for the defense as a secular reformer (he represented Debs in 1894 and he opposed capital punishment) and as a remarkably successful lawyer who had lost only one of his many criminal clients to the executioners. He had just dramatized (1924) that ability as counsel for Nathan Leopold and Richard Loeb, two intelligent and affluent children who had systematically kidnapped and murdered another boy named Robert Franks. They wanted to find out what it would be like to willfully kill another human being. Darrow's brilliant use of psychiatric evidence and analysis and his summation to the jury saved his clients from the death chamber.

In an almost surrealistic scene, Bryan on the stand and Darrow prosecuting for the defense, the two men confronted each other in suspenders, sweat-stained shirts, and no ties in a classic example of cross-examination. The transcript of their long exchanges leaves one with an understanding of how two minds can pass each other in a moment of mutual incomprehensibility as one view of the world is being replaced by another. Having a brilliant and sharply honed intellect, Darrow may well have comprehended Bryan's view of the world, but he gave no evidence that he understood how Bryan could (and did) live a coherent life within that framework. Hence he was ruthlessly uncomprehending of his opponent.

Bryan won his case—the legal outcome was never in doubt—and wrote the epitaph for his cause. The same could be said of the official and unofficial advocates who finally (1927) enabled the ancient State of Massachusetts to execute two Italian aliens, anarchists, and draft dodgers named Nicola Sacco and Bartolomeo Vanzetti. The basic issue of their ordeal is clarified if we grant that there is considerable after-the-fact evidence that at least one of them probably did participate on April 15, 1920, in a robbery and murder at a shoe factory in Braintree, Massachusetts.

For in their own time they were judged, convicted, and executed as aliens who were radicals, as anticapitalist and antiwar activists. The judge was at best incompetent and at worst prejudicial beyond any self-knowledge of his own bias. In the course of it all, Sacco and Vanzetti transcended their initial fears and evasiveness. By the time they were killed by the state (1927), they had admitted their early lies and came to personify the integrity, courage, and radicalism that America ostensibly symbolized.

The trial and the long years of appeal became a rallying point for those who wanted to revive the momentum of reform. Darrow in Tennessee was using the new sciences of Freud and Darwin, and the State of Massachusetts was misusing the infant technology of ballistics identification in presenting its case against Vanzetti and Sacco. Science—and its various uses and abuses—was likewise at the center of the fourth major trial of the era, the 1925 court-martial of an Army Air Corps officer named William Lendrum ("Billy") Mitchell. After enlisting as a private during the Spanish-American War, he rose quickly through the ranks and in 1913 became the youngest officer ever appointed to the general staff. Air power was his life, and after the war he became the director of aviation.

Mitchell understood the revolutionary nature of military aviation before anyone else in the country. He demonstrated that planes could sink battleships and vividly described what they could do to the American fleet at Pearl Harbor. He also developed an antiimperialist strategy of national security: planes based in the United States could block any attempt to invade the country. Orthodox naval officers (and other expansionist groups) fought him bitterly, and he was ultimately found guilty of insubordination.

The general might have won more support if he had used planes to enforce Prohibition by establishing routine surveillance of the bootleggers who smuggled booze into the country and of others who manufactured it illegally at home. The constitutional amendment that outlawed the sale of alcoholic beverages in the public marketplace (ratified on January 29, 1919) dramatized the failure-in-success of the reformers. They won a victory against one group of corporations (the liquor industry) but were soon defeated by the new giants of organized crime. And that process revealed the nature of an even more fundamental change that was proceeding very rapidly in American society.

EXPLORATORY READING

A very useful, but often neglected, study is:

J. M. Clark, *The Costs of the World War to the American People* (1931)

The postwar labor upheavals are discussed in the following volumes:

D. Brody, *Labor in Crisis: The Steel Strike of 1919* (1965)

R. L. Friedman, *The Seattle General Strike* (1964)

G. G. Groat, *Introduction to the Study of Organized Labor in America* (1921)

I. A. Hourwich, *Immigration and Labor* (1912)

Interchurch World Movement of North America, *Report on the Steel Strike of 1920* (1920)

G. S. Watkins, *Labor Problems and the Administration During the World War* (1919)

The most stimulating books about the blacks who moved north are:

H. Cruse, *The Crisis of the Negro Intellectual* (1967)

G. Osofsky, *Harlem: The Making of a Ghetto* (1965)

W. M. Tuttle, Jr., *Race Riot: Chicago and the Red Summer of 1919* (1970)

A. Waskow, *From Race Riot to Sit-in* (1966)

The central place of radicalism is discussed by these authors:

J. S. Gambs, *Decline of the I.W.W.* (1932)

G. L. Joughlin and E. M. Morgan, *The Legacy of Sacco and Vanzetti* (1928)

R. K. Murray, *Red Scare* (1955)

W. Preston, Jr., *Aliens and Dissenters: Federal Suppression of Radicals, 1903–1933* (1963)

F. Russell, *Tragedy in Dedham* (1962)

J. Weinstein, *The Decline of Socialism in America, 1912–1923* (1967)

Foreign policy in general, and the struggle for a peace treaty in particular, are explored in these volumes:

L. E. Gelfand, *The Inquiry, 1917–1919* (1963)

G. G. Levin, *Woodrow Wilson and World Politics* (1969)

A. J. Mayer, *Wilson vs. Lenin* (1959); and *Politics and Diplomacy of Peacemaking* (1965)

R. A. Stone, The *Irreconcilables* (1970)

B. M. Unterberger, *America's Siberian Expedition, 1918–1920* (1956)

W. A. Williams, *Russian-American Relations* (1952)

These books provide a good introduction to the social turmoil of those years:

D. M. Chalmers, *Hooded Americanism: The History of the Ku Klux Klan* (1965)

N. F. Furniss, *The Fundamentalist Controversy* (1954)

R. Ginger, *Six Days or Forever* (1958)

J. Higham, *Strangers in the Land: Patterns of American Nativism, 1860–1925* (1963)

K. T. Jackson, *The Ku Klux Klan in the City: 1915–1930* (1967)

A. S. Kraditor, *The Ideas of the Woman Suffrage Movement, 1890–1920* (1965)

W. L. O'Neill, *Everyone Was Brave* (1969)

A. Sinclair, *Prohibition: The Era of Excess* (1962)

9 AND STILL MORE TURMOIL

THE direct and indirect consequences of Prohibition provide many insights into the corporate America that emerged from the Progressive era and the war. The attempt to enforce the policy, for example, offered a preview of the problems inherent in trying to control large numbers of dissident citizens in a vast continental society long before those difficulties were dramatized by the civil rights movement or the agitation against the war in Vietnam.

To begin with, enforcement required vast amounts of money. The states were spending about $700,000 per year by 1927, and the federal government was contributing $12 million. That was a significant amount for those years, but it was woefully inadequate. Many of the enforcement agents were able and dedicated, and some were also imaginative and possessed of a sense of humor, but all were underpaid and overworked. It was no surprise that some accepted bribes.

The task was impossible without the creation of a massive police force. Americans had always used alcohol—even the Puritans held that the only sin was overindulgence—and the rapid and extensive changes inherent in shifting from agrarianism to industrialism increased the propensity of everyone to seek solace in booze—and other forms of personal pleasure and escapism. President Warren G. Harding, for example, thought that a fully stocked liquor cabinet was an essential part of normal life. As a result, even though many individuals made their own liquor, the business of supplying a national market was rapidly dominated by a few criminal corporations.

Organized corruption, particularly in prostitution and gambling, was well established long before Prohibition. But the mass demand for liquor and the mobility provided by the automobile opened the way for vast profits on a continental scale. Gang wars were part of the competition that produced the syndicates. After many battles, Al Capone of Chicago emerged triumphant in a Darwinian struggle of the most ruthless kind.

As in all efficient business operations, the profits had to be reinvested, and so the criminal corporations began to expand their narcotics operations and to hire policemen, judges, politicians, lawyers, and juries. They also devised a new kind of insurance business. The technique was simple: an agent of a company offered protection to nightclubs, garages, and other solvent enterprises (including labor unions). If they paid the premiums they were not bothered and were also protected against rival criminal firms. If they balked, however, other employees of the insurance company demonstrated their skill in arson, theft, beating, explosive devices, and murder. Crime became an ever expanding corporate enterprise that was never seriously challenged by the Justice Department.

The incorporation of crime on a national scale occurred because most citizens viewed Prohibition as an unfair and irrational abridgment of their rights and liberty. A militant plurality (even a determined minority) can push a conservative or reformist law through the Congress, but it will not achieve the desired result unless the majority agrees with—or acquiesces in—the measure. Those elementary realities of American politics were enough to insure the failure of Prohibition, but there were other factors that reinforced the primary cause of the debacle.

Only a clearheaded and deeply dedicated individual can sustain an effort to change the world over a long period of time, and even small groups—let alone the majority of a society—eventually lose the energy and esprit that supply the impetus for major reform campaigns. Hence it was natural after 1919 for Americans to turn away from social crusades and seek a haven from the other changes that they had endured since 1900, and that reaction was intensified by the great discrepancy between the expectations raised by Wilson and the reality of his performances in Mexico, China, Russia, and Paris.

At the end of the war, moreover, Americans were well into another and more subtle change that further intensified their feelings of unease and turmoil. That shift involved the very nature of property in a capitalist political economy. Property has two dimensions in such a system: personal ownership or possessiveness and as a base of power in the marketplace. Until the late nineteenth century, those two aspects of property generally reinforced each other in the United States.

A person who owned land or a business exerted significant influence in the society. And a majority owned such property.

The rise of the corporation after the Civil War subverted that classic relationship between personal ownership and power in the political economy. Owning a home (even a small farm) or a small shop—let alone a car—meant less and less in the politics of the capitalist marketplace increasingly dominated by corporations. For the great majority of people, therefore, property lost its organic relationship to power and was devalued into a means to indulge personal pleasure.

Debs and other Socialist leaders had invested their lives in explaining that process to Americans. And until Wilson used the power of the government to quash such teachers, the Socialist leaders had gained ever more supporters. With Debs silenced, however, the debate about the nature of property in a capitalist system was monopolized by the corporations and their spokesmen. The result was that the great majority of Americans increasingly confused their individual possession of property for *pleasure* with freedom, liberty, independence, and *power* in their society. Property as power became ever more the pleasure of the corporations.

Faced with such an imbalance in the distribution of property as power, the ordinary citizen became more content with cars and washing machines. The corporations thus proceeded to transform *citizens* into *consumers*. Capitalist leaders had always understood the vital importance of expanding the market, and the most perceptive among them recognized that their situation now called for an appeal to individualistic self-gratification at home while expanding other markets abroad.

TABLE 1 Percentage Shares of Total Income Received by the Upper 1 Percent and the Upper 5 Percent of the Population

Year	Upper 1 Percent	Upper 5 Percent
1919	12.2	24.3
1923	13.1	27.1
1929	18.9	33.5

From *Historical Statistics of the United States:* G 135–136.

The citizenry was slow to sense how property as power was being replaced by property as pleasure. If another Debs had come upon the scene, then America might have provided a truly new vision for the world. But the Socialists—let alone the Communists—could not break free of their traditional approach and analysis. They could think only in terms of the nineteenth-century example of early industrialization;

but the idea of making everything into public property—nationalization on a continental scale—was no longer relevant because it offered nothing more than one massive bureaucracy to replace the corporations.

The shrewdest capitalist leaders thus emphasized the importance of *personal* property. They pushed new fashions in clothes, new car designs, and new appliances for the home. And the citizens, convinced that property was the proof of individual worth, liberty, and freedom, responded enthusiastically. It is easy, therefore, to understand why Americans went wild about Charles Augustus Lindbergh, Jr., who in May, 1927, flew alone and nonstop across the Atlantic Ocean in a single-engined monoplane.

Lindy personified the visceral desire of most Americans to evade the truth that the individual was losing power to the corporations and to preserve their dream of independence in a corporate system. He played a major part in designing and building the unusually beautiful plane (the *Spirit of St. Louis*); he arranged for financing through smaller businessmen; and he alone made the final decisions. And in talking about the triumph in terms of "we"—himself and the plane—he sustained the nineteenth-century dream that the individual could become one with his tools and his work. Even his subsequent marriage to a daughter of a partner in the House of Morgan was interpreted as evidence that the old dreams could still be fulfilled.

Lindy was the last national hero from the past. But most Americans lacked any sense of history and hence did not know how to learn from The Lone Eagle. He had a strong sense of community (his father had been a prewar reformer in Minnesota) and of the necessity for the individual to become part of a process larger than himself, but he was viewed—and lionized—only as proof of the power of one man to beat the system. For that matter, most of the leading intellectuals of the 1920s honored that kind of individualism. They failed to devise a philosophy designed to control the corporations in the name of the general welfare within a community.

That was revealed with superb irony in the career of Henry Louis Mencken. Viewed superficially, he was the most unrelenting, enraged, and biting critic of the old values. As a key figure on the editorial boards of *The Smart Set* and *The American Mercury* (1924–1933), he hurled a steady shower of thunderbolts at those he called boobs, yokels, frauds, and fanatics. Mencken did not, however, offer any vision of a new community, and in reality he did nothing more than project the old individualism into urban corporate America as a way to escape the corporations. Thomas Held's evocative illustrations of that ostensibly good new life in the pages of *Vanity Fair* made it seem uncommonly attractive as a nirvana of unlimited consumerism and endless personal pleasure.

Mencken's close friend and collaborator, drama critic George Jean Nathan, provided a more accurate description of their outlook and attitude:

> The great problems of the world—social, political, economic, and theological—do not concern me in the slightest. . . . What concerns me alone is myself, and the interests of a few close friends. For all I care the rest of the world may go to hell at today's sunset.

The disillusionment with the war and with Wilson's grandiose crusade that fed such individualism dominated the early work of writers as disparate as Ezra Pound, E. E. Cummings, and Ernest Hemingway. Even John Dos Passos, who for a time was a radical, revealed the anger of the postwar artists. He ends his wrenching description of the Unknown Soldier with this embittered juxtaposition: "Where his chest ought to have been they pinned the Congressional Medal. . . . Woodrow Wilson brought a bouquet of poppies." Cummings offered in *An Enormous Room* a numbing account of the loss of identity in the bureaucratic maze.

And Hemingway, who with many other young artists (and would-be artists) left postwar America for Paris, developed the perfect style to express his ostensibly tough, no-nonsense individualism. Here is his account of the return of a marine to his home in Oklahoma. The ex-soldier is forced into exaggerated lies about his truly grisly experiences and the lying leads to nausea. His parents have just told him that he must "settle down to work."

> "Is that all?" Krebs said.
> "Yes. Don't you love your mother, dear boy?"
> "No," Krebs said.
> His mother looked at him across the table. Her eyes were shiny. She started crying.
> "I don't love anybody," Krebs said.
> It wasn't any good. He couldn't tell her, he couldn't make her see it. It was silly to have said it.

Inside the glory of his impersonal style, Hemingway was a classic romantic individualist. So also, at least in the beginning, was F. Scott Fitzgerald. His first novel, *This Side of Paradise* (1920), chronicles the escape into love and pleasure and glamour of those who grew up "to find all Gods dead, all wars fought, all faiths in man shaken." Fitzgerald not only wrote as well (though in a different idiom) as Hemingway, but he revealed—as in *The Great Gatsby*—an appreciation of the limits of romantic individualism in the age of the corporation. His effort to transcend that contradiction produced some moving writing (as in *The Crack-Up*) even as it drove him to an early death.

Fitzgerald's sense of impending doom was honed into a scalpel by three great poets. Robinson Jeffers was a man of wide-ranging intellect who informed his private passions, visions, and fears with monumental resignation. He reacted to the war by accepting violence—individual, sexual, and social—as a major part of life. Concluding that the United States was no more immune to decline and decay than Rome, Robinson took his stand as a craggy (and sometimes cranky) individualist who denied even the possibility of community.

The central figure of modern American poetry began with a similar outlook. Born in Idaho (as was Hemingway), Ezra Pound became an expatriate even before the war after losing his first teaching job because he was too much of a bohemian. His mind was superb: he absorbed, transcended, and integrated all the idioms of modernism— from impressionism through Dada and surrealism—into his own individualism. Yet he always sought community. His voyages into the past created great poetry in the guise of translating classical literature from Italy and China, prompted him to help other writers, and ultimately led him to embrace a reactionary philosophy of community.

Along the way Pound provided crucial assistance in making a good poet into a great spokesman for the conservative insights into the failure of individualism and into the inability of the corporation to create a community. Though his own *Cantos* are brilliant, Pound's most creative act may have been his role in refining the work of Thomas Stearns Eliot of St. Louis, Missouri, into *the* statement of the counterrevolution against the privatizing of social experience.

Eliot was a traditionalist rather than a romantic; the Harvard-educated son of a Unitarian minister, he turned away from his father's individualized faith to a more structured and integrated outlook. He was also concerned with the chaotic and threatening life of the industrial city and deeply involved with the question of good and evil. His first works, *Prufrock and Other Observations* (1917) and "Gerontion" (1920), reveal the talent and the themes that with Pound's critical assistance made *The Waste Land* (1922) a classic. Life as an individual without community and faith was hell: work was pointless and sex was meaningless. The result, as he dramatized in "The Hollow Men" (1925), was life as death. Modern man only killed himself when he asserted that God was dead.

Hart Crane was another young poet influenced by Pound (as were most American writers of the era), but he was determined to refute Eliot's outlook by reasserting the validity of the individual's "ecstatic vision." His conscious effort to write a rebuttal to *The Waste Land*, finally published as *The Bridge* (1930), is a failure as philosophy and as poetry—though some sections, such as the one about the Brooklyn Bridge, are magnificent.

Despite his brilliance, Crane failed in his attempt to deal with the entire American experience, and it is ironic that the attempt was more nearly realized by a less gifted writer named Sinclair Lewis. He dealt powerfully and perceptively with several major aspects of the confrontation between the country and the metropolis during a period of major changes and deep uneasiness.

His first novel, *Main Street* (1920), concerns a midwestern town that is at once a metropolis that exploits the surrounding farmers and a part of the larger country dominated by the eastern industrial and financial metropolis. The ostensible protagonist, Carol Kennicott, comes west to transform the yokels, but finally (after a return to the East) accepts her lot. But Lewis's real anger is focused on the husband (and his associates) who fail to put Carol in her proper place in a positive way by transcending their own stereotypes and creating a new culture appropriate to the new reality.

That anger became cutting satire in *Babbitt* (1922), which is perhaps the best fictional explanation of how the country lost the war with the metropolis by simply accepting its rhetoric of growth and efficiency as reality. In that fashion Babbitt dooms himself to be a minor cog in the economic system and a mindless consumer of the corporation's gadgets.

Lewis also sensed how Fundamentalism contributed to the defeat of the country, and in *Elmer Gantry* (1927) he mounted a ruthless attack on the evangelical preacher (such as Billy Sunday) who was in truth a hypocritical businessman selling God instead of automobiles. It was less a novel than a piece of imaginative sociology based on Sunday and McPherson, but it shocked many people into a greater awareness of reality.

His passion and energy were enormous: *Arrowsmith* (1925), *The Man Who Knew Coolidge* (1928), and *Dodsworth* (1929). *Arrowsmith* is a tough, informative story about the struggle of a medical scientist to maintain his integrity in corporate America and offers one of Lewis's few likable women. Lewis reached his stylistic pinnacle in *Coolidge*, a novel without a story, but a book that told much about America by presenting its citizens through their conversation. And *Dodsworth* was a better book (perhaps his best) about a Babbitt who tried to engage the metropolis in a serious dialectical confrontation. Lewis became in 1930 the first American to be honored with the Nobel Prize for literature (he had earlier spurned the Pulitzer Prize).

William Faulkner, another and dramatically different writer, won that accolade a generation later, but for most of the 1920s he was largely ignored. Faulkner was a far greater artist than Lewis, a true giant of American letters, but they shared the same concern with an America undergoing visceral changes. Faulkner's early novel about the returning veteran (*Soldier's Pay*, 1925) did not attract much attention, but it contains most of the elements that he quickly integrated into his major works: the destructive impact of industrialization upon a once aristocratic and community-oriented South. Faulkner is often difficult to read because of his style. But the effort is worth the labor because he comprehends the intricate process of social change—the vast complexities (and terrors) of the transition from agrarianism to industrialism affecting all classes and colors—better than most sociologists or historians.

Beginning in 1929 with *The Sound and the Fury*, Faulkner matched Lewis's outburst of energy at a much higher level: *As I Lay Dying* (1930), *Sanctuary* (1931), and *Light in August* (1932). In *Sanctuary*, for example, he bares with chilling terror the corruption of small-town youths in an age of Prohibition and criminality. Almost from the beginning, moreover, as through the character Dilsey in *The Sound and the Fury*, Faulkner suggests that the black American's experience and solidarity provide him with a greater resiliency and a deeper sense of community.

CHALLENGING BLACK LEADERS

A firm belief in that idea was at the heart of Marcus Garvey's African nationalism, and it also energized the creative outburst of black artists in the North. The segregation of blacks in northern cities was well under way by 1913, and the war accelerated the process. New York became the center of what was called a Black, or Harlem, Renaissance, however, simply because New York was the center of the white artistic world.

After the collapse of the Afro-American Realty Company in 1907, the migration of New York (and other) blacks into the Harlem area was sustained by churches (which invested heavily in real estate) and smaller businessmen. The population increased by 115 percent (to 327,706) during the 1920s, and what was once an ethnic neighborhood became a racial slum. The black bourgeoisie lacked the economic power required to create a center of black power. Unemployment was high, illness and death rates were high, and crime was high.

But so, too, was the incidence of creativity. Poets, writers, and playwrights were complemented by scholars, actors, dancers, musicians, and rising public leaders. The Lafayette and Lincoln theaters and the 135th Street Library were centers of the vital work of women and men like Countee Cullen, Claude McKay, Gwendolyn Bennett,

Ethel Waters, Paul Robeson, Langston Hughes, James Weldon Johnson, and E. Franklin Frazier. And the *Messenger*, dominated by labor organizer A. Philip Randolph, offered militant socialist leadership.

But the movement lacked a strong economic base and an intellectual leader and was further weakened by the tension between American blacks and West Indian immigrants. The white artist had far more financial support, and the Greenwich Village movement was given vital focus after 1912 by the sophisticated salon presided over by Mabel Dodge at 23 Fifth Avenue. A'Lelia Walker (daughter of Madame C. J. Walker, who made a fortune from ingenious cosmetic preparations designed to make blacks look more like whites) created a rendezvous for blacks, but it was far more a social than an intellectual and cultural center.

While some whites, particularly Carl Van Vechten, helped black writers and other artists gain some measure of the recognition they deserved, the underlying prejudice and weakness meant most black contributions were either absorbed into the existing white cultural explosion (as in Eugene O'Neill's play *The Emperor Jones*) or patronized as a semiprimitive cult of naturalism and free expression. The powerful black theater which began in 1917 with mid-Manhattan performances, for example, was soon relegated to Harlem and often presented white plays.

Perhaps the crowning insult was *Jazz Singer* (1927), the first sound motion picture, which demeaned black religion, black music, and black culture. White artists could create powerful works about their own world, as with O'Neill in his sequence of plays that revitalized white theater; Jerome Kern in musical comedy *(Show Boat)*; the Ziegfeld Follies; and in the classical music of Roy Harris, Howard Hanson, Roger Sessions, and Aaron Copeland. But the blacks were largely denied the opportunity to make their own contribution to a pluralistic American culture.

There were two important exceptions: jazz, and the brilliant social analysis and criticism offered by DuBois, Randolph, Johnson, and Frazier. Through jazz, the black artist established his music as the music of America. It was a subtle and effective victory. For in jazz, for the first time, the white man accommodated to the black man. Five major elements contributed to the music that emerged during the 1920s. It had of course started with the drum in Africa, then it was informed by the white man's religion, and finally consolidated when the blacks obtained various instruments after the Civil War.

Granted all that, jazz began with classic New Orleans Dixieland dominated by King Oliver. Then came the Kansas City style developed by Pete Johnson, Mary Lou Williams, and William

("Count") Basie; the related blues personified by Bessie Smith; the Chicago idiom created by Louis Armstrong, and the genius of William Kennedy ("Duke") Ellington in New York. All of it was vital, much of it was good, and Ellington intergrated the classical and jazz idioms in a way that made him a master of his age. He scored his grand compositions for specific musicians in a way that neither Mozart nor Beethoven had done.

DuBois, Johnson, and Frazier found it much more difficult to penetrate and influence the white world. Johnson's *Black Manhattan* (1930), for example, is brilliant history and cultural sociology; and Frazier's early article in the *Modern Quarterly* (1928) ruthlessly analyzes the pro-British orientation of Garvey's movement, offers a biting class analysis of black American society, and points the way to Black Power. Few white intellectuals were as perceptive or as tough, and even fewer talked about blacks.

CRITICISM OF THE POLITICAL ECONOMY

Thorstein Veblen and Randolph Bourne were devastating about Wilson's foreign policy, however, and Veblen's analysis of the new corporate system (*Absentee Ownership and Business Enterprise in Recent Times*, 1923) was perceptive, even if his dream that engineers could humanize it proved to be a fantasy. The best study of the new order was written by two men, Adolf A. Berle and Gardner C. Means, who remained highly influential well past the middle of the century. Their handbook on the corporate system, *The Modern Corporation and Private Property* (published in 1932 but based on the events of the 1920s), clearly drew on Veblen's pioneering work. Their evidence that the giant corporations were managed by men who did not own them in the classical sense documented one of the major changes between 1890 and 1925, but Berle and Means were mistaken in their conclusion that such managers were less capitalistic than their predecessors. Their noncapitalistic managers were kissing cousins of Veblen's reforming engineers.

Historian Charles Austin Beard was closer to the mark. He argued in his 1916 lectures, published in 1922 as *The Economic Basis of Politics*, that while "the problem of property, so vital in politics, is not as simple as it was in old agricultural societies," it would not do to treat the manager as "an abstract man divorced from all economic interests and group sentiments." Later in the 1920s in *The Idea of National Interest* and *The Open Door at Home*, he analyzed American expansion and suggested a retreat from imperialism.

Another historian named Vernon Louis Parrington offered in his three-volume *Main Currents of American Thought* (1927–1930) a study of the intellectual and social maturation of the nation (largely ignoring females, blacks, and other minorities) that suggested a return to the Jeffersonian-agrarian tradition. It was an impressive reassertion of old values, but it was not a guide to the creation of an industrial community. That was also true of the ideas of a group of southern artists led by the poet Allen Tate and two conservative philosophers, Irving Babbit and Paul Elmer More. With Eliot, they all realized the need for a new outlook, but none of them dealt with the realities of controlling the corporation and creating a new community.

Lewis Mumford, deeply concerned with "the nature of the good life," attacked the abuses of the corporation and exhorted Americans to create a great civilization with the technology at their disposal. His three major works of the era, *Sticks and Stones* (1924), *The Golden Day* (1926), and *American Taste* (1929), cried out for an end to sentimentalism and strained to see the glimmerings of hope in the architecture of Frank Lloyd Wright.

Walter Lippmann, a young Socialist who became a concerned and sophisticated conservative, explained the seeming paradox of indifference and anger in terms of the breakdown of leadership and the lack of any new and viable conception of an American community. And he saw clearly, as early as 1927, that "the New Capitalism" was vastly more powerful, subtle, and pervasive than the old capitalism.

Two patient and thorough, and perceptive and imaginative, sociologists realized that they had caught the essence of the trauma of the postwar years during one interview. Helen and Robert Lynd's study of Muncie, Indiana (*Middletown*, 1929), returns again and again to one remark by one citizen: "These people are afraid of something: what is it?" *It* was a combination of realizing that traditional society was disappearing and that the new corporate system had yet to be humanized and directed toward the creation of a community.

As a result, many middle- and lower-class people clung to the past—or what they thought was the past—or sought solace in booze and other forms of personal pleasure. Others increasingly withdrew from any active participation in the dialectic of the political economy even as they continued their creative activities. The scientists provided a good example of that latter pattern. Many Americans were exceptional: in physics, for example, Robert A. Millikan of the California Institute of Technology won a Nobel Prize in 1923, and in 1927 Arthur H. Compton of the University of Chicago again won that honor. And similar advances in biochemistry were typified by the isolation of vitamin D in 1924 by Harry Steenbock of the University of Wisconsin and Alfred Hess of Columbia University. Equal and related achievements were made in medicine. Philip Drinker and Louis A. Shaw, for example, developed the iron lung in 1927–1928, a sophisticated device that made it possible to sustain the life of people who were afflicted with a variety of respiratory illnesses.

But the physicists and the medical leaders were not guided by a value system that emphasized the importance (let alone the primacy) of *social* responsibility. Neither group concerned itself with the public consequences of its research or the practical applications by the giant corporations or the government. The members of each group were very much like Mencken in being individualists who failed to move beyond the idiom of the nineteenth-century capitalist marketplace. The physicists did not address themselves to the question of how and for what purposes the corporations or the government would use their discoveries, and the medical doctors did not agitate for a system of public health care that would give all citizens the benefits of their knowledge.

Some of the younger engineers displayed more of an understanding of the need for a new approach. As people who applied new scientific knowledge in practical, everyday action, they found it hard to avoid the obvious dilemma. Their expertise opened the way for them to move up the ladder of influence within the corporation, but at the same time, they had been educated to value intellectual honesty above profits. As a result, they were jammed into a corner.

Indirectly and directly, Veblen was their mentor and their conscience. He counted on them to become reformers dedicated to humanizing and democratizing the corporate political economy. It was a noble dream, and nothing more than that. Most engineers were concerned only to use their skills to rationalize the new system: to build better bridges, better cars, and better appliances. Even so, a dedicated minority did try to honor Veblen's ideal.

Led by Morris L. Cooke and Herbert Hoover, two brilliant young and thoughtful engineers, they organized the Founder Societies, groups that were dedicated to accepting collective responsibility for using their knowledge and skills to further the general welfare. As Hoover expressed it, they wanted the engineer to function as a person who would "correct monopolies and redistribute national welfare."

Hoover was very probably influenced by Veblen, but in any event, he had developed his own vision. By the end of World War I he was dedicated to two principles: the decentralization of the corporate system and the active participation of the average citizen in the political decisions affecting the system. Those were terribly demanding criteria. Even under the best of circumstances—if Hoover instead of Taft had succeeded Theodore Roosevelt (or Woodrow Wilson)—he would have found it extremely difficult to translate them into a political movement able to make structural changes in the corporate political economy. But he never enjoyed even that limited kind of opportunity. For, after a short interlude of euphoric prosperity, the corporate economy began to lurch from crisis to crisis.

EXPLORATORY READING

The continuing changes reviewed in this chapter provide an excellent example of the importance of your doing history. There are some fine books about these developments (which I have listed below), but the crucial work involves reading the books and articles written by the protagonists who are named in the text.

The changing nature of property, a fundamental issue, has yet to be explored or discussed beyond the work of the Lynds mentioned in the text. But see, as an introduction to the subject, these two volumes:

K. W. Kapp, *The Social Costs of Private Enterprise* (1971)

C. B. MacPherson, *The Political Theory of Possessive Individualism: Hobbes to Locke* (1962)

The cultural and intellectual ferment is explored in these volumes, all of which are worth your attention:

F. L. Allen, *Only Yesterday: An Informal History of the Nineteen Twenties* (1931)

L. Baritz (Ed.), *The Culture of the Twenties* (1970)

J. Berendt, *The Jazz Book* (1975)

O. Cargill, *Intellectual America: Ideas on the March* (1941)

P. A. Carter, *The Twenties in America* (1968)

M. Cowley, *Exile's Return: A Literary Odyssey of the 1920s* (1934)

F. Hoffman, *The Twenties: American Writing in the Postwar Decade* (1955)

W. Morris, *The Territory Ahead* (1958)

M. Plesur, *The 1920s: Problems and Paradoxes* (1969)

F. Rudolph, *The American College and University* (1965)

G. Schuller, *Early Jazz* (1968)

E. Stevenson, *The American 1920s: Babbitts and Bohemians* (1970)

Twelve Southerners, *I'll Take My Stand: The South and the Agrarian Tradition* (1930)

No one has yet written a first-rate history of American science during this period, but the works of Morton White offer many insights and suggestions. As for the engineers, J. H. Wilson provides an excellent introduction in Chapter II of *Herbert Hoover: Forgotten Progressive* (1975).

10 THE TRIUMPH OF THE CORPORATION

OOVER'S effective leadership as head of the American Food Administration during the war, as the director of major relief programs for Belgium and other countries, and as an adviser at the Peace Conference, led him into an increasingly close relationship with President Wilson. After Wilson's illness removed him from active politics, there was considerable discussion of Hoover as a presidential candidate. A good many Democrats, including Assistant Secretary of the Navy Franklin Delano Roosevelt, thought he would be an excellent choice.

Hoover indicated that he was available but chose to identify with the Progressives in the Republican party. They did not have the power to nominate him, however, and hence Hoover missed his chance to serve during the years when his sophisticated upper-class reformism would have been most useful and beneficial. Although they had lost much of their momentum, the Progressives if led by Hoover might well have developed a new strategy (and programs) and revived their prewar power. For Hoover did understand the new system, and he had important ideas about how to prevent the corporations from dominating it to the detriment of other groups.

Even so, and despite the election of Warren Gamaliel Harding, a handsome, pleasant man who was at best a second-rater, the reformers managed to win some victories after the war. The government's operation of the railroads (and control of other social resources) during the war had been so effective that the unions (and other groups) began to agitate for permanent nationalization of the railways under a plan devised by Glenn E. Plumb, a lawyer representing the Railroad Brotherhoods. That proposal was not adopted, but Congressman John J. Esch and Senator Albert B. Cummings did make some meaningful improvements through the Transportation Act of 1920.

The ICC was given control of intrastate as well as interstate rates, was empowered to propose consolidations for efficiency and service, and was authorized to evaluate railroad property and establish levels of fair return for stockholders. But the Railroad Labor Board, established to handle wage disputes and related issues, was never very effective. Nationalization would have been more efficient and equitable.

Similar limited benefits were gained through the Merchant Marine Act of June 5, 1920, which attempted to create a civilian industry by selling government ships to private lines. About half the wartime fleet of some 15 million tons was kept in operation through a combination of low selling prices, loans, large mail subsidies, special tariff rates on goods imported in American ships, and by giving the trade of American colonies to American shippers. Most of those measures involved subsidies that were paid by the taxpayer. Again, it would have been better to nationalize the industry.

The war also created great concern about oil reserves. The imperial navies of the world were shifting to oil-fired turbines. The resulting scramble for oil that began after the armistice was intensified by a misleading government report of low supplies in the United States. The General Leasing Act (1920) empowered the government to take control of domestic petroleum deposits and granted it the right to arrange contract leases for the exploitation of the fuel as the need arose.

Other natural resources were dealt with in the Water Power Act of June 19, 1920, which organized the secretaries of Agriculture, Interior, and War into the Federal Power Commission (FPC) to control the development of power sites on public lands and navigable rivers. The increasing electrification of industry and services (and of urban homes), which had been accelerated by the war, made the generation of power the focus of the legislation. The FPC could grant 50-year licenses for such facilities, regulate the securities sold to finance them, control the rates on the product, and was given an option to recover and operate the installations at the end of the licensing period.

Many reformers also rallied to the battle launched by Senator Norris to prevent the government from abandoning its great wartime complex of chemical plants and power centers at Muscle Shoals in the Tennessee River valley. Those installations could be used to produce the cheap fertilizer and the electrical power that could improve the life of all the people in the area. Or they could be sold at a loss to private companies, which would then reap enormous profits. In 1921 the Harding administration invited bids on the complex, which included one partially completed dam. The only partially serious offer was made by Henry Ford, but it was ludicrously low. Norris and his allies were able to block the sale, but they did not win their battle to have the government use the tax-financed complex to improve the quality of peacetime life.

Other Progressives moved to extend and improve welfare services for those who were unable to find a profitable place in the corporate system. Their efforts produced the Sheppard-Towner maternity and infant legislation of 1921, and the campaign continued at the state and local levels. The American Association of Welfare Workers was organized in 1922, and its members struggled to provide more assistance to such needy people.

Women reformers were also active in the Progressive Education Association (founded in 1918), which labored to improve and enlarge the school systems. One of its leaders, Helen Parkhurst, in 1920 pioneered the development of a system of individual instruction carried on in a laboratory context. Others, less famous but still influential, supplied much of the pressure for the expansion of education during the decade. High school enrollment jumped 400 percent, to a total of 4.8 million students. The steady climb in the numbers going on to college was even more impressive. That figure rose by about 50,000 per year, and by 1926, one of every eight eligible young men and women was attending university or college.

Hoover was seriously concerned with education and other reforms. More importantly, he considered it reactionary and pointless to talk about returning to laissez-faire capitalism and was firmly convinced that the economy could be controlled and made more equitable without embracing socialism. That was the thrust of his efforts to deal with the sharp postwar depression that occurred while Wilson was too ill to act. The fundamental cause of the deflation was the end of the wartime demand for goods and services. Farmers were hit especially hard. But urban unemployment reached three million early in 1919, which, combined with inflation, caused widespread suffering among additional millions.

Foreign trade, and particularly exports, declined by almost 50 percent. Total national income slipped from $64.5 billion in 1918 to $57.9 billion in 1920, and the drop in national income per gainfully employed worker, which decreased from $1788 in 1920 to $1279 in 1921, was also dramatic. The index for all wholesale prices fell by 21 percent and for farm products by 48 percent. Almost five million workers were unemployed at the depth of the depression.

Hoover responded with two programs. He sought in the long run to help Europe recover in order to expand the market for American exports—and particularly farm products. He tried in the short run to generate private and public recovery programs at home. A close associate once calculated that Hoover had been involved in almost 1000 meetings arranged for that purpose. His proposals stressed three themes: increased efficiency, cooperative action at local and state levels, and public works projects to sustain the economy and provide the demand that would cut unemployment and lead to recovery.

If Hoover had won the Republican nomination, he would have been in a good position to translate those ideas into policies. As it happened, however, he appeared as a caretaker for the defunct Wilson administration and hence had little power (or influence) as an innovator. Failing to nominate Hoover, the Republican reformers had no fallback position because Hughes flatly refused to consider another campaign. As a result, the party was torn by factionalism.

There were three main groups fighting for control. The reformers were concentrated in the Congress, but most of them came from states that lacked significant power in the electoral college. The sophisticated upper-class urban Progressives had been on the defensive ever since Theodore Roosevelt had handed the presidency to Taft. That left the conservatives and reactionaries in the driver's seat. They nominated Harding knowing that he was so weak that they could control the basic decisions.

The election was something of a farce because the Democrats—still mesmerized by the magic of Wilson—nominated James M. Cox (governor of Ohio) to lead yet another crusade for the League of Nations. The explanation of Harding's overwhelming victory (16.2 million votes to 9.2 million) can be summarized in two episodes. The first involves a story, probably apocryphal, about Harding. In a moment of exasperation, so it goes, Harding's father exploded: "Warren, it sure as hell is a good thing you're not a woman. You'd be in the family way all the time—you can't say no!" No doubt about it, Harding was the master of the maybe, but in that situation it worked to his advantage: maybe yes to the reformers, and maybe yes to the conservatives. Maybe yes to the league, and maybe yes to the opponents of the league.

The other tale has to do with his stroke of ungrammatical genius. At one point in the campaign he encapsulated all those maybes in a ringing cry for "normalcy," which meant—if it meant anything—an end to the crusades, failures, and turmoil that were upsetting so many Americans. But Harding was not incompetent and exhibited his own kind of shrewdness in picking his cabinet: Hoover at Commerce, Hughes at State, Andrew W. Mellon at Treasury, and Henry C. Wal-

Newly enfranchised, the women of the United States were courted by candidates in the national election of 1920. Hoping for political preferment, a host of new suitors gave Miss Suffrage an exciting role as "The Belle of the Ball." James Donahey drew for the Cleveland Plain Dealer.

THE BELLE OF THE BALL
—Donahey in Cleveland *Plain Dealer*

Reprinted in *Current Opinion*, vol. 68, April, 1920, p. 7.

lace at Agriculture. Agree or disagree with their policies (which were often in conflict), they were nevertheless knowledgeable and impressive leaders with ideas of their own, and in selecting them Harding outfoxed the mundane and orthodox conservatives who thought they had him in their pocket.

But a man who has sex with his mistress in a White House closet amid coats and overshoes, with the Secret Service standing guard outside the door, is not a man in charge of his own life—let alone a president capable of controlling the corporations in the name of the general welfare. The vast changes that matured during the 1920s are often referred to as "a second industrial revolution" or the "New Economic Era." Those are useful, if exaggerated, concepts because they serve to emphasize the social and political aspects of the economic process that had been going on for two generations.

Beginning at the end of 1921, the industrial sector of the economy revived rapidly and entered a period of general expansion that lasted about six years. Many people benefited from those gains. The 1920 census revealed, for the first time, that a majority of Americans (51.4 percent) lived in cities and towns of more than 2500 inhabitants and that there were almost 100 urban centers of more than 100,000 people.

The construction, clothing, and food industries were key areas in the industrial economy. In terms of dollar output, the food-processing and textile industries ranked first and second at the beginning and the end of the decade. The construction industry, however, was more important in generating economic growth. As a market for the rest of the economy, for example, it used materials worth $12 billion in 1919 and $17.5 billion in 1928. And at the height of the boom, in 1926, the construction industry paid 7.5 percent of all salaries and wages.

The interplay between the automobile and trucking industries and the construction boom was a particularly dynamic growth factor, but there was much other activity. Many existing corporations built new plants, and new industries required facilities. Central Manhattan was largely rebuilt, and other cities followed the trend toward skyscrapers. And there were land booms around cities like Detroit and Cleveland, as well as in California and Florida.

Manufacturing also expanded extensively. During the postwar depression, the volume of manufacturing dropped 21 percent, but from 1921 to 1923 it climbed 54 percent, and the net gain from 1919 to 1924 was 22 percent. That growth continued, and output increased about 50 percent from 1920 to 1929. At the same time, the man-hours required per unit of production fell by almost 40 percent, and as a result the real income of workers who were employed on a regular basis rose by 26 percent.

During those years, the United States accounted for 50 percent of the world's output and national income. And it supplied more capital for overseas investments than was provided by all other creditor countries combined. Ford's assembly line was producing a finished car every ten seconds in 1925, and by the end of the era there was one car for every five people (almost one for every family, though they were not distributed on that basis). In related industries, the production of tires jumped 200 percent, and gasoline consumption soared by 400 percent. There was tremendous activity in chemicals, the electrical industry, and the far-flung complex of activities based on the automobile industry. The increase in the production of automobiles was 255 percent; in rubber products, 86 percent; and in chemicals, 94 percent.

The productivity of the auto industry quickly led to a search for the overseas markets that became a central part of its operations. It became necessary, particularly after 1926, for the companies to find foreign markets in order to maintain steady and profitable operations. Even before that, in the early 1920s, as much as 20 percent of truck production was sold abroad. The figure for passenger cars reached 12.7 percent in 1925, and climbed to about 17 percent in 1928 and 1929. In the latter years, the United States produced 53.7 percent of the world's automobiles.

The petroleum-refining industry also introduced important technological innovations and mass production systems. Almost all of the continuous-flow thermal cracking plants that were in operation in 1929 were installed after 1918, and they accounted for nearly 90 percent of the output of gasoline. That process increased the efficiency of capital investment in the petroleum industry by about 40 percent. And the development of oil furnaces for heating and for generating power added to the profits of the oil companies—and contributed to the problems of the coal industry.

The growth in petroleum was also aided by the great expansion of the chemical industry. That involved the production of nitrates and similar items used by other manufacturers and the development of new synthetics. Rayon remained a staple, but the invention of celanese led to an even better artificial silk. Bakelite became a staple of the mushrooming radio and telephone industries: phone installations zoomed from 1.36 million in 1900 to 20.2 million by 1930, and the sales of radios in 1929 totaled $852 million. Cellophane quickly became a standard packaging material after DuPont introduced it in 1924, and the same corporation's development of fast-drying paints drastically shortened the production time in the automobile industry and transformed the production of paint.

The chemical corporations used enormous amounts of electricity, but all industries were turning to that source of power. Almost half of the steam engines in America were abandoned during the 1920s, and by 1929 the industrial system was 70 percent electrified. Part of that growth resulted from new applications developed and perfected in the research laboratories of the major corporations. Following General Electric's creation of such a center in 1894, the practice spread rapidly throughout American industry. The DuPont Corporation created its research complex in 1902; Westinghouse, in 1910; the United States Rubber Company, in 1913; and by 1918 there were more than 300 such laboratories.

During the 1920s such research operations began to become a quasi-independent industry concentrated in corporations and characterized by a close interconnection between the corporations and universities, private foundations, and the government—all of which supplied additional funds. Even so, the continuing importance of the individual genius like Thomas Edison (who organized his own corporation) was dramatized by the work of George Washington Carver. Born of slave parents, Carver worked his way through Iowa State College and became one of the world's most brilliant agricultural chemists. His research on peanuts and sweet potatoes, which ultimately produced plastics, dyes, medicines, and face creams, generated new industries and helped to move the South away from its dependence on cotton.

Individuals such as Carver could not, however, slow the onward rush of corporate power. General Electric and Westinghouse merged in 1919, for example, to become the Radio Corporation of America. That corporation, in turn, began to operate in broadcasting, as well as in the manufacture of radios and the research that led to television, and soon became a giant in the economy. Serious commercial broadcasting quickly blossomed after KDKA of East Pittsburgh aired the results of the 1920 voting on the night of the election. Within a decade, 40 percent of American homes contained a radio.

But using public airspace to make a private profit (and to control information) raised serious policy questions involving the manipulation of a captive (and entranced) audience. Largely through the efforts of Secretary of Commerce Hoover, the public interest was initially protected by relatively strong controls. "It is inconceivable," Hoover declared in 1922, "that we should allow so great a possibility for service, for news, for entertainment, for education, and for vital commercial purposes to be drowned in advertising chatter. . . . It is a public concern impressed with the public trust."

Hoover's philosophy influenced the establishment (1927) and early operations of the Federal Radio Commission. Broadcasting licenses were granted only after a review of the programs offered by the stations and companies, and the standards were specific and fairly tough.

"Advertising," the commission ruled, "should be only incidental to some real service rendered to the public, and not the main object of a program."

ENTERTAINMENT AND SPORTS INDUSTRIES

The broadcasting industry competed for the family's entertainment dollar (and time) with the movie industry, the growing sports industry, the car, and the avalanche of other new products. The availability of so many options steadily eroded the traditional pattern of life. The average attendance at movies in 1930, for example, was 100 million people per week. Husbands and lovers had to compete with Douglas Fairbanks, Sr., and Rudolph Valentino (barbershops reported a jump in the sales of hairdressing to copy his sleek look). Wives, mistresses, and sweethearts had to cope with the examples set by Greta Garbo, Lillian Gish, Gloria Swanson—and by the largely unclothed females in various semiorgiastic films of the era. But everyone was happy to pay to laugh at the antics of Harold Lloyd, Charlie Chaplin, Buster Keaton, and at the zany activities in the animated cartoons created by Walt Disney.

Others, 91,000 of them, paid more than $1 million to watch a tough, ruthless fighter named Jack Dempsey dispose of the Frenchman who was then the world champion in four rounds. They paid even more to see the subsequent classic encounters between The Mauler and Gene Tunney, whose fighting style involved speed and intelligence, as well as power. But the boxing industry provided stark testimony to the continuing prejudice against blacks.

No one can say, despite the efforts of the most sophisticated computers, who was the best heavyweight. But surely "Jack" Johnson would qualify as one of the very few atop the mountain reserved for the greats. He was graced with a magnificent body and a mind that could respond in a microsecond. John Arthur Johnson, born in 1878 into racism and poverty in Galveston, Texas, became heavyweight champion of the world for a short period before World War I. As he made clear in his autobiography, written in 1926, the boxing industry was racist to the core. It defeated him and fought an effective rearguard action against further black champions for another generation.

All the athletic heroes were white. Consider golf, in some ways the most demanding game invented by man. Blacks had no access to golf, so Bobby Jones, a young middle-class white, became the star. The same was true of tennis, where Bill Tilden, a man who lived in the mortal fear of exposure as a homosexual, ironically transformed the game into one that idealized the strong, powerful male.

The big money was in professional baseball and amateur football.

Babe Ruth was the classic hero: despite his drooping belly and tooth-pick legs, he could pitch, steal bases, and hit home runs. He and his astute Yankee owners agreed that the 'home run served their mutual advantage. So he became a specialist on the field and a hedonist when he left the home-run factory. He once (only?) bedded every employee in a whorehouse during one visit and did his considerable best to keep the bootleggers busy.

The student amateurs lined other people's pockets by playing college football well enough to attract all classes into stadiums on Saturday afternoons. The Four Horsemen of Notre Dame provided vicarious satisfaction for Protestants and agnostics, racists and Polish immigrants, as well as for Catholic true belivers. Harold ("Red") Grange of the University of Illinois played his game as well as The Babe played his. Smashing 60 home runs in a season is impressive, but so is running for four touchdowns in the first 12 minutes of a game against the University of Michigan. Small wonder that by 1929 the universities were collecting $21 million from the sale of football tickets or that Grange was the man who provided professional football with its first star attraction.

Many of the people in the stadiums, moreover, had the money to buy wristwatches and cigarette lighters. The seats were probably built of a new material called reinforced concrete, and many of the spectators would go home to meals cooked in Pyrex dishes. If they lived in the northern part of the country, then the vegetables were probably delivered fresh from the South or the West. If not, they came from a can. The ability to have a tasty meal that had been harvested by poor farmers (black and white) and then either canned or transported fresh symbolized the triumph of the corporation.

Food was increasingly being processed and marketed by the large operators. The Great Atlantic and Pacific Tea Co., for example, was a giant chain of retail outlets that quietly forced thousands of independent neighborhood storekeepers out of business. And the corner drugstore was becoming a corporate enterprise that sold perfume as well as ice cream, and contraceptives as well as prescription drugs. That industry was dominated by Drug, Inc., a mammoth corporation that owned the Rexall, Liggett, and Owl retail chains, as well as such manufacturing firms as Vick Chemical, Bayer Aspirin, and Bristol-Myers.

The trucking industry was beginning to challenge the railroads for the contracts to haul steel, food, and drugs. Trucks had been used prior to World War I, but they had not proved satisfactory because the poor design, poor technology (as in the steel for springs), hard tires, and poor roads (and weak bridges) severely limited their reliability. When the railroads were unable to handle the supply problems of the war, however, the automobile manufacturers solved those problems. Cross-country truck caravans were commonplace by 1918, when more than 250,000 trucks were in operation. The industry grew very rapidly during the 1920s and exerted considerable pressure on state legislatures (and the Congress) for the construction of all-weather highways.

The government (meaning the taxpayers) also aided the aviation industry. Airmail service was established between Washington, D.C., and New York in 1918, and cross-country and Western Hemisphere routes appeared in 1920. During the early years, while commercial companies were struggling to maintain reliable schedules, individual barnstorming pilots were acquainting the public with the experience of flying, and some of them began to transport corporation executives around the country on a regular basis. One of the key figures in the development of scheduled flights was Juan T. Trippe, who entered corporate aviation in 1921 after his graduation from Yale. He became president of Pan American World Airways in 1927 and promptly demonstrated his ability by winning an exclusive contract from the government for overseas airmail service.

That kind of government aid was of major importance. It involved direct and indirect subsidies and the enforcement of safety and performance standards. The contracts for military aircraft and the Kelley Act of 1925, under which airmail contracts were awarded to private firms, provided the most direct kind of economic assistance. The government also began, in 1925, to finance navigational aids. That kind of help, similar to the subsidies given to the automobile industry through road-building programs, was extended in the Air Commerce Act of 1926. By the end of the decade, 7500 planes were being produced each year, and 112 airlines were fighting each other for passengers.

Most of the passengers were carried by a few large companies, and that pattern was typical of the new corporate economy. The consolidations and the mergers of the decade were not as spectacular as those that had occurred between 1897 and 1904, but they were equally important. Despite the nation's economic growth, there were approximately 65,000 fewer entrepreneurs in 1929 than there had been in 1920. The four largest copper firms, for example, extended their share of the market from 20 percent to 80 percent. Even at the beginning of the period, when less than one-third of all the manufacturing enterprises were corporations, that minority hired 86 percent of all the labor in manufacturing and turned out 87 percent of all the products.

By 1927, at the height of the era's growth, the 200 largest nonfinancial corporations held over 45 percent of industrial wealth, received over 40 percent of the total corporate income, and accounted for nearly 20 percent of the total national wealth. Samuel Insull's utility empire produced one-eighth of all electrical power generated in the country.

Bethlehem Steel and Youngstown Sheet and Tube increased their capacity—and share of the market—by acquiring smaller firms. Similar consolidations in the railroad industry were carried through by the Van Swerigen brothers of Cleveland. The chain store system, which had been established by Frank W. Woolworth prior to World War I (more than 1000 stores in 1911), also expanded very rapidly. Other leaders in that movement were Montgomery Ward, the First National Stores, and the S. H. Kress system.

The same pattern was apparent in finance. At the end of the decade, almost 50 percent of the nation's banking resources were controlled by 1 percent of the banks. Most of the giants (like Morgan and Chase National) were located in New York, but a newcomer in the West offered a strong challenge. Amadeo Peter Giannini's operation based in San Francisco, the Bank of America National Trust and Savings Association, had become the fourth largest bank in the country. During and after World War I, however, the banks lost the kind of control they had exercised over industrial corporations during the years of finance capitalism.

The key to that change was the tremendous profits earned by the industrial firms during the war. Their cash reserves were almost 250 percent greater in 1918 than they had been in 1914, and hence when the banks began in 1921 to press them to pay their notes, they were able to do so without undue strain (or further borrowing). The corporations continued to use the banks to facilitate their routine commercial operations, but they did not depend upon them for basic capital.

Instead, they financed themselves from their own profits. More than 80 percent of the money required for the large programs of plant expansion undertaken in 1922 and 1927, for example, and 47 percent of all the expansion of the decade was financed by internal profits. Corporations also drew funds from the sale of their securities in the domestic market and from the profits earned by their overseas branches and subsidiaries.

Control of the corporations took several forms: complete ownership by an individual or group; control by a majority of investors; control by a minority of stockholders; control by management personnel; or control exercised by a group through a legal device. The bankers did not immediately lose all of their influence, but by virtue of their day-to-day operational authority, corporation executives increased their power.

Some observers argued that the public sale of voting stock meant that ownership and control were separated and that the managers were the effective owners because they directed the routine operations. That interpretation could be questioned on the evidence that revealed that important blocks of stock continued to be held by a few individuals or groups. But the basic question could not be answered by that kind of data: the central point was that the managers—regardless of their individual or collective holdings of stock—thought and operated as though they owned the corporations and behaved as marketplace entrepreneurs. They acted as owners even though they were not owners. As for the ordinary individual stockholders, they exercised little influence even when they tried. They were too divided and too ignorant of the real workings of the system.

Many big-corporation leaders introduced important measures of reorganization and rationalization during the 1920s. That was not true of all firms; the United States Steel Corporation, for example, did not become a highly integrated operation until the next depression (and effective competition) induced it to initiate such change. But others modified their form and policies to meet specific crises, to increase efficiency, to expand their existing market, to control labor, to expand overseas, or to diversify their production and markets.

The interrelated history of the DuPont Corporation and General Motors illustrates the basic pattern. Within the DuPont firm, the death in 1920 of Eugene du Pont ended a period of personalized leadership. Alfred du Pont met the challenge by consolidating and centralizing management and by improving and diversifying production. At the same time, however, the DuPont investments in General Motors were threatened by the inability of William C. Durant to compete effectively against Ford and other companies like Olds and Chrysler.

The postwar collapse dramatized Durant's troubles. He played a vital role in the initial organization of General Motors but lost control of his system of divisions and, as one Du Pont remarked, "there was no control of how much money was being spent." In response to Durant's request for help, Pierre du Pont took charge. With the assistance of others like Alfred Sloan, Donaldson Brown, and John Lee Pratt, he corrected the failures and created the basis for the vast growth of the company in subsequent years.

In the early years of the century, the car was a novelty that sold itself, but as General Motors, Chrysler, and others began to compete effectively with Ford, the automobile industry joined the rush to use advertising to persuade the citizen to buy a particular product. From the outset, the ad business was based on the theory of behavioral psychology developed by John B. Watson. The idea of dealing with human beings in terms of stimulus-and-response patterns naturally appealed to a firm interested in motivating people to buy its products in preference to those of other companies, and in creating a sense of need for an item never before considered useful or desirable.

The capitalistic marketplace relationship between the assembly line and the advertising agency is obvious: the more that is produced, the more there is that must be sold to turn a profit. But there was also a more subtle connection involving the definition and organization (even manipulation) of people. And in that respect Frederick Winslow Taylor did for the assembly line what Watson did for advertising.

Taylor began as a shrewd engineer who realized that the profitability of machine tools (such as unattended lathes programmed to produce an endless stream of bolts and nuts) depended upon the quality of the steel fed into the machines. With important help from J. Mannel White of the Bethlehem Steel Company, Taylor developed a high-speed carbon steel that could withstand the tensions and the temperatures of that process.

Then Taylor turned his attention to the problem of producing workers who could match the materials. He studied the motions required to do a job and clocked the time taken to make those moves. Then he reorganized people to fit the demands of the assembly line. He was at once ruthless (forcing the workers to push themselves to the limit) and subtle (organizing them into friendly and compatible groups). It was an impressive example of the logic underpinning corporate capitalism, and even the reform lawyer Brandeis became an enthusiastic supporter of Taylor's approach.

The early advocates of advertising, who were almost as much concerned to sell the public on the virtues of the corporation as to induce them to buy its goodies in the marketplace, employed the same techniques. The pioneers in that process, like Ivy Lee and George Harvey, simply transferred Taylor's principles of the scientific management of workers to the organization of consumers. Their successors, who came to the fore in the 1920s (having learned much from the way that the Wilson administration sold its policies), created a burgeoning new industry.

There is no solid evidence about how much money was spent on advertising during the 1920s, but one estimate suggests that the total for 1929 was about $1.8 billion. One basic strategy was to encourage consumers to think of their existing goods as old-fashioned. The clothing industry was perhaps the first to substitute the issue of style for the question of quality, but that strategy was rapidly applied to cars, furniture, and other items that had formerly been used for many years.

Advertising also played a major role in changing the public's food-buying habits. By the end of the era more than half the families in the nation had stopped purchasing bulk groceries in favor of buying trade-name and packaged units of such items as cheese, bacon, butter, soap, and coffee. The effectiveness of such advertising was a major cause of the rapid concentration of power in the food and drug industries and in the business of distributing to the retail market.

The advertising industry also accelerated the process of creating a

national market and a new national consciousness. A classic convergence of those two developments occurred in 1925, when Henry B.
Luce began publishing *Time* as a national newsweekly carrying great
amounts of advertising copy. The publishing industry had founded
The Saturday Review of Literature the previous year, and in 1926 it
added the Book-of-the-Month Club and The Literary Guild to expand
its retail market.

The survival and growth of those ventures was another indication
(along with the steady sale of cars, radios, and movie tickets) that many
Americans shared to some degree in the prosperity of the corporations.
But it was a much smaller share. The income of urban labor increased
11 percent from 1923 to 1929, but corporate profits and dividends
jumped more than 60 percent. The union movement was too weak to
secure a more equitable division of the economic pie. And several
important industries, particularly coal, leather, and textiles, did not
benefit from the boom. Neither did the blacks in *any* industry. As for
agriculture, it never recovered from the sharp deflation caused by the
loss of wartime markets.

Hoover broadly agreed with the view of most farm leaders (on the
left as well as the right) that the long-term solution involved the expansion of export markets. But that was a complex matter, and in the
meantime the agricultural agitation produced several domestic reforms. The Packers and Stockyards Act of August 15, 1921, sought to
correct weaknesses and abuses in that part of the domestic market. It
outlawed unfair and discriminatory practices, such as control of prices,
that tended to create a monopoly in the meat-processing industry.
Similar regulations were applied to poultry and dairy operations. Next
came the Grain Futures Trading Act of August 24, 1921, designed to
regulate all markets selling grain for future delivery and thereby prevent the manipulation of the market by any combination or monopoly.

That law was ruled unconstitutional in 1922, but the Congress
quickly passed a similar bill that met the legal requirements by tying
the controls to the commerce clause of the Constitution. Additional
help had been provided in the meantime through the Cooperative
Marketing Act (February 18, 1922), which exempted agricultural producers, including cooperatives, from prosecution under the antitrust
laws.

In terms of immediate assistance, however, the most useful law was
the Intermediate Credit Act of March 4, 1923, which provided aid for
financing crops. The legislation created 12 banks (one in each FRS
district) under the control of a Federal Farm Loan Board. Each bank
was provided with $5 million in capital by the government. As with
similar private banks authorized by the law, the government-backed
institutions could make loans over a period of six months to three years

to cooperatives and other producing and marketing associations. Those laws offered some help to the farmers, but they did not solve the market problem and they did not produce any sustained improvement in agricultural prices or general farm conditions.

President Harding was concerned about the farmers, but he was far more impressed with the corporate elite and its spokesmen. Those men emerged from the war with a new confidence that they could work with and through the government to accomplish their objectives. Bernard Baruch, the speculator and financier who had directed the WIB, made the point with typical understatement: "What was done in those war years was never to be completely forgotten."

Such men did not always agree on policy matters, but they were generally arrayed against the laissez-faire conservatives. They fought the reformers on some issues, compromised on others, and in the process developed their own programs for the new corporate system. The dramatic scandals of the Harding administration—which involved personal corruption in the Departments of Justice, the Interior, and the Navy, and in the Office of the Alien Property Custodian—often obscure the continuing struggle to rationalize the new order.

EXPLORATORY READING

The best book (and with an excellent bibliography) on the subject of this chapter is:

G. Soule, *Prosperity Decade: From War to Depression, 1917–1929* (1968)

But also consult:

W. E. Leuchtenburg, *The Perils of Prosperity* (1958)
J. Prothro, *The Dollar Decade* (1954)

Other studies of the corporate society are:

M. Heald, *The Social Responsibilities of Business* (1970)
R. Sobel, *The Great Bull Market: Wall Street in the 1920s* (1968)

The politics of Harding are explored in:

R. K. Murray, *The Harding Era* (1969)
A. Sinclair, *The Available Man* (1965)

The various effects and consequences of the triumph of the corporation are examined in:

I. Bernstein, *The Lean Years* (1969)
W. H. Chafe, *The American Woman: Her Changing Social, Economic, and Political Roles, 1920–1940* (1972)

C. A. Chambers, *Seedtime of Reform: American Social Service and Social Action, 1918–1933* (1962)

P. H. Douglas, *Real Wages in the United States, 1890–1926* (1930)

P. J. Hubbard, *Origins of the TVA: The Muscle Shoals Controversy* (1961)

J. S. Lemons, *The Woman Citizen: Social Feminism in the 1920s* (1973)

T. Saloutos and J. D. Hicks, *Twentieth Century Populism: Agrarian Discontent in the Middle West* (1951)

S. D. Spero and A. L. Harris, *The Black Worker: The Negro and the Labor Movement* (1931)

R. Zieger, *Republicans and Labor, 1919–1929* (1969)

On the importance of Taylor, see:

F. B. Copley, *Frederick W. Taylor* (1923)

C. B. Thompson (Ed.), *Scientific Management* (1914)

11 THE POLITICS OF THE CORPORATE POLITICAL ECONOMY

THE scandals that plagued—and almost destroyed—the Harding administration (and the Republican party) did not involve the corruption of the basic constitutional and political processes. That kind of subversion occurred two generations later. The shame of the Harding years involved greedy men abusing their public trust to stuff their pockets with money: ordinary men committing ordinary crimes. Their misbehavior was not incidental (even though the punishment was minor), but the crucial story of those years concerns the battles over policy.

One small and thoughtful group of Progressives, personified (and in general led) by Hoover, was struggling to devise and implement an interrelated set of policies that would humanize as well as rationalize the corporate political economy. They were capitalists, to be sure, but they knew that the corporations had to be controlled. They also recognized that any effort to accomplish that objective by creating a national bureaucracy centered in Washington, D.C., would ultimately undermine democracy and community.

Hoover's experiences as a presidential administrator during the war had given him a keen understanding of the dangers of building a system in which the corporations would exercise equal power with the Congress and the executive in directing the political economy. He deeply feared that the corporations would emerge—and sooner rather than later—as the dominant element in such a coalition of the powerful. At the same time, he had become ever more impressed with the dangers—and inefficiencies—of centralizing power in the government.

The wartime practices had led others, however, to favor more extensive coordination and controls. A good many of those men were upper-class leaders like Baruch, Gerard P. Swope, and Owen D. Young of General Electric. But men from other social groups also shared that outlook, men such as Donald Richberg, a Chicago lawyer; Otto T. Mallery of the Pennsylvania State Industrial Board; and Matthew Woll, a leading intellectual in the AF of L. Many of those people favored various social reforms, and in that sense they were progressives in the broad sense of the term. But, as Hoover realized, their approach to the political economy pointed toward a kind of nonterroristic fascism in which corporation leaders would dominate an integrated national system.

The antitrust wing of the Progressive movement, symbolized by Senators LaFollette and Borah, agitated for assistance to agriculture (and, to a lesser extent, to labor) and for limitations on the power of the industrial and financial corporations. Other major spokesmen of that group, such as Senators Norris and Johnson, persistently resisted the movement toward an integrated, corporate, and centrally managed society.

The conservatives were almost as divided as the Progressives. The minority, typified by the Du Pont family, would have repealed most if not all of the major Progressive legislation. A strong plurality, however, had either accepted or acquiesced in the work of the prewar reformers. Those people had three broad objectives: to block further regulations and controls, to emasculate those bureaus (such as the FTC) that they found troublesome and limiting, and to proceed with the profitable development of their own operations within the existing framework. As revealed in the attack on the FTC, that group included bankers like George B. Roberts, businessman-politician William E. Humphrey of Washington, and others like Vernon S. Van Fleet of the NAM.

A third and smaller number were in some respects moving toward an accommodation with the Swope group of upper-class Progressives. Despite his militant opposition to labor unions, for example, Elbert H. Gary of United States Steel accepted other reforms and stressed the need for responsible leadership— if only to avoid more radical measures. So did others like Theodore N. Vail of the Bell Telephone System and John D. Rockefeller, Jr. Perhaps the most significant member of that group, however, was Andrew William Mellon. Mellon capped his career as a Pittsburgh banker and capitalist who had played a central role in financing the steel, electrical, oil, and aluminum industries by serving as secretary of the treasury from 1921 through 1932.

Mellon was a nonacademically trained advocate of manipulating the monetary system to generate economic activity. His basic idea was to free capital funds for investment in order to facilitate recovery from the postwar depression and to sustain prosperity thereafter. The first step in creating such a system came in June, 1921, with the Budget and Accounting Act. The Bureau of the Budget, headed by a director appointed by the president, was created within the Treasury Department. The director was responsible for submitting a detailed budget to each Congress, along with recommendations for raising the required money through taxes and loans. The allocation of the funds was placed under the comptroller general, who headed the General Accounting Office.

Mellon then won, in the Revenue Act of November 23, 1921, an endorsement of his basic approach to monetary policy. The excess profits tax was terminated, and the maximum surtax was cut to 50 percent. Those features were attacked by Progressives like LaFollette on the grounds that they favored the wealthy. Partially in response to that criticism, but also in line with Mellon's general ideas, individuals were given income tax relief. And the tax on corporate net profits was raised from 10 percent to 12.5 percent.

Mellon's broad strategy was further developed and articulated by the increasingly able and sophisticated men who staffed the bureaucracy of the FRS. The Federal Reserve Board's annual report for 1923 outlined a monetary policy that was one of the earliest attempts to devise a system of controls to maintain prosperity and prevent serious unemployment. It represented the influence of quasi-public bodies like the National Bureau of Economic Research, but it also grew out of the Reserve Board's own successful handling, beginning in April, 1923, of the inflationary pressures associated with recovery from the postwar depression. It carried through a successful deflation, thus in all probability preventing a panic like the one in 1907, and then tried to provide enough credit for sustained growth.

Old-line conservatives fought those new ideas, and another battle occurred within the executive department over Hoover's effort to control the overseas operations of the investment bankers. He viewed overseas economic expansion as an essential ingredient of prosperity but wanted to prevent such operations from involving the government in political or military interventions. Given the inherent dynamics of a capitalist political economy, Hoover was probably trying to resolve the irreconcilable, but he did make a brave effort. He proposed, after failing to persuade the bankers to regulate themselves, that the government should assert its power to block all loans that were not peaceful and economically productive. The first White House conference on May 25, 1921, attended by banker Thomas Lamont, Secretaries Hughes and Mellon, as well as by Hoover and Harding, made it clear that the president was unwilling to override the opposition. The bankers continued to do as they pleased—which included making many loans for unproductive and military purposes.

Harding followed a similar course in accepting the shipping industry's proposals for subsidization. Vessels that had cost the taxpayers about $250 million, for example, were sold to private firms for less than $25 million. But Hoover and others did win some victories in the fight over the tariff. That battle, which produced the Fordney-McCumber Law of September 21, 1922, hinged on the delegation of power by the Congress to the president to enable him to bargain for reciprocal advantages in the world marketplace.

The postwar depression, along with strong pressure from various industries and the farmers, created a predisposition in favor of high rates. The reformers might have concentrated on lowering the rates but chose instead to fight for the reciprocal provisions. The central figure in the modernization of the Blaine-McKinley approach was William S. Culbertson, the leader of the Progressive bloc on the Tariff Commission created during the Wilson years. "The principle of the Open Door," Culbertson noted, "is an accepted feature" of American policy, and the power to use the tariff as a club would enable the United States to win "equality of treatment."

Section 317 of the law of 1922 gave the president authority to raise or lower tariffs up to 50 percent of the existing figure, and the State Department promptly launched a campaign to win the second objective of the reformers—extensive concessions from Great Britain, France, the Netherlands, and Japan. Those battles proved far more difficult than anyone anticipated, but the principle of flexibility—and the related bargaining power in negotiations—was an important part of later successes.

The push for overseas markets and raw materials was a major aspect of American diplomacy during the 1920s. Owen D. Young of General Electric provided one of the best explanations of the stress on exports even in industries where the percentages involved might seem small. "Fifteen percent was a most material contribution to our prosperity," he pointed out. (Corporation leaders like Young formed an interlocking directorate in organizations such as the Foreign Trade Council, the Foreign Bondholders Committee, the American Manufacturers' Export Association, and the Pan-American Society.)

The bankers shared that outlook. The *Acceptance Bulletin*, a key financial journal, provided a typical summary of their thinking: "It is useless to attempt to further develop our own country until a satisfactory market is created for our surplus products." Total foreign invest-

When the Congress began tinkering with the tariff schedules once again in the 1920s, "Ding" Darling, cartoonist for the New York Tribune, recalled another day when Congress wandered into the same wilderness. The driver of the coach enjoys relating the story to the new passengers on the same trek.

A NICE LITTLE SUMMER OUTING FOR CONGRESS

From the *Tribune* © (New York)

Reprinted in the *Review of Reviews,* vol. LXIV, September, 1921, p. 252.

ment jumped from $6.96 billion in 1919 to $17.01 billion in 1929; and in some countries, such as Cuba, the percentage increase was almost 500 percent.

There was a related effort to control raw materials. Edward N. Hurley of the Shipping Board revealed one of the arguments behind that drive in a long letter to Bernard Baruch at the end of World War I:

> The more we study world conditions, with respect to commerce, the more convinced I am that world peace in the future, as well as moral leadership, will swing upon the pivot of raw materials. . . . In what better way could we be of real service than by the use of our financial strength to control the raw materials for the benefit of humanity.

Various other countries, industrial powers like Great Britain as well as underdeveloped nations like Brazil and Mexico, took a different view of such American predominance. The result, as in the oil industry, was vigorous opposition to American expansion in Eastern Europe, the Middle East, and Latin America. Foreigners were likewise skeptical of the export of American industries.

Some of that expansion occurred through licensing foreigners to use American patents and other technological advances in return for royalty payments on every article that was produced. In most cases, however, it involved the construction or purchase of branch factories in other nations. That reduced labor and transportation costs and made it easier to adapt the product to the culture of the specific foreign country. The branch factories also provided a way to evade tariff barriers erected by European nations, for the profits earned from goods made and sold abroad could be returned to the United States without any losses.

Such overseas expansion was strongly supported by most federal bureaucrats. Under Hoover's leadership, the Department of Commerce emphasized that objective. And in the State Department, the career officials who generally favored a similar policy consolidated their position and power through the Foreign Service Act of May 24, 1924. That legislation, known as the Rogers Act, combined the diplomatic and consular branches into one professionalized foreign service system. One of the leaders of that bureaucracy, Joseph C. Grew, made the expansionist point very simply in describing and defending the new system: "We must get it out of the mind of the public that the consular service is the only one that looks after that side. Rather, the diplomatic service, in its commercial activities, paves the way for the consular service to function at all." Perhaps no one, however, described the relationship between economics and diplomacy more succinctly than Secretary of State Hughes: "All political questions . . . broadly, have some economic force lying back of them."

Presidents Harding and Coolidge shared that view. As early as 1915, for example, Harding told the NAM that the goal was "commercial supremacy." He warned that the end of the war would bring tough competition and asked the country to moderate its internal differences in order to achieve *"the peaceful commercial conquest of the earth."*

Coolidge was more militantly and righteously nationalistic. "There can be no peace with the force of evil," he declared in 1923. The United States was the leading force for good, and he thought it "perfectly obvious" that if any conduct was "wrong . . . within the confines of the United States, it is equally wrong outside our borders." As for America's economic expansion, that was part of "the natural play of the forces of civilization." "Our investments and trade relations are such," he explained, "that it is almost impossible to conceive of any conflict anywhere on earth which would not affect us injuriously." "The one great duty that stands out," he concluded, "requires us to use our enormous pressure to trim the balance of the world."

The major diplomatic maneuvers of the early 1920s involved the problems the war created in the Pacific and in Europe. The objective in Asia was to check Japan while furthering America's overseas economic expansion. At the same time, Secretary of State Hughes was sympathetic with the campaign for disarmament that had been launched by Senator Borah. His resolution calling on the president to convene an international conference for naval disarmament was overwhelmingly endorsed by the Congress in the early summer of 1921.

Hughes began immediately (July 8, 1921) to arrange such a meeting in Washington and tied it to a general review of the problems in the Pacific. He opened the conference on November 12, 1921, with a dramatic and stunning speech telling each major power how much of its existing navy was to be scrapped and how many vessels it could build in the future. He destroyed a total of 66 ships (30 American, 19 British, and 17 Japanese) in his first volley from the rostrum. A British spokesman documented the effectiveness of the Hughes strategy: "It is an audacious and astonishing scheme, and it took us off our feet."

France and Japan, in particular, recovered their balance and fought back vigorously, but Hughes never fully lost the initiative. By the time the conference ended, on February 6, 1922, nine treaties had been negotiated and signed (and all were ratified by the Senate). Japan formally agreed to withdraw its troops from Siberia, to evacuate Shantung (though it kept favorable economic rights), and to give America the right to build a cable station on the island of Yap. Even more significantly, it had to acquiesce in the destruction of its alliance with Great Britain and the termination of the Lansing-Ishi agreement.

The Five Power Naval Armaments Treaty signed by America, Britain, Japan, France, and Italy declared a ten-year naval holiday during which no capital ships would be built and established a ratio of 5:5:3:1:1.67:1.67 for vessels displacing over 10,000 tons for armed with guns of more than eight-inch caliber. Japan and France vigorously opposed the place given them in the descending order of strength (3 and 1.67) but finally acquiesced. The Four Power Pact involved America, Japan, Great Britain, and France. They agreed to respect each other's rights in various Pacific island groups and to consult over disagreements that arose in the future.

Finally, in the Nine Power Treaty, the United States won formal recognition of the Open Door policy. The signatories bound themselves to respect "the sovereignty, the independence, and the territorial and administrative integrity of China," and to honor "the principles of the Open Door." That was more than even the United States had done during the conference, however, for China's wishes and suggestions were largely ignored.

That had also been the case with Germany during the Versailles peace negotiations, but the situation changed rapidly as its economy began to collapse. That development threatened the entire European system and raised the possibility of more Communist revolutions. The United States had two options: cancel the debts owed by England and France ($7.7 billion), with the understanding that they would forgo the reparations they claimed from Germany, or use more loans to revive Germany. Most American leaders opposed the first policy because of their marketplace outlook and because they wanted to use the debts as bargaining counters in other negotiations (as for reciprocity agreements).

Hughes and Hoover took the lead in using the other option to meet the crisis. The Germans found it impossible to make full payments on their debts ($33 billion), and the French and Belgians retaliated in January, 1923, by occupying the Ruhr Valley, the industrial heart of the German economy. The resulting drop in German production only intensified the problems.

Hoover and Hughes were primarily concerned with strengthening Germany against the threat of a Communist revolution and with reviving the European economy as a market for American exports. The ensuing negotiations produced a broad program generally known as the Dawes Plan because of the central role played by Charles G. Dawes, who handled the official negotiations in Europe and was a key figure in obtaining the participation of private American financial corporations like the House of Morgan.

The final arrangements, negotiated during the spring of 1924 and put into operation on September 1, were designed to underwrite the recovery of the German economy and then to siphon off a reasonable amount of the resulting surplus production as reparations. The German Reichsbank was reorganized under Allied supervision, and an international loan of $200 million was provided to revive the German economy. Payments to the Allies were placed on a sliding scale determined by German production. American financiers and other investors provided $110 million, and an American banker, Parker S. Gilbert, was appointed as agent general of reparations.

By that time President Harding had died (August 2, 1923) amidst persistent rumors of the scandals that were shortly exposed by various congressional committees. Charles R. Forbes, chief of the Veterans Bureau, and Thomas W. Miller, alien property custodian, were convicted of fraud, bribery, and conspiracy. Attorney General Harry W. Daugherty was charged with bribery and failure to prosecute other offenders. He resigned upon the request of President Coolidge but escaped conviction in court. The major conspiracy to defraud involved the attempt to transfer navy oil holdings, known as the Teapot Dome and Elk Hills reserves, to private businessmen.

That swindle was uncovered by a congressional committee headed by Montana senator Thomas J. Walsh. The central figures were Secretary of the Interior Albert B. Fall, Harry F. Sinclair of the petroleum industry, and Edward L. Doheny. Sinclair wanted the oil and the others wanted money. The resulting litigation dragged on for three years before the oil reserves were returned to the government. Fall was convicted of bribery, but Doheny and Sinclair were acquitted (although the latter was fined and sentenced for contempt of court).

In addition to firing Daugherty, President Coolidge appointed Harland Fisk Stone to handle the prosecution, and Stone's quiet, effective work did much to avoid political disaster for the Republicans. Coolidge's own reputation as a proper New Englander also helped, and he moved quickly and effectively to secure his own nomination for president. Even so, he might have failed if either Hoover or Hughes had chosen to campaign, but both declined to rock the boat.

POLITICAL PROBLEMS FOR THE PROGRESSIVES

That was understandable, but it weakened the Progressives. Without Hoover or Hughes the reformers had no candidate strong enough to recapture control of the party. Earlier organizations like the Committee of Forty-Eight and the American Labor party were still active, and the Conference for Progressive Political Action (CPPA), called in February, 1922, by the Railroad Brotherhoods, had proved effective in electing Progressives in some local and state elections. But none of the leading Republican senators—Borah, Johnson, Norris, or LaFollette—could muster enough support within the party to replace Coolidge.

Failing there, LaFollette chose to run as an independent candidate nominated in July, 1924, by the CPPA convention. The Democrats were bitterly divided by three issues: the rise of new urban leaders like Alfred E. Smith of New York; the question of racism; and the larger problem of creating a coalition that included urban and labor

The LaFollette run for the presidency in 1924 was derided by Charles Sykes in the Philadelphia Evening Public Ledger. *The gallant steed of progressivism was only a kiddy-car; the issues will hardly fly at all as a kite of third-party talk; and the force of discontent is delivered by a hand bellows. The climate was unkind to LaFollette and his colleagues.*

"LET'S GO!"
—Sykes in the Philadelphia *Evening Public Ledger*

Reprinted in *The Literary Digest*, vol. 81, April 19, 1924, p. 15.

interests as well as southern agriculture. City leaders generally backed Smith, an exuberant Irish-Catholic reformer who opposed the Klan and Prohibition. William G. McAdoo was his first and strongest opponent, but neither of them survived the long convention battle. Smith won a platform denunciation of the Klan, but a Wall Street lawyer named John W. Davis was finally nominated on the 103rd ballot.

Coolidge had no such problems, winning the Republican nod on the first ballot. As had occasionally happened in the past, the vice-presidential candidate exerted some influence on the final outcome. That was due in considerable degree to the strategy devised by Hoover. Even as the Dawes Plan was being negotiated, he took the lead in presenting it as a program to counter the rising militance of the farmers. Hoover's argument was simple but persuasive: the revival of the German economy through American loans would produce general European prosperity, and that would create an expanding market for America's agricultural surpluses. It would do so directly, through European purchases of food and fiber, and indirectly, through the expansion of America's industrial exports, which would in turn increase the domestic market for farm products. Dawes, who had developed his own political base in the Midwest, won the vice-presidential nomination.

Hoover's logic was used to counter the two-price, parity proposal introduced in Congress on January 16, 1924, by Senator Charles L. McNary and Congressman Gilbert N. Haugen. That bill was designed to improve the position of farmers who raised wheat, cotton, wool, cattle, sheep, and hogs. A federal farm board would purchase the surpluses of those items (along with flour and processed meat products) at the parity price and then hold them off the market or sell them abroad. The difference between the world price and the fixed domestic parity price would be partially recovered by an equalization fee collected from the farmers.

The fight over that proposal, which all knew (even if they did not admit it publicly) would involve direct government subsidies from tax receipts, was symbolized by the split within the cabinet. Secretary of Agriculture Henry C. Wallace of Iowa backed the bill as part of his fight to keep Hoover from centralizing all market expansion programs in the Department of Commerce. The Hoover group opposed it, and their arguments based on the Dawes Plan helped defeat the bill in the House of Representatives on June 3, 1924.

The Republicans got most of the credit for the Agricultural Credits Act in August, 1924, which provided federal loans to enable dealers and cooperatives to hold farm surpluses off the market when prices were unusually low. The objectives were to put a floor under prices and to halt the rising number of farm bankruptcies. More than $300 million was advanced between 1924 and 1932. That was not enough to save either the farmers or the economy, but it did help Coolidge.

Hoover also moved to blunt the restlessness of labor, which had not been cowed by the defeat of the steel strike in 1919. The United Textile Workers of America, for example, prevented the owners from pushing them further down the wage scale, and Julius Emspach of the United Electrical Workers continued to build a strong base for future negotiations—or strikes. But other union leaders turned toward cooperation and negotiated compromise. Gompers, growing old, remained committed to the craft union approach, and others were discouraged when the recovery from the postwar depression cut deeply into the membership of the AF of L (down from 4 million in 1921 to 2.9 million in 1929).

The prewar idea of union-management cooperation reached a peak in the agreement of 1922–1923 between the Baltimore and Ohio Railroad and the Railroad Brotherhoods (copied by the Chicago and Northwestern Line and the Milwaukee Railroad) and in similar arrangements negotiated by the ACW. There were more than 400 company unions operating in 1926, and a good many of them provided various benefits for workers even though they were not independent organizations. Such conservatism was perfectly illustrated when the AF of L refused the request by General Electric to organize all its workers in one industrial union.

But like the farmers, the workers in the depressed parts of the industrial economy were not so passive. John L. Lewis of the UMW led the miners out of the pits in the spring of 1922, after the operators began to cut wages by as much as 33 percent, in a strike to obtain steady work, a six-hour day, and a five-day week. Violence promptly erupted in such places as Herrin, Illinois, when the owners tried to maintain production with nonunion labor. From the outset, Lewis received a good deal of behind-the-scenes support from Hoover.

Such maneuvers brought the operators to a White House conference in July, and they agreed to arbitration and to reopen the mines on the terms existing prior to the strike. Hoover renewed his support for the workers in 1924, and that helped influence the election. A Coolidge with a Hoover looked better than a Davis without a Smith; and while LaFollette's antitrust strategy might have worked in 1904, it was largely irrelevant in 1924 because the corporations were too strong and had become too cozy with the regulatory agencies of the federal government.

Neither women nor blacks played a significant role in the election. Some females did organize pressure groups that were sometimes effective: the Women's League for Peace and Freedom; the National Consumer's League; the League of Women Voters; and the Women's

Joint Congressional Committee. People like Carrie Cutt continued the old struggle and were joined by others like Dorothy Detzer, Jessie Hooper, Lucia Mead, Mary Woolley, and Caroline O'Day. But winning the right to vote did not lead on to a movement by women to vote according to feminist or reform principles. Divided against themselves—or indifferent to public issues—women failed to challenge the political economy of corporate capitalism.

The most quietly subversive women were Margaret Sanger and Mary Dennett. Sanger was the brave pioneer, creating in 1914 the National Birth Control League. She was promptly prosecuted for distributing her magazine, *Woman Rebel,* through the mails and made a tactical retreat to Europe. Dennett took charge of the battle, creating (in 1918) the Voluntary Parenthood League. Then Sanger returned and in 1921 organized a rival group called the American Birth Control League. Dennett became a radical, arguing that a more liberal attitude toward sex was the key to a candid and effective approach to birth control.

Her loving and moving explanation of sex, first written to and for her son in 1915, provoked a national scandal when the postmaster general prosecuted her for circulating it through the mails. She was ultimately vindicated in a memorable decision by Justice Augustus N. Hand (1930) and joyfully continued her campaign for a more humane approach to sex. Dennett was the precursor of later attitudes and behavior, but Sanger nevertheless encouraged women to change their sexual attitudes—and relationships. But none of that influenced elections or challenged corporate power.

The blacks were no more successful. The determined efforts of Chandler Owen and A. Philip Randolph (who organized the Pullman Porters' Union) won some gains for a few black workers. And DuBois continued his noble efforts. He confronted the sex issue bluntly by asking white males the basic challenge: "Who in hell asked to marry your daughters?" Then he defined the ultimate choice: the only way to keep black Americans "in their place" was "by brute force." Charles S. Johnson, the unusually able leader of the NUL, described the fate of the black urban male with majestic simplicity. The black worker "is a buffer between the employers and the unions. . . . His relation to his job takes on the nature of a vicious circle. In the unionized crafts he may not work unless he belongs to a union, and the most frequent, specious argument advanced by the unions is that he cannot become a member unless he is already employed. The result is frequently that he neither gets a job nor joins a union."

Most blacks were indifferent to the 1924 election. Coolidge won, Davis was second, and LaFollette was a distant third. Coolidge would have won even if the latter two had combined their votes, and he thus became the last old-line conservative president, an orthodox man who suppressed in public his rather delightful sense of wit and humor. He supported Secretary Mellon, lowered many taxes, and appointed laissez-faire businessmen (like William E. Humphrey) to direct regulatory agencies. It was like putting the cat in the canary cage. Their philosophy was to help "business to help itself."

Except for the farmers. Coolidge twice vetoed the McNary-Haugen legislation after the Congress approved it by strong majorities, but he offered no positive alternative. He also killed the bill that Senator Norris and other reformers passed in May, 1928, that would have directed the government to undertake the long-term development of the Tennessee Valley around the facilities at Muscle Shoals. Coolidge called that socialistic. But he approved the Jones-White Act of 1928 that provided more subsidies to the shipping industry.

The reformers did win a few victories, as when they blunted the nationalistic and interventionist outlook of Coolidge and other conservatives in foreign affairs. Aided by pressure from Senator Borah and organizations like the Women's League for Peace and Freedom, for example, Secretary of State Frank B. Kellogg and State Department officer Nelson Johnson defeated those who demanded intervention against the ongoing Chinese Revolution.

Encouraged and aided by the Bolsheviks in Russia, the Chinese Communists had reinforced the nationalism and antiforeignism of the revolution that Sun Yat-Sen had initiated in 1911. President Wilson and Secretary of State Hughes ignored Sun, but the movement he created survived their opposition. The resulting tension erupted on May 30, 1925, and the old order dominated by warlords steadily lost ground to the nationalist (or Kuomintang) forces that were influenced by Communist ideas and Russian advisers.

Secretary Kellogg had been a secondary Progressive figure before the war, and Borah effectively appealed to that tradition to prevent the secretary from surrendering to the interventionists. The senator argued that China was "dominated in all matters which are essential to a nation's prosperity and growth by foreign powers" and that the "problem at bottom is nationalism coming into the presence of imperialism." The two men agreed that the United States should revise the treaty system while refusing to intervene. That policy was vigorously opposed, however, by business interests and a significant group of bureaucrats in the State Department. The American Chamber of Commerce of Shanghai called for armed intervention in April, 1927, for example, and that proposal was backed by various foreign service officers. But Kellogg refused to buckle under their pressure.

The reformers also influenced policy toward Mexico. Secretary of State Hughes had reached a modus vivendi with the Mexican Revolution in 1923: the United States recognized the government headed by President Alvaro Obregon on the basis of a promise that Article 27 of the new constitution, which nationalized subsoil resources, would not be applied retroactively against American holdings in oil, silver, and agriculture. But President Platarco E. Calles, determined to sustain the momentum of the revolution, withdrew those assurances. The oil companies, and others such as the Catholics who opposed the revolution because it attacked the power of the church, immediately raised a clamor for intervention.

President Coolidge and the American ambassador to Mexico, James R. Sheffield, took a tough line. "There is a vast amount of policing to be done in this world," Sheffield asserted; and the president was adamant:

> We have only one question there and that is the question of whether American property is going to be confiscated. . . . It is very difficult for me to see how anyone in this country can see that there is more than one side of that question.

Progressives like Borah and Johnson modified that attitude. They played a key role in Coolidge's decision of September, 1927, to send Dwight Morrow to Mexico as a special representative to ease the tension and negotiate a compromise. His easy acceptance of the Mexicans as equals and his upper-class reform outlook enabled Morrow to reach an agreement: there would be no expropriation of holdings that had been worked prior to the promulgation of the new Mexican Constitution. That did not solve all the problems between the two countries, but it indicated that the reformers were pointing the way toward a more rational policy.

The reformers won, and then lost, a similar battle over relations with Nicaragua. The last of the marines that had been sent by Wilson in 1912 were finally withdrawn in 1925, after the loans from American bankers had been repaid. But the conservatives of that country promptly revolted and seized power. The liberals, behind the brilliant guerrilla leadership of General Augustino Sandino, responded with an insurrection. Coolidge and State Department officials relanded the marines. The Progressives were outraged. "Oh, Monroe Doctrine," cried one Democratic critic in the House of Representatives, "how many crimes have been committed in thy name!" The president in reply reinvoked his policy toward the strike by Boston policemen: "We are not making war on Nicaragua any more than a policeman on the street is making war on passersby." The marines were not withdrawn.

The reformers did, however, win a battle for an idea whose time had not yet come—and has still not come. The campaign to outlaw war was one of the great expressions of romantic idealism in modern history. The romanticism was best revealed by Borah's support: he was a man who spoke with gutsy realism about imperialism and revolution and yet voted for a treaty that was an act of faith. The Coolidge administration fought hard to defeat the prime movers of the idea, Professor James T. Shotwell of Columbia and Chicago lawyer Solomon O. Levinson, but in the end they accepted (1928) a document that— except for defensive purposes—outlawed war as "an instrument of national policy."

But the concept of defense is notoriously open to infinite interpretations. And the United States later invoked the treaty to impose a victor's punishment upon the leaders of Nazi Germany and Imperial Japan. A good many conservatives and radicals, as well as middle-of-the-roaders, opposed that action as a self-serving abuse of the idealism that had motivated the people who forced the treaty upon their reluctant leaders in the belief that the law was to be honored—not twisted.

At the time, however, the twister that counted was the hurricane of 1926 that destroyed the Florida land boom. The resulting regional deflation, marked by many bank failures, underscored the more general signs that the postwar boom was coming to an end. As the economy staggered, labor became more militant. Communists, Socialists, and other radicals regained some of their old influence among the miners and the fur and textile workers. And a bit later, the United Textile Workers launched an organizing drive among poorly paid workers in the South.

That combination of economic difficulties and working-class militance had a significant impact on the elections of 1926. Progressive Republicans displaced conservative members of the party in the Midwest, and those victories, combined with Democratic gains, gave the Progressives a strong position in a Senate formally divided 48 to 47 in favor of the Republicans (with one Farmer-Laborite member). And some of the Democrats, such as Robert F. Wagner of New York, were strong and effective reformers. And even in the House, where the Republicans boasted a formal edge of 237 to 195, there was a similar atmosphere of uneasiness.

And with good reason. The Republicans had failed to exploit a golden opportunity to assert themselves as a party with leaders who could control and direct the corporate political economy. For by 1926 the society was riven by gross inequities and by a growing retreat into pleasure-seeking individualism; and the economy was manifesting clear signs of structural weakness. It is easy, beginning with their limited moral and intellectual vision, to recite the weaknesses of men like Harding and Coolidge (and many of those they appointed to positions of power), but the basic reasons for the developing crisis involved more fundamental factors.

The underlying cause was the structural imbalance of the corporate system. Far too many groups in the society—farmers, miners, blacks, and women, to name a few—lacked the power required to elevate themselves into a dialogue among equals with the corporations.

Second, most corporation leaders did not have any broad, inclusive conception of an industrial society as a community in which all the elements were involved with each other in mutually responsible relationships. Corporation executives persistently made it clear by their actions that they were primarily concerned with the exploitation of human and material resources to earn the largest possible profits. In the elementary sense, of course, there was no reason to expect them to behave in any other way: they were talented and tough (even brilliant and ruthless) capitalists playing the game according to the fang-and-claw rules of the marketplace. As one of them remarked: "Do unto before you are done unto." But that kind of short-run rationality usually breeds serious long-range problems. And the economic downturn that began in 1927 underscored such lack of vision.

Third, most Progressives proved unable or unwilling to confront the truth that their reforms were insufficient to prevent the developing crisis. The evidence increasingly suggested that the only meaningful choice was between effective decentralization (very tough application of the antitrust principle) and sophisticated socialism. But the great majority of reformers continued their search for a middle ground defined by the government accepting and discharging the public responsibilities neglected by the corporations.

Fourth, the minority of perceptive upper-class leaders failed to go for broke. They had a vision (we will moot its limitations), but they refused to challenge either the leaders of the corporations or the mediocre politicians like Harding and Coolidge. Hughes should have confronted Harding in 1920, and four years later Hoover should have challenged Coolidge. Shakespeare said it all:

There is a tide in the affairs of men,
Which, taken at the flood, leads on to fortune;
Omitted, all the voyage of their life
Is bound to lie in shadows and in miseries.

Hoover missed his flood tide and as a result went ashore in the shallows of the Great Depression and suffered the related miseries.

EXPLORATORY READING

The published source materials dealing with the politics and the policies of the 1920s are so extensive that they offer a marvelous opportunity for all to do their own history of their favorite subject. The congressional debates are entertaining as well as illuminating; the State Department documents are unusually revealing; and the memoirs and diaries are chockablock with useful material. I urge you to dig into those sources.

The following books (Wilson's contains an excellent contemporary bibliography) offer the most useful overviews of the period:

S. H. Adams, *Incredible Era* (1939)

J. Braeman (Ed.), *Change and Continuity in Twentieth Century America: The 1920s* (1968)

J. D. Hicks, *Republican Ascendancy, 1921–1933* (1960)

J. H. Wilson, *Herbert Hoover: Forgotten Progressive* (1975)

The underlying problems are extensively explored in these two massive volumes that were initiated by Hoover:

Recent Economic Changes in the United States: Report of the Commission on Recent Economic Changes of the President's Conference on Unemployment (1929)

Recent Social Trends in the United States: Report of the President's Research Commission on Social Trends (1933)

These volumes are helpful in connection with particular political themes (see in particular Link's chapter on progressivism during the 1920s):

D. Burner, *The Politics of Provincialism: The Democratic Party in Transition, 1918–1932* (1968)

A. S. Link, *The Higher Realism* (1959)

K. C. MacKay, *The Progressive Movement of 1924* (1947)

D. R. McCoy, *Calvin Coolidge: The Quiet President* (1967)

B. Noggle, *Teapot Dome: Oil and Politics in the 1920s* (1962)

G. C. Zilg, *DuPont: Behind the Nylon Curtain* (1974)

There is no first-rate history of American foreign relations between 1920 and 1929, but these studies open the way to an understanding of those years:

D. Borg, *American Policy and the Chinese Revolution* (1968)

J. Brandes, *Herbert Hoover and Economic Diplomacy* (1962)

C. Chatfield, *For Peace and Justice* (1971)

B. Glad, *Charles Evans Hughes and the Illusion of Innocence* (1966)

A. Iriye, *After Imperialism: The Search for a New Order in the Far East, 1921–1931* (1965)

C. Lewis, *America's Stake in International Investments* (1938)

M. Tate, *The United States and Armaments* (1948)

J. H. Wilson, *American Business and Foreign Policy, 1920–1933* (1971)

B. Wood, *The Making of the Good Neighbor Policy* (1961)

12 STAGNATION AND BREAKDOWN

DESPITE the warning signs that appeared in 1926 and 1927, the threat of a serious economic downturn did not affect the election of 1928. Hoover and others were privately very concerned, however, about the continuing financial troubles in England and Germany, and they worried about such domestic developments as the continuing inflation, the overextension in capital goods, the collapse of the Florida real estate boom, and the persistent woes of agriculture. One shrewd observer of the economy, Congressman Cordell Hull of Tennessee, flatly predicted a major crisis unless there was a great expansion of foreign markets. Banker Paul M. Warburg repeatedly asked the FRB to curb speculation, and Dwight Morrow of the House of Morgan financed a campaign to persuade the Congress to put Hoover's 1921–1922 public works program on a standby basis.

The farmers were the only ones to have any significant political impact. They first threw their support to Frank O. Lowden of Illinois for the Republican nomination. His limits as a conservative-interest-group politician soon became apparent, however, and the agricultural bloc reluctantly accepted Hoover. He won the Republican nomination on the first ballot (with important help from Borah) and promised the farmers more government assistance. They were skeptical, even after Senator Charles Curtiss of Kansas, a one-time agrarian militant, was selected as vice-presidential candidate, and hence continued their lobbying during the Democratic convention.

The Democrats were in a paradoxical position. They were stronger in many states than they had been for years, but they lacked national leadership capable of creating an effective coalition that included agriculture. The increasing dominance within the party of the northern city machines from Chicago eastward to Boston was not in and of itself the cause of the trouble. The difficulty was that those centers had not produced any candidates to challenge Smith, and as a result he had become a quasi-untouchable symbol of urban strength within the party. Franklin Roosevelt made the point very neatly: the failure to nominate Smith, whatever his limits or weaknesses, "would alienate from the party for a long time a tremendous vote in the eastern and middle western states."

The Democrats were going through the same difficult process of building an alliance between the city and the country that the Republicans had successfully done during the 1890s. But the Democrats in 1928 had no strategic master like Blaine, and Smith lacked McKinley's ability to appeal to conflicting groups. Even so, the Democrats made a significant contribution to America's political maturation by nominating Smith, a man who challenged majority views on religion and secular mores.

But Smith never exploited the farm depression to overcome his handicaps as an urban spokesman, a Catholic, and a wet. He very probably would have lost the election in any event, but he made no sustained effort to induce the farmers, who as a group were Protestant and dry, to vote their pocketbooks instead of their traditions. Instead, he chose John J. Raskob of General Motors as his campaign manager and made it clear that he was not going to attack the corporations. That antagonized many workers despite their opposition to Prohibition.

Hoover ran a subtle and effective campaign. He ignored Smith personally (as well as his background and religion) and emphasized that he was not a Coolidge conservative. Hoover was not a charismatic figure, but his approach was effective over the radio, which was used extensively for the first time in a presidential election.

Smith's failure to woo the farmers was underscored by the election results, for his aides, who invested great amounts of money and energy in the Midwest, produced a significant increase in the Democratic vote in such states as North Dakota and Wisconsin (where the gain was almost 700 percent). Smith won majorities in the largest cities and might have won by giving more attention to agriculture. But Hoover carried 40 states and topped Smith by more than six million popular votes.

Hoover immediately dramatized his differences with Coolidge by embarking on a goodwill tour of Latin America. Through his personal manner, as well as in his speeches, he made it clear that he intended to terminate America's military interventions in Latin America and to initiate a far less bellicose policy. He was the originator, for example, of the phrase "Good Neighbor," and he developed the theme in the way it was later used by President Franklin Roosevelt and other New Deal spokesmen. Nor was it merely talk.

That became clear when Hoover selected Henry Stimson as secretary of state and when he bluntly referred in his inaugural address to the American troops still in Nicaragua and Haiti with the remark that "we do not wish to be represented abroad in such a manner." Hoover and Stimson accepted the arguments against earlier bellicosity and intervention advanced in 1928 by Under-Secretary of State J. Reuben Clark. Clark, a close friend of Senator Borah, had assisted Dwight Morrow during the latter's effective diplomacy in Mexico and returned impressed by the dangers of militant intervention and by the possibilities of accommodation. His *Memorandum on the Monroe Doctrine* attacked the use of the doctrine as a cloak for intervention and asserted that Theodore Roosevelt had gravely distorted the meaning and spirit of the original document. Defense, not expansion, was the only justification for intervention. Hoover (unlike Coolidge) published the *Memorandum* as part of his effort to settle differences "by the orderly processes of conciliation and arbitration."

Hoover's approach to foreign policy and his paradoxical actions during the depression can only be understood in terms of his broad analysis of American society. He knew more about the corporate system that had been created after 1892 than any other president—those before him as well as those who came later. His knowledge was that of the poor boy who gets to the top: detailed and extensive. Hoover did not like much of what he had seen and learned and was deeply concerned to control the corporate order and make it more equitable.

He revealed his reform outlook as early as 1909 when, in an important book on mining engineering, he devoted considerable space to a critique of the corporation. He may well have been influenced by Thorstein Veblen, but in any event, he wanted "to diminish the opportunity of the vulture so far as possible," and he viewed labor unions as the "normal and proper antidotes for unlimited capitalistic organization."

Hoover analyzed his own era as one of transition from "extremely individualistic action into a period of associational activities." Arguing that human beings were subjected to an inherent tension by the contrary pull of "the immutable human qualities" of "selfishness" and "altruism," he looked to education as a way of enlisting man's intelligence on the side of altruism. First in a series of speeches during 1921–1922 and then in a small book, *American Individualism* (1923), he outlined a broad program for Progressives.

"We have long since abandoned the laissez-faire of the eighteenth century," he explained, and then he warned that the real problem was to control the corporate system. He admitted the appeal of socialism but decided against it because the nationalization of all economic activity would create a tyranny. But he also opposed allowing the corporations to run free with the kind of liberty that individuals enjoyed under laissez-faire. That would produce "fascism," "where dominant private property is assembled in the hands of the groups who control the state."

Yet Hoover also feared the development of "a syndicalist nation on a gigantic scale," by which he meant a system in which highly organized interest groups—corporations, bankers, workers, farmers—used the government to help themselves and for punitive action against the other groups. Under that approach, the bureaucrats would gain enormous power beyond effective control by the citizen and the interest groups would increasingly "dominate legislators and intimidate public officials."

Hoover's solution to the dilemma was to view the government as "the umpire in our social system" rather than to allow it to become the tool of either the corporation (fascism), labor (socialism), or the interest groups (syndicalism). The way to maintain that delicate balance was to encourage private and public cooperation in order to solve the basic economic problems. That cooperation, of course, had to be guided by a concern for the general welfare and the common good.

He therefore found himself in the midst of a swirling intellectual and political struggle. On the one hand, he opposed corporation leaders like Gerard Swope who favored a political system controlled by the corporations. On the other hand, he argued against proposals that would turn the federal government into the dominant element in the political economy. He faced the same dilemma in foreign policy.

Hoover accepted the necessity of overseas economic expansion. The "export market becomes of peculiar importance to us in maintaining a stable and even operation of our domestic industries. It has an importance in that regard far beyond the percentage of our exports to our total production." But he also knew that market expansion had led to imperialism and wars in earlier years, and he was opposed to both for idealistic and pragmatic reasons.

His principles were religious (Quaker) and humanitarian; hence he actively wanted to help other people—as well as simply not hurt them. His practical point was simple: imperialism was self-defeating. "A large part of the rest of the world," he accurately observed in 1921, "has come to believe" that the United States was "a new imperial power intent upon dominating the destinies and freedoms of other people." He brought the two approaches together in his commitment to the principle of self-determination: "The American people cannot say that we are going to insist that any given population must work out its internal social problems according to our particular conception of democracy."

That enabled him to assert that "It ought not to be the policy of the United States to intervene by force to secure or maintain contracts between our citizens and foreign states or their citizens." "In stimulating our exports," he added, "we should be mainly interested in development work abroad such as roads and utilities which increase the standards of living of people and thus increase the demand for goods from every nation, for we gain in prosperity by a prosperous world [and] not by displacing others."

Hoover largely honored his principles in foreign policy, but he became a victim of his own perceptions in handling domestic affairs during the depression. Seeing all the dangers and fearing the consequences of all the options, he was ultimately overwhelmed. But the massive economic collapse that followed the stock market crash of October 29, 1929, would have checkmated any president. For in truth Franklin Roosevelt's New Deal did not revive the system. It recovered only through a global war against Germany, Italy, and Japan. And in the process a new America was created—a highly centralized form of corporate state capitalism that combined many of the features that Hoover had opposed so deeply.

Prior to the crash, Hoover tried in several ways to forestall a major deflation. First he warned the public about the dangers of continued speculation in the stock market, and then he tried to persuade Secretary Mellon, the leaders of the stock exchange, and the FRB to institute strong measures. Mellon agreed to push investments in bonds rather than stocks, but the exchange did little to control the manipulation of stocks. The Reserve Board responded more favorably, raising the rediscount rate to 6 percent by June, 1929, and refusing discounts to banks that were deeply involved in the dangerous stock market speculation.

The president also acted to help agriculture. Keeping his campaign promise to Senator Borah, he called the Congress into special session and specifically asked for higher tariffs on farm products and for a cooperative system to improve the marketplace position of agriculture. Farm leaders (such as those in the Grange) replied with a demand for export bounties. After defeating that proposal, along with the parity plan of McNary and Haugen, the administration offered its own legislation.

The Agricultural Marketing Act of June 15, 1929, was based on the proposition that indirect government assistance would enable the farmers, if they coordinated their own efforts in cooperatives, to improve their prices and incomes. It created the Federal Farm Board, in charge of a revolving fund of $500 million to be used in loans to cooperatives and authorized private corporations. Those organizations, each one dealing in a single commodity, were to be controlled by the voting membership. They could use the money to trade, store, or process the commodity in whatever way they thought best and most effective in controlling the surplus.

The board itself was assigned the responsibility of coordinating the activities of the various associations in a way that would raise all farm prices. Had it been passed in 1920 or 1921, Hoover's farm program might have developed the institutional strength required to produce significant improvements. It had no such chance in 1929. The National Grain Corporation came into existence on October 29, 1929, the day that 16 million shares of stock changed hands as the market value of 50 top firms dropped almost 40 points.

The effort to revise the tariff, which had begun hopefully under the moderate leadership of Congressman Willis C. Hawley of Oregon, turned into a brawl among those fighting to secure protection from the ravages of the depression. In the broader sense, Hoover never had an opportunity to translate his ideas into a coherent program.

The visceral impact of the depression is best revealed by individual experiences rather than by statistics. Paper money, for example, became highly suspect. New Yorkers used their large bills to buy commuter tickets to Newark and then redeemed the tickets in silver coin. A man tried to buy a razor and shaving cream with a $50 bill and was told to grow a beard. In Wisconsin, a wrestler was paid with a peck of potatoes and a can of tomatoes. A New York State politician took his own food to the legislative session—a side of pork and 12 dozen eggs. And in Illinois, a boy who had saved 11,357 pennies to help pay his way through college found his house surrounded by businessmen who demanded the hard money in return for bills.

Thousands of men, including businessmen who had failed, signed up for jobs in the Soviet Union. Others simply wandered away from their homes and families and were never seen or heard from again. The psychological pressure on marriages increased drastically (as did separations and divorces) as men abandoned their search for work, moved in with relatives or with their own children, and often lost all sense of purpose or of identity. There was a rapid rise in the diseases that feed on desperately weakened bodies. Many who survived did so only by eating roots, dandelions, and food scavenged from refuse piles. And in Iowa, one justice of the peace spent an entire day hearing and dismissing charges brought by a railroad against children and their parents who walked the right-of-way picking up bits of coal to heat their homes.

Such were the human realities behind the 50 percent decline in industrial production between 1929 and mid-1932, the thousands of business failures, and the steady progression of bank failures: 1352 in 1930, 2294 in 1931, and 1456 in 1932. Unemployment jumped from 1.8 million persons in 1929 to more than 4 million in 1930; and then, with a devastating shock, to more than 12 million in 1932. One of the clichés about the depression involves people selling apples on street corners. But those were the fortunate ones. Thousands were squatting by fires in hobo camps, struggling as much to hang on to their self-respect as to find a bit of food and warmth.

Banker Frank A. Vanderlip bluntly described the highly skewed economy: "Capital kept too much and labor did not have enough to buy its share." That truth was dramatized even as the stock market raced toward the precipice. The National Textile Workers Union, led by militant radicals, including Communists, staged a major strike in Gastonia, North Carolina, in April, 1929, in an effort to win better wages. It failed after seven Communists were convicted on a second-degree murder charge in the death of the chief of police. A similar strike in Marion, North Carolina, also ended in violence when a sheriff's posse murdered five pickets.

Hoover first called numerous conferences to secure the kind of cooperation and self-regulation that he preferred. On November 21, for example, he spoke bluntly with Henry Ford, Walter Teagle of Standard Oil, Owen D. Young of General Electric, and Pierre du Pont. Warning them that "labor was not a commodity, it represented human homes," he urgently pressured the corporations to maintain their investment programs and to refrain from cutting wages. He also reactivated his old plans for public works and won increased appropriations to build roads, dams, and public buildings, and for river and harbor improvements.

Seeking to free capital for investment and consumption, the president then recommended a tax cut. That came quickly (by mid-December), but it unfortunately did not induce a construction boom. He was no more successful in his attempt to help the farmers. In response to Hoover's request, the Congress provided an extra $100 million to help the Farm Board purchase more commodities. He also acted promptly to provide relief to the victims of the severe drought that hit the lower Mississippi Valley and neighboring states. But the Farm Board's efforts to sustain prices proved unsuccessful because it lacked enough funds and because the farmers refused to cut their production. Then came the tariff fiasco. The crash turned the tariff debates into a wild orgy among protectionists, and the average rate was kicked up to 40 percent.

Although the reaction against the tariff debacle contributed to

Hoover's troubles in the midterm election of 1930, his principal difficulties stemmed from the continuing decline of the economy and the
increased effectiveness of the Democrats. Guided by Charles Michel-
son, an astute publicity man, the Democrats organized a sustained
attack on Hoover. The president was blamed for the depression,
damned as an enemy of labor and the farmer, vilified as cruel and
heartless for not providing more relief, and—where it was useful—
cursed for being responsible for a man being unable to buy a drink to
drown his sorrows. The Republicans lost control of the Congress to the
reformers of both parties in the Senate and to the Democrats in the
House (220 to 214).

*In spite of statements that were intended to promote patience and maintain
confidence in the economy, the depression worsened. Proposals seemed to call
for an advance in all directions. Jerry Doyle of the Philadelphia* Record *cartooned Hoover's policies and leadership as out of phase with the Congress.*

Kidding Himself

——Doyle in the Philadelphia "Record."

Reprinted in *The Literary Digest*, vol. 106, July 19, 1930, p. 6.

HOOVER ATTACKS THE DEPRESSION

The pressure from the Democrats and the insurgent Republicans undoubtedly played a part in Hoover's renewed efforts to counter the depression. But other factors were more important. The president proved willing to take further action on his own when it became clear that the economy was not improving, asking in December, 1930, for another public works appropriation of $150 million. The president was also affected by the rising militance of labor unions. The UTWA strike at Danville, Virginia, in the fall of 1930 was defeated, but it seemed to be a clear indicator of future trouble. So did the manifesto of the AF of L, which demanded "a federal labor board."

Hoover did provide considerable help for agriculture after the drought of 1930. The Federal Land Banks were given an extra $125 million to underwrite recovery, new road programs were undertaken, and $45 million was appropriated as direct relief. Perhaps even more important, the surplus food supplies of the Farm Board were tapped: the Red Cross distributed 85 million bushels of wheat and 844,000 bales of cotton to needy families. The farmers might have won even more if they had been able to agree on one program, but they continued to bicker among themselves over the McNary-Haugen approach, the export subsidy plan, and other proposals to restrict production.

The veterans of World War I were far more effectively united behind their demands. They wanted the government to loan them 50 percent of the bonus that had been authorized by earlier legislation. That plan won quick approval in Congress after the election of 1930, but Hoover vetoed the bill on February 26, 1931. The Congress promptly overrode his action on the next day, and the law created a small, limited, and selective relief program. One of the main reasons that Hoover vetoed the proposal was that signs of recovery had appeared in January, 1931: the decline in retail sales was halted, for example, and textile production turned upward. The president was even more encouraged by the rise in exports and by the surprising strength of investments in building branch factories. During March and April, moreover, the indices of production, employment, and payrolls showed steady strength.

The cautious optimism engendered by those improvements was demolished by the collapse of the European economy. French bankers put heavy economic (and political) pressure on Germany and Austria by demanding immediate payment of extensive short-term loans. British advances postponed the crisis for more than a month, but the largest Austrian bank went under on May 11, 1931, and the economy of Central Europe seemed doomed.

Hoover countered on June 20 by proposing a one-year moratorium on all international governmental debts (including reparations). The French stalled, and Germany sank deeper into the morass. Then, after agreeing to the moratorium, French bankers began to withdraw their large gold deposits from British banks. With help from the United States, the Bank of England survived until September 21, 1931, when it defaulted on gold payments.

Those events rocked the American economy. American financiers had to demand payment on their domestic loans to meet the withdrawals by Europeans, and the loss of capital for domestic investment was intensified as Europeans liquidated their stocks and other securities. The European depression also drastically cut the market for American industrial and agricultural exports. That further lowered production and employment. The result was another panic. The stock market sank, and depositors began to withdraw their money from banks. Wheat slumped from 68.1 cents to 39.1 cents a bushel, and cotton dropped from 9.5 cents to 5.7 cents a pound.

The atmosphere of failure and fear was intensified by the concurrent crisis in the Far East. That eruption of violence was particularly jarring because of the seeming success of the London Naval Conference of 1930, during which the United States and Great Britain had agreed to allow Japan to improve its strength in all secondary ships of the line except cruisers. Parity in submarines was accepted and, continuing the pattern established by Secretary Hughes in 1922, the three nations agreed to scrap some capital ships.

The world was stunned on September 18, 1932, therefore, when Japan attacked Chinese forces at Mukden, Manchuria. The Japanese army rapidly moved to occupy the entire province. Secretary of State Stimson initially hoped that the moderate Japanese leaders would force the militarists to begin "crawling back into their dens," but he changed his mind on October 8, when the Japanese bombed southern Manchuria. "I am afraid," he noted in his diary, "we have got to take a firm ground and aggressive stand toward Japan." The president, however, had no intention of running a bluff or of going to war.

As the Japanese continued their assault, taking Chinchow and completing their victory on January 3, 1932, Stimson argued for a public stand against the conquest. Hoover agreed "to take that risk," and the United States formally told Japan on January 7 "that it cannot admit the legality of any situation de facto nor does it intend to recognize any treaty or agreement . . . which may impair the treaty rights of the United States or . . . the Open Door policy." The American action did not deter Japan from attacking Shanghai on January 29, 1932, however, and Stimson advocated stronger action.

Like many Progressives, Stimson was a vigorous advocate of defending and extending what he called "the traditional and standard American doctrine toward China of the Open Door." He thought Hoover lacked the proper "appreciation" of that policy and "had a set-to" with the president over the wisdom of strong action. Hoover remained adamant: he would not risk war.

In the president's view, the armed forces had one purpose: to guarantee "that no foreign soldier will land on American soil." Japan's actions were of course "immoral," but "the United States has never set out to preserve peace among other nations by force." Those "acts do not imperil the freedom of the American people, the economic or moral future of our people. I do not propose ever to sacrifice American life for anything short of this." And, finally, to intervene "would excite the suspicions of the whole world."

Neither was the president ready to follow Senator Borah's suggestion to bring pressure on Japan by recognizing the Soviet Union. He had opposed recognition in 1917–1918, and, though he had helped organize a food relief program during the Russian famine of the 1920s, he had continued to resist such a routine accommodation. A combination of reformers and businessmen, led by Raymond Robins, Alexander Gumberg, and Borah, had created considerable pressure for recognition, however, and in the end—with the help of the depression—they pushed Hoover very close to de facto recognition.

That occurred as part of Hoover's last big push to generate recovery. He was not only challenged by the renewed downward course of the economy but by alternative courses of action vigorously advocated by several individuals and groups. The most directly political competitor was Franklin Roosevelt, governor of New York. Though crippled by polio, he had emerged as a charismatic and energetic figure and as a pragmatic reformer. When it became clear by the end of the summer of 1931, for example, that the economy had again turned downward, Roosevelt established the New York State Temporary Emergency Relief Administration (September, 1931). And his obvious ambition to win the Democratic presidential nomination dramatized the need for Hoover to act more decisively.

By the time Roosevelt acted on relief, historian Charles A. Beard had offered a broad plan calling for changes in the structure of the political economy. It was an ironic moment for Beard and his collaborator (and wife) Mary: they had published in 1927 a majestic history of the country called *The Rise of American Civilization,* and then four years later they were taking a cue from the Soviet Union in order to deal with the seeming collapse of American civilization.

Beard's proposal that appeared in the July, 1931, issue of *Forum,* "A 'Five Year Plan' for America," did not advocate socialism or communism. But it did indicate how the depression and the Soviet approach had strengthened the corporate wing of the Progressive coalition originally led by Brooks Adams, Mark Hanna, Herbert Croly, and Theodore Roosevelt. Beard called for the government to rationalize and direct the political economy based on large corporations. That view soon came to be called "liberal" rather than "progressive," but it represented the triumph and fulfillment of one of the major themes of Progressive thinking as it developed prior to World War I.

Beard began by arguing that the modern American economy was based on technology and that technology had an inner logic and momentum that was "rational and planful." Planning was therefore necessary: it was "hazardous" because of its inherent tendency to create a centralized power structure, but it "must be faced." Dismissing antitrust prosecutions and radical confiscation of private property as equally futile and harmful, he proposed a syndicalist-corporate organization of the economy under a national economic council. Beard broke with the classic Progressive drive for overseas economic markets, however, on the grounds that it led to intervention and war.

His program pointed toward the kind of syndicalist bureaucracy that Hoover considered destructive of freedom and democracy. But the proposal advanced by Swope in September was even more disturbing: he advocated the organization and control of the economy by trade associations dominated by the large corporations. Developed with the assistance of Owen D. Young and Newton Baker, the program also called for a national workmen's compensation act and a system of insurance, pension, disability, and unemployment benefits enforced by the trade associations.

The Swope plan was supported by such men as Henry I. Harriman and Silas Strawn of the Chamber of Commerce, William W. Atterbury of the Pennsylvania Railroad, and Nicholas M. Butler, president of Columbia University. Even Leo Wolman, then an economist at Columbia who later became a vigorous New Dealer, thought it was "constructive." Hoover was appalled. Swope had not only failed to offer any proposals to help agriculture, but the plan was "the most gigantic proposal of monopoly ever made in this country"—"sheer fascism and merely a remaking of Mussolini's corporate state."

Hoover counterattacked in August, 1931, when he established the Presidential Unemployment Relief Organization to strengthen and coordinate local and state efforts. Then, on October 4, he initiated a series of high-level and high-pressure conferences with top economic leaders. His objective was to create a credit pool of at least $500 million to stimulate the economy and to obtain a commitment to halt the foreclosure of mortgages by life insurance companies. The response was poor. As for the Democrats, most of them were busy hustling votes for the 1932 elections. One old-time Progressive, Senator Hiram Johnson, was so disgusted with the failure of the Democrats that he called them "the weak and timid echo of the Republican party." His point was established when the Congress spurned Hoover's request for a strengthened, centralized Public Works Administration (PWA).

Hoover then proposed on December 8, 1931, to create a government lending agency to underwrite the recovery of banks and railroads. That would in turn produce an upswing in industry and agriculture. The Congress promptly passed legislation establishing the Reconstruction Finance Corporation (RFC) with an authorization to borrow up to $2 billion. The agency quickly loaned $1 billion to agricultural credit corporations, banks, and life insurance companies and also financed large cotton exports to Russia.

A related measure, the Glass-Steagall Act, authorized about $750 million for similar actions by modifying the rules of the Federal Reserve System. Next came a pro-labor act sponsored by Senator Norris and Democratic Congressman LaGuardia. Their Anti-Injunction Act of March 23 outlawed actions by the courts designed to prevent boycotts, picketing, or strikes or to support antiunion employment policies and practices. Then came a struggle over relief, which increasingly became the focus of the attack on Hoover.

Senator Wagner of New York and Congressman John N. Garner of Texas pushed through a bill to further relief activities by extending the federal employment service, but Hoover vetoed it on July 11, arguing that it would weaken state and local efforts to meet the unemployment problem. The president then offered a counterproposal to enlarge the activities of the Reconstruction Finance Corporation. That legislation, known as the Relief and Construction Act of July 21, 1932, empowered the RFC to loan money to state and local governments for public works and to supply as much as $300 million in emergency aid to finance state relief programs. The law also provided more aid to agriculture.

The Congress next passed another measure that had first been recommended by the president in December, 1931. The Federal Home Loan Act of July 22, 1932, was designed to reduce foreclosures and to stimulate new construction (and home ownership) by providing loans through regional banks to be established and controlled by the Home Loan Bank Board.

Though it was not apparent at the time, Hoover had initiated most of the measures that would come to be known as Franklin Roosevelt's New Deal. But he refused to take the last steps into the kind of corporate state capitalism that he feared would destroy democracy. That doomed him politically and for many years made him the patsy for the massive failure of corporate capitalism. If there had been a strong Socialist movement in 1931–1932, its challenge to Hoover would have been dramatic and potentially the most creative confrontation in

American history. But there was no such Socialist movement, and the Communists were even weaker.

That left it open for the Democrats. They were still divided: not only was Smith embittered by the rise of Roosevelt but Garner had much southern support. And Huey Long of Louisiana attracted many reform votes. But Long stuck with Roosevelt, and the dramatic New Yorker (aided by astute associates like Louis Howe and James A. Farley) won the nomination on the fourth ballot. He dramatized his victory by flying to the Chicago convention to make his acceptance speech and by pledging "a new deal for the American people."

The campaign was more than a bit like *Alice in Wonderland.* On any given morning, for example, farmers might dump milk along the highway in the forlorn hope of raising prices or take their shotguns to a sheriff's auction to redeem a friend's farm for a dime, but in the afternoon they would be down at the railroad station cheering Roosevelt's mundane remarks delivered from the observation platform of his private train. Hoover opposed a general relief program for a country with 13 million unemployed workers on the ground that it would lead to tyranny. Roosevelt promised massive emergency aid *and* a balanced budget.

Hoover refused to intervene against a developing revolution in Cuba but then allowed an ambitious general to stage a battle in Washington against poor, unemployed, and desperate veterans. Roosevelt talked about the end of the frontier and then militantly asserted the need and responsibility to help China against Japan. Everyone seemed to be running faster and faster in order to stay in the same place.

From the outset, Hoover was on the defensive. Three years of pain and hunger and trauma do not reelect a president. But if he had any chance to fill an inside straight, he lost it by not controlling General Douglas MacArthur. The general, an arrogant man who referred to himself in the third person, clearly enjoyed his power as chief of staff and was contemptuous of the ragged group of veterans who came to Washington to demand another bonus payment.

When ordered to restore order after an encounter between the veterans and police, he mustered an imposing force of cavalry, infantry with fixed bayonets, machine guns, and tear gas against people living in a shantytown. MacArthur won the battle and lost the war. The veterans were dispersed, a baby killed, and the shanties burned. The veterans straggled home and voted for Roosevelt.

Hoover made several impressive and moving speeches near the end of the campaign, but the Democrats had effectively blackened his reputation by presenting him to the public as a bumbler personally responsible for the depression and as a callous millionaire indifferent to the suffering of the poor. That enabled Roosevelt, an upper-class charmer with a sense of noblesse oblige, to promise many things to many people: a balanced budget and massive relief, and reforms that would save corporate capitalism even as they helped the farmer and the workers. Most citizens had been so passive for so long (no serious, sustained unrest or radical ferment for three years of increasingly desperate depression) that they responded to a man who promised to "do something—anything." Roosevelt won by 22.8 million votes to 15.8 million votes, and the Democrats dominated the congressional elections (60 seats to 35 in the Senate, and 310 to 117 in the House).

There were some signs, through the summer and fall of 1932, that led a few observers to predict serious social unrest. Farmers in Nebraska bluntly warned the state legislature to act promptly or they would "tear that new state capitol building to pieces." Miners in Wyoming occupied company property, sank their own shafts, and began to market the ore on a cooperative basis. Fearing violence if they did not act, the authorities in Minnesota halted all mortgage foreclosures. And various politicians came to share the feeling of conservative Senator Theodore Bilbo of Mississippi that the country was becoming "restless."

But that was as far as it went. The editors of the ILGWU periodical, *Justice,* were closer to the mark: "We are just sodden with panic, cloggy with doom." In what was probably their most serious domestic crisis since the Civil War, the American people damned the bankers instead of mounting a national campaign for reform or revolution.

The downward plunge continued through the winter of 1932–1933. The financial system staggered through the crisis in October, 1932, but the closing of Detroit banks in February, 1933, triggered a national panic. By March 4, when Franklin Roosevelt took the oath of office, 38 states had been forced to declare bank holidays. And on the morning of the inauguration, the New York Stock Exchange and the Chicago Board of Trade closed their doors.

EXPLORATORY READING

The best way to understand the human side of the depression is to listen to the members of your family (and their friends) who endured and survived the suffering, pain, and fear of that desperate time. Most of them will romanticize it a bit, but if you ask tough questions in a gentle and friendly way, you will learn how truly terrible it was for almost everyone.

Then read the newspapers and magazines of those years—and do not skip the classified advertisements, which reveal far more than most historians have recognized. As for the raw politics of those years, start with the records of the Congress. And not just the *Record.* Read the hearings before the various committees.

An excellent guide to further sources, and a fine book in its own right, is:

D. A. Shannon (Ed.), *The Great Depression* (1960)

On the economics of the crash, consult these volumes:

J. Brooks, *Once in Golconda: A True Drama of Wall Street* (1969)

L. V. Chandler, *America's Greatest Depression* (1970)

S. Chase, *Prosperity: Fact or Myth* (1929)

B. Mitchell, *Depression Decade* (1947)

The most stimulating way to learn about Hoover is to read Hoover and the contemporary record of his various ideas and proposals. But in addition to the volume by Wilson mentioned at the end of the previous chapter, it is helpful to read the following:

H. G. Warren, *Herbert Hoover and the Great Depression* (1959)

W. A. Williams, *The Contours of American History* (1961); and *Some Presidents: From Wilson to Nixon* (1972)

Political and social developments are reviewed and occasionally interpreted in a stimulating fashion by these writers:

E. A. Moore, *A Catholic Runs for President: The Campaign of 1928* (1968)

A. M. Schlesinger, Jr., *The Crisis of the Old Order, 1919–1933* (1957)

J. Shover, *Cornbelt Rebellion* (1965)

R. C. Silva, *Rum, Religion, and Votes: 1928 Re-examined* (1962)

D. Wecter, *The Age of the Great Depression* (1948)

13 RELIEF, REFORM, AND THE EMERGENCE OF CORPORATE STATE CAPITALISM

"I don't know about this Roosevelt," a mine worker observed during the campaign of 1932. "His heart seems to be in the right place as far as labor is concerned. But he has two dangerous hobbies—battleships and big dams." It was a perceptive and insightful remark. Roosevelt was an upstate New York aristocrat with an honest (if limited) sense of noblesse oblige: he did care about the poor, and he was willing—when pushed—to provide more equity for workers and farmers. But he was not particularly concerned about women, blacks, or other minority groups, and his hobbies, as the miner called them, provided greater benefits for the corporations than for the workers.

The president's greatest contribution to American society was to restore the nation's faith in itself and in its ability to cope with its many troubles and weaknesses. His strong personality (and great élan) infused millions of people with hope and trust and made them believe in a better tomorrow despite the dreariness and hardships of the present. And he could persuade, wheedle, and force men of vastly different outlooks and temperaments into a working partnership to save the country from total collapse.

One of countless stories about him catches the magic of the man. During a reunion at Harvard after he was elected, Roosevelt had a candid private talk with a group of classmates and other alumni who feared that he was going to destroy the system even as he tried to save and rationalize it. His candor, charm, and persuasiveness won the respect of all, and even the support of many, who were present. But the clincher was the remark of one who remained staunchly conservative: "If the son of a bitch had talked another 15 minutes, he'd have had me voting for him, too!"

A sentence from his 1932 inaugural speech reveals his strengths and weaknesses. "The only thing we have to fear," he cried, "is fear itself." That half-truth rallied a depressed and frightened people, but it was a poor substitute for the ideas and programs required to create a social movement that would honor *all* Americans and help them to create a community of equals. He revealed his true colors by moving first to save the banks.

He could have nationalized the financial and monetary systems, but after declaring a bank holiday, he sent the Congress a bill written by financiers such as George Hamilton and Treasury Department officials. Passed the same day it was introduced, the law delegated broad powers to the president to control currency, gold, silver, credit, and foreign exchange. Its purpose, which was to underwrite the existing financial system, provoked a bitter protest from William Lemke, a left-wing farm leader. "The president drove the money changers out of the Capitol on March 4—and they were all back on the ninth." But most people were relieved by the revival of the banking system. Almost 75 percent of the FRS banks promptly reopened, and the stock market enjoyed a modest upturn.

The Beer and Wine Revenue Act of March 22 provided a psychic lift. It amended the Volstead Act to legalize 3.2 percent beer, ale, and wine (by weight); placed a tax of $5 per barrel on the products; and delegated most of the enforcement problems to the states. The constitutional action to repeal Prohibition, which was proposed on February 20, 1933, was completed on December 5 with the ratification of the Twenty-first Amendment.

Then came two important measures that combined relief with broader objectives. The first was the Civilian Conservation Corps Reforestation Relief Act of March 31, 1933. The president was interested in conservation, but his initial proposal did not envisage vast public expenditures to create jobs for the unemployed. Administration leaders like Secretary of Labor Frances Perkins and White House adviser Harry Hopkins, along with western senators like Robert LaFollette, were responsible for broadening the program. As in many instances throughout the history of the New Deal, pressure from congressional and other spokesmen forced or persuaded Roosevelt to liberalize his originally conservative attitudes and policies.

In the case of the Civilian Conservation Corps (CCC), that influence first created a program to provide work for 250,000 men between the ages of 18 and 25. Work camps under the general authority of the army

*The whirlwind of social legislation during the New Deal's "First 100 Days"
sent Ding Darling of the* New York Herald Tribune *to his drawing board to
show that FDR had taken Uncle Sam from a home of rugged individualism,
based upon a morality of Prohibition and the gold standard, to a questionable
future of socialization and government regulation.*

Reprinted in the *Review of Reviews*, vol. LXXXVIII, July, 1933, p. 47.

were established to undertake projects in flood control, soil erosion, road construction, reforestation, and the improvement of national parks. The pay was $30 a month, with allotments sent to dependents. By the time it was terminated (in 1941) more than two million men had been employed. On balance, it was the most creative and productive relief project undertaken by the New Deal (and a classic example of how the army could be used for peaceful purposes).

The second major relief bill (May 12) created the Federal Emergency Relief Administration with an initial fund of $500 million; half went directly to the states, and the rest was assigned on the basis of one dollar of federal money for three dollars appropriated by a state. Roosevelt appointed Harry Hopkins to run the program. Hopkins was an Iowa-born New York social worker who looked like a cagey race-track tout and who was in action a shrewd, effective administrative politician. He soon became one of the president's most intimate advisers. His style of operation was revealed by his first move after being appointed. He left the White House, went to work at a desk in the halls of the RFC, and spent $5 million in the first two hours.

Roosevelt shortly installed a man of a vastly different background, but of equal verve, as head of the RFC. Jesse H. Jones, a Texas banker and general entrepreneur, handled that agency as if it were a frontier land-and-oil-boom office. It became the biggest bank and the largest single investor in the national economy. He also created a vast network of subsidiary agencies extending from the Export-Import Bank to federal home mortgage agencies, and from the Commodity Credit Corporation to the Electric Home and Farm Authority. As a result, the RFC played a central role in helping to sustain the corporations with government funds that came from the pocketbooks of the ordinary citizens, who also supported the corporations whenever they purchased their products in the store.

Many farmers were shrewd enough to perceive the inequitable nature of that program, and their anger carried them to the edge of open revolt. Spurred on by Milo Reno, the militant leader of the Iowa Farmer's Union, they formed the Farmers' Holiday Association and set May 13 as the date for a national strike. The Roosevelt administration had not been indifferent to agriculture, but it had not developed a consensus about the most effective policy. Secretary of Agriculture Henry A. Wallace of Iowa leaned most heavily on a group of advisers, headed by Milburn L. Wilson of Montana State College, who favored a system of restricted production to raise prices. But another group stressed export markets; and still others, who steadily gained support through March, wanted an inflationary policy based on the free coinage of silver.

Amid the currents of controversy that circled around the New Deal, the Civilian Conservation Corps steadily increased its popularity. Reg Manning of the Phoenix Arizona Republic *presented the three "Cs" towering over the wreckage created by the Supreme Court with its invalidation of the NRA and the AAA.*

By Manning, in the Phoenix *Arizona Republic*

Reg Manning in the *Arizona Republic*. Reprinted in the *Review of Reviews*, vol. 93, February, 1936, p. 42.

Roosevelt was warned that he would have to compromise, and he did so with abandon, accepting the remonetization of silver and the use of greenbacks, and announcing on April 19 that the country had gone off the gold standard. The final agricultural legislative proposal was a hodgepodge that accurately reflected the crosscurrents of the time. Known as the Agricultural Adjustment Act (AAA), it was rushed through on May 12 in an obvious effort to forestall the threatened strike.

The AAA was based on three principles: parity prices, federal subsidies, and expanded credit. The years 1909–1914 were taken as the base for prices of corn, wheat, hogs, cotton, rice, and dairy products; and the years 1919–1929, for tobacco. The farmers were paid for reducing their plantings from taxes collected from processors. And credit for refinancing mortgages was extended through the Land Banks.

The AAA began infamously when it financed the destruction of ten million acres of cotton and the slaughter of some seven million pigs. The public outrage lasted for decades—people *were hungry and cold*—but the law proved moderately effective after several modifications. One of those came in the Farm Credit Act of June 16, 1933, which followed the earlier (March 27) consolidation of all rural credit agencies. It provided low-interest, long-term loans for mortgages, and within 18 months at least 20 percent of all farm mortgages were refinanced in that manner. The Commodity Credit Corporation was created on October 18, and the loans it extended against crops helped to raise cotton prices by avoiding a glut on the market.

Many southern farmers also ultimately benefited from the operations of the Tennessee Valley Authority (TVA). Roosevelt's experience in enlarging the New York State planning measures instituted by Charles E. Hughes prior to World War I led him to expand Senator Norris's idea of operating the Muscle Shoals power complex. The president wanted a vast program to handle flood control, soil erosion, land reclamation, and to encourage the diversification of the region's entire economy.

The TVA was created by a law of May 18, 1933, as a public corporation. David E. Lilienthal became the driving force of the transformation of the Tennessee Valley region, including parts of seven states from North Carolina to Mississippi and from Georgia to Kentucky. Empowered to build and operate power dams, the TVA electrified the region as well as produced nitrogen fertilizer and explosives. The law also provided that its operations would serve as a guide for judging and regulating other utilities in the production and transmission of electric power. In many ways, the TVA was the most significant innovation of the New Deal; it was a program that generated long-range structural improvements in a significant part of the American political economy.

After the passage of the TVA legislation, the Roosevelt administration turned back to financial problems. The Federal Securities Act of May 27, 1933, provided for the regulation of new public securities issues by compelling full disclosure of all relevant data through registration with the FTC. Then came the Banking Act of June 16, which guaranteed individual bank deposits up to $5000 and separated deposit banks from investment houses. It also strengthened the power of the FRB to control speculation and allowed savings and industrial banks to enter the system.

Along the way, the Congress created (June 6) a national employment system that linked federal and state agencies. It then expanded Hoover's effort to help homeowners. The Home Owners Refinancing Act of June 13 created a federal corporation with capital exceeding $2 billion to underwrite urban home mortgages (and advance cash for taxes, repairs, and maintenance).

The Emergency Railroad Transportation Act of June 16 was the first move to deal directly with the industrial side of the economy. It was designed to end unnecessary duplication of services, to simplify supervision of the companies, and to encourage financial reorganization. The ICC won authority over railroad holding companies, and a new office, the Federal Coordinator of Transportation, was created to supervise the operation of the law and to initiate studies for future improvements.

Four factors explain the failure of the Roosevelt administration to produce basic recovery legislation for industry prior to the National Industrial Recovery Act of June 16, 1933. The first was the necessity of providing relief. The second was the strong public feeling against the financiers, which led the president and others to concentrate their attention in that area. The third was the pragmatic and political need to help agriculture. And the fourth was the lack of any consensus on what to do to help industry beyond enlarging the operations of the RFC.

Senator Wagner, financier Paul Warburg, and Raymond Moley (a member of that group of Roosevelt advisers known as the brain trust) tried to induce Roosevelt to act more quickly, but he refused. Typifying its initiative and pressure during the period, the Congress moved to make policy. The Senate passed the Black Bill, which called for a 30-hour week. Firmly opposed to that approach, Roosevelt responded with a proposal more in keeping with his own experience with the trade association movement of the 1920s (when he had worked with Hoover) and with his own desire to develop "cooperation with business."

The ensuing legislation (as well as the president's organization of the Business Advisory Council, a permanent liaison group between government and business) was the result of several factors. One was the general weakening of the antitrust movement in the face of the depression and the ongoing consolidation of the economy by the large corporations. Another was the pressure from labor union leaders like John L. Lewis and Sidney Hillman. Lewis wanted "to organize and stabilize the coal operators themselves and the industry" as part of strengthening the union. He also favored "a national economic council" with the authority to regulate production and to guarantee "workers the right to organize and bargain collectively." Hillman agreed, calling for "the substitution of plan and system for chaos, disorder, and social irresponsibility."

A third influence was exerted by a group of industrial leaders like Gerard Swope of General Electric. And, finally, administration spokesmen like Rexford Tugwell and Secretary of Labor Perkins favored a system based on the "obligation and duties of one group to the other group and to the common good." Matthew Woll of the AF of L was basically accurate in describing the resulting system as one that

Observers around the world watched FDR's efforts to lessen the impact of the depression. The Daily Express *in London carried this cartoon with Roosevelt steering the vehicle of Recovery along difficult pathways. He admits to Uncle Sam and the Congress that he is a stranger at the wheel and that he has no knowledge of the brakes.*

ROOSEVELT (on Prosperity Drive): "Strong brakes?
I can't say, Sam, I've never driven this car before."

Reprinted in the *Review of Reviews*, vol. LXXXVIII, October, 1933, p. 45.

"borders closely upon the corporate or syndicalist form of organization characterized by fascism in Italy."

The National Industrial Recovery Administration (NRA), brought into being on June 16, was based on the principle of self-regulation by industry armed with government authority. Each industry was granted wide powers to establish its own rules. When those arrangements were approved by the NRA, often after long bargaining sessions, the resulting code became enforceable by law and the companies were exempt from prosecution under antitrust legislation. Labor won, in Section 7-A of the law, recognition of the right of workers "to organize and bargain collectively through representatives of their own choosing." And, to reinforce industry's own power to act once it had structured the marketplace through the codes, the law provided for government investment through the PWA. That agency was funded at $3 billion to finance the construction of roads, buildings, and other large public facilities.

THE NEW DEAL STRENGTHENS THE TIES BETWEEN GOVERNMENT AND LARGE CORPORATIONS

The legislation of the first three months made it clear that the centralizing, rationalizing, regulative, and corporate strand of thought that had always been strong among Progressives had become the basis of the new liberalism. From the outset, the New Deal strengthened the convergence and coordination between the government and the large corporations. Whatever the rhetoric of liberalism, the substance of the political economy was a corporate state capitalism increasingly financed by the taxpayer and controlled by a bureaucratic and political elite drawn from the upper class.

Old-line conservatives like the Du Ponts, along with the noncorporate Progressives like Smith and Borah, fought a long, often embittered, and sometimes effective rearguard action against the new system. But the primary and consequential conflicts—political, economic, and social—occurred within the new framework and involved the basic issues of equity and participation for the weaker elements of the corporate order. The NRA was too poorly conceived and too formalistic to be effective in the throes of a devastating depression (and was shortly abandoned), but it opened the way for labor to launch a major campaign for greater influence within the corporate order.

Labor leaders generally interpreted Section 7-A of the NRA legislation to mean that industry was required to engage in direct collective bargaining. That view was not shared by President Roosevelt and many corporation executives, however, and new unions often collapsed due to opposition from management and from their own poor organization. But there were important gains, one of which involved the mine workers and the emergence of John L. Lewis as national leader.

Lewis invested the last of the UMWs' treasury in a massive organizational drive in the summer of 1933, and within a year he had increased membership from 150,000 to 500,000. Ship workers in New Jersey scored a similar success, as did James Carey at Philco Radio. Organizing behind the façade of a social club, Carey took over the company union and then won a closed-shop agreement and a sizable wage increase.

The union struggle for parity with the corporation was aided by the code of administrative law that the National Labor Board developed under the chairmanship of Senator Robert Wagner. Supported by Francis Biddle, an upper-class financial leader from Philadelphia, and Lloyd Garrison of the University of Wisconsin Law School, Wagner established two basic principles: union elections would be secret, and the vote of the majority would determine which union would be certified to negotiate for all workers in the given plant.

The full impact of those decisions came later. In the meantime, during the spring of 1934, Minnesota workers supplied leadership for the rising labor unrest. Much of the trouble centered in Minneapolis, where in April a group of 6000 workers attacked city hall with lumps of coal and other missiles to emphasize their demands for work at a decent wage (or more relief). Then come one of the nation's most important—and bloody—strikes, by Minneapolis truck drivers. Despite continued opposition by the police and deputized townspeople, who shot more than 50 workers in one episode, the union finally won the union shop and wage benefits.

By the summer of 1934, the nation was rocked with strikes. West Coast stevedores closed ports from San Diego to Vancouver, and their determined show of strength finally provoked the shippers to try to open the docks of San Francisco. Behind the leadership of Harry Bridges, a tough, honest, and extremely capable radical, the unions united in a general strike that shut down the city in July and won recognition for the union. Then textile workers walked out on Labor Day and closed the entire industry for three weeks. But the owners, retaliating with violence all along the East Coast mill strip, finally won a costly victory.

Another general strike occurred in Terre Haute, Indiana; and the cabdrivers in Philadelphia and New York burned cars in the course of their militant demonstrations. Similar violence erupted during the strike of streetcar workers in Milwaukee. The electricians in Iowa began their walkout by pulling the master lighting switch in Des

Moines. Similar militance was displayed by the workers in the copper mines of Montana. And one of the most bitter confrontations came in Toledo, Ohio, where radicals A. J. Muste and Louis Budenz led a strike at the Electric Auto-Lite plant. They faced tear gas, bayonets, and bullets, but held on and won most of their demands.

The strength and openly radical nature of much of the labor activity during 1934 encouraged John L. Lewis and other union leaders to challenge William Green for control of the AF of L. Lewis was by no means as radical as men like Bridges or Muste, but he was far more aggressive and effective than Green. In less than a year, AF of L leaders lost 94 percent of the steelworkers they had recruited as union members. Lewis did not win in 1934, but he laid the foundation for later victory, and he left no doubt that labor would make extensive demands on Roosevelt.

Farm labor was far less organized and effective. Southern share-croppers and tenants, black and white, along with the Mexican-American migratory workers who harvested crops from Ohio to California, were not helped by the AAA. The landlords in the South and the owner-operators in other regions used the AAA codes against those people, and many administrators were almost as unsympathetic and unhelpful. The southerners, led by Socialists, were the first to organize. A group in Arkansas formed the Southern Tenant Farmers' Union in July, 1934, and were immediately met by a campaign of landlord terrorism that included murder as well as flogging and trumped-up jail sentences.

Northern farm businessmen, though white and at least pseudo-owners of their land, also moved to the left. Governors Floyd Olsen of Minnesota and Reno of Iowa, for example, were impatient and out-spoken. Olsen proudly proclaimed his radicalism and supported indus-trial workers as well as farmers. Such people were strong in their own states, but their followers increasingly looked to Senator Huey Long of Louisiana for national leadership. Earlier, as governor, he had attacked the corporations and bosses and had instituted a public works program that provided jobs and pride. He also subtly helped the blacks.

Long was a complex mixture of sincere populist reformer and am-bitious, egoistic demagogue. He is best portrayed by another south-erner, Robert Penn Warren, in the novel *All the King's Men*. He could use sarcasm and satire as well as Roosevelt, and he shrewdly pre-sented himself as a common man who was weary of selfish, bumbling aristocrats. He made his move in January, 1934, by organizing a na-tional campaign to win support for his "Share the Wealth" program.

After confiscating all large fortunes, Long proposed to distribute the surplus by giving every family enough to buy a radio, car, and home; by providing a pension for old people; and by sending all able young

By the summer of 1934, the administration had fought a frustrating battle against the depression only to know that it was still there. H. I. Carlisle of the Des Moines Register cartooned FDR, Uncle Sam, and the Congress desperately trying, still trying, to launch recovery into a steady orbit. Sympathy can attend their cry: "Isn't the blamed thing ever going to take off?"

By Carlisle, in the Des Moines *Register*

ISN'T THE BLAMED THING EVER GOING TO TAKE OFF?

Reprinted by permission of the Des Moines *Register*. Reprinted in the *Review of Reviews*, vol. 90, July, 1934, p. 46.

males to college. Those actions, he argued, would generate recovery, and prosperity would be sustained through a vast public works program, a national minimum wage, a short workweek, and a farm policy designed to balance production with market demand.

Long was also shrewd and demagogic enough to use the appeal of a Catholic priest of Royal Oak, Michigan, the Reverend Charles Coughlin, who was as effective a radio speaker as President Roosevelt was. Coughlin was a popular philosopher who preached the virtues of the Catholic corporate system as the basis for a moral, prosperous society with welfare for all. His particular target was the financial elite, which he increasingly linked with the Jews in an anti-Semitic campaign. That mixture (with the anti-Semitism played down in the early years) won him a mass audience almost as soon as he began his radio sermons in 1926. The depression reinforced and extended his appeal, and by 1933 he was reaching upwards of 40 million adults every week.

The most extreme conservative attack on the New Deal was led by R. M. Carpenter and John J. Rascob, two leaders of the DuPont Corporation. Rascob, who had campaigned with Smith in 1928, wanted to educate the people in the virtues of the old capitalism—encourage them "to get rich." The resulting organization, incorporated as the American Liberty League in August, 1934, was dedicated to the proposition that "business which bears the responsibility for the paychecks of private employment has little voice in government."

The league at first attracted a rather diverse group of businessmen and politicians, although the hard core was composed of those who worshiped the principles of traditional laissez-faire. But early membership included such different figures as Al Smith and corporation leaders like Will H. Clayton, head of a mammoth cotton brokerage firm, and William S. Knudsen of General Motors. The latter two men ultimately accepted the kind of state capitalism created by the New Deal, however, and became important government officials in later Roosevelt administrations.

The president's inherent conservatism was revealed not only by his reluctant and limited support for labor but by the lack of dynamic leadership after the initial burst of activity during the "First 100 Days." The legislation of 1934 was largely derivative and supplemental: more laws concerning gold and silver; generous bankruptcy laws for businessmen, corporations, and farmers; more help for those raising peanuts, sugar, and tobacco; additional assistance for homeowners and the construction industry; and (sparked by the kidnapping and murder of the Lindberghs' child on March 1, 1932) legislation against crime.

One of the few significant bills established the Securities and Exchange Commission (SEC) to regulate the stock market. The commission was charged with regulating the entire operation and in particular with controlling the kind of speculation that had contributed to the 1929 crash. And more direct relief was provided through the Civil Works Emergency Act. That program employed 2.5 million people during 1934–1935, before direct relief programs began to be handled through state and local agencies.

The failure to deal with other pressing problems not only enabled Lewis, Long, and Coughlin to build their followings, but it sparked two other movements that also challenged Roosevelt. One was organized in January, 1934, by Francis Townsend, an older resident of California who had been hit hard by the depression. He proposed to generate recovery through a 2 percent turnover tax on all business transactions; the money would be used to provide a monthly pension for all people over 60. Townsend incorporated his campaign as the Old Age Revolving Pensions, Ltd., and by September, 1934, he had chartered more than 1000 member clubs. Townsend was thus responsible for one of the most important changes in the dynamics of American political power that occurred during the Roosevelt era. Americans over 60 became a force that every politician had to deal with, a truth that Long soon recognized by including a pension plan in his "Share the Wealth" program.

The protest movement that posed the most immediate threat to Roosevelt, however, was organized in California by Upton Sinclair, the old Progressive muckraker and novelist. Under the catchy title of EPIC, he proposed to organize all unemployed people in producer cooperatives and thereby End Poverty in California. He won the Democratic nomination for governor by the whopping margin of 436,000 to 288,000. Conservatives were terrified, but most Democrats were also upset. The president had no intention of dealing with the depression along the lines proposed by Sinclair. Hence he withheld his personal support from Sinclair while California New Dealers organized a coalition to help conservative Republican governor Frank Merriam. Sinclair was defeated by the state capitalists.

Roosevelt's combination of personal politics and effective party organization produced a smashing victory in the elections of 1934: the Democrats dominated the House of Representatives by 322 to 103, and their 69 senators gave them the largest majority in the history of the Congress. Hopkins and other New Deal leaders were elated. "Boys—this is our hour," he cried. "We've got to get everything we want—a works program, social security, wages and hours; everything—now or never."

But the president offered little positive or sustained leadership during the winter of 1934–1935. He did create the Civil Works Administration on November 8 as another emergency relief agency, and Hop-

*The Townsend Old Age Revolving Pensions plan was one of the more
spectacular utopias spawned in the depression years. Gene Elderman of the
Washington* Post *pictured the good doctor leading the two political parties to
his life stream of recovery and commanding them to drink.*

By Elderman, in the Washington (D.C.) *Post*

Elderman—The Washington *Post.* Reprinted in the *Review of Reviews,* vol. 93, February, 1936, p. 43.

kins, who knew the gravity of the crisis, quickly funneled another $1 million into the economy. But Roosevelt's annual message of January 4, 1935, sounded no clarion call for immediate or extensive reforms. He asked for better conservation measures; legislation to provide help against the ravages of unemployment, old age, and illness; bills to supply better housing; and a new relief program. Having made those requests, he became almost passive. He did not even display any great concern or anger when the Supreme Court ruled in January against one of the NRA codes (*Panama Refining Company* v. *Ryan*).

The president exerted himself only to win the kind of relief measure that he desired and in behalf of his request for social security legislation. Roosevelt wanted to terminate relief as rapidly as possible, and to that end he proposed to pay less than the prevailing wage on government projects, to require a means test for employment in those jobs, and to turn direct relief back to the states and local agencies. That approach provoked the anger of organized labor and such reformers as Senators Wagner and Black, as well as the opposition of Coughlin and Long. They demanded that the government pay marketplace wages to all who were hired.

After a long battle, however, the president won the fight. As finally signed on April 8, 1935, the Emergency Relief Appropriation Act had two distinguishing characteristics. It was the largest single appropriation (nearly $5 billion) in the history of the world, and it was a

Figure 3   Government spending for goods and services, 1929–1954. (From A. O. Dahlberg, *National Income Visualized,* New York: Columbia University Press, 1956, p. 13. By permission of the publisher.)

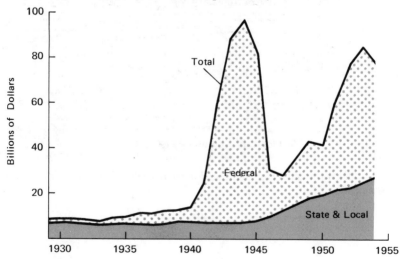

watershed in the delegation of congressional authority to the executive. The president was empowered to spend the money as he desired. His fundamental decision was unfortunately open to grave question.

Roosevelt gave control of the money to Hopkins rather than to Secretary of the Interior Harold Ickes. That meant it was spent on many direct relief projects rather than on a fewer number of large public works. The president was influenced by his personal relationship with Hopkins, who stressed the immediate social benefits of his approach, and by the greater political advantages to be gained from the Hopkins strategy. He was not persuaded, probably because he did not enjoy any great understanding of economic theory, by the Ickes argument that money invested in major construction projects would generate recovery throughout the entire economy.

Hopkins did employ a large number of people through the Works Project Administration (WPA) that he headed after May 8, 1935. His payroll climbed to about 3.5 million people by March, 1936, and he spent 95 percent of the money on wages and salaries. That left between seven and ten million men still unemployed, however, and much of the work done by the WPA was redundant, irrelevant, and wasteful.

THE CREATION OF A SOCIAL SECURITY SYSTEM AND SUBSEQUENT BATTLES

Roosevelt asked the Congress to create a social security system on January 17, 1935, but then largely withdrew from the battle. As a result, the fight was carried by Senator Wagner and Maryland Congressman David Lewis. Conservatives attacked the proposed legislation as an inducement to laziness and as a threat to white supremacy in the South. The real pressure to write a strong bill came not so much from New Deal leaders, and certainly not from the White House, but rather from Townsend and his battalions. California Congressman John McGroarty introduced an alternate proposal based on the Townsend demand for a monthly pension of $200, and the vigorous support for that idea impressed all congressmen with the necessity for action. The House defeated the McGroarty bill, but finally passed the administration bill in April by a vote of 371 to 33.

The president made no effort to move it rapidly through the Senate. Instead, he helped defeat an effort to aid sharecroppers and tenant farmers. Jerome Frank sought to make such reforms by persuading his superior, Chester Davis, director of the AAA, to require better treatment of those workers as part of the conditions for the owners to obtain federal aid. Roosevelt knew of the terrible conditions affecting poor farmers, but he declined to antagonize southern conservatives and approved the firing of Frank.

In a similar way, the president persistently refused to help Senator Wagner obtain a better and more extensive housing program. In truth, he encouraged the private interests in that fight. He also openly supported management in the continuing flurry of labor disputes and appeared in person before the Congress to read an angry speech vetoing a bonus bill.

Roosevelt's behavior during those months is not inexplicable. He was first and last an upper-class aristocrat: not at all a vigorous reformer and most certainly not an advocate of broad economic planning. Given that outlook, it seems very likely that the president hoped the economy would recover without further intervention and regulation. The resulting prosperity would end the need for relief and at the same time take care of agitators like Long and Coughlin. He could then perfect the reforms that had been made, add others if the occasion arose, and serve out a second term in relative domestic tranquillity while devoting primary attention to foreign affairs.

It became increasingly apparent after February, 1935, however, that the economy remained in very poor condition. There were at least ten million unemployed, and countless others were living on the edge of subsistence. Confronted by that harsh and unhappy truth, the president had little choice but to extend government intervention. Several factors influenced the timing of Roosevelt's decision to act. He was undoubtedly annoyed, if not actively provoked, by the rising tide of criticism about his passivity and conservatism. The growing strength and boldness of Long and Coughlin created more direct pressure, and Roosevelt was warned specifically in mid-February by his trusted aide Louis Howe to "watch very carefully" the growing support for Long. The Louisiana senator was gaining strength among urban workers, western businessmen, Iowa farmers, and even college professors. His increasing cooperation with Coughlin further intensified the concern of the administration.

In typically indirect fashion, the president moved on May 1 to mollify those who criticized his part in firing Frank over the issue of aid to sharecroppers and tenant farmers. He created the Resettlement Administration by executive order and appointed Rex Tugwell to direct an effort to help impoverished rural families by creating new urban-rural complexes. The action signaled an increasing use of the executive order as a method of starting reforms. But, also characteristically of many such measures, it produced few concrete gains because Roosevelt did not follow through to provide continuing support. Tugwell was able to move less than 4500 families.

Roosevelt's next maneuver, timed as a response to harsh criticism by the United States Chamber of Commerce, was to create the Rural Electrification Administration (REA) on May 11, 1935, through another executive order. Under the driving leadership of Morris L. Cooke and John Carmody, the REA changed the substance and style of life for many farmers by integrating them into the modern world. When Cooke took charge of the program, only one in ten farms had electricity. He built power lines when private utility companies refused to make such investment, and, working through farm cooperatives, he and Carmody strung wires into the backcountry of the South, into the forests of the Northwest, across the plains of the Middle West, and up the crags of the mountain states. Thanks to the REA, the ratio of farms with lights and power was reversed (9 out of 10) in 15 years.

The House of Representatives responded to the president by passing a banking bill prepared by Marriner Eccles, the newly appointed governor of the FRB, who was a strong advocate of using monetary policy to control the economy. It quickly became clear, however, that the bill would be changed drastically by conservative Senator Carter Glass of Virginia. But at that point, the Supreme Court angered Roosevelt and he reasserted himself vigorously.

Announcing its decision on what came to be known among New Dealers as Black Monday, May 27, 1935, the Court unanimously invalidated the NRA. In a case initiated by the A.L.A. Schechter Poultry Corporation, the judges ruled the legislation unconstitutional because it delegated too much power from the Congress to the executive and because it grossly exceeded the constitutional power to regulate interstate commerce. Since the NRA was a failure, dying on its feet, the administration was not upset by the first aspect of the decision, but the Court's interpretation of the commerce clause, if projected to other New Deal measures, would weaken or destroy much of the administration's program for state capitalism.

Roosevelt responded early in June by telling the Congress that it could not adjourn until it dealt with social security, labor unions, the banking system, taxes, and the power companies. To emphasize the point, and to flaunt delegated power in the face of the Supreme Court, he created the National Resources Committee on June 7 through another executive order. It was charged with developing plans for the rational conservation and use of the nation's resources. Largely through the efforts of a few men like the economist Gardner Means, the agency blazed the trail for a coordinated effort to rationalize and manage the economy. Not by intent, but rather by the creative energy of Means and others, it prepared the way for the ultimate creation of the president's Council of Economic Advisers.

Between that move and the end of August, when he allowed a weary Congress to adjourn, Roosevelt directly and indirectly aided the new liberals to pass nine pieces of significant legislation. The first was the National Labor Relations Act, which was largely the creation of the revived labor movement and the persistent efforts of Senator Wagner and Francis Biddle. Roosevelt did not like the legislation, but he finally agreed not to oppose Wagner in the Senate. When Wagner won, 63–12, Roosevelt added his endorsement and it easily passed the House.

The law created the National Labor Relations Board (NLRB) and in effect compelled employers to accept unionization and engage in collective bargaining. The board was empowered to hold and supervise elections and to act against unfair labor practices. The law was in truth a state capitalist charter that legitimized organized labor in the corporate political economy as an equal with industry and agriculture and institutionalized its interaction with those elements through the government.

The Banking Act of August 23 was a victory for the Eccles drive to win more control over the financial system and over monetary policy. It provided for the regulation of credit, for authority over the reserve requirements of Federal Reserve Banks (and over their top officials), and required large state banks to join the FRS within seven years. It was a major step in centralizing and extending the power of the executive to rationalize and control the political economy.

The Public Utility Holding Company Act of August 28 had a similar effect. It was supported by old Progressives, conservationists, and public power advocates. Roosevelt, who personally disliked the industry, tried to win approval for a clause that would have enabled the government to destroy any holding company that could not prove it was needed for effective operation. He lost that battle but won the war.

The law dissolved all holding companies that operated more than two organizational steps above the firms that generated the power and gave the SEC authority to destroy others if such action was deemed in the public interest. It also gave the FPC authority to regulate the interstate transmission of electricity. The measure forced many giant holding companies to divest themselves of their satellites.

The social security legislation of August 14 was far weaker, less equitable or advanced than similar legislation in Europe. The government, for example, accepted no responsibility to contribute funds under the law, and vast numbers of workers were excluded from the benefits. The entire cost of the compensation to be paid after the age of 65 was to be supplied by taxes levied on the worker's wage or salary and on the employer's payroll. Furthermore, the system of unemployment compensation was created as a joint federal-state operation in which each state administered its own program. Even so, weak, inequitable, and economically unsound as it was, the bill did provide some help.

The Bituminous Coal Stabilization Act of August 30 represented an effort to rationalize that industry by controlling production and by creating a special labor board. Another farm mortgage act (August 29) provided a three-year moratorium during which bankrupt farmers could keep the title to their land by paying a reasonable rent determined by a court. The Wagner-Crosser Railroad Retirement Act (also August 29) established a pension system headed by a three-man administrative board. And the Motor Carrier Act of August 9 placed the bus and trucking industries under the regulative authority of the ICC.

New Dealers also managed to shift a small part of the tax burden to the rich. Outraged opposition from conservatives, which Roosevelt did not fight very vigorously, kept the bill basically weak, but it did increase estate, stock, and gift taxes, and imposed an excess profits levy. It was a gesture: it raised little new revenue and did not produce any significant redistribution of income. For that matter, the share of the national income received by the richest 1 percent of the country actually increased after the Revenue Act of 1935 because the New Deal's tax system was generally regressive and operated—directly and indirectly—to extract more revenue from the lower-income groups.

The law did not cripple business. Beginning near the end of February, 1936, and gaining momentum rapidly through March, the industrial sector of the economy enjoyed a revival that produced a gain of 30 percent within a year. Part of that improvement was generated by technological developments, such as new abrasives and semiautomatic and automatic control systems, that changed and revitalized the machine tool industry. Chemicals also continued their growth, particularly in plastics. And the steady introduction of electric power and service systems and the increasing market for appliances stimulated that industry.

Contrary to the dire forecasts of the diehard conservatives, the militance of organized labor did not derail the limited recovery. The union push began in October, 1935, when John L. Lewis forced a showdown with the tradition-bound leadership of the AF of L. He and other more radical leaders were ready to exploit the favorable situation created by the Wagner Labor Law, but they wanted to organize on an inclusive basis in order to gain bargaining power. Lewis lost his battle to win charters from the AF of L for industrial unions, but his one-punch knockdown of "Big Bill" Hutcheson, president of the narrowly craft-oriented carpenters' unions, was a more revealing indicator of what was to come.

Over breakfast the next day, Lewis joined other militants to establish the rival Congress of Industrial Organizations (CIO). His key allies were Sidney Hillman, Max Zaritsky, and David Dubinsky, who led the clothing workers; Charles Howard of the typographers; and Thomas McMahon of the textile unions. Within a month they launched an organizing drive in every major industry from steel to automobiles. They also turned away from the AF of L policy of holding aloof from overt, organized political action. It quickly became clear that the CIO would give money as well as votes to reelect Roosevelt.

Additional help to that end, though unintentional, was provided by the Supreme Court. It opened the year by striking down the AAA legislation (*United States* v. *Butler, et al.,* January 6, 1936). Farm prices immediately went into a severe slump, and Iowa farmers hanged the six majority judges, headed by Justice Owen J. Roberts, in effigy. The Roosevelt administration counterattacked on February 29, 1936, with the Soil Conservation and Domestic Allotment Act. That law combined slapdash emergency subsidies for restricted production with a serious effort to deal with the problem of conservation that had been dramatized by the terrible dust storms of the decade. Those catastrophes, which covered the Midwest and Southwest with dirt, and even carried vast clouds of dust and red snow to the Atlantic Coast, had evoked a belated concern with preserving the nation's topsoil. The key provision of the act authorized cash payments to farmers who planted soil-preserving crops.

At that point, Roosevelt again relaxed. He wanted to give business a breathing space (he still hoped to pull more industrial and financial leaders into his coalition), and he did not desire to weaken the economic revival. In addition, he felt politically more at ease after the September, 1935, assassination of Huey Long because Father Coughlin was incapable of rallying Long's following to his own movement.

Before it adjourned, however, the Congress passed three other important bills. The first, the Federal Anti-Price Discrimination Act of June 20, 1936, represented an initial effort to deal with the system of administered prices that the large corporations (led by DuPont) had begun to develop in the 1920s. Through the use of a complicated formula, firms manipulated prices in order to limit competition and operate their own plants at the most profitable level. Such control enabled them to use price wars as a tactical device, and the 1936 law was aimed specifically at the chain stores employing that maneuver to weaken independent operators and smaller corporate rivals.

The Walsh-Healy Act of June 30 required all firms handling government business to pay their workers the prevailing minimum wage in that industry (or service) as determined by the secretary of labor and to limit the workweek to 40 hours. It also outlawed the employment of

convicts or children. The measure undoubtedly reinforced the drive
by unions to improve wages and to establish a standard workweek.

The Merchant Marine Act of June 26 created the United States
Maritime Commission as an independent agency to regulate and revive (with government aid) the merchant marine. It provided straight
subsidies calculated on the difference between domestic and foreign
operating costs. An attempt was also made to improve the working and
safety conditions aboard ship. The law was also significant in revealing the Roosevelt administration's increasing emphasis on overseas
economic expansion.

That issue was not debated during the presidential campaign of
1936. Roosevelt ran on the record of the New Deal in providing relief,
in offering temporary work for some unemployed and hope for the
remainder, in instituting reforms that balanced and rationalized the
political economy, and in generating a modest recovery. In launching
his campaign on September 29, he offered an evaluation of the New
Deal that, for insight and accuracy, can hardly be surpassed. "The true
conservative," Roosevelt explained, "seeks to protect the system of
private property and free enterprise by correcting such injustices and
inequalities as arise from it."

That not only sounded like a paraphrase of one of Theodore
Roosevelt's famous speeches, but it accurately described what the
Progressive coalition had sought to do from its beginnings in the 1890s
and what the New Deal tried to accomplish during its first term in
office. The only questions were whether or not it had succeeded and
whether or not, as Hoover had feared, its methods would produce a
system of centralized power controlled by a new corporate elite. Such
questions did not engage the American people during the election of
1936.

The Republican candidates, Alfred M. Landon and Frank Knox, did
try to raise those issues. Hoover was far more effective, though Landon
exhibited a sense of history and a perception of the tendencies inherent in the domestic and foreign policies of the New Deal that proved
more than a little prophetic. But his insight into the long future was no
match for Roosevelt's command of the present. Landon and the Republicans were overwhelmed by a liberal coalition of farmers, workers, blacks, and many large as well as small businessmen.

The president won by more than ten million votes and carried every
state except Maine and Vermont. The Democrats dominated the Senate
by 77 seats to 19 and the House of Representatives by 328 to 107. But
even those majorities failed to provide the New Deal with either the
ideas or the power to cope with the troubles that awaited Roosevelt as
he prepared his second inaugural address. He himself knew, as he said
on January 20, 1937, that one-third of the nation was still "ill-housed,

ill-clad, ill-nourished." The country did not recover from the Great Depression until it had become involved in another world war.

EXPLORATORY READING

The literature on Roosevelt and the early phase of the New Deal would fill a village library. The most interesting items are:

J. M. Burns, *Roosevelt: The Lion and the Fox* (1956)

P. K. Conkin, *The New Deal* (1967)

The Editors of the *Economist, The New Deal: An Analysis and Appraisal* (1937)

D. Fusfeld, *The Economic Thought of Franklin D. Roosevelt* (1956)

W. E. Leuchtenburg, *Franklin D. Roosevelt and the New Deal* (1963)

E. Robinson, *The Roosevelt Leadership, 1933–1945* (1955)

E. Roosevelt, *This I Remember* (1949)

A. M. Schlesinger, *The Coming of the New Deal* (1958)

R. E. Sherwood, *Roosevelt and Hopkins* (1948)

R. Tugwell, *The Democratic Roosevelt* (1957)

Roosevelt's critics and opponents are discussed in these volumes:

D. H. Bennett, *Demagogues in the Depression* (1969)

A. Bingham and S. Rodman (Eds.), *Challenge to the New Deal* (1934)

R. Moley, *After Seven Years* (1939)

J. T. Patterson, *Congressional Conservatism and the New Deal* (1967)

T. H. Williams, *Huey Long: A Biography* (1969)

The following books provide a helpful introduction to the basic economic issues of the period:

D. V. Brown *(et al.), The National Recovery Administration* (1935)

A. W. Crawford, *Monetary Management Under the New Deal* (1940)

A. Hansen, *Full Recovery or Stagnation?* (1938)

E. Hawley, *The New Deal and the Problem of Monopoly* (1966)

H. V. Hodson, *Slump and Recovery, 1929–1937* (1938)

D. Lynch, *The Concentration of Economic Power* (1946)

M. N. Rothbard, *America's Great Depression* (1973)

The experiences of workers, employed and otherwise, is movingly reviewed by these authors:

E. Abbott, *Public Assistance* (1940)

I. Bernstein, *The New Deal Collective Bargaining Policy* (1950); and *Turbulent Years* (1970)

E. W. Blake, *Citizens Without Work; The Unemployed Worker* (1940)

M. Derber and E. Young (Eds.), *Labor and the New Deal* (1957)

W. Galenson, *The CIO Challenge to the AFL* (1960)

E. Levinson, *Labor on the March* (1938)

The attempts to deal with the personal and structural aspects of the breakdown of agriculture are dealt with in:

D. E. Conrad, *The Forgotten Farmers: The Story of the Sharecroppers in the New Deal* (1965)

G. Fite, *George N. Peek and the Fight for Farm Parity* (1954)

R. Lord, *The Wallaces of Iowa* (1947)

E. Nourse (Ed.), *Three Years of the Agricultural Adjustment Act* (1937)

While there are many, many books dealing with special aspects of the depression and the New Deal, these offer especially important leads into your own research on such subjects:

R. Lubove, *The Struggle for Social Security, 1900–1935* (1968)

R. Martin (Ed.), *TVA: The First Twenty Years* (1956)

J. Salmond, *The Civilian Conservation Corps, 1933–1942* (1967)

P. Selznick, *TVA and the Grass Roots* (1953)

R. Wolters, *Negroes and the Great Depression* (1970)

14 COMMUNITY AND CREATIVITY DURING THE CRISIS

ROOSEVELT'S smashing triumph in 1936 cannot wholly be explained by his charisma, the support from a newly militant labor movement, the effective organization of the Democratic party, and the relief programs that were followed by limited recovery. As with the earlier legislative victories, the crucial factors were the energy, ideas, and resiliency of countless people throughout the country. They revealed, whether as a feisty young congressman full of concern and ideas like Maury Maverick of Texas or as a farmer who kept the family together after losing his land, a spirit of community and creativity that was inspiring and pragmatically effective.

At the heart of it all was the family, that elementary social unit based on a commitment to the idea (and ideal) of creating a civilization in microcosm. Not too many years later, of course, corporate state capitalism largely subverted that kind of family, but it was a dynamic element in the social vitality of the depression period. In those years, at any rate, it was a network of relatives and neighbors which played important roles in the larger community.

Aunts and uncles helped less fortunate sisters and brothers. Neighbors shared garden vegetables and child care. A person would feign illness to give another person a week's work. Judges handed down suspended sentences for stealing food or clothes. Theater managers looked the other way when kids opened the exit door to admit a friend from "the wrong side of the tracks." Dedicated teachers often worked for a pittance. Local grocery store managers understood why people grew food on land that had once been a lawn and carried charge accounts to—and sometimes over—the edge of bankruptcy. It was a time when parents secretly handed a storekeeper the 50 cent piece that was then paid to a child for sweeping the floor that had been walked on by ten customers. It was a time of caring and concern.

Also, true enough, it was a time when the pain and the pressures disrupted community. When men out of work hated to go home because their wives were waiting to berate them (or deny them sex)—or because they were ashamed that their wives were earning the money for food and shelter. But even those terrors involved an affirmation of community. That was the case, for example, with the early 1935 riot in Harlem. An initially minor incident between a young Puerto Rican black and a white store clerk triggered a wild outburst against the denial of community—indeed, the abuse of community—by the property power of white corporations.

Among blacks as well as whites, moreover, women were at the center of the community during the depression years. A few years later, radical feminists would argue that such a life for women was limited, demeaning, and destructive. But in the 1930s the issue was survival—not a second or third car—and women were at the center of success. John Steinbeck forever dramatized that aspect of the era in *The Grapes of Wrath*, the powerful novel about a family driven off its land in Oklahoma by the dust storms. He memorialized the indomitable family, led by a woman, as the primary social unit. Without Ma Joad (and there were millions like her), many other people would have slipped off into a state of funk. The Ma Joads had a magic unknown to Franklin Roosevelt: he could rouse the masses, but the Ma Joads were at the heart of the units that composed those masses.

One of the ways to stay humane and sane in a time of trouble is to dance, and Steinbeck understood that dancing was an important element of community during the depression. Some people did hoedowns to country and western music; others preferred to revive the waltz or the square dance; but *the* music of the depression era was swing, and the moves were known as "trucking" and "The Big Apple." Swing was a form of jazz played by big bands (14 to 18 people) directed by a talented musician and featuring instrumental and vocal soloists in a dynamic relationship with the larger community.

Big-band swing was a classic example of nongeneric community. Its foundation involved blacks and whites in a common—if tension-scarred—enterprise. The jazz of the 1920s would not have become swing without the driving, slashing ensemble treatment of the Dixieland idiom by Chicago whites like the Austin High School Band and Benny Goodman. But that was not enough. Their intensity had to be disciplined. That was first accomplished by Fletcher Henderson, a black artist whose talents are usually lost in the glow surrounding such names as Goodman, Artie Shaw, Tommy Dorsey, Count Basie, and Duke Ellington.

Henderson's genius was to transform a nice but routine tune into a concerto for a swing band. He could take an ordinary song, say *Tea for Two*, and score it in counterpoint for reeds, brass, and percussion—and in the process (like Mozart) leave creative openings for individual musicians and vocalists. Ellington later proved to be the master of that idiom, scoring the songs for specific people, but Henderson was the man who changed the music.

The big bands were a beautiful example of community. The members did not simply follow the leader. One of the most neglected aspects of the history of the so-called ordinary man, for example, concerns the unheralded blacks and whites who wrote or arranged the music association with the name of the man out front. On balance, Ellington was the most honest about that aspect of the community of the band: he honored Billy Strayhorn and others throughout their careers.

At its best, as with the Goodman-Krupa version of *Sing, Sing, Sing*, Shaw's *Begin the Beguine*, and Basie's *One O'Clock Jump*, swing was art in the true sense of that much abused term. Those bands, along with Ellington, also created a larger community. Two of them, Goodman and Shaw, broke the color line. Shaw even dared to tour the South with blacks in the band: he was an incipient radical in a time of reform, and he ultimately walked off the stage in disgust over the commercialization of his music.

Shaw was thus a key white man in the music that created a greater community. There were no age or class lines on the dance floor (and, in some places, no color line, either), and the big swing bands created a cultural movement very similar to the one later generated by rock. Shaw's sensual treatment of *Begin the Beguine* gave millions a vision of a different life. And Ellington's *Black, Brown, and Beige* was a stunning evocation of the great dignity and beauty of black Americans in the face of prolonged mistreatment.

Life as it was also defined the art of John Stewart Curry, Grant Wood, and Thomas Hart Benton. As realistic painters, they were the heirs of the Ashcan school that had flourished during the second and third decades of the century. But those earlier men, led by George Luks and John Sloan, had freely used European techniques and dealt with a wide range of subjects. Benton, Curry, and Wood, on the other hand, were far less bold and imaginative. Some of their work was extremely powerful, but others, particularly Georgia O'Keeffe, George Bellows, and Edward Hopper, used realism in far more effective ways.

Though overshadowed by the realists, and by those like William Cropper and Ben Shahn whose work contained biting social commentary, other artists sustained the modern movements of abstractionism, expressionism, and cubism that had made such a disturbing impact during the early years of the century. John Marin's one-man show at the Museum of Modern Art in 1936, for example, was a triumph for American modernism. And Alexander Calder's magnificent mobiles, perhaps the best-known works of modern American sculpture, were directly inspired by the abstractions of Piet Mondrian.

The Europeans encouraged the modernists, but they were also aided by the Federal Art Project created as part of the WPA. It provided employment for Jackson Pollock and Willem De Kooning, as well as for realists and other artists. One significant result of such work was *Index of American Design,* an excellent history of the nation's creative work from the time of the first settlers. Perhaps the major achievement, however, involved reviving the art of murals and providing them for many of the public buildings constructed as part of the recovery programs.

The WPA also aided other parts of the cultural community. The most controversial was the Federal Theater Project headed by Hallie Flanagan of Vassar College. Employing major figures like Elmer Rice, it performed a wide selection of plays: Marlowe's *Dr. Faustus* and Shakespeare's *Hamlet,* modern verse drama by Eliot, and an adaptation of Sinclair Lewis's novel about fascism in America, *It Can't Happen Here.* More importantly, it offered live drama to millions of people in all parts of the country who had never before seen a play: the total attendance was somewhere near 30 million adults and children. But it was attacked for the strong social criticism in many of the plays and for a striking innovation called "The Living Newspaper." That new idiom dramatized current issues, such as poverty in the South, and hence generated embittered (and frightened) opposition. Roosevelt let it die.

The commercial theater, as usual centered in New York, offered its own kind of social realism. The Group Theater, organized by a community of actors, gave Clifford Odets a chance to write instead of act, and he produced several moving plays: *Waiting for Lefty* (1935), *Awake and Sing!* (1935), *Golden Boy* (1937), and *Rocket to the Moon* (1938). Odets was more romantic than radical, but his *Rocket to the Moon,* for example, is a powerful evocation of the way poverty destroys human potential.

Lillian Hellman was more truly radical. Her personal life was centered around a long, tempestuous, nonmarital involvement with Dashiel Hammett, the first master of the novel of social criticism masquerading as a detective story. Her own plays, especially *The Children's Hour* (1934) and *The Little Foxes* (1939), are moving critiques of American capitalism. So, too, were the works of Maxwell Anderson, who was in important ways a T. S. Eliot who stayed home. His plays in the idioms of verse and tragedy, like *Valley Forge* (1934) and *Winterset* (1935), were unusually effective. *Winterset,* for example, dealt with the Sacco-Vanzetti case in a way that matches the power of O'Neill's *Mourning Becomes Electra*—or even *Long Day's Journey into Night.*

Some of the younger writers, consciously or otherwise, explored the frontiers between the theater and the novel. One has the feeling when reading Nathaniel West—*Miss Lonelyhearts* (1933) or *The Day of the Locust* (1939)—that he was writing movies or plays in the guise of the novel. West was Hemingway without the romanticism. His Hollywood had no trace of the gory glory of the bullring. A similar ability to use dialogue and flat description characterized the early work of James Cain.

The romantic individualism of Hemingway gave way in the 1930s to the social romanticism of Thomas Wolfe and the more intellectual community of southerners around Allen Tate. Though drastically different men, Wolfe and Tate nevertheless revealed and honored the tensions and the traditions of the South as it struggled to come to terms with the new corporate society. To oversimplify it: Tate said "No" and Wolfe said "Yes." Tate argued that there was "no escape." Wolfe asserted that *You Can't Go Home Again,* and then went on to celebrate the intellectual and social joys—including sensuous Jewish women—of life outside the South.

Both men were right. The noble best in Tate's Old South was dying along with its horrific worst (though it proved to be an excruciatingly slow process), and Wolfe's premature vision of indulgent affluence would ultimately become a reality that was a waking nightmare. Others were closer to the truth suffered by the general community. James T. Farrell told his readers how it was in the cities *(Studs Lonigan),* Robert Cantwell was far better on strikes than Steinbeck (or anyone else), and William Faulkner remained the master of describing how corporate industrialism destroyed an earlier culture.

Many writers were helped by the Federal Writer's Project headed by Harry Alsberg. That effort did not subsidize the great American novel, but it did underwrite the creativity of many people who never became famous, even though they told us much about ourselves. The series on Life in America, for example, and the 100 volumes on the states, territories, and cities were generally magnificent. And the books on ethnic groups, such as the Italians in New York or *The Negro in Virginia,* were excellent.

And, thanks indirectly to Huey Long, ever more American youth were being exposed to those aspects of American culture. Harry Hopkins used one of Long's ideas to establish (in June, 1935) the National

Youth Administration (NYA). Headed by Aubrey Williams of Alabama, the NYA helped more than 500,000 people to enter or stay in college and at least 1.5 million who might otherwise have dropped out of high school. The program also financed other aspects of education, such as an observatory at the University of Nebraska and a study of social welfare legislation by students at Connecticut College.

In the broader sense, the predominant influence in education was Dewey's pragmatic instrumentalism. After the creation of the Progressive Education Association in 1918, his ideas gained wide acceptance. His program to educate people for progressive citizenship through experimentation and peer group cooperation influenced millions of people: directly through the students he trained at the University of Chicago and Columbia University and indirectly through the students they educated. But his hope that the approach would create a community of concerned citizens who would mold nature and the social environment into a humanitarian society was not fulfilled.

Part of that failure was due to the inherent weaknesses of Dewey's pragmatism and reformism. In a crucial sense, therefore, the limitations of Dewey's educational reform symbolized the entire Progressive movement of the twentieth century. The issue is not whether improvements had been made, for many reforms had been accomplished during the half century after the 1880s. The point is best stated by Frederick C. Howe, a leading Progressive who sadly concluded that American reformers were fundamentally limited by an "evangelical-mindedness that seeks a moralistic explanation of social problems and a religious solution for most of them."

CORPORATIONS INFLUENCE EDUCATION

Howe did not deny that a moral outlook (including the humanism espoused by Dewey) offered a useful way of looking at the world, but he did come to realize that it did not provide a basis for analyzing and changing the political economy. Instead, Dewey's educational reforms were absorbed by corporate state capitalism. Even critics of Dewey, like Robert Maynard Hutchins who advocated a return to the classical ideal, were overwhelmed. The corporations financed the kind of education they deemed vital to the sustenance of their power. They did so indirectly by hiring specialists rather than people who obtained a broader education and directly through their membership on boards of trustees, their financial grants, and the research foundations that they subsidized.

The first such organization, the National Industrial Conference Board, had been created in 1916 through the efforts of Mangus Alexander of General Electric. A more reformist group of businessmen, headed by Edward A. Filene and Henry S. Dennison, followed in 1919 with the Twentieth Century Fund. Then came the National Bureau of Economic Research, the Brookings Institution, and the Foreign Policy Association; and finally, spawned by the depression, the National Economic and Social Planning Association. As its name suggests, the latter was the most militantly reformist, but even its proposals did not challenge the essentials of the corporate system.

The National Bureau of Economic Research, created through the efforts of Columbia University economist Wesley C. Mitchell and Malcolm C. Rorty of the American Telephone and Telegraph Company, was probably the most important foundation during the interwar years. Mitchell was speaking for all when he candidly defined the outlook and purpose of the National Bureau: "To develop the best possibilities of our existing institutions." That philosophy, as well as the more general tendency of education to buttress the status quo, provoked Columbia sociologist Robert S. Lynd to issue an angry and militant manifesto. His *Knowledge for What?* (1939) charged—and illustrated—that education was prostituting itself as a servant of power rather than honoring its fundamental commitment to devising and exploring new alternatives to the status quo.

Lynd could have stressed even more forcefully the point that the foundations—within their own framework—were ignoring vital institutions that needed drastic reforms. One of the most striking examples involved the First Americans. Neither early Progressives nor later liberals offered much help to the Indians who survived their final defeats in the late nineteenth century. The Pueblos did muster enough support during 1922–1923 to defeat an attempt to transfer their land to whites, and a year later they won their battle for compensation. And all First Americans were finally (1924) given full citizenship in the white man's corporate system. But two years later the Indian Bureau opened a concerted campaign to deny the Pueblos the right to practice their religious ceremonies.

Finally, in 1928, the Brookings Institution published a report *(The Problem of Indian Administration)* that argued for reform. The resulting Indian Reorganization Act of 1934 did return some land to the tribes, but it offered the First Americans no opportunity to revive and sustain their own cultures—or, if they chose, to enter the corporate system as equals. Some Indians also benefited sporadically from various relief and recovery programs, but the New Deal did not change the reality that the First Americans had become the Forgotten Americans.

Perhaps the Indians made their greatest gains through the favorable backlash created among young people by the treatment of Indians in the movies. The perennial loser, who is also presented as a bad guy, ultimately generates a pervasive sympathy. And in choosing sides for the afternoon, or Saturday morning, game of cowboys and Indians, a good many children preferred to be a First American (and that idiom even affected the game of hide-and-seek). It was somehow a better life *and* a better death. But no children played the game of land owners and migrant farm workers. Perhaps because children sensed that there was no way to make a game out of that miserable reality.

There were two categories of migrant workers: Americans driven off their land by bankers and corporations and by the climatic changes that created dust bowls, and Mexican-Americans (Chicanos). The first group was memorialized in *The Grapes of Wrath* (book and movie) and in the photographs of Dorothea Lange. Those people were the primary focus of the investigation conducted by Senator Robert LaFollette during the late 1930s, even though his Senate committee dramatized the hellish existence of both groups. The mean annual income of migrants was $574 in 1937, 30 percent had poor shelter, and "on the average there was one toilet unit for every 24 persons."

The Mexican-Americans (probably about two million in 1930) were near the bottom of the economic ladder. Big ranchers and corporation farm managers preferred to hire them because they were desperate: they had no hope at home, were usually illegal immigrants ("wetbacks"), and could not qualify for relief programs. They had no choice but to work for a pittance and keep their mouths shut. The standard joke of the era described their breakfast as "a cigarette and a piss." Carey McWilliams, a brave and radical intellectual, tried to do for them what LaFollette and Steinbeck did for the migrants from within the United States, but his moving book (*Factories in the Field*, 1939) did not provoke either photographers or legislators to confront—let alone deal with—the horror of their lives.

The president's reference in 1937 to "one-third of a nation ill-housed, ill-clad, ill-nourished" provided an accurate description of such workers and others who existed in the area from Oklahoma east to Georgia. Their efforts to improve their condition, most militantly expressed through the Southern Tenant Farmers' Union established in 1934 in Arkansas, were generally as unsuccessful as the government programs. Their condition was revealed for all to see in a classic neo-documentary of reportage and photos by James Agee and Walker Evans, *Let Us Now Praise Famous Men* (1946). Agee's agony over the plight of the people emerges in a fantastic series of verbal portraits that convey the reality of the lives of the tenants almost as powerfully as the starkly simple photographs by Evans. Robert Coles documented the failure of *any* leaders to change that situation in his books (published in the late 1960s) under the general title of *Children of Crisis*.

In many respects, the documentary was *the* artistic idiom of the depression era, and it did much to reveal the full nature of that trauma to all Americans. The photojournalism of the period was clearly influenced by earlier experiments in Soviet Russia and Germany (and by those who fled that country after Adolf Hitler's rise to power), but American artists quickly adapted and extended the idiom. Some of the best work, such as Pare Lorentz's *The River* and *The Plow That Broke the Plains,* was supported by the WPA and other government agencies like the Farm Security Administration. Other photojournalism, like the *Workers' Newsreels* produced by the Workers' Film and Photo League, was done by independent operators. And some, as with the various studies in *Life,* resulted from commercial assignments.

As usual, however, American blacks were not featured in this work. Some of them were helped by such New Deal programs as the Federal Employment Relief Administration and by a few high officials like Secretary of the Interior Ickes, but the administration's performance was basically poor. That truth was documented by many blacks. As he became more radical, resigning as editor of *The Crisis* in 1934, for example, DuBois also became more subtly visceral. His moving pamphlet celebrating the centennial of Texas independence *(What the Negro Has Done for the United States and Texas)* began with this elegantly ironic sentence: "The meaning of America is the possibilities of the common man." After reviewing the contributions of blacks as crucial members of the labor force (chattel slaves and wage slaves), in music and the arts, as soldiers, and in religion, he concluded that even more participation was possible if the whites would extend "justice and freedom and understanding" to their fellow Americans with black skins.

The footnotes for his judgment appeared as letters written by individual blacks to government agencies: "It is a well-known fact that one cannot live without food and clothes. . . . We must have something at once"; "nothing in my house to eat and no close to wear"; "My boy went up in town to sign to get on the releaf work. . . . I am a poor widder woman with a house full of little childrens and a cripple girl. . . . The white peoples knocked him down run him out of town . . . [and] got after him agin about a hundred head of white mens with knives and they run him all over town. . . . He left in the night walking with no money. . . ."

Blacks in northern cities knew their own hells. The city was even then failing to function as a community of neighborhoods. Harlem was well along the road to becoming a nightmare of decaying buildings, overcrowding, unemployment, and crime. Those and similar aspects of the life of northern blacks were recounted with devastating realism and tearful anger by Richard Wright in *Uncle Tom's Children, Native Son,* and *Black Boy.* Other black leaders like Mary McLeod and

Robert C. Weaver gained political recognition by the New Deal and tried to push the government into more active and extensive programs.

Even so, the Urban League's low-key evaluation was devastating: "The Roosevelt record is spotty, as might be expected in an administration where so much power is in the hands of the southern wing of the Democratic party." The league acknowledged that the government had made an effort to include blacks in most of its programs, particularly in low-cost housing and the WPA, but nevertheless concluded that federal "policies in many instances have done Negroes great injustices and have helped to build more secure walls of segregation."

A classic example was the way that Robert Moses, ostensibly a liberal planner, destroyed the neighborhoods of New York—Italian and Jewish, as well as white and black—in order to build freeways and other conveniences for the middle and upper classes. His orders bulldozed countless homes and left thousands of people isolated in high-rise apartment buildings that denied individualism—let alone community. The so-called model playgrounds became surrealistic stage sets for robbery, mugging, and rape.

Even though they lost in the short run, the activist blacks built a more creative and lasting monument than Moses. The Urban League, the NAACP, and radical leaders like A. Philip Randolph laid the foundation for future gains that would involve large numbers of blacks. For that matter, they generated enough strength by the end of the decade that their threat to stage a massive demonstration in Washington forced President Roosevelt to begin the long process of treating blacks as equals in the armed forces and in war industries.

The president's wife, Eleanor, was a strong advocate of equality for blacks and other minorities, as well as for women. Mrs. Roosevelt was not a radical feminist, but she did a great deal to help women and to encourage them to participate more actively as citizens in their society. In many respects, the shift in her own life symbolized the changes that were beginning to affect all women during the decade.

In her early years, Eleanor was a rather homely, quiet, and deferential person. Franklin was handsome, debonair, and ambitious, and his mother dominated the marriage. Mother wanted son to retire from public life after his legs were paralyzed by polio, and in the ensuing battle Eleanor asserted her independence and became a strong helpmate in Franklin's renewed political career. But it seems improbable that she would have developed into the powerful public reformer she became without the deep fissure in her emotional relationship with Franklin caused by his long and intense liaison with Lucy Rutherford, an unusually warm and attractive woman.

The marriage survived, and indeed became one of the most effective partnerships in American political history, but Eleanor increasingly gave herself to the struggles for equality and equity. Her activities initially provoked much criticism and opposition, but she refused to be cowed. She helped children, she spoke for the poor, she helped women (personally, for example, securing the appointment of more than 4000 as postmasters), and she badgered the president about all those matters—and about the problems of the blacks. And in the course of all those battles her soul transformed her into a radiantly beautiful person.

There was a similar, if less extensive and powerful, development in the treatment of women in American movies. There was more than enough of the usual nonsense: "Me Tarzan—You Jane"; the cowboy and the rancher's daughter; Shirley Temple sitting on somebody's lap and being waited on or entertained by the "good" black who knew his place; and Snow White as the model of femininity. But some movies of the 1930s, despite the censorship of the Hays office, did offer a deeper reality.

Frank Capra knew that he did not have to film copulation in *It Happened One Night*. He made the point by having Clark Gable strip off his shirt and go to bed separated from Claudette Colbert by nothing more than a blanket suspended from a wire. A bit later, in *Gone With the Wind*, Gable as Rhett Butler told Scarlett O'Hara that the old romanticism was gone with the Old South: "Frankly, my dear, I don't give a damn what you do."

One can argue, of course, that Gable's remark was classic male chauvinism. And perhaps it was; yet it embodied the recognition that individualism cuts both ways. To be equal does carry the chance of being left out. There was a latent recognition of that truth in a number of the movies of the 1930s. Many women protagonists had jobs and careers as well as pretty faces and seductive bodies, and if they married they did so by choice. Even the major sex symbols, such as Jean Harlow and Mae West, made it clear that they went to bed only on their terms. West was so sure of herself, indeed, that she provoked otherwise mundane congressmen to debate her threat to the Republic.

Most women were not public figures—political or otherwise. They were mothers or grandmothers, wives or would-be wives, or young females becoming involved with young males. There were exceptions: most notably among upper-class and middle-class women who engaged in social services and political action. And some working women were involved in union activities. Those who fought alongside Mary Anderson and Mary Van Vleeck for an equal rights amendment to the Constitution seemed for a time (especially in 1935–1936) to have a good chance of success, but the campaign lost its power when it concentrated on trying to influence party politicians.

The League of Women Voters was more effective in blocking various attempts (local and federal) to limit the hiring of married women. It was also successful in promoting improvements in the social security system. Other groups, such as the Women's League for Peace and Freedom and various religious organizations, agitated vigorously— and for a time effectively—against an imperial foreign policy. All those activities provided the women who were involved in them with the reality of community, as well as the satisfaction of individual achievement.

Other women, and men, fulfilled those needs through religion. The depression did not generate the kind of boom in church participation that many people anticipated—or hoped for—but there was a significant revival. One of the era's best sellers, for example, was *Return to Religion*, in which Henry C. Link asserted the utilitarian value of Christianity in a time of trouble and pain. Others found help through less orthodox churches. Many middle-class whites joined the Oxford Group, which used an early form of group therapy to revive flagging spirits. And some blacks in Harlem gained solace and some material help through the messianic movement headed by Father Divine. But most religion had become so secularized around the idea of God revealing himself through material progress that much of the old commitment to religion (and the related psychological satisfaction) manifested itself in more pragmatic activities.

Perhaps the strongest sense of community emerged with the revival of the labor movement. One of the organizing songs makes the point:

If you want to form a union, here is what you've got to do:
You've got to talk to the fellows in the shop with you.

The CIO adopted an old Wobbly song, *Solidarity Forever*, as its official anthem. The common effort to deal with common problems created a kind of solidarity that was unique. That was enhanced, moreover, because most workers had never been organized, and the funny and frustrating efforts to create a union and then use it to win better wages and working conditions were the very essence of building a community.

The blacks like Jessie Reese who were involved in unionization faced great problems—physical violence as well as the usual racism and discrimination—but nevertheless did great work. On his first assignment, Reese was met with a classic line: "I love Negroes, but I like to see 'em in their place." When the time came, Reese gave it back: "Brothers, I agree with him. The place of black people is in the labor movement and officiating in their place, and I'm going to see that everyone out here can be put in his place." And when the company's owners threatened to hire a foreman who was a Klansman, Reese shut down the mill. Needless to say, he organized the union.

It was "a great movement of the people," as another worker said of the general drive for unionization, and "that doesn't happen very often in one's lifetime." It was also an extremely powerful movement, as corporation leaders and Roosevelt learned shortly after the election of 1936. Indeed, the crisis of the New Deal began with the spectacular sit-down strike in the Flint, Michigan, plants of General Motors on December 31, 1936, even before the president began his second term.

EXPLORATORY READING

There are many sources for the cultural history of the 1930s, beginning with the members of your family who lived through the depression. The newspapers and magazines of those years also give one a sense of daily life—and again, be sure to read the advertisements. Small-town newspapers are in some ways more revealing than the big-city dailies.

As for books, begin with:

W. Susman, *Culture and Commitment, 1929–1945* (1973)

Then consider the following items:

F. L. Allen, *Since Yesterday* (1940)

W. H. Chafe, *The American Woman* (1972)

P. Conkin, *Tomorrow a New World* (1959)

M. Geisman, *Writers in Crisis* (1942)

L. Gurko, *Angry Decade* (1947)

M. Komarovsky, *The Unemployed Man and His Family* (1940)

J. D. Mathews, *The Federal Theater, 1935–1939* (1967)

D. R. McCoy, *Angry Voices: Left-of-Center Politics in the New Deal Era* (1958)

15 ROOSEVELT'S TIME OF TROUBLES

THE gains that the New Deal had made by 1936 were real, but they were also limited, and they did not mask the strategic weaknesses that still existed in the American political economy. Industrial production had increased, for example, as had wages, but unemployment remained very high and agriculture was still depressed. Roosevelt's great popularity and political strength were not harnessed to any clear and forceful program for full recovery and further reforms. And the social imbalances of the country remained very great, whether between blacks and whites, between other ethnic minorities and whites, or between a small group of very powerful whites and the rest of the population. The country was surviving, and in some ways improving, but it was not developing a momentum toward creating a truly democratic and equitable society.

The improvement that had occurred was not only uneven, it was also incomplete in the abstract, impersonal ways by which economists measure reality. Compared with 1929 (index number 100), for example, real income had recovered by early 1937 to 93.7; but only for those fortunate enough to have a job. Beyond that, of course, was the extent to which the corporations were being underwritten by the government—which meant being supported by the taxpayers. And the tax system was becoming increasingly inequitable.

All that was known at the time. Some businessmen, like Lewis E. Pierson, chairman of the board of the Irving Trust Company, were brutally frank: "There are vast surpluses of unused plant capacity, and the ranks of the unemployed provide a great reservoir of labor await-ing employment." Even the president admitted that there were "tens of millions" who were "denied the greater part of . . . the necessities of life. . . . Trying to live on incomes so meager that the pall of family disaster hangs over them day by day."

New Deal leaders were worried about such problems, but they viewed and tried to deal with them within the framework of corporate capitalism. That was natural, but it was also insufficient. One of their major concerns, for example, was to control the limited recovery be-cause they did not want it to develop into another speculative boom. Policy makers in the FRS were particularly fearful of that possibility, and early in 1937 they increased the reserve requirement for banks by 50 percent, and at the same time, member banks began to buy gov-ernment bonds as a way of limiting inflation.

Secretary of the Treasury Henry Morgenthau argued that business should make a greater contribution to recovery, and in response Roosevelt began to reduce expenditures and to cut the work relief program as a way of balancing the budget and generating confidence among corporate (and other conservative) leaders. That move was so successful that by August 1937 nearly 50 percent of the people in the WPA had been denied its assistance.

The administration did propose (on January 6, 1937) a few more positive programs: an expansion of public housing; modest help for the long neglected tenant farmers; and some improvements in the social security system. But it also asked (a week later) for more cen-tralized power: a reorganization of the executive department to enable it to deal more directly with the problems. That move foreshadowed a subsequent bid for even more power that, together with other political and economic developments, created a serious American crisis.

The ultimate result, as Herbert Hoover had feared, was the evolu-tion of an impersonal bureaucratic system and a society characterized by the few leaders of big government, big capital, big labor, big ag-riculture, and big military dominating millions of other people. But for a time, many workers and others resisted the forces of corporate state capitalism. Some of them were old Progressives like Senator Borah. Others were the incipiently radical farmers who had formed the Non-partisan League in 1915 and continued to seek a working coalition with urban workers. There were also the industrial radicals: the heirs of Debsian socialism and the new Communists. Those people were crucial in helping to win important gains for workers and some minor-ity groups, even though they were often damned, harassed, and jailed for upsetting the social order.

Another group, the old-line conservatives, were often (and with con-siderable reason) criticized for their resistance to change, for their narrow individualism, and for their deep prejudice—or racism—against blacks and other minority groups. But the best of them fought the centralization of power as a matter of principle as well as a threat to their own position. Ironically, some of those views were shared, at least in part, by the rank-and-file workers. Their individualism along with their ethnic antagonisms led them to resist being organized into large, centralized, quasi-corporate unions.

In the end, of course, most of them joined a union, and that was probably the only way that the workers could gain any significant measure of equity within the system. But it is important to realize that the drive for union power between 1936 and 1941 grew out of the activity of many small groups of workers. The president's conservative bias against organized labor became apparent during the years of the NRA. Section 7-A of the legislation was evaded by many industries, and he did very little to keep them from evading the law's intent to support independent unions and the collective bargaining process. Some gains were made, but by the end of 1935, only 30 percent of the workers in industry were organized in independent unions: 20 percent were still represented by company unions and 43 percent were unorganized. Serious union men came to call the NRA the "National Run Around."

That imbalance was partially corrected by the major confrontations between late 1936 and 1941, but those victories grew out of many earlier and smaller battles—often fought against those who later emerged as leaders of big labor as well as against corporate management. That was the case, for example, in the coal and steel industries. A local strike at the Frick mines in 1933—"quickies" as they came to be known—was vigorously opposed by John L. Lewis. And another, during the same year, by Amalgamated steel workers in Weirton, West Virginia, was attacked by Philip Murray as the work of "outlaws."

The growing strength of the union movement was nevertheless fueled by such militant workers. A longshoremen's strike in San Francisco during July, 1934, almost paralyzed the city, and similar action by Alabama textile workers in the same year mushroomed into a walkout by 500,000 workers in 20 states. It was at that time the largest strike in American history, and it provoked the owners and their allies to muster 11,000 militiamen in the southern states alone.

The use of force by corporate management was nothing new (recall only the Homestead strike of 1892), but it was thoroughly documented by the investigations during 1936–1937 of a committee headed by Senator Robert LaFollette. The research revealed that not only was it standard practice to stockpile weapons against union activity, but that the Remington Rand Corporation had developed a broad strategy of opposition. That program, which came to be known as the Mohawk

Valley Plan, involved organizing local police forces and vigilantes, using newspaper and radio leaders to smear union men as dangerous radicals, exploiting the unemployed as strikebreakers, intensifying ethnic antagonisms among workers (and the public), and spending at least $80 million a year to hire spies to infiltrate the union movement.

Frightful though it was, it was not enough to intimidate the workers—who knew, or guessed, most of it long before Senator LaFollette made it public knowledge. If one translates the structural failure of the New Deal into specific episodes, then Roosevelt's time of troubles began in January, 1937, when workers in a General Motors factory in Flint, Michigan, went on strike by taking possession of the corporation's property. That strategy, which quickly became known as the sit-down strike, had been used in smaller confrontations during 1936 by other automobile and rubber workers in Ohio. But the Flint strike jarred the nation—and especially its leaders.

It was a risky move, and one leader probably spoke for all: "I was scared; my knees were shaking in spite of all my experience." The first attempt to remove the workers from the plant was repulsed with bottles and other missiles, and in the second, known as the Battle of the Running Bulls, the police retreated when the strikers turned the factory fire hoses on them.

The managers of General Motors then asked Governor Frank Murphy to use National Guard units. Feeling deeply that the workers had just grievances, and not unaware of their political power, he refused and tried instead to mediate. His attempts were fruitless, and G.M. obtained an injunction ordering the workers to vacate corporation property. They responded with a manifesto that made it clear that any effort to remove them by force would produce a bloodbath.

Roosevelt intervened at that point and began to exert heavy, sustained pressure on General Motors to recognize the union and begin negotiations. His effort was reinforced by the sympathy of the public for the workers and probably even more by management's fear about extensive damage to its plant and equipment. The company gave way on February 11, 1937, recognized the United Auto Workers (UAW), and began contract talks.

The sit-down strategy was quickly adopted by other workers, and by June, 1937, almost 500,000 people had been involved in such strikes. It also prompted some of the better union songs, as in this example:

When the speed-up comes, just twiddle your thumbs,
    Sit down! Sit down!
When the boss won't talk, don't take a walk,
    Sit down! Sit down!

The sit-downs also underscore the vital part played by local union leaders. Some of those people, such as the Mazey and Reuther brothers in the automobile industry, ultimately became national leaders, but all of them were crucial to the gains of the era.

For most people, John L. Lewis became the symbol of the rise of big labor. That was understandable in view of his leadership and his ability to dramatize the issues, but there were many other important figures in the movement. Philip Murray, who began with Lewis in the UMW, became the leader of the steel unions. Sidney Hillman was a central force in the growth and effectiveness of the ACW and was strikingly successful in mobilizing the political power of all workers. David Dubinsky played a similar role in the ILGWU, as did Charles Howard of the typographical union and Harry C. Flemming among petroleum workers.

But Lewis was the first charismatic labor leader since "Big Bill" Haywood and Eugene Debs, and he took most of the headlines. Strengthened by the victory over General Motors, his confrontation with Myron C. Taylor of U.S. Steel ultimately led, in March, 1937, to a significant victory. The union was recognized, and the workers won a good wage increase, an eight-hour day, and a 40-hour week (with time and a half for overtime).

The March sit-down strike against the Chrysler Corporation was more troublesome. Not only did the firm obtain an injunction, but many middle-class people were reacting against what they were coming to view as a threat to all property. Governor Murphy realized that he would very probably have to enforce the injunction if a settlement was not arranged. Lewis took charge of the negotiations and, with help from Murphy, arranged the evacuation of the factories on March 24, and on April 6 signed an agreement with the corporation.

All in all, it was a successful drive: by May 1937 the CIO had won gains through 100 contracts that involved 300,000 workers. Equally impressive victories were won by Hillman and Dubinsky: within the year their 37 unions had organized half the nation's textile workers. And other industries, such as rubber, were also being unionized. By the end of the year, the CIO was a powerful and effective organization of 3.7 million members. Labor's position was also strengthened by two decisions of the Supreme Court (*National Labor Relations Board* v. *Jones and Laughlin Steel Co.*, and *Thornhill* v. *Alabama*) that upheld the right to organize and the legality of picketing during a strike. And the Guffey-Vinson Bituminous Coal Act of April 1937 added further (though insufficient) regulations of that industry.

But neither Lewis nor the CIO won every battle. The Ford Motor Company, for example, was not unionized until 1941, and the so-called "Little Steel" corporations won a bloody Memorial Day battle in 1937. Those corporations were neither small nor powerless. United

States Steel was *the* giant of the industry, but Bethlehem, Youngstown Sheet and Tube, Inland, and Republic were major corporations that could—and did—exert great power in the political economy.

Thomas Girder of Republic led the resistance. He was tough: he said he "would rather dig potatoes than ever sign a contract with any labor organization." And he had enough political clout to control the police, who were tough, organized, and effective. When the confrontation came, the police could have won without an injury to anyone because the strikers "ran like hell." But as one worker said, "The cops make you riot. . . . They chased us and they beat us again. . . . They began to shoot us, club us, gas us . . . ten people died, while 68 were wounded. . . . It was really hell on that field. . . . It dawned on me: They were shooting real bullets. . . . They didn't stop shooting and killing till an hour and a half later." And so the workers lost. The Little Steel corporations were not organized until 1941—like the "little" car company named Ford.

The militant, industrial unionism of the CIO generated other kinds of opposition. The leaders of the AF of L, whose narrow view of the modern factory system had cost them the chance to gain members in the auto and steel industries, launched their counterattack during the negotiations of 1937 for a merger with the CIO. Their refusal to combine led to a wild battle for power that hurt the rank-and-file worker for another generation. The resulting jurisdictional strikes (disputes about which union would represent the laborers in any given plant) did, on balance, extend the power of labor, but they also divided workers against each other and drew increasing opposition from the middle class.

So did the fight over the legislation introduced in May, 1936, that proposed to establish a minimum wage, maximum hours, and severe limits on child labor. The AF of L opposed the bill on the grounds that "minimum wages become maximum wages." Even Lewis said no. But there was enough support to prompt Roosevelt to try again by calling a November, 1937, special session of the Congress. That failed, and still another such meeting in January, 1938, also came to nothing. Then some victories in off-year elections in the South, Claude Pepper in Florida and Lister Hill in Alabama, produced the June, 1938, Fair Labor Standards Act. It established a rising minimum wage, a decreasing workweek, and some restrictions on child labor.

ROOSEVELT'S BATTLE TO CONTROL THE SUPREME COURT

That long battle, along with the sustained labor unrest, typified the frustrations that Roosevelt increasingly felt about the failure of the

New Deal to solve the problems of the economy and restore social tranquillity. Impatient and exasperated, he dramatically proposed to make a basic change in the structure of American constitutional government. Very simply, Roosevelt sought either to outflank the legislative branch by consolidating the Supreme Court as an instrument of the executive or to redefine the Court as an instrument of a political majority that controlled the White House and the Congress. In either case, the Court (and the law) would become the instrument of politics.

The president prepared and launched his assault on the Court in privacy. It seems likely, however, that three considerations were in his mind. The first was the frustration he felt in trying to deal with the urgent problems of the country and to counter the Court's rulings during 1935 and 1936 against New Deal legislation. The second was the confidence created by his resounding victory in the election of 1936. The most intangible factor was Roosevelt's tendency to personalize issues, but he seems to have taken the Court's rulings as a direct attack on himself and his leadership. His secrecy in handling his counterattack indicates that kind of psychological involvement.

Without consulting other Democratic leaders, Roosevelt fired his salvo at the Court on February 5, 1937, in the form of a special message to the Congress. He was disingenuous, for the proposal seemed at first glance to be nothing more than an extension of his earlier request to reorganize the executive department: a plan to expedite federal court proceedings and to prevent the lower courts from interfering with (or delaying) the judicial process in major cases. Three of the proposals were: to direct all appeals on constitutional issues straight to the Supreme Court; to make it mandatory to hear the arguments of the Justice Department before granting an injunction against an act of the Congress if a constitutional question was involved; and to add new judges in district courts that were slow or overloaded.

Roosevelt's major objective became clear, however, in his request for authority to add judges to federal courts (up to a total of 50) when a member continued working after he reached the age of 70, and in that connection to enlarge the Supreme Court to a maximum of 15 members. Roosevelt's closest approach to candor came in his observation that younger judges would help the country adapt to changing conditions. But neither the secrecy nor the camouflage was sufficient to save the president. The opposition was immediate, angry, powerful, and widespread.

Roosevelt lost the support of many reformers and deeply divided his own party. That result is a strong argument against the assertion that the president was engaged from the outset in a calculated strategy of losing the battle and winning the war. It is possible to make that interpretation: that Roosevelt made an exaggerated attack designed

not to win through the formal capitulation of the enemy and the impo-
sition of his own plan but to get what he wanted through the concessions made by the opponent in order to avoid complete defeat. Even if
that was the case, and it seems highly dubious, the president paid an
extremely high price for his success.

He no doubt expected the outrage of the Liberty League, Father
Coughlin, and the Court itself. And the president was supported by
some reformers like LaFollette, who argued that the Court had been
packed for years with men who served "the cause of reaction and
laissez-faire" and who insisted that the proposal was necessary and
constitutional. He was unquestionably correct about the narrow legal
question, but he did not speak to the main points that many people felt
to be at issue. Nor was it enough for the president to say (as he did on
March 4 and 9) that the change was necessary because the "personal
economic predilections" of the Court's conservative majority "cast
doubts on the ability of the elected Congress to protect us against
catastrophe by meeting squarely our modern social and economic
conditions."

The president and his supporters grievously underestimated the extent to which the country was worried that his remedy would be more
catastrophic than the illness. That basic issue had been dramatized by
Sinclair Lewis in his novel *It Can't Happen Here* (1935). Lewis suggested that Americans were mistaken in their easy confidence that
totalitarian or dictatorial government could never develop in the
United States; and the actions of Hitler, who did rise to power by
manipulating a system of representative government, highlighted his
warning. Many people who doubted that Roosevelt himself wanted to
be a dictator nevertheless feared that making the Supreme Court so
directly subject to the will of the president involved a consolidation
and centralization of power that would fatally undermine representative government. The reforms of the New Deal might be legalized, but
so could less humane and benevolent measures.

Roosevelt's harsh use of patronage and personal influence to win
votes for his plan only reinforced that concern. True, his opponents
were moved by particular interests as well as by general ideas, but the
extremely individualistic businessmen of the Liberty League were not
alone in being upset. The economic system relied heavily on the
routine functioning of the law, and a threat to its stability concerned
many corporation leaders who otherwise supported the president. The
more astute businessmen who accepted the increased role and power
of the government in the political economy opposed Roosevelt's court
plan because it threatened to weaken or even destroy their position
and influence in the developing partnership.

The president's offensive against the Court also increased the uneasiness about the rise of corporate labor. That fear influenced many middle-class people, but southern spokesmen were especially worried. They saw the CIO as a threat to their regional labor policies (against poor whites as well as blacks) and also opposed union strength on the broader ground that it weakened their power in the Democratic party. Their political philosophy was predicated upon the contradictory combination of viable local self-government with the invidious racism of segregation: the court plan struck them as a major threat to *their* white South. Important and powerful Democrats such as Carter Glass of Virginia, Walter George of Georgia, and even Vice President Garner revolted openly against the president.

Their decision to form a working alliance with Republican conservatives that extended to other issues was even more consequential for it threw a major roadblock across the path of the New Deal. Both as a specific issue, therefore, as well as a cause that deeply divided the New Deal coalition, the court fight came to dominate the affairs of government. Very little other business was transacted.

The Court was in many ways its own best defender. Brandeis, the oldest as well as the most liberal judge, made no effort to hide his outrage at being labeled incompetent because of his age. Chief Justice Hughes pushed that counterattack in an effective letter written March 21, in which he publicly denied the charges of slowness and inefficiency. Hughes also led a vital dialogue among the justices. He had voted with the liberal Brandeis group in important decisions, and he very probably influenced Justice Owen J. Roberts, a conservative who occasionally supplied a key vote for a liberal interpretation of the Constitution.

Roberts had done precisely that in an important case decided *before* Roosevelt opened his attack on the Court. The decision, in *West Coast Hotel* v. *Parrish,* reversed an earlier ruling and upheld a minimum wage law enacted in the state of Washington. The Court based its logic, furthermore, on broad and general grounds. The decision was announced publicly on March 29, 1937, and had a sharp impact on the debate. The Court looked much less reactionary than Roosevelt and his supporters had maintained. It followed quickly (April 12) with another and even more significant verdict. With Hughes and Roberts again casting crucial votes, the Court upheld the validity of the National Labor Relations Act (in *NLRB* v. *Jones and Laughlin Steel Corporation*).

Then Justice Willis Van Devanter, one of the four staunch conservatives, seized the initiative from Roosevelt. Under sustained though friendly pressure from Senator Borah, who considered the court fight of vast importance to the survival of representative government, Van Devanter announced on May 18 that he would retire shortly. The

Court assembled a week later on decision day and fired another salvo, ruling that social security legislation was constitutional (*Carmichael* v. *Southern Coal Company*). But Roosevelt showed little willingness to accept an indirect victory, an attitude that suggests he was not engaged in a grand bluff. His stubbornness also made his defeat more obvious. Only with the death of Senator Joseph T. Robinson (July 14), who had served as the president's chief aide in the fight to whip the Democrats into line, did Roosevelt finally admit that he was beaten. The Senate promptly (and convincingly, 70–20) buried his bill in committee.

Roosevelt did accomplish two things: he focused great attention on the process of judicial review, and he contributed to the Court's acceptance of more far-reaching regulation of the economy. Beginning with the appointment of Hugo Black to replace Van Devanter, moreover, the president placed five men on the Court during the next 30 months. The others were Stanley Reed, Felix Frankfurter, William O. Douglas, and Frank Murphy. But the justices won the war, and the importance of that victory can easily be overlooked in concentrating on Roosevelt's role. The Court maintained its vital part in the constitutional system *and* its prestige.

Roosevelt paid for his gains, moreover, with coin that was difficult to replace. The fight disrupted the New Deal coalition and turned it away from further reform. The New Deal was very probably running out of intellectual drive and emotional zeal, much as the earlier Progressive coalition had ground to a halt in 1913–1914, but the court fight distracted and divided the alliance that had produced so much legislation between 1933 and 1937.

There were some further reforms. The Bankhead-Jones Farm Act, an attempt to deal with the continued rise in tenancy and sharecropping, attracted enough support among southerners and westerners who had fought Roosevelt on the court issue to become law on July 22, 1937. A report of February had revealed that those categories accounted for 50 percent of the farmers in the South, 30 percent in the North, and 25 percent in the West. The law established the Farm Security Administration to reorganize and strengthen the program handled earlier by the Resettlement Administration. Long-term, low-interest loans were offered to men who wanted to buy land, and other credit was made available for refinancing and education. And, despite opposition from those who exploited such labor, efforts were made to improve the pay and living conditions of migrant laborers. But that part of the program was not generally successful.

The National Housing Act of September 1, 1937, created an authority responsible for improving conditions for the poor. Slum clearance projects and straight housing proposals were eligible for federal assistance in the form of 60-year loans. There was also a provision to adjust rents to low-income levels, but that depended upon local authorities contributing an amount equal to one-quarter of the federal loan. The agency signed contracts for a mere 511 projects during its first three years (to January, 1941), though it became somewhat more active during the war. The program did help some people, but it did not in any way solve the problem. Most projects were taken over by middle-class families.

Such legislation manifested a concern to deal with basic weaknesses in the system and should not be discounted even though it proved insufficient. But the New Deal's loss of momentum became increasingly clear throughout the summer. Congress passed a fair trade bill, for example, that changed antitrust laws so that corporations could legally set and enforce the prices charged by distributors and retail merchants. Roosevelt did not like the law, but he did not feel that he had the strength to sustain a veto.

The shift in power became apparent when the anti-Roosevelt coalition controlled the Congress during the special session called on October 12, 1937. The conservatives blocked action on the president's requests for wages-and-hours legislation, conservation programs, and new agricultural policies. Those measures were part of the administration's rather desperate effort to compensate for the weaknesses and failures of earlier reforms and to cope with another crisis in the economy.

ANOTHER ECONOMIC CRISIS

By the time the Congress convened, the country was confronted by a grave economic recession. The recovery in industrial production that had started in March, 1936, began to slow down in April, 1937, and the economy failed to make further gains. The collapse came in October, and it was almost as devastating as the 1929 trauma. The key index figures in October were: production, 102; payrolls in manufacturing, 104.9; and employment in manufacturing, 110.3. By December they had dropped to 84; 84.6; and 97.7. Prices fell sharply, unemployment jumped upward, and real income (measured against 1929 as 100) dropped from the 93.7 mark it had reached early in 1937. The New Deal was in serious trouble.

Millions of Americans suffered severe deprivation through the winter of 1937–1938 as a result of the recession. That pain dramatized the more general failure of the New Deal to pull the nation out of the depression. Even the depersonalized statistics communicate a sense of the drastic downturn. The steel industry, for example, was using only 19 percent of its productive capacity. Overall industrial activity nose-

Figure 4 *Families living in deprivation, comfort, and affluence, 1929–1960.*
(From *Poverty and Deprivation in the United States. Conference on Economic Progress,* Washington, D.C., 1960, p. 34.)

Millions of Multiple Person Families with Annual Incomes[1]
of $4,000 and Over, Before Taxes, in 1960 Dollars

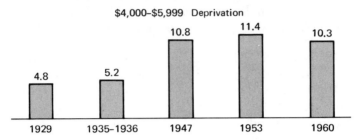

$4,000–$5,999   Deprivation

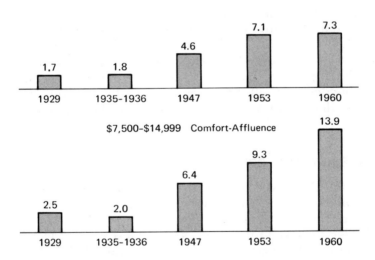

$6,000–$7,499   Deprivation-Comfort

$7,500–$14,999   Comfort-Affluence

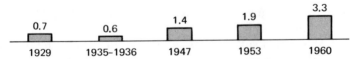

$15,000 and Over   Affluence

[1] Includes in addition to cash income the monetary value of food and fuel produced
and consumed on the farm, and other nonmoney income.
Data: 1929 and 1947–'60, Dept. of Commerce. 1935–'36, Nat'l Bureau Economic
Research. 1960 distribution partly CEP estimated. Conversions to 1960 dollars, CEP.

dived from a level of 102 (October, 1937) to 79 by March, 1938, and as unemployment continued to rise, the WPA rolls increased 200 to 400 percent in some major centers of population. But the relief system broke down in some areas, and people could not get subsistence supplies for as long as two weeks.

The human beings involved were cold, hungry, and miserable. They became ill and died because their bodies were weak and their spirits destroyed. Hundreds of them stood long, shivering hours in line to draw handouts or in the forlorn hope that they would be chosen for the one job that had been advertised—or rumored.

Roosevelt and his advisers floundered. The president first talked with Myron Taylor of U.S. Steel and other economic leaders and on January 4, 1938, spoke as though he was planning to revive the NRA approach. Cartels, so ran the argument, could generate recovery. The president's liberal critics were distraught and disgusted. Secretary of the Interior Ickes remarked bitterly that Roosevelt was "pulling the petals off the daisy with representatives of big business."

The critics had their say when the stock market broke downward again on March 25, 1938: led by Ickes, Hopkins, and Leon Henderson, they insisted that the government had to resume its spending programs. That was the only way, they argued, to overcome the crisis. The reformers did not propose any drastic changes in the system of corporate state capitalism. They were trying to save it by somehow making it work satisfactorily enough to avoid complete collapse, and then, hopefully, well enough to produce significant improvements in the material conditions of life in the United States. Perhaps the most far-reaching suggestion came from presidential adviser Adolf A. Berle, who warned in the spring of 1938 (just before he resigned) that the Roosevelt administration had better prepare itself to nationalize "great blocks of industry" if it wanted to prevent a continuing cycle of recession and partial recovery.

In some respects, at least, that kind of reorganization was happening as a result of the New Deal. It was not nationalization in the nineteenth-century Socialist sense of integrating the existing system into one vast interrelated order in which the government played a primary and guiding role. Instead, the corporations and the labor unions, and to a lesser extent the farm bloc, joined with the government bureaucracy to provide some direction over the political economy.

Herbert Hoover had foreseen that possibility, and his analysis provided the basis for his criticisms of the New Deal. He argued that the public was losing power over its own affairs as a coalition of government and the elite leadership of various organized groups made more and more of the basic decisions outside the framework of representative government. Similar fears led men like Senator Borah to suggest the licensing of corporations by the government. That approach, they argued, would give the government more direct and effective control of the private giants.

Roosevelt opposed that idea but seemed more responsive to the antimonopoly arguments of men like Henderson (an adviser to Hopkins), Assistant Attorney General Robert Jackson, and other New Dealers like Benjamin Cohen and Thomas Corcoran. Those people also supported the Hopkins-Ickes-Eccles drive for more spending, and that coalition finally persuaded the president to act on their recommendations. He may also have been influenced by the Congress: it passed on February 16, 1938, a revised Agricultural Adjustment Act.

That law attempted to cope with the continuing farm crisis by controlling the production and marketing of cotton, wheat, corn, tobacco, and rice. All farmers were eligible for payments in return for decreasing their acreage, but those who raised the specified commodities were given special treatment. Farmers immediately demanded increased payments, but they generally accepted the proviso that enabled the government to buy surpluses and distribute them to school lunch programs and to needy families and individuals.

Roosevelt also asked (April 14, 1938) for vastly expanded relief expenditures and eased credit restrictions. Two weeks later he requested authority and funds for an investigation of monopoly and the concentration of economic power. The administration won much of what it asked, but its proposals were not sufficient to produce sustained recovery. Farmers were undoubtedly helped by the new AAA, but within a year the government was forced to begin paying export subsidies and to dump various surpluses in the world marketplace. The export subsidy on cotton, for example, climbed as high as $7.50 a bale. Such palliatives were helpful, but American agriculture remained depressed until war orders generated recovery.

That was true of the economy in general. The Congress did, through the Emergency Relief Act of June, 1938, provide more temporary aid: the $3.75 billion was divided among the PWA, the WPA, housing programs, more parity payments for agriculture, and other New Deal agencies. And the RFC expanded its loans. The Congress also launched an investigation of concentrated economic power by establishing a joint Temporary National Economic Committee (TNEC) under the leadership of Wyoming senator Joseph O'Mahoney.

But neither the relief measures, the TNEC hearings, nor a related revival of the antitrust approach revived the economy. The TNEC study revealed that the structure of the economy had not changed in any substantive way since the earlier study by Adolf Berle and Gardner Means. A handful of giant corporations dominated the economic system: they limited the alternatives open to the government, as well as to the big labor unions, the farmers, and the consumers. But the congressional committee did not challenge that power; it sought only (and without much passion) to provide a bit more regulation.

One such measure of June 24, 1938, did set certain rules for companies involved in interstate commerce. It was a serious effort to establish and enforce minimum standards of equity in the relationship between employer and workers and to put a floor under the buying power of the consumer, thereby maintaining some level of demand in the marketplace.

And it helped: 750,000 workers began receiving more money in August, 1938, and millions gained increases in later years. But neither it nor other New Deal measures pulled the country out of the recession. Nor did the Roosevelt administration offer any broad, imaginative program for that purpose. Such an attempt might have been limited, even blocked, by the conservative coalition that had emerged from the battle over the Supreme Court. But Roosevelt never tried to organize a serious confrontation of that kind, though he did make one attack on conservative Democrats.

The emerging bipartisan coalition of conservatives proved strong enough by the spring of 1938 to influence much legislation and to create platforms for the members' assaults on the administration. They established the House Committee on Un-American Activities, for example, on May 26, 1938. Ostensibly organized to investigate the activities of Nazi and Fascist groups, as well as of Communist, its conduct quickly made it clear that it was largely concerned with discrediting the New Deal by allegations of radicalism and subversion. The conservatives also heavily influenced the Revenue Act passed on May 27, 1938, which made significant concessions to business. The existing tax on undistributed profits was repealed, as was the progressive normal tax. The substitute provisions lowered the rates and left many loopholes. Other parts of the law favored large corporations against small businesses.

Roosevelt was encouraged by the failure of Governor Philip LaFollette of Wisconsin to rally old Progressives and new reformers behind his National Progressives of America (launched April 28, 1939). LaFollette attacked concentrated corporate power in the economic system, the increasing governmental centralization of the New Deal, and the idea of solving economic problems by restricting production. At the same time, however, he called for more regulatory legislation and even for public ownership. A good many of LaFollette's criticisms of the

New Deal were valid, but the spirit and tone of the movement, which relied on a crude kind of nationalistic and underdog psychology, failed to attract significant backing. The effort collapsed.

Other organizations, however, such as Frank Gannett's National Committee to Uphold Constitutional Government, were building support for conservatives. They concentrated on blocking Roosevelt's government reorganization bill and on providing help for conservatives in the off-year elections of 1938. "Why should Congress continue to surrender and abdicate its legislative function to the chief executive," asked one such member of the Senate, "and leave itself with no more legislative authority than Gandhi has clothing?"

Roosevelt launched his counterattack in June, 1938, with a bold campaign to defeat key opponents in the Democratic party (such as Senator George of Georgia). The president failed. Not only was the purge blocked but the Republicans gained 81 seats in the House, 8 new votes in the Senate (including that of Robert A. Taft of Ohio), and 13 new governorships. The administration retained formal control of the Congress, but the conservative coalition had been immensely strengthened. It was a defeat that could not be disguised or discounted.

One of the Democrats who lost his seat in the House of Representatives offered a candid and generally accurate explanation of the results. "The main reason is the Democrats thus far have failed in their major objective," observed Charles R. Eckert of Pennsylvania. "The New Deal was set up not only to arrest the depression but to lay the foundation for permanent recovery. The prosperity for which the American people have been yearning for more than a decade has failed to make its appearance. It is still around the corner."

Roosevelt acknowledged the end of reform, if not the broader failure to generate sustained recovery and further economic growth, in his message to the Congress on January 4, 1939. "We have now passed the period of internal conflict in the launching of our program of social reform. Our full energies may now be released to invigorate the processes of recovery in order to preserve our reforms." The president offered no program, however, for either the marshaling or the direction of those full energies. He concentrated instead on providing more relief and on asking for more armaments.

His relief request of January 5, 1939, totaled $875 million. The Congress cut that to $725 million and likewise pared the president's later appeals (in February and March) for more money. As a result, the aid administered through the WPA declined: its rolls dropped to just over 2.5 million people by the middle of 1939. The ensuing crisis was met by the Emergency Relief Appropriation Act of June 30, 1939. It allotted $1.5 billion to the WPA, but in doing so it killed the Federal

Theater Project and limited people to 18 months of continuous relief employment. A good many got less than that: they were dismissed for participating in a nationwide strike of WPA workers against the harshness of the law.

Although Roosevelt was becoming ever more deeply involved with foreign policy, a shift in emphasis that rather quickly led to America becoming a belligerent power aligned against Germany, Italy, and Japan, he and other New Deal leaders did secure several other reforms. The Administrative Reorganization Act, finally approved on April 3, 1939, enabled Roosevelt to reshuffle the executive department under three main offices called the Federal Security Agency, the Federal Works Agency, and the Federal Loan Agency. The most important change involved shifting the Bureau of the Budget from the Treasury Department to the executive office of the presidency. Roosevelt and his successors thus gained direct authority over the planning and allocation of federal expenditures.

Such power had been criticized and challenged during the elections of 1938 through charges that the WPA rolls in Kentucky, Maryland, and Tennessee had been manipulated to control votes for Democratic candidates. While all the allegations were not proved, enough evidence was produced to win support for the Hatch Act of August 2, 1939. That law made it illegal for officeholders below the policy-making level of the executive department to engage in political campaigns, to solicit contributions from workers in relief jobs, or to otherwise interfere in federal elections. The law was later extended (July, 1940) to apply to members of state and local governments whose salaries were paid in whole or in part from federal funds.

The people on relief, meanwhile, were helped by the Food Stamp Plan that began operation in Rochester, New York, in May, 1939. Designed to distribute surplus agricultural products to the millions of needy people, the program was ultimately extended to more than 100 other cities. Social security benefits were also extended by the law of July 13, 1939: it provided for earlier payment of old age benefits, extended supplementary assistance to wives, added maritime workers and other categories of labor, and made average wages (rather than total wages) the basis for computing benefits.

As with various other New Deal measures, those laws generated desirable and helpful improvements of life in America. But in 1939, the last year that can accurately be called peacetime, there were still more than nine million unemployed people in the United States. That was about 17 percent of the population. The farmer who had managed to stay on the land was earning an average income of $1000 a year. Such a family could buy a Ford sedan, with license but without oil and gas, for $700. Perhaps that comparison provides the best illustration of the limits of the New Deal. It had done much, but not nearly enough. Recovery came only through a war economy.

EXPLORATORY READING

The nature of the corporate state capitalism that emerged by the end of the 1930s is perceptively discussed by these authors:

W. Adams (Ed.), *The Structure of the American Industry: Some Case Studies* (1961)

J. S. Bain, Jr., *Industrial Organization* (1968)

A. Hacker (Ed.), *The Corporation Take-Over* (1965)

R. A. Lawson, *The Failure of Independent Liberalism, 1930–1941* (1971)

T. Lowi, *End of Liberalism* (1969)

E. A. Purcell, *The Crisis of Democratic Theory* (1972)

B. Seligman, *Permanent Poverty* (1962)

G. W. Stocking and M. W. Watkins, *Monopoly and Free Enterprise* (1951)

The impact on workers, farmers, blacks, and Indians is discussed in these books:

S. Baldwin, *Poverty and Politics: The Rise and Decline of the Farm Security Administration* (1967)

M. Benedict, *Can We Solve the Farm Problem?* (1955)

R. R. Brooks, *Unions of Their Own Choosing* (1939)

E. S. Cahn (Ed.), *Our Brother's Keeper: The Indian in White America* (1969)

S. Fine, *Sit-Down: The General Motors Strike of 1936–1937* (1969)

W. Galenson, *The CIO Challenge to the AFL* (1960)

A. W. Jones, *Life, Liberty, and Property* (1941)

M. Josephson, *Sidney Hillman* (1952)

A. Raper, *Preface to Peasantry* (1936)

W. T. Tabb, *The Political Economy of the Black Ghetto* (1970)

R. Wolters, *Negroes and the Great Depression* (1970)

Many of the best discussions of Roosevelt's attack on the Supreme Court are to be found in the law reviews, but these volumes provide a good introduction to the subject:

J. Alsop and T. Catledge, *The 168 Days* (1938)

L. Baker, *Back to Back: The Duel Between FDR and the Supreme Court* (1967)

S. Hendel, *Charles Evans Hughes and the Supreme Court* (1951)

R. Jackson, *The Struggle for Judicial Supremacy* (1941)

P. B. Kurland (Ed.), *The Supreme Court Review* (1966)

P. L. Murphy, *The Constitution in Crisis Times* (1972)

16 RECOVERY AND CONSOLIDATION THROUGH WAR

THE New Deal's domestic failure was largely forgotten by most people during the war against the Axis powers headed by Germany and Japan. Roosevelt and other key leaders remained acutely aware of the crucial relationship between recovery and war, however, and it exerted a powerful influence on their thinking during and after that global conflict. That was not particularly surprising because the president and other important New Dealers had always revealed a strong—if sometimes subtle—commitment to the economic and political imperatives of the American empire.

Recognizing that imperial thrust, some observers (most notably historians Charles Beard and Harry Elmer Barnes) concluded that Roosevelt turned to war when he failed at home. It seems more likely, however, that the inherent imperialism of the system increasingly defined American foreign policy in terms of war. Given the assumption that American welfare depended upon a world marketplace system open to American economic power—and to the enlightened reformist outlook of the United States—the rise of militant alternatives led naturally to military action to preserve the Open Door policy.

One of Roosevelt's first moves in foreign policy (March, 1933) was to recognize the Soviet Union, and it involved a classic combination of motives: the hope for markets (particularly cotton and machine tools) and a subtle signal to Japan to restrain itself in Asia. Roosevelt's sympathy with China was apparent, even though the depression and the opposition of religious and secular groups restricted his ability to act. In the end, he settled for sending the fleet to Pearl Harbor.

He also used the navy and economic power to support his efforts (1933–1934) to control a revolution in Cuba. It was a fine example of subtle and effective—even relatively generous—imperialism presented in the rhetoric of "The Good Neighbor." The United States was saving the Cubans from their own mistakes. The result was a right-wing authoritarian regime (and ultimately a dictatorship) that was dependent upon the United States. Having learned the lesson, Cuba was rewarded with a guaranteed market for its sugar and with a rising flow of investment capital that, among other things, transformed Havana into a playground for the rich (including the criminal syndicates).

Roosevelt's imperial outlook emerged quite clearly during the 1933 fight over farm legislation, which made it clear that New Deal leaders were going to sustain the traditional policies of the Open Door and overseas economic expansion. An astute British spokesman correctly predicted "an outward drive of American imperialism on a scale and with an intensity which the world has hitherto had no experience."

Secretary of State Cordell Hull, who, despite appearances to the contrary, exercised considerable influence in the policy-making process, was a staunch advocate of the Open Door, of American hegemony in the Western Hemisphere and of the expansion of foreign markets. He immediately revived the Blaine-McKinley program of reciprocity treaties and, with Roosevelt's support, pushed through (June 12, 1934) the new Trade Agreements Act. The law combined the bargaining authority given to the president in the tariff act of 1890 with the 1922 power to manipulate rates up to 50 percent and added the proviso that future agreements did not require congressional approval.

Roosevelt also moved quickly to use relief funds for building new warships. Then, in March, 1934, he won a general authorization (through the Vinson Naval Parity Act) to construct 100 ships and increase the air force to 1000 planes. Another law authorized him to integrate the National Guard into the regular army during an emergency. That expansionist momentum was checked, however, by the rising intensity of the debate about the relationships between economic expansion and war.

One of the early exchanges involved historian Charles Beard and Secretary of Agriculture Henry A. Wallace. Beard's harsh attack on the imperial outlook of the New Deal upset Wallace, who considered the penetration and control of export markets as "one of my own pet hobbies." The secretary, who was a global reformer as well as a shrewd agricultural businessman, admitted that Beard offered a valid challenge: make a clear and open choice between new domestic planning or continue "the old export approach." Wallace did so, arguing bluntly

International trade inside the depressed world of the 1930s required a salesman who not only knew the territory but could also cover it well. Poor Uncle Sam had the products, but he was crippled by shoes that hurt his feet. This was a limitation on his access to the marketplace. Knox presented the agony in the Memphis Commercial Appeal.

Can't Seem to Get Going
—Knox in the Memphis *Commercial Appeal*

Jack Knox, the *Commercial Appeal*, Memphis, Tenn. Reprinted in *The Literary Digest*, vol. 117, May 12, 1934, p. 10.

This cartoon details an old, old story. The annual cry is shrill, fearful, and full of doom—"Nations are spending more on defense than we are, we must catch up." Security depends upon spending more and more and more. The technique is almost perfect, for each year the defense budget is increased. This is J. T. Cargill in the New York Herald Tribune.

And the Military Appropriations Are Coming
—Cargill in the New York *Herald Tribune*

Reprinted in *The Literary Digest*, vol. 121, March 7, 1936, p. 11.

"that the future of capitalism depends on increased foreign purchasing of our exports."

Beard replied that such an approach meant war. "I consider the foreign implications of our domestic policy and the hazards of a futile and idiotic war in the Far East more important than old age pension and all the rest of it." That concern was intensified by the debates over the Vinson Naval Bill. The leader of the opposition was Senator Gerald Nye of North Dakota, who opened the attack on February 8, 1934, with a call for an investigation of the armaments industry. Nye's campaign was strengthened by the editors of *Fortune* magazine, who published a devastating critique of that industry in their March issue, and by pressure from Dorothy Detzer and other peace advocates. After the passage of the naval legislation, the Senate promptly created a special committee to study the arms makers.

Partially because of his own intention to explore broader problems of foreign policy, and also because of the rising pressure for such an inquiry, Nye began to stress the relationship between trade, investments, and war. That question was brilliantly defined by lawyer Charles Warren in a 1934 issue of *Foreign Affairs*. Warren, who had served as assistant attorney general under President Wilson, argued that economic ties pulled nations into war. And he candidly admitted that they would continue to do so unless trade, investments, and loans were limited and controlled.

Nye candidly admitted, however, that the commitment to overseas markets and raw materials was so strong among corporation and government leaders that it was impossible to pass a law that dealt effectively with the problem of maintaining neutrality. Roosevelt underscored that point with a blunt speech at the height of the debate: "Foreign markets must be regained if American producers are to rebuild a full and enduring prosperity for our people. . . . There is no other way if we would avoid painful economic dislocations, social readjustments, and unemployment." The president did not mention—let alone discuss—the dangers and the consequences of tying the welfare of the country so intimately to imperial expansion.

The best that Nye and his supporters could obtain in 1935–1936 were two compromises. One law (August 31, 1935) authorized the president to embargo arms shipments if he ruled that a state of war existed between foreign countries; the other (February 29, 1936) prohibited loans or credits to those defined as belligerents. Neither piece of legislation dealt with the central problem raised by defining the military security of the country in terms of overseas markets deemed necessary for domestic prosperity. Even more ominous was the abdication of power by the Congress. What in later years came to be called the "Imperial Presidency" was aptly named, for while the depression contributed much to the centralization of power in the executive, the crucial factor was the delegation of power to the executive within the expansionist outlook on foreign affairs.

The subsequent arguments over foreign policy, and particularly those that occurred during and after the domestic breakdown of the New Deal in 1937, obscured the main issue: Roosevelt centralized control of an imperial foreign policy *before* Germany or Japan posed any strategic threat to the security and welfare of the United States. Those nations intervened first in the Spanish Revolution, which began on July 18, 1936, when General Francisco Franco led Fascist and other reactionary elements in a move to take over the country in the name of corporate Catholicism.

But the existing government, composed of a coalition of Republicans, Socialists, Communists, and Syndicalists, held firm in Madrid and Barcelona despite Franco's control of most of the army and air force. That success blocked a quick coup and the conflict became a full-scale revolutionary civil war. Germany and Italy began to aid Franco, while Russia, along with radicals and reformers in other countries, supported the Republican government with matériel and advisers.

The conflict generated a heated debate between two groups of Americans. Catholics and other conservatives supported Franco and vigorously opposed aid to the Spanish government, but a liberal-radical coalition agitated vigorously for sending help. The latter group organized a volunteer force, the Abraham Lincoln Brigade, that fought bravely in Spain, and its view of the war provoked Ernest Hemingway to abandon temporarily his romantic individualism and write a moving novel *(For Whom the Bell Tolls)* about the anti-Franco coalition.

Roosevelt was not persuaded by either action. He asked the Congress in December, 1937, to modify the Neutrality Act so that its provisions were specifically extended to civil wars, and that was promptly accomplished (January 6, 1938) with but one dissenting vote. Armed with that discretionary power, the president refused to help the Republican government in Madrid. Franco captured Barcelona in January, 1939, and Madrid in March, and the United States promptly recognized his government.

The anti-Franco campaign probably helped Roosevelt and Hull block the passage of any tougher neutrality legislation. But as one senator explained, the major factor in that battle was the broad consensus among the leaders of the corporate political economy on "the necessity for foreign commerce." As a result, the neutrality law of May 1, 1937, was a pro-administration compromise. The sale and export of munitions were forbidden, along with loans to belligerent powers. Latin-American countries, however, were exempted from those provisions, an action that revealed the growing concern over German economic and political penetration of the Western Hemisphere. Travel on belligerent ships was also made illegal. But the president was given discretionary powers to allow (for a trial period of two years) the export of specified raw materials, such as copper, to belligerents on a cash-and-carry basis. That clearly favored Great Britain and its allies in any conflict with Germany and Italy.

Japan posed the most immediate threat to the Open Door empire, however, when it reopened its assault on China near Peking on July 7, 1937 and then ignored Roosevelt's request for a new pledge to respect the Open Door policy. Many people, despite their sympathy for China (and for Americans who suffered during the attack on Shanghai), seemed ready to let the war take its own course. But others insisted that the United States had to take a strong stand, arguing that a line had to be drawn, and better then than later.

Many of the interventionists felt that the Japanese were going to prevent America from realizing its old dream about the opportunities in China. A Bureau of Foreign and Domestic Commerce report summarized that outlook: "Probably never in its history has China offered greater promise for its future trade, industry, and general economic progress than it evidenced at the end of the first six month's period of the current year and just prior to the outbreak of the present hostilities." The Japanese attack threatened that rosy prospect. It also upset men like Assistant Secretary of State Francis B. Sayre who were generally concerned about America's overseas expansion. "If we lose our foreign markets for cotton, lumber, or any one of a number of major industrial exports," Sayre asserted, "large sections of our country must face disaster."

Another group of leaders argued that the Japanese action was part of a general assault upon America's position in the world, and many were especially worried about Latin America. Corporate spokesmen like George E. Roberts, vice president of the National City Bank, shared that attitude with government figures like Secretary of the Treasury Morgenthau and Ambassador to Mexico Josephus Daniels. The Mexican situation provided a particular focus for their concern.

The long dispute with Mexico, arising from the property and labor provisions of its 1917 Constitution, had been kept under control but it had never been resolved. The Mexicans would not surrender the right to run their affairs in their own way, and neither the American companies nor the American government would relax pressure. The conflict again became serious in 1937 when the corporations refused to meet the demands of Mexican labor unions. The rising tensions scared Morgenthau. "We're just going to wake up," he warned, "and find inside of a year that Italy, Germany, and Japan have taken over

Mexico." He feared that Mexico would of necessity begin making barter deals to obtain the goods, services, and capital that it needed. Daniels agreed and constantly advised Washington to resolve the problems and expand trade.

Roosevelt ultimately compromised in Mexico, but he was primarily concerned with Germany and Japan. Ostensibly in Chicago to dedicate a bridge, the president spoke forcefully about the "problems of world economy, world security, and world humanity." He sounded more than a little like Wilson as he attacked the "international lawlessness" that was creating "international anarchy." Using the metaphor of "the epidemic" to describe those who were "threatening a breakdown of all international law and order," he called for a quarantine of the dangerous elements.

The president was attacked by those who feared he was talking about war or action that would lead to war. The critics made the loudest noise, but the speech received considerable support throughout the country. A good many people called for immediate action, stressing the power of economic sanctions. Senator Burton K. Wheeler, for example, pointed out that that was "the only way Japan can be brought to her knees," and former Secretary of State Stimson called for an arms embargo. Others, including labor unions long worried about low-priced competition, began to boycott silk stockings and other Japanese goods.

Though he was dedicated to the Open Door policy, Secretary Hull thought such actions would only incense the Japanese without stopping them, and he was supported by Joseph Grew, the American ambassador in Tokyo. Others feared that Russia would gain the most if Japan was weakened. Roosevelt may have been doing nothing more than venting his own opposition to Japan and taking a sounding of public opinion in the process, or he may have had vague thoughts of a joint protest with other nations, but he clearly had no plan to impose sanctions or otherwise move against Japan.

He made that clear during the Far Eastern Conference held during November, 1937, in Brussels. The Soviet Union asked how far the United States was willing to go in order to stop Japan, and its foreign minister, Maxim Litvinov, warned that he and other Russians who favored cooperation with the West "had taken some terrible beatings" as a result of the failure of the West to respond. A few Americans, such as Assistant Secretary of State Sumner Welles, correctly interpreted that remark as a signal that Russia might ultimately turn toward an agreement with Germany and Japan as the best way of insuring its own security.

His superiors thought that such an arrangement was so improbable as to be impossible. They preferred to use the Brussels meeting to arrange a compromise between China and Japan. Roosevelt agreed with that approach. But the Chinese ignored Tokyo's bid for bilateral conversations, and in reply the Japanese stepped up their military operations. The Roosevelt administration's unwillingness to take strong measures did not mean that it approved Japanese actions. That became apparent when Japanese planes sank the American gunboat *Panay* and three Standard Oil tankers in the Yangtze River on December 12, 1937. The United States promptly demanded a formal apology, full reparations, and a guarantee against similar episodes in the future. The Japanese government did not want war, and it immediately apologized and promised to comply with the other demands. The reparations amounted to $2.2 million and were unofficially supplemented by gifts from thousands of Japanese in an outburst of sincere concern and friendship.

PRELIMINARY PREPARATIONS FOR WAR

The attack encouraged Roosevelt to begin making a stronger response to Germany, Italy, and Japan. But it also galvanized those who opposed intervention that led to war, and Congressman Louis Ludlow of Indiana reintroduced his resolution calling for a constitutional amendment to change the process of declaring war. He proposed a national referendum except in cases of invasion. Ludlow had been defeated in earlier attempts, but this time he mustered very strong support. One public opinion poll indicated that 70 percent of the country favored his resolution.

The same poll also revealed, however, that people were worried about America's defenses. Roosevelt appealed to that sentiment in his counterattack. He first warned on January 3, 1938, that "we must keep ourselves adequately strong in self-defense." Three days later, in a letter written to be read in the Congress, he opposed the resolution on the grounds that it "would encourage other nations to believe that they could violate American rights with impunity" and that it would hamper the president's ability to cope with such challenges.

Ludlow had posed a central issue. The president had enormous power, some of it constitutional and much of it accumulated informally, to influence and direct the course of foreign affairs. He could act, and all presidents had so acted, in ways that seriously restricted the choices open to the Congress and the public. He could even maneuver, as President Polk did in his dealings with Mexico in 1846, in a way that left the country no choice but to go to war. A good many Americans were increasingly concerned with the issues of presidential responsibility and the weakening of representative government due to the concentration of power in the executive, and their uneasiness generated much of the support for Ludlow's amendment. Roosevelt's direct and vigorous intervention in the fight was probably decisive. The final vote, January 10, 1938, returned the resolution to committee by a very slender margin. It would have passed if 12 men had voted differently.

Roosevelt wasted little time in exploiting the victory. He asked the Congress on January 28, 1938, for a vast increase in defense appropriations (for industry as well as the army) and a major boost in naval construction. Such military spending was a crucial factor in finally pulling the economy out of the recession that threatened by January, 1938, to become another depression. The president also moved to strengthen and expand American influence in Latin America by using the Export-Import Bank to make governmental loans.

Those two aspects of foreign affairs began to converge into a general strategy after Hitler absorbed Austria into Germany during the first part of March, 1938. A good many people, both then and later, raised the question as to whether—and to what extent—the Roosevelt administration turned to foreign affairs as a way of dealing with the recession. Democratic congressman Maury Maverick of Texas, a vigorous domestic reformer, was especially blunt: "The reason for all this battleship and war frenzy is coming out," he charged on the floor of the Congress. "We Democrats have to admit we are floundering. The Democratic administration is getting down to the condition that Mr. Hoover found himself [in]. We have pulled all the rabbits out of the hat and there are no more rabbits."

It seems more likely that Roosevelt's most serious disingenuousness involved his unwillingness to be candid about his developing opinion that the United States would ultimately face a showdown with Germany, Italy, and Japan. He was clearly moving toward that conclusion during the latter part of 1937, and that attitude was behind his large armament requests in January, 1938. The long debate over that legislation made it clear, moreover, that the administration and its supporters were thinking about the conflict in broad economic and political terms.

Senators, State Department personnel, and congressmen all talked about the need to protect and expand America's position in the world economic system (including raw material imports as well as export markets). On that basis, they then warned that the Germans and the Japanese threatened to isolate the United States economically even if they did not appear bent upon a direct invasion of the Western Hemisphere or the United States.

There were also significant references in the debate to the way rearmament would help the economy, so there is no doubt that many American leaders made a connection between the two problems. In any event, the Naval Expansion Act of May 17, 1938, authorized the expenditure over a ten-year period of $1,090,656,000 to construct a two-ocean navy. Aircraft carriers were to be expanded to a total of 175,000 tons; capital ships to 660,000 tons; and cruisers to 412,500 tons.

Yet Roosevelt soft-pedaled foreign affairs through the summer of 1938, seemingly having decided to make one last effort to stabilize the world situation on the basis of accepting some changes in Europe and Asia. That approach culminated in his support for the Munich settlement of September, 1938. Hitler's late-summer pressure on Czechoslovakia to give up the German-speaking area of Sudetenland prompted the Czechs to mobilize and prepare to fight. France also seemed ready to take a strong stand, and there was considerable speculation that Britain would join France in an alliance with the Soviet Union.

But the English, under the leadership of Prime Minister Neville Chamberlain, preferred to compromise with Hitler. The country was not prepared for a major war, and the Conservatives' basic reluctance to side with the Soviets was reinforced by their agreements with (and sympathy for) conservative governments in Eastern Europe. Those leaders were not willing to let the Red Army cross their borders and establish logistic support systems across their countries in order to defend the Czechs.

Roosevelt threw his influence on the side of a compromise with Hitler, and after the settlement dismembering Czechoslovakia had been reached (September 29–30), he sent the British prime minister a terse telegram of congratulations: "Good man!" He also threatened the French with an arms embargo if they acted to bring on a war. A bit later, on October 5, the president explained his position in a longer message to Chamberlain: "I fully share your hope and belief that there exists today the greatest opportunity in years for the establishment of a new order based on justice and on law."

Despite that hope and belief, or perhaps because he felt it was necessary to support them with force, Roosevelt moved on October 11 to strengthen America's armed power. He announced a $300 million expenditure on military expansion, and the navy formed a special Atlantic Squadron. At the same time (October 6), the United States protested vigorously to Japan over its continued violations of the Open Door policy in China. That pattern of action was reinforced when Hitler opened a new and particularly vicious campaign against German Jews at the end of November, 1938. The United States withdrew its ambassador in a strong gesture of disapproval. He never returned.

The administration's long concern with German and Japanese competition and rising influence in Latin America produced a strong drive for countermeasures at the Inter-American Conference that opened in Lima, Peru, on December 9, 1938. The American delegation won approval for its proposal to take a formal stand against Axis penetration of the Western Hemisphere and to consult on defense measures. And at the end of the year, in response to Japan's blunt announcement that it considered the Open Door policy "inapplicable" to its new order for Asia, the Roosevelt administration tersely rejected Tokyo's assertion and at the same time extended a $25 million loan to China.

President Roosevelt's attack on "aggressor nations" and his call for still more armament appropriations in his January, 1939, message to the Congress previewed his revealing remark, later that year, that the New Deal was going to war. But the failure of the Munich agreement to lead on to a general settlement provoked a serious division of opinion among American leaders. James T. Ferrell of the steel industry argued that "no compromise seems possible" with nations that were "closing the Open Door over a great part of our former Chinese market," creating an "unfavorable situation in Mexico," and generally blocking "the opening of new markets." Secretary of State Hull agreed with that estimate: it was necessary to stand firm against the countries that threatened the American trading system throughout the world.

Other leaders accepted the broad proposition that America had to maintain and expand its overseas operations but argued that it could be done by compromising with Germany and Japan. "It is of paramount importance," banker Winthrop W. Aldrich insisted, "that the efforts of the diplomats and of the heads of governments should speedily be reinforced by measures of economic appeasement." Ferrell, Hull, and Aldrich could agree (and did, at the end of 1938), therefore, on a vital point: corporate leadership should act "to assure American business a proportionate and equitable share in the normal trade. . . . The door of equal opportunity to all trading areas should be kept open."

The debate concerned the most effective means to attain the agreed upon objective. There were three general proposals. The initially smallest, but nevertheless influential, group led by Stimson maintained that it would very probably be necessary to go to war. A much larger group, ultimately led by men like William Allen White and Clark Eichelberger, admitted (if pressed) that war might be necessary, but they argued that the best way to avoid it was to help Great Britain, France, and China stand firm against the Axis.

The third group, which was finally organized as the America First Committee headed by General Robert E. Wood, held that a realignment of power in Europe and Asia presented no necessary or intermediate threat to the vital interests of the United States. Hence the best policy for America was to consolidate its position in the Western Hemisphere, strengthen its defenses, and deal with the pressing domestic problems.

Many critics increasingly attacked President Roosevelt for being disingenuous, if not simply dishonest, as well as mistaken. Clearly enough, Roosevelt was not candid with the American people about his own analysis of the situation or about his actions. And, ultimately, he involved the country in belligerent acts without a congressional declaration of war. The president's behavior is often explained as the result of the fear that his critics could have blocked his maneuvers if the issue had been clarified and discussed in an open forum. That defense only raises the even more central issue, however, of whether or not the highest leader in a system of representative government is justified in using devious means to impose his own best estimate of the situation on the country.

Hitler's occupation of the remainder of Czechoslovakia in March, 1939, prompted Roosevelt on May 19, 1939, to bypass the Senate and try to win repeal of the arms embargo in the House. Led by Congressman Sol Bloom of New York, the maneuver was almost successful. Repeal lost by two votes, 159 to 157. Other events encouraged Roosevelt to feel that the decision could be reversed. One of Stimson's campaigns, organized as The American Committee for Non-Participation in Japanese Aggression, had generated support for embargoing oil and scrap iron shipments to Japan, and even some of those who were opposed to involvement in war, such as Senator Arthur K. Vandenberg, supported that move on the grounds that it would stop the Japanese.

Encouraged by such developments, Roosevelt made a calm, reasoned public appeal on July 14, 1939, to reconsider and repeal the arms embargo. But after polling the Congress, Vice President Garner gave Roosevelt the bad news: "Well, Captain, we may as well face the facts. You haven't got the votes, and that's all there is to it." But the president could and did (at the end of July) advise Japan that the commercial treaty between the two countries would be terminated in six months. Japanese leaders realized that the United States was moving from rhetorical to practical opposition to their expansion, but they also felt that they were being offered the narrow choice of accepting Washington's interpretation of the Open Door policy or a continuing confrontation pointing toward war.

During the same months of 1939, moreover, American leaders moved vigorously to settle their differences with Mexico, and as part of the ultimate compromise they agreed to aid the Mexican economy. Similar assistance was extended to Brazil as part of a general attempt to develop an economic program that would attract the support of other countries. At the same time, the State Department exerted tremendous pressure to halt and then reverse German influence (particularly in the airline and other key areas of the hemispheric economy).

Those efforts were never abandoned, but primary attention was focused on Europe and Asia. The Russo-German nonaggression treaty of August 23, 1939, made it apparent that Hitler was about to launch a war. Welles and other Americans had warned of that possibility if the Western powers failed to reach an accommodation with Moscow, but most Americans felt (both then and later) that the Soviets were almost as responsible for the war as the Germans.

Those who had been sympathetic toward the Russians were disillusioned and embittered, and they sustained their antagonism into the postwar era. Actually, the Russians acted not to help Hitler but to protect themselves after the failure of their attempts to form a united front with Britain and France. As for Hitler, he made the decision to move into Poland long before he negotiated the treaty with Stalin.

ON THE DOORSTEP OF WAR

During the last months before the Nazi attack on Poland (September 1, 1939), President Roosevelt took two actions that made it clear that he anticipated war and expected the United States to become involved. First, during the summer, he ordered research started on the possibility of creating an atomic weapon. Then in August the president created the War Resources Board to develop a plan for industrial mobilization. And when the war began he invoked the neutrality law and convened a special session of the Congress to repeal the arms embargo so that the United States could help Britain and France.

Roosevelt personally encouraged Carl Eichelberger and William Allen White to open a major campaign for aid to the Allies. They did so on October 2 as the Committee to Defend America by Aiding the Allies. The opposition was not as well organized (or financed), but it counterattacked with considerable effectiveness. Senator Borah insisted with his usual bluntness that repeal of the arms embargo meant American intervention and that the issue ought to be discussed candidly without misleading palaver about defense. Senator Harry S Truman spoke for those who wanted to preserve American power for later crises. "The role of this great public," he proclaimed, "is to save civilization; we must keep out of war." And Charles Lindbergh, who later became involved with the America First Committee (and suffered from serious misrepresentation by people who disagreed with him), advocated making a stand in the Western Hemisphere.

Labor leader John L. Lewis was one of the small group of men (including Charles Beard) who placed the fight over the arms embargo in a broader framework. Arguing that "the 'Open Door' is no more" in Asia, Lewis advocated the vigorous development of an American system in the Western Hemisphere. Tying the push to repeal the neutrality law to the domestic failure of the New Deal, he argued that the country was headed for war unless Latin America was accepted as the basis of a new policy. "Unless substantial economic offsets are provided to prevent this nation from being wholly dependent upon the war expenditures," he warned, "we will sooner or later come to the dilemma which requires either war or depression."

The battle produced a compromise that generally favored Roosevelt. The new law (November 4, 1939) authorized the export of many articles of war and restored the cash-and-carry rule. Those provisions were more important than the clause that forbade American ships to enter a war zone defined as extending from the North Sea west beyond Ireland and then south to the border between Spain and France. The legislation favored the Allies, even though there were many disputes over the blockade they established and extended from time to time during 1940 and 1941. Those arguments, like the ones with Britain between 1914 and 1917, did not change the pro-Allied stance of the Roosevelt administration.

Roosevelt opened 1940 with a request for almost $2 billion for military purposes. He met serious opposition until Hitler attacked Denmark and Norway on April 9, an action that encouraged Roosevelt to use the ever growing powers of the presidency without recourse to congressional approval. German economic assets in the United States were seized, and on April 18 the president declared a virtual protectorate over Greenland under the provisions and authority of the Monroe Doctrine. A day earlier, Secretary of State Hull had warned the Japanese that an attack on the Dutch East Indies would raise the danger of war.

Then, as the Germans drove deep into France and pushed the British off the continent at Dunkirk between May 28 and June 4, Roosevelt extended his commitment to the Allies. He called for 50,000 planes a year and then requested another $2 billion and authority to mobilize the National Guard and the Reserve Corps. Two days before France was defeated on June 20, Roosevelt formed a coalition cabinet by appointing Republicans Henry Stimson and Frank Knox as secretaries of the War and Navy departments. After the Congress approved tax increases and raised the national debt limit, the president directed the RFC to spend some of the anticipated revenue for defense plants. Another executive order authorized the sale of old military equipment to Britain and other anti-Axis nations.

The Congress and the Supreme Court also became more militant. The Alien Registration Act of June 28, 1940, was aimed at all critics, left as well as right, and was designed to harass domestic groups as well as the aliens who were required to register with the federal government. The Supreme Court, speaking through liberal Justice Frankfurter, upheld the expulsion from school of two children who had refused, on religious grounds, to salute the flag *(Minersville School District* v. *Cobitis).*

Despite the biases of some of their members against workers, blacks, and Jews, the America First Committee and other critics did challenge Roosevelt on basic issues. Pointing to such actions as the inclusion of Greenland under the Monroe Doctrine and arms sales by the government to the Allies, they argued that all-out aid to Britain and France would end in war. On that basis, they insisted that Roosevelt was obligated to take the issue openly to the people.

Roosevelt persistently evaded that challenge, even as he moved the United States ever closer to belligerent status. He signed a huge navy bill on July 20, 1940, and then acted against Japan by prohibiting the export of all petroleum products and all forms of scrap iron. Opposition within the cabinet forced him to retreat a bit, and the order as issued applied only to aviation gasoline and the highest grades of scrap iron and steel.

Up to that time, Roosevelt had not been attacked on foreign policy issues by Wendell L. Willkie, the Republican candidate for president. An open, jovial, hulking bear of a man who had earned his reputation and wealth in the utility industry, Willkie won the nomination with the backing of the northeastern wing of the party that favored an activist foreign policy and that understood and accepted the need for many of the recovery and reform measures of the early New Deal. His supporters had defeated the traditional party leaders by packing the galleries of the Republican convention with a crowd that chanted "We want Willkie" in a rhythmic frenzy.

Willkie's corporate reformism, however, left him little to offer except the promise that he and the Republicans could do a better job of running the New Deal. The attention of the country, moreover, was focused on the Battle of Britain through the early part of the election campaign. The Germans opened the assault on August 8, 1940, relying on their 2600 fighters and bombers to destroy the Royal Air Force. But the radar defenses developed by the British, combined with excellent fighter aircraft and superbly brave and skillful pilots, kept the Germans from winning the control of the air that was necessary for an invasion.

The emphasis on foreign policy served only to underscore the initiative that Roosevelt enjoyed in the campaign. That advantage was a good part of the reason that the Democratic party broke with tradition and nominated him for a third term. But he had helped his own cause by preventing any potent rival from emerging after the assassination of Huey Long. He might well have run, even if there had been no war, in order to block the conservatives, but the war made the nomination a formality.

The campaign was dull until the president made the United States a belligerent power through the unilateral use of his executive powers. He took that momentous step in response to a request by British Prime Minister Winston Churchill on May 15, 1940, for 15 old American destroyers to help counter the rising threat of the Nazi submarines. A small group of militant interventionists inside the White committee proposed trading the destroyers for British real estate in the Western Hemisphere, and the deal was completed on September 3, 1940. The British took title to 50 old destroyers in return for 99-year leases on various British possessions stretching from Newfoundland south to British Guiana. The illegal action, which was handled secretly and deviously, made the United States a belligerent ally of Britain and consolidated even further the control of foreign policy in the executive department.

Two weeks later, on September 16, a vigorous campaign by interventionists produced the first peacetime draft in the nation's history (the Selective Training and Service Act). The campaign for conscription was launched in May by veterans of the volunteer training program that had been started before America entered World War I, and by June the key figures, New York attorney Grenville Clark and *New York Times* publisher Julius Ochs Adler, succeeded in having a bill introduced in the Congress. The Japanese helped their efforts by moving deeper into China on August 1, and the Roosevelt administration provided its own push on August 31 by federalizing units of the National Guard. Opponents fought the measure bitterly but managed only to limit the length of service to one year and to restrict the draftees' duty assignments to the Western Hemisphere.

Just before the measure was passed (September 12), the American ambassador to Japan, Joseph C. Grew, recommended, in what came to be known as the "Green Light Message," a stronger stand in Asia. He had long opposed such action on the grounds that it would strengthen the military and expansionist groups in Japan, and his reversal strongly influenced Hull and Roosevelt. The first response, on September 19, was to embargo shipments of all scrap iron and steel, a move the president had proposed in June.

Willkie responded with a blunt attack: "You may expect we will be at war." Roosevelt was stung. He made a blanket denial, or so it seemed at first glance. "I have said this before," he replied, "but I shall say it again, and again, and again. Your boys are not going to be sent into any foreign war." It was at best a disingenuous and misleading remark and probably involved knowing and defiant deceit, yet Roosevelt presented it as a sincere promise. The president's performance, along with Willkie's hammering on the issue in the last days of the campaign, may have helped Willkie poll more votes than any previous loser. But the president carried 38 states and won the popular race by almost five million votes.

Having won at home, Roosevelt continued his anti-Axis moves abroad. A $100 million loan to China was announced on November 30, and that was followed by private assurances that planes and men would be made available to strengthen Colonel Claire L. Chennault's squadron of Flying Tigers that was leading China's meager air war against the Japanese. And then, in December, Washington extended the embargo on exports to Japan to include iron ore, pig iron, and many kinds of finished steel (copper and brass were added in January, 1941).

At the same time (on December 30), the president created the Office of Production Management under the direction of William S. Knudtsen of General Motors to speed the output of war goods and expedite their delivery to the Allies, as well as to the expanding armed forces of the United States. Shortly after Christmas, on December 29, Roosevelt exhorted Americans to make the United States "the great arsenal of democracy."

He did not, however, repeat his promise not to send Americans to fight in foreign wars. The truth, of course, was that the United States had become a belligerent power with no serious hope of avoiding combat operations. But there was one bit of good news: because of the rapidly expanding war effort, the real income of the American people had finally climbed back to the 1929 level. Going to war had ended the depression and consolidated the system of corporate state capitalism in the office of the presidency.

The more perceptive American leaders were already worrying about how conditions would be at the end of the war. Most were fearful that the economy would slide back into another depression, but all of them recognized the imperial future. Virgil Johnson, president of the National Industrial Conference Board, caught the spirit of the time:

> America has embarked on a career of imperialism, both in world affairs and in every other aspect of her life. . . . At best England will become a junior partner in a new Anglo-Saxon imperialism. . . . Southward in our hemisphere and westward in the Pacific the path of empire takes its way, and in modern times . . . the scepter passes to the United States.

The struggle for the scepter, however, was long, bitter, and costly. It required almost five years of sacrifice and blood to defeat the Axis. And the struggle never would have been won without the courage and fortitude of the British and the bravery and determination of the Russians.

EXPLORATORY READING

The literature on New Deal foreign policy is enormous. These volumes will introduce you to the subject and to various interpretations, and most contain bibliographies to guide your further research:

T. A. Bailey, *The Man on the Street: The Impact of American Public Opinion on Foreign Policy* (1948)

C. Beard, *President Roosevelt and the Coming of the War* (1948)

D. Borg, *The United States and the Far Eastern Crisis of 1933–1938* (1964)

W. S. Cole, *Senator Gerald P. Nye and American Foreign Relations* (1962); and *America First: The Battle Against Intervention, 1940–1941* (1953)

R. N. Current, *Secretary Stimson: A Study in Statecraft* (1954)

D. Detzer, *Appointment on the Hill* (1948)

R. A. Divine, *The Illusion of Neutrality* (1962); and *The Reluctant Belligerent* (1965)

A. A. Ekirch, Jr., *The Decline of American Liberalism* (1967)

T. R. Fehrenbach, *F.D.R.'s Undeclared War* (1967)

H. Feis, *The Road to Pearl Harbor* (1950)

L. C. Gardner, *Economic Aspects of New Deal Diplomacy* (1964)

A. Guttmann, *The Wound in the Heart: America and the Spanish Civil War* (1962)

M. Jonas, *Isolationism in America, 1935–1941* (1966)

W. L. Langer and S. E. Gleason, *The Challenge to Isolation: The World Crisis of 1937–1940 and American Foreign Policy* (1952); and *The Undeclared War, 1940–1941* (1953)

A. Offner, *America's Appeasement of Germany* (1968)

B. M. Russett, *No Clear and Present Danger: A Skeptical View of the U.S. Entry into World War II* (1972)

P. Schroeder, *The Axis Alliance and Japanese-American Relations, 1941* (1958)

E. Tupper and G. McReynolds, *Japan in American Public Opinion* (1937)

L. Wittner, *Rebels Against War: The American Peace Movement, 1941–1960* (1969)

17 A LONG WAR FOR THE OPEN DOOR

THE Roosevelt administration's increasing momentum toward military intervention in the war was starkly dramatized by the president's third inaugural address of January, 1941, in which he talked about the ultimate peace settlement. "In the future days, which we seek to make secure," he asserted, the United States would use its strength to establish "four essential freedoms . . . everywhere in the world." He defined two of them as the active freedoms of speech and religion, and the others as the release from the pressures that cramp and inhibit all people: the freedom from fear and the freedom from want.

The paradoxes of extending freedom by force were far less pressing at the time, however, than the challenge of German power in the Atlantic Ocean. Having failed to subdue England by air power, the Nazis shifted to the strategy of wolf-pack attacks by submarines. Deploying the subs in groups and using surface attacks at night to minimize various detection devices, the German navy took a frightful toll of Allied shipping.

During his post-election vacation in the Caribbean, Roosevelt was warned by Prime Minister Churchill (on December 9, 1940) that the English position was grave and growing desperate, and he asked for money and active military assistance against the submarines. The president responded with the idea of Lend-Lease. This proposal, which was introduced into the Congress on January 10, 1941, authorized the president "to sell, transfer title to, exchange, lease, lend, or otherwise dispose of" any matériel to "any government whose defense the president deems vital to the defense of the United States." It involved a massive delegation of initiative and power to the executive, and that engendered almost as much opposition as did the clear indication that it carried the United States a long step toward military intervention. It was finally passed, 260 votes to 161 in the House, and 60 to 31 in the Senate, and signed on March 11, 1941. The first appropriation was for $7 billion.

By that time, the American and British chiefs of staff had been discussing the best global strategy against the Axis for more than a month. The basic American position, stated by Secretary of State Hull on April 14, amounted to a demand for Japan to retreat from the territory it held in China as a *precondition* for a general settlement. Japan was also to repledge itself to the principles of the Open Door policy: territorial integrity, noninterference in the affairs of other nations, and equal economic opportunity as the basis for stabilizing the Far East. The United States never retreated from those demands, and Japan ultimately decided that it had no choice but to surrender or go to war.

Roosevelt meanwhile directed the preparation of naval units for convoy duty in the Atlantic. Bases were secured through an executive agreement of April 9 with Danish leaders that opened Greenland to American military and naval forces. Two days later the president told Churchill that he had authorized aggressive patrols eastward to the mid-Atlantic, which was termed "the sea frontier of the United States." Shortly thereafter, the Nazi battleship *Bismarck* sank what everyone had thought was the British supership, H.M.S. *Hood,* and prepared to terrorize Allied shipping in company with the *Scharnhorst* and the *Gneisenau.* The *Bismarck* was finally found and eventually sunk (May 27), but the scare prompted Roosevelt to declare an "unlimited national emergency" on the grounds that German power threatened "the immediate safety of portions of North and South America."

The American economy was also being mobilized. The National Defense Mediation Board, headed by William H. Davis, was created in March to deal with labor disputes and to maintain production in defense industries. The Office of Price Administration and Civilian Supply was established on April 11, and Leon Henderson became the first of many men to wrestle with the difficult problems of controlling inflation and keeping the civilian population supplied with butter while the military obtained the guns it needed. And on June 25, 1941, Philip Randolph and other black leaders finally forced the New Deal to act against racial discrimination. A Fair Employment Practices Commission was created to attack job discrimination in the government and in war industries.

Hitler's massive assault on the Soviet Union, launched on June 22, posed the question of whether or not American leaders would discriminate among Axis enemies on ideological grounds. A good many Americans were either opposed, reluctant, or indifferent to aiding the Russians. Senator Harry S Truman, for example, thought it would be wise to let Hitler and Stalin bleed each other white and then perhaps aid one side in return for broad concessions. Another group, including many key leaders in the government, argued it was pointless to help Russia because the Soviets would be defeated within three months. And others considered it more important to help Britain and move to a direct confrontation with Germany and Japan.

Roosevelt's decision to provide assistance was made easier by Churchill's bold promise that England would supply all the material it could spare to help the Soviets. But American aid was very slow in becoming effective, and the Red Army stopped the Nazis at the gates of Moscow without any help from the United States.

Japan responded to the German attack on Russia with more firmness and vigor, launching an offensive in southern Indochina on July 24. The next day the president froze all Japanese assets in the United States. Ambassador Grew accurately interpreted the meaning of both acts: "The obvious conclusion is eventual war."

Roosevelt and Churchill discussed their many problems during a conference aboard ships off the Newfoundland coast between August 9 and 13, 1941. The agenda included aid to Russia, the shipping crisis, how to meet the Japanese thrust, and the best approach to postwar security. Their public declaration, known as the Atlantic Charter, generally followed the traditional lines of the Open Door policy. It committed all anti-Axis forces to a program of no territorial conquests and no territorial changes without the consent of the people involved, the right of people to choose their own government, a system of open trade and access to raw materials, freedom of the seas, and the creation of a "permanent system of general security."

The private discussions were more revealing. Churchill, for example, pushed Roosevelt hard about entering the war. The President replied rather impatiently that, if offered a clear choice, the Congress would debate the issue for three months—adding that it was not "truly representative of the country." Roosevelt then said that "he would wage war, but not declare it, and that he would become more and more provocative. . . . Everything was to be done to force an 'incident.'"

The United States exerted strong pressure to force Britain to abandon, or at least modify extensively, its imperial economic preference system that limited American markets, investments, and control of raw materials. The drive to apply the Open Door policy to the British

Empire continued throughout the war and was ultimately successful. For the moment, however, the British fought an effective rearguard action.

As for policing the world after the war, Roosevelt thought that task should be handled by the United States with assistance from Great Britain. Churchill agreed, and the two men explored the problem without seriously considering the possibility that the Soviet Union would be involved. Their attitude, and the vast confidence in American power that it revealed, was a central feature of all subsequent dealings with Russia. It immediately caused friction, moreover, when the United States indicated its unwillingness, shortly after the Atlantic Conference, to agree to even the most elementary settlement of postwar boundaries in Eastern Europe.

As the conference terminated, the Congress ended its long and embittered wrangle over renewing the draft law. That battle represented the last stand of the antiinterventionist forces, and they lost by one vote in the House of Representatives. The legislation, revised to provide for 18 months' service, passed the Senate 45 votes to 30, and the House 203 to 202. With 1 million men in service and the assurance of more to come, the armed forces moved in September, 1941, to implement their strategy for victory in a two-front war.

First priority was given to Europe, where at the moment the United States was very much on the defensive. As part of its cooperation with the British fleet, the American destroyer *Greer* finally provoked a Nazi submarine commander to retaliate. After being trailed for three hours and having his position reported to the British, he attacked the *Greer* with torpedoes. The ship was not sunk, but Roosevelt disingenuously used the incident (omitting the *Greer*'s provocation) to arouse the American public and to begin convoying all Allied ships to Iceland. He also authorized full combat operations against what he called "the rattlesnakes of the Atlantic." By the end of October, 1941, when the destroyer *Reuben James* was sunk, the United States was openly engaged in an undeclared war with Germany.

During the same month, Secretary Hull told the Japanese that they would have to withdraw from Indochina as well as China if they wanted peace with the United States. In a curious coincidence, both countries made their decisions for war on November 5, 1941. The Japanese decided to fight unless America gave way and reduced its demands, and in the United States, the joint board of the army and the navy agreed on war if the Japanese moved beyond a line drawn south and westward around existing Japanese holdings in the Pacific.

The attack on Pearl Harbor was the result of the decision by Japanese leaders that the nation could not meet its needs and satisfy its desires in the face of America's adamant insistence on maintaining the

Open Door policy in Asia. The assault itself was conceived and executed as a brilliant tactical maneuver to place the United States on the defensive in the Pacific and to allow Japan to complete and consolidate its basic strategic expansion before a counterattack could be launched.

The great effectiveness of the Japanese strikes (in the Philippines as well as Hawaii) was due to human errors, but none involved the knowing or willful exposure of American forces to a one-sided and extensive defeat. Leaders in Washington functioned very poorly in coordinating intelligence data gathered by breaking the Japanese code, but the crucial failure came in Hawaii. The army and navy commanders were simply not alert and prepared. The Japanese planes came in unopposed at 7:55 A.M. and sank or disabled 19 ships, destroyed over 100 planes, and inflicted 3513 casualties (2335 killed). Nine hours after the attack on Pearl Harbor, the Philippine command headed by General Douglas A. MacArthur was still unready. It lost half its planes on the ground in the first Japanese attack. That was an even graver failure of leadership.

Although the loss of equipment was severe, the cost in men was far more crippling. Most of them were long-term regulars of great experience and esprit de corps: men who functioned as well-trained and integrated crews. Among all the books that have been written about Pearl Harbor, perhaps the novel by James Jones, *From Here to Eternity*, best captures the feel of that tragic moment and the way in which the garrison responded to the attack.

While it was a major tactical success, the attack on Pearl Harbor was a strategic failure for the Japanese. It united a nation that was still divided over the question of military intervention and charged it with the volatile emotions of fear, anger, and revenge. One of the first results of that combination, unfortunately, was a terrible violation of the American traditions of civil rights and civil liberties.

After the turmoil of the years before World War I, the Japanese-American citizens (and their children) of the western states made significant contributions to the development of that region. Discrimination against them continued, but their abilities, poise, and courage enabled them to prosper and gain some degree of acceptance. But the attack on Pearl Harbor released all the jealousies and prejudices of white westerners, and the Japanese-Americans became the target of a bitter campaign of intimidation and anger. People who wanted to take over their lands and businesses joined with those who seriously feared an attack on the West Coast and with still others who just wanted somehow to strike back at Japan in a demand that the Japanese-Americans be imprisoned, deported, or otherwise removed. As one woman, who was then a teen-ager in Oregon, later recalled, "We went to school each day expecting our friends to have just disappeared. It was very scary."

The Japanese-Americans did disappear. President Roosevelt gave way to the pressure and on February 19, 1942, authorized the military to act. Making no effort to be selective, to act only against those who had given some concrete evidence of disloyalty, General John L. De-Witt ordered all Japanese-Americans removed from the western one-third of Washington and Oregon, the western one-half of California, and the southeastern quarter of Arizona. All were abruptly and arbitrarily uprooted, and many were incarcerated in miserable desert camps. Their lives were irrevocably scarred, twisted, and thwarted. Perhaps even more damaging to the spirit of America was the Supreme Court decision upholding the action (*Korematsu* v. *U.S.*, 1944), which indicated that similar action could and would be repeated in a future crisis.

The defeat of the Japanese-Americans was the only victory that the United States enjoyed for many months. Roosevelt and Churchill met in Washington after the U.S. declarations of war against Germany and Italy on December 11, 1941, but their only significant announcement concerned the future. The Declaration of the United Nations was signed by 22 nations, including China and the Soviet Union, on January 1, 1942, and offered some hope that the problems of establishing a world order would be resolved before the fighting stopped.

TENSIONS AMONG THE ALLIES

The Roosevelt administration indicated very clearly, however, that it wanted to delay serious negotiations until it could exert the greatest possible influence on its allies. That strategy led to immediate and sustained difficulties with the Soviet Union. As the Russians stopped the Germans before Moscow and began the long, bloody, and terribly costly process that Churchill later called "tearing the guts out of the German army," they asked for assurances that their 1939–1940 western frontiers in Europe would be restored as protection against another German assault. "It is very important for us to know," Stalin told British Foreign Minister Anthony Eden early in 1942, "whether we shall have to fight at the peace conference in order to get our western frontiers." The English, who had signed a 20-year alliance with Russia, were inclined to view the request as understandable and reasonable. Eden also reminded the United States that Russia's adherence to the Atlantic Charter "was undertaken upon the understanding that the Soviet Union was to be regarded as being entitled to its 1940 frontiers."

Many military experts later came to feel that the Russian stand before Moscow was the crucial battle of the war, and in a similar way it may be that the American response to Stalin's request for a guarantee of Russia's 1940 frontiers was the crucial decision that led to a generation of tension and conflict with the Soviet Union. Roosevelt and Secretary Hull refused to make such a commitment and left the British with the unpleasant task of coping with Stalin. He was not easy to handle: "Surely this is axiomatic," he told the British. Eden bluntly told the president that his attitude would "surely appear to Stalin so uncollaborative a state of mind as to confirm his suspicions that he can expect no real consideration for Russian interests from ourselves or the United States" and that as a result the future "may be seriously endangered." Roosevelt and Hull were adamant, but they did invite Soviet Foreign Minister Vyacheslav M. Molotov to Washington in May, 1942, to discuss strategy and aid.

Emphasizing that Russia was deeply dissatisfied over the handling of the boundary question on which it "had very definite convictions," Molotov pressed Britain and America to open a second front in Western Europe. "What answer shall I take back?" Roosevelt was vague, if not simply evasive. He "answered," so the record shows, "that Mr. Molotov could say that . . . we expect the formation of a second front this year."

One adviser promptly warned Roosevelt that his answer was very apt to cause serious trouble because the Russians would take the remark to mean a firm commitment, even though it was certain that there could be no invasion of Europe in 1942. As a result, the Soviets would lose confidence "in our sincerity of purpose." The warning and advice were correct and accurate. The United States and Britain were wholly on the defensive throughout 1942, and Stalin had to be told in August (by Churchill and W. Averell Harriman) that there would be no second front. Stalin was angry, and neither he nor other Soviet leaders forgot the episode, which left a bitter legacy of suspicion between Moscow and Washington.

That was underscored by the dependence of the Western powers upon the courage of the Red Army. The United States first concentrated on blunting the Japanese offensive in the Pacific. The brave troops in the Philippines, led by Jonathan M. Wainwright after Douglas MacArthur was evacuated to Australia to assume overall command, played an important role in that effort. The Japanese took Manila on January 2, 1942, but the army units fought a stubborn and valiant delaying action and did not surrender for another four months.

The first effective American counterattack came during May in the Battle of the Coral Sea. That engagement, the first ever fought entirely by carrier-based aircraft, stopped the Japanese drive to take Port Moresby, New Guinea, as part of their plan to invade Australia.

The Japanese, nevertheless, opened a strategic assault in the Central Pacific. They would have succeeded, moreover, except for two factors: the American navy made far better use of the information it gained from having cracked the Japanese code than it had at Pearl Harbor, and the men of the fleet displayed great skill, incredible energy, and exceptional courage. The ships (including submarines) that defeated the Japanese in the Coral Sea raced northward in time to intercept a major Japanese task force moving in to take Midway Island as a base from which to neutralize or invade Hawaii.

The Battle of Midway (June 3–6, 1942) was a wild and deadly melee in which Americans had to drive home their attacks with a ferocity and indifference to life that was later (and mistakenly) thought to be a unique attribute of Japanese kamikaze (suicide) pilots. But they stopped the Japanese, sinking four carriers and downing 275 planes, and made it possible to concentrate on keeping the Japanese from sustaining their offensive in the southwestern Pacific.

That long and bloody process began when the marines landed on Guadalcanal on August 7, 1942, and managed to seize and hold the vital airfield before they were contained (and badly mauled). The crucial battle developed at sea (November 12–15, 1942) when a major Japanese task force steaming to reinforce and hold the island was intercepted and destroyed. The Japanese garrison fought a tough, costly rearguard action, but it finally abandoned the island on February 9, 1943.

Even so, the Japanese maintained pressure at both ends of the Pacific; and the ability of the United States to mount an offensive in the Pacific, as well as to join Russia in ground operations against Germany, depended on mobilization at home. That had begun in 1940, long before Pearl Harbor, but it nevertheless proved very difficult to produce all the matériel and train all the people required to defeat the Axis.

President Roosevelt established the War Production Board, headed by corporation executive Donald M. Nelson, in January, 1942, and charged it with the responsibility for increasing production and coordinating resources with the requirements of the global battle fronts. Large corporations dominated the economy at the start of the war, and they increased their power and influence through their near monopoly (directly and through the subcontracting system they controlled) of war production.

Senator Truman's investigation of the process, which revealed how it strengthened an existing and powerful elite of top industrial, military, and other governmental leaders, and how it squeezed the small businessmen, was a particularly revealing inquiry into the structure of the American political economy. It did little, however, to slow the process of consolidation and centralization.

Nelson halted nonessential residential and highway construction on April 8, 1942, and instituted specific allocation priorities for all strategic materials in June, but he failed to control the economy. James F. Byrnes resigned from the Supreme Court and took charge as head of the new Office of War Mobilization and Reconversion (October 3, 1942). He was tougher and more effective, as were Jesse H. Jones of Texas and William M. Jeffers of the Union Pacific.

The military exerted great influence on the economy through its power over research programs, as well as through its authority to award contracts. It even directed the supersecret Manhattan Project, organized under Brigadier General Leslie R. Groves to produce a nuclear weapon. The first sustained chain reaction occurred at the University of Chicago on December 2, 1942, without any contribution from the military, but Groves, who considered the scientists under his command "a bunch of crackpots," then took charge of production of the weapon. Despite his talents and drive, however, the project would never have succeeded without the contribution of J. Robert Oppenheimer, who provided catalytic personal leadership as well as key scientific knowledge.

The military likewise moved directly into civilian policy matters through the June, 1942, creation of the Office of Strategic Services (OSS). The OSS gained considerable (and sometimes exaggerated) exotic fame for its cloak-and-dagger operations under the direction of William J. ("Wild Bill") Donovan, but its routine intelligence activities were more important. Through its control of information at the source, the military also influenced the operations of the Office of War Information, established on June 13, 1942, to handle domestic as well as overseas news.

Such continuing centralization of power increased the public's uneasiness and testiness about the domestic effects of the war. Americans were neither unpatriotic nor laggards, and their discontent stemmed from a healthy kind of concern to improve the country. It was their energy and skill, after all, that boomed the economy from a gross national product (GNP) of $91.3 billion in 1939 to $166.6 billion at the end of the war in 1945. The increases by major sectors were: manufacturing, 96 percent; agriculture, 22 percent; and transportation, 109 percent.

SOCIAL AND ECONOMIC CHANGES INITIATED BY THE WAR

Women made vital contributions in all those areas, as well as in the armed forces. America was not prepared for females to be mustered into combat units, but they served with distinction as members of the army, navy, and marines. And some of them, along with nurses and Red Cross workers, were exposed to enemy fire. Others, who participated in the programs of the United Service Organization, kept many a young man from deserting or going into a state of funk before he went into battle. But the women in the factories performed equally important work and played a key role in a vast social transformation.

As with many social changes, the dramatic postwar women's liberation movement began quietly on the assembly line during the war. Many women had worked before 1942: in colonial times, on the farm, as secretaries, and in textile factories. But never before had the government actively encouraged them to enter the industrial marketplace. The campaign was more than a bit romantic—the public image of Rosie the Riveter glossed over the true nature of factory labor—but it was effective. In five years, 1940–1945, the percentage of women in the work force jumped from 25 percent to 36 percent (more than six million).

The increase was particularly impressive in the federal bureaucracy (four females were hired to one male), and the states also hired women for better jobs. Even black women shared in the gains. National child care programs facilitated the change from housewife to worker and enabled other women to participate in political activity. They continued to suffer, however, from discrimination on the job, and President Roosevelt's periodic intervention did not prevent employers from paying women less for doing the same (or more demanding) work as men. Perhaps the UAW did the most: the union agitated for women's rights from 1941, and its Women's Department (1944) fought hard for equality.

The social consequences of large numbers of women entering the corporate marketplace are difficult to estimate with any confidence, and the problem is further complicated because it happened during a war. But it seems probable that the combination affected three important areas of American life: the extended family; sexual behavior; and life-style expectations. The war severely disrupted traditional family life: sons and daughters left home, many of them never returned; parents and relatives went off to other places to earn more money; and, at the end, everyone wanted to relax and fulfill themselves after the traumas of depression and war.

Wars traditionally subvert existing sexual mores. That is reinforced, particularly on the job, by two other forces. Actors have a telling expression for one of them: "The propinquity of skin." Males and females engaged in sustained but initially nonsexual associations do tend to pair off for intercourse, whatever their primary emotional commitments. Second, the spirit of camaraderie in a common effort, such as factory work for the war, produces the same result. Thus what was later recognized as and called the *sexual revolution* very probably began during the war.

But camaraderie on the job—in riveting or in combat—also leads to talk about nonsexual matters, and as a result of such discussions many Americans came to feel that they were not being treated fairly. The great majority of them, for example, reacted against the failure to control inflation and the great increase in taxes. Because of such weaknesses, and because of the impersonal character of government and business, a significant number of citizens began to treat the system as something to be beaten for individual gain rather than as the basis of a common and shared life as members of a community. The process started in small ways, as in individual blackmarket operations, in stealing from the plant, or in doing less than one's best on the job, but it gradually came to affect the general attitude.

Inequity and inflation sustained that process. The pre-Pearl Harbor effort to control inflation failed, and by the end of 1941 prices were rising at the rate of 2 percent per month. The Emergency Price Control Act of January 30, 1942, authorized price and rent ceilings. But the farm bloc held out until its prices rose to 110 percent of parity, and there was no tough attempt to hold the line. Food prices, for example, rose 11 percent in 1942.

Rationing, which began on December 27, 1941, was not immediately effective, though the Anti-Inflation Act of October 2, 1942, led to some improvement. The president finally took strong action on April 8, 1943, and slowed the rate of increase for the remainder of the war. The performance was still not good, and consumer prices jumped by 31 percent by the end of the war.

Long before that, labor became restive and militant. The National War Labor Board, created on January 12, 1942, did maintain the organizing and bargaining rights won during the depression, and six months later it offered some economic help by tying wages to the cost-of-living index and authorized a 15 percent increase to bring them somewhat into line with inflation.

Knowing they were still behind in real wages, and also dissatisfied with working conditions, many workers went on strike. The total number of such stoppages (14,731), was misleading, however, for the overall loss in production was very small. Three of the biggest difficulties involved the UMW, the railroads, and the Sears Roebuck management (which refused, until taken over in December, 1944, to honor directives from the War Labor Board). On balance, however, the government moved more vigorously against the unions than against management.

The coal miners walked out of the pits on May 1, 1943. The ensuing struggle between the workers and the owners (who were in effect supported by the government) and within the government itself won the miners a wage increase, but it produced an antilabor reaction that led to restrictive legislation. The War Labor Disputes Act of June 25, 1943, was so stringent that it had to be passed over Roosevelt's veto. It authorized the president to seize plants, ruled strikes in such plants illegal, and made unions liable for damage suits unless they gave 30 days notice of proposed strikes in war industries. Despite his veto, however, Roosevelt used the law on December 27, 1943, to seize the railroads. They were promptly returned to the owners on January 18, 1944, after the strike danger had passed.

Most railroad workers who were black belonged to the union led by the dynamic A. Philip Randolph, who played a central role in the rising militance of black Americans. As with the largely neglected beginnings of the revolt of women, the growth of Black Power during the war was generally ignored—or dismissed as the result of special circumstances. One of the keys to the mounting disaffection of blacks during the war was an organization of the depression years called the National Negro Congress. It emerged from the concern and labor of a strange assortment of people: among the leaders were Ralph Bunche, a professor at Howard University; John P. Davis, an able and energetic radical; Lester Granger of the Urban League; the indefatigable Randolph; and the writer Langston Hughes.

The moving spirit was best stated by Randolph. "The Negro should not," he wrote Davis, "place his problems for solution . . . at the feet of his white sympathetic allies . . . for in the final analysis, the salvation of the Negro . . . must come from within." If the American black was to be saved, he added, "he must depend upon his own right arm."

The National Congress was particularly effective at the local level. One person who recognized the significance of the organization in creating a sense of awareness and confidence and in training leaders was the Swedish scholar Gunnar Myrdal. He thought it was the most important black group in many parts of the country, and his conclusion, in *An American Dilemma* (1944), that the war would forever change race relations was based in part upon the impact of the congress. It ultimately fell victim to the reaction against the Communists after the Nazi-Soviet pact of 1939, but its influence was clearly apparent during the war.

Large numbers of blacks, more than a simple majority, viewed the war effort as a test of American democracy. And they were not impressed. They were segregated in the armed forces. They were given inferior jobs in industry. Even their donations to the blood bank were segregated despite the key work of a black physician in developing the entire program. And the state of Mississippi ruled that textbooks for black children must omit any references to voting, elections, and democracy. The issue was stated with eloquent clarity by the editors of the journal of the NAACP:

> *The Crisis* is sorry for brutality, blood, and death among the people of Europe, just as we were sorry for China and Ethiopia. But the hysterical cries of the preachers of democracy for Europe leave us cold. We want democracy in Alabama and Arkansas, in Mississippi and Michigan, in the District of Columbia—in the Senate of the United States.

The wonder is not that there were riots; the wonder is that there were so few. Aware of the explosive dangers in the situation and constantly badgered about the issue by his wife, Eleanor, President Roosevelt strengthened the Fair Employment Practices Commission on May 27, 1943, through an executive order making nondiscrimination clauses mandatory in all war contracts. That was not enough, even if it had been rigorously enforced. The guts of it all were laid bare by a young black officer's account of his ordeal for democracy on a bus from a southern training camp to Washington, D.C.:

> "Hey, all nigras sit in the black of the bus," the driver yelled.
> "I made up my mind right then," the officer recalled, "that I had taken the last insult from crackers I was going to take."

Blacks in Detroit, in Beaumont, Texas, in Philadelphia, and in New York agreed. The riots in those cities during 1943 grew out of the fear and resentment of whites in the face of black competition and success. In Detroit, for example, the riot of June 20 was preceded for several months by walkouts by white workers in defense plants. During the fighting that erupted out of a confrontation at an amusement park, Detroit policemen killed 17 of the 25 blacks who died and in other ways helped whites who were beating and stabbing black citizens. The New York uprising of August 1 erupted after the shooting of a black soldier by a white policeman. Harlem burst into fighting and flames: five people were killed, 307 injured, and the property damage was over $5 million.

Some blacks were also caught up in the outbreak of racial violence during June in Los Angeles, but most of the white attacks were directed against Mexican-Americans. The traditional prejudice against them was intensified by the Hearst newspaper campaign that unjustly blamed them for a crime wave. The performance of the press became so scandalous that the government had intervened in August, 1942, in an effort to prevent trouble.

The papers did stop using the word Mexican, but they began featuring photos of Mexican-American youths dressed in zoot suits. The garb was a typical fad that featured very long jackets with wide lapels, pants that were oversized at the knees and tiny at the bottom, a porkpie or pancake hat, and an exaggerated watch chain (often draped down to the knee) that was twirled in the hand as the supreme gesture of sophistication. It was zany and fun, an effective bit of counterculture, and it predictably annoyed many whites.

The trouble began with the beating of a group of peaceful zoot suiters after they had been talking with policemen about how to prevent trouble in their neighborhood. That incident opened a three-day assault by white-citizens (especially soldiers and sailors) on any and all Mexican-Americans: they were pulled out of theaters and bars and stripped on the streets, beaten, and knifed. As in Detroit, the police did little to prevent or stop the violence, and the press grossly distorted the outrage by presenting the whites as acting in self-defense.

Some Mexican-Americans, along with some blacks and other minority citizens (and poor whites), were able to use the war effort as a way of improving their position. There were more and better jobs, and service in the armed forces (though marred by extensive prejudice and discrimination) gave many of them more education and money then they had ever known. After Pearl Harbor, the draft law was revised to include men through the age of 44 (although not many that old were called after the early months), and the term of service was extended to end six months after the conclusion of the war. Of the 31 million men registered, 9,867,707 were inducted. That number was swelled by volunteers to a grand total of 15,145,115 men and women in service (including the female auxiliary corps, largely in the army, 100,000; and the navy, 86,000). That was a larger force than any previous American effort, but it was smaller than the totals mustered by other major belligerents. Russia lost at least 20 million *killed;* Germany mustered 17 million under arms; and Great Britain's total of 12 million in the service was only slightly smaller—and much larger proportionately.

Americans did suffer higher taxes. Roosevelt accurately called the Revenue Act of October 21, 1942, the "greatest tax bill in American history." Middle- and low-income families were swept into the net like herrings: 50 million people paid income taxes for 1942 as compared with 13 million for 1941. To facilitate collections and to prevent (and apprehend) offenses, the payroll deduction system was instituted in 1943. Even so, much of the cost of the war was passed on to future generations.

Despite excess profit levies of up to 95 percent, moreover, and a minor shift in the distribution of income toward those in the lower income levels that resulted from such procedures, the war did not significantly change the distribution of power or wealth in the American economy. A good many people made more money than ever before, but the corporations still controlled the political economy. The increase in wages and salaries, even if some of it was used to purchase voting stock, did not buy any significant influence or authority in the process of making decisions within the system of corporate state capitalism.

By the end of 1942, the tremendous productivity generated by the mobilization of the nation's people and resources began to pay military dividends. An invasion force led by General Dwight D. Eisenhower went ashore on November 8 at Casablanca, Oran, and Algiers, to help the British complete the defeat of a Nazi army that had invaded North Africa to capture the Suez Canal. And four days later, the navy blocked a major Japanese effort to reinforce its troops on Guadalcanal. Neither operation engaged the main forces of the enemy, but each demonstrated the growing ability of the Allies to wage effective transoceanic campaigns.

They also reinforced the traditional confidence of American leaders (and people) that the nation had the power to accomplish its traditional objectives. Roosevelt and Hull expected that victory would finally make it possible to establish the principles of the Open Door through an international organization that would provide an institutional framework for economic as well as political stability and for military security.

Congressman J. William Fulbright of Arkansas was particularly concerned to avoid the kind of embittered struggle that had defeated the League of Nations Treaty in 1919. His efforts, along with those of Senators Joseph Ball, Carl Hatch, and Tom Connally, played a vital part in committing the Congress during the fall of 1943 to participation in the postwar United Nations organization.

During those debates, Roosevelt and Churchill met in Casablanca (January 14–24, 1943). They gave little time to postwar plans, concentrating instead on strategy for an invasion of Europe and on adopting the American doctrine of unconditional surrender. That policy was not a new departure in American history: General Ulysses S. Grant made the same demand of the Confederate forces at Fort Donelson in 1861, and President Wilson followed its essentials in dealing with the Germans at the end of World War I. It was criticized during and after the war for being unnecessarily harsh and tending to strengthen the will of the enemy. Whatever the opposition, the decision grew out of the strong reaction against Nazism and the Japanese attack at Pearl Harbor.

PLANS, AGREEMENTS, AND BATTLES
THAT ENDED THE WAR

Roosevelt and Churchill agreed on the necessity of a massive attack to engage and defeat the Nazi army but disagreed over strategy. Churchill favored an invasion through what he called "the soft underbelly of Europe," followed by a drive north into Germany. He was concerned about casualties, and thought his plan would block the Red Army from driving into Central and Southeast Europe as it forced the Nazis westward. Americans preferred the cross-Channel strategy largely on military grounds, although some realized that a southern invasion would allow the Russians to move west along the Baltic Coast. The United States finally won the argument and the Normandy coast of France was selected during conferences in Washington (May 12–25, 1943) and Quebec (August 11–24, 1943).

Armed with their plans for a second front in Western Europe and with their position seemingly strengthened by the invasion of Italy on September 3, 1943, the British and Americans opened discussions with the Russians on October 9. Secretary of State Hull and British Foreign Minister Anthony Eden eased the serious tension with Russia by assuring Stalin that the invasion of France was scheduled for May 1, 1944, and for his part, Stalin promised Hull that the Soviet Union would join the war against Japan after Germany was defeated.

But there was no agreement about Eastern Europe. The Polish government in exile, which had established itself in London after Hitler's victory in 1939, was fiercely nationalistic and antagonistic to the Soviet Union. It was not willing to accept the boundary line the Russians wanted, and which they had established in 1939–1940, because it involved the loss of considerable territory. The Poles rejected the argument that a very similar line had been proposed by a commission headed by an Englishman after an extensive study of the problem in 1919, and they ignored the argument that it would be wiser to compromise with Moscow in 1943 than to allow the Red Army to resolve the issue.

As a result, the Soviets ignored the exile government and instead worked with Poles who were more willing to accept Russian predominance in Eastern Europe. The United States refused to recognize those Poles or to force the London exiles to compromise, even though it recognized that the Russian argument had some substance. American leaders wanted a non-Communist government in postwar Poland, and they were confident enough of the power of the United States to believe that they could ultimately drive a satisfactory bargain with the Russians.

Roosevelt next met Churchill in Cairo. By then (the talks ran from November 22 through December 6, 1943), Allied forces had taken the offensive. The United States marines and the navy had destroyed Japanese power in the Solomon Islands, and the day before the conference began they struck Tarawa in the Central Pacific's Gilbert Islands. That operation marked the first application of the leapfrogging strategy evolved by General MacArthur. His plan was to take key points that controlled large regions of the Pacific, thus moving closer to Tokyo while leaving the Japanese forces that were bypassed to die on the vine. The approach was ultimately effective—but it was also bloody because the Japanese fought determinedly for every island.

The Germans were equally tough in Italy. They met General Mark

Clark's Fifth Army with heavy firepower when it came ashore at Salerno on September 9, and their stubborn defense enabled them to seize Rome and use Mussolini as the puppet head of their government. Gradually, at great cost, the Allies enlarged their beachheads and pushed eastward and northward across Italy. Though it never received the attention given to other campaigns, the Italian war was particularly grisly. The German resistance was bitter and effective, and the Allies were not able to drive a line across Italy until the end of 1944.

As that campaign began, Roosevelt and Churchill met for the first time with Generalissimo Chiang Kai-Shek to discuss the war in the Pacific. Churchill was not impressed by China's contemporary importance or future significance, but Roosevelt and other American leaders honored the traditional vision of a strong and independent China allied with (and responsive to) the United States. As a result, the agreements reached in Cairo were designed to defeat Japan and restructure the Asian world in keeping with the Open Door policy.

Japan would be forced to surrender unconditionally and lose all its Pacific possessions. The arrangements represented for Chiang the highpoint of his career, which had from the beginning been based on an alliance with Western interests and governments. The Cairo agreements also made it clear that Roosevelt wanted to block any Russian effort to regain its late-nineteenth-century influence in China.

The difficulties of that approach arose almost immediately, however, when Roosevelt and Churchill moved north to Teheran, the capital of Iran, for discussions with Stalin. Some critics have argued that Roosevelt was either naïve or too casual in his dealings with Stalin. That view ignores, to begin with, the strong bargaining position enjoyed by Stalin. The Russian army had demonstrated its ability to sustain a continental offensive against the bulk of the German army. And, Roosevelt aside, the great majority of American leaders either assumed or concluded, on the basis of their knowledge of the great weaknesses of Russia, that the United States could ultimately get what it wanted from the Soviets.

Stalin agreed to coordinate a major Russian offensive with the cross-Channel invasion of occupied France and reaffirmed his earlier commitment to attack Japan. He raised the question of a warm-water outlet in the Far East, and Roosevelt moved to deflect the thrust with the suggestion that Dairen, Manchuria, might be reserved as a free port. No firm decision was made. Perhaps the most important agreement settled the Polish eastern border along the line enforced by Russia in 1939–1940. The Poles were promised compensation with land taken from German territory in the west.

As usual, it all depended upon the men who went into combat. They bled and died and began to win the war. Russians clawed deeper into the guts of the German Wehrmacht. Marines waded ashore in the Marshall Islands. And the British and American armies gave their guts (and souls) to push the Germans back in Italy. Two of the best novels about the war came out of those costly and discouraging experiences. One of them, *A Walk in the Sun,* by Harry Brown, is a wrenching account of an American infantry patrol encountering death on a day that was meant for love. And in his bigger novel, written 20 years after the war, Joseph Heller captured in *Catch-22* the horror of modern warfare that drove men into seemingly irrational behavior as a way of retaining their humanity and sanity.

Those pressures and tensions also affected the highest officers. William Haines wrote a perceptive novel about that side of the war in *Command Decision,* a story of the men who directed the massive air offensive against Germany. The first 1000-plane raid was flown on May 30, 1942, by the British against Cologne, but the nightly storms of death and destruction began in earnest during the winter and spring of 1943–1944. It was usually forgotten, after the use of the atom bomb against Hiroshima and Nagasaki, that such massive saturation attacks killed millions of people. One raid on Dresden, later chronicled by Kurt Vonnegut in *Slaughterhouse Five,* burned, suffocated, and otherwise destroyed 125,000 people, and a similar fire-bombing of Tokyo claimed 80,000 lives. The atom bomb did involve a qualitative difference, but the attitude that led to its use was apparent among American (and British) leaders long before it was perfected.

Such raids were not decisive in the war against Germany and were not used by the Russians—or even by the Allies in Italy. The miserable war in that country liberated Rome on June 4, 1944, and was then largely forgotten. Two days later, under the supreme command of Eisenhower, Allied forces fought their way ashore along a 60-mile stretch of the Normandy coast. Then on June 23 the Russians launched their promised offensive on a front stretching 800 miles south from Leningrad. Within a month, almost one million men and about 170,000 vehicles were landed. The Nazis were in the vise.

Japan was also on the defensive. The B-29 Superfortress bombers made their first raid on June 16, 1944, the day after the marines had invaded Saipan in the Mariana Islands. Then the navy delivered a crippling blow to the Japanese fleet in the Battle of the Philippine Sea (June 19–20), another engagement fought entirely by carrier-based aircraft. The succession of defeats forced the resignation of Admiral Hideki Tojo as premier (along with his entire cabinet) on July 18, 1944, and his successor was greeted by an assault on Guam.

In Europe, meanwhile, the Allies captured St.-Lô on July 18 and opened their drive for Paris. Two days later a group of German officers and other officials attempted to assassinate Hitler and take over the government. They failed, and Hitler tightened his control and prepared to fight to the end. Shortly after the Allies struck north up the Rhône River valley from a beachhead opened on August 15 between Nice and Marseilles on the southern coast of France, the Germans began firing their V-2 rockets into England. And their development of jet fighters and rocket-powered interceptors made it clear that they were not defeated.

Americans finally entered Germany on September 12, but the northern end of the Allied line was slowed by heavy and effective German defenses. They also stiffened in the south. The First Army launched its attack on Aachen on October 2, but it took almost three weeks of bitter fighting to penetrate the Siegfried line and take the city. By that time, the Red Army had entered East Prussia and had joined Yugoslav forces to recapture Belgrade.

Many novels have been written about the European war. The two most famous ones are probably Irwin Shaw's story of the violent convergence of a young German and a young American, *The Young Lions,* and Konstantine Simonov's moving account of the Soviet stand at Stalingrad, *Days and Nights.* But *The Deathmakers,* by Glen Sire, is in many respects the best. His recreation of a tank battle fought through the rubble of a destroyed German village is unsurpassed. And his accounts of how combat extracts its deadly toll even from those who survive and of the irrationality of the war-making process are classic.

No novelist has done as well with the Pacific war. That conflict jumped into the headlines on October 20, 1944, when Americans invaded the Philippines by striking Leyte in the center of the islands. The Japanese offered fierce, determined resistance and might have repulsed the assault if the effectiveness of their fleet had not been destroyed in the crucial Battle of Leyte Gulf (October 23–25, 1944). The three separate but interrelated surface-and-air engagements that composed that battle marked the climax of the naval war. Both sides made mistakes and suffered losses, and some experts have concluded that the United States was fortunate to escape with the victory. But the Japanese lost four carriers, two battleships, and 18 other ships of the line, and that was enough to give the United States effective control of the Pacific.

Perhaps the best novel about the western war is *The Naked and the Dead,* by Norman Mailer, an account of a battle for an island coupled with a dialogue between Mailer and the reader (as well as between the protagonists) about the dehumanizing and undemocratic character of war and the armed forces. But *Beach Red* by Peter Bowman and *Away All Boats* by Kenneth Dodson are powerful accounts of the nature of the Pacific way of death.

The Japanese fought tenaciously, though they never launched a powerful counteroffensive. But the Germans made a serious effort to reverse the flow of the war at the end of 1944 under the leadership of General Karl von Rundstedt. His forces launched a vigorous assault along an 80-mile front in the Ardennes sector that was held by an insufficient number of American troops, many of whom lacked combat experience. Striking suddenly on December 16, the Germans broke through and drove rapidly toward Liege and Antwerp. American forces suffered heavy losses in the ensuing Battle of the Bulge (8000 killed; 48,000 wounded; and 21,000 captured or missing).

But the Germans lost their momentum when Bastogne held out even though surrounded. It took the Allies another month, however (until January 21, 1945), to restore their original line and resume the offensive. The Russians had meanwhile launched a general assault from their winter line in eastern Poland. They took Warsaw on January 17 and reached the Oder River a week later. The Allies crossed the Saar River on February 22 and penetrated the Ruhr Valley the following day.

The Japanese fiercely resisted a similar fate. They made effective use of the tiny volcanic island of Iwo Jima, 750 miles southwest of Tokyo, to counter B-29 raids on their homeland, and the American decision to assail the island produced one of the goriest battles of the war. It took the marines of the Fourth and Fifth divisions almost four weeks (February 19–March 17, 1945) to conquer the Japanese garrison, and it cost almost 5000 men killed or missing and more than 15,000 wounded.

The Japanese clearly retained the capacity to inflict heavy casualties on Allied forces as they retreated toward their home islands, and that power influenced American leaders as they planned for the last phase of the Pacific war. But it was nevertheless apparent by the end of February, 1945, that both Axis nations would be defeated, and American discussions about specific problems were carried on within a general framework that defined America very largely in terms of the world. The ideological, political, and economic elements that had always influenced the country's dealings with other nations became fused or intertwined to a degree that made foreign policy far more of a purpose than a means. Or, to phrase it differently, the ends and the means merged in a conception of America as the American empire.

The pervasiveness of that attitude is nicely illustrated by the remarks of three quite different leaders. Henry Luce, the wealthy and conservative publisher of *Time, Life,* and *Fortune,* hailed the birth of "The American Century" in 1941; a bit later Secretary of State Hull called for the United States to construct "a new system of international relationships in trade and other economic affairs . . . primarily for reasons of pure national interest"; and Vice President Henry Wallace, a liberal reformer, proclaimed in 1944 that America's "new frontier extends from Minneapolis . . . all the way to Central Asia." The underlying outlook that is so apparent in those remarks was the determining element in subsequent American actions.

EXPLORATORY READING

The detailed military history of World War II can only be found in the multivolumed series published by each service. They are official accounts, but many of the writers produced excellent studies. These are the most useful general introductions to the subject:

A. R. Buchanan, *The United States in World War II* (1964)

K. R. Greenfield (Ed.), *Command Decisions* (1959); and *American Strategy in World War II* (1963)

U. Lee, *The Employment of Negro Troops* (1966)

R. F. Weigley, *The American Way of War* (1973)

There are many studies of the home front, but two of the very best are:

J. M. Blum, *V Was for Victory: Politics and American Culture During World War II* (1976)

M. Weglyn, *Years of Infamy: The Untold Story of America's Concentration Camps* (1976)

Both authors have drawn upon the following excellent studies, which are also worth your serious attention:

K. Archibald, *Wartime Shipyard: A Study in Social Disunity* (1947)

Bureau of the Budget, *The United States at War* (1946)

B. Catton, *The War Lords of Washington* (1948)

E. S. Corwin, *Total War and the Constitution* (1947)

R. Daniels, *Concentration Camps: USA* (1971)

H. Garfinkel, *When Negroes March* (1959)

A. Girdner and A. Loftis, *The Great Betrayal* (1969)

J. Goodman (Ed.), *While You Were Gone* (1946)

S. Harris, *Price and Related Controls in the United States*; and *Inflation and the American Economy* (both 1945)

R. Havighurst and H. G. Morgan, *The Social History of a War-Boom Community* (1951)

H. C. Mansfield, *A Short History of the OPA* (1947)

F. E. Merrill, *Social Problems on the Home Front* (1948)

H. Northrup, *Organized Labor and the Negro* (1944)

R. E. Paul, *Taxation for Prosperity* (1947)

R. Polenburg, *War and Society: the United States, 1941–1945* (1970)

J. Seidman, *American Labor from Defense to Reconversion* (1953)

R. Shogan and T. Craig, *The Detroit Race Riot* (1964)

R. Weaver, *Negro Labor* (1946)

W. W. Wilcox, *The Farmer in the Second World War* (1947)

The best studies of wartime diplomacy are:

R. Beitzell, *The Uneasy Alliance* (1972)

R. A. Divine, *Second Chance: The Triumph of Internationalism* (1967)

G. C. Herring, Jr., *Aid to Russia, 1941–1946* (1973)

G. Kolko, *The Politics of War, 1943–1945* (1970)

W. H. McNeill, *America, Britain and Russia, 1941–1946* (1953)

R. G. O'Connor, *Diplomacy for Victory: FDR and Unconditional Surrender* (1971)

18 VISIONS OF A BENEVOLENT AMERICAN EMPIRE

THE conception of America that emerged from the discussions and debates of the period from 1939 to the end of the war involved a subtle but far-reaching modification of the traditional outlook that had emerged during the 1890s. The earlier expansionist view of the world that produced the Open Door policy was based on the assumptions that America was so powerful that it could transform the world without becoming a classically imperial nation and that its vast economic strength would gradually and peacefully dominate the world marketplace. By the end of the war, however, American leaders had significantly modified that outlook.

It was not a sudden or dramatic shift but the result instead of various experiences over the preceding half century. It quickly became apparent after 1900 that the Open Door system required more active intervention in nonindustrial countries in order to facilitate American penetration and to change those societies so that they would become profitably integrated into the American economy.

Expansionist leaders also recognized, even before the outbreak of World War I, that other industrial powers understood the objectives of the Open Door policy and were prepared to resist being absorbed into the American system. The revolutions in Mexico and Russia and the revival of the Chinese Revolution posed two further difficulties. Those upheavals made it clear that the nonindustrial world was rising against the domination of the Western capitalist metropolis just as the United States was consolidating its preeminence in that metropolis. And it was apparent that all such changes—conservative or radical, indigenous or informed and influenced by Marxist doctrine—challenged American capitalism.

The cumulative effect of those developments became apparent on a sustained and growing basis during the 1930 debates over neutrality and over naval rearmament. Perhaps the most striking example came in the admission by the advocates of strong neutrality legislation that they could not secure such laws because of the vast involvement of American corporations in the world marketplace. To change that economic pattern of empire would involve drastic modification of the entire political economy.

During the winter of 1939–1940 American leaders became increasingly preoccupied with the question, as an editor of *Fortune* phrased it, "of whether the American capitalist system could continue to function if most of Europe and Asia should abolish free enterprise." Hence the problem was to organize "the economic resources of the world so as to make possible a return to the system of free enterprise in every country" after the Axis had been defeated. By the winter of 1943–1944, the subtle change was complete: American leaders had defined the United States as the imperial metropolis of the capitalist world marketplace.

Assistant Secretary of State Francis B. Sayre, for example, bluntly asserted that the United Nations would handle colonial or semicolonial areas along American lines: "The Open Door policy is made a binding obligation in all trust territories." Secretary of War Stimson repeatedly emphasized "the importance of the Open Door policy." And a position paper on American policy in Eastern Europe was equally explicit: the objective was "to permit American nationals to enter, move about freely and carry on commercial and governmental operations unmolested in the countries in question."

American leaders revealed two basic attitudes as they discussed structuring the world in terms of the Open Door policy. One was a deep sense of urgency born of their depression experiences and the other was the assumption that the United States had enough power to accomplish the objective. The testimony before the congressional committees created to probe the question of extending Lend-Lease and to formulate recommendations for postwar economic policy and planning provided a clear expression of both views.

Senator Joseph C. O'Mahoney offered a revealing summary of the general outlook. The "tremendous increase of our industrial activity" that produced prosperity, he pointed out, was the result of providing "public money . . . from the federal treasury" through the war effort. The government was "purchasing more than 50 percent of all the goods and services that are produced. . . . Obviously, when the federal government withdraws from the market, we must have some other purchases. . . . If that doesn't happen, it is impossible to see how a depression can be avoided much worse than any depression which the country has ever known."

The potential crisis was dramatized by an expert from the Department of Labor:

It unfortunately is a fact that for the majority of the people in the United States the thing we have liked to refer to as the American standard of living is only possible in situations where two people in the family are working— that is, to get the kind of an income which will allow them to buy adequate food, reasonably decent clothing, and have just a little margin for expenditures which might be regarded as comforts or luxuries, depending upon how you classify them.

Some of the most significant testimony came from Assistant Secretary of State Dean G. Acheson, an upper-class lawyer from Yale. The central danger, he pointed out, was the very real possibility of sliding into another depression. If that happened, he warned, "it seems clear that we are in for a very bad time, so far as the economic and social position of the country is concerned. We cannot go through another ten years like the ten years at the end of the twenties and the beginning of the thirties, without having the most far-reaching consequences upon our economic and social system."

Acheson admitted that the problem could be solved through some form of socialism. In his mind, however, and in the minds of other American leaders, that was unthinkable. They all agreed with him that it was impossible to have freedom under socialism:

That would completely change our Constitution, our relations to property, human liberty, our very conceptions of law. And nobody contemplates that. Therefore, you find you must look to other markets, and those markets are abroad. . . . My contention is that we cannot have full employment and prosperity in the United States without the foreign markets.

The assumption about American power seemed to be verified, moreover, by the continuing defeat of Axis forces on the field of battle and by the gains won at the conference table. The old struggle with Britain for world markets was sustained through the war by using the Lend-Lease agreements and regulations to help American businessmen. The British complained bitterly, but Assistant Secretary of State Will L. Clayton continued to do all he could to eliminate such competition. And the rivalry was carried into the United Nations Monetary and Financial Conference held in July, 1944, at Bretton Woods, New Hampshire.

The United States was not particularly upset when Russia declined to participate because it felt that the Soviets were so weak that they

TABLE 2   Percentage of Money Income Received by Each Fifth of Families and Individuals and by Top 5 Percent

Families and Individuals Ranked from Lowest to Highest	1947	1957	1962	1967	1968
Total	100%	100%	100%	100%	100%
Lowest fifth	4	4	3	4	4
Second fifth	11	11	11	11	11
Middle fifth	17	18	17	17	17
Fourth fifth	24	25	25	24	25
Highest fifth	46	43	44	44	44
Top 5%	19	17	17	16	15

Herman P. Miller, *Income Distribution in the United States*, Government Printing Office, 1966, page 21; and unpublished data. (From H. P. Miller, *Rich Man, Poor Man*, New York: Crowell, 1971, p. 50.)

would ultimately have to accept whatever arrangements were agreed upon, and American leaders were primarily concerned to establish the kind of a system that would facilitate American expansion under American control. The British delegation headed by Lord Keynes fought hard for a more flexible plan less dominated by American power. But Keynes lost, and the conference established an international monetary system designed to implement the Open Door policy.

The Russians caused more difficulties at the conference held at Dumbarton Oaks (a Harvard-owned estate near Washington) to prepare a draft charter for the United Nations. The long discussions, August 21 to October 7, 1944, failed to resolve the disagreement over the power of the major nations designated to hold membership on the Security Council. Roosevelt had modified his earlier idea of having an Anglo-American force police the world, at least to the extent of including the Russians as a partner, but the United States was vigorously opposed to allowing a member of the Security Council to use the veto power in any dispute to which it was a party. The Russians refused to accept that limitation and the matter was left moot.

PLANNING FOR PEACE

The Soviets were not present during the talks between Roosevelt and Churchill held in Quebec (September 11–16). Those two Western leaders completed plans for the final assault on Germany and discussed the division of that country for the purposes of occupation and postwar control. They belatedly recognized General Charles de Gaulle as the spokesman of France and agreed to allot France a zone of occupation in Germany and a voice in postwar decisions. Roosevelt offered, and won tentative agreement for, a very tough policy toward Germany.

That proposal, variously known as the Morgenthau Plan or the "potato patch policy," called for the wholesale deindustrialization of Germany. Some critics charged that it was advanced by people who were sympathetic to the needs or wishes of the Soviet Union. There were a few such men in the government, but none of them possessed authority to make final decisions. The plan for Germany was approved by Secretary of the Treasury Morgenthau, who was clearly motivated by his intense emotional opposition to the Nazis, but it was so harsh that it evoked widespread criticism, and Roosevelt quietly dropped it within six weeks.

Similar opposition had developed within the government toward the request by Russia for a large loan to help it recover from the war. The Soviet interest in such aid became known during 1943, and the question was periodically discussed during the next two years. One group of leaders, led by Donald M. Nelson and Eric Johnston, argued that such a loan would provide a bargaining lever for reaching political agreements with the Soviets and open a vast market for American surpluses (and make it possible to obtain important raw materials).

Others, though they knew that the Russians "were anxious to come to a prompt understanding," disagreed. Their attitude became clear in 1944 when Stalin made a formal bid for a $6 billion loan. Led by W. Averell Harriman, they argued that Russian weakness ought to be exploited to obtain all possible concessions. "I am opposed to granting her that credit," Harriman bluntly explained. "I would apportion that credit out piecemeal, demanding in return concessions on the political field." Though they shared Harriman's confidence in American power, a few more perceptive policy makers warned that the Russians could not be pushed around so easily. The Soviets wanted security in order to "turn to industrialization and development," cautioned Admiral William H. Standley, who served as ambassador to Russia during the first part of the war, adding that they would "proceed on their own to provide it" unless the United States accepted its share of the responsibility for working out acceptable guarantees.

Churchill began early in 1944 to nag Roosevelt on the same issue. The westward advance of the Red Army made it vital to reach agreements with the Soviets before the situation was settled by military occupation. The failure of the Polish government in exile to reach an understanding with Moscow underscored that point, as did Russia's unilateral decision, on July 27, 1944, to recognize the Committee of National Liberation (organized by Poles in Moscow) as the government of Poland. Roosevelt initially accepted the prime minister's argument that it was necessary to agree upon a clear division of authority. Then, just as Churchill left for Moscow, the president reversed himself and asserted that he must retain "complete freedom of action" regardless of any agreements reached with Stalin.

Churchill knew that that was impossible. There was no point in going to Moscow to talk about "complete freedom of action" for the United States. "The moment was apt for business," Churchill recalled, "so I said, 'Let us settle about our affairs. . . . Don't let us get at cross-purposes in small ways.' " Stalin accepted Churchill's proposals: Rumania, 90 percent interest to Russia; Greece, 90 percent interest to Great Britain and the United States; Yugoslavia and Hungary to be divided 50–50; and Russia to have a 75 percent preference in Bulgaria. "Might it not be thought rather cynical," Churchill then remarked, "if it seemed we had disposed of these issues, so fateful to millions of people, in such an offhand manner? Let us burn the paper." "No, you keep it," Stalin said, and pushed it back across the table to Churchill. He kept it, and printed it in his memoirs; hence there is no doubt about the bargain.

Stalin honored the agreement when the British intervened in Greece through the winter of 1944–1945 to suppress a revolution against a dying monarchy. Roosevelt was aware of all those events when he met Churchill and Stalin early in February, 1945, in the Crimean peninsula. He was also a tired man whose health was failing, and the results of the Yalta Conference have often been explained as the result of his fatigue and his naïve failure to stand up to Stalin. The argument is not persuasive. Despite the strains of his early illness, increased by the strain of the depression and the demands of the war, Roosevelt had undoubtedly been revived and encouraged by his November, 1944, election victory over Thomas E. Dewey.

The elements within the Republican party that had nominated Willkie in 1940 and supported his urban and reforming outlook consolidated their position during the next four years. Their influence helped to win 46 seats in the House and nine in the Senate in the off-year elections of 1942. And in securing the nomination of Dewey at the Chicago convention (July 20), they placed the party in a strong position despite the obvious difficulties of trying to unseat the commander in chief of a vast and successful war effort.

Dewey was young and attractive, and the Republicans were further encouraged by the split within the Democratic party over Vice President Henry Wallace. He was too liberal for Democratic businessmen, as well as for most Southern politicians, and the city bosses dismissed him as a utopian. Those groups forced Roosevelt to drop Wallace, but organized labor blocked the nomination of James F. Byrnes, the first choice of conservatives as a replacement. Roosevelt broke the deadlock by suggesting Senator Truman, a popular New Dealer in the Congress and a loyal party man.

Truman was acceptable to labor, which campaigned vigorously for the Democrats. The CIO, functioning through its Political Action Committee, delivered a large, and perhaps decisive, bloc of working-class votes. Dewey made an effective appeal to middle- and upper-class groups during the late summer and early autumn campaigning, and the president's routine efforts offered little active opposition. He did not even do much to exploit the vote-getting appeal of the Servicemen's Readjustment Act (the GI Bill of Rights) that the Congress passed on June 22, 1944, to provide extensive educational and economic assistance to returning servicemen.

But Roosevelt came zestfully alive, attacking Dewey and promising a return to the New Deal program after the war, in a late September speech before a wildly enthusiastic crowd of the teamsters union. He exploited that success in Chicago and the cities of the East, and his exhilaration—and effectiveness—reached a climax in a full-day tour of New York City. Despite a steady, drenching rain, he waved and smiled to the entire city from an open car. Dewey ran close in the popular vote (22 million to 25.6 million), but Roosevelt carried 36 states and the Democrats retained control of the Congress.

The president did not enjoy that kind of power base, however, in his negotiations with the Russians at Yalta. Having declined to make firm agreements with Russia about Eastern Europe in 1941–1942, Roosevelt did not have many options when he met Stalin. The Red Army had driven the Germans back into Germany, and its strength was considered necessary to defeat Japan. Given those circumstances, the United States had four alternatives. It could threaten to use, and if necessary actually employ, its great military power to force the Soviets to accept American policies. It could use the combination of Russian weakness and American economic strength to attain its most important objectives. It could simply acquiesce in the consolidation of Russian influence westward to the Oder River in Germany. Or it could negotiate short-run compromises in the confidence and expectation that American power would ultimately be decisive.

Roosevelt thought in terms of the last alternative. He did not threaten the Russians, but neither did he discuss firm agreements involving economic aid for concessions in Europe and Asia. And he did not acquiesce in all their proposals. They demanded $20 billion in reparations from Germany, for example, and Roosevelt simply refused. The president also made it clear that the United States would control the reconstruction of Japan. He likewise won an ambivalent understanding to broaden the provisional Polish government, and his agreement to accept the Ukraine as a member of the United Nations did not give the Soviet Union any more effective power in that organization.

In other respects, the Yalta accords confirmed earlier arrangements. Poland's new borders were set by the Curzon line in the east and the Oder River in the west. The agreements concerning the Far East, which provoked considerable criticism when they were made known after the war, were either in line with the general policy of restoring the *status quo ante* in the Pacific or the result of the concern to insure Soviet help against Japan.

The major weakness of the Yalta agreements was that too many agreements had been left vague and indeterminate. That was dramatized when Roosevelt died in Warm Springs, Georgia, on April 12, 1945, of a massive cerebral hemorrhage. The nation was stunned and saddened, and it mourned him with deep emotion as decisions passed into the hands of other leaders.

Millions wept openly, and many of his most embittered critics admitted his greatness. Even the pathetic diehards who declared they were glad he was gone acknowledged his significance and influence. He was a great leader who had rallied a people at the edge of their despair and saved their confidence in a system that had carried them into a disastrous depression. The involvement with Roosevelt had been warm and deep, and Americans honored him as a beloved aristocrat who had done his best to discharge the obligations of wealth and power.

Harry Truman was a man of vastly different talents, attainments, and style, and his knowledge of the stark contrast between himself and Roosevelt left him temporarily overwhelmed. Few men could have stepped easily and confidently into Roosevelt's place, and Truman was additionally handicapped by the failure of Roosevelt to keep him even moderately well informed about government affairs. Truman had to begin making important decisions even before an intense briefing program was fairly under way.

The only real breathing space he had was provided by the war effort, which had sufficient momentum to sustain itself during the first crucial weeks. The assault northward from Iwo Jima toward Japan was resumed just before Roosevelt died. After extensive air attacks and naval bombardment, the marines and the Tenth Army invaded Okinawa on April 1.

Japanese resistance was awesome. Their heavy air attacks, including the most organized and sustained use of suicide flights of the war, took a heavy toll of ships and men. And their ground forces fought with the wily toughness that American units had come to expect and dread. But the beachhead was secured, and the Japanese cabinet resigned on April 5, after it had become apparent that the American forces could not be driven into the sea. The price of victory was staggering: 11,260 dead and 33,769 wounded. Those costs reinforced the feeling among American leaders that they needed help from the Russians during the final attack on the Japanese home islands.

Progress in Europe was more spectacular. Cologne was captured on March 7, and the next day American forces took the bridge across the Rhine at Remagen before it could be destroyed by the Germans. Men and armor streamed across, and on April 25 American and Russian forces met at Torgau on the Elbe, one day after the Red Army had entered Berlin. The Americans could have met the Russians farther east, and they might even have been the first to enter Berlin. German resistance in the west was weaker because—with considerable reason—they feared the vengeance of the Russians. Churchill argued that it was worth the cost in lives to race headlong to the east and stop the Russians as soon as possible. But it is extremely doubtful that his advice would have worked out as well in practice as it appeared in theory after the fact.

Eisenhower constantly had to prod the British to move the northern end of the Allied line eastward in order to secure the Baltic coastline against a Russian flanking maneuver to drive around the Nazis to the Atlantic Coast. If all the resources of the Western Allies had been concentrated on a thrust into Central Europe, the Red Army would have enjoyed a cakewalk across the northern rim of the continent. Churchill was a magnificently charismatic leader of an empire during a war, but he failed to perceive that the empire was disintegrating in its finest hour. He mistakenly thought that the problem was a matter of deploying power whereas the real issue involved the limitations of rapidly decreasing power. But he was not alone. American leaders also thought that they could shape mankind in their own image.

President Truman very rapidly concluded, if he did not already believe, that the only effective way to deal with the Russians was to be tough. The briefings that he was given after he became president reinforced his own strong inclinations in that direction. Harriman warned him, for example, that the Soviets posed the threat of "a barbarian invasion of Europe," but went on to assure him confidently that American power could keep them under control. Truman's basic attitude became clear when the Russians raised reservations about going ahead with the United Nations conference that had been scheduled before Roosevelt died.

After discussing the question of postponement with the cabinet, Truman announced that he felt "our agreements with the Soviet Union so far [have] been a one-way street" and that he could not continue: it was now or never. "We have got to get tough with the Russians. They don't know how to behave. They're like bulls in a china shop. They're only 25 years old. We're over 100 years old and the British are centuries older. We've got to teach them how to behave."

The Russians were not intimidated. They were already suspicious and angry about American negotiations with the Nazis in Italy, and they arrived in San Francisco insisting upon their view of the veto power in the Security Council. They also opposed the American willingness to admit nations (like Argentina) that had not cooperated against the Nazis and America's policy on regional treaty organizations and other issues. The situation was not eased when the United States canceled all Lend-Lease allocations and shipments to Russia. Stalin thought the action "brutal" and warned that if it was "designed as pressure on the Russians, to soften them up, then it was a fundamental mistake." The order was temporarily modified, and Truman sent Harry Hopkins to Moscow to resolve the differences over the U.N. and Poland.

The Russians gave way on the veto question, and on June 25, 1945, the charter for the United Nations was approved. The secretary-general, the administrative head of the organization, was to be elected by the member nations, all of whom were given one vote in the General Assembly. The Security Council, a special organization meeting in continuous session to handle major disputes, was dominated by the five permanent members: the United States, Russia, Great Britain, France, and China. Members to fill the six other seats were elected for a term of two years.

The Economic and Social Council (composed of 18 members elected by the General Assembly) was created to deal with problems of economic development and fundamental human rights. The General Assembly was also empowered to join the Security Council members in electing the 15 judges of the International Court of Justice. Finally, a Trustee Council was established to handle various dependent and conquered territories. The United States secured unilateral control over former Japanese islands in the Pacific. That decision, in which the Russians acquiesced, created a precedent that the Soviets used in handling matters in Eastern Europe.

CONFRONTATION AT POTSDAM

The division of authority over Germany was meanwhile institutionalized on June 5, 1945, through the creation of the European Advisory Council. The country was divided into zones ruled by Britain (west), Russia (east), and France and the United States (each had a zone in the south). Each of the four Allies also occupied part of Berlin, located inside the Russian zone, and the administration of the city was assigned to an Allied military Kommandatura. That arrangement did not resolve the differences over reparations, however, or the questions pertaining to Eastern Europe, and the leaders of the Big Three met in Potsdam (a suburb of Berlin) between July 17 and August 2, 1945, in an effort to reach agreements on those issues.

American leaders went to Potsdam concerned to reaffirm and implement the Open Door policy in Central and Eastern Europe as well as in Asia. Secretary of War Stimson repeatedly and forcefully emphasized that objective in his correspondence and discussions with President Truman and Secretary of State Byrnes. His diary tells the story. Stimson saw Truman on July 14 and 16, and "went over with him carefully" the issue, "again and again warning him to be absolutely sure that the Russians not block off our trade." He talked with Byrnes on July 17: "I impressed on him the importance of the Open Door policy." And, after still another meeting on July 18, Stimson reported that Truman "was confident of sustaining the Open Door policy." The president also agreed with Stimson's plan to block the Soviets from any significant part in the occupation of Japan.

A similar approach was outlined for Europe. Harriman's recommendations centered on "the development of the commerce and trade of the United States." Truman was "greatly interested" in applying the Open Door principle to the Danube River waterway system. The broad objective was to win "access, on equal terms, to such trade, raw materials and industry, and appropriately to modify existing arrangements" to secure that access. That meant, in keeping with the traditional Open Door approach, that the United States intended "to insist on the reorganization of the present governments" in Europe, "or the holding of free general elections."

The Russians were primarily concerned with reparations and with security against a future attack by a resurgent Germany. Stalin left no doubt that he expected the conference to settle the reparations issue. "This council," he bluntly announced in his opening remarks, "will deal with reparations." Soviet leaders feared "they would be left with very little equipment as reparations in spite of the fact that the Germans had destroyed Soviet industries." As for the question of security, Stalin considered that a matter "of high policy. The purpose of such a policy was to separate these countries from Germany as a great power. . . . [To] rally the satellites around them and to detach them once and for all from Germany."

American leaders were well aware of the "intense popular feeling and fresh experience" that lay behind Soviet policy. Despite such knowledge, they did not move to meet such Russian desires in return for compromises about the Open Door in Eastern Europe and Asia. Secretary Byrnes remarked almost casually that "reparations do not seem to the United States to be an immediate problem." That attitude was reinforced by the news of the successful test of the nuclear bomb.

The scientists and technicians at the secret desert laboratory near Los Alamos, New Mexico, triggered the first nuclear explosion at 5:30 A.M. on July 16, 1945. Awestruck and apprehensive, they knew they had forever changed man's life on earth. Some of them acknowledged the shift by talking about their new and intimate knowledge of original sin. One put it more bluntly: "Well, we're all sons of bitches now." A significant number of them joined a campaign to prevent the terrible weapon from being used. Another group argued that only by using it could men be shocked into making the changes in attitude and the practical compromises that were necessary to prevent its future use. Most of them wanted to use it as soon as possible. That was the decision of American policy makers in Potsdam when they were informed of the successful test.

The report on the effectiveness of the bomb had a dramatic effect on President Truman, Secretary of War Stimson, and Secretary of State Byrnes. Stimson reported that the president was "immensely pleased" and "tremendously pepped up by it." It "gave him an entirely new feeling of confidence," and he was "greatly pleased" with the idea of using the bomb quickly.

American leaders welcomed the bomb as a weapon that would defeat Japan without the invasion of the home islands that was scheduled for November *and* as a means of checking the Russians. Truman immediately asked whether there was any need for help from the Soviet Union against Japan, and Stimson advised him that "with our new weapon we would not need the assistance of the Russians." Byrnes later explained the strategy very directly: "We wanted to get through with the Japanese phase of the war before the Russians came in." As part of that effort, the United States told the Chinese to stall their negotiations with the Russians concerning the agreements on the Far East that had been made at Yalta. "If Stalin and Chiang were still negotiating," Byrnes explained, "it might delay Soviet entrance and the Japanese might surrender. The president was in accord with that view."

American leaders were reluctant to tell Stalin about the bomb. That was in keeping with the earlier decision by Churchill and Roosevelt on September 18, 1944, not to inform the world about the weapon. They had opted for secrecy even if it meant a failure to obtain "an international agreement regarding its control and use." Truman told Stalin in a very casual, cryptic, and vague way that the United States had a new and powerful weapon that it would use against Japan.

The Russians already knew about the bomb from information given them by the British scientist Klaus Fuchs. Fuchs felt that the Soviets, as allies, had a right to know of the weapon, and he also believed that there would be a greater chance for peace after the war if the bomb was not the monopoly of one power. Even if they had been wholly in the dark, however, the Russians would have realized from Truman's changed manner that something very important had happened.

Churchill left a dramatic account of the way the news of the bomb affected the president. The prime minister "noticed . . . that Truman was evidently much fortified by something that had happened and that he stood up to the Russians in a most emphatic and decisive manner, telling them as to certain demands that they absolutely could not have and that the United States was entirely against them. . . . When he got to the meeting after having read this report he was a changed man. He told the Russians just where they got off and generally bossed the whole meeting." Churchill added, in a remark that reveals the general attitude of American and British leaders, that "we possessed powers which were irresistible." At least they seemed that way to those who possessed them, if not to those who sat across the table.

Confident in that power, Truman bluntly told the Russians that the United States would not recognize the existing governments in Eastern Europe. "When those countries were established on a proper basis, the United States would recognize them and not before." American leaders took the same kind of position on reparations. Unwilling to give the Soviets any major assistance, Byrnes proposed "each country taking reparations from its own zone." He added, as had Truman, that "there can be no discussion of this matter."

Some American advisers warned Truman and Byrnes that such an approach would create a de facto division of Europe. Molotov saw and made the point very directly. "Would not the secretary's suggestion mean," he asked, "that each country would have a free hand in [its] own zones and would act entirely independently of the others?" Byrnes admitted "that was true in substance." "Perhaps the demarcation line between the Soviet and Western zones of occupation should be taken as the dividing line," Stalin suggested, "and everything west of that line would go to the Allies and everything east of that line to the Russians."

Truman asked if Stalin "meant a line running from the Baltic to the Adriatic." The Russian "replied in the affirmative." After further discussion that made it clear that the agreement between Stalin and Churchill of October, 1944, would be honored in such a division, "the president said that he agreed with the Soviet proposal." As far as economic matters were concerned, therefore, the United States accepted temporary Soviet control throughout Eastern Europe on the assumption that America's great economic and military powers would enable it to prevent the Soviets from extending that control into political authority and from making it permanent.

That confidence was strengthened by the effectiveness of the nuclear bomb in ending the war against Japan. The argument of the scientists who opposed using the weapon, at least until its terrible powers had been demonstrated on an uninhabited island, was dismissed without serious consideration. The weapon was dropped first on Hiroshima on August 6, 1945. It obliterated more than four square miles of the city and killed or injured over 160,000 human beings. All that remained of some people was the shadow they had cast on a concrete wall at the instant they were vaporized. They had protected that portion of the wall from the full fury of the radioactive fireball, and hence it remained darker than the exposed sections. Perhaps the classic account of the disaster has been provided by John Hersey in his moving essay *Hiroshima*. An excellent report on how the Japanese felt about the experience 20 years later is offered by Rafael Steinberg in *Postscript from Hiroshima*.

The Russians launched their promised attack in Manchuria two days later. The United States promptly dropped another bomb on August 9, inflicting vast death and destruction on Nagasaki. The Japanese, affected by the Russian assault to a greater extent than Americans generally recognized, surrendered unconditionally on August 14. The war was officially terminated the next day, an event marked by general rejoicing and by uninhibited street celebrations in many of the larger cities of the United States.

"WHY CAN'T WE WORK TOGETHER IN MUTUAL TRUST AND CONFIDENCE?"

David Low, *Years of Wrath. A Cartoon History: 1931–1945*. With text by Quincy Howe. New York: Simon & Schuster, 1946. (The cartoon and the text appear on the page following the introduction. The pages are not numbered.)

For many, of course, the triumph was bittersweet. More than 300,000 Americans had been killed and more than twice that many wounded. Though air power played a significant part in the conflict (and 36,700 fliers had been killed), 70 percent of all casualties were suffered by the infantry. Faster and better care—and new medicines such as penicillin, sulfa drugs, and blood plasma—had reduced the death rate among the wounded to less than half of what it had been during World War I. Even so, 41,322 of the 170,596 casualties in the Pacific theater were either killed outright or died despite medical aid.

The United States acted rapidly to exploit the victory in Asia. The occupation of Japan began on August 27, 1945, and the surrender terms were signed aboard the battleship *Missouri*, anchored in Tokyo Bay, on September 2, 1945. American forces also moved quickly into China to help Chiang Kai-Shek consolidate his position against Mao Tse-Tung, the revolutionary heir of Sun Yat-Sen. It is often overlooked that the United States exercised the same kind of power in Asia that the Soviet Union displayed in Eastern Europe. The Russians were effectively excluded from any meaningful share in reshaping Japan, and their occupation zone in Korea was far less significant than comparable Western positions in Germany and Austria. They had gained some influence in Manchuria, but even there they posed no serious threat to a strong and effective Chinese government.

The trouble was, of course, that Chiang Kai-Shek was neither strong nor effective. He had failed to rally and inspire the country even before the Japanese attack in 1937, and he did not offer bold and imaginative leadership after their defeat. He was immediately confronted, moreover, by the challenge of a peasant-based Communist movement led by people who were honest and capable of building a powerful revolutionary social movement. Misreading the situation, American leaders were confident that their aid would enable Chiang to reestablish himself as the leader of a restored and vital China.

Even as the victory over Japan was being won, however, Secretary of War Stimson began to doubt that American policy would produce a benevolent empire. He had played a central part in developing the strong attitude and tough posture toward the Russians, but he courageously concluded that the United States "was on the wrong path" in its approach to the Soviets. The failure of his efforts to modify the existing assumptions and policy meant that the confrontation with Russia would define the context and the character of the next decade.

EXPLORATORY READING

The history of ideas, world views, and visions is buried in the private manuscripts of the protagonists. Hence the place to go is to those papers and to the published expressions of their thoughts and ideas in newspaper interviews, in magazine articles, and in the published versions of their memos, conversations, and recommendations. Begin with the State Department volumes on the conferences at Yalta and Potsdam, which contain many revealing comments.

The two most exciting books are:

L. C. Gardner, *Architects of Illusion* (1970)

M. J. Sherwin, *A World Destroyed: The Atomic Bomb and the Grand Alliance* (1975)

But these volumes challenge you to make your own sense out of the facts:

G. Alperovitz, *Atomic Diplomacy* (1965)

S. E. Ambrose, *Rise to Globalism* (1971)

D. S. Clemens, *Yalta* (1970)

H. Feis, *The China Tangle* (1953); and *Between War and Peace: The Potsdam Conference* (1960)

W. L. Neuman, *After Victory: Churchill, Roosevelt, Stalin and the Making of the Peace* (1967)

W. A. Williams, *The Tragedy of American Diplomacy* (second revised edition, 1972)

19 EMPIRE AS A WAY OF LIFE

THERE is a fascinating paradox about American society between 1945 and 1964, the years when the United States dominated world affairs. American leaders invested great thought and resources in an imperial foreign policy, but they committed far less energy and money to programs to improve the substance and quality of life at home—and the vast majority of citizens acquiesced in that imperial ordering of priorities. There is no simple explanation of that striking phenomenon, but three factors do help in understanding how it occurred.

Two generations of Americans composed the majority of the population that emerged from the war: the adults of the depression decade and their children. By 1945 each group had undergone three social traumas: the depression; the war; and the related decline and fall of most extended families because of those disruptions and because of the families' own impotence in the face of the power and seductiveness of corporate state capitalism. The psychological and social fatigue caused by those crises and the desire of the survivors to enjoy life prompted most to retreat even farther into the individualism that was so crucial to the power of the corporate upper class.

Secondly, the ruling class effectively used American ideals and traditions to evoke public support for its imperial policies. However questionable the purposes (or the benefits), American citizens responded from the best of motives—and the elementary human need to be part of a social relationship with people outside their immediate, nuclear home. In a very real sense, therefore, the cold war against communism served as an imperial substitute for an indigenous social reform movement, such as Debs had created between 1900 and 1920, designed to honor American values in domestic life.

Finally, a significant number of middle-class Americans did reap some benefits from imperialism. The political economy of empire created jobs and left people alone to enjoy their privatization of life so long as they did not challenge the system. And for many, at least for a time, that was enough: a tolerable bargain in the marketplace. They wanted to indulge themselves after the depression and the war, and the imperial foreign policy enabled them to do so.

TABLE 3   Characteristics of Family Dwellings" in the United States, by Place of Residence, 1940 and 1950

	Percentage of Dwellings with Specified Facilities							
	United States		Urban		Rural Nonfarm		Farm	
Facilities	1940	1950	1940	1950	1940	1950	1940	1950
Electric lighting	79	94	96	99	78	90	31	78
Running water in dwelling	70	86	93	98	56	73	18	47
Flush toilet in dwelling	65	77	91	92	45	57	11	29
Central heating	42	50	58	62	27	32	10	17
Mechanical refrigerator	44	80	56	86	39	72	15	61
Gas or electricity for cooking	54	73	78	85	33	59	6	37
At least one room per person	80	85	84	87	77	81	79	78

Series H-44, No. 4, December 29, 1944; and No. 6, February 14, 1945. Series H-45, No. 1, April 28, 1945. Series HC-5, No. 1, February 17, 1951; No. 2, June 10, 1951. (From E. E. Hoyt *et al.*, *American Income and Its Use*, New York: Harper & Row, 1954, p. 353.)

" The 1940 data for lighting and plumbing facilities relate to all dwellings, whereas the 1950 data relate to occupied dwellings. Since the vacancy rate was low in 1950, for the most part the figures are the same for these two categories of housing. The greatest difference occurs in rural-farm places, the vacancy rate being greater there. The 1950 census of housing reported 4 percent of the urban and 9 percent of the rural farm dwellings to be vacant, and 55.5 percent of all farm dwellings had no piped running water.

But not all Americans were that passive. The hundreds of thousands of veterans who used the GI Bill to attend college changed campus life in many ways, for example, even though they did not engage in mass demonstrations. Not all of the impact was good. Far too many of them were simply job and marriage oriented, and thus unknowingly helped the corporations further distort education into job training—it became ever more a public subsidy for the corporate system. On the other hand, such students did force many academics to face the implications of their lectures and improve their pedagogy, and in that sense, university life became more serious and consequential.

Ironically, however, those college graduates created a life-style of middle-class values that ultimately influenced many of their children to revolt against the contradiction between the values they had been taught and the reality of American corporate society. And still other Americans, black and brown, female as well as male, did fight for more

TABLE 4 Personal-Consumption Expenditures, Personal Taxes, and Personal Savings in the United States, Percentages, 1929 and 1951

Item	1929	1951
Personal-consumption expenditures		
Food		23.9
Alcoholic beverages		3.3
Total of above	23.1	27.2
Clothing	12.9	9.7
Personal care	1.3	1.0
Housing	13.4	8.6
Household operation	12.4	10.8
Medical care and death expenses	4.2	4.0
Personal business	6.1	3.7
Automobile	6.8	7.2
Other transportation	2.1	1.3
Recreation	5.1	4.5
Tobacco	2.0	1.9
Private education	.8	.7
Religion and welfare	1.4	.8
Foreign travel and remittances	.9	.5
Total personal-consumption expenditures	92.5	81.9
Taxes, personal	3.1	11.4
Savings, personal	4.4	6.7
Total of all	100.0	100.0

From E. E. Hoyt *et al.*, *American Income and Its Use*, New York: Harper & Row, 1954, p. xvii.

equitable treatment during the years of empire. They won some improvements and, perhaps even more importantly, they sustained the traditions of resistance, protest, and reform.

Others who ultimately became critical of the imperial political economy did not view themselves even as reformers—let alone as radicals. But they slowly began to oppose a system that increasingly defined the nature of their lives and claimed their children for military interventions and another war. Some of those citizens, after one or two unsuccessful efforts to change the system, acquiesced in the fact of established power, but others became vigorous reformers.

The women reformers were as different as sea and desert: famous ones like the writer Lillian Hellman or politician Helen Gahagan Douglas, and those not famous like Elizabeth Link of Wisconsin and Lisa Von Borowsky of Florida who bravely fought imperialism and racism and poverty despite being isolated and demeaned by others in their communities. Such white women had a taste of the ashes that formed the diet of the blacks who opposed the empire. For even the great ones, such as DuBois, Randolph, and Paul Robeson, suffered much more, and the unknowns in unions and the South endured hell to realize at home the ideals that were being trumpeted around the globe by American leaders.

White male radicals also took their lumps. Even academic reformers like Charles Beard and Harry Elmer Barnes were vilified by their colleagues. Other more radical figures like A. J. Muste, David Dellinger, and Norman Thomas were harried, harassed, and imprisoned, though their dedication and courage ultimately proved effective. In the short run, however, the issues were kept alive in the public arena by a strange group of liberal and conservative leaders. That tiny band, personified by Secretary of War Stimson, former Vice President Wallace, Senator Robert Taft, and the once despised Herbert Hoover, sustained the nonimperial conception of America and provided a basis for legitimizing such views among those who initially went along with empire as a way of life.

The specific and general influence of such people poses one of the most difficult problems for historians. Yet sometimes the inability to be certain about one connection enables us to be reasonably certain about another relationship. No one can say for sure that Hoover induced Stimson to change his views, but we can assert with considerable confidence that the failure of Hoover *and* Stimson *and* Wallace to change the outlook of Truman and other top leaders meant that the policy-making elite was knowingly embarked upon an imperial venture.

Truman's initial insecurity led him to ask for advice from Hoover, and that invitation led to a series of memos and conversations with various people in the executive branch of the government that culminated in a May 25, 1945, discussion between Hoover and Truman. Hoover's advice, quite in keeping with his ideals and earlier performance as president, was against imperialism: "We could not go to war with them [the Russians] and we should never bluff. Our position should be to persuade, hold up the banner of what we thought was right and let it go at that."

Hoover detested communism (and the distortion of it that had been created in the Soviet Union), but he defined America in terms of its basic security against invasion and the quality of life at home. Thus he also detested the corporate state capitalism that had emerged during the New Deal and had been consolidated during the war. He was true to his own conception of America in opposing imperialism—whatever the rhetoric of saving the world for democracy—and in emphasizing the importance of creating a community at home. Four months later, well aware of Hoover's recommendations, Secretary of War Stimson urged Truman to take a different approach to the Russians.

Stimson shifted his ground in a long memorandum of September 11, 1945, calling for a direct and sympathetic effort to establish a relationship with Russia based "on co-operation and trust." *"For if we fail to approach them now,"* he emphasized, *"and merely continue to negotiate with them, having this weapon rather ostentatiously on our hip, their suspicions and their distrust of our purposes and motives will increase"* (italics in original). That attitude, he warned, would lead to an "armaments race of a rather desperate character."

Stimson's powerful appeal may have prompted Truman to reconsider his attitude, but the president did not change American policy. The London Conference, called to write peace treaties for Italy, Bulgaria, Hungary, and Romania (September 11–October 2, 1945), foundered on what editors of the London *Times* accurately described as an American determination to "claim a right of intervention even in regions especially affecting the security" of the Soviet Union. Byrnes verified the analysis: his objective, he told the Congress, was "the maintenance of the Open Door in the Balkans."

The confrontation between Byrnes and Molotov in London foreshadowed the full development of the cold war. As Stalin had made clear in December, 1941, the Soviet Union sought three principal (and largely nonrevolutionary) objectives. It wanted military security, primarily against Germany, which had attacked Russia twice since 1917. It sought economic assistance to help repair the terrible devastation of the war, which seriously threatened all the gains that the Soviets had made since the 1920s. And it wanted to obtain certain traditional Russian objectives, such as reliable access to warm-water outlets to the Mediterranean Sea and the Pacific Ocean.

Stalin was not indifferent to increased Communist influence around the world, but, as he made clear to Chinese and Yugoslavian Communist leaders, he was not ready to risk Russia (or his own power) for that cause. He was basically conservative and cautious in foreign policy, not at all the aggressive international revolutionary described by American leaders for purposes of creating support for their own policy. Hence the cold war could probably have been avoided if the United States had either accepted Russian predominance in Eastern Europe or had used its economic power to negotiate Russian withdrawal in return for help in reconstruction and a mutual security alliance. It declined to act on the first option because it desired to apply the ideological and economic principles of the Open Door policy in Eastern Europe, and it refused to follow the other choice because it believed that its power was great enough to force the Russians to withdraw.

Thus the Soviet request for a large reconstruction loan was "lost," while the French and the British were treated in a relatively generous manner. The negotiations with England for a loan of $3.75 billion, for example, revealed a great deal about American objectives. "A general purpose of the loan," explained Senator Fred M. Vinson, was to boost exports because "the prosperity of this country is closely linked with our export trade." A related objective, as with the later Marshall Plan, was to strengthen the world capitalist system against indigenous radical social movements.

The effort to consolidate the Open Door in China, however, was not successful. Nationalist forces were effective against Mao's Communist movement in Manchuria during the latter part of 1945, and the Communists announced on November 28 that there was no necessity for a civil war. They even offered to participate in a coalition government. During those months, moreover, the Russians offered Mao little encouragement or assistance.

Despite their advantages, however, the Nationalists failed to consolidate their position, and Truman sent General George Marshall to China in December to arrange a compromise before the Communists exploited Chiang's weaknesses and indecision. Marshall faced three obstacles. One was Chiang's unwillingness to compromise. The second was the growing appeal of Mao, which gave him a strong bargaining position in 1945–1946 and ultimately carried him to power in 1948–1949.

The third was self-imposed and consisted of two ideas: (1) the traditional view that the United States had a special, quasi-fatherly relationship to China, and (2) the newer conviction that all Communist movements were controlled by Moscow. Both made it difficult for Americans to view the conflict as what it was—a revolutionary civil war in which the Chinese were going to decide their own fate regardless of American or Russian preferences. And, in a narrower sense, the second assumption led most policy makers to view Russian actions in Manchuria as part of a deep plot to help Mao. The Soviets had ransacked Manchuria after the defeat of Japan, but their primary objective was to obtain reparations for themselves. What they left did provide some aid for the Chinese Communists in the short run, but it was not a determining factor in the civil war.

The Russians were more active in seeking access to some of the oil in the Middle East and in trying to obtain a larger part in controlling the access to—and egress from—the Black Sea. But they retreated when Truman told Stalin that we would "send troops" if the Russians did not ease their pressure on Iran. The president reinforced that message by warmly applauding the March 5, 1946, anti-Soviet speech delivered by Churchill in Truman's home state of Missouri. Stalin called that militant attack "a dangerous act," and it undoubtedly increased the tension between the two countries.

Two months later the United States twisted the screw a bit more. Arbitrarily and without prior notice it terminated even the small, almost token, reparations to the Soviet Union from the American zone of occupation in Germany. It was one of the crucial acts of the postwar period: a Russian official who later defected to the West called it "one of the pivotal events" in turning Moscow toward a policy of maintaining indefinite control over Eastern Europe. That was indicated at the time through the first all-out Soviet propaganda attack on the United States.

The action on reparations was underscored by the nature of the American plan for dealing with nuclear power and weapons. First drafted in 1946 by Dean Acheson and David E. Lilienthal, the proposal was then revised under the direction of Bernard Baruch. He translated it into a plan (offered in June, 1946) whereby the American bloc in the United Nations would enable the United States to supervise the global development and use of nuclear energy.

Robert Oppenheimer, a key figure in developing the atom bomb, candidly testified that the plan was developed by those who "saw in the problems of atomic energy . . . an opportunity to cause a decisive change in the whole trend of Soviet policy." Such leaders, he explained, were acting on "the notion of a trusteeship" for the world. The assumption of superiority bordered on arrogance. American decision makers were fully aware that the Russians were reducing their ground forces, that they had no means of delivering a sustained nuclear attack on the United States, and that the Soviet Union and the areas it dominated "were all devastated as badly or worse than our Allies."

Even Secretary of the Navy James V. Forrestal, who was so militantly anti-Soviet that some people thought the obsession drove him insane, candidly noted the weakness of the Russians in his diary, though he did not speak publicly with equal candor. "The Russians would not move this summer," he wrote on June 10, 1946, "—in fact not any time." Eisenhower and others agreed. And Baruch admitted that the American plan asked too much: the Soviets could not be expected to allow their economy "to be placed under foreign control."

Secretary of Commerce Wallace was fully aware of that top-level assessment and deeply concerned that the imperial thrust of American policy would subvert reforms at home even if it did not lead to a nuclear war. Wallace was not isolationist, and many of his proposals involved (knowingly or not) American penetration of other societies, but he considered it essential to accommodate to the reality of Communist power. He courageously and forcefully criticized Truman's policies in September, 1946, calling publicly for a peace treaty with Russia. "Getting tough," he argued, "never brought anything real and lasting—whether for school yard bullies or world powers. The tougher we get, the tougher the Russians will get."

The president promptly dismissed Wallace from the cabinet and created a new bureaucracy to investigate and certify the loyalty of government employees. That action (which opened the door for another Red scare) may have been influenced by wild-eyed and persecution-minded conservatives who argued that the premises of the cold war ought to be pushed to their logical conclusion. To the degree that the president responded to the pressure of such zealots, then the best that can be said is that he was willing to curtail freedom at home in order to extend it abroad.

The harsh European winter of 1946–1947 intensified the existing sense of urgency among American leaders. There is no reason to discount or demean the honest desire to help people in trouble; it was real and consequential. The vital questions involve which people are helped and the terms of the assistance. The aid supplied through the United Nations to Russia and Eastern Europe was terminated in a ruthlessly imperial decision. Then England was helped to disengage from its empire as America slipped into command. Finally, the Western capitalist metropolis, reorganized around Washington, mustered its resources for the confrontation with Russia and China.

TENSION IS CRYSTALLIZED IN THE COLD WAR

It happened quickly. Britain told America during the winter of 1946–1947 that it could no longer honor its imperial commitments in Greece and Turkey. That news was received in an intellectual context largely defined by an influential foreign service bureaucrat named George Frost Kennan, who had been urging Forrestal and others to deploy American power to reform the Russians (and therefore the world). He argued that the Soviets could only be understood by analogy: they were a toy automobile, powered by Marxist ideology, that moved across the room (world) until they ran into a wall (America). The quicker the wall was built, the sooner they would be stopped. Once halted, their regime would disintegrate.

Few people responded forcefully to Kennan when his grandiose analysis was finally made public (July, 1947). The most powerful critique was offered by Walter Lippmann, who argued in a series of newspaper columns (later published as *The Cold War*) that Kennan was advocating an implausible crusade more apt to weaken the West than to unhorse the Soviets. But Kennan's influence within the government had already done much to consolidate the consensus for an imperial policy. He later complained that Truman and others had carried his ideas too far, but he did not make that criticism publicly at the time (and even decided not to mail a letter he.had written to Lippmann).

Truman meanwhile rejected Russian claims for reparations and moved dramatically to replace the British in Greece and Turkey. He revealed that decision on March 12, 1947, in a speech that went far beyond a specific and limited aid program. He dramatically called for a global program to help all "free peoples who are resisting attempted subjugation by armed minorities or by outside pressure." That misleading description of what was happening in Greece, which involved a largely indigenous rebellion against a reactionary government, marked the final redefinition of self-determination by American policy makers. They would measure a nation's self-determination first and primarily by the degree to which it accepted and supported American policies and preferences.

Some conservatives like Senator Taft, as well as reformers like former Secretary of Commerce Wallace, opposed the narrow and anti-Russian emphasis on the evolving campaign. They were highly skeptical of what Senator Arthur Vandenburg called the need "to scare hell out of the American people" (as well as the domestic consequences of that approach) and felt that the policy might well provoke rather than intimidate the Russians. That kind of thoughtful conservatism also led Taft and a few others to criticize the vengeful and ex post facto justice that led to the imprisonment or execution of various Germans and Japanese as war criminals.

But most Americans approved those trials in Nuremberg and Tokyo, just as the Congress supported Truman on May 22 by appropriating the first installment of $400 million (for Greece and Turkey) in what shortly became a mammoth foreign aid program. A week later the United States moved to consolidae the Western occupation zones of Germany and to revive its industrial power. And two days after that, on May 31, further aid was extended to Italy, Greece, and the Western occupation zones of Austria. Secretary of State Marshall then proposed (on June 5, 1947) a general assistance program in a commencement address at Harvard University. England and France responded quickly, and the Russians were also invited to attend an exploratory conference in Paris. The United States said publicly that it was willing to allow the Soviets to participate if they accepted the conditions and controls that went with the help, but officials later admitted that the terms were designed to insure Russian refusal. That maneuver was successful. Stalin withdrew from the preliminary talks, and the plan involved only capitalist countries.

After tough and intensive negotiations with England and other Western nations that continued into the fall, Truman convened the Congress on December 17, 1947, and asked it to provide the money. It first passed an Emergency Foreign Aid Act, and then it began the work of preparing the massive European Recovery Program. Long before that, on June 24, a new Selective Service Act had been passed, and the long struggle to unify and rationalize the armed forces under a secretary of defense had begun with the July 26 approval of the National Security Act.

No such dramatic aid programs were proposed, however, for Latin America, China, or other areas of the world. In keeping with their definition of Soviet Russia as the enemy, American leaders generally supported the efforts of the Western European powers to reassert and maintain control of their empires. They helped the French to maintain their power in Indochina, for example, and gave similar assistance to the Dutch and the British. Some aid was given to Latin-American countries, but it was designed to support the traditional aristocratic governments in those countries—and the established pattern of relations with the United States.

American aid proved least effective in China. Chiang Kai-Shek was unable to reestablish the authority of his government: the inefficiency and corruption of his regime accentuated and dramatized its more fundamental loss of confidence and élan, and it rapidly lost the support of the Chinese people. A small group of non-Communist reformers tried to rally resistance to the growing appeal and military effectiveness of Mao Tse-Tung's Communist movement, but China was involved in a major social revolution and Mao was both the symbol and the agent of a profound transformation.

General Marshall's effort to mediate the conflict was terminated on

January 27, 1947, and the Truman administration dispatched Lieutenant General Albert C. Wedemeyer to evaluate the situation. While his report of August 24 condemned the Communist use of force, it also documented the failure of Chiang to carry through the economic and political reforms that were so desperately needed. By that time, moreover, it was apparent that Mao's forces were taking control of large areas of the country.

Americans generally deplored that turn of events, but few of them seriously proposed the kind of massive military intervention that would have been necessary to save Chiang. For that matter, the Congress was not even willing to appropriate the full amount of economic aid that Truman proposed. He requested $570 million, but the decision in April, 1948, was to grant only $400 million. However much they disliked it, most American leaders sensed in 1948 that the future of China was beyond the direct control of the United States. The issue did not play a significant part, therefore, in the elections of that year.

That was not the case, however, with other developments in foreign affairs. President Truman gained considerable support from the Jewish community, for example, by promptly recognizing Israel on May 14, 1948, the day it declared its existence as a nation. A few American leaders were perceptive enough to see the dangers of such a one-sided alignment in the Middle East, but they were unable to modify the administration's view. Truman was unquestionably influenced by domestic political motives: large numbers of Jewish-American voters were concentrated in important states, and they made generous campaign contributions. But he was also acting in the Wilsonian tradition of saving the world for democracy.

American policy was also influenced by the interrelationship between the secular idea of self-determination and the Judeo-Christian religious tradition, as well as by the traditional American view of the Arabs—part of its attitude toward most colored and nonindustrial societies—as dirty, heathen, backward people who were wholly dependent on the capitalist metropolis. Both outlooks contributed to the refusal to consider a more balanced policy. That classically imperial outlook continued to plague American policy making for many years.

Another such central idea, likewise fundamentally mistaken as a guide for policy making, held that Stalin's Soviet Russia was very similar—if not identical—in all important respects to Hitler's Nazi Germany. That view was first advanced in the mid-1930s by disillusioned Communists, but it gained increasing acceptance after Russia refused in 1938 to go to the aid of Czechoslovakia without help from France and England, and it became widely held after the Nazi-Soviet pact of 1939. It underpinned the thought advanced in 1941 by Truman and others, for example, that the United States should let Germany and Russia destroy each other.

The postwar confrontations with Russia consolidated that interpretation long before the Czech Communists, who were supported by about 40 percent of the population, seized control of the government in a February, 1948, coup. That event was dramatized by the death of Eduard Beneš, the hero of the modern Czech movement for independence. American leaders promptly damned the communist exercise of power as a repeat performance of Hitler's 1938 invasion.

The analogy was imperfect and misleading, but it generated a powerful reaction that seriously affected American attitudes and behavior. American leaders were determined to avoid what they considered the mistakes of appeasement and were strongly inclined to explain the effectiveness of the Communists in terms of conspiracy and subversion. That attitude was strengthened by the revelations of Russian spying in Canada, and it was dramatized by the question of espionage in the United States.

Another confrontation arose over the American and British efforts to revive and strengthen West Germany. That crisis was triggered by American proposals for economic and administrative changes in Berlin. Impatient of reaching an agreement with the Soviets, the United States in June, 1948, unilaterally instituted currency reform measures. Charging that the action violated the Potsdam agreements, the Russians retaliated on June 24 with a tight blockade of all land traffic from Western zones of occupation into Berlin. The United States then organized a massive airlift to sustain the 2.1 million people of western Berlin who relied upon the United States and its allies.

The blockade was finally ended after 321 days (on May 12, 1949), but it drastically intensified the strong anti-Russian feeling in the United States. That was the context when, on August 3, 1948, Whittaker Chambers admitted that he had been a Communist and a Soviet agent, and named Alger Hiss as a Communist who had passed government documents to him during the late 1930s for delivery to the Russians. Because of his continued service in the government, which included a secondary part in organizing the United Nations and an even less significant role during the Yalta Conference, Hiss offered the more rabid members of the House Committee on Un-American Activities (led by an ambitious and devious young man named Richard M. Nixon) an opportunity to popularize their argument about the danger of subversion in the United States.

When Hiss charged him with libel, Chambers dramatically produced hitherto undisclosed microfilm he had hidden in a pumpkin on his farm and asserted that it contained copies of the documents Hiss had provided in the 1930s. After he denied spying before a New York grand jury, Hiss was charged with perjury and ordered to stand trial. He was never indicted for treason, but the public rapidly came to view the case in those terms and the government did not counteract that erroneous impression.

The Hiss case, and the events that provided its context, undoubtedly influenced the campaigns of 1948. Truman lost some votes over the Hiss affair and because of the frustration over the failure to bring the Russians quickly to terms. But he gained from the patriotic tendency to rally in support of the government during a crisis. The man who lost most from the developing spy hysteria and from the difficulties with Russia was Henry Wallace. His criticism of official policy initially evoked a significant response, but many of those supporters were disturbed by the Communist support for his campaign for the presidency. Rather than fight for control of the movement, however, most of the non-Communists left the Wallace campaign. As a result, Wallace failed to realize his primary objective of attracting enough votes to defeat Truman.

The president's narrow victory in the election served to consolidate the consensus on foreign policy. For that matter, given the triumph of many conservative senators and representatives, the cold war was intensified. The Berlin crisis provided a clinching argument for the creation of a military alliance among the Western powers. That came on April 4, 1949, in the form of the North Atlantic Treaty Organization (NATO) dominated by American power and commanded by General Eisenhower. NATO was designed to add conventional muscle to the Atlas-like strength of nuclear bombs and thus to support Kennan's imperial conception of containment and the related strategy of "negotiation from strength."

That definition of diplomacy was endlessly emphasized by Dean G. Acheson after he succeeded Marshall as secretary of state. Acheson was a brilliant and able graduate of Yale who made his mark in the high echelons of corporation law before he entered the government during the New Deal period. He offered a classic example of the way that upper-class leadership had become institutionalized in the corporate political economy. He moved in and out of government offices with routine aplomb (and ambition), and even when ostensibly practicing law he remained a highly influential adviser.

He was a tough advocate of American supremacy who stressed the necessity of marketplace expansion, and he possessed the temperament to ingratiate himself with Truman. Thus the aristocrat from Yale and the middle-class businessman and politician from Missouri became an impressive imperial partnership. Their strategy was simple: muster the nation's economic and military power in order to force the

Russians, the Chinese, and others to accept various American proposals as a *precondition* for negotiations.

The result, as with a similar American policy toward West Germany, was ironic. Freed from wasteful military expenditures, Japan ultimately became a powerful competitor of the United States in the international capitalist marketplace. Long before that became apparent, however, the Russians made it clear that they, too, could negotiate from strength. They exploded their first atom bomb on September 24, 1949, an achievement only incidentally related to knowledge gained by espionage. Then Mao forced Chiang to flee to Formosa (December 8), a triumph that should have made it clear to American leaders that the Open Door policy was no longer relevant to the realities of the world. And, in truth, some policy makers were initially willing to adapt to the new circumstances.

Those people, including one group of businessmen in China, for example, thought that the United States might work out a satisfactory relationship with Mao's Communist government. A few of them, along with some State Department bureaucrats, knew that Mao and his associates had earlier expressed a serious willingness to explore the possibility of working with the United States instead of tying themselves to Stalin's Russia. But the government nevertheless supported Chiang's conquest-in-defeat of Formosa (the native population was ruthlessly suppressed) and prevented Mao's new Chinese government from being seated in the U.N. Security Council. The Russians seized the opportunity to strengthen their ties with Mao by stalking out of the council on January 13, 1950, in a dramatic gesture of protest.

The victory of Mao, combined with the failure of Russia to collapse, raised serious questions about American policy. Acheson was arrogant and disingenuous. There was no reason to worry: after all, America had the bombs and the planes to deliver them on Moscow. The fundamental problem was "to maintain the volume of exports which the free world needs"—and which were vital to the American political economy of corporate state capitalism. But the assumptions that underpinned the imperial system inherently pointed toward two options. One tiny group, which included powerful civilians as well as star-shouldered military officers, followed the logic to recommend a preemptive war against Russia and China.

Truman and Acheson remained confident that American power would force the Communists to change their ways without war. So, at any rate, they told the public. But they secretly proceeded to develop the hydrogen bomb, an even more awesome weapon than the atom bomb. The imperial irrationality of the decision was exquisitely revealed by Oppenheimer. He recognized the moral absurdity and the practical irrelevancy of the project, but nevertheless went along because the scientific solution to the problem was "so technically sweet." There is no more visceral footnote to document the nature of empire as a way of life.

Even so, some people wanted more. The most nearly successful leader of that crusade was Senator Joseph R. McCarthy of Wisconsin. Richard Nixon ultimately proved more effective, but McCarthy was the interim American master of the big lie, the nasty innuendo, and the false syllogism. He was a mediocrity who had won election to the Senate by deceit, and for a time he became the ruthless commander of the anti-Communist hysteria.

McCarthy defined Russia and China as the sources of all evil (an argument first advanced by men like Truman and Acheson), and he pushed that argument to its logical conclusion. Speaking in West Virginia on February 12, 1950, he explained everything by asserting that the State Department was riddled with more than 200 people who were "either card-carrying members or certainly loyal to the Communist party." He then extended the argument to include almost every other aspect of American life: schools, radio, television, sexual mores—even the army.

WAR IN KOREA

He was given a formidable assist by the North Korean Communists, who underestimated the will of American leaders as badly as they overestimated their appeal in South Korea. At the end of the Pacific war, the United States and Russia had casually and arbitrarily divided the occupation of Korea along the 38th parallel of north latitude. The decision artificially disrupted the economy of Korea and then, in the context of the developing tension between Washington and Moscow, led to the creation of two ruthless and bitterly antagonistic governments. Mao's victory in China intensified the resulting problems.

One group of American advisers, satisfied with the Asian base provided by Japan, were inclined to get out of a bad situation and let the Koreans settle their own future, and some observers mistakenly read one of Acheson's speeches to mean that he had accepted that approach. But other policy makers argued that South Korea was important as a staging area on the Asian mainland and as proof of America's power and credibility in the struggle with Russia and China. They seemed to have won the debate when, in the spring of 1950, the Truman administration sent John Foster Dulles, a Republican corporation lawyer who had become a militantly anticommunist foreign policy adviser, to reassure the South Koreans of continued American support.

The two Korean governments had engaged in mutual provocations for many months, and the southern leaders had begun to talk ever more stridently about liberating the north. They may have gone too far during the days of June 22–23, 1950, or (and more probably) the North Koreans may simply have decided to terminate the division of the country. In any event, on June 24, the northerners launched a full-scale offensive across the 38th parallel.

President Truman was so dedicated to the anti-Communist crusade he had launched in 1947 that, ignoring the Constitution and the Congress, he personally ordered American military units into combat within 24 hours. He did not even wait for the United Nations to approve the action. The early defeats in Korea helped conservatives and reactionaries in the United States to pass a piece of repressive legislation known as the Internal Security Act that was designed to harass or imprison reformers and radicals who challenged the imperial foreign policy. As a result, McCarthy and his allies gained a forum and more power for their assault on such critics.

In the war itself, the United States (aided by a handful of reluctant allies) managed to stabilize the front in southeastern Korea. They then opened a counterattack with an imaginative amphibious assault on Seoul, the capital of South Korea. That brilliant maneuver, which involved an extremely tricky and difficult coordination of men with nature (ships and tides), was conceived by the marines, who had to fight a long preliminary battle to convince MacArthur to approve the plan. The general was of course given public credit for the victory.

Strategically outflanked, the North Koreans rapidly retreated northward across the 38th parallel. Thus the avowed objective of the policy of containment was achieved: military aggression by the Communist satrapies of Moscow was thwarted, and it would be only a matter of time until Stalin's empire collapsed. But Truman and his advisers could not resist the imperial temptation. They ordered MacArthur on September 27, 1950, to advance north across the 38th parallel to destroy the North Korean government by force of arms. As Kennan later admitted, the policy of containment had honored its implicit logic by becoming a strategy of rollback. The United Nations approved the action on October 7, and thereby documented its subservience to American policy.

China warned the United States, at least as early as October 1, that it would not acquiesce in such aggression to its borders. Truman was worried enough to fly to Guam on October 14, 1950, to discuss the issue with MacArthur. The general condescendingly assured the president that everything was under control and proceeded to move northward to the Chinese border. A few days later (on November 1), in one of those terrifying and macabre acts of desperation by the underlings that illuminate the nature of the empire, two Puerto Rican nationalists tried unsuccessfully to assassinate Truman. Then on November 26, the Chinese crossed the Yalu River with roughly 850,000 men and began to drive American forces back to the 38th parallel.

MacArthur was beaten, though he tried to save his career by becoming a candidate for president. He appealed to the cold war extremists, some of whom had just been elected to the Congress, and called publicly for the bombing of China. Truman responded with a warning about the possibility of using nuclear weapons, declared a national emergency, and mobilized the economy for a protracted conflict. Those moves extended the militarization of American thinking about foreign affairs and thereby undercut MacArthur's appeal. The general also aroused those who were concerned with maintaining civilian control of the policy-making process—however militant the policy.

Even so, the president and those who agreed with him were in trouble. China's dramatic display of power made it clear that there were limits to the ability of the United States to reform the world in its own image. MacArthur evoked an emotional response from those who failed to recognize, or were unwilling to acknowledge, the inherent restrictions of empire in an age of nuclear weapons. But that group of extremists was countered by critics who raised the basic questions. Senator Taft, for example, won considerable support for his opposition to sending American troops to Europe. Herbert Hoover sharply denounced the conception of a global empire and called for a policy dedicated to improving life in the United States within a strategic concept of defense based on controlling the air and sea approaches to the Western Hemisphere.

Hoover's vigorous attacks generated extensive public debate and upset the Truman administration. The president and his supporters (Republican conservatives like John Foster Dulles as well as Democratic reformers like Adlai E. Stevenson) struck back hard. They reasserted the necessity and wisdom of the existing policy and at the same time took various actions that made it seem effective. The president removed MacArthur from command in April, 1951, reaffirmed American support and control of Chiang's imperial enterprise on Formosa, belatedly signed a peace treaty with Japan that ratified its special relationship with the United States, and through the FBI and the Central Intelligence Agency (CIA) stepped up the government's covert activities against critics at home and abroad.

But none of those moves quelled the growing opposition to the Korean War. That was a strange phenomenon, not at all like the later resistance to the Vietnam conflict. Radicals and some students were involved, but there were few large demonstrations and no major confrontations in the streets. From the beginning, moreover, the movement included farmers and other middle-class citizens who were angry over the endless killing in Korea and otherwise disillusioned with the imperial policies of the administration.

That opposition contributed to Truman's decision not to run for reelection. He could have done so, for he was explicitly excluded from the two-term provision of the Twenty-second Amendment (finally ratified February 26, 1951), but instead he threw his support to Adlai Stevenson, the articulate and witty reform governor of Illinois, who was nominated on the third ballot. Stevenson's sharp counterattack on Hoover made it clear that he generally supported the policies that had evolved during the 1940s, but he did reveal a sense of restraint and patience lacking in most other imperial leaders.

A campaign between Stevenson and Robert Taft might have produced a significant dialogue about the need to limit the arms race with Russia and the desirability of restricting America's global activities. But Taft lost the Republican nomination to Eisenhower, and the charming and able general declined to engage in such a debate. He did promptly reveal, however, a kind of restraint and deep concern about war that characterized his presidential decisions. When Dulles began during the campaign to talk about rolling back communism and to imply taking military action in Eastern Europe, for example, Eisenhower bluntly told him to stop forthwith. And his promise to go to Korea as part of an effort to bring the war to "an early and honorable end" foreshadowed his refusal to involve the United States in another such venture.

The commitment to end the war in Korea undoubtedly contributed to Eisenhower's impressive victory (33.8 million popular votes to 27.3 million, and 442 to 89 in the electoral college), and he promptly embarked on the arduous effort to negotiate an armistice. That was not achieved, however, until five months after Stalin died in February, 1953. The agreement was signed on July 27, after 37 months of fighting that had killed over 25,000 Americans and inflicted more than 100,000 additional casualties. Korea remained divided along a line very close to the original boundary at the 38th parallel.

Washington's response to Stalin's death illustrated the general rigidity of American policy, as well as the particular paradox of Eisenhower's handling of foreign policy. In selecting Dulles to be secretary of state, the president picked a man whose militant crusading zeal contrasted sharply with his own relatively relaxed and low-key manner. Dulles had been active in the economic and political aspects of American foreign policy since the 1920s, but he was extremely doctrinaire and inflexible. He viewed the Soviet Union very narrowly in terms of the rhetoric of Lenin and Stalin, and hence he was particularly ill-prepared to respond to the new Russian leaders. But so were most other American policy makers, and hence the United States missed an important opportunity to ease the tensions of the cold war and to begin the long process of responding creatively to other important changes throughout the world—and to problems within the United States.

The successful transfer of power in Russia to Georgi Malenkov and the Soviet explosion of a hydrogen bomb in August, 1953 (less than a year after America's first test of such a weapon in November, 1952), made it clear that the assumptions behind the tough policy had been mistaken. Neither the weaknesses of the Soviet Union nor the pressures exerted on it by the United States through the policy of containment had led to the collapse of its system or forced the Soviets to acquiesce to America's plans for the postwar world.

The Russians probably gained some help in making their first nuclear weapons from the information supplied by Klaus Fuchs, for example, but Soviet scientists proved their own impressive and independent abilities by devising a different technique for producing a hydrogen (fusion) explosion. The American slowness in grasping the truth about Russian ability was perhaps more costly than the loss of information through espionage. For one thing, it increased the hysteria about spies. Spying was an inherent part of America's relationships with other countries by the end of World War II, yet most Americans acted as though it was carried on only by other nations.

The climax of such irrationality came in the prosecution of Julius and Ethel Rosenberg, who were charged in 1950 with passing vital information about the first atom bomb to the Russians. The evidence was at best highly controversial and, even if true, the data passed along was pragmatically worthless. The grossness of the entire affair was characterized by the absurd conclusion, offered by the presiding judge, that the Rosenbergs were personally responsible for the outbreak of the Korean War. Their conviction and execution in 1951 said far more about the American imperial state of mind than about the Rosenbergs.

The Russians, meanwhile, benefited from the generally negative reaction around the world to the execution of the Rosenbergs. More positively, many non-Americans realized that there were forces in Soviet society that could, given favorable circumstances, begin to exert pressures for positive and humane changes in Russian life. Those developments indicated the wisdom of a shift in American attitudes and actions. Stalin's successor, Premier Malenkov, made it clear, for example, that the Soviets desired to relax the tension between the two countries in order to concentrate on internal development, as well as to decrease the danger of a nuclear war.

The end of the fighting in Korea presented a similar opportunity to reopen a dialogue with China. The opening was not as dramatic as the one available with Russia, but it was nevertheless real and meaningful. Mao's government had demonstrated that its power was secure in China and that it had effectively mobilized the spirit and resources of that country for the first time in at least two centuries. The acceptance of a stalemate on the battlefield offered an opportunity to acknowledge that turn of events, establish regular lines of communication, and begin the process of accommodation.

A change in policy toward Russia and China was made even more desirable because those nations exerted important influences on the poor, nonindustrialized societies that composed the majority of the world's population. World War II accelerated the disintegration of the empires that had been established by Western European nations during the eighteenth and nineteenth centuries, and the suppressed peoples looked to Russia and China as guides for their own struggles for independence and development.

The British were pushed out of India and increasingly lost their hold in Africa. Their authority over the great crown colony of Hong Kong continued only at the pleasure of China, as the Korean War made clear. Their position in the vast peninsula of Southeast Asia, once symbolized by the great naval and trading center of Singapore, likewise crumbled under the pressure of militant nationalistic movements in Burma, Siam, and Malaya.

The French were also on the defensive. Spurning various proposals for compromise at the end of the war, they attempted to reassert their power in Indochina. The result was a war for independence and a revolutionary movement to reorganize that society. The Algerians and other French subjects in Africa mounted their own drives for freedom. The Dutch encountered similar resistance throughout their vast island empire that centered in Sumatra and Java, and they rapidly lost their power to the Indonesian nationalists.

AMERICAN IMPERIALISM ENCOUNTERS RESISTANCE

American leaders faced four principal difficulties. One involved the relationship with the Philippines, Cuba, Puerto Rico, and Panama: they were not formal colonies, but they were protectorates whose development was defined and limited by American influence and policy. The first uprising came in the Philippines, where the radical Huk program of land reform, social equality, independence, and more balanced economic development attracted a significant body of supporters behind its rallying cry of the Philippines for the Filipinos. The resulting guerrilla warfare against the government won control of significant areas before it was finally suppressed with extensive American aid.

The second problem was far more extensive because it involved the vast informal empire that had been created during more than 50 years of America's overseas economic expansion. That imperial system grew enormously after 1939, and by the end of the 1950s the overseas assets and investments held by American citizens were approaching $100 billion. The government's holdings of foreign real estate and its other overseas operations boosted the total wealth far beyond that figure. Though earlier concentrated in Latin America, overseas expansion between 1943 and 1960 involved the Near East and Africa, Europe and Southeast Asia.

Such activity was undertaken for the traditional imperial purposes of acquiring markets and raw materials, and it was supported by the United States government. The government provided help through the Export-Import Bank, the Development Loan Fund, the Agricultural Trade Development and Assistance Act, the International Bank for Reconstruction and Development, the International Finance Corporation, and the Marshall Plan.

The International Bank, for example, specified that its loans would generally be dependent on the willingness of a borrowing country to undertake "such reforms in fiscal and monetary matters and general economic policies as we consider an essential prerequisite . . . and conducive to all private investment." The Congress openly declared that the Development Loan Fund was designed to support "a compet-

Figure 5   National defense and total budget outlays, 1940–1970. (From U.S. Department of Commerce, *Statistical Abstract of the United States, 1970,* Washington, D.C., 1970, p. 244.)

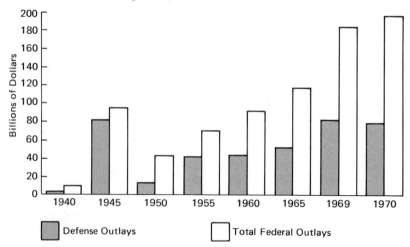

itive free enterprise system." The agricultural program was described with similar candor: "The most important tangible benefit Congress had in mind [was] development of new and extended commercial markets for American agricultural products." And the Department of State explained that loans for general improvements were geared to create "those basic public facilities on which private enterprise depends."

Other loans were extended through various military assistance acts designed to strengthen the foreign governments that accepted the American Way. That help became increasingly necessary because the American programs did not generate rapid or effective economic development in the poor nations. As a result, the existing governments were challenged by revolutionary movements. American expansion, as one Brazilian official admitted, "has brought sudden wealth to a small number of people; [but] it has changed very little the lot of three-fourths of the population. In fact, the peasants and industrial workers are worse off now than they were before in relation to other classes in society."

Such imperial expansion created an ever more centralized political economy within the United States. Eisenhower recognized that possibility at the close of World War II, and at the end of his second term warned the public about the great power of "the military-industrial complex" spawned by that conflict and then pampered into a giant by lush contracts derived from the confrontation with Russia. But in truth it was an imperial complex that involved workers and farmers, clerks and truckers, and housewives and career women, as well as generals and corporation executives. An empire is in the long run no more equitable at home than it is abroad, but for a time it functions in a way that involves a significant number of citizens in its general expansion. That is why the rhetorical criticism of the military-industrial complex took so very long to produce any important changes at home.

Ironically, the European nations began to resist the policies of the United States before serious opposition developed in America. That third source of difficulties developed in response to the power that American companies (aided by the government) deployed inside the economies of those nations. The corporate giants not only exported their surpluses from America but built branch factories or simply bought established facilities.

Finally, the United States encountered a fourth problem because it defined the poor and needy countries so largely in terms of its own conflict with the Soviet Union and China. American leaders increasingly aided only those governments that resisted the steadily mounting demands for noncapitalist reforms. The result was that more and more of the nationalist and reform movements turned toward socialism and communism as guidelines for their own thought and action and at the same time increasingly resorted to violence against the status quo.

The challenge posed by the poor and nonindustrial nations called upon the United States to honor its commitment to independence and self-determination and to supply proof that the expansion of the American economic system could produce as much benefit for the poor countries as it did for the United States. And it also demanded that Americans deal with the populations of the rest of the world as people with their own legitimate existence instead of viewing them so largely as secondary and dependent actors in the struggle with Russia and China.

Eisenhower did help Americans to recognize those problems, and he was personally less intense and inflexible than most other top-level leaders. Paradoxically, however, his attitude of live and let live allowed the militant cold warriors to block any long-term shift in American attitudes and policies. That became apparent, for example, in his handling of the hysteria created by Senator McCarthy. The president was deeply angered by McCarthy's assault on the loyalty of General Marshall and disgusted by the senator's overall behavior. But he argued that McCarthy would destroy himself and that any direct confrontation would demean the office of the president. Those arguments had some weight, and they would have had more if the liberals and the conservatives, such as Taft, had launched a vigorous counterattack against McCarthy. But they did not, and the vicious demagogue continued his destructive rampage through the fabric of American society.

He was ultimately stopped at the end of 1954 after he had extended his attack to the army. That was too much for the editors of *Time* magazine, for example, and they belatedly assaulted McCarthy for weakening America's ability to resist communism. A more fundamental attack was made on March 9, 1954, by Edward R. Murrow, the first charismatic television commentator. Then Eisenhower finally spoke out, criticizing McCarthy as a man trying "to set himself above the laws of our land," and other public figures joined the counteroffensive. Finally, in December, 1954, the Senate condemned McCarthy by a vote of 67 to 22.

The senator was done, but his legacy was not uprooted. The scientist Robert Oppenheimer, for example, was removed (in April) from his position on the Atomic Energy Commission for his radical associations and because he had not been enthusiastic enough about developing the hydrogen bomb. And Dulles did not reinstate the honest and perceptive State Department officials who had been discharged in response to McCarthy's attacks. In the broader sense, the end of the senator did not mean the end of the vast system of domestic surveillance by the FBI and other agencies that infringed upon the constitutional rights of countless citizens and underpinned the pattern of smear and intimidation that cost many of them their jobs.

The persistence of the imperial outlook, and the related institutions and behavior, was nowhere better revealed than in the relationship between Eisenhower and Dulles. While the president was deeply concerned to avoid another war and to ease the tensions of the cold war, he was nevertheless far too inclined to follow the advice offered by Dulles and to allow the secretary (and other militants) to push matters to a crisis that he then had to resolve before it became unmanageable.

In itself, the appointment of Dulles is not difficult to understand: he was an able and ambitious leader of the eastern Republicans who had secured the nomination for Eisenhower. Beyond that elementary bit of politics the relationship becomes more complex, but the following factors appear to be at the center of interaction. The first involves the question of basic strategy. The Soviet production of an atom bomb did not immediately undercut America's nuclear (let alone economic) supremacy, but it did reopen the basic question of how to deal with the Russians. The United States could turn away from global confrontation toward a relaxation of tension and accommodation with the Soviets, or it could try to maintain its overpowering superiority.

Eisenhower was clearly attracted to the first approach while Dulles talked constantly about the need for fearless face downs at the brink of war in order to sustain the American empire and prevent the spread of godless communism. Or, to use the term that became popular later, Dulles stressed the need to establish and maintain credibility—to convince the Russians that the United States *would in truth go to war* to prevent its empire from being nibbled to death or if confronted with a demand for outright surrender. The president understood the logic of that argument, but, unlike many others, he also revealed a sense of its dangers and limitations. At the same time, he was strongly anti-Communist, concerned about oil and other raw materials, and inclined (from his military experience) to delegate authority.

The interplay between those variables produced a strange foreign policy that oscillated between various kinds of intervention and almost magisterial overtures to the Russians. The CIA was used, for example, to overthrow governments in Iran (1953) and Guatemala (1954), and the marines were landed in Lebanon (1958) in a show of force designed to intimidate Communists and other radicals.

On the other hand, Eisenhower's refusal to become involved in another operation like the Korean War became apparent in 1954 through his handling of the Indochina crisis. The Truman administration had committed the United States to paying about 80 percent of the cost of the French effort to reimpose its imperial power, but that investment was gravely threatened when the forces led by Ho Chi Minh of Vietnam surrounded the French forces attacking Dien Bien Phu. Dulles and other militants proposed military intervention by carrier-based planes using small nuclear bombs.

That plan was opposed by a coalition in the Congress led by Senator Lyndon Baines Johnson. Eisenhower no doubt considered that criticism, but his refusal to approve the plan was based on his own unwillingness to start another war of indefinite duration. But he did not follow through by preventing Dulles from undercutting the negotiations at the subsequent Geneva Conference that produced a temporary end to the conflict. The secretary of state began an ultimately successful effort to subvert those agreements, and in the meantime organized an alliance system (South East Asia Treaty Organization) to preserve what remained of the imperial system. He followed that in February, 1955, by signing military treaties with Iraq, Iran, and Pakistan.

In the almost schizophrenic counterpoint of the era, Eisenhower then told the country that the combination of the hydrogen bomb and ballistic systems capable of delivering the weapon anyplace in the world meant that compromise was the only basis for security. His July, 1955, meeting with the leaders of France, Great Britain, and the Soviet Union in Geneva did reduce the tension, although it did not produce any final settlements. But the clear differences between Eisenhower and Dulles reassured America's allies, as well as the Russians.

Then the president was incapacitated by a heart attack on September 24, 1955, and Vice President Nixon's views were far closer to those of Secretary Dulles. Hence the opening provided by the Geneva talks was never exploited. Eisenhower recovered in time to assert his control during the multiple crises of 1956, a move that helped him to win reelection as well as to avoid a major war.

The trouble began just as the president was hospitalized. The smoldering Egyptian movement for independence and reform, additionally inflamed by Arab opposition to the creation of the state of Israel, erupted in a successful revolution headed by Gamal Abdel Nasser. He was determined to free Egypt from its long colonial ties to Britain and the West and to strengthen the Arab world against Israel. Hence in September, 1955, he signed a barter agreement with the Soviet Union whereby he obtained arms (and some economic aid) in return for cotton.

The United States responded by bidding against the Russians to help Nasser build a massive dam on the upper Nile River at Aswan as a dramatic move to develop Egypt. The project was involved and demanding and was seriously questioned on purely economic and practical grounds, and the United States could have quietly withdrawn for those reasons. But Dulles suddenly opposed the project in an effort to discipline Nasser and trap the Russians.

It was a gross blunder. Nasser seized the Suez Canal in July, 1956, and moved to consolidate his position with the Soviet Union. While Dulles fumed, Britain, France, and Israel plotted to overthrow Nasser. Israel struck first on October 29, and the European countries joined the assault on the next day. The United States knew of the plan, but made no serious effort to stop the attack.

The ensuing crisis was further complicated because the Russians were simultaneously engaged in military intervention to suppress a rebellion against the existing Communist government in Hungary. The world seemed literally to have reached the brink of nuclear war. Fortunately, Eisenhower took command. He made it clear that the United States would not intervene in Hungary and that it would not tolerate the continued invasion of Egypt. The Russians simultaneously announced they would support Nasser and warned Israel, Britain, and France to withdraw. The American pressure was more influential, but in any case the attack was halted. Nasser ultimately proved capable of operating the Suez Canal, and the British grudgingly accepted the inevitable.

Dulles was again criticized for his blustering behavior in support of Chiang's provocative use of the tiny islands of Matsu and Quemoy, located a few miles off the China coast near the important center of Amoy. In a calculated move to involve the United States, Chiang garrisoned about one-third of his aging army on the islands. Mao's forces began to shell those troops on August 23, 1958, and Dulles appeared ready to fight if the bombardment led to an invasion of Quemoy. The Chinese backed off, but so did the secretary. His opponents forced him to join Chiang in a formal statement (October 23, 1958) renouncing the use of military force to reestablish Chiang as the ruler of China.

That crisis was immediately followed by Russia's declaration in November that it was preparing to hand its part of Berlin over to the Communist government of East Germany within six months. To ease the blow, Premier Nikita Khrushchev proposed that all Berlin be united as a free city. While they worried about that proposal, American leaders were shaken by the January, 1959, triumph of Fidel Castro in Cuba. Castro's victory not only reinforced the mounting anti-Americanism throughout Latin America but it also dramatized the failure of American policy in a nation it had dominated for two generations.

American leaders soon made it clear that they were unwilling to compromise with the Cuban revolution. Castro was thus put in the position of having to make serious changes in his program or to proceed in the face of American opposition. He might have moved left to an alliance with the Russians in any event, but American policy played a significant part in causing that alignment. Eisenhower did not seize the opening created by the resignation of Dulles (who was dying of cancer) to reestablish a dialogue with Castro.

But the president did move to ease tensions with Russia by inviting Khrushchev to the United States. Their meeting during September, 1959, produced an agreement to continue negotiations, which would include the British and the French, in Paris in May, 1960. Both countries, however, had allowed the Berlin issue to harden in a way that might have disrupted the conference even if it had been held. But it was subverted before it began in a way that dramatized the imperial assumptions and momentum of American foreign policy.

The crisis was caused, at least in the narrow sense, by the CIA. It had long been involved in covert operations in many countries, and its successes created a sense of omnipotence among many American leaders. The agency shared that confidence, and it had been using an

Figure 6 Total investment of government and private funds in facilities used by certain aircraft companies during 1955. (From G. R. Simonson, Ed., *The History of American Aircraft Industry,* Cambridge: MIT Press, 1968, p. 221. Reprinted by permission of the publisher.)

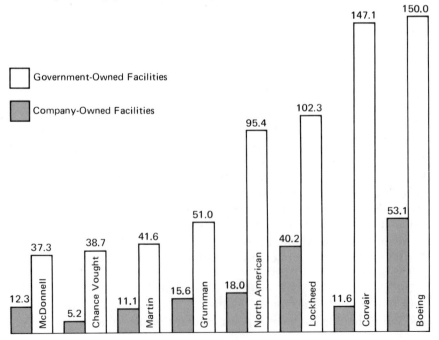

exceptionally long-range and high-altitude plane (the U-2), developed by Lockheed Aircraft Corporation, to photograph Russia for about five years. Despite its knowledge of the impending conference and its awareness that the Russians knew of the flights and were trying to destroy the planes, the CIA decided to fly one last mission before the Paris meeting.

The plane crashed 1200 miles inside Russia. The State Department first denied any responsibility, but then Eisenhower accepted responsibility for the flights and asserted that they were necessary to prevent another Pearl Harbor. The Soviets exploded, and in reply the president announced that the flights would not be continued. But the concession came too late to mollify Khrushchev and the scheduled Paris Conference collapsed.

American leaders were further upset when Castro signed a trade pact with the Soviets on February 13, 1960. That move dramatized the late 1959 outbreak of violence against American control of Panama. Then the Russians launched the first space satellite on October 4, 1959, and a bit later fired a missile that traveled almost 8000 miles to a test target in the mid-Pacific. The Russian use of that ocean seemed to upset some Americans, and many leaders began to campaign for drastic changes in American education and to build ever more nuclear weapons.

Given the psychology of empire as a way of life, those were potent political slogans. The president had avoided involving the country in another war, for which he deserved high praise, but he had not redefined America in terms of its own balanced and equitable development. That failure ultimately produced a powerful reaction against the imperial outlook.

EXPLORATORY READING

There is a vast literature about American foreign policy from 1943 to the present and hundreds of thousands of pages of published primary sources—such as memoirs, diaries, and other documents. Along with the volumes by Gardner and Sherwin that were noted in the previous chapter, the following volumes offer the best places to start in making a detailed examination of the history of imperial America and of the different ways of making sense of the evidence:

C. V. Crabb, Jr., *Policy-Makers and Critics: Conflicting Theories of American Foreign Policy* (1976)

T. Kent, *Theories of Imperialism* (1967)

W. LaFeber, *America, Russia and the Cold War: 1945–1975* (3rd ed., 1976)

T. G. Paterson, *Soviet-American Confrontation: Postwar Reconstruction and the Origins of the Cold War* (1973)

The following books will introduce you to various special aspects of the policy:

S. E. Ambrose, *The Supreme Commander: The War Years of General Dwight D. Eisenhower* (1972)

R. J. Barnet, *Intervention and Revolution: The United States and the Cold War* (1968)

G. Barraclough, *An Introduction to Contemporary History* (1964)

J. M. Blum, *The Price of Vision: The Diary of Henry A. Wallace, 1942–1946* (1973)

C. D. Bohen, *Witness to History, 1929–1969* (1973)

J. L. Clayton (Ed.), *The Economic Impact of the Cold War* (1970)

B. Cochran, *Harry Truman and the Crisis Presidency* (1973)

H. S. Dinerstein, *Fifty Years of Soviet Foreign Policy* (1968)

H. and F. Duncan, *Atomic Shield, 1947–1952* (1970)

R. Freeland, *The Truman Doctrine and the Origins of McCarthyism* (1971)

D. Green, *The Containment of Latin America* (1971)

R. Griffith, *The Politics of Fear: Joseph R. McCarthy and the Senate* (1970)

M. Gurtov, *The United States Against the Third World: Antinationalism and Intervention* (1976)

L. Halle, *The Cold War as History* (1967)

S. P. Huntington, *The Common Defense* (1957)

A. Iriye, *The Cold War in Asia* (1974)

G. F. Kennan, *American Diplomacy, 1900–1950* (1952); and *Memoirs, 1925–1950* (1967)

B. Kuklick, *American Policy and the Division of Germany* (1972)

J. Lukacs, *History of the Cold War* (1966)

P. Lyon, *Eisenhower* (1974)

E. R. May, *Lessons of the Past: The Use and Misuse of History in American Foreign Policy* (1973)

A. Myrdal, *The Game of Disarmament* (1976)

R. E. Osgood, *N.A.T.O.: The Entangling Alliance* (1962)

G. D. Paige, *The Korean Decision* (1968)

J. Patterson, *Mr. Republican* (1972)

W. R. Polk, *The U.S. and the Arab World* (1975)

H. B. Price, *The Marshall Plan and Its Meaning* (1964)

R. Radosh, *American Labor and U.S. Foreign Policy* (1969)

H. H. Ransom, *The Central Intelligence Agency and National Security* (1958)

M. Rogin, *The Intellectuals and McCarthy* (1968)

T. B. Ross, *The Invisible Government* (1964)

L. and M. Schwartz, *American Strategy* (1966)

A. K. Smith, *A Peril and a Hope: The Scientists' Movement in America, 1945–1947* (1969)

J. W. Spanier, *The Truman-MacArthur Controversy* (1959)

E. Stillman and W. Pfaff, *Power and Impotence: The Failure of America's Foreign Policy* (1966)

R. J. Walton, *Henry Wallace, Harry Truman, and the Cold War* (1976)

A. Whiting, *China Crosses the Yalu* (1960)

M. Wilkins, *The Maturing of Multinational Enterprise: American Business Abroad from 1914 to 1970* (1974)

S. G. Xydis, *Greece and the Great Powers, 1944–1947* (1963).

20 INSIDE IMPERIAL AMERICA: MUCH FOR THE TOP, SOME FOR THE MIDDLE, AND A LITTLE FOR THE BOTTOM

THE citizens of the metropolis of an empire generally live better than most of the people who reside in the colonies, protectorates, and other dependent or formally independent areas that contribute economically to the center. The only significant exception to that rule involves the small governing elites of the dependent regions—they live very well and wield considerable local power. The United States proved to be no exception to that historical pattern. It suffered no major depression for a generation (1944–1974), enjoyed a dramatic increase (despite inflation) in overall production and wealth, enacted some reforms, produced significant work in the arts, and provided many conveniences and pleasures for the largely white upper and middle classes.

It must also be recognized that American leaders, by presenting their imperial policies as the expression of the nation's best ideals and tradition, generated among many citizens the élan of being associated with great enterprises. However mistaken it proved to be, or however more desirable to have it grow out of other common purposes, that esprit provided a kind of psychic income that cannot be ignored in understanding the support for imperial programs or even in evaluating the nature of life in America. It is also true that a later generation educated in those ideals and traditions used them to attack the imperial system.

But other aspects of life inside America proved more revealing of the nature of empire. The vast growth of national wealth, for example, did not involve any significant redistribution of income, which remained grossly unbalanced and inequitable. And though many people had more money, it increasingly bought less in terms of quality—and therefore involved more and more waste. That in turn created further dangers to the balance within society and between society and nature that was essential to survival.

There were also economic dislocations that affected many people, and whose effects were not offset by either the reform legislation or the charity of the powerful. In addition, there was political repression and gross racial injustice. And so, also, a decrease in opportunity and mobility that helped explain the steady increase in crime and violence. Despite the rewards of imperialism, it became impossible not to recognize that a chant of black sharecroppers during the 1930s depression remained painfully relevant in the 1960s:

There is mean things happenin' in this land;
There is mean things happenin' in this land.
Oh, the rich man boasts and brags,
While the poor man goes in rags,
There is mean things happenin' in this land.

President Truman knew more at first hand about those mean things than either Franklin Roosevelt or most other New Deal leaders. He *did fail* as a small businessman in the marketplace, and he *did live in Missouri*, where he dealt directly as a politician (and judge) with farmers, workers, and blacks—with the poor as well as the more powerful (some of whom were involved in sophisticated crime and injustice). He honestly desired to put an end to those mean things.

But he could only imagine doing that within the existing system and within the framework of an imperial confrontation with the Soviet Union. The second condition reinforced—and ultimately extended—the limits of the first outlook, but in the meantime, on September 6, 1945, he sent the Congress a 21-point reform program that provided the substance of what came to be known as the Fair Deal. Probably the most significant recommendation concerned measures to guarantee full employment through action by the federal government. Truman was also concerned to improve the condition of blacks and other minorities and asked the Congress for a permanent fair employment practices commission. He meanwhile used his presidential powers to begin the long effort to end discriminatory practices within the federal government, including the armed forces.

Other proposals called for improving and expanding social security coverage, raising the minimum wage from 40 cents to 60 cents an hour, providing federal money for slum clearance and low-cost public housing, extending conservation programs, undertaking more public works programs on the scale of the TVA, and subsidizing scientific research. He later added requests for aid to education, for the St. Lawrence Seaway, for an improved health insurance and medical care system, and for an agricultural program that would overcome the failures of the New Deal approach to that problem.

The government also acted to shift from a wartime to an imperial economy. One of the most significant contributions to that transition was provided by the GI Bill of Rights, which kept millions of men and women out of the labor market while the economy was readjusting and also trained them for new jobs. The legislation also underwrote many small business ventures and established the principle of government aid to education. Overall, the program pumped at least $35 billion into the economy between 1945 and 1952: a mini-Fair Deal in itself.

Redundant war contracts totaling $35 billion were terminated even before Japan surrendered, and the War Assets Administration (established in January, 1946) sold hundreds of war plants at large discounts, usually to the corporation that had managed them, and disposed of vast surpluses to individuals as well as to corporations. At the end of the war, the Defense Plants Corporation owned 90 percent of all firms engaged in the production of synthetic rubber, aircraft, magnesium, and in shipbuilding; 70 percent of the capacity for aluminum production; 50 percent of machine tool facilities; and approximately 4000 miles of pipeline for the continuous-flow transportation of petroleum products. Such facilities were turned over to private operators at a fraction of their original cost, and the tax cut provided by the Congress in November, 1945, provided corporations and consumers with an additional sum of nearly $6 billion.

The resulting shift in emphasis led to the production within 18 months of 6.2 million refrigerators, 14.6 million radios, and hundreds of thousands of new houses and other buildings. The television industry began its fantastic growth, and by the end of 1948 automobile companies were rolling out five million cars a year. The government's action was the direct result of its visceral concern to avoid sliding back into the depression of the 1930s, and that fear also played a large part in the passage of the Maximum Employment Act of 1946.

The initial legislation was introduced early that year by Senators James E. Murray and Robert F. Wagner after consultation with President Truman. They proposed the creation of a joint congressional committee, acting in cooperation with a group of presidential advisers, to maintain such "federal investment and expenditure as will be sufficient to . . . assure a full employment volume of production." Some businessmen and politicians were frightened by what they mistakenly considered a giant step toward socialism, but a majority of those leaders grasped the essential distinction between socialism and corporate state capitalism: the latter system subsidized the corporate elite through public taxes.

The final legislation established a three-man Council of Economic Advisors charged with the responsibility of constantly studying the economy and with making annual reports and recommendations, and created a joint House-Senate committee to propose legislation on the basis of such continuous research and analysis. As strengthened in subsequent years, the law of 1946 provided the basis for routine government action that attempted to control the business cycle and insure prosperity.

The Truman administration was not as effective in handling other transitional problems. The National War Labor Board was abolished and replaced by the Wage Stabilization Board in December, 1945, but it was so ineffective that the Office of Economic Stabilization was created in February, 1946, under the direction of Chester Bowles. By that time, however, the discrepancies between demand and supply had created a serious inflation that accentuated the drop in wages caused by the end of wartime production. There were shortages in everything from stamping presses to stockings and steaks. And the worker who had been making an average of $46.35 per week in June, 1945, was down to $35.60 by September.

The strikes began in the fall of 1945 with the walkout of 150,000 UAW men at General Motors. They ultimately won a raise of 18 cents per hour, but they were still earning less than they had during the war. Other strikes came in rapid succession. Production was stopped at General Electric and Westinghouse in January, 1946, and by June there was a total of 31 strikes, each involving 10,000 or more workers (a total of 4.6 million). More man-hours were lost through strikes during the first half of 1946 than in any previous year in American history.

There was also serious trouble in the steel industry. The union demanded a raise of 25 cents per hour to restore wartime levels of take-home pay, but the industry, under the leadership of Benjamin F. Fairless, president of U.S. Steel, refused to accept that figure unless the government allowed it to raise prices by $7 per ton. Truman first offered the corporations an increase of $4 if they raised wages 18.5 cents per hour. The union accepted the recommendation, but Fairless refused. Truman then gave ground. He insisted that labor deserved raises to match the 33 percent rise in living costs since January, 1941, but left the way open for the steel companies to boost prices. In the end, the workers got 18.5 cents per hour and the companies took $5 per ton.

Then came strikes in the coal industry and by the Brotherhood of Engineers and Trainmen. John L. Lewis took the miners out of the pits on April 1, 1946, demanding drastic (and long overdue) safety improvements, a health-and-welfare fund, and a wage hike. To blunt the public's anger and Truman's opposition, the miners went back to work for 12 days in May. By that time, the railroad unions were ready to close down what was then the nation's basic transportation system. The trucking industry had expanded rapidly since 1941, but it was not capable of handling the industrial traffic of the country. With one eye on the confrontation with Russia and the other on the public, Truman asked for power to seize the rails, threatening to draft stubborn workers. The Congress immediately authorized such action.

The trainmen surrendered, but Lewis continued his fight. Truman took over the mines, and Lewis was ultimately fined $10,000 for contempt of court. The massive levy against the union of $3.5 million was later reduced to $700,000. It was a steep price, but the workers won almost all their demands during subsequent negotiations. The coal and rail strikes, however, did a great deal to turn the nonunion public against labor. Ever more people were becoming white-collar (and white-blouse) workers as new techniques and machines changed the nature of production, and such people were inclined to consider themselves as a separate and superior group, even allied with management.

As for the managers themselves, they concentrated on removing the remainder of the wartime controls over their operations. Under counterpressure from Truman, labor unions, and reformers who favored regulation, the Congress in June, 1946, passed a weak control law. Truman vetoed it, and prices zoomed upward during the first half of July. Basic commodities jumped 25 percent and top-grade beef increased from $18 to $22 per hundred pounds in one day. By the time partial (and largely ineffective) controls were restored on July 25, 1946, real income had dropped 12 percent below the high point in July, 1945.

Reformers did win a victory of sorts in the law to control nuclear energy. Led by Senator Brian McMahon, those who were uneasy about the increasing power and influence of the military established the principle of civilian control in the legislation of October 1, 1946. The AEC was created as a civilian board of five men holding a monopoly of fissionable materials and exercising firm control over all research and production. The military had to work through the AEC, and the president was given sole power to order the use of nuclear weapons.

While the McMahon Act did set limits on the military's direct authority over nuclear energy, neither that legislation nor any other law prevented civilians from adopting a quasi-military outlook on world affairs. That attitude, typified by Truman's remark of January 5, 1946, that World War III was inevitable unless Russia was "faced with an iron face and strong language," undercut the intent of the law.

THE CONSERVATIVE COALITION

The congressional elections of 1946 consolidated the coalition of conservative Democrats and Republicans that had begun to emerge at the end of the 1930s, a group of people who could and did block many needed reforms—or weaken initially helpful proposals and thus make them ineffective. A powerful bloc of those men, more properly called reactionaries, wanted to restore as much as they could of the past (especially in racial and labor matters) while continuing to subsidize the corporate giants. The less extreme conservatives argued that the existing system would deal effectively with the problems and needs of the country, and on that basis they were extremely skeptical of any broad reform measures. Another small group, often led by Senator Taft, seriously tried to devise a rational alternative to the New Deal liberalism that had created the vast federal bureaucracy interlocked with the corporations.

Taft's skepticism about Truman's foreign policy was based on his concern about distorting and overextending the economy, as well as on his fear of provoking the Russians. The senator also upheld the elementary right of radical—even Communist—critics to participate freely in the public dialogue about all issues. And his positions on public housing, labor, and equality for blacks and other ethnic minorities were far less doctrinaire and negative than his critics often charged.

But the majority of the conservative coalition did not follow Taft. They blocked his proposal for housing, refused to support more aid for education, declined to extend social security benefits, effectively sustained the gross discrimination against blacks, Indians, and Mexican-Americans, cut appropriations for reclamation and power programs, and hounded all critics of the American empire. They were even unwilling to help agriculture unless a program provided vastly disproportionate subsidies to the big operators.

The war reinforced the propensity of New Deal legislation to consolidate American agriculture. Profitable operations depended upon ever more capital investment in equipment, labor, fertilizer, and land. The small and marginal operators clamored for help through subsidies and foreign markets. But the large farmers (including corporate operations) increased output by 48.6 percent between 1946 and 1956 and thereby increased their real income. Investment per worker in agriculture climbed so fast that by 1960 it was $21,300—more than $5,000 higher than in the industrial sector. Farm income dropped 15 percent in 1946, and by 1953 the agricultural share of the gross national income had slipped from 49 percent to 35.6 percent. And farm mort-

Figure 7 Poverty among farm workers, 1959. Annual money wages for both farm and nonfarm work of wage-earners who worked at least 25 days on farms. (From *Poverty and Deprivation in the United States. Conference on Economic Progress*, Washington, D.C., 1960, p. 52.)

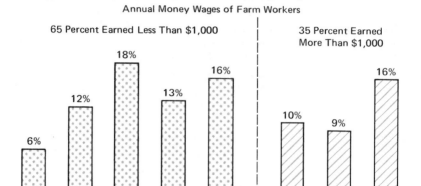

Annual Money Wages of Farm Workers

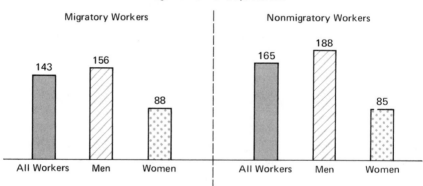

Average Number of Days Worked

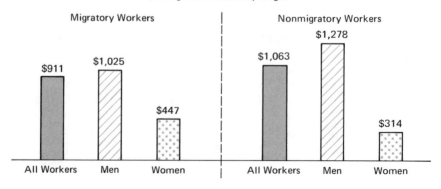

Average Annual Money Wages

gages, which had dropped during the war boom, began to rise toward the 1950 total of $5.4 billion.

The big farms grew bigger and richer, while the others struggled to survive. The agricultural legislation of 1948 and 1949, which maintained the parity principle and adjusted the base for such payments to compensate for inflation, did no more than hold the line. None of the laws did much to help nonwhite farmers, over 70 percent of whom were tenants (and most of those, southern black sharecroppers), or the Mexican-American migrant labor that harvested many of the crops west of the Mississippi River. They remained poor, ill-educated, and shabbily treated.

The conservative coalition was also effective in helping the corporations control organized labor. While the vast majority of labor leaders accepted the system of corporate state capitalism, they did not think that labor had achieved parity with business. But the conservatives, encouraged by the public anger over the postwar wave of strikes, as well as by Truman's occasional militance, were determined to end what they considered the special privileges and exceptions of labor and to root out the radicals within the union movement. Enough liberals supported those objectives to pass a law initially introduced by Senator Taft but modified by Congressman Fred Allan Hartley, Jr., and others in the course of the action by the Congress.

The final result, the Taft-Hartley Act of June, 1947, was more severe than Taft's first proposal. It banned the closed shop, required a 60-day cooling-off period prior to strikes, called for public financial statements from unions, forbade union contributions to political campaigns, terminated the checkoff system under which employers had collected union dues in the same way they withheld income tax payments, and authorized employers to sue unions over broken contracts or for damages sustained during a strike. It also empowered employers to agitate their point of view among workers and to petition the NLRB for redress of grievances. Some union procedures were prohibited as unfair, including jurisdictional strikes, secondary boycotts, and failing to bargain in good faith.

The law was an attempt to deal realistically with the truth that unions had become highly institutionalized organizations firmly integrated into the routine operations of the political economy of state capitalism. Far from being inclined toward socialism, union leaders adamantly opposed any suggestion to use their power to win a share in making management decisions. They accepted the role of handling the labor side of the corporate system and concentrated on winning a larger share of the returns from that way of organizing production and distribution. But they justifiably complained that some provisions of the law—such as forbidding the kind of organized political action that corporations regularly practiced and the closed shop—were unfair.

Truman agreed and vetoed the law on June 20, 1947, but the Congress promptly and overwhelmingly overrode his action. The House vote was 331 to 83, and in the Senate the margin was 68 to 25. The law in operation was not as damaging as union leaders and other critics had feared, and Truman further eased its impact by appointing men to the NLRB who were generally sympathetic to labor. The long fight over the law revived some of the crusading zeal that had characterized labor during the 1930s and improved Truman's political prospects for election in his own right.

Union labor remained strong, but the strikes of 1948 did not win enough monetary gains to compensate for the increase in the cost of living. Retail prices, for example, moved upward at about 3 percent per month. Truman finally asked, on July 26, 1948, for authority to halt inflation, increase the excess profits tax, and create a system of priorities and a rationing program. But the antiinflation legislation that the Congress approved on August 16 was a feeble compromise measure that did little even to ease the problem. The economy continued to slide downward into what became by 1949 a painful recession.

During those months preceding the election, moreover, Truman became even more of an imperial leader and less of a reformer. The reactionary southern Democrats, led by Governor Strom Thurmond of Georgia, who was a crusader on three fronts—anti-Communist, anti-black, and antireform—took the field as a third party waving Confederate flags. Truman walked a narrow ledge: hedging enough to keep the votes of the marginal conservatives but not enough to lose the vital votes of the northern blacks (and other minorities) and white liberals.

He was a fighter at home as well as abroad, and by the end of the 1948 campaign his rousing cry of "I'm going to give 'em hell"—reminiscent of his telling the Russians that they could "go to hell"—won him a narrow victory over Republicans Dewey and Earl Warren. But he was even more beholden to the conservatives (Thurmond had won 38 electoral votes), a truth that he overlooked in his mistaken notion that the sympathy for him as an underdog could be translated into votes for reform. That became clear during the renewed struggle for agricultural legislation.

Secretary of Agriculture Charles Brannon wanted to help farmers in two ways. Those who produced nonperishable commodities would be aided through price supports, loans, and the storage of surpluses. The people who grew perishable crops would sell their produce at the current market price, which would hopefully help the consumer, and the federal government would pay the producer the difference between that figure and the parity price. The plan was vigorously opposed by large farmers and others, who felt it would lead to regimentation. As a substitute, the Congress in October, 1949, passed a law continuing the traditional 90 percent parity program through 1950, at which point prices would be tied to a scale that moved between 75 percent and 90 percent of the parity figure.

Southern conservatives continued to cultivate future crises by opposing the president's efforts to extend freedom and opportunity for black Americans. Truman did what he could (within his outlook) through executive orders, but no serious civil rights legislation was approved by the Congress. The president was somewhat more successful in other areas. The minimum wage was raised to 75 cents an hour. Social security benefits were extended to ten million more workers and were increased by nearly 80 percent. Rent control was extended to April, 1951, and the National Housing Act of 1949 authorized the construction of 810,000 units. The latter program did not end the terrible slum conditions and the attempt to control rents failed, but the law did open the way for more action in the future.

Perhaps Truman's most significant domestic contribution involved health and medical care. He fought hard for that program, even though the social irresponsibility of the American Medical Association (AMA) defeated his proposals. The poor continued to go untreated except in grave emergencies. The middle class continued to use medicine as a necessary evil rather than as an institution of health. And the aged (who were often also poor) died sooner and in greater pain than was necessary. For all its wealth and despite its important contributions to the techniques and skills of easing life, the United States remained far behind other countries in providing for the health of its citizens.

Only the respectable rich and the criminal rich could count on enjoying regular access to expert doctors. Based on their shrewd investment in providing booze during the Prohibition era, the leaders of organized crime had created their own version of the highly sophisticated and profitable corporate world. The criminal had become a corporate businessman, though when the relations between that shadow system and the public system became too obvious, there was a scandal. The Truman administration was a victim of that periodic surfacing of the whale of corruption. Measured against the far greater distortion and misuse of American ideals through racism and empire, such episodes were minor. But they did make for interesting politics, high profits for newspapers and TV, and an occasional good joke.

The vast military and other contracts subsidized by the Truman administration opened the door to what was—on balance—a minor kind of corruption: a world of scribbly middlemen who took 5 percent for minor services. The country was inundated with wry, envious, and sexy stories about what that commission could provide—for anyone involved. Some of it was funny, but most of it was largely misdirected. Organized crime was the real issue, and it was a parallel culture with enormous power. Senator Estes Kefauver's 1950–1951 investigation of that problem was justifiably given extensive and effective television coverage by the major networks. It was an early and memorable example of how television could inform the public and move it to demand action—though in this case the government failed to respond with an effective program.

The formerly shadowy (and hence exotic) conception of the corporate criminal system was starkly clarified. Some of those who appeared on camera confirmed the popular impression that the big-timers enjoyed the favors of sexually attractive females, but both sexes revealed a benumbing dullness along with their ruthless contempt for the government and ordinary citizens.

Kefauver destroyed some of the romantic respectability that criminal leaders had sought so hard to acquire and maintain, and he also clarified the vast and interlocking nature of their operations and laid bare some of the ways they influenced politics from the ward level to the federal bureaucracy. It became apparent that the money lost on a bet placed by a middle-class man in Chicago or a lower-class man in Brooklyn was often used to defeat his political candidate in the next election. The Bureau of Internal Revenue, already a prime target for most citizens, took a particular beating during the testimony. Top officials in St. Louis, Boston, Brooklyn, and San Francisco, along with 31 others, were fired for accepting bribes and other abuses.

Kefauver parlayed his Senate hearings on crime into considerable popular support for the 1950 Democratic nomination for the presidency. But Truman and labor combined to select Stevenson. It was one of those situations in which the professional politicians were wiser than the populace, for Kefauver was not smart enough, big enough, or tough enough for the White House. But Eisenhower's public appeal would have beaten any Democrat, so the professionals were largely irrelevant. For that matter, Stevenson was probably a better critic than a commander, though he was by no means wishy-washy or irresolute.

Eisenhower could be a decisive leader, but his determination to avoid another war and his sense of the need to reach an accommodation with the Russians were not matched by an understanding of the dynamics of corporate capitalism. Elected by a landslide in 1952, he became a good man unable to act effectively on his desire to strengthen the power and improve the life of the citizenry. Eisenhower's mistake was to believe that the corporate leadership of the country cared first about the welfare of the people and to think that the profitable operations of the corporations would automatically improve the lives of all Americans.

The president sought, for example, to increase the production of electrical power by the TVA by contracting with a private syndicate for a steam power complex instead of enlarging the capacity of the government side of TVA. That led to a scandal in 1954 when it became apparent that the profits demanded by the syndicate (the Middle South Utilities, Inc. and The Southern Co.) would far exceed any short-run savings to the taxpayer.

The success of President Eisenhower's effort to keep the presidency insulated from politics was dependent upon the wisdom of Sherman Adams and others. The Republicans had presented themselves to the public as the paragon of purity. Adams's usefulness vanished when disclosures revealed that he had accepted gifts from friends who were seeking government favors. Ike's anguished "I Need Him" brought this cartoon from R. A. Lewis in the Milwaukee Journal, *July 7, 1958.*

'I Need—'

JULY 7, 1958

By R. A. Lewis of the *Milwaukee Journal. The Cartoons of R. A. Lewis/Milwaukee Journal.* Edited and Annotated by George Lockwood. Milwaukee: The Journal Company, 1968, p. 56.

The Eisenhower administration was not wholly passive in domestic affairs. Hoover's ancient project for a St. Lawrence Seaway to connect Chicago and Milwaukee with the ports of the world was finally approved in 1959, for example, and during the same year the Congress passed various labor reforms, granted statehood to Alaska and Hawaii, and created an agency to begin the exploration of space. But neither the president nor other Republican leaders confronted the central issues with positive and imaginative programs or policies.

ECONOMY ADVANCES FAVOR THE MAJORITY

The fundamental problem of the corporate political economy was obvious: neither the vast technological changes nor the dramatic increases in production had led to a trouble free economy or a more equitable distribution of the wealth. Therefore millions of whites, blacks, and other minorities continued to live in powerless poverty. Herman P. Miller, probably the most knowledgeable student of income data, made the point with devastating clarity. "When the actual dollar amounts are adjusted for price changes," he reported, "there appears to have been no increase in the average family's real income since 1944. On the contrary, the figures indicate a slight decrease in the purchasing power of the average family during the period after World War II." He also revealed that more than one-fourth of all individual workers received less than $1000 a year and that half of them were earning less than $2000. That meant, as he pointed out, that "many of the middle-income families would probably be at lower income levels if they depended entirely upon the income of one wage earner."

The condition of agriculture provided a particularly revealing example of how the changes in the economy failed to help many people. The consolidation and centralization in that part of the corpo-

TABLE 5   Poverty Income Threshold: 1968

Size of Family	Nonfarm	Farm
1	$1,748	$1,487
2	2,262	1,904
3	2,774	2,352
4	3,553	3,034
5	4,188	3,577
6	4,706	4,021
7 or more	5,789	4,916

U.S. Bureau of the Census, *Current Population Reports*, Series P-60, No. 68, p. 11. (From H. P. Miller, *Rich Man, Poor Man*, New York: Crowell, 1971, p. 118.)

rate system was staggering: there were only 4.8 million farms in 1955, and 1.1 million of those ceased operations during the next four years (a drop of 23 percent). By 1962 a mere 3.7 percent of the farms controlled 49 percent of the land, and approximately the same group (3 percent) produced more than the bottom 78 percent.

Agriculture had become a highly organized, corporate economic enterprise. In California, for example, 6 percent of the farms contained 76 percent of the farm acreage. "Farming here," explained the Los Angeles *Times,* "is usually an intensive, specialized, commercial undertaking conducted for the purpose of obtaining income from the employment of labor, managerial ability, and capital." Appropriately enough, a new word—*agribusiness*—was coined to describe the result. Such consolidation subjected hundreds of thousands of people to serious pain and loss. An average farm worker in 1961 received only $881, and the extra he could earn brought his income to a mere $1054. The migrant field hand managed to pocket only $677. Government aid programs helped to consolidate the power of the giants, for the richest 15 percent received 50 percent of all federal subsidies to agriculture.

Those who were forced to leave the land because they could not compete with the giants, and because government subsidies helped the big farmers far more than they aided the small family operator, were thrown on the labor market at an advanced age and without adequate training. The national decrease in the number of farms was 39 percent between 1940 and 1959, but southerners were hit even harder (45 percent), and blacks the worst of all (60 percent). The issues thus involved not only whether (and how) to help those who wanted to stay on the farm but also how to assist those who had already been driven into the cities.

Similar challenges were posed by the changes in the industrial sector of the economy. Steel had been the king of the system at the turn of the century, but it had slipped to fourth place in manufacturing by the 1950s, falling behind chemicals, the airframe industry, and motor vehicles—and only just ahead of the burgeoning electronics industry. Some of the most dramatic growth in electronics occurred in television and in the computer industry. Television had established itself by 1948, when the presidential nominating conventions were covered for the first time for the owners of the 200,000 sets then in use. Transcontinental networks (with some color broadcasting) were operating by 1951, and by 1960 the number of receivers had zoomed to 70 million.

The computer industry, like television, was a product of developments that began in the 1920s and 1930s. The highly sophisticated range finder systems created during World War II, which provided continuous solutions to complicated mathematical problems involving many variables and multiple equations, accelerated that progress. The first digital computer using traditional vacuum tubes was produced at Harvard in 1944, but the real breakthrough came with the fabrication of transistors and other electrical improvements that made them smaller, more versatile, and more reliable. Significant applications in business and government did not occur until the 1950s, and even so only 25 were sold in 1954. In the next decade, however, 4500 computers were installed, and increasing numbers of firms and bureaus began to integrate them into their operations.

The most obvious benefits from computers involved their accuracy and speed in solving complex problems that could be reduced to numbers and other symbols. But the most far-reaching and portentous effect was to make it possible for decision makers to play the game of "As If" in a very abstract manner. By reducing human problems to variables that could be handled by the machines and then by changing the combinations of those variables, estimates could be made of the results that would occur under various conditions. To the extent that human factors could be so reduced to symbols or to the degree that decision makers displayed the will and the lack of imagination to act as though they had been so reduced, the computers thus opened the way to a vast manipulation of man's environment—including man himself.

The petroleum industry, which supplied basic raw materials to the chemical and plastic industries, and underpinned the automobile and aviation corporations, benefited from various government favors that extended its marketplace power and profits. One basic subsidy, ostensibly designed to encourage exploration and production, allowed the companies to deduct 27.5 percent of their gross income from federal income taxes: in 1968 their taxes were less than 8 percent of their income. Standard Oil reported profits of $1 billion for that year. The government also allowed the industry to organize cartels and other forms of cooperation that further enhanced the tremendous power of the companies.

The activities of the oil cartels and other corporations in foreign countries became so extensive that they developed quasigovernmental authority and at times transcended effective control by the American government. The International Telephone and Telegraph Corporation, another giant that operated in many areas in many countries, routinely intervened in the internal affairs of those nations and often cooperated in such ventures with various agencies of the American government. All those giants (which came to be called *multinational corporations*), as well as smaller companies, were further subsidized by the taxpayer through a government insurance company (the Overseas Private Investment Corporation) created to repay them for various kinds of losses incurred when the weaker countries took actions to reform or curtail their operations in order to protect their own economies.

American reformers became understandably concerned about such power and its uses. Their anxiety was heightened by the continuing centralization of power in business and government. Between 1947 and 1958, for example, the 50 largest corporations increased their share of the industrial system from 17 percent to 23 percent and the biggest 200 upped their share from 30 percent to 38 percent. Part of their greater power came through expansion into new areas of production and service, but they also bought control of other corporations. The 500 largest industrial firms were involved in 3404 mergers between 1950 and 1961, and the top 200 dominated over half (1943) of those combinations.

Such economic power was directly related, moreover, to the increasingly intimate connection between the corporations and the government. The most visible sign of that relationship, of course, was the large and growing number of economic leaders who participated actively in high-level politics and who served in key administrative posts throughout the government. In a similar way, successful politicians (and military leaders) moved across to important jobs in industry and finance. Even a few labor leaders became part of that policy-making elite.

The economy had become significantly dependent upon the high level of government expenditures that had begun in the 1930s. Federal spending alone supplied 24.2 percent of the GNP in 1942, and it remained at that level after the war (24.4 in 1950, and 26.5 in 1957). Some of that money, all of which was gathered through the taxing process, reached the corporations (and other businesses) through consumer purchases by people on welfare, pensions, unemployment compensation, and other such payments. But a vast amount of it was channeled to a relatively few of the largest companies through government purchases. Much of that occurred through foreign aid programs and procurement for the armed forces and the space program. The Defense Department spent more than half of the federal budget in 1961 and operated various facilities valued at more than $32 billion.

The ten biggest corporations were awarded 36.8 percent of prime military contracts in 1959, and the top 25 firms held over half of the total. Or, looked at in another way, all corporate profits in the third quarter of 1960 stood at $42.2 billion, as compared with $45.1 billion spent by the government during the same period for security purposes. The heavy reliance on military expenditures not only skewed the economy and concentrated increasing power in a small part of the political economy but it also played a key role in various states. Defense plants accounted for the following share of all employment in manufacturing in these states in 1960: Kansas, 30.2 percent; Washington, 28.6 percent; California, 23.3 percent; Arizona, 20.6 percent; Utah, 20.4 percent; Colorado, 17.8 percent; and Maryland, 12.2 percent.

Even the private philanthropic foundations, which prided themselves on providing independent leadership, were subject to the same pressures and processes. Not only were they controlled by the same group of economic leaders who were tightening their relationships with the government, but they were also increasingly dominated by a few giants such as the Ford and the Rockefeller foundations. By the 1960s, for example, 176 foundations controlled more than 75 percent of all such assets. Their grants were certainly helpful, and in some cases encouraged serious independent research and reflection, but for the most part they were concerned with projects closely tied to the functioning of the existing system. Furthermore, the practice of turning to the foundations and research centers for answers to questions of public policy removed the power of decision making even farther from the citizenry.

Some astute commentators began to echo Hoover's much earlier warnings about the system of corporate state capitalism. Herbert H. Lehman, who knew how it worked from his experience as a senator, warned bluntly that the corporate giants were close to dominating not just the economy but also the government and the entire culture. August Hecksher dramatized that point by questioning "whether the independent being, the individual of conscience and conviction, is any longer to have a place in our society." He added, in an especially perceptive insight, that the reformers treated the individual "too abstractly," and that, in accepting the corporate order, they left themselves with no effective power base and no program except various proposals to tinker with the system.

Organized labor did not offer much more in the way of responsive and creative leadership. Its broad acceptance of the postwar political economy limited its outlook and largely confined its objectives to wages, hours, and fringe benefits. Walter Reuther of the UAW, who had been a militant leader in the 1930s, in 1955 obtained a guarantee that Ford and General Motors would pay 60 percent of regular wages through 26 weeks of unemployment and won a contract in 1968 that tied wages to the government's consumer price index. But neither Reuther nor other leaders offered striking innovations or new goals, and the merger of the AF of L and CIO in December, 1955, reinforced labor's conservative attitudes and policies.

The head of the new organization, George P. Meany, made that clear by supporting the imperial foreign policy and by proudly disclaiming any inclination toward radicalism. "I never went on strike in my life," he boasted in 1956, "never ran a strike in my life, never ordered anyone else to run a strike in my life, never had anything to do with a picket line. . . . In the final analysis," he continued, "there is not a great difference between the things I stand for and the things that NAM leaders stand for. I stand for the profit system. . . . I believe in the free enterprise system completely." It was hardly surprising, therefore, that the labor movement made few efforts to deal with the problems of poverty and racial discrimination, or to change the imperial foreign policy.

THE LIMITS OF IMPERIAL SUCCESS

The relatively prosperous middle class offered even less leadership. The vast majority of its members were content to retreat into a nuclear family and spend their money, time, and energy in largely personal pursuits. It was a privatizing of life that ignored social problems—and opportunities—in favor of subsidizing the boom in professional sports, gadgets, and the automobile culture. And despite the increasing number of married women who worked (up from 15 percent in 1945 to 30 percent in 1960), the feminist movement remained weak.

It was another decade, for example, before Simone de Beauvoir's magnificent reassertion of female equality, *The Second Sex* (1952), generated serious response. Some of the orthodox women's organizations continued their activities, but a surprising number—including the Women's Trade Union League—either disbanded or became dormant. And one classic disagreement within the movement remained as divisive as ever. One group, which included the National Federation of Women's Clubs, agitated for an equal rights amendment, but another bloc, led by the League of Women Voters and women in the labor movement, campaigned equally hard in opposition.

Most women responded to another image of the ideal American female. She was pictured as one who married early and made a happy home for her husband and children. Her responsibility was to be cheerful, efficient, sexy, and permissive. The mother's cult book of the era was Dr. Benjamin Spock's volume, *Baby and Child Care* (1946), which advised her to substitute love and understanding for direction and discipline, rather than to combine the two approaches. As for community activities, they should be limited to neighborhood projects, the Parent-Teachers Association, afternoon shopping sprees, and perhaps one annual participation in a volunteer project.

Women were increasingly encouraged, however, by many movies as well as by the advertising industry, to develop a more relaxed attitude toward sex. The general acceptance of a freer and more permissive approach to sex had its roots in the popularization of Freudian doctrines that began prior to World War I. But that conflict, and particularly World War II, along with the simultaneous fragmentation of the older social fabric by the modern industrial system, contributed more to the change than the ideas of Freud. The new economic order weakened the integrated and extended family and subverted the authority of the home. Perhaps more importantly, it functioned to depersonalize life and to make relationships more casual and transitory.

Perhaps nothing illustrated the mood of the era as well as the appearance of sex manuals and the magazine *Playboy*. The development of greater sensuality and sexuality between lovers is a healthy and creative part of such relationships, but the manuals distorted and reduced those qualities to various techniques of arousal and intercourse—usually in terms of the male acting on the female. *Playboy* was blatantly male-oriented and reduced women to sexual toys to be selected largely on the basis of their youth and large breasts. All of it was a travesty on true sexuality and women—indeed, on love and life.

So was much of the entertainment offered by the television and movie industries. In a world of poverty, revolution, racism, and war, those corporations offered Doris Day's cute sex, Marilyn Monroe's faint echo of Mae West, and shows that glorified middle-class existence and extolled violence in support of the status quo. There was some truth to the theory that television, in particular, mesmerized people regardless of the message being delivered, but in the end that argument evaded the essential point—*what* mesmerized them was crucial.

The educational system developed in a similar way, concentrating more and more on training people to slip into niches in the existing corporate order. More people were educated, and some of the techniques—particularly in the primary and secondary schools—were effective adaptations and extensions of ideas first offered by John Dewey. But despite the fact that Dewey would have accepted the existing system—he was a reformer, not a revolutionary—he would have been appalled at the conservative uses of his pedagogy. The result, as Paul Goodman bluntly commented, was an institutional pattern for *Growing Up Absurd*.

As had become apparent during the 1920s, the corporate political economy depended on the willingness of the people to privatize their lives except as it needed them for its own larger purpose. The educational system functioned within that framework. So also did a good part of the intellectual and artistic creations of the era. Some of the novels and poems about World War II and the Cold War were implicitly anticorporate, but that meaning was usually lost in the drama of combat—or in the narrow focus on military life.

Women's rights acquired a new cutting edge with the militancy of the Women's Liberation Movement of the sixties and the seventies. Bill Mauldin celebrated a new triumph for women in an old setting with this cartoon, which appeared in the Chicago Sun-Times.

'My woman's okay. She says she don't wanna be my equal.'

Copyright © 1975 The Chicago *Sun-Times*. Reproduced by courtesy of Wil-Jo Associates, Inc., and Bill Mauldin.

Most postwar literature was infused with a romantic or tragic individualism. Hemingway, for example, offered in *The Old Man and the Sea* a moving (if somewhat sentimental) account of a man's inner triumph despite being defeated by an implacable environment. Tennessee Williams probed the inner torments and horrors of people trying to assert their essential humanity in such plays as *The Glass Menagerie* and *A Streetcar Named Desire.* The subjectivism in those works was echoed by Saul Bellow. His protagonists, as in his novel *Seize the Day,* struggled desperately to survive in the face of forces that pushed them toward passivity and fantasy.

A few writers spoke more directly to the broader issues. Though he did not repeat his brilliant performance at the end of the 1920s, Faulkner continued to attack modern industrialism and to emphasize the importance of community. So did Harvey Swados, whose *On the Line* remains one of the best novels about union laborers in modern industry. A similar emphasis on the necessity of common action is apparent in Sol Yurik's *Fertig.*

The more powerful efforts to display the inherently self-defeating weaknesses of individualism came from Arthur Miller and Wright Morris. Miller's first play, *All My Sons,* dramatized how a man's whoring after an extra dollar for his family led him into dishonesty in producing equipment for the war effort and how that in turn devastated the sons he was trying to help. Then Miller offered an electrifying play, *Death of a Salesman,* that dealt viscerally with the destruction of a man who tried to create a meaningful life by honoring the corporate rules.

Morris was equally powerful in two of his novels: *The Field of Vision* and *Ceremony at Lone Tree.* His central theme was the irrelevance of the frontier interpretation of American history—and of life in general—in a world where the frontiers were erupting in revolution against the imperial metropolis—not just the irrelevance, indeed, but the destructive fantasy of such an outlook on life. At the end of *Ceremony,* a dying old man sits alone in the abandoned railway station of a deserted town, looking west for a frontier that no longer exists.

Others looked inward for a similar frontier. Such intense subjectivity in the graphic arts had been reinforced during the war by European immigrants like Max Ernst, Marc Chagall, and Piet Mondrian. The movement was then strengthened by the work of Franz Kline and Willem de Kooning, who were also affected by surrealism, and came to full expression in the work of Jackson Pollock, a romantic individualist from Wyoming. "The source of my painting is the Unconscious," Pollock explained. "When I am painting, I am not much aware of what is taking place." His inventive representations of personal battles between despair and hope produced a sequence of powerful statements, between 1942 and his death in 1956, that oscillated between dark and concentrated terror and open and flowing rhythms and clarity.

The subjective romanticism inherent in abstract expressionism also appeared in postwar films, most notably in the cases (and cults) of James Dean and Humphrey Bogart. In his life, as well as in his films (*Rebel Without a Cause, East of Eden,* and *Giant*), Dean personified the desperate search of the adolescent for identity and meaning in a modern and rapidly changing bureaucratized society that intensified the traditional problems of family life and the gap between the generations. Bogart's appeal was more subtle and indirect: he was at once the man the adolescents wanted as their father and the man they dreamed of becoming—the antihero who refused to be destroyed by the system. But neither the fathers nor the sons struggled to change the system.

In one respect, at least, the new jazz musicians did accomplish that objective. Dizzy Gillespie, Thelonius Monk, Miles Davis, and Charlie Parker revolted against the commercialization of the 1930s swing idiom and boldly created new rhythm patterns and striking melodies and harmonics. Parker personified the defiant and creative assertion of the black artist in a society that was oppressive. The feel and thrust of the entire movement was perhaps most bluntly expressed by Parker's reaction to the effort to commercialize the new jazz through concerts and festivals: "Evil, man, evil."

Those jazz artists were in truth cultural revolutionaries (as was the poet LeRoi Jones), for they instilled a new self-consciousness and pride in the younger generations of black Americans. That played a subtle but vital part in their ultimate eruption in anger against the white corporate system. They were the first of the poor—including the poorest of the poor—to revolt against the gross domestic inequities of imperial America. A society in which the profits *after* taxes of one corporation, General Motors, were greater than the revenues of 90 percent of the nation's state governments—and whose total sales exceeded the GNP of all but nine nations in the world—could hardly expect to avoid indefinitely some social unrest.

In one sense, at any rate, being poor is like being rich: both can be measured by the figures behind the dollar sign, but in truth neither can be understood in terms of money. The crucial differences involve poverty and wealth: contrasting conditions of life that revolve around the opportunities to realize one's potential. The poor are routinely powerless to flower as people or influence the world they inhabit. They are subjects and objects until and unless they act together for a common purpose. Though it is possible to be rich without being wealthy (stars of the entertainment business provide a good example), most people who have great amounts of money are also powerful. That was certainly the situation in postwar America.

In 1947, for example, the lowest 10 percent on the money scale received 1 percent of the money income. That share for the very poor remained the same throughout the following two decades while the top 10 percent retained their 30 percent during the same period. But 36 percent of all individual workers earned less than $2000 in 1947, and as late as 1960 there were 40 million people who existed below the *government's* own standard of $4000 for a family of six people. As one of the poor blacks explained in a wrenching bit of honesty that was also poetry:

> They lucky to have [milk] twice a month.
> And there are days without meat, or vegetables, or
> fruit. And days with only one meal or two—or three, and
> they aren't really meals.
> And the children go to bed hungry.
> Sometimes they cry.

Part of the poverty was caused by the persistent unemployment despite the vast expenditures for defense, public works, and foreign aid, or the continued growth and expansion of the economy. Official figures revealed that between 6 and 10 percent of the labor force was jobless during the first postwar decade. But those estimates were admittedly low, and many more people were out of work during the periodic recessions. Blacks and other minority groups, moreover, suffered unemployment that was often more than twice as high as the national average.

TABLE 6   Percentage of Wives in the Labor Force and Median Age of Wife, by Earnings of Husband: March 1969

Earnings of Husband	Percentage of Wives in Labor Force	Median Age of Wife
$1 to $999	33	55
$1,000 to $1,999	38	50
$2,000 to $2,999	42	41
$3,000 to $3,999	44	39
$4,000 to $4,999	45	38
$5,000 to $5,999	47	39
$6,000 to $6,999	47	39
$7,000 to $7,999	45	39
$8,000 to $9,999	41	39
$10,000 to $14,999	35	40
$15,000 to $24,999	26	42
$25,000 and over	18	45

U.S. Bureau of the Census, *Current Population Reports*, Series P-60, No. 66, Tables 20 and 21. (From H. P. Miller, *Rich Man, Poor Man*, New York: Crowell, 1971, p. 225.)

The shifting structure of the corporate economy also destroyed some areas, as in West Virginia. Senator Jennings Randolph reported that the region "has for approximately ten years suffered from extreme and chronic unemployment." And in January, 1964, the Department of Labor reported that there were at least 573 other areas "of substantial and persistent unemployment." The people involved in those disasters, as with others who lost jobs when they were older, found it very difficult to find new work. They lacked both the training and the experience for different jobs, and they did not learn or adapt as rapidly as younger men and women.

Still another cause of poverty involved the increasing sophistication of the new machinery and of production techniques. The equipment permanently displaced people. In mining, for example, production increased dramatically between 1947 and 1963, but the number of workers declined by 300,000. And between 1958 and 1963 similar changes produced a net loss of 425,000 jobs in manufacturing. During the same period, moreover, the total labor force increased by 3.8 million workers, but the productivity, or output, per man increased by 12.5 percent. That meant, as the Department of Labor explained, that the economy had to produce the equivalent of 11.3 million new jobs. It failed to do so, falling short by 1.1 million (or approximately 10 percent).

The results of such weaknesses in the economy meant, even as late as 1960, and according to government figures that were optimistic, that 23.1 percent of all families had an income of less than $4000 per year. An even higher number of individuals, 36.6 percent, received less than $2000. Although most of the growing concern with poverty focused on the ghettos and the slums, the largest number of the poor lived in small towns or in rural areas.

At the same time, the American city was failing to maintain its creative role in modern industrial society. While it remained the center of much business activity, including manufacturing, it had not sustained itself as a social system of neighborhoods that integrated the entire population. Part of that failure was due to the unprofitability of maintaining old buildings. Landlords could make more money by renting to poor people instead of renovating to keep middle-class tenants. Increasingly, moreover, only the large corporations could afford to erect new structures, and they used that space for management and service offices rather than for production. Most white employees did not want to live in, or next to, ghettos and slums. And the population growth, accentuated by the internal migration to urban centers, demanded more space than the existing cities could provide.

The interaction of those factors produced a downward spiral nowhere more dramatically illustrated than in New York City. It increasingly became a place inhabited by the rich and the poor and only worked in—or visited—by other groups in society. The great majority of middle-class families moved out to the suburbs because they could not afford what they considered adequate housing, because they wanted lily-white education for their children, and because they did not want to live next to—or among—the white or black poor.

The resulting sprawl outside the cities not only created such monstrosities as the urban ooze of Los Angeles, with its related and fantastic transportation problems, but it also meant that the city proper ceased to be a cross section of the population. The rich and the poor increasingly existed within their own limited worlds, and the culture of the poor became more and more isolated, confined, unsatisfactory, and frustrating. Their environment was not only ugly and negative but it also offered fewer and fewer avenues of escape, and fewer and fewer ways of becoming a functioning member of the larger American society.

It was understandable that blacks and other nonwhite groups explained their inferior position in the North, as well as in the South, as the result of racism. That attitude certainly existed and clearly guided the action of many people throughout the country, but discrimination in the narrow sense of antagonism unrelated to anything except color and ethnic origin was not the only cause of the problem. Many white people were equally prejudiced against poor white people and equally opposed to living next door to them or having their children share the same educational and recreational facilities.

THE STRUGGLE FOR CIVIL RIGHTS

Color served to dramatize basic class differences. The blacks became *the* problem and *the* threat because they were more starkly visible and unavoidable, and because they began to act during the 1950s to win long overdue improvements in their position. Many whites became increasingly concerned and antagonistic as they realized that the changes that were necessary to improve the position and the life of the poor—white or black—would force them to modify their own lives. Helping the poor not only involved higher taxes, it also meant competition for jobs. Extending civil rights to the blacks and to other ethnic minorities also created votes for change in the North as well as in the South. That was why many northerners began openly, as well as covertly, to support southerners who were digging in to preserve the system of discrimination.

Southerners had been spurred to action by black agitation during the late 1930s and by the blacks' wartime movement into the armed forces and better jobs, and three other developments near the end of the war further upset the conservatives and reactionaries. The large corporations that began to move into the South cared less for the color line than they did for profit margins. They wanted a cheap and reliable labor force, and hence they began—without any crusading zeal or rhetoric—to hire black workers. During the same years, moderate and liberal southern whites who believed in equality organized (Atlanta, 1944) the Southern Regional Council to work for desegregation. And the Supreme Court ruled in *Smith* v. *Allwright* (1944) that the exclusion of blacks from the Democratic party in Texas was unconstitutional. That decision was not praised or damned as dramatically as later decisions involving race issues, but it was a vital breakthrough that opened the way for blacks to gain political power.

Those events help to explain the strong opposition to Truman's creation in December, 1946, of the Commission on Civil Rights. The bipartisan coalition against desegregation also fought his recommendations to strengthen the Justice Department division on civil rights, his request to reorganize the Fair Employment Practices Commission on a permanent basis, and his call for the Congress to pass legislation outlawing lynching and poll taxes. Lacking strong support from northern whites, the president lost those battles.

Once again the Supreme Court finally acted when it became apparent that other leaders were timid, indifferent, or opposed to elementary equality. Led by Chief Justice Earl Warren, it ruled unanimously in May, 1954 *(Brown et al.* v. *Board of Education of Topeka, et al.)*, that segregated schooling was unconstitutional. Holding that "education is perhaps the most important function of state and local governments," because "it is doubtful that any child may reasonably be expected to succeed in life if he is denied the opportunity of an education," the Court held that "separate educational facilities are inherently unequal." It then ordered desegregation to proceed gradually but inexorably.

The opponents (northern as well as southern) launched a bitter and all too effective campaign of resistance and delay. It is possible that the reformers made a serious strategic error at that juncture. They refused the proposal, supported by many southerners, to integrate the schools one grade at a time over the next 12 years. Most liberals balked, but it could well have accomplished the objective more effectively, and perhaps with less violence, than the alternate strategy of fighting for immediate and total integration.

The school issue seemed to galvanize blacks to assert and exercise *all* their rights as American citizens. That great battle began spontaneously in 1955 in Montgomery, Alabama, when a woman, as weary of

The Supreme Court's decision to integrate the schools of the nation was followed by a compliance that was all deliberation and very little speed. By 1960 the gains were minimal. Mauldin's cartoon represents the massive opposition giving way only an inch at a time.

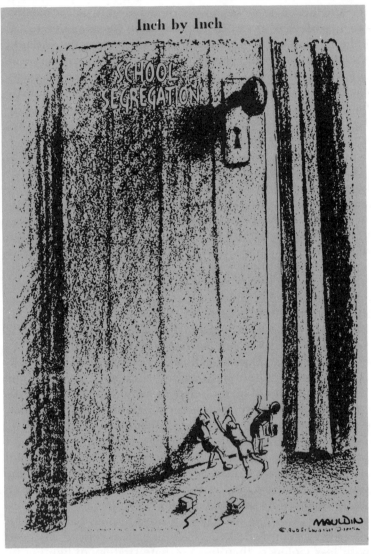

the oppression of segregation as she was tired from her day's labor, refused the driver's callous order to move to the back of the bus. That magnificently courageous act of dignity touched off a determined boycott of the city's bus system by all blacks. The Reverend Martin Luther King, Jr., emerged during that confrontation as a symbol of the determined bid to win "Freedom Now." King's leadership was particularly effective, and difficult for southern opponents to deal with, because it was based on the practice of nonviolence. The dramatic pictures of southerners using force, dogs, and gas on passive victims did much to win national support for the campaign.

Eisenhower was not a bigot, but he was slow to use the power of the government to speed the process of ending segregation and other forms of discrimination. But when the crunch came, as it did in 1957, he refused to be cowed by the coalition of southerners and northerners—Republicans and Democrats—who opposed even rudimentary equity for black Americans. The attempt in 1956 to integrate the University of Alabama provoked riots that led to the withdrawal of the black student. She had no chance in the face of such irrationality. Eisenhower did not intervene in that crisis, but he did approve the law to provide federal protection for blacks and other minority citizens in the political process.

The president was reluctant to use federal power for two reasons: he feared a general outbreak of violent resistance, and he felt that effective and substantial equality could only come as the white majority truly accepted blacks as fellow citizens. In the latter sense, of course, Eisenhower was correct, but he seriously underestimated the need to maintain firm pressure on those who actively fought the spirit as well as the letter of the law. However, he did act firmly in the fall of 1957 when mobs supported by local and state officials threatened to prevent the integration of public schools in Little Rock, Arkansas. He dispatched federal troops that enforced desegregation. But by the long delay in demonstrating beyond a doubt that the government would enforce the Constitution, the president and other American leaders gravely weakened the credibility of the corporate system.

That truth, which soon became visible in the streets of the North as well as in the school yards of the South, was recognized at the time by James Reston of the *New York Times*.

> There is an overwhelming feeling here [in Washington] that somehow we have lost our way. Nobody seems to know just how or why, but everyone feels that something's wrong. . . . An impression of haphazard greed, and a system debased and out of balance.

It was a time, he added, "for searching criticism . . . of the whole society."

EXPLORATORY READING

Three of the best detailed reviews of domestic history between 1945 and 1960 are:

J. Brooks, *The Great Leap: The Past Twenty-five Years in America* (1966)

C. Solberg, *Riding High: America in the Cold War* (1973)

L. S. Wittner, *Cold War America: From Hiroshima to Watergate* (1974)

The following authors offer particularly challenging interpretations of the era:

N. Birnbaum, *The Crisis of Industrial Society* (1969)

K. L. Nelson, *The Impact of War on Life* (1971)

R. Theobald, *The Challenge of Abundance* (1961)

R. H. Wiebe, *The Segmented Society: An Introduction to the Meaning of America* (1975)

The nature and dynamics of the postwar corporate political economy are described and analyzed in these studies:

W. Adams and H. M. Gray, *Monopoly in America* (1955)

R. J. Barber, *The American Corporation: Its Power, Its Money, Its Politics* (1970)

R. J. Barnet, *The Economy of Death* (1969)

R. Gilman (Ed.), *Power in Postwar America* (1971)

M. Gort, *Diversification and Integration in American Industry* (1962)

S. A. Greer, *Urban Renewal and American Cities* (1966)

W. Karp, *Indispensable Enemies: The Politics of Misrule in America* (1973)

S. Lens, *The Military-Industrial Complex* (1970)

A. J. Matusow, *Farm Policies and Politics in the Truman Years* (1970)

S. Melman, *The Permanent War Economy; American Capitalism in Decline* (1974)

C. W. Mills, *White Collar* (1951); and *The Power Elite* (1962)

L. Mumford, *The Highway and the City* (1958)

J. O'Connor, *The Corporations and the State* (1974)

W. Proxmire, *Report from Wasteland: America's Military-Industrial Complex* (1970)

M. D. Reagan, *The Managed Economy* (1963)

A. Shonfield, *Modern Capitalism* (1966)

L. Soth, *Farm Trouble in an Age of Plenty* (1957)

H. G. Vatter, *The U.S. Economy in the 1950s* (1963)

A. Yarnell, *Democrats and Progressives* (1974)

The life and times of postwar workers are discussed by:

R. Balzer, *Life In and Outside an American Factory* (1976)

H. Braverman, *Labor and Monopoly Capital* (1974)

W. M. Leiserson, *American Trade Union Democracy* (1959)

J. Seidman, *American Labor from Defense to Reconversion* (1953)

B. J. Widick, *Labor Today* (1964)

The highly skewed distribution of money and wealth is described in these volumes:

P. M. Blau and O. D. Duncan, *The American Occupational Structure* (1967)

M. Harrington, *The Other America* (1962)

R. J. Lampman, *The Share of Top Wealth-Holders in National Wealth, 1922–1956* (1962)

H. P. Miller, *Rich Man, Poor Man* (1971)

The struggle for civil rights and liberties is the subject of these volumes:

N. Bartley, *The Rise of Massive Resistance* (1969)

W. Berman, *The Politics of Civil Rights in the Truman Administration* (1970)

A. Blaustein and C. Ferguson, Jr., *Desegregation and the Law* (1962)

T. Emerson, *The System of Freedom of Expression* (1970)

G. Grebler, J. W. Moore, and R. C. Guzman, *The Mexican-American People: The Nation's Second Largest Minority* (1972)

D. Lewis, *King: A Critical Biography* (1970)

L. Lomax, *The Negro Revolt* (1963)

C. McWilliams, *North from Mexico: The Spanish-Speaking People of the United States* (1968)

A. Meier and E. Rudwick, *From Plantation to Ghetto* (1970)

M. S. Meier and F. Rivera, *The Chicanos* (1972)

C. H. Pritchett, *Civil Liberties and the Vinson Court* (1954)

S. Steiner, *LaRaza* (1970)

B. M. Ziegler, *Desegregation and the Supreme Court* (1958)

Intellectual and cultural matters are explored by these writers:

J. I. Baur, *Revolution and Tradition in Modern American Art* (1951)

D. J. Boorstin, *The Image: or What Happened to the American Dream* (1962)

R. Coles, *Children of Crisis* (1967—.)

B. and J. Ehrenreich, *The American Health Empire* (1971)

P. Goodman, *Growing Up Absurd* (1960)

M. Gordon, *Sick Cities: Psychology and Pathology of American Urban Life* (1963)

J. L. Hess and K. Hess, *The Taste of America* (1976)

S. Hite, *The Hite Report* (1976)

R. Hofstadter, *Anti-Intellectualism in America* (1964)

M. Mayer, *The Schools* (1961)

R. B. Nye, *The Unembarrassed Muse: The Popular Arts in America* (1970)

W. Pomeroy, *Dr. Kinsey and the Institute for Sex Research* (1972)

D. Riesman, *The Lonely Crowd* (1950)

B. Rose, *American Art Since 1900* (1967)

B. Rosenberg and D. M. White (Eds.), *Mass Culture* (1957)

L. S. Silk, *The Research Revolution* (1960)

L. Valdez (Ed.), *Aztlan: An Anthology of Mexican-American Literature* (1972)

W. H. Whyte, Jr., *The Organizational Man* (1956)

R. C. Wood, *Suburbia* (1959)

21 THE IMPERIAL FRONTIER UNDERMINES DEMOCRACY AT HOME

RESTON'S advice, the troubled, somber recommendation of a a distinguished conservative commentator, was not heeded by American policy makers. Any "searching criticism . . . of the whole society" would of necessity have had to begin with a ruthless reevaluation of the ideas advanced during the late 1880s and the 1890s by the spokesmen of the agricultural, industrial, financial and intellectual sectors of the political economy. All of them—whatever their differences of idiom and emphasis—concluded that expansion was the cornerstone of American democracy and prosperity.

Seventy years later, only a few leaders challenged that analysis, and as a result, the nation continued on down the imperial road to Vietnam and Watergate. The frontier-imperial definition of the United States as either the world or nothing dominated American thinking until, ultimately, other nations began to impose various limits upon the United States. And even then it remained an open question as to whether or not Reston's perceptive warning (and anguished cry) would lead on to the kind of changes that were necessary to avoid breakdown or catastrophe. As a result, the years from 1960 to 1976 were all of a piece despite the different personalities of the men who occupied the White House.

Eisenhower had a visceral sense of the need to redefine America as America, and before Dulles died (May 24, 1959) the president had acted on that insight by attempting to moderate the cold war. Even Richard Nixon, who had so long personified the most militant and irresponsible kind of anticommunism, seemed to sense the necessity for change. He supported the idea of a relaxation of tensions with this explanation: we want a thaw "because we realize that if there is none we will all be eventually frozen in the ice so hard that only a nuclear bomb will break it."

That comment foreshadowed some of Nixon's later actions, but Eisenhower put his finger on the reason that many Americans failed to take the remark seriously. "Dick," he told key Republican leaders in 1959, "just isn't presidential timber." That proved to be an astute reading of Nixon's character, but in 1960 the vice president enjoyed all the advantages of the insider who was accepted by the party regulars. He placated the belated opposition of the liberal wing of the party by allowing Nelson A. Rockefeller, the governor of New York, to play a major role in writing the platform and was routinely nominated on the first ballot at the convention.

Four Democratic leaders fought it out in the primaries and a fifth (Adlai Stevenson) mustered his remaining supporters in the hope of staging a blitzkrieg at the convention. The early favorite was Senator Hubert H. Humphrey of Minnesota, an intense, vigorous, and dedicated New Dealer who for many years had advocated reforms designed to help the unemployed and the blacks even as he thumped the drums of the cold war. That gave him a strong advantage over two of his rivals, Senators Stuart Symington of Missouri and Lyndon Baines Johnson of Texas, who were handicapped by their southern traditions and connections.

Senator John Fitzgerald Kennedy of Massachusetts, the fourth challenger, was a handsome, dashing Irishman who had an eye (and the time) for the ladies and who chanted the praises of a New Frontier. His grandfather had gone into Boston politics to achieve social status as well as power, and his father (Joseph P. Kennedy) had added a vast fortune to that commitment to respectability. John Kennedy became the chosen instrument of his father's ego and drive for power after his older brother was killed in the war. John soon established his psychological independence within the family structure (which was a modern version of the ancient clan), and as a congressman and a senator he made it clear that he differed with his father on various policy issues. But he did not turn his back on the family fortune or break with his father's visceral commitment to capitalism.

Kennedy prided himself on being pragmatic rather than philosophical, but he failed to recognize that pragmatism had become the American philosophy of corporate capitalism and that his advocacy of the expansionist outlook was likewise based on a philosophical position. His campaign for the nomination also made it clear that he was an elitist who viewed the presidency as the center of power for directing national and international affairs.

Combined with the almost limitless funds at his disposal, Kennedy's efficient organization (led by Lawrence F. O'Brien and Kenneth O'Donnell) overwhelmed his rivals. Humphrey provided an apt description of the Kennedy machine after he had been defeated in the West Virginia primary: "It was like the corner grocer running against a chain store." (In similar fashion, Kennedy later shunted Stevenson aside as the administration's errand boy at the United Nations.)

Those characteristics, which had become increasingly apparent by the time he was nominated, generated considerable public uneasiness about him, and northern liberals were particularly upset about his choice of Johnson as the vice-presidential candidate in an obvious maneuver to outflank Nixon in the South. Despite Eisenhower's failure to provide an enthusiastic endorsement, Nixon generally led the opinion polls until he became ill in September and lost his momentum. Then came the first of the televised debates, prompted by Kennedy's challenge, which proved to be disastrous for Nixon. He was weak and tired, as well as nervous, and gave a poor television performance against the apparently relaxed, robust, and vigorous Kennedy.

In truth, Kennedy was burdened by his own psychological and physical problems, but appearances were crucial in that first encounter. Kennedy appeared much younger, and his energy and intelligence—and his upper-class verve and style—attracted many people of all ages. Those characteristics not only clouded Kennedy's stand on many issues during the campaign but also ultimately created a myth in place of the reality of the man. He appeared, both at the time and after the fact, to do more and different things than he actually did. The image created an excitement and a sense of progress that was not supported by the record.

Nixon fought back vigorously, however, and actually scored more heavily in the following three debates. He was also aided by the nagging skepticism about Kennedy generated by his failure to denounce Joseph McCarthy's demagoguery during the 1950s, his father's wealth and shady reputation, his Catholicism, his elitism, his harsh criticism of Eisenhower, and his aggressive foreign policy. Kennedy helped his own cause significantly, however, by handling the religious issue with candor and dignity. After a group of bigoted Protestant leaders attacked him as a potential tool of the Vatican, he calmly replied that he would resign as president if faced with a conflict between his religion and his constitutional oath of office.

The most striking aspect of Kennedy's campaign involved his almost demagogic attacks on the Republicans for being soft on com-

Richard Nixon's first debate with John F. Kennedy in the presidential campaign of 1960 did not go well for him. Angry friends of Nixon blamed the "makeup" job for his appearance of fatigue and discomfort. Later assessments pointed to the debate as a turning point in favor of Kennedy. Bill Mauldin cartooned this comment.

"IT'S POSITIVELY FRIGHTENING. THESE HANDS CAN CHANGE HISTORY."

Copyright © 1960 St. Louis *Post-Dispatch*. Reproduced by courtesy of Bill Mauldin.

munism. He had begun criticizing Eisenhower as early as 1958 for failing to stand up to the Russians, and he continued the assault with increasing militance. Asserting that "the hopes of all mankind rest upon us," he issued apocalyptic warnings of a terrifying missile gap that favored the Soviet Union and invoked the image of Churchill to dramatize his own argument that any relaxation of cold war tensions amounted to another sellout like the one to Hitler at Munich.

He gave no indication that he knew about—let alone understood— the rupture of relations between Russia and China. Those revolutionary bedfellows (never very comfortable together) had dumped each other on the floor between 1958 and 1960 over the issues of the revision of Marxist ideology in the Soviet Union, the terms of economic aid provided by Moscow, and the decision by Khrushchev not to help China develop nuclear weapons.

Mao's old suspicions about the Soviet Union were verified by those policies, and he became very angry after Khrushchev talked candidly with Eisenhower at Camp David. Kennedy ignored what had happened to the so-called monolith of communism and instead reiterated the traditional argument that "our frontiers today are on every continent" and defined Cuba as "a source of maximum danger." To emphasize the latter point, he called for a campaign to overthrow Castro.

Kennedy also attacked the Republicans for failing to solve America's persistent economic problems by generating ever more growth. The issue was real, even though his solution was debatable. As for other important signs of domestic trouble, he and his advisers displayed a nice sense of political expediency rather than any grasp of the social forces threatening to disrupt the status quo. On February 1, 1960, for example, black students began their nonviolent assault on segregation. A handful of them sat down on the plastic covered stools of the F. W. Woolworth store in Greensboro, North Carolina, and ordered coffee. They were refused, but they stayed until closing time, despite taunts and mild physical annoyances.

They returned the next day, and their brave example triggered similar action by other blacks in Tennessee, Florida, Virginia, and South Carolina. White youths quickly undertook supporting action against Woolworth and other stores in the North. Kennedy ignored them. He also discounted the white students in northern California who on May 13, 1960, protested the efforts of the House Committee on Un-American Activities to harass or imprison various citizens who criticized American foreign and domestic policies. Those students rapidly became the nucleus of the Free Speech Movement on the Berkeley campus of the University of California, and that in turn led to agitation that challenged the role of the university in sustaining corporate capitalism.

The contest for the presidency found both Kennedy and Nixon sharply critical of U.S. foreign policy. Promising something new and vigorous, each sought support of the voters. Bill Mauldin questioned the wisdom of such tactics that left the foreign policy of the Eisenhower administration in verbal shambles.

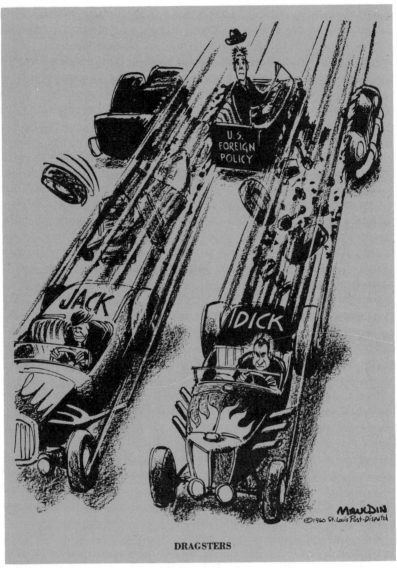

DRAGSTERS

Copyright © 1960 St. Louis *Post-Dispatch*. Reproduced by courtesy of Bill Mauldin.

But those developments were of minor concern to the pragmatic elitism of Kennedy. He did not confront such domestic social issues until Nixon (with belated but effective help from Eisenhower) began to pull even in the polls. Then, running scared, Kennedy moved to win support from the blacks. Martin Luther King, Jr., who had become the symbol—but not the moving force—of the nonviolent protest movement, was again arrested and sentenced to four months of hard labor. Kennedy made a sympathy call to Mrs. Coretta King, and his brother Robert persuaded the southern judge to release King on bail.

It was a shrewd move but, even so, Eisenhower's active campaigning almost won the election for Nixon. Maybe it did: no one will ever know because Nixon declined to demand an investigation into the strongly supported allegations of fraud by the Democratic machines in Illinois and Texas. In keeping with his campaign slogan to "get this country moving," Kennedy marched on into the New Frontier. He knew, as he stepped to the podium to deliver his inaugural address in January, 1961, that the Soviets had made repeated overtures that "stressed the urgency of negotiations," but he emphasized the need for all citizens to subordinate themselves to the state—and hence to the elite that made policy: "Ask not what your country can do for you; ask what you can do for your country."

Kennedy's most revealing early act involved his response to being advised that there was no missile gap. The president had appointed Robert S. McNamara, a Republican who had distinguished himself as an intelligent, hard-driving modern corporation executive of the Ford Motor Co., as secretary of defense, and he quickly began to use sophisticated techniques of analysis and management in an effort to rationalize and control the Pentagon. McNamara quickly learned that there was no missile gap, that instead the United States "possessed a marked advantage over the Soviet Union" in strategic weapons, and he promptly said so in a public statement. Kennedy blandly replied through his press secretary that McNamara did not know what he was talking about and proceeded to launch a huge increase in America's military might. He was proud that one million Americans were serving overseas, and he moved to expand and strengthen that imperial force.

Turning for advice to men like army general Maxwell Taylor, who was concerned "to keep the peace on our terms," Kennedy opened a powerful campaign to create a striking power that could "intervene effectively and swiftly in any limited war anywhere in the world." Sometimes known as the doctrine of 2.5 wars, the plan involved overkill nuclear superiority vis-a-vis Russia, the power to wage a conventional war in Asia, and the capacity for counterrevolutionary supremacy in Latin America or other similar areas.

In a determined display of political pressure, the president rammed the program through the Congress. Ignoring the advice of experts who argued that it was time to negotiate with the Russians (and even the Chinese), he increased the military budget by a total of $7 billion during his first year in office. He asked for and received more missiles, more submarines armed with nuclear warheads, more conventional weapons, a domestic bomb-shelter program, the vast expansion of special counterrevolutionary forces known as the Green Berets—and the CIA was given 50 percent more money than the State Department. By the end of 1963 the Russian military budget was less than 60 percent of the American outlay.

KENNEDY'S CRUSADING FOREIGN POLICY

As that program developed, Kennedy moved against Castro's government in Cuba. During the last months of the previous administration, while Eisenhower had concentrated on reducing tensions with Russia, Vice President Nixon and the CIA had developed a plan to infiltrate anti-Castro Cuban guerrillas into Cuba and see what happened. It was at best a romantic scheme that violated the basic American commitment to self-determination (as well as international law) and at the same time revealed Washington's progressive loss of perspective about world affairs.

At some point, however, the CIA decided—in its monumental arrogance and incomprehension of the changes taking place in the world—that a small orthodox invasion by the Cubans would trigger a mass uprising against Castro. That fundamental change in strategy was never cleared with Eisenhower, who almost certainly would have vetoed it with withering criticism. Kennedy approved the plan, however, and the result was a disaster. A pathetically small band of anti-Castroites invaded Cuba on April 17, 1961, at the Bay of Pigs and was quickly contained; the men were either killed or captured.

Kennedy publicly apologized for the failure, but not for the intention to overthrow Castro. He revealed no understanding that Cuba had a fundamental right to an indigenous revolution or that Castro—whatever his failings—had implemented a program of land and tax reforms and of improvements in housing, health, and wages. Instead, the president emphasized, as one observer phrased it, that "the only danger to America lay outside its borders." The deep roots of that imperial outlook were shortly revealed in several different kinds of action.

He moved first, on March 1, 1961, to institutionalize an idea initially advanced by the socially conscious novelist Harvey Swados (*On the Line*), who had proposed that idealistic Americans be sent abroad to help the poor peoples of the world. The resulting Peace Corps Program, which involved old as well as young people, improved education, health, and agriculture in Latin America and other regions. At the outset, the goodwill of the volunteers and those who organized the program obscured the degree to which it was part of the Kennedy administration's strategy of outflanking Castro and other radicals. But the effort soon lost much of its people-to-people character, was subverted by the CIA and distorted by other pressures, and became ever more a counterrevolutionary enterprise.

A similar fate befell the Alliance for Progress that was launched on March 13, 1961, as a dramatic undertaking to aid Latin-American

John F. Kennedy was hardly comfortable in the White House before the Bay of Pigs disaster occurred in April. He was made aware of the plan to invade Cuba in December before he was inaugurated. Having approved the project, Kennedy accepted the full responsibility for an acutely embarrassed nation. Duncan Macpherson, a Canadian cartoonist for the Toronto Star, *captured the surprise and discomforture in the old exploding-cigar routine.*

Reprinted with permission of the Toronto *Star.*

countries (other than Cuba) in reforming and modernizing their political economies. While the plan did follow an Eisenhower initiative of 1960, Castro could legitimately claim most of the credit for the overture. It was clearly a move to prevent more social revolutions in the hemisphere. He could not be saddled with the responsibility for its rapid failure, however, because that was due to Washington's insistence that the aid money must be spent in the United States, to its concern to protect the huge investments of American corporations, and—fundamentally—to its unwillingness to accept and support those groups who wanted to modernize Latin America with a primary emphasis upon social democracy. That became clear when the Kennedy administration used its economic and political power to prevent Juan Bosch (who had been elected president with 60 percent of the vote) from establishing such a government in the Dominican Republic. Washington rejoiced when he was overthrown (September 25, 1963).

By that time, of course, the Kennedy administration felt secure enough to do almost anything it wanted in the Western Hemisphere. That confidence (however ultimately misleading) had been generated by the superficially decisive defeat of the Soviets during the Cuban Missile Crisis. That terrifying confrontation grew out of Kennedy's invasion of Cuba in 1961, his determination to enhance America's nuclear superiority, and his failure (unlike Dulles) to understand that the permanent division of Germany was an essential part of any strategy to avoid a nuclear holocaust.

The integration of West Germany into NATO during 1955 and its subsequent rearmament had increasingly alarmed the Soviet Union. The Russians had twice been invaded and almost fatally wounded by Germany since 1914, and they were determined to prevent a third assault—and to integrate the other half of Germany into their Eastern European imperial system. They were also trying, however fitfully and reluctantly, to correct the worst abuses of Stalin's rule and to stabilize world affairs within the context of America's strategic nuclear superiority in order to proceed with domestic development.

But Kennedy and his policy advisers displayed little comprehension of those interrelated and ticklish matters. Hence when the president met Khrushchev in Vienna in June, 1961, he misread the premier's insistence upon a series of prompt compromises. Kennedy also ignored the Russian spokesman who later sent word to the White House that "all we want to do is to have a chance to discuss these things." And so the president, who had belligerently criticized Dulles for risking too much in nuclear confrontations, leaned so far over the brink of such a war that only the Russians could save the world.

The crisis began sometime during the summer of 1962 when Khrushchev, despairing of any meaningful negotiations (and no doubt

The mania of the United States to sell and distribute arms around the world drew this comment from Bill Mauldin's pen.

"It's beautiful, but we were sort of hoping for a plow."

May 16, 1961

pushed by his own hard-liners), decided to deploy some short-range missiles in Cuba. The confrontation came in mid-October, on the eve of the off-year elections, when American espionage flights over the island revealed the presence of the weapons. Secretary of Defense McNamara advised Kennedy to "sit tight" because the missiles did not change the strategic balance of power. But the president viewed the situation as a personal and a political challenge and so chose to force a showdown. Disdaining direct talks with Khrushchev, Kennedy and his personally selected group of intimate advisers spent most of their time discussing plans for air strikes and invasion, but they finally agreed to try a blockade (which was of course an act of war against Cuba).

As Attorney General Robert Kennedy later admitted, "what hope there was now rested with Khrushchev's revising his course." The Soviet leader displayed the courage to retreat, and war was avoided. He may well have undertaken the gambit with the primary purpose of dramatizing the dangers of nuclear war. In any event, the crisis was resolved: Kennedy pledged not to invade Cuba, Russia effectively divided Germany by building a wall between East and West Berlin, and Kennedy moved reluctantly toward compromise through an agreement to end atmospheric testing of nuclear weapons (signed July 25, 1963). The president also revealed that he had at least been forced to question his assumptions about the global supremacy of the United States.

Compared with his earlier remarks (private as well as public), his speech of November 16, 1961, at American University suggested that he had finally glimpsed the meaning of Eisenhower's restraint. "We must face the fact," admitted Kennedy, "that the United States is neither omnipotent nor omnipresent. . . . There cannot be an American solution to every problem." It was not so much an end to the psychology and philosophy of the New (Old) Frontier, however, as it was a first shock of recognition that the traditional American outlook might have to be changed.

On the next day, however, the president vigorously reasserted the conventional global definition of America: "Other countries look to their own interests. Only the United States has obligations which stretch ten thousand miles across the Pacific, and three or four thousand miles across the Atlantic, and thousands of miles to the south." It was not only a strange and contradictory remark from a man who had repeatedly argued that only the Russians (or Chinese or Cubans) were imperial powers but it also revealed his persistent refusal to concentrate on the difficulties *within* America.

Kennedy and his advisers were not indifferent to domestic problems, but they approached and dealt with those issues within the framework of America as an imperial power whose overseas activities were more important. Shortly after his inauguration, for example, the president spoke to a group of powerful corporation leaders in the idiom of Woodrow Wilson: "Our success [is] dependent upon your profits and success. Far from being natural enemies, government and business are necessary allies. . . . We seek the spirit of a full-fledged alliance." He added, a bit later, that "we are anxious to do everything we can to make your way easier."

The relationship was not all wine and roses. Kennedy could do nothing to stop the government's conflict of interest suit against the Chrysler Corporation or the price-fixing prosecution against General Electric and Westinghouse because those had been started under Eisenhower. All the firms were found guilty, though the punishment was as a slap on the wrist as compared to what was meted out to those who robbed a corner grocery store. An even more revealing example of the double standard of justice was provided when Kennedy became outraged when the United States Steel Corporation tried to raise its prices in the aftermath of White House intervention to settle a strike in the industry.

The president handled the conflict with a combination of inside pressure (including the midnight use of the FBI to intimidate the corporations) and public exposure. The steel companies backed down (in the short run), rescinding their price hikes, but continued to reap long-range benefits from the armaments program. Kennedy also provoked some opposition from the corporate community by his proposals to extend social security benefits, to raise the minimum wage (to a modest $1.25 per hour), to provide a temporary extension of unemployment benefits, to help women workers through a meager day care bill, to add some federal assistance to various housing programs, and to provide special help for health care and assistance for those who lived in areas where the unemployment rate was above the national average.

But astute corporation leaders realized that he was trying to help them maintain their position (and profits) within the system. The president did not attack the oil companies, backed away from an agricultural program that offended the agribusiness farmers in the South and the Midwest, and exerted strong pressure for legislation to expand exports. The Trade Expansion Act of 1962, for example, the only major bill pushed by the White House during that year, was designed to support American penetration of European markets, and it further centralized power over economic decisions in the executive department. As for Kennedy's education proposals, they provided help for the construction industry but did not challenge the pragmatic definition of education as training for employment in the corporate system.

Nor could the corporations complain about Kennedy's legislation to reduce taxes: the law grossly favored the rich. Likewise, the administration's attempt to establish a system of wage and price controls emphasized the need to control wages. And it handed the new frontier of satellite communications over to private corporations like the Bell Telephone System even though the average taxpayer had funded the research that made it possible. For that matter, Kennedy's dramatic call in May, 1961, to put a man on the moon before 1970 provided a vast public subsidy for the largest aerospace companies. To the degree that the Kennedy administration got the country moving, it did so by emphasizing a militant foreign policy, a grandiose space program, and other subsidies to the giant corporations.

The administration might at least have recommended more extensive reforms if the labor movement had exerted pressure for such policies, but, having become junior partners of capital in the corporate political economy, most labor unions (and their leaders) ceased to agitate for social change. That acceptance of the system as it emerged from World War II was largely due to the prosperity underwritten by the cold war and related overseas economic expansion and to the loss of intellectual vigor and moral outrage among top labor spokesmen. Walter Reuther stopped talking about socialism, for example, and John L. Lewis concentrated on protecting as many jobs as he could when new mining machinery was introduced—and on establishing a pension fund for the remaining miners.

Those were not irrelevant objectives (and were soon taken up by other unions), but they symbolized the emphasis on security. Despite the flurry of radicalism under Eugene Debs before the First World War and the militance of Lewis and Reuther during the Great Depression, the American labor movement remained true to the vision of business unionism first offered by Samuel Gompers at the turn of the century. Not unexpectedly, two of the secondary results of that commitment involved the centralization of power in the top echelons and the rise of shady practices and outright corruption.

That kind of misbehavior principally involved behind-the-scenes deals between union leaders and corporation executives and the kind of criminal activity that was called white-collar crime when practiced by management personnel. Such activities were documented in many unions—the miners, bakers, and distillery workers, for example—but the classic example was provided by the International Brotherhood of Teamsters.

For many years, truck drivers were miserably underpaid and overworked as the automobile industry effectively lobbied the government to downgrade the railroads in favor of a publicly financed system of interstate (and urban) highways that increased their profits. If the truckers had elected socially conscious leaders (and there were some), they might have dramatized—even won—some vital confrontations over policy. But they were understandably if regrettably more upset over their wages and conditions of work than about the broad social issues. Hence they elected men who responded in kind.

The result was a scandal that revealed much about the Kennedy administration. As chief counsel for a Senate investigating committee, Robert Kennedy had led the 1957 attack on Teamster president David Beck and his successor James Hoffa. Kennedy continued that assault after he became attorney general, and he finally put Hoffa behind bars for conspiracy and fraud in mismanaging (and stealing from) the union pension fund. But neither the attorney general nor his brother the president followed through by proposing a fundamental reevaluation of the nation's transportation system.

KENNEDY AND CIVIL RIGHTS

In a similar way, the Kennedy administration was slow to offer moral or political leadership in the black struggle for civil rights and other realities of equality. Kennedy entered the White House with a poor record on that fundamental issue and had been booed by blacks during the 1960 Democratic convention. Even King, who had benefited from Kennedy's intervention on the eve of the election, remained skeptical. "I'm not concerned with the New Jerusalem," King remarked with pointed and bitter sarcasm about Kennedy's imperial foreign policy. "I'm concerned with the New Atlanta, the New Birmingham, the New Montgomery, the New South."

King and other black leaders were divided among themselves, however, which weakened their pressure on Kennedy. The NAACP, which had long been the cutting edge for black civil rights, was being shoved aside by the more militant Congress for Racial Equality and the Student Non-Violent Coordinating Committee (SNCC). The latter two organizations were far more overtly aggressive than the NAACP, and young leaders like John Lewis barely contained their impatience with King's more religious and philosophical approach—let alone with the passivity of the Kennedy administration. They were contemptuous, for example, of the Kennedy effort to pacify the white South by appointing a group of antiblack judges.

The radicals forced the issue. A Supreme Court decision early in 1961 ordered the desegregation of all phases of interstate travel, and on May 4 a group of blacks and whites of all ages began a program of Freedom Rides designed to force Kennedy to get the country moving at home, as well as in Cuba and Berlin, and on the way to the moon. Primarily concerned, as one insider commented, "to keep control over the demand for civil rights," the president and his brother hung back until they were forced to provide federal officials to enforce the law. By that time, however, hundreds had been beaten to the edge of death.

Kennedy was even slower to help the blacks establish their rights to vote and obtain an equal education. Late in 1961 the leaders of SNCC opened a drive to register black citizens in Atlanta, Georgia. King joined the campaign, but the administration offered no meaningful help. When the movement refused to fold and Kennedy remained quiescent, many young blacks embraced the quasi-revolutionary doctrine of Black Power. It was another year before the Kennedys acted firmly to help James Meredith enter the University of Mississippi (September 30, 1962) and to attack the problem of segregated housing (November 20, 1962).

Northern white critics of the system were also ignored. The young women and men who organized the Students for a Democratic Society in June, 1962, were motivated by an idealistic belief that they could reform the corporate political economy. They were slow to attract significant support, even on the college campuses, and in the meantime SNCC launched a major attack on segregation in Birmingham, Alabama. The police easily contained the first peaceful marches (arresting many children in the process), but the demonstration on May 3 was so impressive that it provoked whites into a vicious display of violence that once again aroused the rest of the country.

The Kennedy administration finally acted with vigor and decisiveness. It deployed its considerable resources to influence northern white corporation leaders who had investments in the South and also used federal power in Alabama (and other southern states). The result was a compromise that led to the desegregation of downtown Birmingham stores and more local employment opportunities for blacks. The White House sustained that momentum by outflanking the dramatic efforts of Governor George C. Wallace of Alabama to block the admission of black students to the state university. And, finally (June 11), the president publicly acknowledged for the first time that the crux of the issue involved the moral question of freedom for all citizens: "This nation, for all its hopes and all its boasts, will not be fully free until all its citizens are free."

That was an ironic commentary on American foreign policy, dramatized a few hours later when Medgar Evers, the NAACP field secretary in Mississippi, was murdered from ambush by whites as he returned to his home. Obviously shaken, the Kennedy administration finally called for a civil rights law. The president refused, however, to cancel a trip to Europe in order to take part in a massive demonstration in Washington. Foreign affairs continued to take priority.

The administration demanded, moreover, that the movement control its more radical and militant members. In particular, the speech proposed by John Lewis, a courageous and oft-beaten young leader, was censored of such phrases as "Listen, Mr. President" and of his blunt talk about a revolution. It would have been better for Kennedy to have stayed home and listened to Lewis, but failing that, he should have been there to hear Martin Luther King, Jr. For on August 28, 1963, standing before the Lincoln Memorial, King said all the things that Lincoln should have said a century before. "I have a dream," cried King, and he went on to document all that had to be done before equality would become reality.

Kennedy returned from talking tough in Europe to reassert the vitality of the New Frontier in Asia. As far back as 1956 he had described the issue in Indochina (and in particular Vietnam) as one defined by the United States offering those peoples a better revolution than the one that was under way: "far more peaceful, far more democratic, and far more locally controlled." When it became clear that the Vietnamese revolutionaries were determined to make their own future, moreover, Kennedy reiterated his determination to control the outcome. Twice within a week (September 2 and 9, 1963) he spoke forcefully about maintaining a dominant American presence: "I don't agree with those who say we should withdraw. That would be a great mistake." He subsequently approved a defoliation campaign that "became an exercise in wholesale crop destruction" and sent more American advisers who took part in ever more combat operations.

The president also reassured veterans of the fiasco at the Bay of Pigs that he would help them return to Cuba. Indeed, he persistently talked about removing Castro, and the CIA mounted several efforts to kill the Cuban leader. Shortly after a particularly militant anti-Castro speech in Miami, the president flew to Texas to arrange a compromise between the feuding factions of the Democratic party in that state. And there, at midday on a sunny street in Dallas, he was murdered. Shot dead in his open car sitting near his beautiful wife and Governor John Connally.

Quite in keeping with his imperial outlook, Kennedy was on his way to a trade exposition to deliver a speech calling for the vigorous expansion of foreign trade and investment. In the aftermath, many people of various ideologies offered different explanations of the assassination. All of those hypotheses can be reduced to two propositions: either the president was killed by Lee Harvey Oswald, a loner who had become imbalanced by his personal problems and his opposition to Kennedy's persistent talk about overthrowing Castro, or he was the victim of conspirators yet unknown who used Oswald as a patsy.

The official board of inquiry, headed by Chief Justice Earl Warren, faced an awesome choice: to function as a ruthless detective in the classic American idiom of Sam Spade or to examine the evidence with

The enigmatic involvement of the United States in Southeast Asia invited Duncan Macpherson's pen to portray the wizardry of Dean Rusk (secretary of state) as a sorcerer with all the magic of a rabbit in the hat and a CIA as part of the bag of tricks.

Sorcerer's Apprentice

Reprinted with permission of the Toronto *Star*.

one eye on the need to avoid a trauma that would further weaken the domestic social fabric and subvert America's imperial position in the world. Given that option, which clearly informed their reading of the evidence, the members of the Warren Commission concluded that Oswald was solely responsible for killing Kennedy.

Someday, perhaps, another investigation—or a solitary historian—will prove them wrong. According to some sources, even the new president, Lyndon Baines Johnson, was inclined to explain the murder as the work of a conspiracy. He did not reopen the inquiry, but instead emphasized the need for Americans to compromise their differences and embark upon a broad program of domestic reform. As one of his aides remarked, Johnson "wishes the rest of the world [would] go away and we could get ahead with the real needs of Americans." That insight was verified a bit later by the president's perceptive wife, Claudia Alta Taylor ("Lady Bird"): "I just hope that foreign problems do not keep mounting. They do not represent Lyndon's kind of presidency."

There is a story about Johnson that offers a sense of what might have been—of the possibility that he could have changed America's conception of itself and thereby led the country into a different outlook and pattern of behavior. He remarked, shortly after the election of 1960, that Kennedy should recognize the Chinese government headed by Mao Tse-Tung "and be done with it." The tale has the ring of truth because it reveals Johnson's realism, his astute sense of political timing, and his visceral understanding that America needed to concentrate upon domestic problems.

Historians and sociologists are already debating whether Johnson came from a truly poor, or merely a lower-middle-class, family. And the first psychological biography presents him as a man driven by a need for love and security. Those matters are relevant, but they become meaningful only within a broader framework. Johnson was a Texan (a special kind of southerner), he was shaped by the Great Depression, and his heroes—in particular, Franklin D. Roosevelt—were men who acted vigorously to deal with concrete problems even if their immediate solutions later had to be modified almost beyond recognition.

VICTORIES AND DEFEATS OF JOHNSON'S PRESIDENCY

As the first southerner to occupy the White House in more than a century, Johnson was initially and understandably on the defensive. He was additionally cautious because he had not been elected and because he knew that many northerners viewed him with suspicion—even contempt. Hence in the early months he emphasized his role as the executor of Kennedy's political testament. As he began to revise and move Kennedy's domestic legislation through the Congress, however, he was challenged by an outburst of nationalism in Panama.

Much to the consternation of some advisers, Johnson picked up the phone and called Panamanian president Robert F. Chiari ("What's his name?") to defuse the crisis. Johnson's keen understanding of Chiari's domestic problems (and political ploys), combined with a quiet firmness, led to an agreement in April, 1964, to hand the issues—which concerned control of the canal and the canal zone—over to talented negotiators.

By that time, the president was deploying all his considerable powers to avoid a national railroad strike. He enjoyed two negotiating advantages: (1) neither management nor labor liked the memory of Kennedy's threat in 1963 to impose a compulsory settlement and (2) in intimate situations Johnson could be overpowering when he invoked his personality in support of his vision of Americans working together to solve their common problems. He used a version of Roosevelt's technique of locking the antagonists in a room until they produced a compromise to avert the strike and move out of the shadow of Kennedy.

Johnson seemed almost obsessively concerned—and determined—to bring Americans together in order to improve the general welfare. One of his advisers touched that nerve in a memo that suggested that "we are all liberals, we are all conservatives." The phrase was a rather feeble echo of Jefferson's assertion in his first inaugural address that "we are all Republicans, we are all Federalists," but it caught Johnson's fancy and he made it into his own under the rubric of coming together in a consensus to build The Great Society.

He first outlined that idea on May 22, 1964, in a speech at the University of Michigan and then moved to implement it by forcing the Senate to approve the Civil Rights Bill that the House had passed in February. Deploying all his intelligence, physical presence, charisma, and political clout—"the treatment," as it was known to friend and foe alike—he overrode a southern (and Republican) filibuster and pushed the bill through, signing it on July 2, 1964. The legislation outlawed racial, sexual, and religious discrimination and provided stiff penalties for all violations.

By that time Johnson was embarked upon his own presidency. He had launched a vigorous campaign against poverty in March, and, with the crucial help of Phil M. Landrum of Georgia who bluntly called poverty "social dynamite," he won passage of the Economic Opportunity Act in August. The fight for that legislation was aided by riots in

New York City and Rochester, by deadly violence against civil rights workers in the South, and by the growing concern that George Wallace of Alabama might disrupt the effort to build The Great Society through his demagogic appeals to white middle- and working-class people who felt threatened by social change.

Wallace's principal appeal in the South was overtly racist, but he also attracted support there, as well as in the North, by playing on the theme that "the little man" was being fleeced and misgoverned by an unholy and greedy combination of wealthy easterners, intellectuals, and federal bureaucrats. Johnson did not back away from the challenge, and his vigorous campaign for reform won him the Democratic nomination and secured significant legislation from the Congress. Between July and September, for example, the administration approved an urban transportation act, a food stamp program to help the poor, housing assistance, and a law to preserve wilderness areas for conservation and recreation.

In response, the Republicans offered a muted version of Wallace's program behind the leadership of Senator Barry M. Goldwater of Arizona. Nominated by a convention that displayed a visceral antagonism toward Republican liberals like Nelson Rockefeller (and reform in general), Goldwater campaigned on an appeal to the fear that blacks and other minorities were threatening the white middle class, a promise to break up big government and return to free enterprise, and a foreign policy that stressed military supremacy throughout the world.

As Johnson recognized, he had lost the support of many southerners without gaining the full confidence of northerners and westerners. He put it bluntly: his support was like a river that was "broad but not deep." And he increased the uneasiness among many people by his response to an encounter on August 2 between an American destroyer and North Vietnamese torpedo boats in the Gulf of Tonkin.

Recognizing the dangers—domestic as well as international—of a major intervention in that country, the president had moved cautiously in Vietnam despite the pressure from many advisers to commit American resources on a large scale. It was an extremely ticklish situation because, beginning with the Truman administration, the United States had become increasingly involved in trying to prevent the nationalist and Communist revolutionaries led by Ho Chi Minh from taking power throughout Vietnam. The artificial division of that nation after the defeat of the French put the United States in the position of backing a government in the southern part of the country that proved incapable of attracting mass support.

American forces were becoming ever more involved in combat operations even before Kennedy was killed, but, unlike the piecemeal loss of advisers in the field, the naval exchange in the Tonkin Gulf was too dramatic to ignore. Even so, the episode could have been handled differently: Johnson could have waited until the facts had been established and then openly explained it for what it was—a confused confrontation on a stormy night for which American ships were largely responsible. Goldwater and other hard-liners would no doubt have attacked Johnson for being soft on Communism, but candor would very probably have carried the day with the majority of Americans.

Johnson instead responded as if the North Vietnamese were intentionally trying to humiliate the United States. That reaction was the result of several factors: the president's patriotism and his sense of American mission in Asia and the propensity of all American leaders to think about foreign affairs in terms of avoiding another Munich, maintaining the creditability of American power, and preserving access to raw materials and strategic bases.

Those considerations also guided the members of the Congress who overwhelmingly authorized Johnson to retaliate to protect American forces. He did so by bombing North Vietnamese torpedo boat bases. Emphasizing the limited nature of his response, and warning that Goldwater would have overreacted in a highly dangerous fashion, Johnson survived the crisis and went on to win the election by the largest margin in modern history.

For that reason, as well as because the bombing seemed to impress the North Vietnamese, neither Johnson nor most other policy makers reexamined their fundamental assumptions about American foreign policy. In a very short time, therefore, the president's dream of The Great Society became a nightmare of an increasingly embittered and divided country. Before that disintegration became fully apparent, however, Johnson enjoyed his finest hours as a dynamic domestic leader.

In classic style, the president seized upon a striking event to dramatize his entire program. Martin Luther King, Jr., black militants, and other activists began a voter registration drive in Selma, Alabama, in January, 1965, and the increasingly violent white opposition soon attracted national attention and concern. King moved to capitalize on the situation by scheduling, for Sunday, March 7, a 52-mile "March of Freedom" from Selma to the state capitol in Montgomery. Shortly after they began the trek, the 650 blacks were met at the bridge over the Alabama River by state troopers and a mounted sheriff's posse. Using whips, clubs, and tear gas—and trampling those who went down in blood and pain—the brave defenders of white supremacy stopped the march.

Immediately supported and joined by people from throughout the nation, King planned another march. Johnson rose to the challenge despite his reservations about King and his own dislike of mass demonstrations. In the immediate situation, he outmaneuvered Governor Wallace and insured the safety of the march. Even before that victory, however, he had decided to wage a frontal battle with the white supremacists and their allies. It was not a sudden response: he had long before instructed the Justice Department to prepare a tough voting rights bill, and in October, 1964—in the white heat of the election struggle in the South—he had laid it on the line among Goldwater supporters.

Arriving in New Orleans on October 9, Johnson was met with skepticism and hostility. That night, at the end of a routine speech, he paused, looked around—and into his own soul—and spontaneously gave another speech. He began by invoking the memory of Huey Long: a man "way ahead of them all because he was against poverty, *really* against it, and for the ordinary man, *really* for him." Then, in his inimitable way, Johnson told his still skeptical audience a story about another southern politician.

Near the end of a distinguished career, Johnson explained, Senator Joseph W. Bailey of Texas had expressed the desire, despite his failing health, to "go back down there and make them one more Democratic speech." He was tired, he admitted, but he was even more weary of having the race issue used to exploit the South economically. Southerners had fallen into the trap set by northerners. "All they ever hear at election time is nigra, nigra, nigra."

The rest is best told by historian Eric F. Goldman:

> The audience gasped . . . and for a long few seconds the room was quiet. Then, starting here and there, applause came and people stood up. Tentatively, slowly, the handclapping built into a standing, shouting ovation. . . . It went on, a tremendous roar, for fully five minutes. The nineteen hundred Louisiana Democrats knew they had heard truth, political skill, and audacity combined in one electric moment.

He did it again on March 15, 1965; only this time he was talking to the entire country. Many southern legislators chose to boycott that joint session of the Congress because the word had gone out that the president was going to "get it said, really said." And indeed he did.

> At times history and fate meet at a single time in a single place to shape a turning point in man's unending search for freedom. So it was at Lexington and Concord. So it was a century ago at Appomattox. So it was last week in Selma, Alabama. . . .
>
> For with a country as with a person: "What is a man profited, if he shall gain the whole world, and lose his own soul?" . . .
>
> There is no Negro problem. There is no southern problem. There is no northern problem. There is only an American problem. And we are met here

tonight as Americans—not as Democrats or Republicans—we are met here as Americans to solve that problem. . . .

And . . . we . . . shall . . . overcome. . . .

I never thought . . . in 1928, that I would be standing here in 1965. It never occurred to me in my fondest dreams. . . .

But now I do have that chance—and I'll let you in on a secret—I mean to use it. And I hope you will use it with me.

It was one of the great moments in the history of the United States. As Johnson's daughter Lynda said: "It was just like that old hymn, 'Once to every man and nation comes a moment to decide.'"

The president proceeded to win major domestic reforms and then allowed his imperial foreign policy to undercut all those achievements. With important help from Senators Everett M. Dirksen and Mike J. Mansfield, the voting rights legislation was pushed through the Senate within a month. Led by Congressman Gerald R. Ford, a coalition of northern Republicans and southern Democrats in the House delayed the inevitable until August. In the meantime, however, Johnson had maneuvered the passage of many other reforms. The Office of Economic Opportunity (OEO) was funded to help the urban poor, to retrain people for new jobs, to help younger people in Job Corps training centers, and to encourage local communities to assert their own leadership. Then came major legislation to assist lower-income students to obtain an education and to enable older citizens to secure medical care. The Medicare bill, signed July 30, 1965, after a bitter battle against the AMA, was not only a belated first effort to drag American society into the modern world of public health but it also symbolized Johnson's other victories in housing, tax reduction, aid for Appalachia, regional development, antipollution laws, and farm legislation.

It is easy, and largely correct, to argue that the legislation was long overdue and to add that it did little more than fulfill various promises that Franklin Roosevelt had offered during the Great Depression. But despite its endless rhetoric about endless progress, America has always been a conservative society; hence Johnson deserves credit for trying to push that conservatism as far as possible in the direction of humane paternalism.

From the time of James Madison and Thomas Jefferson, however, the other side of such reform was imperial expansion. Jefferson said it twice in memorable prose. First in his inaugural address: America is "the world's best hoe," and the theory of democracy through expansion "furnishes new proof of the falsehood of Montesquieu's doctrine, that a republic can be preserved only in a small territory. The reverse is the truth." Then, as he was leaving the White House, he said it again: "No constitution was ever before as well calculated as ours for extensive empire and self-government."

But those objectives ultimately proved incompatible, first with Jefferson, and later with Johnson. The Renaissance gentleman from Virginia and the earthy Democrat from Texas both chose to extend or preserve the empire rather than to embark upon structural changes at home. It was an eerie parallel because both leaders revealed that similarity in dealing with revolutions in the Caribbean. Jefferson refused during his first term to aid Santo Domingo revolutionaries, and in 1965 Johnson intervened to abort a later revolution in the same country.

The latter action was the beginning of the end for Johnson: his policies in behalf of the imperial frontier began to undermine his efforts to create The Great Society at home. The deployment of marines in the Dominican Republic dramatically enlarged the opposition that he had engendered by the bombing of North Vietnam in August, 1964, and his subsequent escalation of that war after the February, 1965, attack on an American redoubt in Pleiku.

After the Pleiku episode, Johnson and his advisers had three choices. They could have concluded that it was time to withdraw and allow the Vietnamese to determine their own future. They could have set a deadline, say March, 1966, for the pseudo-government in South Vietnam to establish a viable system and during that interim period used air power to protect key centers of population. Or they could have gone back to the Congress (and the public) and requested a declaration of war and the funds to wage such an imperial struggle. Instead, they launched a massive intervention with ground troops, and, in trying to hide the failure of that strategy, they subverted their credibility, drained away the resources that were needed for domestic reform, and intensified internal tensions.

The intervention proved ineffective and the mounting opposition to the war forced Johnson to withdraw from active politics. Beginning in February, 1965, the protests against the war first centered in college communities. Those favoring the war often asserted that the antiwar sentiment was largely confined to students of draft age, their parents, and a few radical professors. That analysis was belied, however, by the composition of the opposition both at the outset of the campaign and during the months after 1967 when it reached its climax.

Students and professors at the universities of Berkeley, Michigan, and Wisconsin had begun even before 1965 to criticize and demonstrate against the corporations' vast influence over education and other aspects of American society. And the first antiwar activities involved many nonacademic citizens who were concerned with general reforms, as well as with changing foreign policy. One group of students did become increasingly aggressive and violent during 1966–1967, and that ruptured the early alliance between the university community and other citizens. But the subsequent congressional hearings and debates on the war, dramatized by Senator J. William Fulbright's inquiry as chairman of the Senate Foreign Relations Committee, revived and extended the opposition among the public at large.

When the Hollywood film portrayed the violence of the 1920s for receptive audiences of the 1960s, David Levine of The New York Review of Books *caricatured President Johnson and Secretary Rusk as the team of Bonnie and Clyde in the conduct of American foreign policy.*

Drawing by David Levine. Reprinted with permission from *The New York Review of Books.* Copyright © 1966 NYREV, Inc.

In the American mind, Johnson and Vietnam became one and the same. When the president permitted visitors and the television cameras to view the scar resulting from his surgery, David Levine immediately drew the surgical incision line as the boundary of Vietnam. Levine had already given the president a Pinnochio nose for his exaggerations about the military situation in Vietnam.

Let Me Tell You About My . . .

Drawing by David Levine. Reprinted with permission from *The New York Review of Books*. Copyright © 1967 NYREV, Inc.

During those same years, the costs of the war cut deeply into the money available for Johnson's Great Society program. In the summer of 1967, for example, there were major riots in Detroit and Newark and more than 160 other such outbreaks of angry discontent by blacks and others. And in April the antiwar demonstration in New York mustered 100,000, and another 75,000 marched on the Pentagon in Washington.

By that time The Great Society had been subverted by the war. White women as well as black males, and Chicanos as well as Indians, were joining the revolt against the system. Perhaps nothing explained the reasons for that general and increasingly more embittered revolt than the budget statistics. The government allocated its tax moneys this way for fiscal 1965: $76 billion to the military and $15 billion for education, health, housing, and welfare. The OEO was granted a total of $2.8 billion between 1965 and 1973—the equivalent of the cost of the war in Vietnam for one month. More than 14 million Americans were suffering from hunger and malnutrition.

Then came the North Vietnamese Tet offensive of January, 1968, a sophisticated attack that made it clear that the United States could not win the war unless it was prepared to destroy North Vietnamese society. Johnson was done. His deep reluctance to admit that truth in a public speech created the misleading impression that he was driven from office by Senators Eugene McCarthy of Minnesota and Robert Kennedy of New York. McCarthy first challenged the president in the New Hampshire Democratic primary election and on March 12 polled 42.4 percent of the vote against 49.5 percent for Johnson. Four days later Kennedy suddenly found the courage to enter the remainder of the primaries.

Behind the scenes, however, Johnson had been moving to deescalate the war, and on March 31 he announced that he was cutting back on the massive bombing of North Vietnam and withdrawing from politics. It was as close to a tragic public drama as twentieth-century America could provide, but it did not end the time of troubles. In the midst of planning a massive demonstration against poverty scheduled to be held in Washington, D.C., Martin Luther King, Jr., flew to Memphis, Tennessee, to support a local strike by garbage collectors. On the evening of April 4, while he stood talking with friends on the balcony of a motel, he was gunned down. Violence immediately erupted in Boston, Philadelphia, Toledo, and more than 100 other cities (and 200 campuses). President Johnson watched helplessly as parts of downtown Washington were burned to the ground during a week of angry rioting.

Johnson was a beaten man. He did nothing to help the Poor People's Campaign, whose participants built a pathetic plywood village in Washington to dramatize their plight. The Reverend Ralph David

Abernathy, much closer to the working class than King, undertook what he called "a desperate effort to help America save itself" by trying to provide effective leadership for the demonstration. But he worked against impossible odds, and the campaign collapsed under internal dissension and external pressures.

Then, just after he had narrowly defeated McCarthy in the California primary on June 5, Robert Kennedy was assassinated in the kitchen of a hotel. The country seemed to be disintegrating. The extremist wing of the antiwar movement made its contribution to the turmoil by provoking a major riot during the late-summer Democratic convention in Chicago. Lacking any significant sense of history—which they therefore disdained as irrelevant—such so-called revolutionaries became the slaves of their irrational rhetoric about "Revolution for the Hell of It," and for similar reasons, they misread the fears and anxieties of the middle class as signs that the system was ready to topple into its grave.

As a result, they learned the hard and painful way that many leaders of the system were willing and able to beat them to the ground. Indeed, Mayor Richard J. Daley, one of the most powerful men in the United States (as well as in the Democratic party), had turned Chicago into a virtual garrison city in preparation for the confrontation. After the first skirmishes, the grisly and bloody battles were accurately described as a police riot against almost anybody who was mistaken enough to appear in the streets. Displayed to the nation on live television, the carnage almost disrupted the convention and further polarized the country over the issues of race, politics, and the war in Vietnam. Hubert Humphrey, a dedicated liberal from the era of the New Deal, won the nomination, but he lacked the courage to break sharply with the war policy that was creating so much havoc. His campaign slogan, "The Politics of Joy," was so grossly at odds with the reality of America as to provoke little more than a shrug of indifference.

Across the road, on the other side of the much vaunted two-party system, Nixon could afford to indulge his prejudices. He was ostensibly challenged by Ronald Reagan, a Grade B motion picture star turned reactionary politician, but it was all a kind of late-movie rerun. Nixon came on as the sophisticated heavy: an honest man making sly references about his deep prejudices against blacks (and other minorities) and about his obsessive ambition to rule the country.

It was a clever ploy. After losing to Kennedy in 1960, Nixon retreated to California to plot his comeback. He seemed to have lost forever, however, when he was beaten in the 1972 race for governor—nothing left but private life as a wealthy corporation lawyer. Many otherwise astute political commentators forgot about

The horrors of the violent decade of the sixties, including the assassinations of the Kennedy brothers, Martin Luther King, Jr., and Malcolm X, prompted Bill Mauldin to draw "The American Way: A Social and Political History." The cartoon "Bookmarks" was given overwhelming support by the Reports of the U.S. Riot Commission in 1968 and The History of Violence in America *by the Commission on the Causes and Prevention of Violence in 1969.*

him. But two shrewd conservative observers followed him into the cave as he invested his considerable intelligence, paranoia, and energy in planning his campaign to win the White House. He "brooded, dreamed, and schemed for the presidency."

Nixon's seed money came from his as yet unexplained connections with two people: John Mitchell, a onetime corporation lawyer turned bond salesman in New York, and Charles ("Bebe") Rebozo, a nononsense manipulator of Florida real estate. As for political capital, Nixon earned his own way by stumping the country for countless Republican candidates. The rubber chicken dinners turned into the gold of delegate IOUs. And, being no dummy, Nixon realized that there was a southern road to the White House: court the new wealth in Florida, Atlanta, and west through Texas to southern California. As for the raw politics of it, Nixon assured Senator Strom Thurmond of South Carolina that he would help white southerners to delay even the trappings of equality for blacks—and then selected the demagogic Spiro T. Agnew (of Maryland) as his running mate.

He handled it all so well that otherwise intelligent people seriously debated the existence of a "new" Nixon. There was no new Nixon, simply a more sophisticated version of the man who had approved the plan to overthrow Castro and who had said that domestic politics could be left to themselves. Wounded as he was by Vietnam, Humphrey could have won the election if he had attacked Nixon from the beginning for the dangerous man that he was and if he had not been so wishy-washy about the war in Vietnam. Even so, he almost carried the day with a final rush of candor.

The truth of it was, as Nixon realized, that almost half the eligible voters were sour on all leaders, and the other half was almost equally divided about how to deal with the multiple crises at home and abroad. Though he campaigned on the vague promise to "Bring Us Together," Nixon moved promptly to isolate himself at the center of power in order to do what he had determined was right. Hence he quickly proceeded to personalize (and extend) the consolidation and centralization of presidential power that had been the central feature of American politics since the 1890s.

EXPLORATORY READING

Four of the most stimulating books on the contemporary political economy are:

N. W. Chamberlain, *The Limits of Corporate Responsibility* (1974)

A. S. Miller, *The Modern Corporate State* (1976)

L. Mosley, *Power Play* (1973)

K. Sale, *Power Shift: The Rise of the Southern Rim and Its Challenge to the Eastern Establishment* (1975)

On the question of energy, which lies at the center of the viability of contemporary capitalism, see:

B. Commoner, *The Poverty of Power* (1976)

P. R. and A. Ehrich, *Population, Resources, Environment: Issues in Human Ecology* (1970)

S. D. Freeman, *Energy: The New Era* (1974)

H. T. Odum, *Environment, Power, and Society* (1971)

L. Rocks and R. P. Runyon, *The Energy Crisis* (1972)

The most illuminating overviews of the Kennedy-Johnson era are:

A. M. Bickel, *Politics and the Warren Court* (1965)

R. Evans and R. D. Novak, *Lyndon B. Johnson: A Political Biography* (1966)

M. Frady, *Wallace* (1970)

E. F. Goldman, *The Tragedy of Lyndon Johnson* (1969)

J. F. Heath, *Decade of Disillusionment* (1975)

J. L. Sundquist, *Politics and Policy: The Eisenhower, Kennedy and Johnson Years* (1968)

To understand the radical ferment of those years, begin with these volumes:

E. Cleaver, *Soul on Ice* (1967)

R. E. Conot, *Rivers of Blood, Years of Darkness* (1967)

D. Dellinger, *More Power Than We Know: The People's Movement Toward Democracy* (1975)

B. Friedan, *The Feminine Mystique* (1963)

G. Greer, *The Female Eunuch* (1971)

M. Heirich, *The Beginning: Berkeley, 1964* (1970)

J. Hole and E. Levine, *Rebirth of Feminism* (1971)

N. Mailer, *Armies of the Night* (1968)

P. Matthieson, *Sal Si Puedes (Escape If You Can): Cesar Chavez and the New American Revolution* (1972)

A. Meier and E. Rudwick (Eds.), *Black Protest in the Sixties* (1970)

M. Miles, *The Radical Probe: The Logic of Student Rebellion* (1970)

B. Muse, *The American Negro Revolution* (1968)

K. Sale, *S.D.S.* (1973)

C. E. Silberman, *Crisis in Black and White* (1964)

S. Steiner, *The Vanishing White Man* (1976)

It is far too early for any definitive study of Nixon, but the following books do provide important insights to his career and his aborted administration:

R. M. Elman, *The Poorhouse State: The American Way of Life on Public Assistance* (1966)

R. Evans and R. D. Novak, *Nixon in the White House* (1971)

J. McGinniss, *The Selling of the President, 1968* (1969)

R. L. Morrill and E. H. Woldenberg, *The Geography of Poverty in the United States* (1971)

B. Page, *American Melodrama: The Presidential Election Campaign of 1968* (1969)

L. E. Panetta and P. Gall, *Bring Us Together: The Nixon Team and the Civil Rights Retreat* (1971)

G. Steiner, *The State of Welfare* (1971)

G. Wills, *Nixon Agonistes: The Crisis of the Self-Made Man* (1970)

J. Witcover, *The Resurrection of Richard Nixon* (1970)

During the height of the opposition to the Vietnam War, Nixon bluntly remarked that he was watching professional football on television instead of giving any thought to the protesters marching in front of the White House. He hoped thereby to gain sympathy from those who had become addicts of such entertainment. These two books explore the rise of sports, professional and otherwise, as a kind of opium of the American people:

J. Michener, *Sports in America* (1976)

M. Novak, *The Joy of Sports* (1976)

Various aspects of foreign policy from Kennedy through Nixon are explored by these authors:

E. Abel, *The Missile Crisis* (1969)

N. Chomsky, *For Reasons of State* (1973)

C. L. Cooper, *The Lost Crusade: America in Vietnam* (1970)

J. Cotter and R. R. Fagen (Eds.), *Latin America and the United States* (1974)

A. C. Enthoven and K. W. Smith, *How Much Is Enough? Shaping the Defense Program, 1961–1969* (1971)

B. Fall, *The Two Viet-Nams: A Political and Military Analysis* (1967)

F. Fitzgerald, *Fire in the Lake: The Vietnamese and the Americans in Vietnam* (1972)

P. Geyelin, *Lyndon B. Johnson and the World* (1966)

A. L. Horelick and M. Rush, *Strategic Power and Soviet Foreign Policy* (1966)

G. M. Kahin and J. W. Lewis, *The United States in Vietnam* (Rev. Ed., 1969)

R. Kovic, *Born on the Fourth of July* (1976)

D. Landau, *Kissinger: The Uses of Power* (1972)

R. Littauer and N. Uphoff (Eds.), *The Air War in Vietnam* (1971)

W. D. Rogers, *The Twilight Struggle: The Alliance for Progress and the Politics of Development in Latin America* (1967)

J. Slater, *Intervention and Negotiation* (1970)

R. J. Walton, *Cold War and Counterrevolution* (1972)

22 THE UNRESOLVED CRISES OF AMERICAN SOCIETY

THE change of presidents served largely to dramatize the continuity of the basic problems in American society: inflation, unemployment, racial and other social inequalities and tensions, the war in Vietnam, energy and water shortages, and the continuing centralization and consolidation of economic and political power. Nixon had never manifested much interest in domestic affairs (nor any significant ability to deal with them), and he moved quickly the emphasize foreign policy issues. He further centralized the decision-making process in the National Security Council (NSC) and consolidated power in his own hands even more by funneling State Department proposals and comments through Henry Kissinger, a brilliant and ambitious Harvard professor whom the president chose to be chairman of the council. The two men complemented each other in their marked confidence in their own ideas and egos, as well as in their demanding mode of operation. Both recognized that America could no longer dominate the world as it had from 1945 to 1965, and hence they embarked upon what can arguably be called a sophisticated effort to devise and implement a new conservative strategy that was appropriate to the changed realities of world politics.

At home, however, Nixon revealed himself to be a narrow and unimaginative conservative. His three closest domestic advisers—White House aides H. R. Haldeman (an advertising public relations man) and John D. Ehrlichman (a real estate lawyer), and John Mitchell (an expert on municipal bonds appointed as attorney general)—were men of little vision, great prejudices, and impressive inexperience as national leaders. Together with the president, they promptly launched a nasty and illegal assault on such radicals as the Black Panther party and on the antiwar movement, leading Democratic politicians, and a wide assortment of other groups and individuals (including newspapers and the CBS television network) that they labeled as enemies. Within six months, for that matter, they were wiretapping members of their own administration, and shortly thereafter Vice President Agnew opened a running-dog attack on any and all critics of the administration.

With a few exceptions, the president's domestic policy decisions revealed the same outlook. As one of his appointees angrily concluded, the administration "deliberately worked to sabotage the very school desegregation effort it was charged under the law with enforcing." That deeply prejudiced (if not racist) outlook was also revealed in the president's failure to support Secretary of Labor George Shultz's effort to desegregate the construction workers' unions, and it became a national scandal in August, 1969, when Nixon nominated Clement F. Haynsworth, Jr., of South Carolina to be a justice of the Supreme Court.

The president had earlier tapped a respected if not exceptional conservative, Warren Burger, to become chief justice upon the retirement of Earl Warren. But it soon became apparent even to leading Republican senators that Haynsworth was wholly unqualified because of his racial prejudice, his antilabor bias, and various charges of conflict of interest. Even so, Nixon refused their request to withdraw the nomination. When the Senate voted 55 to 45 against confirmation, the enraged president intensified his attacks on critics and nominated G. Harrold Carswell of Florida—an even less qualified man. He, too, was blocked by the Senate, and only then did Nixon begin to nominate routinely qualified conservatives: Harry A. Blackmun, Lewis F. Powell, and William H. Rehnquist.

Despite the grave questions raised by those early actions, Nixon did support (at least for a time) positive conservative proposals in two other areas. The most important move involved a major reform of the welfare system. Many knowledgeable people had criticized the hodgepodge of federal and state laws and bureaucracies that attempted to help people who were in need, but Nixon seems to have been influenced mostly by Patrick J. Moynihan, a conservative academic who occasionally taught at Harvard, and conservative economist Milton Friedman of the University of Chicago.

In its initial form, the Family Assistance Plan could be called almost radical. It was based upon the principle of every citizen's right to a minimum income, offered help to the working poor as well as to the indigent, involved direct cash payments and food stamps, and proposed drastic reductions in the welfare bureaucracy. Such ideas quickly provoked criticism from liberals as well as conservatives, however, and Nixon gradually abandoned the battle. That retreat was foreshadowed by the president's failure to support the vigorous efforts of Senator George McGovern of South Dakota and Dr. Jean Mayer of Harvard to deal with the health problems of the poor. In the end, however, the confused struggle for welfare reform did establish (October 17, 1972) the right of the elderly, the blind, and the disabled to receive supplemental income through direct payments via the social security system.

Nixon's other suggestion for domestic reform involved the idea of sharing federal revenues with states and local agencies of government. In that area, however, the president proved far less prepared with a clear program and demonstrated even less interest and staying power in the battle. As a result, the sharing was minor and the issue was

---

The table immediately below shows the annual rate of per capita disposable income in "current"—or inflated—dollars, quarter by quarter, from the start of 1973 through 1976's third quarter (from figures compiled by the Commerce Department).*

Year	1st Quarter	2nd Quarter	3rd Quarter	4th Quarter
1973	$4,130	$4,238	$4,327	$4,443
1974	4,487	4,579	4,705	4,779
1975	4,809	5,102	5,105	5,227
1976	5,347	5,455	5,528	———

In a four-year period the record adds up to: up 34 percent.

A gain of 34 percent in less than four years, if it represented a rise in real buying power, would delineate a leaping living standard indeed. But that's not the way it is. Unfortunately, it is almost pure mirage.

The following table traces the income figures over the same period of time, but gives them in deflated, or constant (1972), dollars, with the inflation factor removed. These are the figures that represent real buying power.

Year	1st Quarter	2nd Quarter	3rd Quarter	4th Quarter
1973	$4,027	$4,056	$4,074	$4,085
1974	4,006	3,970	3,968	3,923
1975	3,889	4,078	4,009	4,049
1976	4,103	4,143	4,144	———

In a four-year period the revised record is: up 3 percent.

Thus, when the inflation comes out the picture changes drastically. And for many individuals who have not enjoyed a 34 percent rise in inflated-dollar earnings since early 1973, the real buying power of paychecks has actually declined.

---

* John O'Riley, "The Outlook," *The Wall Street Journal*, November 15, 1976, p. 1.

The financial burdens of the nation were not borne equally among its citizens. Many loopholes were available for those who could manipulate the system for personal privilege. Herbert Block of the Washington Post *chose income tax time in April of 1972 to cartoon the inequities.*

From *Herblock's State of the Union,* Simon & Schuster, 1972.

allowed to die from lack of sustained leadership. A similar kind of intellectual weakness and irresolution about policy characterized the administration's efforts to deal with the problems of the economy.

Signs of trouble appeared during the winter of 1970, and by spring it was clear that a serious downturn was under way. As unemployment climbed and real wages declined, the country soon found itself in the worst recession in a decade. Belatedly, in August, 1971, Nixon moved to freeze prices, wages, and rents (but not profits); imposed a 10 percent surcharge on imports; and offered a tax cut for business in the hope of stimulating capital investment. Those meager efforts were ultimately abandoned in January, 1973, and the economy—despite a modest recovery—continued to display signs of structural stagnation compounded by inflation.

The ever growing discrepancy between the rhetoric and the reality of the Nixon administration was dramatically highlighted by the president's grandiose call in January, 1971, for "A New American Revolution." His oratorical fireworks about welfare reform, a health program, environmental protection, a balanced budget, revenue sharing, and governmental reorganization were unimpressive, but he soon stopped talking about such limited visions. Instead, he renewed and extended his attacks on all critics; further weakened the effort to enforce civil and voting rights; vetoed (or otherwise blocked) efforts to improve housing, education, and other social programs; and ultimately refused to spend the moneys appropriated by the Congress for such reforms.

Nixon persistently tried to obscure his ineffective and dangerous domestic performance by emphasizing the drama of foreign policy. He and Kissinger shared an outlook on the world that can best be understood as a realistic conservatism grounded in the necessity of cosurvival with the Soviet Union and the People's Republic of China. Both men recognized the central implication of the Cuban Missile Crisis and China's success in fabricating atomic weapons: relations among the nuclear powers had to be stabilized in order to prevent a holocaust. In their view, that required a high degree of centralized power and secrecy in the conduct of diplomacy; a great emphasis upon the use of military and other instruments of power to convince other nations that the United States was not making an unlimited retreat on all fronts; sustained efforts to prevent developing countries from embracing Socialism or Communism; and a grand attempt to establish America as the nation that controlled the global balance of power between China, Russia, Japan, and Western Europe.

Ten days after his inauguration, Nixon ordered Kissinger to begin the maneuvers that would reopen relations with China and simultaneously began to devise a strategy for withdrawal from Vietnam. They were deeply—almost obsessively—concerned, however, not to lose their credibility as men of power as they shuffled to end that massive drain on American resources. As a result, the antiwar movement became ever more powerful and disruptive, and that in turn increased Nixon's determination to impose his will upon the country.

The national antiwar demonstrations of October, 1969, attracted more than two million citizens, for example, and encouraged ever more congressmen and senators to join the critics. Then, despite the administration's vigorous opposition, a November mass rally in Washington drew 400,000 people. At the same time, open and covert resistance to the draft, along with the breakdown in Vietnam of discipline and the will to fight, placed further pressure on the administration to terminate the war. Nixon and Kissinger accepted the inevitability of that outcome, but they displayed a bloody determination to force the North Vietnamese to accept American terms for ending the war.

That effort led to a series of tactical escalations of violence that further disrupted American society—as well as causing more carnage in Vietnam. The first was a March, 1970, incursion into Cambodia undertaken without any consultation with the Congress. That provoked massive demonstrations around the country and, during one protest on May 4 at Kent State University in Ohio, the killing of unarmed students by a unit of the National Guard. Then, ten days later, the anger and frustration led to further killings by police at Jackson State University in Mississippi. Nixon's response was to intensify his attacks on all critics and to launch more tactical offensives.

At the heart of that policy was the sustained bombing of North Vietnam (along with major portions of South Vietnam). It was a bloody business, only superficially described by saying that it involved more bombs than all those dropped in World War II. Chemical warfare was also employed, leading to the defoliation of vast areas of Vietnam. Even so, the war that upset increasing numbers of Americans involved the traditional kind of combat by the infantry. The television coverage of those operations, along with other excellent reportage and photography, had made it known, for example, that American troops burned villages in the hope of destroying the popular power base of the Vietnamese revolutionaries. And the February, 1971, incursion into Laos was revealed for the failure that it was—all in the average home during the dinner hour.

But the revelation in 1971 of a raid conducted in 1968 left most Americans aghast at the routine carnage. The massacre at My Lai 4 was beyond description—almost everyone in sight was shot down in cold blood—but equally terrifying was the sustained effort by American leaders to suppress all knowledge of the atrocity. The concept, let alone the practice, of self-government according to the principles of liberty and democracy was willfully being subverted in its own name.

That was documented again as the Nixon administration moved against the next demonstration in Washington with the techniques of mass arrests and detentions and then tried to suppress the publication of a Pentagon study of the origins and nature of the war. Ever more upper-class leaders had come to recognize the futility of the war (and the related dangers inherent in Nixon's rule), and that alerted them to the threat it posed to their power position in American society. The most perceptive of those men, such as Robert McNamara, had realized by the end of the Johnson administration that it was essential to end the war, and within that framework they had commissioned a study designed to plot the mistaken course that had been followed.

Though they were seriously incomplete in that they did not draw upon many of the sources available in the executive department and were conceptually flawed because they failed to pose questions about the causes of the war, the resulting volumes nevertheless provided devastating evidence about the deception and death. A formerly enthusiastic supporter of the war named Daniel Ellsberg first tried to persuade his superiors to tell the story to the public. When his plea for candor was spurned, he delivered some of the documents to the *New York Times*.

Ellsberg was at that point (he later became more critical) trying to save the Establishment from its own myopia. It was a brave act. But Nixon was unable either to recognize the wisdom of clearing the decks or of saluting Ellsberg's courage. Instead through many and various illegal actions he sought to destroy Ellsberg and to punish the *Times*. The president ultimately lost both battles, but not until he had caused severe damage to Ellsberg and the body politic. As before and after, Kissinger acquiesced in such betrayals of the democracy he was sworn to uphold.

No less than Nixon, Kissinger considered himself to be above the law (and politics) because of the purity and importance of his motives and objectives. Both men thus confront historians (you as well as me) with difficult problems of interpretation and judgment. Nixon and Kissinger did recognize that the world had changed—that the crude mentality and policies of the cold war were no longer relevant. And their concern to stabilize the world on the basis of a multinational balance of power made an elementary kind of sense. What they failed to understand, however, was more important than their perception, finally, of an insight offered for many years by various critics of postwar American policy. On the one hand, they did not comprehend that they had to take the public into their confidence if they were to sustain the power they needed to carry through their grand design, and on the other hand they did not recognize the vital importance of a coherent economic policy to the success of their global strategy. Both weaknesses were initially obscured by their ability to dominate policy decisions and to present them as effective drama.

First they flew off (February, 1972) to China for talks with Mao that reopened rudimentary political contact with a major Asian power. Then Nixon went to Moscow to discuss trade and strategic weapons. It was a temporarily effective exercise in balance-of-power diplomacy, and it provided the setting for Nixon to ultimately withdraw (August) the last American ground troops from Vietnam. The air war continued unabated.

Those three actions decreased world tensions to some degree and opened the way for the kind of discussions that might someday resolve various disagreements about substantive issues. But the initial agreement between Russia and the United States did little more than establish ground rules for a new round in the arms competition, and there was not even that much progress during the conversations with the Chinese.

At the same time, moreover, Nixon and Kissinger failed to confront either the fundamental problems of the world economy (about which both were very weak) or the necessity to develop a different relationship with the poorer nations of the Third World. Kissinger's policy toward Africa and South America, for example, was predicated upon the assumption that the northern industrial nations led by the United States could maintain their traditional political superiority and economic domination by making minor compromises. The effectiveness of that approach in some countries like Chile (where the elected Socialist president Salvador Allende was deposed with American assistance) was nevertheless belied by the ultimate triumph of the revolutionaries in Vietnam and by the persistent determination of other such leaders and movements to assert their independence and equality.

In a similar way, Nixon continued to resist the demands of various domestic groups—such as women, blacks and other minorities, anti-imperialists, and the poor—for more power and reforms. As the election approached, he launched an illegal and reprehensible campaign of lies and other dirty tricks designed to destroy the position of any leader within the Democratic party who might unite those critical and angry citizens in an effective coalition. His fears were justified because, despite his diplomatic achievements, the United States was not a healthy, equitable, and dynamic society in 1971–1972: the many obvious social tensions were only the most dramatic indicators of the failure of a political economy in which the richest 20 percent controlled 45.8 percent of the national income while the poorest 20 percent received only 3.2 percent of the pie.

Nixon's unconstitutional and subversive politics undoubtedly con-

Henry Kissinger's activities were wide-ranging and full of variety. The remarkably energetic secretary of state was here, there, and everywhere. He moved so rapidly that his record became obscured in the mist that quickly settled over where he had been. Herblock characterized the secretary and the conduct of his office in this cartoon.

Copyright © 1976 by Herblock in the Washington *Post.*

tributed to the disarray within the Democratic party, but in a more significant sense he was effective only because its traditional leaders (such as Senators Edward Muskie and Hubert Humphrey) were far too cautious and unresponsive to the needs and demands of the new dissidents. That left the field open to Governor Wallace and Senator McGovern.

Despite his limited intellect and meager grasp of the vital issues, Wallace appealed to two large (and overlapping) groups of people throughout the country. One was composed of those who were primarily driven by their fear or hatred of blacks, other minorities, and the younger generation; the other involved people motivated more by their sense of impotence in the face of corporate and governmental power. The support of those people enabled Wallace to win five early Democratic primary elections (including Michigan as well as Florida). But in May he was paralyzed by a bullet fired by a would-be assassin, and thereafter McGovern moved steadily toward the nomination despite the opposition of top labor leaders and traditional party bosses.

McGovern was intellectually fuzzy and personally uninspiring, but his transparent dedication and honesty initially appealed to a large number of people. And he opened the party to many of the groups, such as women, blacks, and youth, who had for years been given little more than vague promises that were never honored. He won the nomination on the first ballot and began his campaign for president trailing Nixon in the public opinion polls by a mere 10 percent. Within a few months, however, he began to lose support because his policy proposals were sloppy, because he demonstrated poor judgment (as in his handling of the vice-presidential selection), and because he tried to straddle major issues in ways that failed to satisfy moderates while they antagonized his more reformist supporters.

Long before those weaknesses in the McGovern campaign became apparent, the Nixon administration had extended its criminal activities to include the burglary of the national headquarters of the Democratic party. At least as early as January 14, 1972, Nixon ordered his key associates to discredit Larry O'Brien (the astute and effective Democratic national chairman), and by March 30 they had devised a plan to tap his phones and steal important documents from his files. That was done in May by breaking into O'Brien's office in the Watergate apartment-business complex in Washington, D.C. Seeking even more booty, the political criminals returned on the night of June 17, 1972, only to be surprised and apprehended by the police.

The president and his advisers immediately launched a massive and increasingly feverish effort to cover their tracks. Justifiably fearful that the truth about Watergate would reveal other illegal activities and so drive them from power, they employed all the traditional methods of

The dimensions of the Watergate affair increased with each passing month. The dreary business unfolded slowly through 1973 and 1974. The tapes became available in bits and pieces under the pressure of the Ervin committee in the Senate and the efforts of the special prosecutor's office. Herblock viewed the tortured process of revelation in the cropped-picture sequence.

From *Herblock Special Report,* W. W. Norton & Co., Inc., 1974.

criminals—bribery, lies, and the destruction of records—as well as mundane protestations of outrage and innocence. As Nixon told one key aide, the strategy was "to button it up as well as you can." And despite some nervous moments in October, they succeeded in controlling the situation through the election.

Nixon's overwhelming victory (McGovern carried only the state of Massachusetts and the District of Columbia) made him even more confident of his power to embark upon conservative (even repressive) measures at home while continuing his efforts to manipulate world affairs. He began with the savage bombing of North Vietnam during the Christmas holidays, then tried to determine the outcome of the revolutionary and nationalistic violence on the Indian subcontinent, and again intervened in the Middle East.

The attack on Israel by Egypt and Syria in 1973 was supported by an Arab embargo on oil shipments to the United States and other powers that supported or sympathized with the Zionist state. That action dramatized the rising power of the Third World in inescapable terms, and the initial success of the Egyptians in crossing the Suez Canal and pushing the Israeli forces back toward their 1967 boundaries fractured the illusion of Zionist invincibility. Nixon and Kissinger, together with the resiliency of the Israeli army, managed to stabilize the immediate crisis, but they proved unequal to the task of leading Americans into a creative relationship with the new world situation.

Nixon spoke bold words about a crash program to achieve "self-sufficiency in energy," but did nothing of consequence to move the nation toward that inherently unobtainable objective. Kissinger managed (with vital help from Egypt) to keep the Russians from making any serious intrusion into the Middle East crisis (or was it the Russians who were responsible for not intervening?) but revealed a singular inability to realize that it had become vital to evolve new and imaginative relationships with the poor societies of the world. He was remarkably adroit—perhaps even a genius—at holding the line, but he failed to devise and implement an American strategy for dealing with the new order that was emerging around the globe.

At home, Nixon rapidly lost his ability to govern the country. The criminal attempt to subvert representative government that defined the essence of the Watergate scandal was footnoted by the bribery charges that forced Vice President Agnew to resign his office in October, 1973 (he was succeeded by Gerald R. Ford, nominated by Nixon and confirmed by the Congress in November). And the continued failure of the administration to deal effectively (let alone humanely or equitably) with economic and social problems made it increasingly clear that the president was incompetent as well as undemocratic and criminal. Even minor bureaucrats began to turn against him, a remarkable development best symbolized by the lower functionary who slipped the press evidence that the president had cheated on his income tax returns.

Others revealed far more devastating information about Nixon's complicity in the Watergate crimes. Various newspaper reporters played a dramatic part in those revelations, but three hired hands within the Nixon administration were the crucial figures in the final denouement. The first was James M. McCord, a former CIA operative who was a key member of the group that broke into O'Brien's office.

Paul Conrad of the Los Angeles Times *seized the slogan that was popularized by President Truman and gave it a new twist for the White House desk. The word "truth" was substituted for the word "buck." Nixon's tangle of tapes under the desk emphasizes the caption that "the truth stops here."*

Copyright © 1974, Los Angeles *Times*. Reprinted with permission.

He told Judge John J. Sirica, who took jurisdiction over the case, about the White House involvement.

The second was Alexander P. Butterfield. He was the grandson and son of military officers (and a gutsy, distinguished army flier in his own right) who joined the White House staff as a top assistant to Haldeman. When the chips went down (on Friday, July 13, 1973), he honored the very best in his family and service traditions by telling the congressional investigators that almost all discussions in the White House were recorded on tape. The third was John W. Dean, an able, fawning and extremely ambitious young lawyer who had wriggled his way into the center of the cover-up operation. He liked power, but he liked surviving even more, and so on April 8 he began to reveal his vast and detailed knowledge of the criminal activities in order to save his own skin (a project in which he largely succeeded).

Nixon fought back desperately, bitterly, and obsessively (some even thought suicidally), but he was doomed. By turns pathetic, incoherent, and arrogant, he struggled to retain power, but beginning on July 27, 1974, the House Committee on the Judiciary voted three counts of impeachment. Article I charged that the president "prevented, obstructed, and impeded the administration of justice . . . using the powers of his high office . . . to delay, impede, and obstruct the investigation of [the Watergate burglary]; to cover up, conceal, and protect those responsible; and to conceal the existence of other unlawful covert activities. . . ."

Article II asserted that the president, "in disregard of his constitutional duty to take care that the laws be faithfully executed, has repeatedly engaged in conduct violating the constitutional rights of citizens, impairing the due and proper administration of justice and the conduct of lawful inquiries . . . in a manner contrary to his trust as president and subversive of constitutional government. . . ." Article III added that Nixon had failed, "without lawful cause or excuse to produce papers and things, as directed by duly authorized subpoenas issued by the Committee on the Judiciary. . . ."

Then came the devastating disclosure, ordered by the Supreme Court in a unanimous decision, of the tape of Nixon's conversation with Haldeman on June 23, 1972. One of the president's lawyers said it in four words: "It was all over." For the tape revealed that, only a few days after the Watergate robbery, Nixon had ordered the CIA to block the FBI investigation. Nixon clung to power for a few more days, during which he asserted his reactionary will by vetoing a $13.5 billion appropriations bill for programs involving rural assistance and consumer and environmental programs.

Then came the gentle and not-so-gentle pressure from the movers and shakers of the established system. Even the sophisticated leaders of his white southern supporters told him that he had to leave—otherwise he would risk opening a fatal crack for structural changes in America. And so reluctantly, and at times almost hysterically, Nixon accepted the inevitability of resignation. Understandably, he broke into tears more than once, but finally, on August 9, 1974, he mustered the will to walk out of the White House as the first president of the United States to resign (let alone under threat of criminal prosecution). The traditional abuses of the imperial frontier had surfaced at the center of the empire.

THE UNKNOWN FUTURE

Gerald Ford, who had earlier done his best to stop the congressional investigation of Watergate, almost immediately pardoned Nixon for "any and all crimes"—including those connected with Watergate—that he may have committed during his almost six years in office. Ford did not, however, sweep the White House and the executive department clean of Nixon intimates. That strange pattern of behavior raised

This cartoon by Pat Oliphant commented upon the Ford administration's effort to, in Punky Penguin's words, make the nation "neat an' tidy." But housekeeping that merely sweeps the dirt under the rug has seldom been given the Good Housekeeping Seal of Approval. Pat Oliphant is now with the Washington Evening Star.

Editorial cartoon by Pat Oliphant. Copyright © 1977, Washington *Star*. Reprinted with permission of the Los Angeles *Times Syndicate*.

serious questions concerning an explicit or implied understanding about such a pardon when Ford was being considered for vice president, as well as about his judgment and capacity to serve as president. He further intensified those doubts by nominating Nelson Rockefeller to be the new vice president.

Rockefeller was finally confirmed by the Congress after long and arduous hearings (thus filling the nation's top two offices through a nonelective process), but the evidence revealed during the searing investigation left most citizens with grave reservations about the situation. The most vociferous critics were the embittered conservatives, northern as well as southern, who had supported Nixon and Wallace. They wanted no part of Rockefeller and quickly turned to Reagan as their choice to replace Ford. Others mistrusted Rockefeller because of his upper-class elitism, his deviousness, his belligerence in foreign affairs, and because his reforms in New York had never quite managed to help the lower classes. The classic example was prison reform: Rockefeller talked tall but allowed the miserable conditions to endure even after the wrenching revolt at New York's Attica State Prison. Rockefeller refused even to talk with the prisoners.

The same kind of doubts arose about Ford. He had solemnly vowed, during the hearings to confirm him as Nixon's vice president, that he would not seek the presidency in 1976, but he soon changed his mind. His assets in the service of that ambition included (beyond possessing the interim lease on the White House) his long experience in government as a congressman, his related reputation for opposition to centralized presidential power, his personal openness, and a mind good enough to grasp the essential nature of the problems faced by an imperial executive.

Those advantages were mitigated, however, by his deep political partisanship (which had severely clouded his judgment about several important issues), his lack of imagination, his routinely conservative ideology, and his lack of active sympathy for minorities and other disadvantaged—or dissident—groups. It was not surprising, therefore, that Ford set his course to the right of center or that, under increasing pressure from Reagan, he veered ever more in that direction.

As a result, he was constantly at odds with the Democratic Congress on most major issues. The president stressed the need to limit federal spending in order to cut inflation. The Congress emphasized the importance of creating jobs to decrease unemployment and its attendant suffering. Similar disagreements became apparent in their confrontations over protecting the environment, energy policy, control of corporations, the urban crisis, social issues (as widely varied as abortion and school desegregation), and foreign policy.

Still choking on the dregs of the spills of Watergate, the public watched a new congressional investigation into the operations of the CIA, the FBI, and the IRS. The activities of these agencies were soon in the headlines—activities that were far cry from respect for law and liberty usually associated with the Spirit of 1776. Conrad drew the agencies as sinister figures in black marching to a different drum—the spirit of George Orwell's 1984.

The Spirit of '84

Copyright © 1975, Los Angeles *Times.* Reprinted with permission.

But the Democrats and the Republicans also differed among themselves about most of those issues, and the resulting lack of clear and effective leadership compounded the basic weakness and the problems of the political economy. Intellectually, moreover, the country had been living off the fund of ideas developed during the 1930s, and those concepts and proposals were no longer directly appropriate to, or

The critical shortage of gasoline brought a national proclamation to limit the highway speed of automobiles to 55 miles per hour. While the rate of travel was reduced, the enforcement of the limit proved impossible. Mauldin's request is appropriate because the observance of the regulation depends upon individual morality.

Copyright © 1975 the Chicago *Sun-Times.* Reproduced by courtesy of Wil-Jo Associates, Inc., and Bill Mauldin.

effective in dealing with, the realities of the late twentieth century. As a result, the disagreements over policy did not produce a significant political debate or a stimulating intellectual dialogue.

The most serious effort to generate that kind of public discussion in 1976 was provided by Tom Hayden's campaign to win the Democratic nomination for U.S. senator in California. His pamphlet, *Make the Future Ours*, was based on the recognition that it was first of all necessary to revive the concept and practice of active citizenship if democracy was to be revitalized and if the corporate system was to be brought under control and used for the general welfare. It represented a significant change from politics as usual in offering specific reforms as part of a broad program to transcend the status quo by limiting the vast power of the multinational corporations through an economic bill of rights.

That kind of fundamental politics was not practiced by any of the presidential candidates. Reagan's vigorous campaign to take the Republican nomination away from President Ford was based on a combination of nineteenth-century individualism and antigovernment clichés that would in practice enhance the power of the corporations in the name of freedom. Ford fought back by emphasizing his long service to the party and his personal integrity and by offering a hodgepodge of traditional ideas that amounted to a routinely pragmatic effort to sustain the status quo. After he won the nomination, Ford campaigned on little more than his moderate success in stabilizing the country after the Watergate crisis.

Coupled with the political advantages of being president, that limited and unimaginative approach almost proved effective enough to win one of the most uninformative (and increasingly boring) elections of the twentieth century. The principal significance of the long travail, which started during the winter as the divided Democratic party began its search for a leader in the New Hampshire primary, was that Vietnam and Watergate had made it possible for an extremely ambitious and energetic one-term governor of Georgia—a relative outsider—to become president.

James Earl Carter of the hamlet of Plains, Georgia, decided in 1972 (if not earlier) that he wanted to occupy the White House. He was then halfway through his term as governor and already impatient for a bigger job. Such vast ambition and confidence had long been central to his character: in the course of making the decision to leave his promising career in the navy, for example, he had remarked that even if he remained in the navy, the highest possible position he could attain was chief of operations (or chairman of the Joint Chiefs of Staff). Most men would consider that enough power and prestige for one lifetime, but Carter clearly sought more.

Despite his ever increasing exposure in the course of his determined run for the presidency, Carter remained an enigmatic figure who generated considerable unease despite his nonstop rhetoric about being honest, open, and responsible. Certain things about him, however, did become reasonably clear. He was unusually intelligent and a

Candidates for the presidency in 1976 tried to capitalize on the public's suspicion of and impatience with government. Both Ford and Carter requested the confidence of the voters by assuring them that their support would not be misplaced. This caused Paul Interlandi of the Los Angeles Times *to recall several rules in our political folklore.*

"Never eat in a cafe called Mom's, never play cards with a man called Slick, and never vote for a politician who says, 'Trust me'!"

Interlandi: Los Angeles *Times*, April 2, 1976.

tough administrator. Despite his transparent sincerity as a "born-again" evangelical Southern Baptist who was unquestionably sympathetic toward the poor, he was nevertheless arrogant, patronizing, extremely reluctant to consider or accept criticism, and almost unforgiving of less than perfect performances by his associates.

While he sometimes referred to himself as a populist, and had unquestionably come to accept black Americans as equal citizens, he was also an agricultural businessman of considerable wealth who was committed to the corporate system. And although he sometimes spoke about the need to modify the nation's imperial foreign policies, he at other times used the language of a militant interventionist. Those kinds of ambiguities, along with his persistent refusal to offer a coherent statement of his program, meant that many of his initial supporters turned away in disgusted uneasiness. In their own way, they reached the conclusion offered by a man who had observed him closely in Georgia: "He is an able and determined man, but I have absolutely no idea of what he will—or will not—do if he becomes President."

That kind of skepticism (if not cynicism) undercut Carter's shrewd strategy to exploit Watergate and almost enabled Ford to overcome Carter's early appeal and wide lead in public opinion polls. In the end, the Georgian squeaked through by 51 percent to 48 percent in the popular vote (and by 297 to 235 in the electoral college). It is easy to be distracted by the drama of Carter's victory and thereby overlook some vital aspects of contemporary American society.

Carter's triumph, in an election in which only 52 percent of the eligible voters thought it worthwhile to cast a ballot, actually emphasized the extent to which administrative politics had superseded public politics: *the extent to which politics was concerned primarily with managing the existing system more effectively and efficiently rather than with creating a better or a different society.*

Carter's service as a capable but orthodox engineer in the Navy, and his performance as a one-term governor of Georgia, revealed a strong preference for centralized executive power and an extensive confidence in the correctness of his own ideas and proposals. As a late convert to equality for black Americans, and as a "born-again" Southern Baptist, he displayed more than a touch of Woodrow Wilson's propensity for moralizing and for missionary diplomacy. He spoke boldly, for example, about the failure of various countries, such as Russia, to honor human rights, but seriously undercut his rhetoric (and moral position) by making exceptions for reactionary and repressive regimes that he considered essential to America's imperial system.

Similarly his early proposals to deal with the issues of inflation, unemployment, and energy revealed an inherently conservative approach to economic problems. As an executive of a moderately large

The new president-elect, Jimmy Carter, designated many old hands to government office as the announcements of his appointments came out of Plains, Georgia, during the interim months before inauguration. Engelhardt of the St. Louis Post-Dispatch *explains an old and trusty guideline in our political life.*

'When You Run Against 'Em, They're Tired—
When You Appoint 'Em, They're Experienced'

Englehardt in the St. Louis *Post-Dispatch*, December 13, 1976.

corporation, Carter not unexpectedly favored corporate over public enterprise—unless the entrepreneurs needed help from the taxpayers. His effort to dramatize the energy crisis was highly commendable (even daring), but in substance his proposals offered at best a modest attack on that fundamental problem. As one of his closest associates remarked: "Carter campaigns liberal but he governs conservative."

Some day a historian might be tempted to use that pithy comment as a summary for twentieth-century American history. In any event, well into 1977 the United States continued to bump and grind around the dead center: a once revolutionary society unable to break free of the status quo. Carter might prove to be the prophet and the instrument of a new America, but that had not yet become apparent.

EXPLORATORY READING

Amidst all the words written and spoken about the the Nixon Administration, these volumes speak to the essential parts of the economic and political story:

R. Berger, *Impeachment: The Constitutional Problems* (1973)

J. M. Blair, *The Control of Oil* (1976)

G. Emerson, *Winners and Losers* (1976)

J. A. Lukas, *Nightmare: The Underside of the Nixon Years* (1976)

R. Woodward and C. Bernstein, *All the President's Men* (1974)

You, like the rest of us, will have to write your own histories of Gerald Ford and James Earl Carter.

APPENDIX A

PRESIDENTIAL ELECTIONS, 1789–1976

Year	Candidates	Party	Popular Vote	Electoral Vote
1789	**George Washington**			69
	John Adams			34
	Others			35
1792	**George Washington**			132
	John Adams			77
	George Clinton			50
	Others			5
1796	**John Adams**	Federalist		71
	Thomas Jefferson	Democratic-Republican		68
	Thomas Pinckney	Federalist		59
	Aaron Burr	Democratic-Republican		30
	Others			48
1800	**Thomas Jefferson**	Democratic-Republican		73
	Aaron Burr	Democratic-Republican		73
	John Adams	Federalist		65
	Charles C. Pinckney	Federalist		64
1804	**Thomas Jefferson**	Democratic-Republican		162
	Charles C. Pinckney	Federalist		14
1808	**James Madison**	Democratic-Republican		122
	Charles C. Pinckney	Federalist		47
	George Clinton	Independent-Republican		6
1812	**James Madison**	Democratic-Republican		128
	DeWitt Clinton	Federalist		89
1816	**James Monroe**	Democratic-Republican		183
	Rufus King	Federalist		34
1820	**James Monroe**	Democratic-Republican		231
	John Quincy Adams	Independent-Republican		1
1824	**John Quincy Adams**	Democratic-Republican	108,740 (30.5%)	84
	Andrew Jackson	Democratic-Republican	153,544 (43.1%)	99
	Henry Clay	Democratic-Republican	47,136 (13.2%)	37
	William H. Crawford	Democratic-Republican	46,618 (13.1%)	41
1828	**Andrew Jackson**	Democratic	647,231 (56.0%)	178
	John Quincy Adams	National Republican	509,097 (44.0%)	83
1832	**Andrew Jackson**	Democratic	687,502 (55.0%)	219
	Henry Clay	National Republican	530,189 (42.4%)	49
	William Wirt	Anti-Masonic ⎫	33,108 (2.6%)	7
	John Floyd	National Republican ⎭		11
1836	**Martin Van Buren**	Democratic	761,549 (50.9%)	170
	William H. Harrison	Whig	549,567 (36.7%)	73
	Hugh L. White	Whig	145,396 (9.7%)	26
	Daniel Webster	Whig	41,287 (2.7%)	14

PRESIDENTIAL ELECTIONS, 1789–1976 (Continued)

Year	Candidates	Party	Popular Vote	Electoral Vote
1840	**William H. Harrison** (**John Tyler,** 1841)	Whig	1,275,017 (53.1%)	234
	Martin Van Buren	Democratic	1,128,702 (46.9%)	60
1844	**James K. Polk**	Democratic	1,337,243 (49.6%)	170
	Henry Clay	Whig	1,299,068 (48.1%)	105
	James G. Birney	Liberty	62,300 (2.3%)	
1848	**Zachary Taylor** (**Millard Fillmore,** 1850)	Whig	1,360,101 (47.4%)	163
	Lewis Cass	Democratic	1,220,544 (42.5%)	127
	Martin Van Buren	Free Soil	291,263 (10.1%)	
1852	**Franklin Pierce**	Democratic	1,601,474 (50.9%)	254
	Winfield Scott	Whig	1,386,578 (44.1%)	42
1856	**James Buchanan**	Democratic	1,838,169 (45.4%)	174
	John C. Fremont	Republican	1,335,264 (33.0%)	114
	Millard Fillmore	American	874,534 (21.6%)	8
1860	**Abraham Lincoln**	Republican	1,865,593 (39.8%)	180
	Stephen A. Douglas	Democratic	1,382,713 (29.5%)	12
	John C. Breckinridge	Democratic	848,356 (18.1%)	72
	John Bell	Constitutional Union	592,906 (12.6%)	39
1864	**Abraham Lincoln** (**Andrew Johnson,** 1865)	Republican	2,206,938 (55.0%)	212
	George B. McClellan	Democratic	1,803,787 (45.0%)	21
1868	**Ulysses S. Grant**	Republican	3,013,421 (52.7%)	214
	Horatio Seymour	Democratic	2,706,829 (47.3%)	80
1872	**Ulysses S. Grant**	Republican	3,596,745 (55.6%)	286
	Horace Greeley	Democratic	2,843,446 (43.9%)	66
1876	**Rutherford B. Hayes**	Republican	4,036,572 (48.0%)	185
	Samuel J. Tilden	Democratic	4,284,020 (51.0%)	184
1880	**James A. Garfield** (**Chester A. Arthur,** 1881)	Republican	4,449,053 (48.3%)	214
	Winfield S. Hancock	Democratic	4,442,035 (48.2%)	155
	James B. Weaver	Greenback-Labor	308,578 (3.4%)	
1884	**Grover Cleveland**	Democratic	4,874,986 (48.5%)	219
	James G. Blaine	Republican	4,851,981 (48.2%)	182
	Benjamin F. Butler	Greenback-Labor	175,370 (1.8%)	
1888	**Benjamin Harrison**	Republican	5,444,337 (47.8%)	233
	Grover Cleveland	Democratic	5,540,050 (48.6%)	168
1892	**Grover Cleveland**	Democratic	5,554,414 (46.0%)	277
	Benjamin Harrison	Republican	5,190,802 (43.0%)	145
	James B. Weaver	People's	1,027,329 (8.5%)	22
1896	**William McKinley**	Republican	7,035,638 (50.8%)	271
	William J. Bryan	Democratic; Populist	6,467,946 (46.7%)	176

PRESIDENTIAL ELECTIONS, 1789–1976 (Continued)

Year	Candidates	Party	Popular Vote	Electoral Vote
1900	**William McKinley** (**Theodore Roosevelt**, 1901)	Republican	7,219,530 (51.7%)	292
	William J. Bryan	Democratic; Populist	6,356,734 (45.5%)	155
1904	**Theodore Roosevelt**	Republican	7,628,834 (56.4%)	336
	Alton B. Parker	Democratic	5,084,401 (37.6%)	140
	Eugene V. Debs	Socialist	402,460 (3.0%)	
1908	**William H. Taft**	Republican	7,679,006 (51.6%)	321
	William J. Bryan	Democratic	6,409,106 (43.1%)	162
	Eugene V. Debs	Socialist	420,820 (2.8%)	
1912	**Woodrow Wilson**	Democratic	6,286,820 (41.8%)	435
	Theodore Roosevelt	Progressive	4,126,020 (27.4%)	88
	William H. Taft	Republican	3,483,922 (23.2%)	8
	Eugene V. Debs	Socialist	897,011 (6.0%)	
1916	**Woodrow Wilson**	Democratic	9,129,606 (49.3%)	277
	Charles E. Hughes	Republican	8,538,221 (46.1%)	254
1920	**Warren G. Harding** (**Calvin Coolidge**, 1923)	Republican	16,152,200 (61.0%)	404
	James M. Cox	Democratic	9,147,353 (34.6%)	127
	Eugene V. Debs	Socialist	919,799 (3.5%)	
1924	**Calvin Coolidge**	Republican	15,725,016 (54.1%)	382
	John W. Davis	Democratic	8,385,586 (28.8%)	136
	Robert M. La Follette	Progressive	4,822,856 (16.6%)	13
1928	**Herbert C. Hoover**	Republican	21,392,190 (58.2%)	444
	Alfred E. Smith	Democratic	15,016,443 (40.8%)	87
1932	**Franklin D. Roosevelt**	Democratic	22,809,638 (57.3%)	472
	Herbert C. Hoover	Republican	15,758,901 (39.6%)	59
	Norman Thomas	Socialist	881,951 (2.2%)	
1936	**Franklin D. Roosevelt**	Democratic	27,751,612 (60.7%)	523
	Alfred M. Landon	Republican	16,681,913 (36.4%)	8
	William Lemke	Union	891,858 (1.9%)	
1940	**Franklin D. Roosevelt**	Democratic	27,243,466 (54.7%)	449
	Wendell L. Wilkie	Republican	22,304,755 (44.8%)	82
1944	**Franklin D. Roosevelt** (**Harry S Truman**, 1945)	Democratic	25,602,505 (52.8%)	432
	Thomas E. Dewey	Republican	22,006,278 (44.5%)	99
1948	**Harry S Truman**	Democratic	24,105,812 (49.5%)	303
	Thomas E. Dewey	Republican	21,970,065 (45.1%)	189
	J. Strom Thurmond	States' Rights	1,169,063 (2.4%)	39
	Henry A. Wallace	Progressive	1,157,172 (2.4%)	
1952	**Dwight D. Eisenhower**	Republican	33,936,234 (55.2%)	442
	Adlai E. Stevenson	Democratic	27,314,992 (44.5%)	89
1956	**Dwight D. Eisenhower**	Republican	35,590,472 (57.4%)	457
	Adlai E. Stevenson	Democratic	26,022,752 (42.0%)	73

PRESIDENTIAL ELECTIONS, 1789–1976 (Continued)

Year	Candidates	Party	Popular Vote	Electoral Vote
1960	**John F. Kennedy** (**Lyndon B. Johnson**, 1963)	Democratic	34,227,096 (49.9%)	303
	Richard M. Nixon	Republican	34,108,546 (49.6%)	219
1964	**Lyndon B. Johnson**	Democratic	43,126,233 (61.1%)	486
	Barry M. Goldwater	Republican	27,174,989 (38.5%)	52
1968	**Richard M. Nixon**	Republican	31,783,783 (43.4%)	301
	Hubert H. Humphrey	Democratic	31,271,839 (42.7%)	191
	George C. Wallace	Amer. Independent	9,899,557 (13.5%)	46
1972	**Richard M. Nixon**	Republican	45,767,218 (60.6%)	520
	George S. McGovern	Democratic	28,357,668 (37.5%)	17
1974	**Gerald R. Ford**	Republican	Appointed on August 9, 1974 as President after the resignation of Richard M. Nixon. No election was held.	
1976	**Jimmy Carter**	Democratic	40,828,587 (50.1%)	297
	Gerald R. Ford	Republican	39,147,613 (48.0%)	241

Because only the leading candidates are listed, popular vote percentages do not always total 100. The elections of 1800 and 1824, in which no candidate received an electoral-vote majority, were decided in the House of Representatives.

APPENDIX B

PRESIDENTS, VICE-PRESIDENTS, AND CABINET MEMBERS, 1789-1976

President	Vice-President	Secretary of State	Secretary of Treasury	Secretary of War
1. George Washington 1789	John Adams 1789	T. Jefferson 1789 E. Randolph 1794 T. Pickering 1795	Alex. Hamilton 1789 Oliver Wolcott 1795	Henry Knox 1789 T. Pickering 1795 Jas. McHenry 1796
2. John Adams Federalist 1797	Thomas Jefferson Democratic-Republican 1797	T. Pickering 1797 John Marshall 1800	Oliver Wolcott 1797 Samuel Dexter 1801	Jas. McHenry 1797 John Marshall 1800 Sam'l Dexter 1800 R. Griswold 1801
3. Thomas Jefferson Democratic-Republican 1801	Aaron Burr Democratic-Republican 1801 George Clinton Democratic-Republican 1805	James Madison 1801	Samuel Dexter 1801 Albert Gallatin 1801	H. Dearborn 1801
4. James Madison Democratic-Republican 1809	George Clinton Independent-Republican 1809 Elbridge Gerry Democratic-Republican 1813	Robert Smith 1809 James Monroe 1811	Albert Gallatin 1809 H. W. Campbell 1814 A. J. Dallas 1814 W. H. Crawford 1816	Wm. Eustis 1809 J. Armstrong 1813 James Monroe 1814 W. H. Crawford 1815
5. James Monroe Democratic-Republican 1817	D. D. Thompkins Democratic-Republican 1817	J. Q. Adams 1817	W. H. Crawford 1817	Isaac Shelby 1817 Geo. Graham 1817 J. C. Calhoun 1817
6. John Q. Adams* 1825	John C. Calhoun 1825*	Henry Clay 1825	Richard Rush 1825	Jas. Barbour 1825 Peter B. Porter 1828
7. Andrew Jackson Democrat 1829	John C. Calhoun Democrat 1829 Martin Van Buren Democrat 1833	E. Van Buren 1829 E. Livingston 1831 Louis McLane 1833 John Forsyth 1834	Sam D. Ingham 1829 Louis McLane 1831 W. J. Duane 1833 Roger B. Taney 1833 Levi Woodbury 1834	John H. Eaton 1829 Lewis Cass 1831 B. F. Butler 1837

* No distinct party designations.

Attorney-General	Postmaster General†	Secretary of Navy	Secretary of Interior	Secretary of Agriculture
E. Randolph 1789	Samuel Osgood 1789	Established April 30, 1798	Established March 3, 1849	
Wm. Bradford 1794	Tim. Pickering 1791			
Charles Lee 1795	Jos. Habersham 1795			
Charles Lee 1797	Jos. Habersham 1797	Benj. Stoddert 1798		
Theo. Parsons 1801				
Levi Lincoln 1801	Jos. Habersham 1801	Benj. Stoddert 1801		
Robert Smith 1805	Gideon Granger 1801	Robert Smith 1801		
J. Breckinridge 1805		J. Crowninshield 1805		
C. A. Rodney 1807				
C. A. Rodney 1809	Gideon Granger 1809	Paul Hamilton 1809		
Wm. Pinkney 1811	R. J. Meigs, Jr. 1814	William Jones 1813		
Richard Rush 1814		B. W. Crownin- shield 1814		
Richard Rush 1817	R. J. Meigs, Jr. 1817	B. W. Crownin- shield 1817		
William Wirt 1817	John McLean 1823	Smith Thompson 1818		
		S. L. Southard 1823		
William Wirt 1825	John McLean 1825	S. L. Southard 1825		
John M. Berrien 1829	Wm. T. Barry 1829	John Branch 1829		
Roger B. Taney 1831	Amos Kendall 1835	Levi Woodbury 1831		
B. F. Butler 1833		Mahlon Dickerson 1834		

† Not in cabinet until 1829.

Appendix B (*Continued*)

President	Vice-President	Secretary of State	Secretary of Treasury	Secretary of War
8. Martin Van Buren Democrat 1837	Richard M. Johnson Democrat 1837	John Forsyth 1837	Levi Woodbury 1837	Joel R. Poinsett 1837
9. William H. Harrison Whig 1841	John Tyler Whig 1841	Daniel Webster 1841	Thos. Ewing 1841	John Bell 1841
10. John Tyler Whig and Democrat 1841		Daniel Webster 1841 Hugh S. Legare 1843 Abel P. Upshur 1843 John C. Calhoun 1844	Thos. Ewing 1841 Walter Forward 1841 John C. Spencer 1843 Geo. M. Bibb 1844	John Bell 1841 John McLean 1841 J. C. Spencer 1841 Jas. M. Porter 1843 Wm. Wilkins 1844
11. James K. Polk Democrat 1845	George M. Dallas Democrat 1845	James Buchanan 1845	Robt. J. Walker 1845	Wm. L. Marcy 1845
12. Zachary Taylor Whig 1849	Millard Fillmore Whig 1849	John M. Clayton 1849	Wm. M. Meredith 1849	G. W. Crawford 1849
13. Millard Fillmore Whig 1850		Daniel Webster 1850 Edward Everett 1852	Thomas Corwin 1850	C. M. Conrad 1850
14. Franklin Pierce Democrat 1853	William R. D. King Democrat 1853	W. L. Marcy 1853	James Guthrie 1853	Jefferson Davis 1853
15. James Buchanan Democrat 1857	John C. Breckenridge Democrat 1857	Lewis Cass 1857 J. S. Black 1860	Howell Cobb 1857 Philip F. Thomas 1860 John A. Dix 1861	John B. Floyd 1857 Joseph Holt 1861
16. Abraham Lincoln Republican 1861	Hannibal Hamlin Republican 1861 Andrew Johnson Unionist 1865	W. H. Seward 1861	Salmon P. Chase 1861 W. P. Fessenden 1864 Hugh McCulloch 1865	S. Cameron 1861 E. M. Stanton 1862

Attorney-General	Postmaster General	Secretary of Navy	Secretary of Interior	Secretary of Agriculture
B. F. Butler 1837	Amos Kendall 1837	Mahlon Dickerson 1837		
Felix Grundy 1838	John M. Niles 1840	Jas. K. Paulding 1838		
H. D. Gilpin 1840				
J. J. Crittenden 1841	Francis Granger 1841	George E. Badger 1841		
J. J. Crittenden 1841	Francis Granger 1841	George E. Badger 1841		
Hugh S. Legare 1841	C. A. Wickliffe 1841	Abel P. Upshur 1841		
John Nelson 1843		David Henshaw 1843		
		Thos. W. Gilmer 1844		
		John Y. Mason 1844		
John Y. Mason 1845	Cave Johnson 1845	George Bancroft 1845		
Nathan Clifford 1846		John Y. Mason 1846		
Isaac Toucey 1848				
Reverdy Johnson 1849	Jacob Collamer 1849	Wm. B. Preston 1849	Thomas Ewing 1849	
J. J. Crittenden 1850	Nathan K. Hall 1850	Wm. A. Graham 1850	A. H. Stuart 1850	
	Sam D. Hubbard 1852	John P. Kennedy 1852		
Caleb Cushing 1853	James Campbell 1853	James C. Dobbin 1853	Robert McClelland 1853	
J. S. Black 1857	Aaron V. Brown 1857	Isaac Toucey 1857	Jacob Thompson 1857	
Edw. M. Stanton 1860	Joseph Holt 1859			
Edward Bates 1861	Horatio King 1861	Gideon Wells 1861	Caleb B. Smith 1861	
Titian J. Coffey 1863	M'tgomery Blair 1861		John P. Usher 1863	
James Speed 1864	Wm. Dennison 1864			

Appendix B (*Continued*)

President	Vice-President	Secretary of State	Secretary of Treasury	Secretary of War
17. Andrew Johnson Unionist 1865		W. H. Seward 1865	Hugh McCulloch 1865	E. M. Stanton 1865 U. S. Grant 1867 L. Thomas 1868 J. M. Schofield 1868
18. Ulysses S. Grant Republican 1869	Schuyler Colfax Republican 1869 Henry Wilson Republican 1873	E. B. Washburne 1869 Hamilton Fish 1869	Geo. S. Boutwell 1869 W. A. Richardson 1873 Benj. H. Bristow 1874 Lot M. Morrill 1876	J. A. Rawlins 1869 W. T. Sherman 1869 W. W. Belknap 1869 Alphonso Taft 1876 J. D. Cameron 1876
19. Rutherford B. Hayes Republican 1877	William A. Wheeler Republican 1877	W. M. Evarts 1877	John Sherman 1877	G. W. McCrary 1877 Alex. Ramsey 1879
20. J. A. Garfield Republican 1881	C. A. Arthur Republican 1881	James G. Blaine 1881	Wm. Windom 1881	R. T. Lincoln 1881
21. Chester A. Arthur Republican 1881		F. T. Freling-huysen 1881	Chas. J. Folger 1881 W. Q. Gresham 1884 Hugh McCulloch 1884	R. T. Lincoln 1881
22. G. Cleveland Democrat 1885	T. A. Hendricks Democrat 1885	Thos. F. Bayard 1885	Daniel Manning 1885 Chas. S. Fairchild 1887	W. C. Endicott 1885
23. Benj. Harrison Republican 1889	Levi P. Morton Republican 1889	James G. Blaine 1889 John W. Foster 1892	Wm. Windom 1889 Charles Foster 1891	R. Proctor 1889 S. B. Elkins 1891
24. G. Cleveland Democrat 1893	A. E. Stevenson Democrat 1893	W. Q. Gresham 1893 Richard Olney 1895	John G. Carlisle 1893	D. A. Lamont 1893
25. William McKinley Republican 1897	Garret A. Hobart Republican 1897 Theo. Roosevelt Republican 1901	John Sherman 1897 William R. Day 1897 John Hay 1898	Lyman J. Gage 1897	R. A. Alger 1897 Elihu Root 1899

Attorney-General	Postmaster General	Secretary of Navy	Secretary of Interior	Secretary of Agriculture
James Speed 1865 Henry Stanbery 1866 Wm. M. Evarts 1868	Wm. Dennison 1865 A. W. Randall 1866	Gideon Wells 1865	John P. Usher 1865 James Harlan 1865 O. H. Browning 1866	
E. R. Hoar 1869 A. T. Ackerman 1870 Geo. H. Williams 1871 Edw. Pierrepont 1875 Alphonso Taft 1876	J. A. J. Creswell 1869 Jas. W. Marshall 1874 Marshall Jewell 1874 James N. Tyner 1876	Adolph E. Borie 1869 Geo. M. Robeson 1869	Jacob D. Cox 1869 C. Delano 1870 Zach. Chandler 1875	
Chas. Devens 1877	David M. Key 1877 Horace Maynard 1880	R. W. Thompson 1877 Nathan Goff, Jr. 1881	Carl Schurz 1877	
W. MacVeagh 1881	T. L. James 1881	W. H. Hunt 1881	S. J. Kirkwood 1881	
B. H. Brewster 1881	T. O. Howe 1881 W. Q. Gresham 1883 Frank Hatton 1884	W. E. Chandler 1881	Henry M. Teller 1881	
A. H. Garland 1885	Wm. F. Vilas 1885 D. M. Dickinson 1888	W. C. Whitney 1885	L. Q. C. Lamar 1885 Wm. F. Vilas 1888	N. J. Colman 1889
W. H. H. Miller 1889	J. Wanamaker 1889	Benj. F. Tracy 1889	John W. Noble 1889	J. M. Rusk 1889
R. Olney 1893 J. Harmon 1895	W. S. Bissell 1893 W. L. Wilson 1895	Hilary A. Herbert 1893	Hoke Smith 1893 D. R. Francis 1896	J. S. Morton 1893
J. McKenna 1897 J. W. Griggs 1897 P. C. Knox 1901	James A. Gary 1897 Chas. E. Smith 1898	John D. Long 1897	C. N. Bliss 1897 E. A. Hitchcock 1899	James Wilson 1897

Appendix B (*Continued*)

President	Vice-President	Secretary of State	Secretary of Treasury	Secretary of War
26. Theodore Roosevelt Republican 1901	Chas. W. Fairbanks Republican 1905	John Hay 1901 Elihu Root 1905 Robert Bacon 1909	Lyman J. Gage 1901 Leslie M. Shaw 1902 G. B. Cortelyou 1907	Elihu Root 1901 Wm. H. Taft 1904 Luke E. Wright 1908
27. W. H. Taft Republican 1909	J. S. Sherman Republican 1909	P. C. Knox 1909	F. MacVeagh 1909	J. M. Dickinson 1909 H. L. Stimson 1911
28. Woodrow Wilson Democrat 1913	Thomas R. Marshall Democrat 1913	Wm. J. Bryan 1913 Robert Lansing 1915 Bainbridge Colby 1920	W. G. McAdoo 1913 Carter Glass 1918 D. F. Houston 1920	L. M. Garrison 1913 N. D. Baker 1916
29. Warren G. Harding Republican 1921	Calvin Coolidge Republican 1921	Chas. E. Hughes 1921	Andrew W. Mellon 1921	John W. Weeks 1921
30. Calvin Coolidge Republican 1923	Charles G. Dawes Republican 1925	Chas. E. Hughes 1923 Frank B. Kellogg 1925	Andrew W. Mellon 1923	John W. Weeks 1923 Dwight F. Davis 1925
31. Herbert Hoover Republican 1929	Charles Curtis Republican 1929	Henry L. Stimson 1929	Andrew W. Mellon 1929 Ogden L. Mills 1932	James W. Good 1929 Pat. J. Hurley 1929
32. Franklin D. Roosevelt Democrat 1933	J. Nance Garner Democrat 1933 H. A. Wallace Democrat 1941 H. S. Truman Democrat 1945	Cordell Hull 1933 E. R. Stettinius, Jr. 1944	Wm. H. Woodin 1933 Henry Morgan-thau, Jr. 1934	Geo. H. Dern 1933 H. A. Woodring 1936 H. L. Stimson 1940
33. Harry S. Truman Democrat 1945	Alben W. Barkley Democrat 1949	James F. Byrnes 1945 Geo. C. Marshall 1947 Dean G. Acheson 1949	Fred M. Vinson 1945 John W. Snyder 1946	R. H. Patterson 1945 K. C. Royall 1947

Attorney-General	Postmaster General	Secretary of Navy*	Secretary of Interior	Secretary of Agriculture
P. C. Knox 1901	Chas. E. Smith 1901	John D. Long 1901	E. A. Hitchcock 1901	James Wilson 1901
W. H. Moody 1904	Henry C. Payne 1902	Wm. H. Moody 1902	J. R. Garfield 1907	
C. J. Bonaparte 1907	Robt. J. Wynne 1904	Paul Morton 1904		
	G. B. Cortelyou 1905	C. J. Bonaparte 1905		
	G. von L. Meyer 1907	V. H. Metcalf 1907		
		T. H. Newberry 1908		
G. W. Wickersham 1909	F. H. Hitchcock 1909	G. von L. Meyer 1909	R. A. Ballinger 1909 W. L. Fisher 1911	James Wilson 1909
J. C. McReynolds 1913	A. S. Burleson 1913	Josephus Daniels 1913	F. K. Lane 1913	D. F. Houston 1913
Thos. W. Gregory 1914			J. B. Payne 1920	E. T. Meredith 1920
A. M. Palmer 1919				
H. M. Daugherty 1921	Will H. Hays 1921	Edwin Denby 1921	Albert B. Fall 1921	H. C. Wallace 1921
	Hubert Work 1922		Hubert Work 1923	
	Harry S. New 1923			
H. M. Daugherty 1923	Harry S. New 1923	Edwin Denby 1923	Hubert Work 1923	H. M. Gore 1924
Harlan F. Stone 1924		Curtis W. Wilbur 1924	Roy O. West 1928	W. M. Jardine 1925
John G. Sargent 1925				
Wm. D. Mitchell 1929	Walter F. Brown 1929	Chas. F. Adams 1929	Ray L. Wilbur 1929	Arthur M. Hyde 1929
H. S. Cummings 1933	James A. Farley 1933	Claude A. Swanson 1933	Harold L. Ickes 1933	H. A. Wallace 1933
Frank Murphy 1939	Frank C. Walker 1940	Chas. Edison 1940		C. R. Wickard 1940
Robt. H. Jackson 1940		Frank Knox 1940		
Francis Biddle 1941		James V. Forrestal 1944		
Tom C. Clark 1945	R. E. Hannegan 1945	James V. Forrestal 1945	H. L. Ickes 1945	C. P. Anderson 1945
J. H. McGrath 1949	J. L. Donaldson 1947		Julius A. Krug 1946	C. F. Brannan 1948
J. P. McGranery 1952			O. L. Chapman 1951	

* Lost cabinet status in 1937.

Appendix B (*Continued*)

President	Vice-President	Secretary of State	Secretary of Treasury	Secretary of War*
34. Dwight D. Eisenhower Republican 1953	Richard M. Nixon Republican 1953	J. Foster Dulles 1953 Christian A. Herter 1959	George C. Humphrey 1953 Robert B. Anderson 1957	Sec'y of Defense Est. July 26, 1947 J. V. Forrestal 1947 L. A. Johnson 1949 G. C. Marshall 1950 R. A. Lovett 1951
35. John F. Kennedy Democrat 1961	Lyndon B. Johnson Democrat 1961	Dean Rusk 1961	C. Douglas Dillon 1961	C. E. Wilson 1953 N. H. McElroy 1957 T. S. Gates, Jr. 1959
36. Lyndon B. Johnson Democrat 1963	Hubert H. Humphrey Democrat 1963	Dean Rusk 1963	G. Douglas Dillon 1963 Henry H. Fowler 1965 Joseph W. Barr 1968	R. S. McNamara 1961 C. M. Clifford 1968 M. R. Laird 1969 Elliot Richardson 1973 James Schlesinger 1973
37. Richard M. Nixon Republican 1969	Spiro T. Agnew Republican 1969 Gerald R. Ford Republican 1973	William P. Rogers 1969 Henry A. Kissinger 1973	David M. Kennedy 1969 John B. Connally 1971 George P. Schultz 1972 William E. Simon 1974	Donald A. Rumsfeld 1975 Harold Brown 1976
38. Gerald R. Ford Republican 1974	Nelson A. Rockefeller Republican 1974	Henry A. Kissinger 1974	William E. Simon 1974	
39. Jimmy Carter Democrat 1976	Walter F. Mondale Democrat 1976	Cyrus R. Vance 1976	W. Michael Blumenthal 1976	

* Lost cabinet status in 1947.

Attorney-General	Postmaster General*	Secretary of Navy	Secretary of Interior	Secretary of Agriculture
Herbert Brownell, Jr. 1953 W. P. Rogers 1957	Arthur E. Summerfield 1953	Sec'y of Health Educ. & Welfare Est. April 1, 1953 O. C. Hobby 1953 M. B. Folsom 1955 A. S. Flemming 1958	Douglas McKay 1953 Fred Seaton 1956	Ezra T. Benson 1953
Robt. F. Kennedy 1961	J. Edward Day 1961 John A. Gronouski 1963	Abraham A. Ribicoff 1961 A. Celebrezze 1962	Stewart L. Udall 1961	Orville L. Freeman 1961
Robt. F. Kennedy 1963 Nicholas deB. Katzenbach 1965 Ramsey Clark 1967	John A. Gronouski 1963 Lawrence F. O'Brien 1965 Marvin Watson 1968	A. Celebrezze 1963 John W. Gardner 1965 Wilbur J. Cohen 1968	Stewart L. Udall 1963	Orville L. Freeman 1963
John N. Mitchell 1969 Richard Kleindienst 1972 Elliot Richardson 1973 William B. Saxbe 1974	Winton M. Blount 1969	Robert H. Finch 1969 Elliot L. Richardson 1970 Caspar W. Weinberger 1973	Walter J. Hickel 1969 Rogers C. B. Morton 1971	Clifford M. Hardin 1969 E. L. Butz 1971
William B. Saxbe 1974 Edward H. Levi 1975		Caspar W. Weinberger 1974 Forrest D. Mathews 1975	Rogers C. B. Morton 1974 Stanley H. Hathaway 1975 Thomas S. Kleppe 1975	E. L. Butz 1974
Griffin B. Bell 1976		Joseph A. Califano, Jr. 1976	Cecil D. Andrus 1976	Bob Bergland 1976

* Lost cabinet status in 1971 when U.S. Postal Service was created.

Appendix B (*Continued*)

Sec'y of Commerce and Labor	
Est. Feb. 14, 1903	
G. B. Cortelyou	1903
V. H. Metcalf	1904
O. S. Straus	1907
Chas. Nagel	1909
(Dept. divided, 1913)	

Sec'y of Commerce Est. March 4, 1913	
W. C. Redfield	1913
J. W. Alexander	1919
H. C. Hoover	1921
H. C. Hoover	1925
W. F. Whiting	1928
R. P. Lamont	1929
R. D. Chapin	1932
D. C. Roper	1933
H. L. Hopkins	1939
Jesse Jones	1940
Henry A. Wallace	1945
W. A. Harriman	1946
C. W. Sawyer	1948
S. Weeks	1953
L. L. Strauss	1958
F. H. Mueller	1959
L. H. Hodges	1961
L. H. Hodges	1963
John T. Conner	1965
A. B. Trowbridge	1967
C. R. Smith	1968
M. H. Stans	1969
Peter G. Peterson	1972
Frederick B. Dent	1973
Rogers C. B. Morton	1975
Elliot L. Richardson	1976
Juanita M. Kreps	1976

Sec'y of Labor	
Est. March 4, 1913	
W. B. Wilson	1913
J. J. Davis	1921
W. N. Doak	1930
Frances Perkins	1933
L. B. Schwellenbach	1945
M. J. Tobin	1948
M. P. Durkin	1953
J. P. Mitchell	1953
A. J. Goldberg	1961
W. Willard Wirtz	1962
G. P. Schultz	1969
J. D. Hodgson	1970
Peter Brennan	1973
John T. Dunlop	1975
W. J. Usery, Jr.	1976
F. Ray Marshall	1976

Sec'y of Housing and Urban Development	
Est. Sept. 9, 1965	
Robt. C. Weaver	1966
George W. Romney	1969
James T. Lynn	1973
Carla A. Hills	1975
Patricia R. Harris	1976

Sec'y of Transportation	
Est. Oct. 15, 1966	
Alan S. Boyd	1967
John A. Volpe	1969
Claude S. Brinegar	1973
William T. Coleman, Jr.	1975
Brock Adams	1976

APPENDIX C

CONSTITUTIONAL AMENDMENTS, 1892–1976

AMENDMENT XVI [1913]

The Congress shall have power to lay and collect taxes on incomes, from whatever source derived, without apportionment among the several States, and without regard to any census or enumeration.

AMENDMENT XVII [1913]

The Senate of the United States shall be composed of two Senators from each State, elected by the people thereof, for six years; and each Senator shall have one vote. The electors in each State shall have the qualifications requisite for electors of the most numerous branch of the State legislatures.

When vacancies happen in the representation of any State in the Senate, the executive authority of such State shall issue writs of election to fill such vacancies: *Provided*, That the legislature of any State may empower the executive thereof to make temporary appointments until the people fill the vacancies by election as the legislature may direct.

This amendment shall not be so construed as to affect the election or term of any Senator chosen before it becomes valid as part of the Constitution.

AMENDMENT XVIII [1919]

Section 1. After one year from the ratification of this article the manufacture, sale, or transportation of intoxicating liquors within, the importation thereof into, or the exportation thereof from the United States and all territory subject to the jurisdiction thereof for beverage purposes is hereby prohibited.

Section 2. The Congress and the several States shall have concurrent power to enforce this article by appropriate legislation.

Section 3. This article shall be inoperative unless it shall have been ratified as an amendment to the Constitution by the legislatures of the several States, as provided in the Constitution, within seven years from the date of the submission hereof to the States by the Congress.

AMENDMENT XIX [1920]

The right of citizens of the United States to vote shall not be denied or abridged by the United States or by any State on account of sex.

Congress shall have power to enforce this article by appropriate legislation.

AMENDMENT XX [1933]

Section 1. The terms of the President and Vice-President shall end at noon on the 20th day of January, and the terms of Senators and Representatives at noon on the 3d day of January, of the years in which such terms would have ended if this article had not been ratified; and the terms of their successors shall then begin.

Section 2. The Congress shall assemble at least once in every year, and such meeting shall begin at noon on the 3d day of January, unless they shall by law appoint a different day.

Section 3. If, at the time fixed for the beginning of the term of the President, the President elect shall have died, the Vice-President elect shall become President. If a President shall not have been chosen before the time fixed for the beginning of his term, or if the President elect shall have failed to qualify, then the Vice-President elect shall act as President until a President shall have qualified; and the Congress may by law provide for the case wherein neither a President elect nor a Vice-President elect shall have qualified, declaring who shall then act as President, or the manner in which one who is to act shall be selected, and such person shall act accordingly until a President or Vice-President shall have qualified.

Section 4. The Congress may by law provide for the case of the death of any of the persons from whom the House of Representatives may choose a President whenever the right of choice shall have devolved upon them, and for the case of the death of any of the persons from whom the Senate may choose a Vice-President whenever the right of choice shall have devolved upon them.

Section 5. Sections 1 and 2 shall take effect on the 15th day of October following the ratification of this article.

Section 6. This article shall be inoperative unless it shall have been ratified as an amendment to the Constitution by the legislatures of three-fourths of the several States within seven years from the date of its submission.

AMENDMENT XXI [1933]

Section 1. The eighteenth article of amendment to the Constitution of the United States is hereby repealed.

Section 2. The transportation or importation into any State, Territory, or possession of the United States for delivery or use therein of intoxicating liquors, in violation of the laws thereof, is hereby prohibited.

Section 3. This article shall be inoperative unless it shall have been ratified as an amendment to the Constitution by conventions in the several States, as provided in the Constitution, within seven years from the date of the submission hereof to the States by the Congress.

AMENDMENT XXII [1951]

No person shall be elected to the office of the President more than twice, and no person who has held the office of President, or acted as President, for more than two years of a term to which some other person was elected President shall be elected to the office of the President more than once.

But this Article shall not apply to any person holding the office of President when this Article was proposed by the Congress, and shall not prevent any person who may be holding the office of President, or acting as President, during the term within which this Article becomes operative from holding the office of President or acting as President during the remainder of such term.

AMENDMENT XXIII [1961]

Section 1. The District constituting the seat of Government of the United States shall appoint in such manner as the Congress may direct:

A number of electors of President and Vice President equal to the whole number of Senators and Representatives in Congress to which the District would be entitled if it were a State, but in no event more than the least populous State; they shall be in addition to those appointed by the States, but they shall be considered, for the purposes of the election of President and Vice President, to be electors appointed by a State; and they shall meet in the District and perform such duties as provided by the twelfth article of amendment.

Section 2. The Congress shall have power to enforce this article by appropriate legislation.

AMENDMENT XXIV [1964]

Section 1. The right of citizens of the United States to vote in any primary or other election for President or Vice President, for electors for President or Vice President, or for Senator or Representative in Congress, shall not be denied or abridged by the United States or any State by reason of failure to pay any poll tax or other tax.

Section 2. The Congress shall have the power to enforce this article by appropriate legislation.

AMENDMENT XXV [1967]

Section 1. In case of the removal of the President from office or his death or resignation, the Vice President shall become President.

Section 2. Whenever there is a vacancy in the office of the Vice President, the President shall nominate a Vice President who shall take the office upon confirmation by a majority vote of both houses of Congress.

Section 3. Whenever the President transmits to the President pro tempore of the Senate and the Speaker of the House of Representatives his written declaration that he is unable to discharge the powers and duties of his office, and until he transmits to them a written declaration to the contrary, such powers and duties shall be discharged by the Vice President as Acting President.

Section 4. Whenever the Vice President and a majority of either the principal officers of the executive departments, or of such other body as Congress may by law provide, transmit to the President pro tempore of the Senate and the Speaker of the House of Representatives their written declaration that the President is unable to discharge the powers and duties of his office, the Vice President shall immediately assume the powers and duties of the office as Acting President.

Thereafter, when the President transmits to the President pro tempore of the Senate and the Speaker of the House of Representatives his written declaration that no inability exists, he shall resume the powers and duties of his office unless the Vice President and a majority of either the principal officers of the executive departments, or of such other body as Congress may by law provide, transmit within four days to the President pro tempore of the Senate and the Speaker of the House of Representatives their written declaration that the President is unable to discharge the powers and duties of his office. Thereupon Congress shall decide the issue, assembling within 48 hours for that purpose if not in session. If the Congress, within 21 days after receipt of the latter written declaration, or, if Congress is not in session, within 21 days after Congress is required to assemble, determines by two-thirds vote of both houses that the President is unable to discharge the powers and duties of his office, the Vice President shall continue to discharge the same as Acting President; otherwise, the President shall resume the powers and duties of his office.

AMENDMENT XXVI [1971]

Section 1. The right of citizens of the United States, who are 18 years of age or older, to vote shall not be denied or abridged by the United States or any state on account of age.

Section 2. The Congress shall have the power to enforce this article by appropriate legislation.

APPENDIX D

MEMBERS OF THE SUPREME COURT, 1892–1976*

Stephen J. Field	1863–1897	**Charles E. Hughes**	1930–1941
Joseph P. Bradley	1870–1892	Owen J. Roberts	1930–1945
John M. Harlan	1877–1911	Benjamin N. Cardozo	1932–1938
Horace Gray	1881–1902	Hugo L. Black	1937–1971
Samuel Blatchford	1882–1893	Stanley F. Reed	1938–1957
Lucius Q. C. Lamar	1888–1893	Felix Frankfurter	1939–1962
Melville W. Fuller	1888–1910	William O. Douglas	1939–1975
David J. Brewer	1889–1910	Frank Murphy	1940–1949
Henry B. Brown	1890–1906	**Harlan F. Stone**	1941–1946
George Shiras, Jr.	1892–1903	James F. Byrnes	1941–1942
Howell E. Jackson	1893–1895	Robert H. Jackson	1941–1954
Edward D. White	1894–1910	Wiley B. Rutledge	1943–1949
Rufus W. Peckham	1895–1909	Harold H. Burton	1945–1958
Joseph McKenna	1898–1925	**Fred M. Vinson**	1946–1953
Oliver W. Holmes	1902–1932	Tom C. Clark	1949–1967
William R. Day	1903–1922	Sherman Minton	1949–1956
William H. Moody	1906–1910	**Earl Warren**	1953–1969
Horace H. Lurton	1909–1914	John Marshall Harlan	1955–1971
Charles E. Hughes	1910–1916	William J. Brennan, Jr.	1956–
Willis Van Devanter	1910–1937	Charles E. Whittaker	1957–1962
Joseph R. Lamar	1910–1916	Potter Stewart	1958–
Edward D. White	1910–1921	Byron R. White	1962–
Mahlon Pitney	1912–1922	Arthur J. Goldberg	1962–1965
Jas. C. McReynolds	1914–1941	Abe Fortas	1965–1969
Louis D. Brandeis	1916–1939	Thurgood Marshall	1967–
John H. Clarke	1916–1922	**Warren E. Burger**	1969–
William H. Taft	1921–1930	Harry A. Blackmun	1970–
George Sutherland	1922–1938	Lewis F. Powell, Jr.	1961–
Pierce Butler	1922–1939	William H. Rehnquist	1971–
Edward T. Sanford	1923–1930	John P. Stevens	1975–
Harlan F. Stone	1925–1941		

* Chief Justices' names in boldface type.

INDEX

78 79 80 9 8 7 6 5 4 3 2 1